F.V.

The Economics of Gender

To Bill, Catherine, and Kenneth

The Economics of Gender

Second Edition

Joyce P. Jacobsen
Wesleyan University

Copyright © Joyce P. Jacobsen 1994, 1998

The right of Joyce P. Jacobsen to be identified as author of this work has been asserted in accordance with the Copyright, Designs and Patents Act 1988.

First published 1994
Second edition published 1998

2 4 6 8 10 9 7 5 3 1

Blackwell Publishers Inc.
350 Main Street
Malden, Massachusetts 02148
USA

Blackwell Publishers Ltd
108 Cowley Road
Oxford OX4 1JF
UK

Library of Congress Cataloging-in-Publication Data

Jacobsen, Joyce P.
    The economics of gender / by Joyce P. Jacobsen. – 2nd ed.
      p. cm.
    Includes bibliographical references and index.
    ISBN 0–631–20726–0 (hardcover). – ISBN 0–631–20727–9 (pbk.)
      1. Women–Economic conditions. 2. Women–Social conditions.
    3. Sex roles in the work environment. 4. Sex discrimination.
    I. Title.
    HQ1381 IN PROCESS
    306.3′615–dc21   98–11168
                                                  CIP

British Library Cataloguing in Publication Data

A CIP catalogue record for this book is available from the British Library.

Typeset in 10 on 12pt Sabon
by Graphicraft Limited, Hong Kong
Printed in Great Britain by TJ International, Padstow, Cornwall

This book is printed on acid-free paper

Contents

List of Figures

List of Tables

List of Focuses

Preface

The recent explosion of interest in gender-related issues among economists is reflected in a burgeoning research literature, a concomitant rise in the number of relevant courses in economics departments, and the recent establishment of the International Association for Feminist Economics. Economists are increasingly realizing the need for more effective communication of their analytical skills in order to contribute to the current debates in this area occurring in the pedagogical arena, in multidisciplinary gender and women's studies programs, and in courses outside economics, as well as in the policy arena, where economists are not necessarily included in discussions if the public problem is perceived to be social rather than economic. This book attempts to further the establishment of the economics of gender as a valid area of economic investigation.

Study of the economics of gender provides an excellent opportunity both to introduce economics in a relevant and novel way to a wider audience than is generally reached in economics courses and to encourage those students with some background in economics to try out their analytical skills on problems of social concern. The book is also intended to serve as a source of reliable and recent information about gender patterns for all persons interested in obtaining accurate materials, whether students, economists, social scientists, policymakers, or simply interested individuals.

I attempt to approach this field in a balanced way. My emphasis is on the concept of gender studies as opposed to women's studies or men's studies, and I try to give fair space to men's issues and to issues involving gender in general as opposed to solely women's issues and points of view. However, many issues in all categories involve the reality that women receive a less favorable outcome than men, and so attention is focused on how women might rise to a higher level and achieve parity.

How to use this book

This book has been developed to fit a variety of course formats. It can serve as the primary text for a quarter or semester-length undergraduate course in the economics of gender, or as a supporting text for a course in women's studies, labor economics, or economic policy analysis at the undergraduate or graduate level. The book can also serve a variety of audiences. I have taught the economics of gender to mixed groups of undergraduates, ranging from senior economics majors to persons who have had no previous course in economics. For students who have some background in economic theory (in particular, microeconomic theory), the appendices to Chapters 1, 3, and 4 will serve as review or may be skipped completely. For students with no previous exposure to economics, these appendices will be more critical, and they need to be carefully covered in class. No background in mathematics is assumed other than the ability to do simple numerical calculations and to comprehend statistical tables and graphs. Occasionally, formulas are presented in the main text or in endnotes. However, the concepts expressed in these formulas will also be understandable from the surrounding verbal discussion. The appendix to Chapter 7 on regression analysis is included for students without previous statistical training. If the group is mixed with regard to background, it is probably best to cover appendix material in class in some detail, before or concurrently with the material in these chapters.

Structure

The book is divided into five parts. Part I introduces the student to the main patterns and debates concerning economic gender differences. Part II focuses on labor force participation causes and effects. Part III focuses on explanations for differences in earnings between men and women. Part IV compares gender differences across societies. Finally, Part V considers both changes over time in patterns of gender differences and possible future policy directions. Each part contains two or more chapters, and Parts II and III also contain chapter-length policy analyses that serve to draw together themes running throughout the chapters in those parts.

The first three parts of the book concentrate on developing a picture of conditions in the United States since World War II, while Part IV provides a picture of concurrent conditions in the rest of the world. Part V expands the time frame for the United States: Chapter 14 considers conditions in the United States up through World War II, Chapter 15 considers variations in the historical patterns by race/ethnicity and/or class, and Chapter 16 considers future policy directions. However, examples, statistics, and studies from countries other than the United States and conditions from pre-World War II situations in the United States and other countries are discussed throughout the book when relevant. Also, while I have chosen to concentrate the discussion of gender differences by race, ethnicity, and class into one chapter so as to create a historical context in addressing certain relevant issues, gender differences categorized by these other conceptual categories are presented throughout the book as well where they are notable and manageable within the thread of discussion.

The book weaves together theory and data. It remains grounded in practical concerns, and policy aspects of gender differences are discussed throughout the text. Most chapters end with a "Policy Application," which goes into more depth on the topic of a particular policy or related set of policies that arises in the context of the chapter. Each chapter contains one to three "Focuses," or boxed examples, which serve to amplify points made in the main text and to provoke additional thought.

The questions at the end of each chapter are designed to review concepts, to stimulate discussion, to give students practice at "thinking like an economist," and, in some cases, to lead to possible paper topics. They include a question pertaining to each Focus. Notes throughout the book point the student to additional research sources. Many chapters also contain a list of additional references and statistical sources to aid the student who is researching a paper topic. I continue to refer to the printed versions of sources whenever possible, but readers should be aware that many government statistics are now available in both printed and on-line versions, and may increasingly be available only on-line through internet access points or on CD-ROMs.

Alternative orderings

The book has been designed so that it can be used in a number of alternative orderings. Some sections are core material, while others are optional and depend on the instructor's emphasis. Parts I through III contain the core material, but the chapter-length policy applications that conclude Parts II and III may be dropped. Chapters 14 and 15 may be read before Part IV, and may even follow Part II. Chapters 11 and 16 are shorter and more optional. Several suggested syllabi follow for courses in which the book would be used as the primary text:

One-quarter course:
 Chapters 1 to 9, skipping the chapter-length policy applications
 Chapter 10
 Chapter 14

One-semester course with emphasis on cross-societal comparisons:
 Parts I to III (with or without the policy applications)
 Part IV

One-semester course with emphasis on historical comparisons:
 Parts I to III (with or without the policy applications)
 Part V (with or without Chapter 16)

One-semester course with emphasis on policy analysis:
 Parts I to III (including the policy applications)
 Chapter 13
 Chapter 16

Changes in the second edition

In updating the book, I have tried to reflect changes in both theoretical and empirical thinking on the economics of gender. This has taken the concrete form of revising and expanding the references and suggestions for further reading, and updating the data presented in the text, tables, and figures whenever possible to reflect the most currently available information. Some sections within chapters have been more extensively rewritten to reflect major developments. I have also added some discussion questions and Focuses. The basic structure of the text remains unchanged.

Acknowledgments

As with any project of this nature, persons too numerous to enumerate have provided inspiration, newspaper clippings, and spirited discussions that have contributed to my understanding of the economics of gender. In terms of more concrete obligations, I am indebted to the following people. Both current and former editors at Blackwell – Mary Beckwith, Al Bruckner, Rolf Janke, and Susan Milmoe – have been a source of uplift in their belief in this project. A number of colleagues have provided helpful feedback from their classes on either the manuscript or the first edition; in particular I would like to thank Ronald Bodkin, Peter Kilby, Laurence Levin, Hilarie Lieb, and Mary Young. Victoria Alexander, William Boyd, Jonathan Paul, and Marcia Walton read sections and provided many useful comments. Additionally, the anonymous reviewers for Blackwell gave many helpful suggestions. Dana Peterson, Stacy Sneeringer, Cayce Stapp, Jim Turner, and especially James Pearce were capable and conscientious research assistants. William Jacobsen provided grammatical and bibliographical advice, and Marci Hendrix was an invaluable assistant on the nuts and bolts of manuscript production. Special thanks to Victor Fuchs for introducing me to this area of study, to Rae Moses for providing the impetus for me to develop this area into my research and teaching specialty by arranging for my joint appointment at Northwestern University in economics and women's studies, and to my students in classes on the economics of gender at Wesleyan University, Northwestern University and Rhodes College for serving as patient sounding-boards as I developed my understanding of gender issues through teaching them.

JOYCE JACOBSEN

What Are the Issues in the Economics of Gender?

*T*his introductory part defines the realm in which economists discuss gender issues. Chapter 1 discusses the economic perspective on gender issues, both by comparing it with the perspectives of other academic disciplines and by considering some of the debates about the causes and effects of gender in which both economists and noneconomists are engaging. The appendix to Chapter 1 outlines the fundamental concepts of economics that we will draw upon and add to throughout the book. Chapter 2 presents basic data from the U.S. economy on gender differences and gives an idea of how wide-ranging economic differences by gender are by highlighting some less-well-known differences. These two chapters lay the groundwork for the more detailed work undertaken in future chapters: the tasks of accurately describing gender differences in the economy and developing theoretical frameworks that will lead to an increased understanding of why these differences arise.

Introduction

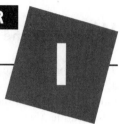

How and why are men and women different? These are questions that almost everyone has thought about. Many scientists have devoted large parts of their careers to attempting to answer them. Since you are reading this book, you have probably wondered about these questions yourself, and may have come to some conclusions already.

The goal of this book is to explain how gender differences lead to different economic outcomes for the sexes, measured in terms of earnings, income, poverty rates, hours of work, and other standards used by economists to determine economic well-being. The field in economics known as the "economics of gender" encompasses this study. This chapter first introduces the field, then contrasts the ways in which different academic disciplines have addressed the area of gender differences. The *how* question will be addressed very briefly in this chapter – just enough to set the tone for the debates to follow. The *why* question will be answered somewhat more in depth as we review the different disciplines' approaches to gender differences. As you will see, people do not always agree, so the basic debates over the nature and influence of gender differences have not been resolved within the boundaries of particular academic disciplines, let alone a consensus achieved among the natural and social sciences.

What is the economics of gender?

Economic agents can be male or female, and they interact in families as well as in firms and in markets. This book explores those areas of economics in which these two facts must be explicitly included for the analysis to be valid. Three types of economic inquiry are discussed: (1) theoretical models that include two sexes, (2) empirical work that addresses similarities and differences between the sexes, and (3) analysis of economic policies that affect the sexes differently. Each chapter in the book generally considers all three types of inquiry.

The questions of how and why men and women are different are amplified throughout this book. Racial, cultural, and class differences in gender patterns are discussed. Although the text focuses on contemporary U.S. patterns, sections are devoted to the comparative study of other developed countries and developing ones, and to gender patterns through history. We take a current perspective in Parts II and III, examining the situation in the

United States in depth for the time period since World War II and using the most current data available. In Part IV, we take a cross-cultural perspective and consider conditions in other societies, categorized as industrialized capitalist, industrialized and nonindustrialized socialist, and nonindustrialized nonsocialist societies. In Part V, we consider the historical situation in the United States, going back as far as the available data allow us and relying on more anecdotal sources of evidence for the earliest times.

Why study the economics of gender?

The economics of gender is an interesting and relevant field to study for several reasons. In all societies, people wonder how and why women and men are different. This book provides accurate and recent information about gender patterns to help inform the debates that arise frequently in modern life concerning roles and rewards for women and men. For instance, did you know that:

- In 1815, U.S. working women made 29 cents for every dollar a man earned; by 1995 they had worked their way up to 74 cents on the dollar, averaging a gain of a fourth of a penny a year.
- Many occupations that are now essentially 100 percent female, such as bank teller and secretary, were for many years 100 percent male.
- A man in his early 30s now is four times as likely to have become divorced as in 1950, even though it is twice as likely that he has not yet married at all.

Economics offers an approach to the broad questions of how and why men and women are different. A number of interesting related questions arise in the course of studying the economics of gender, including:

- Why do women earn less than men?
- Why is there so much occupational sex segregation, and how does segregation relate to the earnings difference?
- Do changes in female labor force participation lead to changes in the home environment (i.e., labor-saving devices, divorce, fewer children) or vice-versa?

Economic analysis is a useful investigative tool for analyzing the evidence for these questions. Although this book has many references to work by noneconomists, the basic assumptions of neoclassical economics as customarily presented in introductory microeconomics classes will be maintained. At various points, reference will be made to the alternative theories of institutionalists, radical economists, and feminist economists, as well as to theories from other disciplines, such as anthropology and sociology.

Economic analysis is also a useful tool for analyzing policies that affect men and women differently. It does not necessarily resolve questions, but it can help elucidate the main points involved. Examples of policy-related questions include:

- Do anti-discrimination policies work?
- What are the pros and cons of implementing comparable worth?
- What are the effects of welfare programs?
- What are the effects of pronatalist and antinatalist policies?
- What are the differential effects of development policies on women and men?

Economists' ways are often at odds with the ways of most people approaching various gender issues. This point will be brought out especially in the discussions of discrimination, of whether or not to implement comparable worth, and of how occupational segregation has arisen. The philosophical and methodological underpinnings of economics will be discussed at more length below and contrasted to those of other disciplines. The appendix to this chapter provides a more formal discussion of the terms and analytical tools commonly used by economists.

Debates between academic disciplines often boil down to disputes over appropriate methodology, and different disciplines focus on different aspects of gender differences – staking out territory, so to speak. Economics is a particularly provocative discipline, in that it is often seen as attempting to encroach on other fields' traditional territory. Economists have only recently started to study gender issues, and many people, both within and without the economics profession, question the appropriateness and applicability of economic assumptions and techniques to gender issues. But this controversy is partly what makes the study of the economics of gender interesting. After you have finished this book, you can decide for yourself whether economics has brought insight into the nature of gender differences – or not.

*H*ow are men and women different?

Differences between men and women can be divided into biological, or sex-linked, differences, on the one hand, and everything else, variously construed as psychological, social, and/or cultural differences, on the other hand. One way to think about this split is to differentiate between sex and gender. Sex can be either female or male; gender can be feminine or masculine. Here we will define *women* as those adult persons having two X chromosomes, and *men* as those adult persons having an X and a Y chromosome.[1] This chromosomal difference leads to biological differences between the sexes, such as women's abilities to bear children and produce milk.[2] We will define *sex characteristics* as attributes of men and women that are created by their biological characteristics, and *gender characteristics* as attributes that are culturally associated with being female and male. Feminine persons look and act in ways that lead observers to classify them as women without directly observing their chromosome pattern; the same assumption is true for masculine persons. This classification can vary in details across cultures, and there may be ambiguity in determining a person's gender (particularly when one is observing persons from a different culture), while there is no ambiguity in determining his or her sex.[3] It is possible to refer to a woman as being a masculine woman and a man as being a feminine man. A person has numerous characteristics, and observers may note some incongruities in the set of characteristics but nonetheless decide to classify the person as being either a woman or a man.[4]

Throughout this book, numerous differences between women and men will be presented. In a statistical sense, the distinction between sex and gender is unimportant in making a statement such as, "Women earn less than men"; this also implies that females earn less than males, because the number of misclassified persons is so small. However, the interpretation of the implications of these differences depends on whether one believes that they are sex or gender characteristics.

Some natural and social scientists argue that there is really no difference between sex and gender, so that the terms may be used interchangeably. Other people argue that the terminology is important, and that the choice of concept – sex or gender – entails an intellectual commitment as to whether or not the terms can be separated. This argument cuts across academic disciplinary boundaries, although it rages more within some disciplines than in others.

In economics, no strong opinion about appropriate terminology has developed, and the terms are used interchangeably with no particular thought about whether they refer to the same concept or not. I chose to use "gender" rather than "sex" in the title of this book because I think that use of "gender" does *not* imply an automatic embracing of the environment side of the debate, but rather implies an open-mindedness as to whether or not gender is separable from sex. In practice, at the level of analysis where economics operates, the difference between sex and gender is generally unimportant, and I often refer to sex differences rather than gender differences, in conformity with whatever source I am using at the moment.

FOCUS

Gender, gender, everywhere

The number of ways in which men and women differ are practically uncountable. This is the case partly because the number of things that psychologists, pollsters, and other observers of society think of to study are practically uncountable. But in considering differences, it is important to differentiate between "statistically significant" differences and "significant" differences. Given a large enough sample of persons, almost any difference, no matter how small, can be said to be measured with confidence as existing. On the other hand, a difference of one percentage point in the answers between women and men may not be much evidence that men and women have different motivations or circumstances. The following are some examples of gender differences, all using recent U.S. data:

Living habits:[5]

- 8 percent of women, 10 percent of men are left-handed.
- Women watch 14 hours, men watch 16 hours of television a week.
- 35 percent of women, 17 percent of men stayed indoors for an entire day in the past week.
- 43 percent of women, 51 percent of men enjoy or look forward to being by themselves.
- 13 percent of women, 8 percent of men frequently talk to themselves.
- 20 percent of women, 18 percent of men frequently sing, hum, and/or whistle.

Dying habits:[6]

- Of those who die in accidents, 34 percent are women, 66 percent are men.
- Of those who die from HIV infection, 14 percent are women, 86 percent are men.
- Of those who commit suicide, 20 percent are women, 80 percent are men.

Crime and criminals[7]

- Of those who are robbed, 35 percent are women, 65 percent are men.
- 33 percent of women, 50 percent of men report having a gun at home.
- Of those in prison, 7 percent are women, 93 percent are men.

Risk-aversion differences:

- 78 percent of women, 68 percent of men believe in heaven and hell.[8]
- 71 percent of women, 92 percent of men have bought a lottery ticket.[9]

And finally, some similarities:

- Of those who own corporate stock, 50 percent are women, 50 percent are men.[10]
- 90 percent of women, 90 percent of men consider themselves happy people.[11]

Why are men and women different?

The heredity versus environment – or nature versus nurture – debate that frames much of scientific discourse is directly relevant to the debate over why men and women are different. The nature side says that gender differences are sex differences: all observed gender differences are biological differences and are therefore traceable to the genetic and hormonal differences between women and men. The nurture side says that gender differences are separable from sex differences and that they are determined by cultural influences. Some of these influences may occur so early in child development as to be hard to distinguish from sex differences, but they are cultural nonetheless. While simple in its dichotomy, the nature-nurture division may not be a useful way to frame the debate over gender differences. One psychologist points out that it may be like asking, "Which determines the area of a rectangle, the length or the width?"[12] However, the implications of these two views are quite strong. For the nature side, it is very difficult – if not impossible – to alter gender differences in fundamental ways. For the nurture side, there are no immutable gender differences.

Consider the widely held belief that motherhood is an important experience for all women to have. The nature side would argue that women are both biologically capable of having babies and genetically programmed to want to have babies. The nurture side would argue that the depth of pronatalist brainwashing/social control that women undergo is truly intensive.[13] Girls are given baby dolls to play with, are made to help with the care of younger children, and are subjected to a wide range of media messages implying that motherhood is, if not the ultimate goal for a woman, at least one of the goals she must achieve to be fulfilled as a woman. While the ability to have a baby is biologically determined, the desire to have one is instilled by the society.

Different academic disciplines have approached this debate using different theoretical and methodological tools, but no consensus has been achieved either within or between disciplines. In the area of the natural sciences, most of the debate has, not surprisingly, occurred within the field of biology, which is the study of the structure and processes of living organisms. Hybrid disciplines have sprung up, notably biopsychology and sociobiology, that attempt to bridge biology and the social sciences. We will first look at biologists' views on gender differences and then take up, in turn, some views of gender emanating from different social sciences. The social sciences (or branches of knowledge dealing with humans) that we will consider are psychology, anthropology, sociology, political science, and economics. These can be loosely defined, respectively, as the sciences of the mind, of culture, of society, of government (or of the state), and of markets.[14]

Biological perspectives

The field of biology has been the scene of much of the most acrimonious debate over the gender aspects of nature vs. nurture. While biologists are the source of most of our knowledge about sex-related differences, after the most obvious physiological differences have been noted, the range of behavior that could be considered "purely biological" is hotly debated. Additionally, while it is clear that men and women have some definite differences, such as different sex organs, many sex differences must be described as ranges or averages, such as height and weight. Many scientists would agree with the statement by Jerre Levy, a biopsychologist, that sex differences are "rather minor compared to differences between people of the same sex: of all the variations we observe among people, eighty to ninety-five percent of them are *within* men and *within* women."[15] If, in fact, the sexes are more alike than different, this fact would cast doubt on the ability of sexual difference to explain much of gender difference.

On the nature side of the debate, the field of sociobiology has developed. Its best-known proponent, the entomologist E.O. Wilson, defines sociobiology as "the scientific study of the biological basis of all forms of social behavior in all kinds of organisms, including man."[16] The roots of this field are in applying principles derived from animal and insect behavior to human behavior. The extreme viewpoint held by some sociobiologists is that all animal behavior (including human behavior) is biologically based, or determined. This is the belief of *biological determinism*.

In the area of male-female relationships, sociobiologists point out the widespread nature of male dominance, both in the animal kingdom and throughout human cultures, and argue that male dominance is biologically based.[17] Arguments for the basis of this male dominance can be grouped by certain common themes:[18]

- aggression arguments: males are more aggressive, due, in humans, to the preponderance of the hormone testosterone in males; inevitably they come to dominate the less aggressive females.
- male bonding arguments: males are able to band together to dominate females; this tendency towards working in groups is a genetic trait that women do not have.
- physical strength arguments: men are stronger than women, so are able to dominate them physically; this leads to social domination as well.
- reproduction-related arguments: women and men take on different gender roles because they support their different roles in reproduction of the species, and specialization of reproductive roles is adaptive for survival of the species.

In each case, sociobiologists back up the argument with the principle of natural selection: males who are weak, submissive, less oriented towards reproduction, and/or less group-oriented are less likely to mate and pass along their characteristics; over time these characteristics are bred out of the males of the species. Women who are weak, submissive, and/or more oriented towards breeding are not killed off in dominance struggles and/or are more popular as breeding partners, so their characteristics persist as well.

There are legions of critics of these views, both within biology and outside it.[19] Problems spotted by critics in arguments for biological determinism include the systematic selection of supporting examples, misrepresentation of examples, improper extrapolation of evidence, and poor theory.[20] Three prominent biologists – R.C. Lewontin, Steven Rose, and Leon J. Kamin – have criticized biological determinism both because they think it is inaccurate and because they find it dangerous in that it politically supports those who seek to justify and maintain the status quo, whom they term the New Right. They characterize the New Right view thus:

> Not only is the [gender] division of labor given by biology, but we go against it at our peril, for it is functional. Society needs both dominant, productive men and dependent, nurturative, and reproductive women . . . .[If] sexual divisions have emerged adaptively by natural selection, as a result of the different biological roles in reproduction of the two sexes, and have evolved to the maximal advantage of both, the inequalities are not merely inevitable but functional too."[21]

While most biologists would not agree with strict biological determinism, in general they are unlikely to fall solidly onto the nurture side in the nature-nurture debate. Instead, they are more likely to espouse *biological potentiality*, the idea that biology shapes our potential, but not our outcomes.[22]

Psychological perspectives

Many studies of sex differences are not obvious in their underlying orientation – that is, are they studying biology, or psychology? Many of the most interesting studies of sex differences bridge this gap. Studies focusing on physiological sex differences are clearly biological in nature. But some biologists are addressing the questions of how thought and actions apparently undertaken under free will are actually affected by biological factors. A field of biopsychology has developed that attempts to synthesize the theory and methods of the two fields, but that by its very existence implies that psychology has some grounding in biology.

Take, for example, studies of intelligence, or scholastic ability. One study gave the math SATs to a group of eighth-grade students who scored high on a standard intelligence test, thereby attempting to control for both IQ and knowledge of mathematics before math coursework patterns by sex began to diverge in high school.[23] Of this sample, over 40 percent were girls, and they were girls who said they liked math. However, there were many more high-scoring boys on the math SAT. This led the researchers to conclude that math ability is biologically linked to sex. This result implies that human ability, while channeled through education, is to a large degree predetermined and linked to sex.

Consider another interesting pattern at the border of biology and psychology. Many more women than men become mental patients. One study found that of the first admissions to private, state, and county mental hospitals in the United States, 139 are women to every 100 men. When Veterans Administration hospitals are included (where the data are considered to be an overestimate of male mental patients), the ratio is still 121 women to 100 men. Among all patients under psychiatric care in general hospitals (including both chronic patients and first admissions), the ratio is 168 women to 100 men.[24] This study does not lead to as strong a biological implication as the former. For instance, women may be more likely than men to be diagnosed as mental patients if they deviate from behavioral norms for their gender.

Two psychologists, Eleanor Emmons Maccoby and Carol Nagy Jacklin, have conducted a thorough review of the psychological literature on sex differences.[25] They come down firmly against biological determinism, and they also argue that the number of firmly established psychological sex differences are few and are outnumbered by beliefs that are unfounded or find only partial support. They found fairly well-established evidence for the beliefs that girls have greater verbal ability than boys, while boys have greater math and visual-spatial abilities and are more aggressive than girls. Differences where evidence is mixed include tactile sensitivity, fear, timidity, anxiety, activity level, competitiveness, dominance, compliance, and nurturing. Unfounded beliefs about girls are that they are more social and suggestible than boys, have lower self-esteem, are better at rote learning, and lack achievement motivation. Neither girls nor boys are more analytic, visually oriented, or auditorily oriented.

In recent years, psychologists and other social scientists have devoted much attention to the question of whether there are sex differences in reasoning, particularly in moral reasoning.[26] While no clear answer has emerged, this topic has been of great interest in the academic feminist community. If women indeed have "different ways of knowing" or "a different voice," as some researchers argue,[27] and if neither sex's way of knowing can be determined to be better or worse, but just different, then there may be strong political arguments for maintaining joint representation of the sexes in critical decision-making positions in society.

Anthropological perspectives

Maccoby and Jacklin note that most psychological studies of sex differences have used white middle class U.S. subjects. Nevertheless, conclusions about universal sex differences have been drawn from these studies. In order to check the validity of these conclusions, there is a need both for cross-cultural work in psychology and for the anthropological viewpoint, which specifically considers cultural differences as an important determinant of human behavior.

Anthropological field work has been an important source of data on the extent and nature of the gender division of labor. A point of general agreement among anthropologists is that evidence for matriarchy, past or present, is lacking; in other words, male dominance is and has been very nearly universal. While there are examples of matrilineal societies (societies where descent patterns are reckoned by mothers rather than by fathers), and while these societies tend to have advantages for women relative to patrilineal societies, men in these societies still hold the prized offices and exercise basic control over resources.[28] However, some anthropologists and others still disagree on this point, arguing either that the data are incomplete or that interpretations of what occurred in particular past societies are biased by the male viewpoint held by most past observers. In fact, anthropology as a field has come under criticism – mostly internally – for showing bias by ignoring women and their activities. Anthropologists have become more sensitive to the importance of both describing and evaluating the importance of women's activities.[29]

In general, anthropologists side with the nurture side of the heredity versus environment debate. As a paradigm for anthropology, more and more anthropologists have espoused the theoretical viewpoint of "cultural materialism,"[30] which one proponent defines as the view that "explanations for cultural similarities and differences lie in the material conditions of human life: how people make a living, how they relate to their environments, and how they reproduce themselves."[31] Therefore, biology, rather than being destiny, is just one factor determining cultural patterns. Ernestine Friedl, an influential advocate of cultural materialism, makes some basic propositions about gender differences that she judges are supported by substantial evidence:[32]

1. The subsistence technology of a society and its social and political organization have crucial consequences for:
    *   the sexual division of labor,
    *   the differential allocation of power and recognition to men and women, and
    *   the quality of relationships between the sexes.
2. The spacing of children and the patterns of childrearing are adjusted to whatever level of work women customarily do (as opposed to vice-versa).
3. The right to distribute and exchange valued goods and services to those outside one's domestic unit confers power and prestige (i.e., it is better to give than to receive); consequently, gender roles are influenced not only by the division of routine labor but also by extraordinary occasions (because those times are when extradomestic exchange occurs most frequently).

We will consider these assertions and their relationship to economic theory later in the book, particularly in Chapter 12.

Sociological perspectives

While anthropology appears to be moving towards acceptance of a paradigm, sociology has long been a field without an established central core of belief. As one sociologist has written, "Sociology's problems stem from its own inability to decide exactly what its subject matter should be."[33] One sociologist has proposed a definition of sociology that attempts to both absorb the lost turf of moral reasoning and to define it relative to economics and political science: it is the social science that teaches both that social practices create moral rules and that "society" is an alternative to markets and states.[34] Other sociologists prefer a definition of the field based on methodology rather than subject matter.[35]

In general, sociologists are inclined to consider environment as more important than heredity and to look for explanations of gender differences that are rooted in social/cultural forces. One view would be that three sociological processes generate observed gender differences: (1) children are socialized into gender roles, which happens at the individual level; (2) gender differences are socially constructed; and (3) socially constructed ideas of gender differences are institutionalized at the societal level.[36] Sociologist Cynthia Fuchs Epstein has synthesized and reviewed the sociological literature on gender differences much as Maccoby and Jacklin did for the psychological literature.[37] In her evaluation, she comes down heavily against biological determinism, although she does not claim to speak for all sociologists,[38] and she decides that women and men are really much more "same" than different. In a vein similar to cultural materialism, some sociologists have focused on the relationship between power and domination and the need to create resource surpluses for survival. One sociologist argues that there is an ongoing tension in dominance relationships due to the economic aspects of the relationships: powerless, slavish, ignorant women (and men) are easier to exploit but do not yield much surplus product for the exploiter; freer, more productive women are more resistant to domination.[39]

Political science perspectives

Political scientists have also considered the causes and implications of gender differences. In particular, political philosophers have considered the question of whether gender differences are just or unjust and what role, if any, the state should have in reshaping gender differences. Susan Moller Okin, in her analysis of the gender implications of recent influential political theories, rebuts two claims made by several political philosophers (all male): (1) the claim that justice is not a primary virtue for the family, that the family is "beyond" justice; (2) the claim that the "nature" of sexual differences makes the demand that families be just not only unreasonable but harmful to society.[40] She argues that political forces generally operate against women, the less powerful of the sexes, at both the family and societal levels. Therefore, a just state would attempt to correct this power balance, in large part through legislation and enforcement that would lead to direct intervention by the state in family situations that are determined to be unjust.

Another group of political scientists reasons that in order to argue that political change can and should have an effect on gender differences, it is necessary to assume that women can shape their circumstances rather than having them determined through biology.[41] In this case, they argue that the government/state should take the role of ensuring that women and men are treated in the public realm as deserving of equal liberty. Under this assumption, the state should have the goal of making the public realm as gender-neutral as possible, rather than allowing special privilege and/or protection for either sex.[42]

We will consider both of these points – whether or not the state should interfere with family situations, and whether or not the state should maintain equal treatment or preferential treatment by sex – throughout the book. Given that a large focus of this book is on policy applications of economics in the realm of gender issues, it is important to keep these basic questions from political science in mind.

Economic perspectives

We now turn at somewhat more length to the economic approach to gender differences, since it is the focus of this book. Economics can be broadly defined as the science of decision making under constraints. Economists stress the concept of scarcity – the need to weigh alternatives with regard to cost, due to an inability to afford everything – as the main constraint affecting individual and societal decision making. Additionally, economists regard humans as rational, in the strongest view, assuming that rationality underlies all human behavior. Rationality involves persons reacting to current conditions in making decisions, using all available information in the decision-making process. Rationality implies both consistency (persons will always act in the same way in identical situations) and foresight (persons will consider long-run implications and indirect effects of their behavior). While people do not need full information and perfect foresight in order to be rational, economists often assume these factors anyway in making predictions about how a person will act. What are the alternatives to rational behavior?

1. Irrational behavior: has no pattern and is apparently completely random in nature, or responds erratically to outside influences.

2. Command-following behavior: is responsive to the desires of others; behavior that does not lead to maximizing one's self-interest but that may be a result of self-interest on the part of others.
3. Customary/traditional behavior: uses one's own past behavior and societal custom as a guide to current behavior, regardless of changing circumstances.
4. Heuristic behavior: routines, "standard operating procedures," and rules of thumb that are acted on but not reflected upon.

One could argue that it may be rational not to disobey a command or custom because one prefers to obey, but then rationality becomes a tautological concept. One could argue that it is rational to follow custom or heuristics so as to reduce the costs of gathering more information, but for particular heuristics that do not appear to have grounds in fact, this is problematic. In order to contrast these types of behavior, consider how a man might react to having a head cold. A command-follower might do whatever his roommate suggests, even if it is something blatantly silly, such as staying out all night dancing. A man exhibiting customary behavior might do whatever he did last time he had a cold, such as taking the same medication, regardless of how the symptoms of this new cold might vary from the last one. An irrational person might do just about anything, including overdosing on a medication. A person following a heuristic might remember the rule, "Feed a cold, starve a fever," and order a pizza for delivery. And a person behaving rationally would analyze the current cold, determine if a new medication (or a visit to the doctor) is needed, and purchase it if necessary.

Economists have skirted the edge of the nature-nurture debate. While they would like to rely on natural selection arguments to argue that rational behavior will generally be favored over other forms of behavior, they also want to argue that people are flexible enough in their behavior to be able to respond to changing conditions. The debate over whether the sexual division of labor is biologically or culturally determined has been of less interest to them than figuring out why segregation is an apparently equilibrium, or economically stable, situation, regardless of the origin of gender roles.

Methodologically, economists rely heavily on statistical data over case studies. This reliance is in strong contrast to the situation in anthropology and political science, which tend to be case-study oriented, and in weak contrast to sociology, whose practitioners rely both on statistical data and on case studies. The economic approach is to have lean theories, with few variables included. Economic theories are not meant to capture all the relevant explanatory elements for a phenomenon, just the most important ones; they are not meant to be fully descriptive theories. While some people consider this characteristic a flaw of economics, economists consider it an asset to have simple analytical models. Additionally, while the models may be simple analytically, they are often fairly complicated statistically, unlike the modeling techniques used in the other social sciences (and in biology).

Recently, economists (and other scientists, both natural and social) have spent a great deal of time considering how to deal with the general and pervasive problem of *sample selection bias*, which occurs when an unobserved variable influences selection of who is observed in a particular category. For example, working women may be significantly different than nonworking women in terms of their motivation and ability to perform paid work. Therefore, results obtained from studying only working women may not apply to all women. These problems are pervasive in economic empirical work because economists try to develop simple models (where they, for instance, do not include measures of motivation) and because of data limitations, but economists have also attempted to develop statistical methods for overcoming them. This issue will come up over and over again in the book as a critique of various interpretations of results from statistical studies.

Economists generally hold that people will act so as to maximize their own outcomes – that is, act in self-interested ways. However, there are several distinct schools of economics that vary mainly in their thinking as to the kinds of constraints people face in their ability to act in their own interests. Neoclassical economists see no constraints other than income, or the ability to earn income. Marxian economists see limits on the ability of most people to further their self-interests due to their position in the class system. Only capitalists have the ability to create enough income through ownership of capital to further their self-interests; working-class persons are able only to earn enough to stay alive, never to move beyond their basic survival level. Feminist economists see limits on women's full participation in the economic system. Institutional economists see constraints in the form of institutions such as governments, unions, and legal and traditional systems; therefore institutions are created not to help people further their self-interests but to satisfy other social goals. Neoclassical economists are more inclined to see institutions as furthering self-interests, at least for particular social groups.

The institution of the family is, perhaps, the area over which the four groups of economists disagree the most as to role and impact. Neoclassical economists tend to analyze the family as if it were one unit maximizing the joint well-being of its members; individual self-interests combine seamlessly into family self-interest. More recent work has considered how bargaining is carried out within families. We will consider alternative interpretations of what happens within families in Chapter 3.

Critiques of the economic approach

The economic approach – in particular, the assumption of rational, self-interested behavior – has been criticized both inside and outside the profession. Much of the criticism from outside the profession, particularly concerning the areas covered by the economics of gender, has taken the form of questioning whether economic analysis is an appropriate tool for studying particular phenomena at all. Also, the hegemony of neoclassical economics and its perceived lack of openness to input from other fields and from alternative approaches within economics has been perceived as a drawback.

Is economics an imperialist science?

Has economics been attempting to take over the traditional subject matter of other disciplines? It is clear that economists have increasingly ventured into studying areas that were traditionally considered to fall within other disciplines. The economic theory of politics, which argues that policymakers continue to act in self-interested ways rather than for the public good, dates from the late 1950s. The economic theory of education, which argues that education is an investment good of which individuals rationally decide how much to purchase, dates from the early 1960s. The economic theory of marriage and divorce, which argues that family formation and dissolution are affected by rational self-interest, dates from the early 1970s. Today, economists routinely write about practically every topic in the social sciences, including sports, crime, poverty, the legal system, and sexuality. But not all economists, including many who work on these "fringe" topics, argue for the universal applicability of the rational self-interest model. However, the Chicago school of economics has been characterized as a "revolutionary movement," in which rational-choice egoism is applied to everything within sight. One critic states that "from the perspective of the Chicago school, there is no behavior that is *not* interpretable as economic, however altruistic, emotional, disinterested, and compassionate it may seem to others."[43]

What determines the boundaries between disciplines, and are there rules that should not be crossed? Ronald Coase, a Nobel prize winner in economics, argued that the binding forces that create a discipline are one or more of the following:[44]

1. common analysis techniques/methodology;
2. common theory or approach to problems;
3. common subject matter.

However, he believes that, in the long run, common subject matter defines the discipline. In other words, while currently people who call themselves economists are making forays into areas traditionally considered to fall in sociology or political science, what will happen is that people who call themselves sociologists and political scientists will increasingly adopt the methodology and theory that economists have been using. In this sense, the disciplines will move closer together in terms of type of methodology and theory used, but people will still define themselves by what they study.

Clearly, then, we also need a definition of economics (and also a definition of sociology and of political science). While many different definitions have been proposed, Coase leans towards use of a somewhat nebulous definition, such as economics as the study of human actions in the ordinary business of life, or economics as the study of the operation of economic organizations, although he realizes that these definitions depend on a shared understanding of what particular terms such as "ordinary business" mean and that they tend to be somewhat circular in nature (for example, what is an economic organization?). He shies away from some of the even broader definitions proposed, such as economics as the science of human choice. This definition, which is one that I favor, implies that the existence of scarcity is the constraint on topics of interest to economists. For example, if there is no shortage of love, then love is not a topic of interest to economists.

Nevertheless, even if Coase is right in the long run, why is it that economists are making forays into other fields, rather than other social scientists foraying into economics? Reuven Brenner, another eminent economist, argues that this is related to the strength of the central theoretical paradigm of rational self-interest in economics.[45] Partly this is just a matter of having the available bodies to lead forays. He argues that, "in fields lacking a paradigm, scientists have to start each time from the very first principles."[46] This is naturally going to be more time-consuming and will lead to the feeling that the field is not building on itself. By contrast, most economists who write research papers assume that all their readers share the same basic understanding of concepts, and they proceed to develop new concepts and expand on the basic ideas of the field. This is a "survival of the fittest" argument: those academic disciplines that are not subject to constant self-doubt have the energy to expand their boundaries and are better able to recruit new followers.

Many observers find the spread of economics very alarming. After all, the economic paradigm, even though it may be an efficient base to build a discipline upon, may not actually be a good description of human behavior. Additionally, the ability of certain fields to feed upon results from each other and therefore "conquer" a wider range of disciplinary opponents is seen as an alarming trend by some observers. One commentator, Barry Schwartz, reviews and criticizes the picture of human nature shared by economics, evolutionary biology (specifically sociobiology), and behavior theory (a branch of psychology that emphasizes the reinforcement mechanism in determining human behavior).[47] He argues that these three fields together have painted a picture of people who are greedy, selfish individualists by *nature*. He contends that it is social conditions that make people this way and that these fields are mistaking local cultural and historical truths about people for natural laws. He points out that, in fact, the earliest economists (Adam Smith being the prime example) assumed that man had a moral side as well as an economic side and that both sides came into play in different circumstances and could be attributed to different causal factors. Instead, over the intervening two centuries since Adam Smith, moral philosophy has evolved into social science. This evolution has led to the widespread belief that morality is developed through nature as well, rather than just through nurture. The implication throughout Schwartz's book is that the rise of these disciplines is an alarming trend because it implies that humans cannot be improved through society, but that society is subject to human nature. If people go around believing this, the train of thought continues, then we will end up in a worse world than if we actively took steps to improve people's moral state.

Criticism within the economics profession

While some critics have characterized economists as being unconcerned with morality and disrespectful of constraints on self-interest, such as love and respect for tradition,[48] most economists in fact believe both that a world composed solely of rational, selfish individuals would be a bad place to live and that the world we live in is not so composed. Additionally, most economists would disagree with the assertion that they are making the world a worse place to live in through espousing basic economic principles. However, they generally do believe that neoclassical economic theory is a useful conceptual starting point for thinking about the world. They disagree about whether it is also an ending point and to what degree evolutionary biology can be coupled with economics in order to strengthen economic predictions. The Chicago school of economics, which has been at the forefront pushing out the boundaries of economics, has also contained the strongest advocates of the general applicability of neoclassical economic theory in these areas is weakened. However, over time, as other economists enter the boundary areas of which the economics of gender is one, the monoculture of neoclassical economic theory in these areas is weakened. In fact, as you will see in this book, many economists use concepts that originated with sociologists, anthropologists, psychologists, and political scientists.

This book attempts to tread the middle ground by presenting a consistent picture of how neoclassical economic theory can be applied to gender issues but also making clear at which points the available empirical evidence does not lend solid support to this body of theory. Additionally, there are many points at which neoclassical economic theory does not give a clear-cut prediction or interpretation of events. For some of these topics, such as labor market discrimination and the role of the family, alternative explanations are available, both within and without economics, and they will be discussed as well.

Other academic perspectives

Researchers in other fields, including geography, history, the humanities, and the natural sciences other than biology, also have theories and evidence to offer about gender differences. Additionally, other fields have constituted an integral part of the interdisciplinary field of women's studies. We will consider geographers' perspectives on gender at several points in the book, as well as historians' perspectives at length in Part V.

Communication between academic disciplines

In general, communication between academic disciplines is limited by the ability of people to comprehend jargon across fields, invest time in reading different academic literatures, and generally overcome the current academic training system, which requires a person both to identify with a particular discipline and to become knowledgeable in only a certain area of that discipline (particularly, given the current criteria for receiving tenure). Nonetheless, most people studying gender issues recognize that knowledge of how other disciplines approach the questions of gender differences is required in order to make real progress in one's own area. Interdisciplinary contacts have become widespread, and the label of "academic feminism" has served as a rallying flag under which people in different academic disciplines have gathered.

The rise of academic feminism

Academic feminism has three main accomplishments to date: (1) it has documented the extent to which academia has excluded women, both as researchers[49] and as subjects; (2) it has begun to redress these shortcomings;[50] and (3) it has opened up the question of how gender shapes scientific inquiry and thought in general. In fact, one prominent academic feminist, Evelyn Fox Keller, argues that "both gender and science are socially constructed categories."[51]

Academic feminism has led to the creation of women's studies as an interdisciplinary field. This has allowed the three parts of the academic feminist research agenda to be brought together, emphasizing the similarity in feminists' approach, regardless of academic discipline: namely, the primacy of gender as a category affecting both human thought and behavior. This has been an extremely successful interdisciplinary field because it combines coherence of subject matter (namely, redressing the lack of attention to women's experience as different from men's experience in the different academic disciplines) with the existence of a central paradigm.

Women's studies has generally remained women's studies rather than gender studies, a fact partly due to the subject emphasis, partly to political constraints. Most of the people working in women's studies are women, and few people are interested in documenting male experiences, arguing that the traditional academic disciplines have been doing just that.[52]

Gender and metaphor in the language of economics

Economists have only recently begun to consider how gender has shaped their discipline.[53] For example, in a session on "feminism and economic argument" at the 1989 American Economic Association meetings (the first ever devoted to the topic at this annual national convention), three economists gave papers arguing that male domination of the field of economics has led to the masculinization of the language and methodology used in economics. The following are some excerpts from their papers:

> As *social* science, economics takes a "feminine" role vis à vis mathematics and the physical sciences. Human behavior is a "softer" subject than abstract math or the natural world, less amenable to quantitative (as opposed to qualitative) description or formulation in terms of "laws." This presents a problem for those economists who, perhaps to maintain a clear-cut gender self-image, need to see their work as consistently masculine. Consider the language used in the statement of purpose of the Econometric Society, which can be found inside the back cover of every issue of Econometrica:
>
> > The Society shall operate as a completely disinterested, scientific organization, without political, social, financial or nationalistic bias. Its main object shall be to promote studies that aim at the unification of the theoretical-quantitative and the empirical-quantitative approaches to economic problems and that are penetrated by constructive and rigorous thinking similar to that which has come to dominate in the natural sciences.
>
> Translated, I suggest that this says, "Hey guys, we want to penetrate and dominate, too!"[54]

> 'What is dear to male economists is not the thing itself but their model of the thing. Disproportionately they scorn the rich and multiple stories of the thing itself. They want to impose their favorite metaphors on the world . . . Male economists sneer at the anecdote, though it gives them most of their factual beliefs . . . self-consciousness about analogizing and storytelling are feminine in our culture; literalism, a belief in The Reality of this or that analogy or story, is masculine.'[55]

> 'In the early neoclassical labor supply literature, there was no question of incorporating the concept of gender into the theory because there were no women. . . . prior to the 1960's women and the economic activity of women were virtually invisible. . . . The definition of labor coincided with men's economic activity. The alternative was called leisure, which ignored the household and childraising activities of women. The very term "women workers" indicates an exception, or an anomaly, requiring a modifier. The term "men workers" seems awkward.'[56]

Divisions in feminist thought

The two broad feminist perspectives on gender divisions in society have been termed the "maximalist" and "minimalist" perspectives.[57] The maximalist perspective, also called *essentialism*, holds that there are basic differences between the sexes. Some proponents believe these differences are biologically determined; others believe that "they are a product of social conditioning (typically set early in life) or lodged in the differing psyche of the sexes by the psychoanalytic processes that create identity";[58] still others are willing to give partial credit to all of these factors. In any case, proponents believe that these differences are deeply rooted and result in different approaches to the world, in some cases creating a distinct "women's culture." The political implications of this view are that these differences benefit society and ought to be recognized and rewarded; an extreme view is that "women's culture" is superior to, or at least less dangerous than, the current "men's culture" that society is subject to, and that women's culture should supplant men's culture, a situation that may require separatism on the part of women.[59]

The minimalist perspective, also called *constructivism*, is that the two sexes are fundamentally similar, and that gender differences linked to sexual functions (e.g., reproduction)are not invariably or necessarily related to psychological traits or social roles. In Fuchs Epstein's words, "This perspective suggests that most gender differences are not as deeply rooted or immutable as has been believed, that they are relatively superficial, and that they are socially constructed (and elaborated in the culture through myths, law, and folkways) and kept in place by the way each sex is positioned in the social structure. This perspective is critical of the notion of a separate women's culture and of the idea that women's psyches or values are different from men's. This view ascribes observed differences in behavior to a social control system that prescribes and proscribes specific behaviors for women and men."[60]

Maximalism/essentialism has also come under attack from feminists who are concerned that race and class differences are obscured by the focus on gender as the critical source of human differences. If, for instance, black and white women differ in many ways, then it becomes less likely that there is a specific women's culture, let alone that it would be desirable to act as if there were one. We will consider the validity of essentialism and minimalism throughout the book, particularly in Chapter 15, which considers different cultural and racial experiences in U.S. economic history.

Summary

The economics of gender is the area in economics that explicitly considers the effects of having two genders as they interact in families, firms, and markets. Economics and many other academic disciplines have considered gender differences, including the question of whether or not gender differences are distinct from sex differences. Two debates run throughout discussions of gender differences: the heredity vs. environment debate about the causes of gender differences and, more recently, the essentialism vs. minimalism debate about the depth of gender differences. While the adage, "Economics is what economists do," can be applied to all the disciplines considered herein, there are useful insights to be gained from considering the bodies of knowledge generated by members of the different disciplines, from thinking about how to define the different fields, and from thinking about how the different fields interact.

Endnotes

1. Adulthood varies in definition across cultures, but the lower limit on adulthood can be set as the onset of puberty.
2. Genetic sex, determined by the chromosomes, is overlaid during human development by hormonal sex, which is determined by the ratios of androgens to estrogens. Hormonal sex is normally, though not always, appropriate to genetic sex. Sex characteristics are therefore determined by both genetic and hormonal sex. Anne Fausto-Sterling, in "How Many Sexes Are There?" *The New York Times* (March 12, 1993): A29, provides an interesting discussion of the range of hermaphroditic outcomes found in humans.

3. I choose not to deal with the rare cases in which a person may have an extra chromosome.

4. There are, of course, many cases, both actual and literary, of persons who manage to pass as a member of the opposite sex. There are fewer cases in which observers are unable to classify a person at all. In the early 1990s, the television comedy show "Saturday Night Live" had a recurrent skit (and a movie was made) involving the inability of observers to determine whether a character named Pat was male or female.

5. Handedness: "Left-handedness: Sinister Origins," *The Economist* (February 15, 1997): 80. Television-watching figures are from John P. Robinson, "I Love My TV," *American Demographics* 12, no. 9 (September 1990): 27, and refer to primary viewing (undivided attention) among men and women ages 18–64 in 1985. The other figures are from Daniel Evan Weiss, *The Great Divide: How Females and Males Really Differ* (New York: Poseidon, 1991): 179, 242, 244; original source is *Roper Reports* (September 1988, December 1988, February 1989).

6. Figures are for 1993; source is *Statistical Abstract of the United States* (1996): 96 (Table 131).

7. Figures are for 1994; source is U.S. Dept. of Justice, *Sourcebook of Criminal Justice Statistics* (1995): 189 (Table 2.79), 232 (Table 3.3), 548 (Table 6.12).

8. Weiss, *op. cit.*: 143; original source is *Roper Reports* (September 1988).

9. Weiss, *op. cit.*: 177; original source is *USA Today* (December 13, 1989).

10. Weiss, *op. cit.*: 108; original source is New York Stock Exchange, *Shareownership 1985*.

11. Weiss, *op. cit.*: 151; original source is R.H. Brustein Associates Market Research, *America in the Eighties* (1985).

12. Personal communication with Marcia Walton, Psychology Department, Rhodes College.

13. See Ellen Peck and Judith Senderowitz (eds.), *Pronatalism: The Myth of Mom & Apple Pie* (New York: Thomas Crowell, 1974).

14. *The New American Webster Handy College Dictionary* (New York: Signet, 1981).

15. Quoted in David L. Kirp, Mark G. Yudoff, and Marlene Strong Franks, *Gender Justice* (Chicago, Ill.: University of Chicago, 1986): 53.

16. See E.O. Wilson, *On Human Nature* (Cambridge, Mass.: Harvard University, 1978): 222. See also *Sociobiology: The New Synthesis* (Cambridge, Mass.: Harvard University, 1975).

17. Cf. Steven Goldberg, *The Inevitability of Patriarchy* (New York: Morrow, 1973).

18. Margot I. Duley, Karen Sinclair, and Mary I. Edwards, "Biology Versus Culture," *The Cross-Cultural Study of Women: A Comprehensive Guide*, eds. Margot I. Duley and Mary I. Edwards (New York: Feminist Press, City University of New York, 1986): 3–25.

19. Cf. Ruth Blier, *Science and Gender: A Critique of Biology and Its Theories on Women* (New York: Pergamon, 1984); Anne Fausto-Sterling, *Myths of Gender: Biological Theories About Women and Men* (New York: Basic Books, 1985).

20. According to R.C. Lewontin, Steven Rose, and Leon J. Kamin in *Not in Our Genes: Biology, Ideology, and Human Nature* (New York: Pantheon, 1984): 158, there are three general areas of difficulty in using analogies to male dominance in other species as supporting evidence for the theory of a biological basis of male dominance in humans:

    1. Inappropriate labeling of behavior, e.g., lion and "harem," where the lionesses are not dependent on the male (the opposite is true).
    2. Partial observations by observer of social interactions, e.g., the position along one dominance continuum need not imply a matching position on other continua.
    3. We have only small numbers of observations on a small number of species in a limited range of environments.

21. Lewontin, Rose, and Kamin, *op. cit.*: 135.

22. Cynthia Fuchs Epstein, in *Deceptive Distinctions: Sex, Gender and the Social Order* (New Haven, Conn.: Yale University, 1988): 6, cites the well-known biologist Stephen J. Gould as one who holds this view.

23. C.P. Benbow and J.C. Stanley, "Sex Differences in Mathematical Ability: Fact or Artifact," *Science* 210, no. 4475 (December 12, 1980): 1262–1264.

24. Walter R. Gove, "Sex Differences in the Epidemiology of Mental Disorder: Evidence and Explanations," *Gender and Disordered Behavior: Sex Differences in Psychopathology*, eds. Edith S. Gomberg and Violet Franks (New York: Brunner/Mazel, 1979): 23–68. Women outnumber men in both psychosis and neurosis admissions.

25. Eleanor Emmons Maccoby and Carol Nagy Jacklin, *The Psychology of Sex Differences* (Stanford, Calif.: Stanford University, 1974). See Anne Fausto-Sterling (1985), Chapter Two, for a reevaluation of Maccoby and Jacklin's discussion of sex-related cognitive differences.

26. The seminal work in this area that has spawned much subsequent debate is Carol Gilligan, *In a Different Voice: Psychological Theory and Women's Development* (Cambridge, Mass.: Harvard University, 1982). See Carol Tavris, *The Mismeasure of Woman* (New York: Simon & Schuster, 1992): Chapter Two, for a critical assessment of Gilligan's findings and subsequent work in this vein.

27. Mary Field Belenky, Blythe McVicker Clinchy, Nancy Rule Goldberger, and Jill Mattuck Tarule, *Women's Ways of Knowing: The Development of Self, Voice, and Mind* (New York: Basic Books, 1986). For a discussion of the influence and critiques of this book, see Daphne Patai and Noretta Koertge, *Professing Feministm: Cautionary Tales from the Strange World of Women's Studies* (New York: Basic Books, 1994): Chapter 7.

28. Ernestine Friedl, *Women and Men: An Anthropologist's View* (New York: Holt, Rinehart & Winston, 1984): 4.

29. Michelle Zimbalist Rosaldo and Louise Lamphere (eds.), *Women, Culture, and Society* (Stanford, Calif.: Stanford University, 1974), is an early attempt to correct bias in anthropological teaching materials towards ignoring women and their activities.

30. Cf. Marvin Harris, *Cultural Materialism: The Struggle for a Science of Culture* (New York: Random House, 1979).

31. Maxine L. Margolis, *Mothers and Such: Views of American Women and Why They Changed* (Berkeley, Calif.: University of California, 1984): 3.

32. Friedl, *op. cit.*: 7–10.

33. Alan Wolfe, *Whose Keeper? Social Science and Moral Obligation* (Berkeley, Calif.: University of California, 1989): 191.

34. Wolfe, *op. cit.*: 188.

35. Personal communication with Victoria Alexander, Sociology Department, Harvard University.

36. Personal communication with Victoria Alexander, Sociology Department, Harvard University. See also Amy S. Wharton, "The Social Construction of Gender and Race in Organizations: A Social Identity and Group Mobilization Perspective," *Research in the Sociology of Organizations* 10 (1992): 55–84.

37. Epstein, *op. cit.*

38. Epstein, *op. cit.*: 15, disapprovingly remarks that "an insistence that gender differences are rooted in the most basic nature of men and women still colors the work of respected scholars in such disciplines as economics, sociology, psychology, and the hybrid field of sociobiology."

39. William J. Goode, "Why Men Resist," *Rethinking the Family: Some Feminist Questions*, eds. Barrie Thorne and Marilyn Yalom (New York: Longman, 1982): 131–150.

40. Susan Moller Okin, *Justice, Gender, and the Family* (New York: Basic Books, 1989).

41. Kirp, Yudoff, and Franks, *op. cit.*: 63; 81.

42. Kirp, Yudoff, and Franks, *op. cit.*: 203.

43. Wolfe, *op. cit.*: 31–32.

44. Ronald H. Coase, "Economics and Contiguous Disciplines," *Journal of Legal Studies* 7, no. 2 (June 1978): 201–211.

45. Reuven Brenner, "Economics – An Imperialist Science?" *Journal of Legal Studies* 9, no. 1 (January 1980): 179–188.

46. Brenner, *op. cit.*: 184.

47. Barry Schwartz, *The Battle for Human Nature: Science, Morality and Human Life* (New York: W.W. Norton, 1986).

48. Wolfe, *loc. cit.*

49. For the case of economics, see Mary Ann Dimand, Robert W. Dimand, and Evelyn L. Forget (eds.), *Women of Value: Feminist Essays on the History of Women in Economics* (Aldershot, United Kingdom: Edward Elgar, 1995).

50. Cf. Dale Spender (ed.), *Men's Studies Modified: The Impact of Feminism on the Academic Disciplines* (Oxford, United Kingdom: Pergamon, 1981).

51. Evelyn Fox Keller, *Reflections on Gender and Science* (New Haven, Conn.: Yale University, 1985): 3.

52. An early exception to the general focus on women is James A. Doyle, *The Male Experience* (Dubuque, Iowa: Wm. C. Brown, 1983), which contains chapters on historical, biological, sociological, and psychological views of male experience.

53. See Frances R. Woolley, "The Feminist Challenge to Neoclassical Economics," *Cambridge Journal of Economics* 17, no. 4 (December 1993): 485–500, and relevant listings in the readings list at the end of the chapter.

54. Julie A. Nelson, "Gender, Metaphor, and the Definition of Economics," *Economics and Philosophy* 8 (April 1992): 108–109. Reprinted with permission.

55. Deirdre N. McCloskey, "Some Consequences of a Feminine Economics," paper presented at 1989 American Economic Association conference (December 1989): 17–18, 23. Reprinted with permission.

56. Lisa Jo Brown, "Gender and Economic Analysis: A Feminist Perspective," paper presented at 1989 American Economic Association conference (December 1989): 6–8. Reprinted with permission.

57. Epstein, *op. cit.*: 25, attributes this terminology to Catherine Stimpson.

58. *Ibid.*

59. An early and influential book espousing this view is Shulamith Firestone, *The Dialectic of Sex: The Case for Feminist Revolution* (New York: Morrow, 1970).

60. Epstein, *loc. cit.* One might still ask why social control exists, but the answer need not be based in biology.

61. Thorstein Veblen, *The Theory of the Leisure Class* (1899; reprinted in New York by Dover, 1994): 3.

62. "The Trouble with Men," *The Economist* (September 28, 1996): 19.

63. Charlotte Perkins Gilman, *The Man-Made World: or Our Andocentric Culture* (New York: Charlton, 1911): 250.

*F*urther reading

Beasley, Chris (1994). *Sexual Economyths: Conceiving a Feminist Economics.* New York: St. Martin's. Comes at the question of what a theory of feminist economics should be from a Marxian background.

Cherry, Robert D. (1989). *Discrimination: Its Economic Impact on Blacks, Women, and Jews.* Lexington, Mass.: Lexington Books. Handbook/textbook; contrasts conservative, liberal, and radical (Marxist) economic views on the causes and effects of discrimination.

Ferber, Marianne A. and Julie A. Nelson (eds.) (1993). *Beyond Economic Man: Feminist Theory and Economics.* Chicago, Ill.: University of Chicago. The first published collection of essays to "examine central tenets of economics from a feminist point of view."

Folbre, Nancy (1994). *Who Pays for the Kids? Gender and the Structures of Constraint.* London and New York: Routledge. Wide-ranging and stimulating discussion of political economy and gender, including useful comparisons of the different economist paradigms.

History of Political Economy (1993). Vol. 25, no. 1 (Spring). Contains a minisymposium: "Feminist Theory and the History of Economic Thought."

Kuiper, Edith and Jolande Sap (eds.) (1995). *Out of the Margin: Feminist Perspectives on Economics.* London and New York: Routledge. The second published collection of essays in feminist economics; very thought-provoking.

Nelson, Julie A. (1996). *Feminism, Objectivity and Economics.* London and New York: Routledge. Interesting discussion of whether and how the study of economics is gendered.

—— (1995). "Feminism and Economics," *Journal of Economic Perspectives* 9, no. 2 (Spring): 131–148. Useful introductory essay on feminist thinking applied to economics.

Peterson, Janice and Doug Brown (eds.) (1994). *The Economic Status of Women Under Capitalism: Institutional Economics and Feminist Theory.* Aldershot, UK and Brookfield, Vermont: Edward Elgar. A set of essays exploring the connections between institutionalism and feminism.

Discussion questions

1. Consider the Focus on gender differences. Which of these strike you as significant? Which appear to be manifestations of deeper differences between women and men?

2. Institutionalist economist Thorstein Veblen wrote in 1899: "There is in all barbarian communities a profound sense of the disparity between man's and woman's work. His work may conduce to the maintenance of the group, but it is felt that it does so through an excellence and an efficacy of a kind that cannot without derogation be compared with the uneventful diligence of the women."[61] What does he mean by this? Is this true in current society?

3. In an editorial on the topic of men's future usefulness, *The Economist* said: "in terms of cultural evolution, men may well have done their job: they have pretty much set up modern civilisations and technologies; they may not be needed to keep them going. Knowledge-based societies, with their stress on brain not brawn, may be safer in women's hands."[62] What types of evidence might lead a journalist to make this sort of statement? Is this an assertion that an economist would make? How might an economist counter this claim?

4. Feminist Charlotte Perkins Gilman wrote in 1911: "We can make no safe assumption as to what, if any, distinction there will be in the free human work for men and women, until we have seen generation after generation grow up under absolutely equal conditions."[63] Is this an assertion that a scientist would make? Is it true? Could conditions ever be absolutely equal?

5. Do you think that the institution of the family is a constraint or a help for individuals in attaining their self-interests? Is it more or less helpful compared with other social institutions?

6. What do you think it means to say that the family is "beyond justice?"

7. Give examples from your life of when you might use traditional, command-following, heuristic, irrational, and rational behavior.

8. What other criteria besides scarcity do you see as affecting individual and societal decision making?

9. What do you see as the major similarities and differences between academic disciplines in their approach to gender differences? If you had to classify disciplines as being more supportive of nature or nurture theories of human differences, how would you rank them?

10. Consider the Focus on gender and metaphor in the language of economics. Is it inevitable that domination by one gender would affect the language and methodology used in a field of study? What factors might this depend on?

Appendix
The repercussions of scarcity

In order to discuss gender-related issues from an economic point of view, some terms must first be introduced. This appendix is the first of the set of appendices in this book that develop the theoretical apparatus necessary to understand economists' views at relevant points in the text. It contains fundamental concepts of economic theory that will be used in the chapters to come.

The basic concept underlying the field of economics is that humans have limited resources but unlimited wants. This leads to the problem of how to allocate those resources – at the individual level, the family level, the societal level, and the world level. This fundamental idea, that there is a problem of *scarcity*, is then expanded into a theory of how to efficiently allocate resources so as to best choose between competing uses. Concepts that then arise include *opportunity cost, marginal benefit* and *marginal cost, marginal utility*, and the tools used to describe market interactions: *supply* and *demand curves* and *competitive* and *non-competitive markets*, such as *monopolies* and *monopsonies*. These concepts are introduced herein and will be reinforced in future chapters with additional examples and applications.[1]

Opportunity cost

To economists, the cost of allocating a resource to a particular use is the lost benefit that would have come from using the resource in its next best alternative. This idea of *opportunity cost* can be readily applied to both time and money, the fundamental resources to be allocated by individuals. In fact, the opportunity cost of time can be measured in monetary terms, and the opportunity cost of money can be measured by how long it took you to earn it. For instance, as students, you are constantly faced with the decision of how to spend your time. Should you spend an evening studying, or watching a movie with friends, or working at your part-time job? If you decide to study, you have determined that the value of the time spent in studying, in its impact on your grades and therefore your eventual probability of getting a well-paying job, is higher than its value in terms of either the money you could earn by working or the enjoyment you forego by not joining your friends at the movies. If you also would have chosen to work over going to the movies if those were the only two choices available, then we can say that the opportunity cost of the time spent studying is equal to the foregone wages plus whatever enjoyment (if any) you would have gained from working. Or, you may need to subtract some value from wages to make up for the lack of enjoyment of working.

The marginal vs. total distinction

An important concept in economics that is critical in determining efficient allocation of resources is the idea of using *marginal* rather than average or total benefits and costs as the basis of decisions about how much of a good or service to purchase. A marginal benefit or cost is the benefit or cost associated with the last unit purchased.

Marginal benefits and costs

It is important to distinguish between the benefit or cost of an action at the margin and the benefit or cost of the total action. The best measure of whether a resource is being properly allocated is to see for the last (marginal) unit of the resource used, if its benefit in a particular use exceeds or is less than its cost. Only when marginal benefit is equal to marginal cost are resources properly allocated. For instance, consider a firm deciding whether or not to hire an additional worker to produce output. The net benefit (change in benefit minus the change in cost) to the firm of the hire will be the increase in *profit* that the worker would generate, where profits are calculated as total revenue minus total costs. If the worker generates an increase in profit, then the firm should hire the worker. The firm continues making this decision for each additional worker until it reaches the point where hiring an additional worker would lead to a decrease in profit.

Marginal utility

A person's satisfaction, or happiness, upon consuming a good or service cannot be directly measured, although we can discover the opportunity cost of the good or service by questioning the person about alternatives. Nevertheless, economists have developed the concept of *utility* to discuss measurement of total and marginal satisfaction generated from consumption of a good or service. The rule for efficient allocation of a person's budget among alternative uses is to judge whether the *marginal utility* (MU), or increment to happiness caused by consumption of a purchase, is higher than for any alternative use of the money. The general rule for a person to follow in, say, allocating money between apples and oranges is to make sure that the marginal utility generated by the last dollar spent is equal across all possible uses of that dollar. In other words, the amount of marginal utility generated by the last piece of fruit eaten divided by the price (P) of that piece of fruit must be equal for apples and oranges:

$$\frac{MU_{apple}}{P_{apple}} = \frac{MU_{orange}}{P_{orange}}, \text{ or } \frac{MU_{apple}}{MU_{orange}} = \frac{P_{apple}}{P_{orange}}$$

If this equation did not hold, then a person could increase utility by shifting purchases towards the fruit that is generating more utility per dollar (or other unit of money) spent.

The number of units already consumed affects the marginal utility of the additional unit. Under the concept of *decreasing marginal utility*, as an individual consumes more and more of a commodity, the additional utility generated by consuming another unit, or the marginal utility, becomes smaller and smaller. This psychological assumption made by economists implies that humans will, in general, diversify their consumption across a range of goods and services. Therefore, if you have already eaten several apples, we would predict that you are more likely to eat an orange than another apple. In applying this concept to time use, if you have already watched several movies today, you are more likely to decide to do some studying or go to work than to watch another movie then if you have not yet seen any movies today.

Markets

In economists' view, *markets* are the critical mechanism for making sure that goods and services are allocated efficiently between persons. A *market* is a situation in which persons come together to buy and sell a particular good or service. There are *product markets*, where outputs of goods and services such as apples, cars, and insurance are sold, and *factor markets*, where production inputs (both goods and services) such as oil, machines, and labor are sold. There are also *financial markets*, where financial instruments such as stocks, bonds, and currencies are traded. These represent claims on outputs of goods and services through the intermediary of money. Since in this book we will be discussing at length markets for different types of labor, market concepts will mostly be illustrated by examples of *labor markets*. In a *labor market,* persons sell their time to firms (both nonprofit and for profit) and governmental bodies. Note that in this era of telecommunications and computers, markets need not necessarily exist physically at any particular location, and even if there is a physical location, all participants need not be at it in order to participate in the market. For instance, while the New York Stock Exchange has a fixed geographical location, people across the country may buy and sell stock over the computer or the telephone.

Markets need to be defined by location, time, and product. For example, at one point in the book we may be discussing the national labor market, which will refer to all persons employed or looking for a job, as well as all firms currently employing or seeking to hire workers, at a particular point in time in the United States. Or a market may be more specific, such as the market for doctors in San Francisco in January 1997. Note that it is difficult, if not impossible, to make sure that we are not being too broad or too narrow in our market definition. Are we talking about all doctors or particular specialties, such as pediatricians? Are there separate markets for male and female doctors? Are we including both hospitals and private practices in San Francisco? What about the surrounding suburban areas? What day in January? What hour? Defining a market is more of an art than a science, but for the purposes of this book, great attention to market definition is generally unnecessary.

The two sides of the market, buyers and sellers, can be described by demand and supply curves, which show for each side of the market what the relationship is between price and quantity demanded or supplied at that price. This graphical depiction of a market will be developed below using the example of a labor market.

The market supply curve

The supply curve for labor shows the relationship between the hourly wage offered and the number of hours persons offer to work at each wage. Each individual has a wage below which he or she will not work at all, called the *reservation wage*. We can draw a supply curve (*S*) for each individual's labor, as is done in Figure 1A.1 (i). The market supply curve is the horizontal sum of all the individual supply curves in the particular labor market, as shown in Figure 1A.1 (ii). If we make the simplifying assumption that all persons work 8-hour days, then the market supply curve shows how many are willing to work at each wage; note the relabelling of the horizontal axis in Figure 1A.1 (iii). The market supply curve for labor is generally upward-sloping: as the wage rises, more people are willing to work.[2]

The market demand curve

The demand curve for labor shows the relationship between the hourly wage offered and the number of hours firms wish to employ persons. Each firm has a labor demand curve that begins at a particular wage, above which the firm is not willing to hire even an hour's worth of labor. The demand curve for labor is downward-sloping: as the wage falls, firms find it profitable to hire more labor. We can draw a labor demand curve (*D*) for each firm,

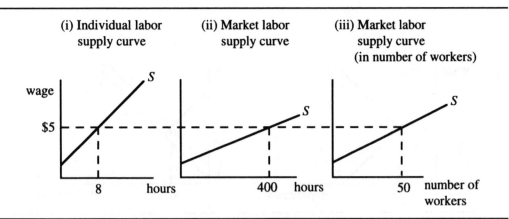

FIGURE IA.I   Individual and market labor supply curves

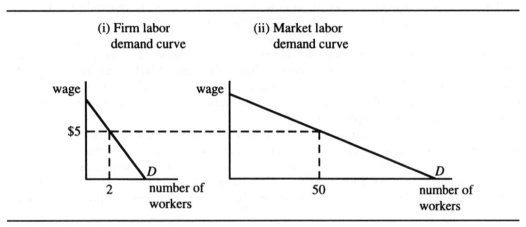

FIGURE IA.2   Firm and market labor demand curves

as in Figure 1A.2 (i), again making the simplifying assumption that the quantity of labor demanded can be measured in 8-hour days, and that an 8-hour day is the standard amount per person hired. The market demand curve is the horizontal sum of all the firm demand curves in the particular labor market, as shown in Figure 1A.2 (ii). If there are 25 identical firms, then 50 workers will be hired at a wage of $5.

Outcomes for competitive markets

Competitive markets are markets in which no buyer or seller can individually influence the price; they are all *price-takers*. Economists often set the condition that a large number of buyers and sellers be present in the market to ensure that it operates competitively; additionally (or alternatively), the assumption is made that buyers and sellers can freely exit and enter the market. In a competitive market, the supply and demand curves are brought together to determine *equilibrium*, or *market-clearing*, price and quantity. This is considered to be an equilibrium point, because only at one price level are the two sides of the market

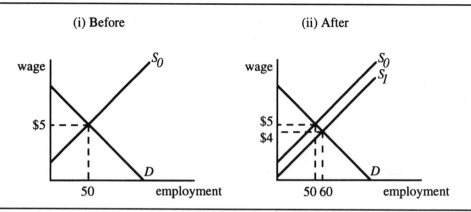

FIGURE IA.3 **Competitive labor market equilibrium before and after a shift in the supply curve**

in agreement as to how much each would like to trade. At prices above equilibrium, sellers want to sell more than buyers want to buy, so the quantity supplied exceeds the quantity demanded; this is the condition of *excess supply*. At prices below equilibrium price, buyers want to buy more than sellers want to sell; this is the condition of *excess demand*. In the case of labor markets, the price of a unit of labor is the *wage*. Market equilibrium is illustrated in Figure 1A.3, before and after the supply curve shifts to the right, indicating that more people are willing to work at every possible wage. This shift reduces the equilibrium wage and increases total employment.

Economists maintain a careful distinction between shifts in the supply or demand curve and changes in quantity supplied or demanded. For instance, a shift of the labor supply curve to the right will lower the equilibrium wage and induce an increase in the quantity of labor demanded. However, the demand curve has not shifted. Shifts in supply and demand curves are caused by a variety of factors and will be illustrated further in following chapters.

FOCUS

The intrinsic value paradox: Are diamonds and water like lawyers and child care workers?

The word VALUE, it is to be observed, has two different meanings, and sometimes expresses the utility of some particular object, and sometimes the power of purchasing other goods which the possession of that object conveys. The one may be called "value in use," the other, "value in exchange." The things which have the greatest interest in use have frequently little or no value in exchange; and on the contrary, those which have the greatest value in exchange have frequently little or no value in use. Nothing is more useful than water: but it will purchase scarce any thing; scarce any thing can be had in exchange for it. A diamond, on the contrary, has scarce any value in use; but a very great quantity of other goods may frequently be had in exchange for it." (Adam Smith, *Wealth of Nations*, 1776, Book 1, Chapter IV)

The problem of reconciling value in use and value in exchange, which Adam Smith noted but did not resolve, continued to puzzle economists well into the nineteenth century, until the distinction between total utility and marginal utility was drawn. When diamonds are inessential and water so essential to human life, why are diamonds so costly and water cheap? Part of the answer is on the supply, or cost side: diamonds are scarce and water plentiful. But the paradoxical part of the problem is explaining how this price difference is reconciled with the fact that people get more total utility from water than from diamonds (for, without water they would die). That is because price is affected on the demand side by marginal utility rather than total utility.

Compare the markets for diamonds and water as shown in Figure 1A.4 (i). Diamonds have a high, steep supply curve, representing the high cost of producing diamonds and the rising cost of finding additional diamonds. Water has a low, flat supply curve, representing the low unit cost of producing water to most communities and showing that increasing the volume of water does not generally raise the unit cost by much. The demand curve for water is higher than for diamonds, but it intersects the supply curve for water at a much lower price and greater quantity than the intersection for diamonds.

A rough measure of total utility is the area under the demand curve up to the point of market equilibrium. This is shown by the shaded areas in Figure 1A.4 (ii). It is clear that the market for water generates much greater total utility than the market for diamonds (think how many more people drink water than own diamonds). But the marginal utility of the last unit of water consumed is much lower than the marginal utility of the last diamond purchased. In the case of perfectly competitive markets, the ratio of the marginal utilities (MU) is equal to the ratio of the market prices (P):

$$\frac{MU_{water}}{MU_{diamonds}} = \frac{P_{water}}{P_{diamonds}} = \frac{1}{1000} \text{ (in this example)}$$

Now consider whether this reasoning is applicable to labor markets. One often hears people assert that various occupations are not paid in accordance with their value to society; for instance, that people working with children, such as teachers and child caretakers, are paid very little relative to the value of their jobs (1996 median weekly earnings for kindergarten and prekindergarten teachers: $361), while other people, such as lawyers, are overpaid relative to the value of their work (1996 median weekly earnings: $1149).[3] Consider whether Figure 1A.4 could be relabelled "lawyers" instead of diamonds and "child care workers" instead of water, and whether this is a useful analysis of the situation that leads to such different wages for the two occupations.

Paradoxically, this analysis implies that one way to increase the value of child care workers, and thereby increase their wages, is for people who care about child care to become lawyers instead of child care workers. By reducing the supply of child care workers and increasing the supply of lawyers, the wages will be driven up in the child care market and down in the market for lawyers. Imagine being lost in the middle of the desert while wearing a diamond ring. If you had been in the desert for awhile and were then given the opportunity to buy a gallon of water, you would be willing to trade your ring for the water. In this situation, the marginal utility of water would exceed that of the diamond.

Noncompetitive markets – monopoly and monopsony

In this section, we will consider two forms of noncompetitive markets: *monopoly*, the case of one seller and many buyers; and *monopsony*, the case of one buyer and many sellers. In each case, if only one party exists on one side of the market, that party can realize gains above the usual level available in a competitive market. These gains are achieved at a cost both to the other side of the market and to society in general.

(i) Supply and demand curves for diamonds and water

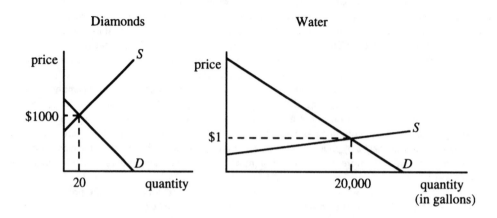

(ii) Measurement of total utility generated by diamonds and water

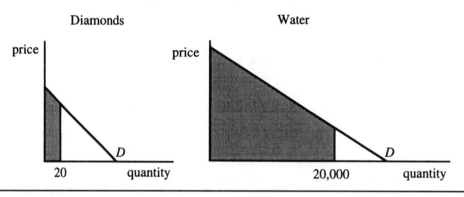

FIGURE 1A.4   Markets for diamonds and water

Monopoly

In the case of a monopoly, the seller is able to set the profit-maximizing price, which is the price corresponding to the quantity where *marginal revenue*, the increment to revenue of an additional unit sold, is equal to *marginal cost*, the increment to cost of another unit produced. Marginal revenue is actually less than price for a monopolist, because in order to sell an additional unit, the monopolist must lower the price, thereby losing revenue on all the units he/she could have sold at a higher price. The outcome under monopoly is a higher price and lower quantity traded than in a comparable competitive market. Unlike a competitive market, where free entry and exit ensures that economic profits are driven to zero for all sellers, a monopolist makes positive profits. Figure 1A.5 compares the monopoly (P_m, Q_m) and competitive (P_c, Q_c) outcomes.

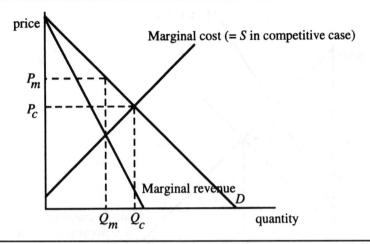

FIGURE 1A.5   Monopoly market equilibrium

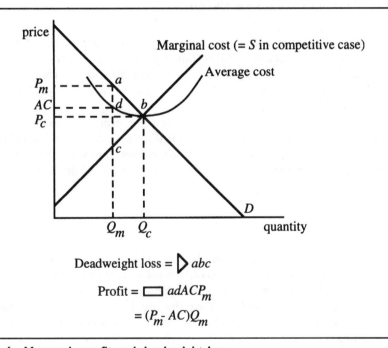

Deadweight loss = ▷ abc

Profit = ▢ $adACP_m$

= $(P_m - AC)Q_m$

FIGURE 1A.6   Monopoly profit and deadweight loss

Figure 1A.6 illustrates the amount of profit the monopolist achieves and the amount of cost this imposes on society. Consumers would like to buy more of the monopolized product and would still be willing to pay more than the competitive market price in order to buy more, but the monopolist is unwilling to lower the price in order to sell additional units, because this will lead to lower profit. They are, instead, forced to spend their money

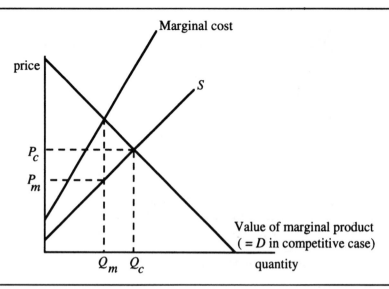

FIGURE 1A.7 Monopsony market equilibrium

on other, less-preferred products. Similarly, since output is below the competitive level, fewer workers and less capital are required in this industry, and these factors are used in areas of the economy where their productivity is lower. *Deadweight loss* is a rough measure of the loss of utility to society (measured in dollar terms) due to this misallocation of resources caused by the monopoly.

While it is hard to think of an industry with just one firm, there are many cases where firms have banded together in a *cartel* to act as if they were one seller and thereby realize higher profits than in the competitive case. In labor markets, unions can act as monopolists, allowing workers to band together and push for higher wages, while the union acts as their agent.

Monopsony

In the case of a monopsony, the buyer is able to set the price, which is the price corresponding to the quantity where marginal cost, the increment to cost of an additional unit bought, is equal to *value of marginal product*, the increment to revenue of another unit purchased. The marginal cost curve lies above the supply curve because the buyer realizes that hiring another worker or buying another unit will raise the cost on all the previous units that he/she could have bought at a lower price. The outcome under monopsony is a lower price and lower quantity traded than in a comparable competitive market. Figure 1A.7 compares the monosony (P_m, Q_m) and competitive (P_c, Q_c) outcomes.

This noncompetitive situation will prove to be particularly important to understand in evaluating arguments made in Part III of this book, where it is shown that economists have disagreed on the extent of monopsony power in the labor market and the level of its influence on wages. The classic example of labor market monopsony is the small town in West Virginia where the only employer in town is the coal mine.

Barriers to entry and exit

What allows monopsonies and monopolies to arise? In each case, the assumption of free entry and exit for the market has been violated. Monopolies are generally dependent upon the existence of *barriers to entry* that keep potential competitors out of the monopolized market. Unions can create barriers to entry by requiring all potential workers in an industry to join the union first. Another barrier to entry is sole control over an important input into production, such as a patent on a production process. Monopsonies generally hinge on "barriers to exit" (although that term is not generally used in economics). In the case of labor markets, people may be unable (or unwilling) to leave their town in order to look for better-paying jobs; this lack of labor mobility leads to the monopsony situation.

Barriers to entry, as we will see in later chapters, are very important in explaining wage differences between occupations and industries. By setting up credentialing systems, professional organizations can limit the supply of labor into an occupation. A cynical economist's view of the American Medical Association would be that its main function is to limit the supply of doctors and thereby raise the wages that doctors earn.

Policy Application: Effects of a minimum wage

Market outcomes can also be affected by various governmental policies that interfere with the market mechanisms determining price and quantity. For example, a quota may be set that artificially reduces quantity supplied and drives the price above the equilibrium level. Alternatively, price may be made subject to a ceiling or floor, which will affect quantity as well as overriding the market price. The analysis of these effects depends on whether the market is assumed to be competitive or noncompetitive. Additionally, we may want to consider the effects of governmental policies on related markets.

Consider the effects of setting a minimum wage in a particular labor market. A minimum wage is equivalent to a price floor for labor. If the current wage is above the minimum wage, then the minimum wage is nonbinding, since employers are paying higher than minimum anyway. However, if the current wage is below the minimum, imposition of a minimum wage will have one of two effects. Figure 1A.8 shows the two possible situations. In a competitive market (i), the minimum wage will lead to reduced employment and increased unemployment. In a monopsony labor market (ii), the minimum wage will lead to increased employment.

The imposition of a minimum wage in one labor market will affect other labor markets as well. First, assume that there is one national market for labor, in which all men and women participate, and that all men and women are equally productive (making them *perfect substitutes* as factors of production). Now imagine that the government enacts a law setting a minimum wage for men only above the current market-clearing, or equilibrium, wage. This has the effect of dividing the national labor market into two markets, one for men and one for women. As shown in Figure 1A.9, the imposition of a minimum wage leads to lower employment and higher unemployment in the *covered* market for male labor (particularly since men cannot move into the other labor market, save at great personal cost), while the *uncovered* market for female labor experiences an increase in labor demand (from D_0 to D_1), generating an increase in employment. Since the female labor supply curve

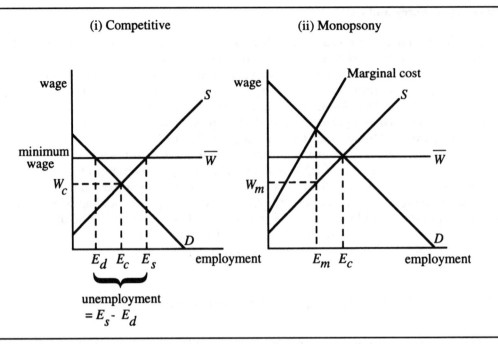

FIGURE 1A.8 Effects of a minimum wage on competitive and monopsony labor markets

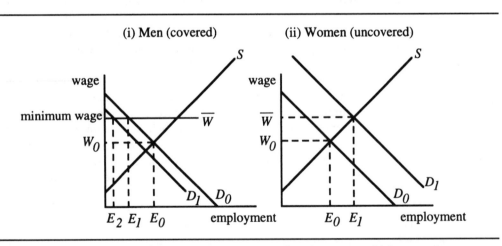

FIGURE 1A.9 Effects of a minimum wage on covered and uncovered labor markets

is upward-sloping, the wage will rise in this market – in fact, if women are perfect substitutes for men, the wage will rise to minimum wage level. We would expect to see overall production decline and the use of other factors of production, such as capital and energy, increase, causing a leftward shift of the demand curve for male labor (from D_0 to D_1). Total employment will decline.

Endnotes

1. For those wishing to see alternative treatments or wordings of the concepts covered in this appendix, there are innumerable textbooks of introductory economics available, all of which cover these topics. Textbooks go through editions so often that I will not refer to a particular year or edition. These concepts are so fundamental that their treatment will not alter much from version to version. Some introductory texts from my reference shelf are Paul A. Samuelson and William D. Nordhaus, *Economics* (New York: McGraw-Hill); Joseph E. Stiglitz, *Principles of Economics* (New York: W. W. Norton & Co.); Richard G. Lipsey and Paul N. Courant, *Economics* (New York: HarperCollins). Any other text you have access to will be suitable.
2. We will see in the appendix to Chapter 4 that an individual's supply curve may be downward-sloping over higher ranges of wages; theoretically this could be true for the market supply curve as well, but empirically labor market supply curves have not been found that display this characteristic; enough people enter at new higher wages to offset reduction of work by people already in the labor market.
3. *Employment and Earnings* 44, no. 1 (January 1997): 206 (Table 39).

Discussion questions

1. Draw a diagram of a labor market in equilibrium, as in Figure 1A.3(i). For each of the following changes, explain whether the supply or the demand curve for labor will shift, in which direction it will shift, and what will happen to wage and employment:

    (a) Men decide to retire at age 60 instead of age 65.
    (b) A new child labor law is passed outlawing work by persons under the age of 16.
    (c) Women are barred from working if they have children under the age of 6.
    (d) All cartels are broken.
    (e) Instantaneous matter transporters are developed that allow people to work anywhere in the world, no matter where they live.

2. As in question (1), explain how each of the following labor markets is affected by the described change:

    (a) Nurses are allowed to assume many of the duties performed by doctors.
    (b) Lawyers are subject to yearly competency exams.
    (c) Child care workers are required to have college degrees.

3. Explain how each of the following labor markets is affected by the described change:

    (a) Pay for doctors is capped at a level below the current equilibrium wage.
    (b) A quota on the number of lawyers is enforced at a level below current employment.

4. Explain how the labor markets for women and men are affected by the described change:

    (a) Mothers are allowed to hold only part-time jobs.
    (b) Parents are allowed to hold only part-time jobs.
    (c) Employers are required to pay child care benefits to working mothers.
    (d) Employers are required to pay child care benefits to parents, regardless of sex.

5. Consider the Focus on lawyers and child care workers. If there are more lawyers than kindergarten and prekindergarten teachers (which was the case in 1996), does this fact change the result that reducing the number of child care workers and increasing the number of lawyers will raise the relative wages received by child care workers?

6. Is it possible for the minimum wage for men to cause women's employment to increase by more than the initial drop (from E_0 to E_1) in men's employment? Is it possible for women's employment to increase by more than the full drop (from E_0 to E_2) in men's employment?

Gender Differences in the U.S. Economy

This chapter outlines the basic economic differences between men and women. U.S. data are presented for the basic variables that economists study, including earnings, labor force participation, and poverty rates. Data are presented as far back towards World War II as they are available. The trends that appear in these data lead to the questions considered in the rest of the book. Data on other economic variables that are not so well-known are also presented, to show how widespread gender differences are. As this book progresses, these many small pieces in the puzzle of how and why women and men differ will be linked together to form a coherent picture of how the organization of human society leads to gender differences on almost all economic dimensions.

How much do men and women work?

The most notable economic trend regarding gender differences is the convergence between gender participation rates for paid work. Table 2.1 displays 10-year averages for several participation measures. The *labor force* is the total of employed and unemployed persons. *Labor force participation rates* are defined as the labor force as a percentage of the population in a demographic group. For example, among all women 16 years of age and over, on average almost 56 percent were either employed or were actively looking for employment during the last ten years. The labor force participation rates for women and men have been converging since 1948 as the male rate has declined and the female rate has risen, but the male rate is still substantially above the female rate. Another participation measure that some economists prefer to use (given ambiguities in the definition of unemployment, as we will discuss below), is the percentage of employed for the population in a particular demographic group. This measure will always be slightly lower than the labor force participation rate but tracks its movement quite closely, also showing a rising trend for women and a declining rate for men since 1948.

The *unemployment rate* is the percentage of the labor force either actively seeking work or awaiting recall from a layoff. In order to be considered as actively seeking work, a person must have made some effort recently to find a job. A person who has not sought work, even if he or she indicates an interest in becoming employed, will be counted as not

TABLE 2.1 Labor force participation, employment, and unemployment rates by sex and proportion of labor force that is female, 1948 to 1996

	% Labor force/ population		% Employed/ population		% Unemployed/ labor force		
	Women	Men	Women	Men	Women	Men	Women/lf
1948–56	34.5	86.0	32.9	82.6	4.8	4.0	0.30
1957–66	38.1	82.4	35.9	78.3	6.0	5.0	0.34
1967–76	44.0	79.1	41.1	75.4	6.5	4.8	0.39
1977–86	52.2	77.0	48.1	71.4	7.8	7.2	0.43
1987–96	57.8	75.7	54.3	71.0	6.0	6.2	0.45

Source: Economic Report of the President (1997): 340 (Table B-34), 343 (Table B-37), 346 (Table B-40). Data are for civilian persons ages 16 and over.

in the labor force. The arbitrary nature of the cutoff on "active search" leads to a certain amount of ambiguity in this definition. However, using the current U.S. criteria, it is interesting to note that the female and male unemployment rates have recently converged, while previous to the 1980s, the female rate was always substantially above the male rate.

Another measure of interest to economists studying gender issues is the proportion of the labor force that is female. Along with the female labor force participation and employment rates, this measure is also trending upward, which is to be expected because the female and male working age populations are roughly the same size.

Labor force participation and employment rates

Figure 2.1 illustrates these trends in the labor force participation rates and percentage of the labor force that is female. While there are small year-to-year fluctuations, the downward trend in the male labor force participation rate and the upward trends in the female labor force participation rate and the female share of the labor force are clear.

It is interesting to delve further into these patterns by considering variations in these trends by demographic group. Three subdivisions of interest are age group, marital status, and presence or absence of children. For men, participation decreases have occurred predominantly among older and younger men. Many younger men have delayed labor market entry, instead investing in further schooling. Even more striking has been the decline in participation among older men, as they begin retirement at earlier ages. The labor force participation rate for men ages 65 and over was 33.1 percent in 1960, but only 16.9 percent in 1996.[1] The decline has also been noticeable among men ages 55 to 64.

Among women, the most striking rise in labor force participation has been among married women with young children. Table 2.2 shows female labor force participation rates in 1960 and 1995 by marital status and age of youngest child. While all groups of women have had an increase in labor force participation, the rise has been much greater among married women, with the rate more than tripling over this period for women with preschoolers.

Much of Chapter 4 will be devoted to considering the reasons behind the rise in the female labor force participation rate. The reasons can be considered in two general classes:

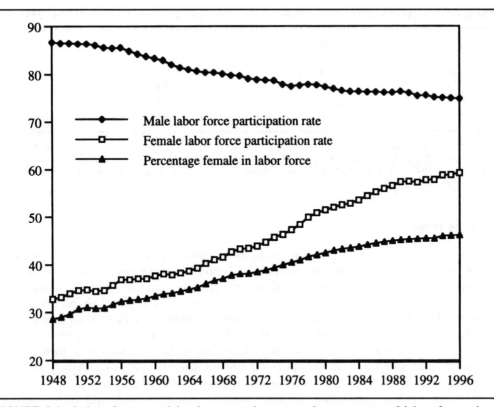

FIGURE 2.1 Labor force participation rates by sex and percentage of labor force that is female, 1948 to 1996

TABLE 2.2 Labor force participation rates for women by marital status and by age of youngest child, 1960 and 1995

	1960	1995
Single, never married	58.6	66.8
Divorced, separated, widowed	41.6	47.4
Married	31.9	61.0
no child under 18	34.7	53.2
child 6–17	39.0	76.2
child under 6	18.6	63.5

Source: Statistical Abstract of the United States (1996): 399 (Table 624), 400 (Tables 626, 627). Data are for civilian women ages 16 and over.

arguments hinging on an increased demand for female labor, which drives the wage up for women and draws them into the labor market; and arguments hinging on an increased supply of female labor (due to such factors as a reduced demand for women to do unpaid household work), which tends to depress wages. Both of these arguments are partial explanations, but deciding which causes have been the most important is not easy.

TABLE 2.3 Part-time workers as percentage of total employed, by sex and overall, 1970 to 1996

	Women	*Men*	*Total*
1970	27.5	9.5	16.4
1980	26.8	9.6	16.9
1990	25.2	10.0	16.9
1996	26.9	10.9	18.3

Sources: 1970, 1990, and 1996 – *Employment and Earnings* 17, no. 7 (January 1971): 131 (Table A-23); 38, no. 1 (January 1991): 171 (Table 7); 44, no. 1 (January 1997): 168 (Table 8); 1980 – *Statistical Abstract of the United States* (1991): 393 (Table 649). Part-time is defined as normally working 1–34 hours per week. Data are for civilian workers ages 16 and over.

Part-time rates

Labor force participation rates give no indication about hours worked; women could be working in greater numbers but for fewer total hours if the number of hours per woman has dropped over time. To this extent, labor force participation rates are misleading measures of the relative amount of work that men and women do, unless their part-time rates are similar. However, Table 2.3 shows that women are much more likely than men to work part-time (defined here as averaging less than 35 hours per week): over a quarter of all employed women work part-time, but only slightly more than 10 percent of men. On the other hand, part-time rates are dropping slightly for women and rising slightly for men, even as the workforce as a whole is more likely to be employed part-time.

Part-time work is considered desirable work by some workers and undesirable by others.[2] When part-time workers are asked why they are working part-time, some say it is by choice and others say it is because they could not find full-time employment. One factor to consider is that many part-time workers do not receive much in the way of fringe benefits such as health insurance and paid vacation time. Therefore, even if the hourly pay is similar for two jobs, one involving part-time and one involving full-time work, full-time work generally entails better average hourly compensation when fringe benefits are included.

Interestingly, there is no significant gender difference in the percentage of workers who are multiple jobholders. In 1996, 6.1 percent of men and 6.2 percent of women held one full-time job and at least one additional part-time or full-time job, which in some cases involved self-employment or working as an unpaid family worker.[3] So "moonlighting" rates are similar by sex.

Unemployment

Figure 2.2 shows yearly unemployment rates by sex. Women have higher unemployment rates than men before the 1980s, after which point the rates become quite similar, and the male rates have actually exceeded the female rates in recent years, starting with the recession of the early 1980s. In general, during recessions, the male rate rises faster than the female rate, reducing the gender gap, while in economic upturns, the male rate drops faster than the female rate, increasing the gap.

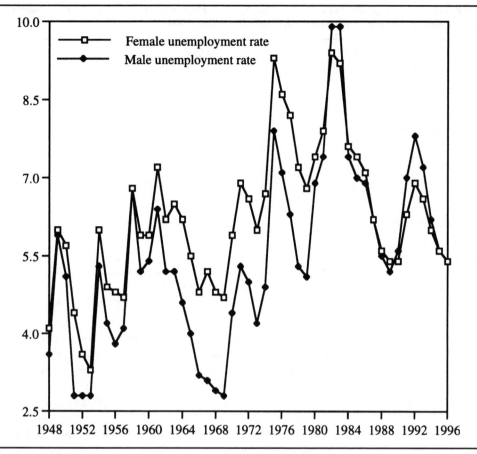

FIGURE 2.2 Unemployment rates by sex, 1948 to 1996

Why do economists care about unemployment? Unemployment is a measure of lost output, of idle resources in the form of people who want to work but are unable to find employment. On a personal level, unemployment is hard on people who are unemployed. While most unemployed persons are eligible for unemployment benefits, these benefits are still less than they would receive in pay. Additionally, the process of looking for work is usually unpleasant and at the very least time-consuming, so unemployed persons are not enjoying their unemployed time as true leisure. It appears from the aggregate rates above that women have until recently been more likely to experience the costs of unemployment than have men.

Again, however, looking in more detail at the composition of the unemployed population allows us to take reasons for unemployment and duration of unemployment into account in considering its costs. Unemployment has different distributional effects if many people experience short spells of unemployment than if a few people experience long spells of unemployment; the same annual average unemployment rate can be generated by either of these patterns. Table 2.4 shows the composition of unemployment in 1996 (a year of low unemployment) by reason for unemployment, as well as several measures of the duration of unemployment by sex. *Mean* is another word for average, so the mean duration is the total

TABLE 2.4 Percentage distributions of reason for unemployment and duration of unemployment, and mean and median duration in weeks of unemployment, by sex, 1996

	Men	Women
Job loser	64.9	41.1
due to layoff	19.6	12.1
Job leaver	10.2	13.0
Labor force re-entrant	23.2	41.5
New entrant	1.6	4.3
Under 5 weeks	35.2	37.9
5–14 weeks	31.4	31.8
15 weeks or more	33.4	30.3
15–26 weeks	14.9	14.1
27 weeks or more	18.5	16.2
Mean duration	17.7	15.6
Median duration	8.7	7.8

Source: Employment and Earnings 44, no. 1 (January 1997): 196 (Table 27), 198 (Table 31). Reason for unemployment data are for persons ages 20 and over; duration data are for persons ages 16 and over.

number of weeks of unemployment experienced by unemployed persons divided by the number of unemployed persons. The *median* shows the value for which half of unemployed persons have a longer period of unemployment, while half have a shorter period.

Men are much more likely than women to be unemployed due to having lost their job; women are much more likely to be a labor market re-entrant who has not yet found employment. Women are somewhat more likely to have short periods of unemployment, men to have long periods of unemployment. The mean duration for both men and women is substantially higher than the median duration of unemployment, showing that a number of people have very long unemployment spells.

These differences imply that the causes and effects of unemployment for men and women are likely to be different, even if their unemployment rates are similar. One study, which decomposes unemployment rate changes from 1968 to 1988, finds that for women, a rise in the probability that a re-entrant was unable to find employment quickly accounts for more than three-quarters of the total rise in female unemployment in the 1970s. For men, the rise in the probability that an employed man would become unemployed accounts for over 40 percent of the rise in male unemployment in the 1970s and almost three-quarters of the rise in male unemployment in the 1980s.[4]

The trend towards greater similarity between the gender unemployment rates appears to be related to the industrial distributions of women and men. Aside from the business cycle effect that men are hurt more by downturns and helped more by upturns, the long-term trend is that women are overrepresented in high-growth industries, so the changing industrial job mix also favors lower unemployment rates for women. Of course this assumes that men continue to be overrepresented in the low-growth and declining industries; men may switch their industry distribution in response to these changing conditions.[5] However, the current structural reconfiguration process of the U.S. economy appears to be causing higher unemployment rates for men.

FOCUS

Will men be tomorrow's "second sex"?

A recent article in *The Economist* called attention to the "growing social problem" in America and Europe of "uneducated, unmarried, unemployed men," making the following statements:[6]

- boys are doing worse than girls at every age in school, except university where girls are narrowing the gap;
- women dominate the jobs that are growing, while men (especially those with the least education) are trapped in jobs that are declining;
- for some reason, men are not even trying to do "women's work";
- there is a loose connection between work and marriage; joblessness reduces the attractiveness of men as marriage partners;
- men do not necessarily adopt "social behaviour" (obeying the law; looking after women and children) if left to themselves; rather, they seem to learn it through some combination of work and marriage (this is a matter of anthropological observation rather than statistical proof); and, hence, putting these claims together,
- that men pose a growing problem. They are failing at school, at work and in families. Their failure shows up in crime and unemployment figures. The problem seems to be related in some way to male behavior and instincts. It is more than merely a mattter of economic adjustment. And (considering the growth in "knowledge-based" employment) it is likely to get worse.

Where do women and men work?

In sorting the different arguments for why the female labor force participation rate has risen so much, it is useful to know whether women are concentrated in particular areas of the economy or whether their representation has risen across a wide range of jobs. In this section of the chapter, we consider various ways of subdividing the economy to see what patterns emerge.

Occupational and industrial distributions

Two ways of subdividing the economy that are commonly used for calculating female representation rates are occupations and industries. Data are available at increasing levels of detail; we will consider only broad categories at present. Tables 2.5 and 2.6 present data on female representation by occupation and industry from 1950 through 1990 at 10-year intervals. For these fairly broad categories, it is clear that women have increased their representation in practically all occupations and industries since 1950, although their rates continue to vary from sector to sector.

While women have increased their representation in all the white-collar occupational groups listed in Table 2.5, they are particularly concentrated in clerical occupations, a feature that exists at all points in the time-series. However, they have made their biggest percentage rise in representation in the managerial occupations. Blue-collar occupations

TABLE 2.5 Percentage female by occupational group, 1950 to 1990

	1950	1960	1970	1980	1990
All workers	28	33	38	44	45
White-collar workers	40	43	48	55	56
professional	40	38	40	46	51
managerial	14	14	17	28	40
clerical	62	68	74	81	80
sales	34	37	39	49	49
Blue-collar workers	24	26	30	34	32
crafts	3	3	5	6	9
operatives	27	28	32	34	26*
laborers	4	4	8	11	—*
private household	95	96	96	97	—†
other services	45	52	55	61	60†
Farm workers	9	10	10	17	16

* Refers to operatives and laborers combined.
† Refers to private household and other services combined.
Sources: 1950–80 – Suzanne M. Bianchi and Daphne Spain, *American Women: Three Decades of Change* (Washington, DC: U.S. Government Printing Office, 1983): 20 (Table 3); 1990 – *Working Women: A Chartbook*, U.S. Department of Labor, Bureau of Labor Statistics, Bulletin no. 2385 (August 1991): 42 (Table A-8).

TABLE 2.6 Percentage female by industry, 1950 to 1990

	1950	1960	1970	1980	1990
All private sector workers	32	35	39	43	46
Mining	2	5	8	12	13
Construction	3	4	6	8	11
Manufacturing	26	25	29	32	33
durable goods	16	18	21	26	27
nondurable goods	36	35	39	41	42
Transportation and public utilities	16	18	22	25	29
Wholesale trade	21	22	24	27	31
Retail trade	41	44	47	51	53
general merchandise stores	68	68	69	70	69
apparel and accessory stores	65	72	66	75	76
eating and drinking places	57	64	62	60	56
Finance, insurance, and real estate	44	49	52	58	63
Services	58	62	63	61	61
health services	74	77	79	76	82
All public sector workers	41	44	47	—	53

Sources: 1950–70 – Census of Population, "Industrial Characteristics," 1950 (P-E No. 1D), 1960 (PC(2) 7F), 1970 (PC(2) 7C); 1980 – Census of Population, Subject Report 7C (Table 4); 1990 – *Working Women: A Chartbook*, U.S. Department of Labor, Bureau of Labor Statistics, Bulletin no. 2385 (August 1991): 43 (Table A-10). Data are for civilian workers on nonfarm payrolls.

TABLE 2.7 Union membership and representation rates by sex and proportion of union membership that is female, 1956 to 1996

	Union members		Represented by union		
	Women	*Men*	*Women*	*Men*	*Women/Unions*
1956	14.9	31.0	—	—	0.18
1976	11.3	27.0	—	—	0.22
1983	14.6	24.7	18.0	27.7	0.33
1986	12.9	21.5	15.5	23.7	0.34
1996	12.0	16.9	13.8	18.4	0.39

Sources: 1956 and 1976 – Linda H. LeGrande, "Women in Labor Organizations: Their Ranks are Increasing," *Monthly Labor Review* 101, no. 8 (August 1978): 9 (Table 1); 1983, 1986, and 1996 – *Employment and Earnings* 32, no. 1 (January 1985): 208 (Table 52); 34, no. 1 (January 1987): 219 (Table 59); 44, no. 1 (January 1996): 211 (Table 40). Earlier data are for persons in the labor force; later data are for wage and salary workers ages 16 and over who are not self-employed.

remain predominantly male, with women actually declining in representation in the area of operatives (which generally refers to factory workers). In services, the proportion of women rose up through 1980, but has more recently stabilized or even started to decline slightly, as men have been shifting out of manufacturing into the service sector.

Table 2.6 shows a rise from 1950 to 1990 in female representation across all industry groups except general merchandise and restaurant/bar retail trade. Female representation has leveled out in services during the 1980s and has actually declined in restaurant/bar retail trade since 1960. In general, the 1960s and 1970s appeared to be the time of the most change in female representation rates, although female representation in construction and transportation and utilities continues to grow at the same absolute pace (while declining in percentage growth terms). However, the variation in female representation across industries in 1990 is notable, as few industries are actually near the overall female percentage of 46 percent, tending to be either much below or much above that figure.

In the public sector, women continue to increase their representation at all levels: women in the federal sector rose from 27 percent of the workforce in 1950 to 41 percent in 1990; at the state level, from 38 to 50 percent; and at the local level, from 50 to 58 percent.

While these tables give some idea of how women and men differ in their daily work experience, female and male worklives vary in many respects within occupations and industries as well, in regard to such factors as working conditions, use of technology, and work schedule. For instance, a 1993 survey found that 52 percent of women were using computers at work, but only 40 percent of men.[7] However, many of these differences are not so easily quantifiable, even though they are important in terms of determining remuneration, upward mobility, and other factors that differ by sex.

Unionism rates

One way in which men and women have both historically and currently differed is in the likelihood of being represented by a union. Table 2.7 presents two measures of unionization by sex: persons who actually belong to a union, and persons who are represented by a union in a collective bargaining process, which leads to a greater measure of union impact. By either of these measures, however, women are less likely to be involved in unionization than are men. This gender difference in unionization is related to gender differences in distributions across industries and occupations; manufacturing is more unionized, while clerical occupations are less unionized. These lower rates of union representation for women have particular repercussions for their relative pay, since union jobs characteristically pay better than comparable nonunionized jobs.

Unions have been declining in both membership and influence. Throughout this period of decline, women have come to comprise a greater proportion of total union membership. There has also been a decline during this period in the gains from joining the unionized sector for women relative to men. One study using job switchers to measure union effects finds that women did as well as men in the early and mid-1970s when they took a unionized job; by the late 1970s and early 1980s, women were receiving a smaller gain in wages measured relative to their previous job than were men.[8]

Other employment categories

Other ways to subdivide the labor force include, by type of employment: agricultural vs. nonagricultural; civilian vs. military; and, among civilians, wage and salary workers, self-employed workers, and persons working in family businesses without pay. Because non-agricultural wage and salary workers are by far the largest category, most research has focused on them. The category of unpaid family workers is the smallest and is declining in importance for both sexes: in 1963, 2.3 percent of female civilian workers and 0.2 percent of male civilian workers were unpaid family workers; by 1996, these percentages had dropped to 0.2 and 0.1 percent, respectively. Self-employment is a larger category: 11.6 percent of male civilian workers were self-employed in 1963; this dropped to a low of 8.2 percent in 1973 and rose to 9.7 percent in 1996. Women similarly had a decline from 6.2 percent in 1963 to a low of 4.4 percent in 1973, and have had a rising rate since, with 6.7 percent in 1996.[9] Self-employment rates by sex generally move together, with the male rate always above the female rate. To the extent that self-employment may be viewed, on the one hand, as a less desirable option than employment with a firm, a rise in the self-employment rate may indicate reduced employment possibilities with firms. On the other hand, self-employment may be viewed as an attractive alternative by those who find work in firms less satisfying or less remunerative.[10]

While this book predominantly focuses on differences among civilian workers, it is interesting to note the extent of female representation in the military. As of 1996, the U.S. military as a whole was 13.5 percent female, including 13.5 percent of officers. This is a striking rise over earlier times, when women were mostly relegated to support positions such as nurses. There is some variation among service branches: the Army and Navy are 13 to 14 percent female, while the Marine Corps is 5 percent female and the Air Force is 17 percent female.[11]

Throughout the book, we will consider questions of how the composition of female and male employment across economic sectors both affects, and is affected by, other factors, such as the relative pay across sectors. But for now, we leave this overview of

TABLE 2.8 Median annual income ratios, women to men, 1947 to 1995

	All persons with income	*Year-round full-time workers*
1947	0.46	—
1950	0.37	—
1955	0.33	0.64
1960	0.31	0.61
1965	0.30	0.60
1970	0.34	0.59
1975	0.38	0.59
1980	0.39	0.60
1985	0.44	0.65
1990	0.50	0.71
1995	0.54	0.74

Source: Current Population Reports Series P-60, nos. 132, 137, 142, 146, 156, 159, 172, 180, 193. Data are for persons with income, ages 14 and over in earlier years, ages 15 and over in later years.

where women and men work and turn to what many economists consider the central topic of interest in the economics of gender: earnings differences.

*H*ow much money do men and women make?

Probably the most widely known and carefully followed gender difference is that in earnings. Measured in either annual or hourly terms, this difference – the *gender earnings gap*, as we will subsequently call it – is wide. Economists and other social scientists have been watching the movement (or lack thereof) in the gender earnings gap in order to gauge the progress of women across societies and over time. We devote Part III of this book to examining causes of this gap.

Table 2.8 displays two of the most commonly followed measures of the gender earnings gap, or ratio of female to male earnings (where the gap equals 1 minus the ratio). The measures are actually based on income rather than earnings, where income may be partly derived from sources other than labor, such as return on investments. However, earnings are the largest component of income, and for subsets of the population such as year-round full-time workers, it is likely to be an even larger component. Income data are generally considered to be more reliable for determining medians than for determining means, because people are likely to report their incomes with some error and because there is topcoding in surveys, so high-earners do not have to report their actual income (and run the risk of being identifiable in supposedly anonymous survey data).

It turns out to be difficult to collect data on wage rates as opposed to earnings or income, although for some purposes we would prefer to use actual hourly wage rates. However, limiting the sample to year-round full-time workers reduces some of the variation in earnings between men and women that is due to differences in hours worked. This measure of the gender earnings gap has been the most widely followed by the press and

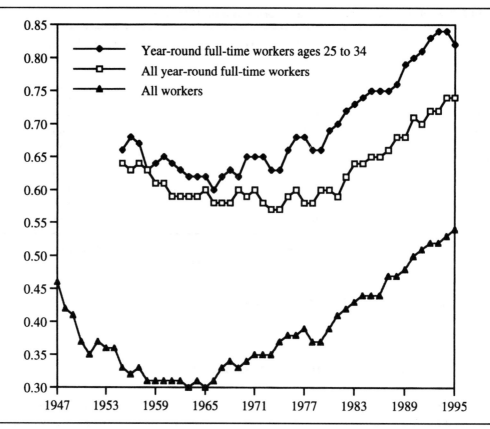

FIGURE 2.3   Median annual income ratios, women to men, 1947 to 1995

other observers. While income for all persons shows a larger gender gap than does income for year-round full-time workers, both display the same pattern of falling female earnings relative to men through the mid-1960s, a period of flat relative earnings through 1980, and rising relative earnings up until the present.[12]

Figure 2.3 plots year-by-year ratios for the two series in Table 2.8, along with ratios for a group experiencing an even more impressive rise: year-round full-time workers ages 25 to 34. In all three series, the same pattern is evident: a downturn in the years following World War II, followed by a long period of only incremental rise, followed by a period of more rapid rise in the 1980s. Interestingly, the series for young workers ends on a slight downtick, dropping from 0.84 in 1994 to 0.82 in 1995.

Table 2.9 contains additional information on trends in the ratios for different age groups. The most noticeable movement towards equality has occurred in the younger age groups, although the largest percentage gain from 1970 to 1995 occurred among women 35 to 44 years of age. However, women ages 45 to 54 actually lost ground from 1970 to 1980 before a net gain by 1990, and in the oldest group, women have actually lost ground since 1970.

TABLE 2.9   Median annual income ratios, women to men, for year-round full-time workers, by age, 1970 to 1995

	1970	1980	1990	1995
15 years and over	0.59	0.60	0.71	0.74
15 to 24 years	—	0.82*	0.90	0.91
25 to 34 years	0.65	0.69	0.79	0.82
35 to 44 years	0.54	0.56	0.69	0.72
45 to 54 years	0.56	0.54	0.61	0.64
55 to 64 years	0.60	0.57	0.62	0.62
65 years and over	0.72	0.72	0.64	0.64

* Average of figures for 15–19 and 20–24 year olds.
Source: Current Population Reports Series P-60, nos. 80 (Table 49), 132 (Table 50), 174 (Table 24), 193 (Table 7).

TABLE 2.10   Median annual income ratios, women to men, for year-round full-time workers, by occupational category, 1960 to 1995

	1960	1970	1980	1990	1995
Professional	0.64	0.67	0.70	0.71	0.70
Managerial	0.58	0.56	0.55	0.64	0.66
Clerical	0.68	0.64	0.60	0.71	0.77
Sales	0.42	0.45	0.49	0.57	0.58
Crafts	—	0.55	0.63	0.71	0.70
Operatives	0.73	0.59	0.60	0.66	0.68
Service workers	0.59	0.57	0.61	0.66	0.69

Sources: 1960 and 1970 – *Historical Statistics of the United States*: 305 (Series 396–405, 408–415); 1980, 1990, and 1995 – *Current Population Reports Series P-60*, nos. 132 (Table 55), 174 (Table 24), 193 (Table 7). Not enough women are in Crafts in 1960 to allow for calculation. Service workers excludes private household workers.

These mixed results or outright losses among older employed women are due in large part to the decreased labor force participation rates among older men. Retirement rates have risen among all older men, but have risen more strikingly among lower-earning older men. Therefore, those men continuing to work into their late sixties tend to be higher-earning men.

Have relative earnings gains for women occurred throughout the economy? Table 2.10 shows the changes in the ratios for different broad occupational categories. Relative earnings for women have risen across the economy since 1960 except for operatives, which (as shown in Table 2.5) is a category in which women have reduced their representation. However, gains have occurred at different rates across categories and have been notably flat since 1980 for professionals.

Why did women's relative earnings rise so much in the 1980s? Five explanations have been suggested by researchers:

1. a rise in the quality of female labor relative to male labor,
2. a decline in labor market discrimination,
3. the shift in the distribution of employment away from unionized, energy-intensive, foreign-trade intensive industries that has hurt men more than women,
4. decline of union wage premiums and other male worker premiums in some sectors, and
5. the convergence of occupational distributions of men and women.

One researcher, looking at data from 1979 to 1984, decided that the most important factor during this period was (5).[13] She also found support for smaller impacts of (1) and (2), and an even smaller impact of (3). Also, while convergence in the industrial distribution of males and females has occurred, it does not appear to have had as big an effect as the occupational convergence. Interestingly, from 1979 to 1984, the returns to education rose for men, but hardly increased at all for women.[14] This implies that factor (1) may become even less important in the future if education implies improved quality, yet women receive a lower payback on quality.

Earnings are only part of the picture of how employment compensation differs by sex; unfortunately, the other components of compensation are more difficult to quantify. It is clear from surveys that women generally have fewer fringe benefits such as health insurance, life insurance, and paid vacation time available to them in terms of total monetary value, partly because more women work part-time and partly because the value of some fringe benefits is directly tied to earnings.[15] The largest monetary difference by sex is likely to be in pension benefits. On the one hand, women live longer: the life expectancy of a person born in 1993 is 72.2 years for men, 78.8 years for women.[16] Many men do not even live until retirement age, although if they do, the life expectancy gap narrows: the average life expectancy in 1993 of a 65-year-old woman is 18.9 years; of a 65-year-old man is 15.3 years.[17] Women therefore can expect to collect pensions for longer periods, but their higher turnover rates and lower earnings reduce their benefits relative to men in defined benefit plans (where a certain percentage of earnings is guaranteed for each year of service). The net effect appears to be that women receive lower total benefits, so taking pensions into account would increase the gender earnings gap. The effect is worse for women the higher the inflation rate, which leads to greater discounting of income received further in the future.[18]

*H*ow well-off are women and men?

This section addresses the questions of whether women or men have higher income variation, and whether women and men have relatively similar household income situations. We consider, in particular, the different rates of poverty for women and men. These are all measures of economic well-being; gender differences in emotional or physical well-being are not addressed here.

Earnings variation

While men have higher median earnings, they may still have greater earnings variation, or *dispersion*, than women. In other words, men may tend to earn either much more or much

TABLE 2.11 Gini indexes of earnings inequality, all workers and year-round full-time workers, by sex, 1948 to 1995

	All workers		Year-round full-time	
	Men	*Women*	*Men*	*Women*
1948	0.360	0.412	—	—
1958	0.398	0.481	—	—
1968	0.394	0.444	0.295	0.256
1978	0.413	0.446	0.296	0.240
1988	0.441	0.451	0.337	0.296
1995	0.485	0.469	0.390	0.322

Sources: 1948–88 Paul Ryscavage and Peter Henle, "Earnings Inequality Accelerates in the 1980's," *Monthly Labor Review* 113, no. 12 (December 1990): 5 (Table 3), 6, 15. 1995 – unpublished data from the Bureau of Labor Statistics. Indexes are calculated using 13 earnings intervals in 1948 and 16 in 1958.

less than the median man, while women may be more tightly clustered around the median, with few very high earners or very low earners. One measure of earnings dispersion is the *Gini index*,[19] which can be calculated as:

$$1 - \sum_{i=1}^{N} [f_i * (Y_i + Y_{i-1})]$$

where persons are ranked in ascending order of earnings into N earnings intervals, f_i = the proportion of all persons in earnings interval i, and Y_i = the proportion of total earnings received by earners in interval i and all lower intervals. It is bounded between 0 and 1, where a value of 0 would indicate complete earnings equality – namely the situation where everyone has the same earnings. The larger the value of the Gini index, the more unequal the earnings distribution – that is, the larger the share held by the top earners.

Table 2.11 contains Gini indexes for all workers and year-round full-time workers by sex. The values are higher for all workers because part-time workers claim a smaller share of total earnings. Among year-round full-time workers, men have greater earnings inequality than women, while for all workers, up through 1988 women have greater earnings inequality, due to the high proportion of female part-time workers; however, this trend has reversed in the most recent data. The trend has been toward increased earnings inequality for all groups over time, with an upturn in the trend in the 1980s, continuing into the 1990s.[20]

Income variation

While both earnings levels and dispersions are important measures of economic well-being, we might be less concerned about women's financial well-being relative to men if they appeared to have access to financial resources beyond their own earnings. Since women's earnings are lower, it follows that women are likely to be worse off than men in terms of

TABLE 2.12 Percentage distribution of household income, median, and mean household income, by sex, 1994

	Men	Women
<$5000	2.0	3.4
$5000–9999	4.5	9.2
$10,000–19,999	13.0	15.6
$20,000–29,999	14.5	14.3
$30,000–39,999	14.0	13.0
$40,000–49,999	12.1	10.8
$50,000–74,999	21.1	18.4
$75,000–99,999	9.6	8.4
$100,000–124,999	5.2	4.4
$125,000–149,999	2.2	1.8
≥$150,000	1.8	1.5
Median income	$40,957	$35,624
Mean income	$49,283	$44,261

Source: Calculated by the author using data from the Current Population Survey, March 1995. The sample consists of persons ages 25 and older.

access to financial resources. However, since men and women form family and household units together, access to monetary resources may better be measured at a family or household level. For instance, if high-earning men tend to be married to low-earning or nonworking women, with the converse being true for high-earning women, then we would expect to see less variation in family and household income between the sexes than in individual earnings.

Table 2.12 demonstrates that this is, in fact, the case. The distributions of men and women by household income are similar, although women are more likely to be in low-income households and men are more likely to be in high-income households.[21] Still, the gender ratio of household median income is 0.87 and of mean income is 0.90, much higher values than the gender earnings ratios shown above.

While earnings are quite different for men and women, household income is quite similar. This implies that household spending patterns for men and women may also be quite similar. The implication is that even if women and men shop for different items, exercise control over different sections of the household budget, and have different tastes regarding consumption, only in a society where a large portion of women and men remain unmarried will gender earnings differences imply much variation in household spending.

There is, however, accumulated evidence that women often pay more than men for a wide range of goods and services (most notoriously, dry cleaning, haircuts, and alterations),[22] implying that their purchasing power is less than that of men for the same level of income. For instance, studies have found that women over age 25 pay the same auto insurance rates as men even though they have fewer accidents, and that women have more tests and drugs prescribed by doctors and are told to come back more times than men for the same illnesses.[23]

FOCUS

Gender differences in charitable contributions

Men and women have different charitable giving patterns. Men give about 2.5 percent of their income to charity, while women give about 2.2 percent. Universities report that gifts from women tend to be at the low and top ends of the spectrum; UCLA found that only 13 percent of donors giving between $1250 and $5000 annually are women.[24] Keller Freeman, a Radcliffe College Alumnae Association trustee, underlines some differences in the ways men and women make charitable donations:[25]

> Over the past months I watched in awe and admiration as my husband and a small band of colleagues raised $42 million for a performing arts center in our small southern town [Greenville, SC]. . . . At roughly the same time, others of us were fundraising for the Emrys Foundation, a local organization whose purpose is the support of women and minorities in the arts. Our campaign came nowhere near its endowment goal of $50,000.
>
> Many of the women on our foundation board were the wives, sisters, daughters, or neighbors of the men on my husband's fundraising committee. So we all fed, so to speak, from the same trough. It became evident, however, that there were critical differences between the two groups of fundraisers. We at the Emrys Foundation thought the women (and men) we solicited would contribute according to their commitment to the goals of the foundation. It didn't occur to us to agonize over who made the solicitation calls, much less over the mode of recognition to be accorded each level of donor.
>
> Different perceptions directed the policies of the performing arts center campaign. There was recognition that who made the solicitation call was a matter of paramount importance. Something like the dominance hierarchy in a band of mountain gorillas was established, so that calls were made peer-to-peer, or superior-to-subordinate. A kind of competition was set up, creating an atmosphere rather like that at a charity auction where people bid against each other for the privilege of giving away the most money. There was an elaborate system of donor recognition, naming everything from dressing rooms to concert halls for contributions at every conceivable level. . . . It was assumed that individuals and corporations would want to stand up and be counted, counted in bills of large denomination.
>
> It was this difference in assumptions, in levels of donor expectation between our two organizations, that caught my attention in a way that literally hit home. My husband and I, who file joint tax returns, eat from a common dish, and make mutual decisions about vacations, responded quite individually to the two hometown philanthropic opportunities described above. My gift to the Emrys campaign was 10 times my usual contribution to causes dear to my heart, including Radcliffe. . . . So I stretched to what I considered my philanthropic limit, even dipping into a small inheritance from my mother so as not to strain unduly the household account. A few weeks later I was stunned to discover that my husband's gift to the performing arts center, which he graciously made in both our names, was precisely 50 times the amount I had pledged to the Emrys Foundation.
>
> I learned first-hand that women and men relate differently to wealth and its distribution. Most of the women I know, or know of, give generously of their time and energy to causes and institutions beyond the circle of the family. But like me, they rarely take responsibility for a comparable fiscal generosity. Anyone who has ever solicited class reunion gifts will probably confirm this observation.

TABLE 2.13 Poverty rates, all, under age 65, and 65 and over, by sex, 1959 to 1995

	All ages			Under 65		65 and over	
	Total	Women	Men	Women	Men	Women	Men
1959	18.2	—	—	17.9	14.2	40.0	33.1
1966	14.7	16.3	13.0	14.5	12.1	32.2	23.8
1970	12.6	14.0	11.1	12.3	10.4	28.5	19.0
1975	12.3	13.8	10.7	13.2	10.6	18.1	11.4
1980	13.0	14.7	11.2	14.1	11.2	18.9	10.9
1985	14.0	15.6	12.3	15.6	12.7	15.6	8.5
1990	13.5	15.2	11.7	15.2	12.2	15.4	7.6
1995	13.8	15.4	12.2	15.7	12.9	13.6	6.2

Sources: 1959 – Richard V. Burkhauser and Greg J. Duncan, "United States Public Policy and the Elderly: The Disproportionate Risk to the Well-Being of Women," *Journal of Population Economics* 4, no. 3 (August 1991): 219 (Table 1); 1966–95 – U.S. Bureau of the Census, *Current Population Reports Series P-60*, nos. 95 (Table 1), 106 (Table 11), 133 (Table 11), 158 (Table 7), 181 (Table 5), 194 (Table 2).

Poverty rates

An area of economic gender differences that has received much attention is the gender gap between poverty rates. Table 2.13 shows poverty rates by sex overall and for younger and older persons separately. Poverty as an old-age phenomenon has become less noticeable, as guaranteed pension programs, social security, and Medicare have combined to improve the financial situation of many older people. The poverty rates for older persons have dropped dramatically since 1959, to the point where the older female rate is slightly lower than that for the general population and the older male rate is dramatically lower than that for the general male population. Among both older and younger persons, however, the female poverty rate remains significantly above the male rate, even as overall poverty has decreased.

Figure 2.4 plots yearly poverty rates to show their fluctuations over the business cycle. Male and female rates move in tandem, so the gender gap remains fairly constant over time, and it shows no sign of closing.

For women of all ages, becoming separated, divorced, or widowed is associated with an increased probability of becoming poor. Elderly women, in particular, are put at greater risk of having a drop in living standards through a change in marital status.[26] The increased number of female-headed households, formed both through divorce and through unmarried motherhood, is a critical factor in understanding the higher poverty rates for younger women.

Men and women are almost equally likely to move up or down the family income distribution, again illustrating that their fortunes are tied together through family structure. From 1987 to 1988, 19.3 percent of men and 19.1 percent of women declined one or more quintiles in the income distribution, 67.2 percent of men and 68 percent of women stayed in the same income quintile, and 13.5 percent of men and 12.9 percent of women rose one or more quintiles.[27] Finally, inheritance patterns are similar by sex, in that both husbands and wives tend to bequeath the bulk of their estates to their spouses, and parents tend to bequeath estates equally to male and female children.[28]

FIGURE 2.4   Poverty rates by sex, 1966 to 1995

*H*ow do men and women allocate their time?

A comprehensive measure of economic well-being would consider the value of time as well as money. Two persons may have the same income, but one may have to work twice as many hours. If women have more leisure time and/or spend more time in unpaid productive activity than men, we may want to credit this time as increasing their well-being relative to that of men.

Table 2.14 presents estimated percentages of weekly time spent on various activities. By far the largest chunk of time for both men and women is devoted to personal care, which includes time spent sleeping, eating, and grooming. Men and women spend almost the same amount of total time on personal care – about 76 hours for women and 75 hours for men out of the total 168 hours of weekly time available – and leisure activities: 39 hours for women and 40 hours for men. The other four categories can all be considered types of work, which means that women and men work the same number of hours per week. Shopping and child care might be considered partly leisure activities by many persons, and paid work and even housework may have pleasurable components as well. Few activities are purely work or purely leisure, even though the economist would like to be able to classify them as such.

These data are probably somewhat surprising to many readers, given the widely held view that most people are operating in a time crunch.[29] Perhaps part of the problem is that some of us expect to have more leisure time at this point in our civilization – in particular, expecting that housework should by now be completely automated. In Chapter 4 we

TABLE 2.14 Percentage distribution of weekly time devoted to various activities by sex, 1985

	Women	Men
Personal care	46	45
Leisure	24	25
Paid work	12	20
Housework	11	6
Shopping	4	3
Child care	3	1

Sources: Calculated by the author from data in John P. Robinson and Geoffrey Godbey, *Time for Life* (University Park, Penn.: Pennsylvania State University, 1997): 95, 105, 112, 126. Personal care includes sleep. Data are for persons ages 18 to 64. Full-time students are excluded from the sample.

TABLE 2.15 Market and nonmarket income in 1983 dollars by sex, 1959 and 1983

	1959		1983	
	Women	Men	Women	Men
Market	4,139	18,776	9,026	22,321
Nonmarket	8,590	5,137	9,810	6,600
Total income	12,729	23,913	18,862	28,920
Women/Men total income	0.53		0.65	

Source: Victor R. Fuchs, "Sex Differences in Economic Well-Being," *Science* 232 (April 25, 1986): 460 (Table 1). Data are for persons ages 25 to 64. Reprinted with permission.

examine the time trend in hours spent on housework and consider whether women's total hours of work have been increasing or decreasing over time. Also, these data refer to a person's primary activity at each point in time. Perhaps the problem is that we have too many activities going on at once, so that much more of child care is performed as a secondary activity along with housework or "leisure."

Additionally, much individual variation is hidden when we examine these averages by sex. Persons who have children spend more time on child care than those who do not, and persons who work spend less time on housework than those who do not work. Additionally, these weekly averages do not capture the fact that leisure time is often taken in week-long or two-week chunks, so that an average workweek might have much less leisure and more work. Finally, another problem for many people may be a perceived lack of flexibility in one's work schedule. Interestingly, men are slightly more likely than women to work with a flexible daytime schedule and significantly more likely to work an evening, weekend or rotating shift: in May 1991, 15.5 percent of male workers and 14.5 percent of female workers were on flexible schedules/flextime; 20.2 of male workers and 14.6 of female workers were on a shift schedule.[30]

Even though hours of work and leisure are remarkably similar for men and women, women are still not able to generate as much economic well-being, because they have lower hourly earnings. Table 2.15 shows measures of income, both market and nonmarket, for women and men at two points in time.[31] In order to impute nonmarket income, time spent

TABLE 2.16 Total number unemployed (in thousands) and percentage-distribution of reason for unemployment, by sex, 1970 to 1996

	Men				*Women*			
	1970	*1983*	*1992*	*1996*	*1970*	*1983*	*1992*	*1996*
Total unemployed	2,238	6,260	5,055	3,880	1,855	4,457	3,885	3,356
Job loser	53.6	69.2	62.3	55.6	33.1	43.2	43.7	36.1
Job leaver	12.6	6.2	10.0	9.6	14.4	10.0	12.1	12.0
Labor force re-entrant	23.8	15.2	18.6	27.7	37.5	32.7	32.4	42.8
New entrant	10.0	9.4	9.1	7.1	15.0	14.1	11.8	9.1

Sources: Statistical Abstract of the United States (1991): 403 (Table 660); (1996): 414 (Table 645); *Employment and Earnings* 44, no. 1 (January 1997): 201 (Table 34). Data are for persons ages 16 and over.

in housework and child care was valued at hourly earnings rates (either the person's own earnings or, if he/she did not do any market work, at the rate of comparable persons in terms of age and education).

This total income measure of economic well-being indicates that women have improved their position relative to men over time, but that they are still at a disadvantage due to their lower wage rate. This measure yields a higher measure of economic well-being for women than market income alone; the median income ratio rose from 0.31 to 0.44 over this same period.

*P*olicy Application: Unemployment policy

It is rare to find discussion among economists of the gender effects of macroeconomic policies, such as fiscal and monetary policies designed to reduce unemployment or reduce inflation.[32] This does not mean that such effects do not occur. For instance, we saw in Figure 2.2 that unemployment rates by sex diverge more during economic upturns than during downturns. Therefore, gender differences in earned income may actually be negatively correlated with the business cycle. Given that women are more likely to be new entrants or re-entrants to the job market, however, maintaining stable employment levels in the economy may allow them to gain additional experience and improve their earnings position relative to men. Recessions are likely to trigger layoffs disproportionately among the most recent hires and cause increased friction among groups of workers who are jockeying for a smaller pool of jobs. Employers who are equal opportunity hirers in good times may not be either equal opportunity hirers or firers during bad times. This tends to imply a positive correlation of the gender earnings ratio with the business cycle, or at least a relationship between low past unemployment rates and current earnings.

We can evaluate the likelihood of these effects by looking at the changes in unemployment composition over the business cycle. Table 2.16 shows the distribution of unemployed persons by reasons for unemployment at different points in the business cycle. In recent times, 1970 and 1996 were low unemployment rate years relative to 1983 and 1992. At all points in the business cycle, unemployed women are more likely to be recent entrants than are unemployed men, but both are more likely to be job losers in recessionary times

TABLE 2.17 Job search methods used by the unemployed by sex, 1996

	Men	*Women*
Contact potential employer directly	66.8	64.7
Sent out resumes or filled out applications	44.5	49.5
Use a public employment agency	20.5	17.9
Answer help wanted ads	17.7	17.8
Use friends/relations as contacts	19.6	15.3
Use a private employment agency	7.2	6.8
Other methods	9.0	6.9
Average number of methods used	1.86	1.79

Source: Employment and Earnings 44, no. 1 (January 1997): 201 (Table 34). Data are for persons ages 16 and over. Multiple responses are possible, so columns add up to more than 100 percent.

and re-entrants in good times. Still, the percentage and absolute number of job losers is much higher at all points in the business cycle among men than women.

This conclusion, combined with the fact that men have experienced higher unemployment rates than women during recent economic downturns, seems to support the idea that women may actually improve their position relative to men during downturns. Nevertheless, this result is sensitive to the definition of unemployment; women may be more likely to withdraw completely from the labor force than to remain unemployed after losing their jobs.

Some government employment policies concentrate on the methods people use to find jobs, attempting to raise the probability of employment and thereby lower the unemployment rate. For instance, fiscal policy can take the form of government spending on job training programs, and job training programs often have a job-finding component in which persons are trained in how to answer job advertisements, fill out applications, and act during interviews. If women and men currently have different search methods, such training programs may help to narrow the unemployment gap – and the earnings gap – between women and men by making their search methods more similar.

In fact, the search methods used by those unemployed in an attempt to find work do not appear to differ substantially for women and men, implying that they use similarly effective (or ineffective) strategies. As shown in Table 2.17, the use of search methods is generally similar for women and men. However, men do rely more heavily on friends and relations and on employment agencies, while women rely more heavily on sending out resumes and filling out applications. Given the basic similarities in search behavior, it is unclear whether government policies attempting to narrow the gender differences in job search behavior could greatly influence the gender difference in unemployment, but particular search methods – in particular, use of contacts – may lead to better-paying jobs, thereby having a direct effect on the gender earnings gap.[33]

Summary

This chapter has introduced the variables that economists study as they relate to gender differences, mostly relating to the labor market. Levels and trends in the data back to the 1940s and up to the 1990s have been examined, and several patterns clearly emerge.

While male and female labor force participation rates have been converging, they are still quite far apart, with men still much more likely to be engaging in paid work than women. Male and female unemployment rates have converged in recent years, with various economic forces leading to the prediction that female rates will actually fall permanently below male rates. Male and female occupational and industrial distributions have also converged over time, with women increasing their representation in almost all economic sectors, but women and men are still concentrated in different areas – women in clerical work and men in blue-collar work.

The gender earnings gap has been reduced from its widest point in recent memory in the mid-1960s, but the recent rise in women's earnings relative to men's earnings has still only brought female earnings to approximately 74 cents to every dollar a man makes among year-round full-time workers. While income dispersion is lower than earnings dispersion due to income pooling within families, women are still disproportionately represented among those persons below the poverty level. Finally, while women and men have similar distributions of time among alternative uses, the lower returns to women from both market and nonmarket work leave them with less total income than men.

These trends are amplified, clarified, and explained in the chapters that follow. They provide the basic themes for our study of the economics of gender.

*E*ndnotes

1. U.S. Department of Labor, Bureau of Labor Statistics, *Working Women: A Chartbook*, Bulletin no. 2385 (August 1991): 39 (Table A-3); *Employment and Earnings* 44, no. 1 (January 1997): 160 (Table 3).
2. See Chris Tilly, *Half a Job: Bad and Good Part-Time Jobs in a Changing Labor Market* (Philadelphia, Penn.: Temple University, 1996).
3. *Employment and Earnings* 44, no. 1 (January 1997): 203 (Table 36).
4. Wayne J. Howe, "Labor Market Dynamics and Trends in Male and Female Unemployment," *Monthly Labor Review* 113, no. 11 (November 1990): 3–12.
5. Larry DeBoer and Michael Seeborg, "The Female-Male Unemployment Differential: Effects of Changes in Industry Employment," *Monthly Labor Review* 107, no. 1 (November 1984): 8–15.
6. "Tomorrow's Second Sex," *The Economist* (September 28, 1996): 23–26. © The Economist Newspaper Group, Inc. Reprinted with permission. Further reproduction prohibited. See also the editorial, "The Trouble with Men," *The Economist* (September 28, 1996): 19.
7. *Statistical Abstract of the United States* (1996): 423 (Table 657).
8. Dwight W. Adamson, "Differences in Union Relative Wage Effects Across Gender and Race: A Longitudinal Analysis," *Journal of Economics* 19, no. 2 (Fall 1993): 79–91.
9. *Employment and Earnings* 44, no. 1 (January 1997): 180 (Table 15).
10. See Robert L. Aronson, *Self-Employment: A Labor Market Perspective* (Ithaca, N.Y.: Institute for Labor Relations, 1991), for further discussion of the phenomenon of self-employment and its differences by sex.
11. Department of Defense, *Selected Manpower Statistics* (1997): (Tables 9 and 10).
12. Another series, collected in the May Current Population Survey, is median weekly earnings for full-time wage and salary workers ages 16 and over and is published in *Employment and Earnings*, January issues. This series, while collected for a shorter time (1967, and continuously since 1969), shows a similar upturn in earnings, but indicates a smaller gap at each point in time. For both 1995 and 1996 it shows a ratio of 75 cents on the dollar (1997 – Table 37).
13. Elaine Sorensen, *Exploring the Reasons Behind the Narrowing Gender Gap in Earnings* (Washington, D.C.: Urban Institute, 1991): 16–18. June O'Neill and Solomon Polachek, "Why the Gender Gap in Wages Narrowed in the 1980s," *Journal of Labor Economics* 11, no. 1, part 1 (January 1993): 205–228, attribute one-third to one-half of the narrowing to (1) and also find support for (4); they also cite an increase in returns to experience for women, which may be

caused by (2). Francine D. Blau and Lawrence M. Kahn, "Swimming Upstream: Trends in the Gender Wage Differential in the 1980s," *Journal of Labor Economics* 15, no. 1, part 1 (January 1997): 1–42, attribute much of the change to (1), (4), and (5) and point out that men benefited relative to women among high-skilled workers.

14. Sorensen, *op. cit.*: 44.
15. Cf. Janet Currie, "Gender Gaps in Benefits Coverage," National Bureau of Economic Research Working Paper no. 4265 (January 1993); Janet Currie and Richard Chaykowski, "Male Jobs, Female Jobs, and Gender Gaps in Benefits Coverage," National Bureau of Economic Research Working Paper no. 4106 (June 1992).
16. *Statistical Abstract of the United States* (1996): 88 (Table 119).
17. *Ibid.* Male life expectancy is currently rising more rapidly than female life expectancy.
18. James E. Pesando, Morley Gunderson, and John McLaren, "Pension Benefits and Male-Female Wage Differentials," *Canadian Journal of Economics* 24, no. 3 (August 1991): 536–550.
19. The Gini index, or coefficient, is named after economist C. Gini, who proposed it in 1912 as a measure of inequality.
20. See Frank Levy and Richard J. Murnane, "U.S. Earnings Levels and Earnings Inequality: A Review of Recent Trends and Proposed Explanations," *Journal of Economic Literature* 30, no. 3 (September 1992): 1333–1381, for a comprehensive discussion of this issue and alternative measures of earnings inequality. See also Paul Ryscavage, "Gender-Related Shifts in the Distribution of Wages," *Monthly Labor Review* 114, no. 7 (July 1994): 3–15.
21. Patterns for families, which are defined by the Census as related subgroups within households, are quite similar.
22. Frances Cerra Whittelsey, *Why Women Pay More* (Washington, D.C.: Center for Responsive Law, 1993); Joan E. Rigdon, "State May Ban Bias in Pricing Hairdos, Wash," *Wall Street Journal* (May 11, 1994): B1; B10.
23. Diane Duston, "Women Often Pay More for Services," Associated Press Wire Service article in *The Commercial Appeal* (May 18, 1993): A2.
24. Liz McMillen, "College Fund Raisers See Their Alumnae as Untapped Donors," *Chronicle of Higher Education* (April 1, 1992): A32.
25. Keller Freeman, "The Gender Gap in Philanthropy," *Radcliffe Quarterly* 77, no. 4 (December 1991): 3–4. Reprinted with permission.
26. Richard V. Burkhauser and Greg J. Duncan, "United States Public Policy and the Elderly: The Disproportionate Risk to the Well-Being of Women," *Journal of Population Economics* 4, no. 3 (August 1991): 217–231. See also Karen C. Holden, "Women's Economic Status in Old Age and Widowhood," *Women's Life Cycle and Economic Insecurity: Problems and Proposals*, ed. Martha N. Ozawa (Westport, Conn.: Greenwood, 1989): 143–169.
27. "Transitions in Income and Poverty Status: 1987–88," *Current Population Reports Series P-70*, no. 24: 5 (Table 2).
28. Paul L. Menchik, "Inheritance: The Treatment of Women," *Women's Life Cycle and Economic Insecurity: Problems and Proposals*, ed. Martha N. Ozawa (Westport, Conn.: Greenwood, 1989): 141–142.
29. See John P. Robinson and Geoffrey Godbey, *Time for Life: The Surprising Ways Americans Use Their Time* (University Park, Penn.: Pennsylvania State University, 1997), for discussion of people's perceptions versus reality concerning the availability of time.
30. *Statistical Abstract of the United States* (1995): 410 (Table 647).
31. Victor R. Fuchs, "Sex Differences in Economic Well-Being," *Science* 232 (April 25, 1986): 459–464. Joyce M. Manchester and David C. Stapleton, "On Measuring the Progress of Women's Quest for Economic Equality," *Journal of Human Resources* 26, no. 3 (Summer 1991): 562–580, contend that Fuchs overestimates the number of nonmarket hours worked by women. If true, this means that the nonmarket income for women is an overestimate, so they would have even lower total income than men.

32. Almost no economists have considered the effects of inflation on gender differences. The only study I have seen finds that the rise in female labor force participation is correlated with the rise in the Consumer Price Index: Beth T. Niemi and Cynthia B. Lloyd, "Female Labor Supply in the Context of Inflation," *American Economic Review* 71, no. 2 (May 1981): 70–75. The authors speculate that this may be due to money illusion, relative price movements, or the perception that two-earner families are necessary to maintain rising living standards in inflationary times.

33. See Susan Hanson and Geraldine Pratt, "Job Search and the Occupational Segregation of Women," *Annals of the Association of American Geographers* 81, no. 2 (1991): 229–253, for a discussion of how women's search techniques perpetuate segregation.

34. Menchik, *op. cit.*: 142.

35. Penelope Wang, "Brokers Still Treat Men Better Than Women," *MONEY* (June 1994): 108–110.

36. Bettina Berch, *The Endless Day: The Political Economy of Women and Work* (New York: Harcourt Brace Jovanovich, 1982): 133–134.

*F*urther reading and statistical sources

American Demographics. Monthly issues containing articles and short news items featuring statistics about American habits, mostly culled from opinion polls and other large statistical samples, including time use surveys and the Consumer Expenditure Survey. Many of these statistics are broken down by sex.

Bianchi, Suzanne, and Daphne Spain (1996). *Balancing Act: Motherhood, Marriage, and Employment Among American Women.* New York: Russell Sage Foundation. Presents a demographic picture of the U.S. economy through approximately 1992, using a mixture of Census Bureau data and more frequently collected series; has sections addressing the major issues introduced in this chapter.

—— (1996). "Women, Work, and Family in America," *Population Bulletin* 51, no. 3 (December). Updates many of the trends and series in their book through 1995–1996.

Blau, Francine D. (1998). "Trends in the Well-Being of American Women, 1970–1995," *Journal of Economic Literature* 36, no. 1 (March): 112–165. Comprehensive survey article of economic research and empirical trends during this period.

Economic Report of the President. Published annually; contains a statistical appendix including data on U.S. labor force participation, employment, and unemployment series based on the same data as *Employment and Earnings.*

Jacobs, Eva E. (ed.) (1996). *Handbook of U.S. Labor Statistics.* Lanham, Maryland: Bernan. Compendium of statistics from a variety of U.S. and foreign sources. Contains historical data on major series. Based on the discontinued series *Handbook of Labor Statistics* published by the U.S. Bureau of Labor Statistics.

U.S. Department of Commerce, Bureau of the Census. *Current Population Reports Series P-20: Population Characteristics.* Several titles per year on different topics, including recurring editions on household composition, marital status, fertility, geographical mobility, and educational attainment. Regular reports are issued focusing on the black population and the farm population. Uses data from the Current Population Survey, which asks recurring questions about labor force participation and earnings, as well as occasional questions on a wide variety of socioeconomic topics. The Census Bureau operates a useful website (www.census.gov).

——. *Current Population Reports Series P-23: Special Studies.* Several titles per year on different special nonrepeating topics, including youth, women, the older population, and summaries of results published in other *Current Population Reports* series. No. 174 (July 1991) is a subject index for all the *Current Population Reports* series through June 1990 (through no. 445 in Series P-20, no. 167 in Series P-23, no. 167 in Series P-60, and no. 18 in Series P-70).

——. *Current Population Reports Series P-60: Consumer Income.* Several titles per year on different topics, including recurring editions on income, noncash benefits, and poverty. Uses data from the Current Population Survey.

——. *Current Population Reports Series P-70: Household Economic Studies.* Several titles per year on different topics, including transitions in and out of poverty and between income levels. Uses data from the Survey of Income and Program Participation, which asks recurring questions about employment, income, participation in government programs, and noncash benefits; periodic questions are asked about school enrollment, marital history, migration, child care, disability status, work history, fringe benefits, and asset holdings.

—— (1975). *Historical Statistics of the United States: Colonial Times to 1970.* Two-volume set containing data as far back as available on all major statistical series available, including guidelines on how to extend those series that are still being collected.

——. *Statistical Abstract of the United States.* Annual compendium of statistics from a variety of U.S. sources that includes information on original sources for all tables. The entire volume is available on-line at the Census Bureau's website.

U.S. Department of Labor, Bureau of Labor Statistics. *Employment and Earnings.* Monthly issues containing labor force statistics, including unemployment rates and earnings. The January issue contains averages for the preceding year. Uses data from the Current Population Survey and data from a monthly survey of establishments. The Bureau of Labor Statistics operates a useful website (www.bls.gov).

——. *Monthly Labor Review.* Monthly issues contain a variety of research articles utilizing recent labor-related data, often from questions included in the Current Population Survey on an occasional basis and from topical modules included in the Survey of Income and Program Participation.

—— (1988). *Statistics Derived from the Current Population Survey, 1948–87.* Historical series of statistics from this household survey.

Discussion questions

1. Consider the pros and cons of requiring firms to provide full fringe benefits for part-time positions. Will women as a group be better or worse off under such a requirement?

2. A current puzzle in labor economics is why unemployment rates increasingly appear to vary across regions. For example, in June 1997 the national unemployment rate was 5.0 percent, but local unemployment rates varied from a low of 1.7 percent in Portland, Maine, to a high of 18.5 percent in the metropolitan area of McAllen-Edinburg-Mission, Texas. Economists generally assume that workers will move from areas without work to areas with work, thereby pushing unemployment rates to be similar across regions. Instead, there are areas where it is hard to find work and areas where it is hard to find workers. How does the existence of an increased number of two-earner households provide a partial explanation for this phenomenon?

3. Consider the Focus on men as the future "second sex." How might one statistically prove that men learn social behavior through some combination of work and marriage? Would women adopt social behavior if left to themselves? Do you believe that men pose a growing problem? Are there appropriate social and economic policy responses to these claims?

4. Why might women as a percentage of union members rise as union membership as a whole is dropping? Could this be a cause or an effect of unions becoming less powerful, or both?

5. Are women and men likely to become self-employed for different reasons? Would you expect women or men to make more money being self-employed relative to working in a firm?

6. The income ratios shown in Table 2.10 declined through 1980 before rising for managerial and clerical workers, while they steadily rose for the other groups. Can you come up with a theory for why there were these different patterns?

7. If women had more control over financial resources, would they spend their money differently than rich men currently do?

8. Assuming that the Gini index is greater for men than for women, but that median income is equal for women and men, if you choose a woman at random, is she likely to have more or less income than a man chosen at random? What if median income is greater for men than for women?

9. Evidence shows that parents tend to bequeath estates in equal shares to their children, but one economist has written, "The equity principle seems to dictate that daughters should inherit more than their proportionate share."[34] What is the empirical basis for this remark?

10. As more people remain unmarried for longer periods of time, how would you expect this pattern, along with the continued gender earnings gap, to influence consumption patterns?

11. Why might the prices that women and men pay for similar or identical goods and services vary? How might women combat the pattern of paying more than men? What effect might you expect passage of an Equal Pricing Act banning gender and race-based price discrimination to have?

12. A 1994 survey by *MONEY* magazine found that brokers tended to recommend higher-risk, higher-return investments to men than to women.[35] Why might this be the case?

13. Consider the Focus on gender differences in charitable contributions. As women give less of their income in percentage terms than men, can we conclude that they are less generous? In what ways might women appear more altruistic than men?

14. One commentator on the economic position of women wrote in 1983: "If the government maintained a full employment economy . . . affirmative action hiring could become the basis for the greater integration of women in the labor market on a long-term basis. Similarly, women's unemployment burden could be reduced and women's poverty status improved. In this sense, women and minorities have a greater stake in full-employment economic policies than anyone else."[36] Comment on the assumptions behind this statement. Is this statement true today?

Why Do Women and Men Work?

*T*his part of the book examines why men and women work, how they decide to divide their time between market and nonmarket work (that is, between work for pay and work at home without pay), and what the repercussions of both types of work are for family structure.

Chapter 3 discusses why households and marriages form and how the division of labor within living groups occurs. Reasons for the traditional division of labor, in which women have performed mostly nonmarket work and men have performed mostly market work, are discussed. The appendix to Chapter 3 discusses some related economic concepts, including the gains from trade, modeling of preferences and consumption choices, and relationships between product markets.

Chapter 4 considers why the traditional division of labor has been changing, as more and more women have been doing market work. The trends in labor force participation are studied in more depth, and the various causes of the rise in female labor force participation are considered. The appendix to Chapter 4 discusses the economic theory of labor supply.

Chapter 5 addresses the question of how changing labor force participation patterns have affected household and family structure. Changes in the composition of the household are presented and discussed. In particular, the relationships between rising female labor force participation and declining marriage, rising divorce, and declining childbearing rates are considered.

Part II concludes with a policy application that draws on material from all three chapters: – that is, the question of how the U.S. welfare system might be improved.

The Household as Economic Unit

A *multi-person household* is two or more persons sharing noninstitutional living quarters.[1] Why do multi-person households form, and why do different household members perform different tasks? Throughout this chapter, we develop a rational choice model of household formation and dissolution. The benefits and costs of living in multi-person households, living in family households, and entering into marriage are considered. We also consider critiques of the rational choice model.

Household and marriage formation

Table 3.1 displays recent data on U.S. household composition. Three-quarters of U.S. households contain more than one person; 54.4 percent contain a married couple. Most U.S. households are family households. Many persons who are currently in nonfamily households have lived or will live in a married couple household at some point in their lives, and most people will live in a multi-person household for a large percentage of their lives.

In a society in which people choose their living arrangements, including whether or not to marry and whom to marry, we will assume that they consider the various factors

TABLE 3.1 Percentage distribution of households by type, 1995

Family households	70.0
married couples without children	28.9
married couples with children	25.5
other families	15.6
Nonfamily households	30.0
women living alone	14.7
men living alone	10.3
other nonfamily households	5.0

Source: Current Population Reports Series P-20, no. 488 (Table A). Children refers to own children under the age of 18.

associated with a particular living arrangement before deciding whether or not to enter into it. Let us model a person's decision as to whether or not to enter into a particular living situation as:

If $B(X) > C(X)$ then enter into X.

If the *benefits* (B) of entering into living situation X are greater than the *costs* (C) of living situation X, then enter into situation X; otherwise don't.[2]

One possible living situation is marriage. Let us model a person's decision to marry as:

If $B(Y) > C(Y)$ then marry Y.

If the benefits associated with marrying person Y are greater than the costs associated with marrying Y, then marry Y; otherwise don't. The trick is to figure out what all the benefits and costs are. In particular, the costs of marrying person Y include the opportunity cost of the next-best alternative, whether that is staying single, marrying a different person, or opting for some other living arrangement. However, the benefits of marrying person Y include not having to continue to incur search costs in looking for a mate.

Benefits and costs of both marriage and alternative living arrangements can include psychic factors such as love, distrust, desire to please or annoy one's parents, and sexual desire. Additionally, they include the monetary factors of expected monetary gain from the arrangement and expected monetary outlay for maintaining the arrangement. We are assuming that all these different types of benefits and costs can be weighted and then summed in order to arrive at a decision. In the case of living arrangements, we are assuming that the other persons involved are willing to enter into living arrangement X. In the case of marriage, we are assuming that person Y is willing to marry the person making this decision.

We will first consider the benefits of living with others as opposed to living alone. We will also consider whether it is actually necessary to enter into a legal contract such as marriage in order to reap certain benefits of living with others. Since we observe that the vast majority of people in most societies do marry at some point, either the benefits of marriage outweigh the costs at some time for most persons or, if we find that the costs of marriage appear higher than the benefits, we must come up with a different model.

Several types of potential benefits will be discussed in turn. These types are: (1) economies in production; (2) internalization of externalities (including provision of public goods); (3) reduction of transactions costs; and (4) reduction of utility fluctuations through resource pooling. For each type, we will also discuss how living with other persons can actually increase one's costs relative to living alone.

Economies in production

The economic model of what families and households do is that they produce various commodities which increase the utility of the household members who consume these household commodities. The primary input into household commodity production is household members' time. Some of this time is traded for money, as household members perform work for pay. Money may then be used either to purchase intermediate goods (e.g., laundry detergent), which are used as inputs along with time spent doing nonmarket work (e.g., time doing laundry) to produce final products (e.g., clean clothes), or to purchase final products (e.g., new clothes). Some households have access to money without having to work, such as interest income, pensions, and transfer payments from the government (e.g., welfare payments). Some commodities may also be received without having to trade time for them, such as free school lunches for poor children.

There are several ways in which multi-person households can save time and/or money relative to single-person households producing per capita quantities of final products:

1. realization of volume discounts on intermediate goods,
2. lower average fixed costs of capital,
3. production process economies of scale,
4. higher output from division of labor/specialization, and
5. lowered costs through complementary production processes.

But there are ways in which single-person households may be able to reap these benefits as well. Let us examine these sources of potential cost differences.

1. Volume discounts: Larger households can buy intermediate inputs in bulk and thereby realize per unit savings. In particular, a single person will be unable to realize as low per capita food costs for perishable food items as a larger household. For nonperishable items, however, a single person with storage space can also realize per unit savings. It is hard to think of how single persons might have lower buying costs than multi-person households, but they may be able to join buying clubs, in which a number of households band together to do their shopping, and thereby realize volume discounts. While larger households often may have higher per capita food costs because they are poor and therefore cannot afford to buy in bulk (and because they live in areas of town where it is harder to find volume discounts), this condition is related to income level rather than to household size.

2. Lower average fixed costs of capital: By maintaining higher capacity utilization and/or spreading the costs of a piece of physical capital over more persons, a multi-person household should have significantly lower per capita capital costs. Many household appliances fall into this category (e.g., dishwashers and irons). Note that people need not live together in order to share ownership. For instance, several families may share ownership of a motorboat, taking turns using it. However, for items that do not require a large investment of money relative to time spent using them, sharing is generally not worthwhile.

3. Production process economies of scale: Many household activities have declining marginal cost measured in time (e.g., cooking for two is only slightly more time-intensive than cooking for one). It is possible to have diseconomies of scale as well. For example, a multi-person household may require elaborate home-cooked meals, while a single person may eat sandwiches standing up at the counter.

4. Higher output from division of labor/specialization: In a multi-person household, persons can specialize in activities and subdivide activities into smaller parts that can be done with greater efficiency, thereby increasing total output available to the household. For instance, if one household member is more efficient at cooking and another at cleaning, they can divide up the household chores in this manner. A single person may be able to hire persons to perform tasks at which he/she is less efficient (e.g., hire a cook), or substitute intermediate goods for time in the production process (e.g., purchase more prepared food and eat out more often). However, he/she may incur additional costs from having to purchase these inputs on the market, and some household commodities may not have market substitutes available – i.e., they are nontraded commodities, or commodities for which only imperfect substitutes exist. For example, is a perfect substitute for a "home-cooked meal" available for purchase?

The ability to specialize and thereby increase per capita output available to household members is the factor most cited by economists in considering the economic rationale for household formation. The appendix to this chapter contains a graphical/numerical example to illustrate that specialization and trade between persons leads to increased production and therefore to the possibility of increased consumption by both parties. However, it is not obvious in this example that it is necessary for persons to live together in order to reap the benefits from specialization and trade. This model is also applied to trade between countries, but does not imply that countries should also merge their legal and social systems and operate as one nation.

There are also disadvantages to specialization if the dimension of time is taken into consideration. We will discuss further the effects of specialization below. Also, this simple model says nothing about whether women or men are more likely to specialize in particular areas. We will consider the forces creating and maintaining the "traditional" division below (i.e., wives specializing in nonmarket work, husbands in market work).

5. Complementary production processes: Economies of scale exist not only in production of a particular commodity but also in producing multiple commodities in tandem. For instance, if a household member has to drive to the shoe repair store to drop off shoes, the additional time involved in also dropping off a videotape for another household member at the video rental store is less than if the other household member had to make a separate trip. Also, particular household commodities, such as minding a sleeping child while doing the laundry, may be practically costless. On the other hand, some activities, such as writing a novel, may take longer if one also has to watch a child who is awake. A single person would be less likely to experience conflicting time uses, but it is hard to see how a single person would be able to reap the cost reductions involved in coordinating chores with other household members.

Overall, it appears that multi-person households are likely to enjoy reduced costs of production over single-person households. However, it is not obvious that it is necessary to enter into marriage in order to reduce living costs. Households of persons related through family relationships other than marriage, living groups where persons are not related at all, including roommate groups, and institutional living situations such as dormitories and old-age homes, can also realize many of these savings.

Internalizing externalities

Externalities are events in which one person's production or consumption activity directly affects another person's production or consumption. A *production externality* occurs when one person's production or consumption activity influences another person's costs of production. A *consumption externality* occurs when one person's production or consumption activity influences another person's utility. *Positive externalities* increase a person's utility or reduce their costs of production; *negative externalities* decrease utility or increase costs of production. The existence of positive externalities increases the benefits of living in a multi-person household. An example of a positive production externality is the benefit to other members of the household when one person cleans his or her bedroom, because there will be less dirt in the house to be tracked into their rooms. An example of a positive consumption externality is enjoyment from hearing your roommate singing in the shower. An important category of positive consumption externalities is linked happiness: if you become happy through seeing other people who are happy, the good fortune of one member of your household will increase your utility as well.

Multi-person households can also have negative externalities that increase their costs relative to single-person households. An example of a negative production externality is living with a messy household member, who increases the time it takes you to keep your part of the house clean. An example of a negative consumption externality is hearing the radio in your roommate's bedroom through your wall. Also, if you become unhappy through seeing other unhappy people, an unhappy family member will decrease your utility.

There are household commodities that have the property of being able to provide streams of services simultaneously to several persons. Television is perhaps the best example of this situation. If one person is watching a television show and another person starts watching as well, the first person's utility may not be affected at all, while the other person will now have increased utility. This is an example of a *public good* (sometimes called a *club good*). This is a particular type of positive consumption externality in which everyone consumes the same amount of the good, although different persons may receive different amounts of utility from consuming the good. A *pure public good* can provide utility to an infinite number of people without diminishment of utility to any person already consuming the good. For most goods, increased congestion in use will reduce the utility gained for earlier persons (e.g., if too many people are watching the same television set, some people may find their view partially obscured). Multi-person households will be able to generate more utility per capita from jointly owning public goods than will single-person households. They also will generally be willing to provide more of the public good than will single-person households (e.g., a large household may be more likely to purchase a large-screen color television; a single person may purchase only a small black and white set).

Many people find that the negative externalities generated by living with other people outweigh the positive externalities. There is no clear advantage to multi-person households in this category. In particular, very large multi-person households and institutional situations may generate large amounts of negative externalities due to crowding, conflicting tastes among group members, and the difficulty of coming to an agreement about the optimal level of externalities among a large group of persons. However, families (in particular, married couples) may have an advantage over unrelated individuals who live together in being able to generate the optimal level of externalities. They may be better able to negotiate compromises in cases of negative externalities because it is harder to dissolve their living arrangements. Additionally, they may be better able to encourage additional production of positive externalities, again due to the difficulty of dissolving their living arrangements. The difficulty of dissolving the living situation may, however, lead to one person creating a higher level of negative externalities for family members than for nonfamily members (e.g., a child who acts irresponsibly, knowing that the parents will not throw him out of the house, would be thrown out by roommates for the same behavior). However, if family members have more similar likes and dislikes than unrelated individuals, they may be less likely to create negative externalities for each other and more likely to create positive externalities.

Reduction of transactions costs

Transactions costs are costs incurred in negotiating a contract or agreement. There are many examples of how transactions costs (also known as *contracting costs*) can be reduced through living with other persons. For example, many household consumption activities require more than one person, such as playing a board game. In these situations, it is generally easier – and therefore cheaper in terms of time – to find other people to engage in the activity within the household than to gather people from other households. Additionally, many household production activities are time-consuming to contract for separately. In order to duplicate the activities of one household member performing nonmarket activities, it may be necessary to hire a maid, cook, butler, plumber, and others. There are often substantial monetary costs involved as well, such as the plumber who charges a fixed amount per service call as well as an hourly rate. Search costs are included in this category, such as the costs incurred in finding a plumber to make a repair. Some activities may have such prohibitive transactions costs that single-person households will be unable to perform them at all (e.g., finding an escort on short notice).

In households, such as families, where people live together for long periods of time, members may have explicit or implicit contracts that do not require constant renegotiation and that cover a wide variety of activities. At the same time, members of households may develop more sources of discord and have more trouble coming to agreement on contracts.

The effects of household size on transactions costs may be positive or negative. On the one hand, a larger household size tends to reduce search costs by improving the possibilities of finding someone to contract with for an activity. In particular, large households have improved possibilities of being able to undertake activities that require many persons as inputs. On the other hand, it may be difficult to get a large number of people to agree to a contract, and transactions costs may increase. Even with these caveats, multi-person households appear to have a clear theoretical advantage in the category of transactions costs over single-person households, which appear to have reduced opportunities to negotiate low-cost contracts.

A particular subset of potential transactions cost reduction that has been emphasized recently by economists attempting to explain the phenomenon of marriage is the reduction of shirking.[3] Costs can be incurred in trying to verify that a party is living up to a contract; these are known as *monitoring costs*. For many production processes, it is difficult to measure the contributions of the persons involved and, therefore, difficult to tell whether they are shirking or not. For example, if a child is well-behaved, it is unclear how to apportion the credit. How much of the child's good behavior is due to the mother's actions, the father's actions, or some other person's actions? A child's parents may end up sharing equally in the praise, even though one parent spent much more time and effort on raising the child. Each parent has incentives to shirk (e.g., playing golf with friends instead of watching the child's baseball game) if the rewards are not directly related to the input provided by the parent. This type of situation will, in general, lead to underprovision of the jointly produced good; while the child may be a model citizen, he/she might have been even better had one or both parents put in more effort.

By living together, people who are engaged in a joint production activity may be able to reduce their monitoring costs. Consider the case where a couple marries, h is a child, and then divorces. The parents share residential custody, so the child spends half of his/her time with each parent. One parent remarries and has another child with the new spouse. The other parent suspects that the remarried parent is spending less time and money on their child due to this new living situation, but is unable to monitor the remarried parent's behavior. One economist has argued that the existence of this type of transaction cost is a justification for state intervention in order to lower these costs and increase the amount produced of these goods (i.e., high-quality children) by making divorce more difficult and costly.[4]

TABLE 3.2 Percentage distribution of married-couple families by labor force status of spouses, 1995

Husband and wife in labor force	55.7
Husband in labor force, not the wife	21.9
Neither spouse in labor force	16.8
Wife in labor force, not the husband	5.6

Source: Current Population Reports Series P-20, no. 488 (Table 15).

Reduction of risk through resource pooling

A final category of possible cost reductions arises from the ability multi-person households have to smooth consumption patterns through resource pooling. For instance, if two members of the household are working but both experience occasional bouts of unemployment, income pooling will, in general, improve their utility by reducing their risk of having no income available at any point in time.[5] Additionally, by pooling funds available for investment, household members are better able to diversify their investment portfolio, reducing the level of risk to which they are exposed.

The phenomena of income and investment pooling are not confined to groups of people who live together. Family members who live in separate households often practice at least some income pooling, and single persons are also able to enter into resource pooling practices. However, they may experience higher transactions costs in setting up resource pooling contracts.

One problem is that living with other persons, particularly in marriage and other family situations, may increase the level of risk to which an individual is exposed. In fact, persons in a multi-person household may engage in riskier behavior than they would living alone. This is the problem of *moral hazard*. For example, a person may smoke in bed, counting on other members of the household to catch any fires that may occur.

*F*orces determining the division of labor

There are clearly many potential sources of cost savings through forming multi-person households, family households, and marriages. While there are also many potential sources of increased costs through living in groups, economic theory has provided a list of rationales for why persons would enter into these living arrangements. We will now consider whether economic theory can also help us explain why households have particular divisions of labor between market and nonmarket activities.

As shown in Table 3.2, what many people think of as the traditional division of labor for a married-couple family – the husband in the labor force while the wife is not – is found in a minority of families in the U.S. Even among families where at least one person works, only 26 percent maintain the traditional division of labor. The most common form currently is to have both spouses in the labor force.

However, Table 3.3 shows that the husband is generally the main contributor of income. In 80 percent of households outside of retirement age, the husband is the sole or higher earner. In only 15.7 percent of these households is the wife the sole or higher earner, and the median income for households where the wife is the sole earner is significantly lower than for other types of working households.

TABLE 3.3 Married couple households, percentage distribution by earner type and median income, 1990

	Percentage of households	Median income
Husband higher earner	56.8	$48,658
Husband sole earner	23.2	$36,100
Wife higher earner	12.8	$43,700
Wife sole earner	2.9	$24,000
Both nonearners	2.2	$10,528
Equal earnings	2.1	$48,000

Source: Calculated by the author using data from the Census of Population and Housing 1990, Public-Use Microdata 1/100 Sample. Data are for couples ages 25 to 59.

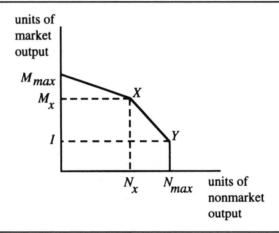

FIGURE 3.1   The household's production possibility frontier

Let us now consider the forces causing households to choose different patterns. Consider a married-couple household. Assume that one spouse is more efficient at producing market goods. There is also some *nonearned income* available (e.g., investment income, retirement benefits) of amount I. Figure 3.1 shows the household's *production possibility frontier*, the different combinations of market and nonmarket output that they can produce *and* consume.[6] (See the appendix to this chapter for a fuller discussion of production possibility frontiers.) Earned income, gained by selling one's time at an hourly wage, is combined with nonearned income to "produce" units of market output indirectly by using income to purchase them. Nonmarket output is produced directly using one's time. M_{max} is the amount of market output that the household can consume if the couple spends all their time in paid work. N_{max} is the amount of nonmarket output that the household can consume if the couple spends all their time in nonmarket activities.

In Figure 3.1, point X is the combination of units of market and nonmarket output that is produced by having the husband and wife completely specialize. The spouse who is more efficient at producing market output spends all his/her work time working for pay. This earned income, combined with nonearned income I, allows the household to purchase M_x units of market output. Meanwhile, the other spouse spends all his/her work time

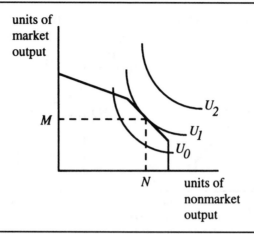

FIGURE 3.2   The solution to a household's utility maximization problem

producing N_x units of nonmarket output. The slope of the frontier becomes steeper at this point, showing that moving beyond this point towards point Y yields less additional nonmarket output for every unit of market output given up by the household, because the person who is less efficient at producing nonmarket output will now spend more time doing nonmarket work. However, the household can pick any combination along the budget constraint, including point Y, where both spouses do not work for pay but instead spend all their time producing nonmarket output. They still have their nonearned income I to spend on market output. If we measure units of market output in dollars, then they are able to purchase I units of market output.

Now, assume a household utility function, which takes the two arguments of units of market commodities and units of nonmarket commodities: $U = f$(market output, nonmarket output). Consumption of market and nonmarket commodities by either household member increases total household utility. This utility function generates a set of *indifference curves*, each of which shows combinations of market commodities and nonmarket commodities that generate the same total utility for the household. (See the appendix to this chapter for a discussion of indifference curves.) Higher indifference curves correspond to higher levels of utility. The household's problem is to maximize household utility, subject to the production possibility frontier.

Figure 3.2 graphs an example of how a household solves this problem. Three representative indifference curves are graphed, corresponding to total utility amounts U_0, U_1, and U_2, where $U_2 > U_1 > U_0$. The household attempts to reach the highest possible indifference curve, while being constrained to remain on the production possibility frontier. U_0 is attainable, but there are still points on the frontier that lie above U_0, so the household can do better than U_0. U_2 is better, but as it lies above the frontier, this level of utility is unattainable. U_1 corresponds to the indifference curve that is just touching the frontier (so the frontier is tangent to U_1); this is the highest attainable level of utility. At this point, the household will produce and consume M units of market output and N units of nonmarket output.

As shown in Figure 3.3, there are four possible forms of the solution, in terms of how the two household members split their time between market and nonmarket work.[7] In each case shown in the figure, the production possibility frontier is identical. The shape of the

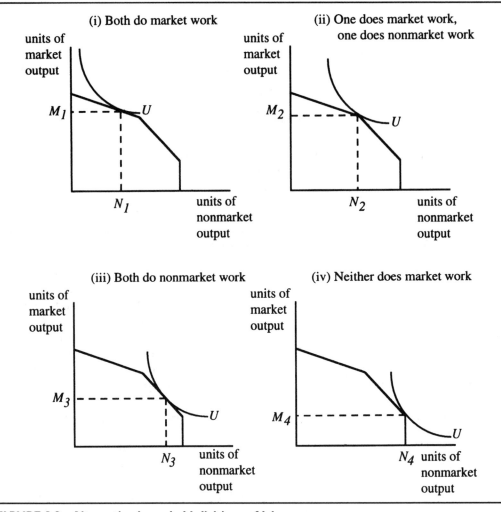

FIGURE 3.3   Alternative household divisions of labor

utility indifference curve is identical in each case as well, but the position on the graph and the slope of the indifference curve where it touches the frontier is different in each case. Different divisions of labor arise because households have different preferences for consumption of market vs. nonmarket output. In case (i), where the household has a strong preference for market output, both spouses do market work, but one spends time doing nonmarket work as well. In case (ii), both spouses completely specialize, one in market work and the other in nonmarket work. In case (iii), both spouses do nonmarket work, but one spouse spends time doing market work as well. In case (iv), where the household has a strong preference for nonmarket output, both spouses do only nonmarket work rather than supplementing their nonearned income in order to buy more market goods.

In cases (i), (ii), and (iii), the spouse that has *comparative advantage* at market work (i.e., is relatively more efficient at market work than nonmarket work) is the one who performs more of it. In order for men to spend more time doing market work, they must have a comparative advantage in market work and women in nonmarket work. Indeed, men are, in general, more efficient at generating units of market commodities than at generating units of nonmarket commodities; the opposite holds for women (see the appendix to this chapter for a demonstration of comparative advantage). Several forces can lead to this situation. First, men generally command a higher wage than women. This may be because they are more productive than women at market work or because discrimination in the labor market leads to men being paid more than equally productive women.

As we saw in Chapter 2, men do generally have higher hourly earnings than women. Of course, the fact that men make a higher wage than women does not necessarily mean that women could not increase their effort so as to earn as high a wage. But, if a person has a limited amount of effort available for work as well as a limited amount of time, he or she may spend time doing both market and nonmarket work, but expend less effort per hour in one work activity than in the other. For example, if a person can average lifting 50 couches an hour for eight hours before collapsing, the total number of couches lifted in eight hours cannot exceed 400, but the hourly rate of lifting couches can vary during the work day. So, too, if a woman is spending much effort on nonmarket work, a limit on total effort will lead her to choose less demanding market work, which may pay less per hour than more demanding jobs.[8] Indeed, studies find that time spent in housework negatively affects wages for both sexes, but more so for women (perhaps because of a nonlinear relationship between time spent in housework and wages, combined with the fact that women spend more time in housework).[9]

Interestingly, married men have much higher hourly earnings than unmarried men – in the range of 10 to 40 percent more. There are three possible forces that can cause this pattern. One is that marriage makes men more productive, either because they can specialize in market work and thereby improve their efficiency in market work and/or because they may exert more effort (perhaps cutting back on the effort they expend on leisure) if they are responsible for supporting a family. Second, discrimination in the labor market may favor married men over both women and unmarried men. For instance, employers, who tend to be married men themselves, may prefer employees who are similar to themselves and/or may be more likely to ascribe positive characteristics to married men. Finally, there may be selection into marriage on the basis of earnings-related characteristics, and married men are the innately more productive men.

One study that attempts to control for this third effect by comparing men's earnings over time (i.e., observing them both when they are single and when they are married) suggests that it is not the major cause of the marriage wage premium; 80 percent of the premium survived this control procedure.[10] The study also finds that married men experience faster wage growth over time than single men. However, controlling for the higher performance ratings from supervisors received by married men, the wage premium disappears. If these performance ratings are not warranted by actual productivity, this is evidence of discrimination in favor of married men. Another study, using data from a 1976 discrimination case involving a New York publishing firm, concludes that firm managers simply believed that married men (particularly those with children) "deserved" higher earnings than equally productive women and unmarried men.[11] The marriage wage premium has been declining since the late 1960s; the cause of this decline is an interesting puzzle that is not yet fully resolved.[12]

Second, women may be more efficient at both market and nonmarket work than men, but they may be relatively more efficient at nonmarket work. This can occur because women are trained to perform nonmarket tasks by their families and by society at large. In general, the training that people receive prior to marriage, as well as the skills they continue to develop, affect the division of chores within the marriage. So far, we have assumed that persons have predetermined levels of relative efficiency. A newlywed couple, however, might be equally efficient at both market and nonmarket work. In this case, the decision of who will work at home and who will work in the market is determined by some other factor, such as the prevailing social norm of women working in the home. After this decision is made, each spouse increases ability in his/her selected area. Through ability development, after some time has passed, the couple will display a comparative advantage pattern that appears to justify their original decision!

The advantages of specialization/division of labor have been couched in terms of increased production of commodities for consumption by household members. One "commodity" produced is satisfaction generated from spending time together. One study comparing single-earner to dual-earner couples finds that single-earner couples spend more time together (3.8 hours of awake time per day, compared with 3.2 hours for dual-earner couples), and that the couples' assessment of their marriage's quality is lower for dual-earner couples than single-earner couples.[13] However, some couples who have similar work patterns may find that their time together generates more utility (perhaps because their choices of leisure activities become more similar), and some couples work together, thereby increasing time spent together (whether they enjoy it or not).

Disadvantages of specialization

There are several disadvantages of specialization/division of labor that must be balanced against the advantages. One is that people may experience declining efficiency as they work more hours at a particular task. While the simple model developed above predicts that at least one person in the family would always be completely specialized, this decline in efficiency could lead to both persons splitting time between market and nonmarket work. This is a simple extension of the model, which still leads to the prediction that, in choosing who will increase nonmarket time by one hour, the person who is relatively more efficient at nonmarket production will be the one to switch.

There are other more important disadvantages of specialization that cannot be so easily incorporated into the simple model. The decision to specialize early in a marriage leads to differential development of skills between spouses, which means that if circumstances change, one or both persons may not be as well off. In particular, divorce or death of a spouse may put a person who has little market work experience and few market work skills in the position of having to do both market and nonmarket work, with a resulting reduction in consumption. The increase in risk from "putting all eggs in one basket" must be balanced against the benefits from specialization during the marriage.

Another important area of costs associated with specialization is the relationship of division of output among household members to division of labor. In particular, greater control over household monetary resources may lead to consumption of a larger portion of total household output. This phenomenon will be discussed below at greater length.

Finally, Charlotte Perkins Gilman, an influential early twentieth-century feminist, wrote: "It is not that women are really smaller-minded, weaker-minded, more timid and vacillating; but that whosoever, man or woman, lives always in a small dark place, is always guarded, protected, directed and restrained, will become inevitably narrowed and weakened by it.

The woman is narrowed by the house and the man is narrowed by the woman."[14] Not only may one's productive abilities be affected by the specialization decision, but also one's personality.[15] This is another cost that must be considered, even though it is hard to quantify.

Government policies affecting the division of labor

There are many government policies that affect household division of labor. In particular, tax codes and social welfare systems often create strong incentives for family households to decrease market work and increase nonmarket work. One basic feature of most income tax codes is that nonmarket output is not taxed. Therefore, a dollar's worth of nonmarket output is still worth a dollar after taxes, while an additional dollar's worth of income is reduced by the family's marginal tax rate. This has the effect of increasing the relative price of market services.

Second, many countries have *progressive* income taxes, which means that the marginal tax rate increases as income rises. The U.S. tax rates currently range from 15 to 39.6 percent; European countries have much higher top rates. Adding an additional market worker can push a family into a higher tax bracket, making it less likely that the family will decide that it is worthwhile to have two persons doing market work.

The tax code can also affect whether or not people marry. For instance, in a progressive income tax system, two persons can end up with more after-tax income by filing taxes separately than together because they can both stay in a lower bracket. Tax systems can compensate for this effect by allowing an additional deduction for married couples or by having a different schedule for married couples. The net effect of such a tax system can be to favor either married couples or single persons. In contrast to most other developed countries, which have individual filing systems, current U.S. tax system has both a "marriage penalty" and a bias against "secondary earners."[16]

Social security systems such as the current U.S. system can also affect the decisions of whether or not to work and marry. A cap on retirement benefits makes it less profitable for either or both spouses to work additional hours. Also, if benefits are determined by the larger of the two spouse's earnings, there is no gain in retirement income by having the lower-earning spouse work. An alternative "earnings sharing" system could credit total lifetime family earnings in determining retirement benefits for both spouses, even if they subsequently divorce. Finally, if a retired person is considering marrying someone who has earnings, that person may lose his/her retirement income, reducing the incentive to marry.

Who to marry and how to share

We have, so far, discussed many possible reasons why people would want to live with other people, as well as reasons why they would want to live alone. Additionally, for those who want to live with other people, the legal contract of marriage can allow for additional benefits by extending the time horizon of the living arrangement. In particular, long-term, costly investments such as houses and children may produce great benefits but be too risky to undertake without the promise of continued partnership that the marriage contract implies. Because there are costs involved in breaking the marriage contract, a marriage is less likely to end than a partnership such as cohabitation or roommate groupings. But we

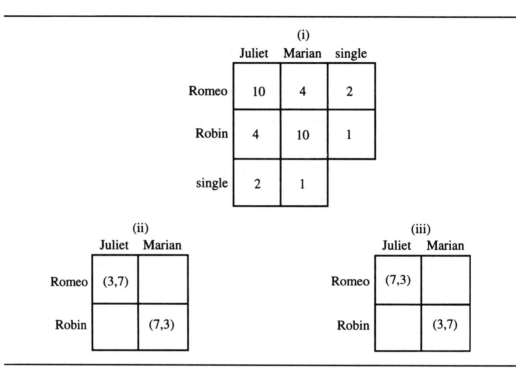

FIGURE 3.4 A marriage market with two stable pairs

have not yet discussed how people choose whom to marry, or who consumes what within a household. We will now use some basic economic concepts in order to discuss the market for marriages.

The neoclassical economic theory of marriage is based on two assumptions: Each person tries to do as well as possible in making a match; and the marriage market is competitive.[17] Under these assumptions, and assuming a large number of potential mates, *assortative mating* will tend to occur (persons tend to marry persons with roughly similar levels of benefits to offer their marriage partner) and partners tend to share equally the returns generated by their marriage.[18]

Consider the situation illustrated in Figure 3.4. Two men and two women are each deciding whether to remain single or not, and if they marry, who to marry. The first matrix, Figure 3.4 (i), shows the total (net) benefit produced by each potential marriage and by remaining single. In order for a marriage to occur, each person must do at least as well as if he/she remained single, and no other potential spouse must be willing to offer either person a better deal. For example, the matrix shows that if Romeo and Juliet marry, the total benefit created is 10, but if Romeo and Marian marry the total benefit is 4. A deal involves specifying how the total benefit produced by the potential marriage will be divided between the partners. The second matrix, Figure 3.4 (ii), shows a particular benefit split, that will lead to a stable marriage situation (where the first number is what the man receives, the second is what the woman receives) where the couples are (Romeo, Juliet) and (Robin, Marian). No one can do better either by remaining single or by marrying the other potential mate. This is not a uniquely stable situation; the third matrix, Figure 3.4 (iii)

	(i)		
	Scarlett	Melanie	single
Rhett	10	5	2
Ashley	5	4	1
single	2	1	

	(ii)		
	Cathy	Isabella	single
Heathcliff	10	9	2
Edgar	9	4	1
single	2	1	

FIGURE 3.5 Different marriage market outcomes

shows an alternative benefit split that maintains the same pairings. Note that the total benefit (10 + 10 = 20) is higher with this set of pairs than for the alternative set (4 + 4 = 8).

Figure 3.5 illustrates some alternative marriage market configurations. Note that in Figure 3.4, no person could be said to be a clearly superior mate, in the sense that he/she would produce more output in conjunction with any potential mate than the others. In Figure 3.5 (i), Rhett and Scarlett are both clearly superior, because they produce more output in conjunction with either of their potential mates than do Melanie and Ashley. Assortative mating will result: (Rhett, Scarlett) and (Ashley, Melanie).

However, assortative mating need not occur: superior mates may marry inferior mates if they can receive a larger share of output in such a marriage. Figure 3.5 (ii) illustrates a case in which the pairings are (Heathcliff, Isabella) and (Edgar, Cathy). Note that the total amount of output produced with this pairing (9 + 9 = 18) is greater than the total produced with the alternative pairing (10 + 4 = 14). Therefore, if Heathcliff and Cathy were thinking about pairing, Edgar could offer a better deal to Cathy and/or Isabella could offer a better deal to Heathcliff, taking into account the additional output generated, and break up the potential pair.

Is there evidence that people do or do not practice assortative mating? One study, using U.S. data from the mid-1970s, found that there appeared to be a positive correlation of traits such as education, ability, and drive among wives and their husbands in managerial occupations, but a negative correlation of traits for wives and their husbands in professional occupations.[19] But note that this does not imply that these couples are or are not practicing assortative mating. Persons may find that more household product is produced by associating with someone who has complementary traits. For instance, men who command a high wage may be better off marrying women who are efficient at producing nonmarket output but who would not receive a high wage doing market work. But a more recent study using Finnish data provides stronger evidence in support of the hypothesis, finding a correlation of both pre-marriage and post-marriage earnings.[20] The study also finds that the correlation has risen from 1970 to 1990, implying an increasing tendency towards assortative mating over this period.

In sparsely inhabited, or "thin" markets, we would expect to see more cases of unequal marriages, where the person with less to offer also takes a lower share of total benefit. We

TABLE 3.4 Numbers (in thousands) of men and women and number of men per hundred women by age group, 1995

	Men	*Women*	*Men per 100 Women*
All ages	128,314	134,441	95
≥16	96,817	104,423	93
20–24	9,087	8,795	103
25–44	41,493	41,848	99
25–29	9,530	9,476	101
30–34	10,902	10,966	99
35–39	11,071	11,178	99
40–44	9,990	10,228	98
≥65	13,689	19,843	69

Source: Statistical Abstract of the United States (1996): 16 (Table 16).

would also expect that the scarcer group in the marriage market would be able to contract for bigger shares of total benefit. Table 3.4 shows 1995 U.S. data for numbers of men and women by age group. Scarcity and market thinness do not appear to be important factors in the national market (although particular geographic submarkets may have sex imbalances and fewer choices – e.g., the larger number of men in rural areas and larger number of women in urban areas may pose a problem to people's marrying at all). During the prime marrying ages – in particular, the 20s – when most people first marry, there are more men than women. Among 25- to 44-year-olds, there are almost equal numbers of men and women. However, at older ages, the number of men drops off sharply, implying that older women are less likely to marry or remarry (assuming that they marry men of the same age or older) and that those who do marry may be less likely to be in equal sharing situations.

Economic theory leads us to categorize single persons as persons who are either better off staying single than taking any available marriage offers or who have too little to offer other persons relative to other available candidates, even if they are willing to strike an unequal bargain.

FOCUS

Is bachelorhood a pitiable state?

In some societies, bachelors cut a sad figure. Consider this description by anthropologist Claude Lévi-Strauss:[21]

> I remember having one day noticed, in a Boróro village of central Brazil, a man about thirty years old, who was carelessly dressed and appeared to be badly nourished, sad, and solitary. I thought at first he was sick. "But no," was the answer to my question, "he is a bachelor."
> ... in a society where work is apportioned between the sexes, and where only the conjugal state permits a man to enjoy the products of women's labor – including delousing, other care of the hair, and body painting, in addition to gardening and cooking ... – a bachelor is half a human being.

Alternative living arrangements

In discussing the marriage market, we did not explicitly consider alternatives to marriage that involve remaining single, but living with other people. Some people are legally single, but are involved in a homosexual or heterosexual live-in arrangement. These households can experience many of the benefits and costs of legal marriage, lacking only the higher cost of dissolving the relationship to help ensure its longevity. We can expand our view of the marriage market to call it a "living arrangement" market instead.[22]

The possibility that sexual orientation is open to choice makes the number of persons on each side of the living arrangement market endogenous.[23] People who are flexible with respect to the sex of their partner will have a larger number of choices than people who are inflexible. Even if there is social disapproval that increases the costs of choosing to live in a same-sex relationship, the living arrangement market will respond to relative supply and demand. For instance, if women were relatively scarce, we might see more men choosing same-sex relationships. Even without the scarcity factor, people may strike better deals through contracting with members of the same sex. And, if social disapproval decreases, we may see more same-sex relationships form.

While the number of nonfamily households is increasing, we know very little about the composition of nonfamily households. Several countries, including Sweden and the United States, have begun to gather statistics and keep records on how many households contain heterosexual cohabiting couples and on the percentage of these households that are long-term arrangements and/or include offspring. However, official economic statistics are not available on how many households contain same-sex couples.[24]

How is power distributed in households?

Earlier in this chapter, we had modeled the household's goal as maximization of the household's utility function. But now we have considered how the living arrangement market creates a situation in which couples bargain with each other over what sharing rule to adopt before becoming a household.[25] A problem in reconciling these two views of how the household works is that many households appear to have sharing rules that cause household members to prefer different points on the household production possibility frontier. For instance, if the sharing arrangement is such that one person receives a larger share of nonmarket production than of market production, then that person has incentive to try to increase the amount of nonmarket goods that the household produces relative to the amount of market goods, while other household members would prefer to see more production of market goods. In this case, who decides what combination of goods is produced? Additionally, why do households appear to have unequal sharing rules in many cases, when we have predicted that the living arrangement market should lead to equal sharing?

Money as power

One possibility is that the partner who provides the greater share of income, whether earned or nonearned, is the one who chooses the mix of products the household produces.[26] One study that compares four types of couples – married, cohabiting heterosexual, gay, and lesbian – finds that for all types except lesbian, "the amount of money a person earns – in comparison with a partner's income – establishes relative power."[27] Power can relate to both who decides the sharing split and who decides what will be produced. This power can be caused by the greater ability of the person with higher market-good producing efficiency to leave the marriage. If money is power in the sense that the person with greater income also commands the larger share of total household market and nonmarket output, then women are generally worse off than men, since they have lower market income. Even after adding in an approximate value of nonmarket output (valued at a woman's foregone earnings) and including this in the calculation of who produces the largest share of *total* income, women appear to be worse off than men under proportionate sharing.[28]

Effects of patriarchy on household sharing

Others, both economists and noneconomists, argue that the whole depiction of a household as a bargaining unit in which women and men rationally choose their sharing rule and where competition drives couples to adopt relatively equal sharing of total production is inaccurate.[29] Economist Heidi Hartmann has been an influential critic of neoclassical economic theory as applied to the household.[30] She argues that the social system of patriarchy means that men can systematically extort women within marriages so as to receive the larger share of household production. For instance, other men (and women) can refuse to support a woman in her bargaining (e.g., family members may refuse to take a wife into their home if she leaves her husband). Additionally, patriarchy, operating through labor market discrimination against women, can reduce a woman's potential earnings and thereby reduce her bargaining power.

Hartmann points out that even when married women do market work, they still do the vast majority of nonmarket work performed in the household, implying that women give up more leisure time than men in order to provide additional income for the household. Since leisure is a nonmarket good, women are receiving a smaller share of total production even if all other household products are split equally. Studies of married-couple households show that women do the majority of nonmarket work performed by the household, whether or not the woman also does market work.[31] In comparing households by how women spend their time, one study finds that, on average, husbands of market-working wives do not have a greater nonmarket contribution, measured either in time units or in monetary terms (where time is valued at the husband's wage), over husbands of wives doing only nonmarket work.[32] Other studies find that even in dual-career couples, wives do the majority of housework, although dual-career husbands do greater amounts of housework only in comparison with husbands whose wives who do only nonmarket work.[33] Interestingly, one study finds that even in cohabiting couples, the women do a greater share of the housework – although not as large a share as in married couples.[34]

Do women care more about children?

Another view of why women end up with the smaller share of household production is that women's greater interest in children puts them at a bargaining disadvantage. If men know that women are more interested in marriage because they derive more utility from having children than do men, then men can receive a larger share of other goods.[35] It is not just that women are able to have children and men are not; this would imply that men would be at a disadvantage in bargaining, because if they cared about having children at all they would need a woman to cooperate with them in order to have them. But once the children are born, either spouse could threaten to walk away from the marriage and leave the other with the children. If men are able to make this threat more credibly, then they will be able to renegotiate household sharing to their favor. Notably, even though joint custody arrangements are becoming more prevalent, women are still much more likely to have residential custody of children following divorce.

FOCUS

The economics of domestic violence

Economists have recently begun to study the phenomenon of domestic violence. Research on this topic has proceeded on several fronts, including measuring the extent and costs of domestic violence, and considering how domestic violence enters into bargaining relationships within the household.

Researchers have found it difficult to establish either the level or the time trend for domestic violence incidence, but it appears to be a worldwide phenomenon that affects a significant percentage of women.[36] Occasional domestic violence may affect as many as ten percent of married women in the U.S. and severe violence may affect around three percent.[37] There are also significant reported levels of violence against married men. In a survey of three villages in India, about one-fifth of the wives admitted to being beaten chronically and severely, with the researchers having difficulty in eliciting admissions of less regular or severe abuse.[38]

Given the difficulty of establishing exact figures on the prevalence of domestic violence, it is also difficult to come up with estimates of its costs, and early research has been limited in scope. One researcher asked 20 formerly battered women to estimate the direct expenses of leaving the abusive relationship, arriving at an estimate of over $14,000 (in 1993 dollars), including medical expenses, legal fees, and lost earnings.[39] This does not include the cost to the government or other agencies of providing shelters, counseling, and other monetary and nonmonetary aid. Another study estimated the annual health-related costs of violence against women (e.g., lost earnings, medical treatment and counseling costs) in Canada at over $1.5 billion (Canadian dollars).[40]

Several researchers have developed economic models in which the threat and/or actuality of domestic violence can be used to affect persons' constraints and subsequent choices, as well as their utilities.[41] It is clear from these models that social institutional responses outside the marriage, such as creation of shelters and how police respond to domestic violence calls, can affect what happens in the relationship.[42] Some of these effects are hard to observe; for instance, shelters may benefit not only those who utilize them, but also those who know that they are available; their very availability changes bargaining positions and may thereby reduce the level of domestic violence.

Renegotiation of sharing rules

In the discussion of the living arrangement market, we implicitly assumed that persons would pick a sharing rule and stick with it throughout their marriage or alternative living arrangement. However, in the case of marriages, in particular, because of the costs involved in dissolving the living arrangement, if one spouse demands a renegotiation of the sharing rule after the marriage has begun, the other spouse may be at a bargaining disadvantage. The factors considered above – the greater portability of market goods-producing skills, patriarchy, and the greater desire of women to produce household goods in the form of children – all imply that men have the advantage and are both more likely to insist on a renegotiation away from equal sharing and to leave the marriage if renegotiation breaks down.[43] In this view, in marriages where equal sharing is maintained throughout the marriage, the woman is receiving more *rents* from the marriage – i.e., benefits in excess of the minimum amount needed to keep the other person from walking away.

FOCUS

Has feminism failed? One woman's viewpoint

Freelance writer Kay Ebeling penned a bitter opinion piece for *Newsweek* in 1990, from which follow some quotations:[44]

> To me, feminism has backfired against women. In 1973 I left what could have been a perfectly good marriage, taking with me a child in diapers, a 10-year-old Plymouth and Volume 1, Number One of Ms. Magazine. I was convinced I could make it on my own. In the last 15 years my ex has married or lived with a succession of women. As he gets older, his women stay in their 20s. Meanwhile, I've stayed unattached. He drives a BMW. I ride buses.
>
> Today I see feminism as the Great Experiment That Failed, and women in my generation, its perpetrators, are the casualties. Many of us, myself included, are saddled with raising children alone. The resulting poverty makes us experts at cornmeal recipes and ways to find free recreation on weekends. At the same time, single men from our generation amass fortunes in CDs and real-estate ventures so they can breeze off on ski weekends. Feminism freed men, not women. Now men are spared the nuisance of a wife and family to support. After childbirth, if his wife's waist doesn't return to 20 inches, the husband can go out and get a more petite woman. It's far more difficult for the wife, now tied down with a baby, to find a new man. . . .
>
> Feminism made women disposable. So today a lot of females are around 40 and single with a couple of kids to raise on their own. Child-support payments might pay for a few pairs of shoes, but in general, feminism gave men all the financial and personal advantages over women.
>
> What's worse, we asked for it. Many women decided: you don't need a family structure to raise your children. We packed them off to day-care centers where they could get their nurturing from professionals. Then we put on our suits and ties, packed our briefcases and took off on this Great Experiment, convinced that there was no difference between ourselves and the guys in the other offices.
>
> How wrong we were. Because like it or not, women have babies. It's this biological thing that's just there, these organs we're born with. The truth is, a woman can't live the true feminist life unless she denies her childbearing biology. She has to live on the pill, or have her tubes tied at an early age. Then she can keep up with the guys with an uninterrupted career and then, when she's 30, she'll be paying her own way on ski weekends too. . . .
>
> Women should get educations so they can be brainy in the way they raise their children. Women can start small businesses, do consulting, write freelance out of the home. But women don't belong in 12-hour-a-day executive office positions, and I can't figure out today what ever made us think we would want to be there in the first place. As long as that biology is there, women can't compete equally with men. A ratio cannot be made using disproportionate parts. Women and men are not equal, we're different. The economy might even improve if women came home, opening up jobs for unemployed men, who could then support a wife and children, the way it was, pre-feminism.

Household and marriage dissolution

So far we have assumed that people rationally consider the various factors associated with entering into a particular living arrangement. We also assume that they continually consider whether or not to continue the situation. Let us model a person's decision as to whether or not to continue in a particular living situation as:

If $B(X) < C(X)$ then leave X.

If the benefits of remaining in living situation X are less than the costs of remaining in living situation X, then leave situation X; otherwise don't.[45] Renegotiation of sharing rules is a factor that can change the benefits and costs of X, but even after renegotiation, a person may still decide to leave.

One possible way to end a living situation is to divorce. Let us model a person's decision to divorce as:

If $B(Y) < C(Y)$ then divorce Y.

If the benefits associated with staying married to person Y are less than the costs associated with staying married to Y, then divorce Y; otherwise don't.

Note that these decisions involve different benefits and costs than the decisions to enter into living arrangements and marriages in the first place. For instance, it is generally costly in terms of both time and money to undergo a divorce. Therefore a benefit of staying married is the avoidance of these costs. Even if a person would not remarry person Y, knowing what he/she now knows about Y, it may still be too expensive for the person to divorce Y. Additionally, popular sentiment against divorce can raise the psychic costs of divorce – e.g., if one's family or religious group has strong sanctions against divorce.

Why do the costs and benefits associated with a particular living arrangement change over time? One possibility is that there exists uncertainty about the exact costs and benefits associated with a living arrangement, and that this uncertainty is resolved after one actually enters into the marriage. For example, you may not realize that your potential mate has various annoying habits, such as snoring loudly, until you have married. You may assess the probability before marriage that the person snores as being low, and this assessment leads you to end up married to a snorer. Some economists have suggested that the majority of divorces result from the existence of uncertainty and the realization of unfavorable outcomes.[46]

Uncertainty over the future course of the living arrangement may include unexpected changes in a household member's situation.[47] For instance, the unexpected illness of one member may affect the viability of the marriage. Another source of uncertainty is imperfect knowledge of one's alternatives to the current marriage. Over time, additional information may be gathered concerning viable alternatives, leading one or both members to opt for divorce. For instance, one's ideal mate may appear only after one has already married someone else, having given up on the existence of the ideal.

Some people may find the costs of waiting for such alternatives, even if they place a high probability on such an alternative arising, too high. For instance, if they do not like living alone, they may marry even though they know there is a high probability they will later decide to divorce. If the costs of waiting for a good match are high and the costs of divorcing are low, then we would expect a number of divorces to take place even in a rational choice system.

We generally expect people to take actions that would reduce the uncertainty associated with marriage, such as getting to know their potential marriage partner well before marriage and trying to assess the availability of other preferable partners (although these two activities may conflict!). However, studies have found that couples who cohabit before marriage, which theoretically would reduce the uncertainty in marriage relative to couples who have not lived together before marrying, have higher divorce rates than average.[48] Creation of a prenuptial agreement, which generally specifies how property will be divided in the case of divorce – and in some cases specifies which spouse will pay various expenses during the marriage, is another way to reduce uncertainty.[49]

In this rational choice model, we would expect government policies that affect the costs associated with divorcing to affect the divorce rate. In particular, the state may force parties to compensate for breach of implicit contract in situations such as the case where one spouse realizes gains from a marriage early in the marriage, while the other spouse plans to realize gains later in the marriage.[50] In these situations, the person who receives high benefits relative to costs and then expects that the marriage will be costly later has incentive to end the marriage after realizing the benefits. An example is the case where one spouse foregoes his/her education and instead works to put the other through school, expecting to be compensated later by sharing in the higher earnings generated from the additional schooling. Once through school, the educated spouse then has incentive to exit the marriage rather than share these higher earnings with the uneducated spouse. While some states have decided that an educational degree is not property, in most states, divorce courts liken marriage to a partnership or an investment and use a variety of legal methods to divide the value of the educational degree asset.[51]

Alimony can serve as an efficient means of redistributing property rights and assets. One study using 1970 data finds that the alimony system as administered at that point in time did act to compensate spouses (in particular, wives who had little market work experience) for these opportunity costs.[52] Interestingly, the study found that states that excluded alimony from divorce arrangements had a lower percentage of ever-married women, aged 25 to 34, and had lower marital fertility, all else equal. This use of the alimony system implies that the granting of alimony will drop over time as women tend to remain in market work situations and as fertility drops, which is what has happened. Notably, a rising number of men now receive alimony, even as the overall incidence of alimony is declining.[53]

There are many details that make it hard for the courts to create rules covering every consideration as to how much income and property rights to transfer to the spouse incurring greater costs from divorce. For instance, some observers have advocated separate standards for short and long marriages. One possibility is to consider the living standard provided during the course of the marriage for short marriages and to use this as the standard for spousal support after the marriage, while long marriages would warrant the possibly higher level of support of an equalized living standard in the two post-divorce households.[54]

Policy Application: No-fault divorce

Economists and other researchers have investigated whether various changes in U.S. divorce laws have had an impact on divorce rates. In particular, they have studied the widespread adoption of no-fault divorce laws in the 1970s.[55] Unilateral no-fault divorce allows a marriage partner to terminate the marriage contract without having to ascribe fault for the termination (the no-fault reason often given is "irreconcilable differences").[56] Before no-fault divorce came into use, even if both spouses desired a divorce, one had to sue the other for divorce on fault grounds, which included desertion, adultery, and cruelty. Starting with California in 1970 (where fault-based divorce was completely abolished)[57] and ending with South Dakota in 1985, all states now allow no-fault divorces, although the laws governing divorce, including grounds for asset division, vary from state to state.[58] The existence of a transition period in which states had very different systems created a "natural experiment" situation for testing the validity of economic theories concerning divorce.

Economist H. Elizabeth Peters has found that during the period in which some states had unilateral no-fault and others did not, the variation in state laws did not cause different divorce rates across states.[59] However, settlements were lower for women in unilateral no-fault states. Both of these findings are consistent with the *Coase Theorem*, which states that if transactions costs are negligible, a change in property rights does not change resource allocation but does influence the distribution of wealth.[60] The lack of difference in divorce rates between states implies that the transactions costs involved in divorcing were not significantly lowered by the switch to no-fault divorce laws. Peters had predicted, based on the Coase Theorem, that no change in divorce rates would occur because marriages would only end when it is efficient to do so – which depends on alternatives to the marriage, not on the law. However, no-fault divorce reassigns the property right of who gets to decide whether or not a divorce will occur. Under fault law, the spouse most wanting to leave must purchase the right to leave. A spouse could exact a large property settlement in exchange for consenting to the divorce. With no-fault, the spouse least wanting to divorce must pay the other to stay, or more likely, will not be able to prevent the divorce from occurring. Since women were the ones to receive smaller settlement amounts after passage of unilateral no-fault, women must be more likely than men to want to stay married.

Subsequently, another economist, Douglas Allen, attempted to replicate these results, doubting their correctness, both because he believed that the transactions costs involved in divorce were large and because he thought that Peters had made some misclassifications of states.[61] He found that no-fault states have higher divorce rates, which is consistent with the idea that the transactions costs were nonnegligible and that no-fault tended to reduce those costs.

Peters then performed a follow-up study, using Allen's reclassifications, finding that whether or not unilateral no-fault divorce laws increase or have no effect on divorce rates depends on whether or not one controls for underlying forces that lead some states (notably California) to have higher divorce rates than other states.[62] These states had higher divorce rates before no-fault laws were passed as well as afterwards. If the higher previous rates are taken into account, it turns out that the passage of no-fault divorce legislation had no effect on divorce rates. In support of Peters, an older study that did not use sophisticated statistical techniques also found no effect on the divorce rate from passage of no-fault divorce laws.[63] The study noted that California and Florida had high divorce rates and were no-fault states, but attributed these rates to socioeconomic differences as well.

What are the possible transaction costs involved in marriage and divorce? According to Allen:[64]

Transaction costs arise from establishing and protecting one's property rights. They result from the possibility of involuntary transfers of wealth, from which marriage is not exempt. Indeed, given the span of married life, the extreme degree of specialization for many women, the difficulty in monitoring a spouse's perform-ance, and the possibility of radical unexpected changes in marriage law, marriage is likely to have very large transaction costs. For example, differences in property-division laws led to huge transaction costs for some couples living in various states when no-fault laws were introduced.

Therefore, *if* property rights in a marriage are perfectly defined, he concludes that transaction costs are zero.

Peters points out that there are different types of transaction costs in negotiating a divorce: (1) technical constraints on bargaining – in particular, indivisibilities for particular types of marital property and the existence of private information, which means that one cannot tell how much the other spouse values divorce; (2) legal costs; and (3) costs associated with *rent-seeking behavior*, which is when one party attempts to gain assets from the other. If (1) is a problem, then one would expect higher divorce rates in no-fault states. With respect to (2), she points out that no-fault divorce is not synonymous with low-cost divorce, so without differential legal costs between types of states, this source of transaction costs alone will not lead to a difference. Finally, she points out that Allen concentrates on the third source of transaction costs, but as with (2), it is not clear that rent-seeking is a bigger problem in no-fault states. Peters notes in looking at the actual motivation for passage of no-fault laws:

> Interest groups of divorcing individuals were basically not involved in the debate over changing divorce laws during the 1970's. . . . The proponents of the change were primarily legal scholars who wanted the letter of the law to better reflect actual practice. The laws were adopted relatively quickly, because there were few conflicting interest groups who participated in the debate.[65]

Summary

Most people live in households – mainly family households. The benefits of forming a household include (1) economies in production, (2) internalization of externalities, (3) reduction of transactions costs, and (4) reduction of risk through resource pooling. Particular activities, such as buying a house and having children, are risky to undertake for nonfamily households, providing an economic rationale for marriage.

The "traditional" division of labor is found in a minority of families. However, men still often have comparative advantage in market work and women in nonmarket work, and women still tend to provide the bulk of nonmarket work, while men tend to provide the larger share of household earnings. This situation may be caused both by choices on the part of individuals and by social forces such as socialization and discrimination. The disadvantages involved in specialization are nonnegligible. Government policies, such as the income tax system, tend to create incentives towards increasing nonmarket work relative to market work.

Competitive marriage markets tend to lead to assortative mating and to adoption of equal sharing rules. However, factors such as access to income, a patriarchial social system, and differential caring about children's well-being may give an advantage to one person over the other, leading to unequal sharing. These factors often relate to the greater ability of one person to leave the marriage and still maintain reasonable living standards. Divorce is modeled as a rational choice along with mar-riage, where the benefits of remaining in a marriage must exceed the costs of leaving it. These costs may be affected by policies such as dropping fault-based divorce and changing property division rules.

Endnotes

1. Institutional living arrangements include dormitories, military barracks, old-age homes, and mental hospitals. For an anthropological/historical perspective on households, see Robert McC. Netting, Richard R. Wilk, and Eric J. Arnould (eds.), *Households: Comparative and Historical Studies of the Domestic Group* (Berkeley, Calif.: University of California, 1984).

2. We will assume that if $B = C$, then the person will not enter into X, on the grounds that he/she will decide in this situation to wait in order to gain more information and break the tie.

3. Douglas W. Allen, "An Inquiry into the State's Role in Marriage," *Journal of Economic Behavior and Organization* 13, no. 2 (March 1990): 171–191.

4. *Ibid.*

5. This assumes that people are risk-averse.

6. I assume that nonmarket goods have no perfect substitutes available for purchase.

7. I am ruling out those solutions that do not fall in the interior of the graph – i.e., solutions in which the household consumes only market goods or only nonmarket goods. Also, they will not choose a point on the vertical portion of the frontier, because those points that involve throwing away some of their unearned income will never be chosen if we assume that people always prefer consuming more to consuming less.

8. Gary S. Becker, "Human Capital, Effort, and the Sexual Division of Labor," *Journal of Labor Economics* 3, no. 1, supplement (January 1985): S33–S58.

9. Joni Hersch and Leslie Stratton, "Housework, Wages, and the Division of Housework Time for Employed Spouses," *American Economic Review* 84, no. 2 (May 1994): 120–125.

10. Sanders Korenman and David Neumark, "Does Marriage Really Make Men More Productive?" *Journal of Human Resources* 26, no. 2 (Spring 1991): 282–307.

11. Paul Osterman, "Sex Discrimination in Professional Employment: A Case Study," *Industrial and Labor Relations Review* 32, no. 4 (July 1979): 451–464.

12. Cf. McKinley Blackburn and Sanders Korenman, "The Declining Marital-Status Earnings Differential," *Journal of Population Economics* 7, no. 3 (July 1994): 247–270.

13. Paul William Kingston and Steven L. Nock, "Time Together Among Dual-Earner Couples," *American Sociological Review* 52, no. 3 (June 1987): 391–400.

14. Charlotte Perkins Gilman, *The Home: Its Work and Influence* (New York: Charlton, 1910): 277.

15. Economists might prefer to say that one's preferences may be affected. See Elaine McCrate, "Gender Difference: The Role of Endogenous Preferences and Collective Action," *American Economic Review* 78, no. 2 (May 1988): 235–239.

16. See Edward J. McCaffery, *Taxing Women* (Chicago, Ill.: University of Chicago, 1997), for a thorough discussion of gender bias in the U.S. income tax system.

17. The classic references for the neoclassical economic theory of marriage are Gary S. Becker, "A Theory of Marriage: Part I," *Journal of Political Economy* 81, no. 4 (July/August 1973): 813–846; "A Theory of Marriage: Part II," *Journal of Political Economy* 82, no. 2, part 2 (March/April 1974): 11–26.

18. Douglas W. Allen, "'What Does She See in Him?' The Effect of Sharing on the Choice of Spouse," *Economic Inquiry* 30, no. 1 (January 1992): 57–67.

19. Paul S. Carlin, "Home Investment in Husband's Human Capital and the Wife's Decision to Work," *Journal of Population Economics* 4, no. 1 (March 1991): 71–86.

20. Maria Cancian and Markus Jantti, "Assortative Mating on Labor Market Characteristics," paper presented at the Allied Social Science Associations Meetings (January 1997).

21. Claude Lévi-Strauss, *The View from Afar* (New York: Basic Books, 1985): 46.

22. However, see M.V. Lee Badgett, "Gender, Sexuality, and Sexual Orientation: All in the Feminist Family?" *Feminist Economics* 1, no. 1 (Spring 1995): 121–139, for a discussion of the

limitations of expanding current gender-based models to apply to lesbian, gay, and bisexual families; also the commentary on this article in the Summer 1995 issue of *Feminist Economics*.

23.   Richard A. Posner, *Sex and Reason* (Cambridge, Mass.: Harvard University, 1991), considers that choice of sexual behavior may be influenced, though not for all people, by the relative benefits and costs of adopting different sexual practices. See also the critical review of this book: Robert M. Anderson, "EP Seeks EP: A Review of *Sex and Reason* by Richard A. Posner," *Journal of Economic Literature* 31, no. 1 (March 1993): 191–198. See also Richard R. Cornwall, "deconstructing silence: the queer political economy of the social articulation of desire," *Review of Radical Political Economics* 29, no. 1 (Winter 1997): 1–130, for an innovative approach to modeling of the social articulation of preferences.

24.   Few papers are available as yet on the subject of variations in economic status by sexual preference. The first American Economic Association session on the topic was held in January 1992, and a general theme was the paucity of data. See M.V. Lee Badgett and Rhonda M. Williams, "The Economics of Sexual Orientation: Establishing a Research Agenda," *Feminist Studies* 18, no. 3 (Fall 1992): 649–657 for background on the session and the issues discussed therein. M. V. Lee Badgett, "The Wage Effects of Sexual Orientation Discrimination," *Industrial and Labor Relations Review* 48, no. 4 (July 1995): 726–739 measures the effect on earnings of sexual orientation, finding that gay and bisexual male workers earned between 11 and 27 percent less than comparable heterosexual males; results for lesbian and bisexual women relative to heterosexual women were inconclusive. Batya Hyman, *The Economic Consequences of Child Sexual Abuse in Women* (Ann Arbor, Mich.: University Microfilms, 1993), using the 1985 National Lesbian Health Care Survey, finds that lesbians who were 'out' to more of their coworkers earned less than those who were out to fewer of their coworkers.

25.   A paper that models the choice of a household sharing scheme as a two-person cooperative game is Marilyn Manser and Murray Brown, "Marriage and Household Decisionmaking: A Bargaining Analysis," *International Economic Review* 21, no. 1 (February 1980): 31–44. Marjorie McElroy and Mary Jean Horney, in "Nash-bargained Household Decisions: Toward a Generalization of the Theory of Demand," *International Economic Review* 22, no. 2 (June 1981): 333–349, fully work out the Nash rule, in which each person tries to do as well as possible, given the other person's choice, and show that the adoption of a household utility function is a special case of adopting this bargaining rule. A fairly technical but interesting set of four papers discussing the empirical implementation of bargaining models can be found in "Symposium on Household Bargaining Models," *Journal of Human Resources* 25, no. 4 (Fall 1990): 559–664.

26.   See Paula England and Barbara Stanek Kilbourne, "Markets, Marriages, and Other Mates: The Problem of Power," *Beyond the Marketplace: Rethinking Economy and Society*, eds. Roger Friedland and A.F. Robertson (Hawthorne, N.Y.: Aldine de Gruyter, 1990): 163–189, for a review of research on marital power.

27.   Philip Blumstein and Pepper Schwartz, *American Couples* (New York: William Morrow, 1983): 53.

28.   Victor R. Fuchs, "Sex Differences in Economic Well-being," *Science* (April 25, 1986): 459–464.

29.   Cf. Amartya Sen, "Gender and Cooperative Conflicts," *Persistent Inequalities: Women and World Development*, ed. Irene Tinker (New York and Oxford: Oxford University, 1990): 123–149, for a critique of simplistic applications of bargaining theory to gender divisions of labor. See also Elaine McCrate, "Trade, Merger and Employment: Economic Theory on Marriage," *Review of Radical Political Economics* 19, no. 1 (Spring 1987): 73–89, for discussion of how power relations within marriage might be modeled.

30.   Heidi I. Hartmann, "The Family as the Locus of Gender, Class and Political Struggle: The Example of Housework," *Signs* 6, no. 3 (Spring 1981): 366–394.

31.   Cf. Sarah Fenstermaker Berk, *The Gender Factory: The Apportionment of Work in American Households* (New York: Plenum, 1985), using time diary data from 1976 for 335 married-couple households; Catherine E. Ross, "The Division of Labor at Home," *Social Forces* 65, no. 3 (March 1987): 813–833, using a 1978 telephone survey of 680 married couples; Beth Anne

Shelton, *Women, Men and Time: Gender Differences in Paid Work, Housework and Leisure* (New York: Greenwood, 1992), using the 1987–88 National Survey of Families and Households; Hersch and Stratton, *loc. cit.*, using data from the 1979 through 1987 waves of the Panel Study of Income Dynamics, including only white employed couples ages 20 to 64.

32. Kathryn E. Walker and William H. Gauger, "Time and Its Dollar Value in Housework," *Family Economics Review* (Fall 1973): 8–13.

33. Donna Hodgkins Berardo, Constance L. Shehan, and Gerald R. Leslie, "A Residue of Tradition: Jobs, Careers, and Spouses' Time in Housework," *Journal of Marriage and the Family* 49, no. 2 (May 1987): 381–390, using survey data from the 1976 wave of the Panel Study of Income Dynamics, including only white couples with both members under 65; Rosalind C. Barnett and Caryl Rivers, *She Works, He Works: How Two-Income Families are Happier, Healthier, and Better-Off* (New York: HarperCollins, 1996), using self-collected interview data from the 1990s.

34. Scott J. South and Glenna Spitze, "Housework in Marital and Nonmarital Households," *American Sociological Review* 59, no. 3 (June 1994): 327–347, using the 1987–88 National Survey of Families and Households.

35. Victor Fuchs, *Women's Quest for Economic Equality* (Cambridge, Mass.: Harvard University, 1988), believes that this difference in caring for children is at the root of the observed economic inequality by sex.

36. United Nations Centre for Social Development and Humanitarian Affairs, "Violence Against Women in the Family" (New York: United Nations, 1989).

37. Murray A. Straus and Richard J. Gelles, "Societal Change and Change in Family Violence from 1975 to 1985 As Revealed by Two National Surveys," *Journal of Marriage and the Family* 48, no. 3 (August 1986): 465–479, using data from the National Family Violence Surveys (NFVS). Another source of information regarding U.S. levels of domestic violence are the U.S. Department of Justice National Crime Victimization Surveys (NCVS), in which lower levels of domestic violence are reported than in the NFVS. The Bureau of Justice Statistics has also started collecting data on domestic violence utilizing emergency hospital admissions, which show a rate of violence about four times higher than in the NCVS.

38. Vijayendra Rao, "Domestic Violence and Intra-Household Resource Allocation in Rural India: An Exercise in Participatory Econometrics," M. Krishnaraj, R. Sudarshan, and A. Sharif (eds.), *Gender, Population, and Development* (New Delhi and Oxford: Oxford University, 1997).

39. Rachel A. Buddeberg, "The Cost of Abuse to Women," paper presented at the Allied Social Science Association meetings (January 1994).

40. Tanis Day, "The Health-Related Costs of Violence Against Women in Canada: The Tip of the Iceberg," Centre for Research on Violence Against Women and Children, University of Western Ontario (1995).

41. Amy Farmer and Jill Tiefenthaler, "Domestic Violence: The Value of Services as Signals," *American Economic Review* 86, no. 2 (May 1996): 274–279; Helen V. Tauchen, Ann Dryden Witte, and Sharon K. Long, "Domestic Violence: A Nonrandom Affair," *International Economic Review* 32, no. 2 (May 1991): 491–511.

42. Helen Tauchen and Ann Dryden Witte, "The Dynamics of Domestic Violence," *American Economic Review* 85, no. 2 (May 1995): 414–418; Farmer and Tiefenthaler, *loc. cit.*

43. Rhona Mahony, *Kidding Ourselves: Breadwinning, Babies, and Bargaining Power* (New York: BasicBooks, 1995), acknowledges these issues and takes the proactive approach of instructing women in how they might become better negotiators.

44. Kay Ebeling, "The Failure of Feminism," *Newsweek* (November 19, 1990): 9. Reprinted with permission.

45. In this case, it is assumed that if $B = C$, the person will stay in X, on the grounds that he/she decides in this situation to wait in order to gain more information and break the tie.

46. Gary S. Becker, Elisabeth M. Landes, and Robert T. Michael, "An Economic Analysis of Marital Instability," *Journal of Political Economy* 85, no. 6 (December 1977): 1141–1187.

47. Allen, *loc. cit.*, considers this case most likely.

48. T.R. Balakrishnan, K.V. Rao, E. Lapierre-Adamcyk, and K.J. Krotki, "A Hazard Model Analysis of the Covariates of Marriage Dissolution in Canada," *Demography* 24, no. 3 (August 1987): 3995–406; Neil G. Bennett, Ann Klimas Blanc, and David E. Bloom, "Commitment and the Modern Union: Assessing the Link Between Premarital Cohabitation and Subsequent Marital Stability," *American Sociological Review* 53, no. 1 (February 1988): 127–138, using Swedish data. For further discussion of what causes this relationship, see William G. Axinn and Arland Thornton, "The Relationship Between Cohabitation and Divorce: Selectivity or Causal Influence?" *Demography* 29, no. 3 (August 1992): 357–374.

49. See Julie Salamon, "Popping the Pre-Nup Question," *New Yorker* (August 25 and September 1, 1997): 70–79, for a provocative discussion of prenuptial agreements.

50. Lloyd Cohen, "Marriage, Divorce, and Quasi Rents; or, 'I Gave Him the Best Years of My Life'," *Journal of Legal Studies* 16, no. 2 (June 1987): 267–303.

51. Andrea J. Melville, "Educational Degrees at Divorce: Toward an Educated Dissolution," *Southern California Law Review* 59, no. 6 (September 1986): 1351–1381.

52. Elisabeth M. Landes, "Economics of Alimony," *Journal of Legal Studies* 7, no. 1 (January 1978): 35–63.

53. Margaret A. Jacobs, "More Men Get Alimony, and More Women Get Mad," *Wall Street Journal* (July 30, 1997): B1.

54. Herma Hill Kay, "Beyond No-Fault: New Directions in Divorce Reform," *Divorce Reform at the Crossroads*, eds. Stephen D. Sugarman and Herma Hill Kay (New Haven, Conn.: Yale University, 1990): 23.

55. See Allen M. Parkman, *No-fault Divorce: What Went Wrong?* (Boulder, Col.: Westview, 1992) for a thorough discussion of these changes in divorce law and their apparent effects.

56. This is sometimes referred to as "pure" no-fault. Another form would be bilateral no-fault, in which marriage partners could divorce by mutual consent without ascribing fault, but if only one partner wanted to divorce, a showing of fault would have to be cited in order to obtain the divorce.

57. Other states continue to allow a variety of fault-based grounds for divorce along with no-fault. The California divorce law revisions have been studied at length for their effects on relative well-being of the spouses after divorce, notably by Lenore Weitzman, *The Divorce Revolution* (New York: Macmillan, 1985). See Susan Faludi, *Backlash: The Undeclared War Against American Women* (New York: Crown, 1991), for a critique of some of Weitzman's methods and results. Weitzman later admitted her figures were wrong regarding the degree of decline in women's post-divorce standard of living; see Richard R. Peterson, "A Re-Evaluation of the Economic Consequences of Divorce," *American Sociological Review* 61, no. 2 (June 1996): 528–536 and the ensuing discussion (pp. 537–540) between Weitzman and Peterson.

58. Doris James Freed and Timothy B. Walker, "Family Law in the Fifty States: An Overview," *Family Law Quarterly* 24, no. 4 (Winter 1991): 309–405. This article contains state-by-state charts on the rules concerning support order enforcements, child support criteria, alimony, spousal contribution in professional degrees, factors considered in property distribution, property division rules, and grounds for divorce. An updated version of this survey is published every winter.

59. H. Elizabeth Peters, "Marriage and Divorce: Informational Constraints and Private Contracting," *American Economic Review* 76, no. 3 (June 1986): 437–454.

60. Technical note: The Coase Theorem also requires no income effects, and given that the transfers here can be large relative to each individual's total income, the Coase Theorem might not hold for this reason.

61. Douglas W. Allen, "Marriage and Divorce: Comment," *American Economic Review* 82, no. 3 (June 1992): 679–685.

62. H. Elizabeth Peters, "Marriage and Divorce: Reply," *American Economic Review* 82, no. 3 (June 1992): 686–693.
63. Gerald C. Wright and Dorothy M. Stetson, "The Impact of No-Fault Divorce Law Reform on Divorce in the American States," *Journal of Marriage and the Family* 40, no. 3 (August 1978): 575–580.
64. Allen, *op. cit.*: 684.
65. Peters, *op. cit.*: 691.
66. "More than Two Live More Cheaply Than One," *Wall Street Journal* (February 10, 1995): B1.
67. Karl A. Egge and Robert L. Bunting, "Divorce Settlements: How to Divide Human Capital Assets," *Trial* 21, no. 8 (August 1985): 27–29.

Further reading

Becker, Gary S. (1991). *A Treatise on the Family*. Enlarged Edition. Cambridge, Mass.: Harvard University. The most thorough application of the neoclassical economic, or rational choice approach, to the family. Epitomizes the Chicago school approach.

Bryant, W. Keith (1990). *The Economic Organization of the Household*. Cambridge, United Kingdom: Cambridge University. Upper-level textbook on economics of the family, developing the basic neoclassical economic model of the family.

Cigno, Alessandro (1991). *Economics of the Family*. Oxford: Clarendon. Upper-level economics textbook that discusses marriage markets and family formation.

Dwyer, Daisy and Judith Bruce (eds.) (1988). *A Home Divided: Women and Income in the Third World*. Stanford, Calif.: Stanford University. Essays dealing with inequality and negotiation in households; theoretical critiques of economic modeling and case studies.

England, Paula, and George Farkas (1986). *Households, Employment, and Gender*. New York: Aldine. Covers many of the issues discussed in this book from the sociologist's viewpoint in an attempt to blend the sociological and economic perspectives on gender issues, along with a large dose of demography.

Ferber, Marianne A. (1987). *Women and Work, Paid and Unpaid: A Selected, Annotated Bibliography*. New York: Garland. Contains many classic references to the literature on economics of the family.

Folbre, Nancy (1986). "New Perspectives on Households and Economic Development," *Journal of Development Economics* 22, no. 1 (June): 5–40. Critical review of economic literature on household and family, including useful discussion of intrafamily events from various empirical studies.

Grossbard-Shechtman, Shoshana (1993). *On the Economics of Marriage: A Theory of Marriage, Labor, and Divorce*. Boulder, Colo.: Westview. Derives new hypotheses regarding marriage, divorce, and cohabitation from a theoretical framework of marriage in the tradition of Becker, along with providing empirical evidence.

Hart, Gillian (1995). "Gender and Household Dynamics: Recent Theories and Their Implications," M.G. Quibria (ed.), *Critical Issues in Asian Development: Theories, Experiences, and Policies*. Oxford: Oxford University, 39–74. Review essay on recent economic literature on the household.

Lundberg, Shelly and Robert A. Pollak (1996). "Bargaining and Distribution in Marriage," *Journal of Economic Perspectives* 10, no. 4 (Fall): 139–158. Clear introduction to types of economic models used in discussion of household interactions.

Pollak, Robert A. (1985). "A Transaction Cost Approach to Families and Households," *Journal of Economic Literature* 23, no. 2 (June): 581–608. Essay explicating the transaction cost approach to explaining how families and households function.

Discussion questions

1. In a society in which parents arrange marriages for their children, how would you expect the benefit-cost analysis of whether or not to marry to differ from one in which people choose their own mates?

2. What role would dowries and/or bride payments play in a society where marriages are arranged?

3. Can you draw cost curves for a household as you would for a firm? What are the appropriate labels for the axes? Sketch what an average fixed cost curve, an average variable cost curve, a marginal cost curve, and an average total cost curve might look like. What factors determine the slopes of the curves?

4. According to the Bureau of Labor Statistics' consumer expenditure survey data, larger households spend more, but their per capita expenses are much lower, with the largest households spending about 60 percent less per capita than a single-person household.[66] Is this evidence of lower household production costs in large households? Can you think of any problems with interpreting the data in this way?

5. What are the advantages and disadvantages of the "traditional" division of labor for a family?

6. Describe the division of labor and bargaining patterns in your family.

   (a) Who does what work?
   (b) How are large purchases decided upon?
   (c) How are day-to-day purchasing and work assignment decisions made?
   (d) Is your family's behavior consistent with the rational choice model?
   (e) If your family does not fit the rational choice model, how would you explain the patterns you observe?

7. Give examples for a household of a positive production externality, a negative production externality, a positive consumption externality, and a negative consumption externality.

8. Many people believe that government policies should be as neutral as possible with respect to effects on family formation and source of income. For instance, a neutral income tax code would require that both market and nonmarket "income" be taxed. What are the pros and cons of a tax system of this type?

9. Consider Figure 3.1. Show how the diagram would be altered in the following cases.

   (a) The tax on earned income is increased.
   (b) The tax on earned income is decreased.
   (c) A tax is levied on nonmarket output.

10. Consider Figure 3.3 (ii). For any of the above three cases, is it possible to say for sure whether or not the spouses will continue to specialize completely?

11. Explain the advantages and disadvantages of switching to an "earnings sharing" system for determining social security benefits.

12. For the marriage markets depicted in Figure 3.5, give a sharing scheme in each case that will lead to stable pairings.

13. Consider the following marriage market:

	Carol	Alice	single
Bob	6	8	2
Ted	10	12	2
single	2	2	

(a) Who will marry whom?

(b) Give one possible sharing scheme that will lead to stable pairings.

14. Consider the Focus on bachelorhood. Why would a society want to make life so miserable for bachelors by, for instance, maintaining strict sex segregation for critical tasks?

15. Consider the Focus on the economics of domestic violence. What would be some of the indirect costs created by domestic violence? Who bears them? Which would be part of deadweight loss for a society?

16. Consider the Focus on the failure of feminism. Do you agree or disagree with the statement that the economy would improve if more women "came home"?

17. Why might couples who cohabit prior to marriage have higher divorce rates than couples who do not?

18. One problem in divorce settlements is how to compensate a spouse who has given up a particular career in order to support the other spouse through providing nonmarket work.[67] One suggestion is that before division, a sum should be deducted from the pool of family assets which will cover the cost of putting the career-disadvantaged spouse back on the career path that he/she would have attained had there been no marriage. This sum would include foregone earnings during training, plus the difference between his/her earnings after entering the career and what he/she would be currently making had he/she entered the career earlier in life. What are the advantages and disadvantages of this method of compensation? What factors make this idea difficult to implement?

19. There has been a notable increase in the use of prenuptial agreements in the United States. Why might this be? Is this trend likely to be good or bad for women relative to men? Do you think existence of a prenuptial agreement increases or decreases the likelihood of divorce for a couple?

Appendix
Consumption and production relationships

This appendix discusses three sets of concepts that can be applied to household production and consumption. The first set of concepts formalizes the idea of gains from trade, in which persons can exploit their differing abilities so as to produce more output through coordinating with one other than they can produce operating separately. Second, the choice of what mix of products to consume can be shown graphically using the tools of *budget constraints* (which show the sets of products that a household or individual can afford to purchase) and *indifference curves* (which describe the household or individual's preferences between sets of products). Finally, the concepts of *substitutes* and *complements* are introduced, in which a price change for one product can affect usage of other products. These concepts are useful in discussing household production and consumption patterns, as well as for other topics in the economics of gender.

Gains from trade

The following model is used by economists to show why persons and countries should specialize in production and engage in trade with other persons and countries specializing in producing different goods. Through specialization and trade, all parties are made better off. This model can be applied to explaining specialization within a family as well.

Take two persons, Jack and Jill, and two types of output, market-produced and nonmarket-produced. Table 3A.1 has two hypothetical cases for Jack and Jill's productivity rates. In case (a), Jill can produce more in one hour of either kind of output than Jack can. Therefore she has *absolute advantage* in market and nonmarket work. In case (b), Jill can produce more nonmarket work in one hour, but Jack can produce more market work in one hour. Then Jill has absolute advantage in nonmarket work, while Jack has absolute advantage in market work.

In case (a), even though Jill is better than Jack at both types of work, she is *relatively* better than Jack only at nonmarket work. In order to produce 4 units of market output, Jill

TABLE 3A.1 Jack and Jill's productivity rates per hour of work

(a) Jill has comparative advantage in nonmarket work, Jack has comparative advantage in market work; Jill has absolute advantage in both.

	Market work	Nonmarket work
Jack	3 units of output	3 units of output
Jill	4 units of output	6 units of output

(b) Jill has absolute and comparative advantage in nonmarket work, Jack has absolute and comparative advantage in market work.

	Market work	Nonmarket work
Jack	3 units of output	3 units of output
Jill	2 units of output	6 units of output

must forego producing 6 units of nonmarket output. So 1 unit of market output costs her 1.5 units of nonmarket output. In order to produce 3 units of market output, Jack foregoes 3 units of nonmarket output. So 1 unit of market work costs Jack only 1 unit of nonmarket output. Measured in terms of nonmarket output, Jack is more efficient than Jill at market work. This is an application of the opportunity cost principle: value is measured in terms of foregone opportunity. This means that Jack has *comparative advantage* in market work. Therefore, Jill must have comparative advantage in nonmarket work. Indeed, 1 unit of nonmarket output costs Jill two-thirds of a unit of market output, while 1 unit of nonmarket output costs Jack 1 unit of market output.

In case (b), the pattern of comparative advantage is the same as the pattern of absolute advantage. One unit of market output costs Jill 3 units of nonmarket output, but costs Jack only 1 unit of nonmarket output, so Jack has comparative advantage in market work. On the other hand, 1 unit of nonmarket output costs Jill only one-third of a unit of market output, but costs Jack 1 unit of market output, so Jill has comparative advantage in non-market work.

No one person can have comparative advantage in all types of work, even if he/she has absolute advantage in all types of work. This situation is what creates the opportunity for trade. If each person specializes in producing the product for which he/she has comparative advantage, total output available for both persons' consumption will increase.

Let us consider what Jack and Jill's opportunities are if they do not trade with each other and if each works 8 hours each day. Every day, Jack and Jill each face a constraint on their total consumption of market and nonmarket goods. This constraint is known as the *production possibility frontier*. The production possibility frontiers for Jack and Jill from case (b) above are shown in Figure 3A.1, parts (i) and (ii).

The *joint production possibility frontier*, which is formed if Jack and Jill combine resources, is shown in Figure 3A.1 (iii). Moving from left to right along the frontier, for each additional unit of nonmarket output desired, first Jill gives up time producing market output and switches to producing nonmarket output, because the opportunity cost for her to do so is lower than for Jack. If more than 48 units of nonmarket output are desired, Jack will have to give up time producing market output as well.

Jack and Jill can now consume more output apiece than they could previously. Consider the hypothetical initial use of time for each person as shown in Table 3A.2. In an 8-hour day, each person divides time between market and nonmarket production. If each person specializes according to the pattern of comparative advantage, market output increases by 2 units, from 22 to 24 units, while nonmarket output increases by 6 units, from 42 to 48 units. This gain can be divided between Jack and Jill, making both better off.

Alternatively, if Jill continued to work in the market one hour a week, nonmarket output would stay at 42 units, while market output would increase to 26 units. This would again be better for both Jack and Jill than not pooling their resources. The decision as to which point to pick depends on whether Jack and Jill value additional units of market or nonmarket output more highly.

*B*udget constraints and indifference curves

The production possibility frontiers in Figure 3A.1 show the points Jack and Jill (acting either alone or together) can produce. It also shows us what they can consume – namely,

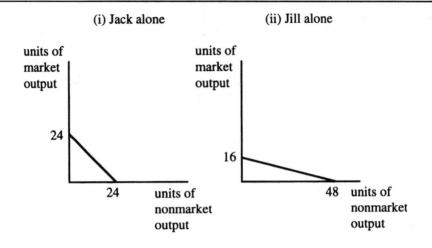

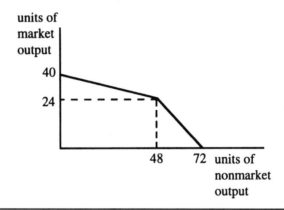

FIGURE 3A.1 Separate and joint production possibility frontiers

TABLE 3A.2 Jack and Jill's production and consumption under separate and joint production

(a) Separate production

	Market work	Nonmarket work
Jack	6 hrs*(3 units/hr) = 18 units	2 hrs*(3 units/hr) = 6 units
Jill	2 hrs*(2 units/hr) = 4 units	6 hrs*(6 units/hr) = 36 units
Total	22 units	42 units

(b) Joint production

	Market work	Nonmarket work
Jack	8 hrs*(3 units/hr) = 24 units	0 hrs
Jill	0 hrs	8 hrs*(6 units/hr) = 48 units
Total	24 units	48 units

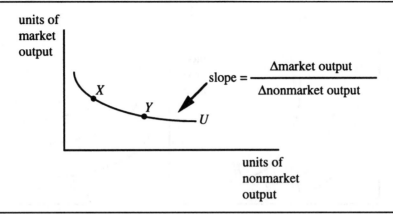

FIGURE 3A.2 An indifference curve for Jill

any point on or below the production possibility frontier. In economics, we assume that people prefer points on the frontier to points below the frontier, for some point on the frontier will always provide more of both products than any given point below the frontier, and we assume that people always prefer more to less. So, although we can safely say that Jack and Jill will pick a point on the production possibility frontier, we cannot predict which point they will pick without knowing something about their preferences. To model different people's preferences, we use *indifference curves*. An indifference curve connects *consumption bundles* – sets of goods – which a person likes equally well. In Figure 3A.2, Jill is indifferent between bundle X and bundle Y, where X contains relatively more market output and less nonmarket output than Y. The slope at any point along the indifference curve shows the maximum amount of market output that Jill is willing to give up for an additional unit of nonmarket output.

Saying that Jill is indifferent between X and Y is the same as saying that she receives the same total utility (amount U_1) from consuming bundle X as from consuming bundle Y. This means that in moving along the indifference curve from X to Y, total utility stays constant, so the loss in utility from giving up market output is balanced by the gain in utility from receiving nonmarket output:

$$MU_{\text{market output}}*\Delta\text{market output} + MU_{\text{nonmarket output}}*\Delta\text{nonmarket output} = \Delta U = 0.$$

Note that the change in market output is negative as we move from left to right along the indifference curve, so the first term in the equation is negative. Rearranging, we get

$$-\frac{MU_{\text{nonmarket output}}}{MU_{\text{market output}}} = \frac{\Delta\text{market output}}{\Delta\text{nonmarket output}},$$

where the right-hand side of the equation is the slope of the indifference curve. So, the slope of the indifference curve is equal to the ratio of the marginal utility of market output divided by the marginal utility of nonmarket output.

As we move from left to right, the indifference curve becomes flatter. This is the same as saying that an additional unit of nonmarket output is valued less and less relative to a unit of market output. In other words, as Jill gains relatively more nonmarket output, an

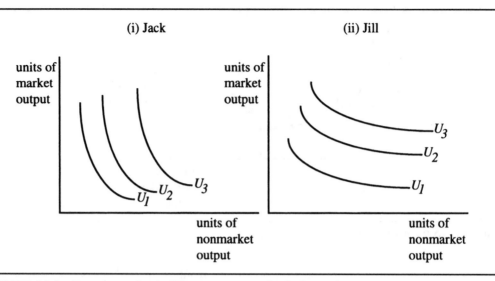

FIGURE 3A.3   Representative indifference curves for Jack and Jill

additional unit of it becomes less valuable to her, and as she gives up more market output, her remaining units of it become more valuable to her.

Each person has a set of indifference curves that completely cover all possible combinations of goods and that correspond to higher levels of utility as they move to the northeast. Additionally, different people will have different preferences for market vs. nonmarket goods, which will be reflected in different slopes of their indifference curves. Figure 3A.3 shows some representative indifference curves for Jack and Jill, where Jack prefers more consumption of nonmarket goods relative to market goods than does Jill at any corresponding point in the graphs.

By combining indifference curves in the same diagram as the production possibility frontier, we can now show how people choose which bundle to produce and consume along the frontier. Figure 3A.4 shows Jill's indifference curves and production possibility frontier. In this case, the highest indifference curve that Jill can reach and still be on her production possibility frontier is U_2, which touches the frontier at point X. This corresponds to 12 units of market output and 12 units of nonmarket output. Referring back to Table 3A.1, case (b), we see that in an eight-hour day, Jill will spend 6 hours in market work and 2 hours in nonmarket work.

Note that the slope of the production possibility frontier shows the tradeoff in terms of time required to produce each type of good. Since Jill is three times as productive at nonmarket work as market work, a unit of market output costs three times as much as a unit of nonmarket output in terms of time. At the chosen consumption bund.e X, the slope of the indifference curve U2 is equal to the slope of the production possibility frontier. Therefore, since the slope of the indifference curve is equal to the ratio of marginal utilities, the ratio of marginal utilities is equal to the ratio of the unit costs of nonmarket and market output:

$$\frac{MU_{\text{nonmarket output}}}{MU_{\text{market output}}} = \frac{P_{\text{nonmarket output}}}{P_{\text{market output}}} = \frac{1}{3} \text{ (in this example)}$$

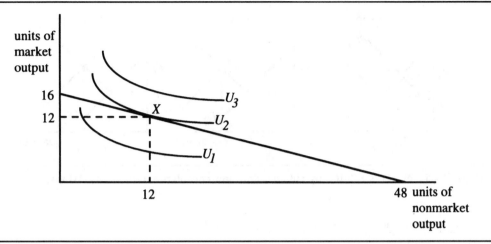

FIGURE 3A.4 Jill's choice of a consumption bundle

This is the rule for efficient allocation of a person's budget among alternative uses that was presented in the appendix to Chapter 1.

In this context, Jill's production possibility frontier is also Jill's *budget constraint*.[1] In other words, it shows the maximum that she can consume of each good, given the current prices of each good. In this case, prices are measured in terms of the time it takes to produce each good. This concept can be used more generally to model the choice between any two goods or groups of goods, where prices are measured in money terms.

Substitutes and complements

In general, for good X, if the price of good X falls, more of good X will be consumed, and if the price of good X rises, less of good X will be consumed:

$$\frac{\Delta Q_x}{\Delta P_x} < 0.$$

This is the same as saying that demand curves are downward-sloping.

We can also consider how the quantity purchased of one good is affected by the price change of another good. For two goods, 1 and 2, good 1 is a *substitute* for good 2 if

$$\frac{\Delta Q_1}{\Delta P_2} > 0,$$

where Q_1 is the quantity demanded of good 1 and P_2 is the price of good 2. This says that if the price of good 2 rises, the quantity of good 1 rises as people purchase the relatively cheaper good 1 in place of the more expensive good 2. Similarly, if the price of good 2 falls, the quantity of good 1 falls as people switch to purchasing the relatively cheaper good 2.

Good 1 is a *complement* for good 2 if

$$\frac{\Delta Q_1}{\Delta P_2} < 0,$$

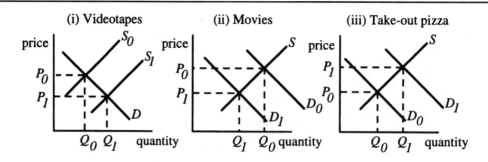

FIGURE 3A.5   Markets related by substitution and complementary relationships

so if the price of good 2 rises, the quantity of good 1 falls, and vice-versa.

In the case of

$$\frac{\Delta Q_1}{\Delta P_2} = 0,$$

the two goods are considered to be unrelated.

Goods may be complements or substitutes in both production and consumption relationships. For instance, in food consumption, jam may be a substitute for butter and a complement for bread. In manuscript production, personal computers may be a substitute for typewriters and a complement for secretaries.

These relationships mean that changes affecting one market can have measurable effects on other markets through both production and consumption complementary and substitution relationships. The distinction between consumption and production becomes blurred when discussing household production, and it is not generally important to maintain. For instance, an increased number of women working may increase the demand for faster methods of food preparation, thereby increasing the demand for microwave ovens. Microwaveable frozen dinners are a complementary input to microwave ovens in the process of food production, so the demand for them will increase as well. Microwaveable meals are a substitute for more laboriously prepared meals, so the demand for prepared meals will decrease.

Price changes for good 2 in the above formulas may be caused by shifts in either the supply or the demand curve. Quantity changes for good 1 are then caused by a shift in the demand curve. Figure 3A.5 illustrates this using the markets for three related goods. The invention of home videotape technology is experienced in the videotape market as a rightward shift in the supply curve (more tapes are available at any market price), which leads to a decline in the price of watching movies at home (i). As the price of home videotapes declines, people substitute watching movies at home for watching movies in the theater, which leads to a decline in quantity and price in the movie theater market (ii). However, people order more pizzas as a complement to watching movies at home, leading to a rise in price and quantity in the pizza market (iii). $\Delta P_{\text{videotapes}} < 0$ and $\Delta Q_{\text{movies}} < 0$, so

$$\frac{\Delta Q_{\text{movies}}}{\Delta P_{\text{videotapes}}} > 0,$$

and movies are a substitute for videotapes. $\Delta P_{videotapes} < 0$ and $\Delta Q_{take\text{-}out\ pizzas} > 0$, so

$$\frac{\Delta Q_{take\text{-}out\ pizzas}}{\Delta P_{videotapes}} < 0,$$

and take-out pizzas are a complement for videotapes.

Endnote

1. This is because we have assumed that nonmarket goods cannot be traded; otherwise, production and consumption would be separable, so Jill could produce nonmarket goods and then sell them.

Discussion questions

1. Using the productivity rates from Table 3A.1 (a):
    (a) Graph the individual and joint production possibility frontiers, assuming 8 hours of work per person.
    (b) Show that if each currently spends six hours doing market work and they do not combine output, Jack and Jill can increase their total output by deciding on production together.

2. If Jill considers a unit of nonmarket output to have the same value as a unit of market output, no matter how many units of each she has, what would her indifference curves look like? Given the production frontier in Figure 3A.4, where would Jill choose to produce and consume in this case?

3. If Jill prefers to have equal amounts of nonmarket and market output and gets zero utility from having unmatched units of either form of output (e.g., she makes right shoes at home and buys left shoes in the market), what would her indifference curves look like? Given the production frontier in Figure 3A.4, where would Jill choose to produce and consume in this case?

4. Suppose Hansel and Gretel have the following potential output units for eight hours of work:

	Nonmarket output	Market output
Hansel	20	8
Gretel	30	15

    (a) Graph their individual production possibility frontiers.
    (b) Who has absolute advantage in nonmarket work? Who has comparative advantage in nonmarket work?
    (c) Graph their joint production possibility frontier.
    (d) Give an example, as in Table 3A.2, that demonstrates that Hansel and Gretel can be better off if they specialize (at least somewhat) and trade output.
    (e) Given that Hansel and Gretel are both more productive at nonmarket work, why would they choose to produce any market output at all?

5. As more women work, what happens to the market for nannies? What markets are affected through substitution relationships with nannies? What markets are affected through complementary relationships with nannies?

6. As more women work, what happens to the market for housekeepers? If fewer men work, would an opposite effect occur? Why or why not? What am I implicitly assuming stays the same in each case?

Labor Force Participation:
Analysis of Trends

*I*n this chapter, we examine the trends in U.S. labor force participation since World War II, in particular, the rise in female labor force participation and the fall in male labor force participation. We consider various theories of why these trends have occurred. The chapter closes with an analysis of the current state of child care in the U.S. and the effects of subsidizing child care.

*T*rends in labor force participation

In Chapter 2, we saw that the female labor force participation rate has been rising, while the male rate has been falling. Let us examine these trends by considering variation in participation by several demographic variables that economists and other social scientists consider important. We can use these data both to compare changes over time for different groups and to compare different groups at points in time.

Table 4.1 contains data on participation rates by sex, educational attainment, marital status, presence of small children (for women), and age group. It is clear from this table that the overall pattern of rising rates for women and falling rates for men is true for subgroups as well, although different demographic groups have had greater or smaller changes. Only the very oldest women and youngest men deviate slightly from these patterns. The huge increase in married women's participation, particularly for those with young children, is noteworthy.

Figure 4.1 plots participation rates for men and women by educational attainment. Participation tends to rise with educational attainment. The most striking trend for men is the steep decline in participation among those with low education, although high school graduates have also had a noteworthy decline, leading to greater divergence among participation rates by education. Meanwhile, all groups of women, save those with the lowest level of education, have had steep rises, although the gap between male and female labor force participation rates is large even among college graduates. The divergence between women with some college and those with only a high school degree has increased.

TABLE 4.1   Labor force participation rates by sex and demographic group, selected years

	Women		Men	
	1948	1996	1948	1996
Overall	32.7	59.3	86.6	74.9
By educational attainment	*1970*	*1995*	*1970*	*1995*
not a high school graduate	43.0	47.2	89.3	72.0
high school graduate	51.3	68.9	96.3	86.9
some college	50.9	77.3	95.8	90.1
college graduate or more	60.9	82.8	96.1	93.8
By marital status	*1947*	*1995*	*1947*	*1995*
single (never married)	65.7	66.8	77.6	73.7
married, spouse present	20.4	61.0	92.5	77.5
Married, by age of youngest child	*1948*	*1995*		
no child under 18	28.4	53.2		
child 6–17	26.0	76.2		
child under 6	10.8	63.5		
By age group	*1963*	*1996*	*1963*	*1996*
16–19	38.0	51.3	52.9	53.2
20–24	47.5	71.3	86.1	82.5
25–29	37.4	75.8	96.4	92.9
30–34	37.0	74.7	97.8	93.4
35–39	42.0	76.5	97.6	92.7
40–44	47.8	78.6	97.3	92.0
45–49	50.4	78.0	96.5	90.8
50–54	50.8	71.9	94.9	86.9
55–59	45.6	59.8	91.3	77.9
60–64	32.9	38.2	80.1	54.3
65–69	16.5	17.2	40.9	27.5
70–74	8.6	8.8	26.9	17.3
≥ 75	3.6	3.1	15.3	7.3

Sources: Rates overall, ages 16 and over: *Economic Report of the President* (1997) 343 (Table B-37). Rates by educational attainment, ages 20 and over; marital status, ages 16 and over, and married women by age of youngest child: 1947, 1948, and 1970 – *Labor Force Statistics Derived from the Current Population Survey, 1948–87* (Tables C-9, C-12, C-23); 1995 – *Statistical Abstract of the United States* (1996) (Tables 618, 624, 626, 627). Rates by age group: 1963 – *Labor Force Statistics Derived from the Current Population Survey, 1948–87* (Table B-4); 16–19 year olds – *Working Women: A Chartbook*, Bulletin no. 2385 (August 1991): 39 (Table A-2); 1996 – *Employment and Earnings* 44, no. 1 (January 1997): 160 (Table 3).

Figure 4.2 shows that the relationship between marital status and labor force participation differs by sex, with married men having a higher rate than never-married men, while never-married women have a higher rate than married women. However, there is a notable convergence for all four rates since World War II. The never-married rates trend downward from 1949 to the mid-1960s before rising, while married rates maintain steady trends over this 40-year period.

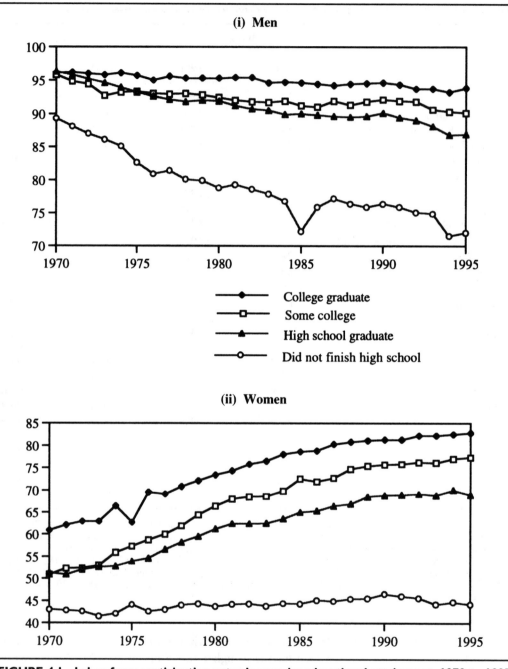

FIGURE 4.1   Labor force participation rates by sex, by educational attainment, 1970 to 1995

Sources: 1970–87 – Labor Force Statistics Derived from the Current Population Survey, 1948–87 (Table C-23); 1988–95 – *Statistical Abstract of the United States* (1991): 382 (Table 634); (1992): 382 (Table 611); (1996): 395 (Table 618). Data from 1994 on are not strictly comparable with data for earlier years.

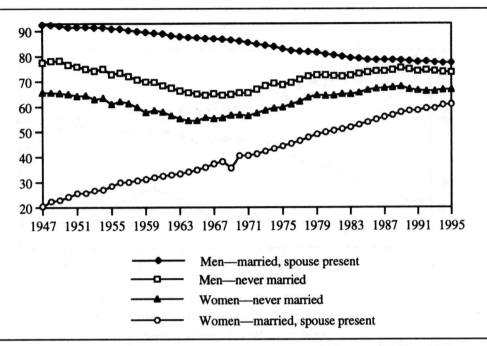

FIGURE 4.2 Labor force participation rates by sex, by marital status, 1947 to 1995

Sources: 1947–87 – Labor Force Statistics Derived from the Current Population Survey, 1948–87 (Tables B-7, C-23); *1988–95 – Statistical Abstract of the United States* (1991): 399 (Table 641); (1992): 387 (Table 618); (1996): 399 (Table 626). Data for 1947–54 are March data adjusted to match the annual series that begins in 1955. Data beginning in 1990, and again in 1994, are not strictly comparable to data for earlier years.

Figure 4.3 displays the divergence in rates by race over this time period for the two largest racial groups in the U.S. – whites and blacks. Black and white men display the same general trends towards convergence of married and never-married rates, but the rates for black men are lower than the rates for white men, particularly for never-married blacks. The female rates are more disparate, with black married women displaying a substantially higher rate than white married women, while the never-married black women's rate is substantially below the never-married white women's rate, as well as being below the married black women's rate.

Table 4.2 displays more detailed participation rates by marital status and allows us to examine differences by race and marital status simultaneously. Here the data are for nonwhites rather than blacks, because the nonwhite data allow us to go back further in time and to look at widowed and divorced persons separately.[1] Much of the available data on widowed and divorced persons is presented in combined form, which confounds trends for two very different groups. Widowed persons are much older on average than divorced persons, and in general their rates are much lower than those of other groups and dropping over time, while divorced rates are much higher than for widowed and have been rising over time. Combining these two groups makes their combined rate very flat over time.

Rates by race have changed over time in their relative relationship. Among women, the rise over time in participation has been less remarkable for nonwhite women than for white women, since the nonwhite married women had started from a higher base. Notable

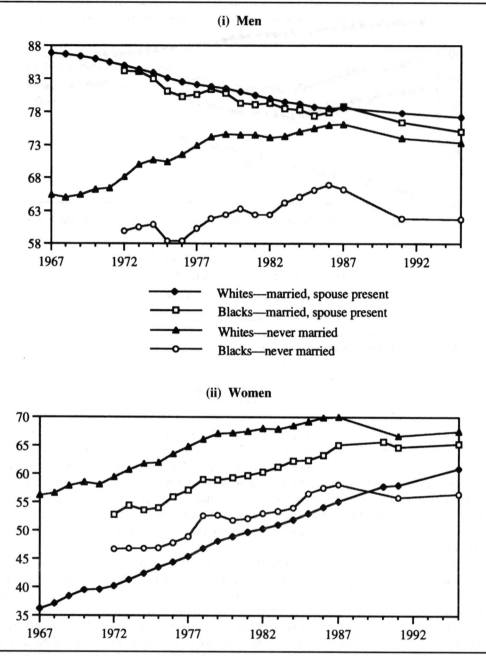

FIGURE 4.3 Labor force participation rates by sex, by marital status and race, 1967 to 1995

Sources: 1967–87 (whites), 1972–87 (blacks) – Labor Force Statistics Derived from the Current Population Survey, 1948–87 (Table B-7); 1990 (married women) – Working Women: A Chartbook, Bureau of Labor Statistics Bulletin 2385 (August 1991): 47 (Table A-15); 1991 and 1995 – calculated by the author using data from the Current Population Surveys, March 1991 and March 1995.

TABLE 4.2 Labor force participation rates by sex and race, by marital status, 1965 and 1995

| | Women | | | | Men | | | |
| | 1965 | | 1995 | | 1965 | | 1995 | |
	White	Nonwhite	White	Nonwhite	White	Nonwhite	White	Nonwhite
Never married	41.8	31.1	67.5	56.7	50.9	46.4	73.3	63.6
Married	33.6	46.7	60.8	62.3	87.6	88.3	77.1	77.7
Divorced	60.5	60.6	71.2	66.4	70.3	69.0	78.5	71.2
Widowed	26.0	33.1	16.7	22.2	33.1	37.7	20.8	21.6

Sources: 1965 – *Labor Force Statistics Derived from the Current Population Survey, 1948–87*(Table C-11); 1995 – calculated by the author using data from the Current Population Survey, March 1995.

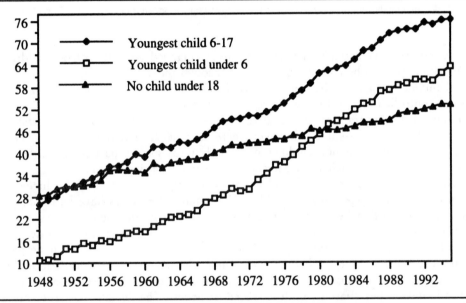

FIGURE 4.4 Labor force participation rates for married women by presence of children, 1948 to 1995

Sources: 1948–87 – *Labor Force Statistics Derived from the Current Population Survey, 1948–87* (Table C-12); 1988–95 – *Statistical Abstract of the United States* (1991): 400 (Table 643); (1992): 388 (Tables 620, 621); (1993): 400 (Table 634); (1994): 402 (Table 627); (1995): 406 (Table 639); (1996): 400 (Tables 626, 627).

convergence has occurred in the rates for divorced and never-married women, with higher rates for white women. The rates for married women have tended to converge. Rates for married and widowed men are remarkably similar by race, while rates for divorced and never-married men, while rising, have diverged.

Figure 4.4 illustrates the most striking trend in the data on participation, which is the increase in participation rates among married women with children under age 18. The rates

TABLE 4.3 Labor force participation rates for women, by marital status and age of youngest child in the household, 1975 and 1995

	1975	1995
All women with children under 18	48.9	69.1
married	45.0	69.8
with child under 2	31.5	58.7
with child 2–3	39.9	65.3
with child 4–5	41.9	67.7
with child 6–17	52.4	76.2
single	60.0	67.7
with child under 2	46.3	53.9
with child 2–3	55.2	61.2
with child 4–5	61.4	66.5
with child 6–17	63.3	73.3

Sources: Calculated by the author using data from the Current Population Surveys, March 1975 and March 1995.

for these women have actually crossed the rate for married women with no children less than 18 and appear to be continuing upwards through the 1990s. There appears to be no effect of number or age of children on participation rates for men once age and marital status are controlled for, and these figures are not widely reported.

In general, it appears that the negative effect of children on labor force participation rates of mothers has dissipated. However, there is evidence that the interaction between presence of children in a household and marital status affects participation. Table 4.3 shows more detailed participation rates for women by marital status and age of child. While single women (which includes all women currently not married) had a higher participation rate for every age range of child in 1975, married mothers have had such a large rise in participation that by 1995 their rates surpassed those for single mothers.

Turning to participation rates by age, Figure 4.5 compares participation rate patterns by age at several points in time: 1963, 1980 (for women), and 1996. The male patterns continue to display a single-peaked pattern that is characteristic of male patterns by age across most societies, although the steep drop-off after age 50 is more characteristic of industrialized societies than nonindustrialized societies. The female patterns display a double-peaked pattern that is found in many societies, but the dip between the peaks has become less pronounced over time, so that the 1996 pattern is approaching the male pattern.

Figure 4.6 illustrates differences by racial group in participation rates by age for 1996. For every age group among men, the black participation rate is lower than the white rate. This pattern is found in earlier years as well. Among women, young black women have lower participation rates, but the rates are almost equal for 30-year-olds and over. All groups have low participation during ages 16 to 19.

The problem with discussing the effect of various demographic factors on the participation rates in isolation from each other is that it is clear that various trends are confounded. For instance, part of the observed racial differences can be attributed to differences in marital status and education levels between the races. In particular, the effects of age

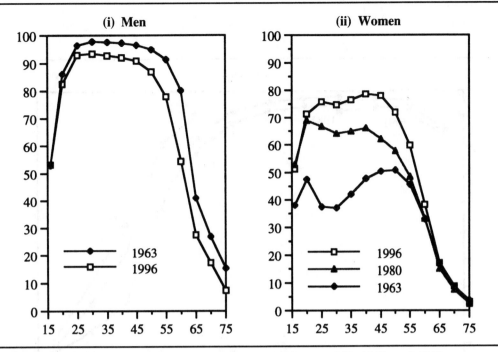

FIGURE 4.5 Labor force participation rates by sex, by age, 1963, 1980, and 1996

Sources: 1963, 1980 – Labor Force Statistics Derived from the Current Population Survey, 1948–87 (Table B-4); 16–19 year olds – *Working Women: A Chartbook* , Bulletin 2385 (August 1991): 39 (Table A-2); 1996 – *Employment and Earnings* 44, no. 1 (January 1997): 160 (Table 3).

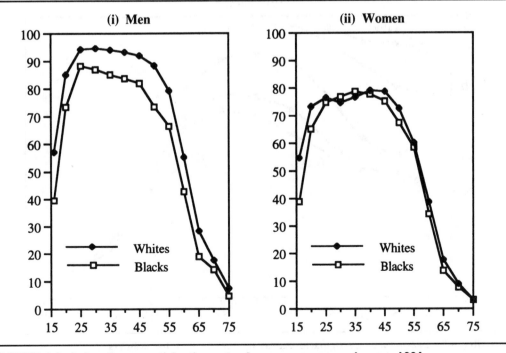

FIGURE 4.6 Labor force participation rates by race–sex group, by age, 1996

Source: Employment and Earnings 44, no. 1 (January 1997): 161–62 (Table 3).

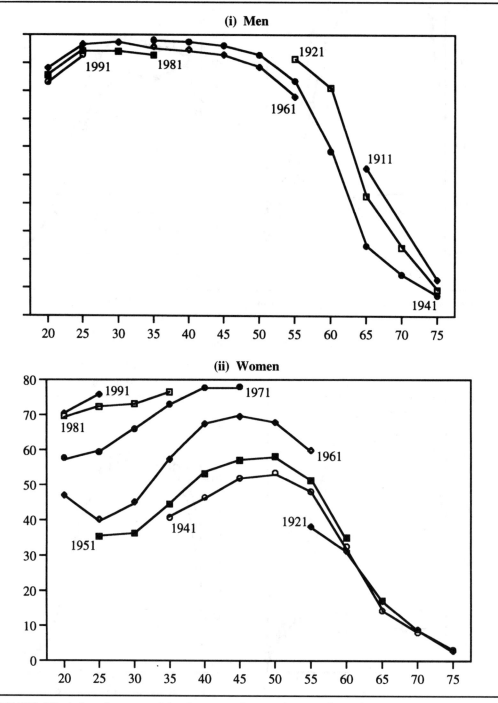

FIGURE 4.7 Labor force participation rates by sex, by age, for cohorts

Sources: 1957–86 – *Labor Force Statistics Derived from the Current Population Survey, 1948–87* (Table B-4); 1991–96 – *Employment and Earnings* 39, no. 1 (January 1992): 164 (Table 3); 44, no. 1 (January 1997): 160 (Table 3).

may be confounded with other trends. For instance, persons with higher educational attainment – as well as mothers of young children – are likely to be young adults. Additionally, it is important to separate out the effect of aging on participation rates from the effect related to which *cohort* one belongs to. A cohort is a group of people who enter a stage of life at the same time, generally measured in five-year intervals. For instance, a birth cohort is a group of people born at the same time, while a college class is a cohort of persons who enter college at the same time. While Figure 4.5 and Figure 4.6 provide snapshots of the labor force participation behavior of many different birth cohorts at one point in time, we can also compare the age-related patterns for different cohorts as they move through time.

Figure 4.7 illustrates this technique using selected five-year cohorts, labeled by the year when they were ages 20 to 24 (which is the time when they first have high participation rates). The usefulness of this technique is limited by the availability of data: for older cohorts, we only have data for their later years, while for younger cohorts, we have yet to observe their behavior when they are older. Nevertheless, it appears that subsequent male cohorts have had lower participation rates throughout their lives, while subsequent female cohorts have had rising participation rates up until ages 60 to 64, when the experience of different cohorts converges.

In summary, it appears that female and male participation rates have been converging over time, due to the tremendous rise in female participation rates and the less notable drop in male rates. However, differences by demographic group remain. We will now turn to an examination of economic and social factors that can help us understand the forces behind these trends.

What has caused these trends?

Why have female labor force participation rates risen and male labor force participation rates fallen? When employment changes, economists look for shifts in labor demand and supply curves. The wage is determined, along with employment, jointly by labor supply and demand. Therefore the wage appears as a factor in both the labor demand and supply functions, along with a host of other factors that cause these curves to shift. A shift in a labor demand or supply curve means that at any given wage, more or less labor is either demanded or supplied. Figure 4.8 illustrates possible shifts in the curves that could have led to this pattern. One possibility is that labor demand curves have shifted: the demand for female labor may have risen (case i), and the demand for male labor may have fallen (case iii). Secondly, the labor supply curves may have shifted: the supply of female labor may have risen (case ii), and the supply of male labor may have fallen (case iv). Most likely, both curves have been shifting simultaneously over time for both men and women, the net wage change shows which curve has shifted more. For instance, if female labor demand shifts more than female labor supply, women's wages will rise over time.

As one form of labor becomes relatively expensive, we would expect employers to substitute the cheaper form of labor for the more expensive form. Therefore a supply curve shift in one market can cause an offsetting demand curve shift in the other. For instance, if men are supplying less labor and driving up the wage for male labor, employers will substitute relatively cheaper women for more expensive men, driving the male and female wages closer together.

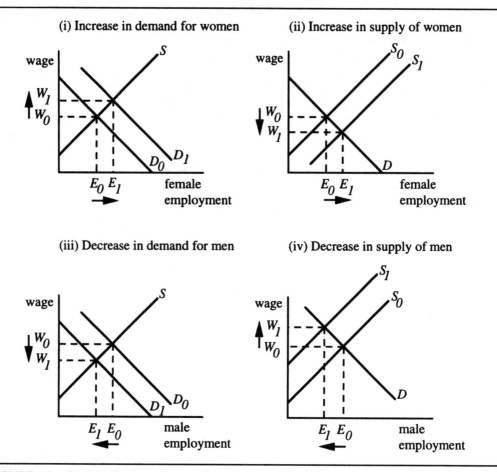

FIGURE 4.8   Changes in the labor markets for women and men

In the remainder of the chapter, we will consider various forces that appear to have led to shifts in the supply and demand curves for various forms of labor. Discussing how demand for various forms of labor arises on the part of firms will help us understand the relationships between male and female labor and the shifts in demand that appear to have occurred in industrialized countries. Examining the factors that affect individuals' decisions as to how much time to spend in market work will help us understand why participation rates vary by factors such as age, education, marital status, and presence or absence of children.

Factors affecting labor demand

The demand for labor is derived from the demand for the goods and services that firms produce. As labor becomes more efficient and cheaper per efficiency unit, firms have incentive to substitute it for other inputs into the production process – in particular, for

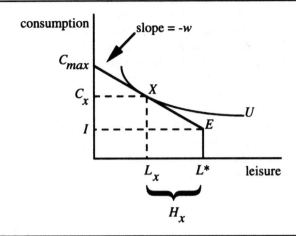

FIGURE 4.9 An individual's labor supply decision

physical capital. Some forms of labor are substitutes for capital (and vice-versa), while other forms – in particular, skilled labor – are complements to capital (and vice-versa). For instance, robots can be used to replace assembly line workers in car factories, but operators are needed to run the robots, and repairers are needed to maintain the robots in working condition.

In order to explain changes over time in the demand for labor and differences between groups of workers, we need to look for several types of changes in the economy: (1) changes in demand for various goods and services; (2) changes in the productivity of different groups of workers; (3) changes in the price of other inputs – in particular, capital, but also land, energy, and raw materials; (4) changes in the level of competition in the economy, for firms with monopoly power may produce less output than if they were competitive, therefore requiring less labor; and (5) changes in the technology of production processes.

Factors affecting labor supply

The labor market supply curve is the sum of individual labor supply curves. Therefore, in order to understand movements in the labor market supply curve, we need to understand how an individual chooses how many hours to work, if any. (See the appendix to this chapter for a discussion of the economic model of labor supply.) As shown in Figure 4.9, an individual chooses the combination of market (H_x) and nonmarket (L_x) hours that maximizes utility, subject to the constraint on total time available (L^*). The hourly wage rate (w) and availability of nonearned income (I) determines the individual's potential maximum market good consumption (C_{max}), where actual consumption of market goods (C_x) equals the amount purchasable using nonearned income plus earned income (equal to w times H_x). The budget constraint slopes down from C_{max} to point E (which shows the individual's *endowment* of time and nonearned income), with a slope equal to $-w$, where w represents the opportunity cost of an hour of nonmarket time.

In order to explain changes over time and differences between demographic groups in their supply of labor, we need to look for two types of changes: (1) changes in the budget constraint that individuals face, and (2) changes in the relative shape and position of the indifference curves, which reflect the individuals' changing tastes for market and nonmarket goods. Changes in the budget constraint are of two general types: changes in nonearned income, and changes in the wage. Changes in the demand for labor are communicated to individuals through their effect on wages. Therefore, wages are the link from the demand to the supply side of the labor market.

We now turn to considering the particular phenomena that have been observed since World War II: the rise in female labor force participation and the fall in male labor force participation. In each case, we consider demand and supply-side factors that could have caused these trends, and we weigh the evidence as to which factors have had the greatest effects.

Explanations of the rise in women's labor force participation

Many economists, having studied the rise in women's labor force participation, have attempted to enumerate the various causes of this rise, particularly among married women, and to figure out which are the most important factors.[2] Factors can be divided into demand-side and supply-side factors. Demand-side factors influence individual labor-supply decisions by increasing the wage that women can potentially earn. As women's wages have risen, the only way to realize gains from the rising wage is to work, so we would predict a rise in women's labor force participation. While women who are currently working may reduce their hours due to the increase in wages, they will remain employed, so the net change in female labor force participation is positive. Many analysts have argued that real wage growth can explain most of the increase in female labor force participation between 1950 and 1980.[3]

Demand-side factors

There are three demand-side factors that are generally cited as of primary importance in explaining the rise in female labor force participation: (1) the general rise in the demand for labor, (2) the rise in labor demand in particular sectors, and (3) the rise in education of women.

1. **The general rise in labor demand:** Demand for labor has been rising over most of this century, subject to business-cycle fluctuations around the long-term upward trend. Since labor demand is derived from the demand for goods and services, as the volume of traded goods – both domestic and international – has risen, more labor has been needed to produce these goods and services. Technological innovations have led to increased demand for labor as production techniques have become more efficient, leading to increased output per worker.

2. **The sectoral rise in labor demand:** Over time, as the economy evolves, different forms of labor are required, reflecting the changing mix of goods and services. Additionally, technological change can influence the substitutability and complementarity relationships between labor and other input factors, and changes in the prices of other inputs influence the demand for labor as well. Demand for particular types of labor has fallen, in

particular unskilled farm labor (where other inputs, in particular capital, have been substituted for labor) and both skilled and unskilled labor for use in manufacturing (where some capital substitution has occurred and growth in demand for manufactured goods has been lower than growth in demand for services). Meanwhile, demand for other types of labor has been growing faster than average, in particular for clerical and service occupations. One analyst argues that the economy has shifted to requiring "female occupations" that require skill, but do not require either long-term commitment to work or specialized geographic location.[4] These occupations may be "female" in the sense that they are compatible with women remaining in the role of primary provider of nonmarket output for their families over their lifetimes, and because married women in these occupations can accompany their husbands on moves for higher-paid work without undue trouble in their own search for new employment.

3. **The rise in education of women:** Education turns unskilled labor into skilled labor and can be viewed as an investment in capital embodied in a person, or *human capital*. Educated persons receive both a payment for their time spent in work and a rental payment for allowing a firm to use their human capital during working hours, which payments are combined into a wage for skilled labor. As women have become more educated, the consequent rise in their wage relative to that of unskilled labor has made it more profitable for them to enter into market work. Additionally, shifts in demand for goods and services and the complementarity between capital and skilled labor – along with the substitutability of capital for unskilled labor – have led to increased demand for skilled workers relative to unskilled.

The increase in women's education is due to multiple causes, including a relaxation of social restrictions on appropriate levels and types of education for women, and greater resources on the part of families who might previously have had to ration higher education among their children. The increase may also be tied to the rise in life expectancy for women (and for men, as well), which means that investment in education has a longer payback period and becomes more profitable to undertake. There are also feedback effects from rising expected wages to education.

Supply-side factors

In addition to demand-side factors operating through the wage to cause movements along the female labor supply curve, there are three groups of supply-side economic factors that must be considered that could shift the supply curve: (1) changing technology of nonmarket production, (2) changes in family composition, (3) lower male earnings, translating into less nonearned income available for married women.

1. **Changing technology of nonmarket production:** Changes in the technology of nonmarket production have two aspects: the greater availability of market-produced substitutes for nonmarket goods and increased efficiency of nonmarket production, particularly housework. As more market substitutes are available for nonmarket goods at lower prices, this will have the effect of increasing labor supply because the efficiency of market production has increased – i.e., the real purchasing power of money wages has increased. In the individual's labor supply diagram (Figure 4.9), this will be shown as a shift in preferences, leading to flatter indifference curves and an increased probability of picking points further to the left on the budget constraint.

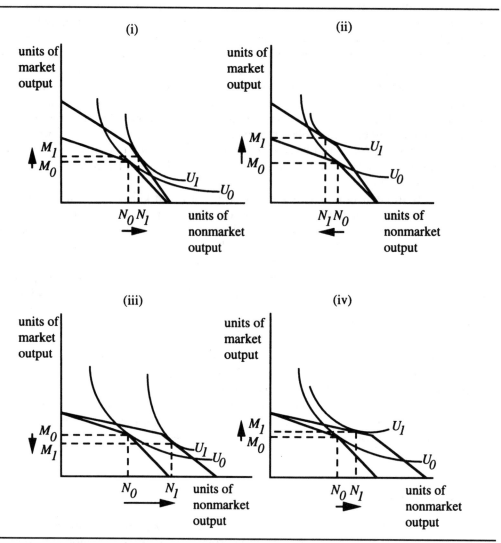

FIGURE 4.10   **Effects of an increase in the efficiency of market or nonmarket production**

However, consider the effect of changes in production efficiency on the household production frontier for a married couple when the wife currently does only nonmarket work and the husband does only market work. We will assume that both market and nonmarket production are *normal* goods, so that when potential income rises, more of both will be consumed. Then economic theory does not tell us whether increased efficiency in either form of production will lead to more or less time spent in the relatively less efficient form of production.

Figure 4.10 illustrates the possible effects on this family of a rise in efficiency of one or the other type of production. Due to the opposite directions of the substitution and income effects, we cannot predict the exact direction in change for the good that becomes relatively more expensive. (See the appendix to this chapter for a discussion of substitution

TABLE 4.4 Meal preparation time by ownership of equipment among Indiana families, 1968

Equipment	owners (%)	Owners		Nonowners	
		Minutes/meal	*Hours/week*	*Minutes/meal*	*Hours/week*
Mixer	98	8	10.3	7	9.6
Electric skillet	68	9	9.9	8	11.0
Pressure cooker	41	8	10.6	8	10.0
Freezer	81	9	10.5	8	9.1
Dishwasher	20	8	10.7	9	10.1

Source: S. Manning, "Time Use in Household Tasks by Indiana Families," Purdue University Research Bulletin no. 837 (January 1968): 9.

and income effects.) If market efficiency increases – e.g., if the wage rises for both family members, the substitution and income effects of this wage change cause an unambiguous increase in consumption of market goods, but nonmarket goods can either increase (case i) or decrease (case ii), depending on whether or not the income effect dominates the substitution effect. We cannot tell if the wife will now participate in market work. Similarly, if nonmarket efficiency increases, there will be an unambiguous increase in consumption of nonmarket goods, but market goods can either decrease (case iii) or increase (case iv), and we cannot tell whether the wife will participate in market work.

During the twentieth century, technology has been widely adopted that has enabled families to produce nonmarket output at lower cost. In particular, we have seen the spread of market goods and services that serve as critical inputs into nonmarket production. In 1920, one-third of homes had electricity; by 1930, over two-thirds were electrified (although only 10 percent of farm homes); by 1960, practically all homes were electrified. By 1940, 70 percent of homes had running indoor water (17 percent of farm homes, 93 percent of urban homes); by 1970, 90 percent of rural homes had running water.[5]

However, it appears that many supposedly time-saving innovations have been widely adopted with no apparent significant saving of nonmarket time. Table 4.4 shows results from a study of time used in meal preparation among a sample of Indiana families. No significant drop in time appears for families who own various "time-saving" household appliances; if anything, the time spent in meal preparation rises. The implication is that families who own these appliances must be creating higher-quality meals than those who do not, for they invest both more capital and the same amount (or more) of time in meal preparation. This appears true for other categories of appliances as well, such as washers and dryers: potential time savings through use of these labor-saving (and generally literally effort-saving) devices have instead been converted into increased output.[6]

It is difficult to analyze fully the trend in time spent on nonmarket work in order to determine if the data in Table 4.4 are typical of households in general and of all types of housework. Data on housework hours, such as meal preparation and cleanup, clothing maintenance, house cleaning, and yard upkeep, are collected much less frequently than data on market work. The main contemporary source of national data on housework hours and on use of time in general outside of market work is a set of three surveys conducted at 10-year intervals, in 1965–66, 1975–76, and 1985–86.[7] Table 4.5 presents results from these surveys. They show that time spent by women on housework has actually been

TABLE 4.5 Weekly hours spent in housework by sex, various demographic groups, 1965, 1975, and 1985

	Men			*Women*		
	1965	*1975*	*1985*	*1965*	*1975*	*1985*
All	4.6	7.0	9.8	27.0	21.7	19.5
Employed	4.4	5.8	8.1	17.8	14.8	14.7
Nonemployed	9.6	10.8	14.7	34.0	26.3	23.6
Married	4.5	6.8	11.1	31.6	24.2	22.4
Unmarried	4.7	7.9	7.9	15.5	17.1	14.9
No children at home	4.7	7.1	10.4	21.3	20.3	17.9
child 5 or over	5.3	7.6	10.4	30.3	23.9	19.9
child under 5	3.9	5.9	9.0	32.0	25.1	22.5

Source: John P. Robinson, "Who's Doing the Housework," *American Demographics* 10, no. 12 (December 1988): 24–28, 63.

TABLE 4.6 Women's housework hours per week from time-use studies, various years

	1924–28, Rural	*1930–31, Urban*	*1965, Urban*	
Tasks	*Nonemployed*	*College-educ. nonemp.*	*Nonemp.*	*Employed*
Food-related	22.8	15.1	16.0	8.2
Clothing-related	11.5	7.9	8.7	3.9
Home care	9.6	7.4	10.2	5.0
Family care	4.1	9.8	9.7	3.3
Shopping and management	2.4	5.2	5.2	3.9
Other, including travel	1.2	2.7	5.6	3.9
Total	51.6	48.1	55.4	28.2

Source: Joann Vanek, "Household Technology and Social Status: Rising Living Standards and Status and Residence Differences in Housework," *Technology and Culture* 19, no. 3 (July 1978): 374 (Table 3). Reprinted with permission of the University of Chicago Press, © 1978.

dropping since 1965, while men's time has been rising.[8] However, women still spend much more time in housework than do men. The total amount of housework done in married-couple families appears to be dropping.

A set of about twenty smaller-scale time-use studies, done under U.S. Bureau of Home Economics guidelines from the 1920s through 1960s, has been used by researcher Joann Vanek to examine housework patterns further back in time.[9] Table 4.6 shows some results from these studies and uses data from the National Time Use survey of 1965–66 with her same definition of housework for comparison. Vanek finds that the number of hours of housework performed by nonemployed women has been remarkably stable throughout this period, staying in the range of 48 to 56 hours per week. Time spent on food preparation and cleanup has gone down, while time spent on shopping and family managerial tasks has gone up.

Vanek's numbers for 1965 are so much higher than those in Table 4.5 because her definition of housework is broader. This implies that the downward trend in women's housework found in Table 4.5 may be offset by a rise in other categories of nonmarket work.

FOCUS

What is higher-quality housework?

An influential line of feminist critique of the increasing quality theory for why housework hours have not declined substantially is that for nonemployed women, chores expand to fill available time. This keeps women inefficiently occupied in the home, reducing their market work. Analyses of reading material meant for a female readership tend to support the views that much of housework is "make-work" and that social standards for housework are unnecessarily strict.

Anthropologist Maxine Margolis has concluded that there is a tendency in women's magazines and newspaper sections to emphasize activities in the home that have visible results, such as home decoration. She believes that the purpose of this emphasis is to validate the importance of housework and that it thereby supports this inefficient housework system.[10] She analyzed a sample of 200 hints taken from 70 "Hints from Heloise" columns published in January–March 1975.[11] She concluded that of these hints, 37.5 percent were needlessly time-consuming, 40 percent were neutral with regard to time use but were often superfluous activities, and only 7.5 percent were actually time-saving ways of performing useful chores. Of the hints, 11.2 percent involved economizing on money (where this category did not have a big overlap with the time-consuming category).[12]

Another researcher, Bonnie J. Fox, analyzed advertisements for household appliances in the prominent women's magazine *Ladies Home Journal*, measuring the percentage of ads that extolled the labor-saving character of household appliances.[13] She surveyed ads at 10-year intervals, starting in 1909–10 and concluding in 1979–80. In 1909–10, 21 percent of the ads stressed the labor-saving nature of their product; the percentage dropped to 13 percent in 1919–20 and 1929–30; rose to 19 percent in 1939–40 and to 20 percent in 1949–50; and fell to between 5 and 6 percent in both 1969–70 and 1979–80. She concluded: "More *Journal* ads featured directives about housework than descriptions of the product; they emphasized work performance far more frequently than liberation from housework, and they also promoted service to family . . . advertiser's [sic] efforts to create a market for household appliances and other means of domestic labor involved promotion of an ideology about housework that reinforced women's dedication to it."[14]

2. Family composition changes: Changing demographics can affect the labor supply decision by causing changes in tastes and changes in availability of nonearned income. In particular, trends in marriage, family size, and divorce are critical determinants of labor supply. It appears that during the 1950s and 1960s, there were fewer young unmarried women available for work due to an increase in the proportion of married women and a drop in women's age at first marriage. Therefore, employers who had an increased demand for female labor would have had to turn to married women as a source of labor, recruiting them actively and offering them better wages.[15] This compositional change in marital status can help explain the increase in the participation rates for married women during this time period.

This explanation for rising female participation appears less viable as the median age at first marriage began to rise in the 1970s and 1980s, and the proportion of single women

TABLE 4.7 Likelihood that marriages of a given duration will end eventually in divorce, 1980

Number of years a couple has been married	% who will divorce at some point in the future
0	49.6
1	48.8
2	46.8
5	38.8
10	26.8
15	17.8
20	11.4
25	6.6
30	3.5
35	1.8
40	0.9
50	0.6

Source: James A. Weed, "National Estimates of Marriage Dissolution and Survivorship: United States," *Vital and Health Statistics*, series 3, Analytical Studies no. 19 (1980) (Table 1).

increased. However, for single persons, nonearned income in the form of spouse's earnings is reduced, and the ability to increase nonmarket production through division of labor is absent. These factors can explain why the participation rate for single women is higher than for married women. Therefore, a shift in composition back towards more single women can help explain the continuing rise in overall female participation rates during the 1970s and 1980s. As the median age at first marriage for women has leveled off in the 1990s (see Figure 5.1), there is interest in whether this signifies a lessening of the rise in female participation as well.[16]

Another trend concerns the effects of changing family size on labor force participation. People with dependents (children and/or elderly relatives) in their household may place a higher valuation on nonmarket time. For instance, complementarity of production processes can mean that their efficiency in producing nonmarket output increases (e.g., being able to simultaneously guard children while they nap and prepare dinner). Therefore, we would expect to see female labor force participation rates decline with increases in the number of children. However, as family size is decreasing, this factor should be decreasing in importance as well. The decline in family size in the 1970s and 1980s can help explain rising participation rates during this period. However, family size rose in the 1950s and 1960s, but participation rates rose as well.

The rise in the divorce rate since 1960 provides another explanation for why female labor force participation would increase. In the simple economic model of labor supply, a switch from marriage to divorce tends to reduce lifetime nonearned income for women, which has the income effect of increasing their market work. Therefore, not only will divorced women have a higher rate of labor force participation than do married women, but married women may increase their labor force participation in response to the increased probability of becoming divorced. Table 4.7 shows that the probability of divorce is very high. Currently, the median duration of marriage is slightly over seven years.[17] While the probability of divorce drops off with the length of marriage, even after ten years of marriage there is a greater than one in four chance that the couple will subsequently divorce. One study found a positive lagged relationship between increases in the divorce rate and increases in the labor force participation rate of married women with young children since WWII.[18] Another study found that women who subsequently divorce increase their labor supply in the three years prior to separation.[19] These researchers calculated that the rise in the divorce rate can account for about 2.6 percentage points out of the 15-percentage-point rise in female labor force participation from 1960 to 1980.

Several researchers have attempted to determine if the introduction in the 1970s of no-fault divorce has contributed to the increase in the labor supply of married women since 1970. This increase in female labor supply could then explain the slower real wage growth. Two studies using 1979 data both conclude that residence in a unilateral divorce state has a statistically significant positive influence on whether a married woman is in the labor force.[20] Another study, using 1972 data, concludes that being in a unilateral divorce state in that year had a negative effect on the labor supply of married women.[21] The 1979 data are probably more appropriate to use both because the innovation took time to spread after its introduction in California in 1970 and because it could have taken time for women to consider the implications of the change in the divorce rules. Since there are several implications of the switch to no-fault divorce, the exact cause for this finding of a positive relationship between unilateral divorce law passage and female labor supply is unclear. One researcher argues that the lack of compensation for marriage-specific investment at divorce creates an incentive for married women to increase their more general market-oriented human capital during marriage by entering the labor force. Another researcher argues that this response is due to a lack of compensation at divorce for married women's reduced human capital (i.e., their future earning capacity) rather than their marriage-specific investment.

3. Falling male wages: In the period after 1970, the female labor supply growth rate rose, while the real wage growth rate fell. Although the percentage growth in real wages averaged over 2 percent per year from 1956 through 1970, the growth rate from 1971 to 1975 slowed to 0.5 percent per annum; and from 1975 to 1980 the rate of change was negative (−0.6 percent per annum). Nonetheless, the female labor force participation rate rose by about 2.5 percent per annum throughout the 1970s, as it had on average throughout the late 1950s and early 1960s.[22] Several researchers have cited the high levels of uncertainty associated with future income streams in the 1970s as an important factor in married women's increased labor force participation.[23] In particular, an increasing degree of uncertainty associated with future wages and, therefore, future household income contributed by husbands appears to have contributed to the growth in married women's participation in that decade.[24]

One way in which this uncertainty may be reflected is in an increasing inelasticity of labor supply with respect to husband's current income. One study finds such a decline from 1960 to 1980 in the sensitivity of married women's labor force participation to husband's income, although a negative relationship still exists.[25] However, this weakened link could be due to uncertainty either about future earnings or about the future of the marriage.

*E*xplanations of the fall in men's labor force participation

Economists have also studied the fall in men's labor force participation and have attempted to enumerate the various causes of this decline, particularly for older men. Factors can again be divided into demand and supply-side factors. Demand-side factors influence labor-supply decisions by decreasing the wage that men can potentially earn.

There are two important possible links from the rise in female participation to the fall in male participation, although in each case it is also possible that the causality runs the other way. One possible link is that the rise in female participation may have led to a fall in male participation as females displaced males in jobs. Alternatively, the fall in male participation may have led to a rise in female participation – that is, as men were less willing to work in particular jobs, women were hired to fill these vacated positions. The second possible link is that the rise in female participation may have led to a fall in male participation as women's earnings were used to finance increased schooling for younger men and earlier retirement for older men. Alternatively, the fall in male participation may have led to a rise in female participation as married women were forced to offset the drop in men's contribution to household income by increasing their market hours.

Demand-side factors

Two demand-side factors are generally cited as of primary importance in explaining the decline of male participation: (1) the sectoral decline in labor demand in sectors where men are predominantly employed, particularly the manufacturing sector; (2) the increased substitution of female for male labor. These effects of changes in labor demand have been discussed above in the section on demand-side factors for women. To the extent that women and men have different skills, they are not perfect substitutes in production. The possibility of increased substitution of female for male labor increases with changes in technology that allow for this substitution to occur and with relatively high wages for male labor, which can be caused by unionization in male-dominated occupations. It appears that the elasticity of labor demand for men is lower than that for women, implying that male wages would have to be fairly high relative to female wages to lead to a large decline in demand for male labor. Also, several studies have found that women predominantly have been substituted in production for young men, in particular for young black men, while prime-age white males have not been replaced by women.[26] So, reduced demand for men does not appear to be a primary reason for the long-term trend in overall male participation rates. However, in the late 1970s and throughout the 1980s, a decline in male labor demand, reflected in declining real wages for men, appears to be responsible for the decline in participation among prime-age men, particularly for less-educated men.[27]

Supply-side factors

There are two supply-side factors that appear to be of primary importance in explaining the drop in male labor force participation: (1) rising real wages, through their effect on lifetime potential income, and (2) the rise in available nonearned income for men, through pensions, disability insurance, and female earned income. These factors appear to be particularly influential before the mid-1970s, after which point real wages and nonearned income have not risen as uniformly for men as a group.[28]

1. Rising real wages: The particular pattern of male labor force participation, especially the fact that the largest drop has occurred among men over 50, implies that reduced labor supply for men takes the form of earlier retirement. If wages have been rising over time for some groups of men, this leads to an increase in their lifetime potential income.

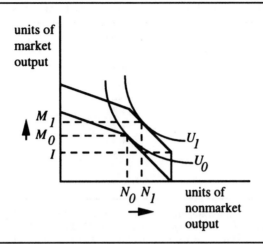

FIGURE 4.11 Effects of an increase in unearned income

If one cannot borrow against future rises in expected income, workers cannot tap this increased income in order to reduce market work early in their lives. Instead, workers have increased nonearned income later in life in the form of interest payments on accumulated assets and will reduce their market work due to the income effect of these payments. Changes in nonearned income for households have the unambiguous effect of reducing market work hours, as shown in Figure 4.11 for a household that originally has only one member performing market work and no nonearned income. While purchases of market output increase, this person will reduce market work (shown as a move to the right of the kink point along the production frontier) and will even stop working entirely if the increase in nonearned income (I) is large.

2. **Rises in nonearned income:** The widespread adoption of pension programs and disability insurance has led to an increase in nonearned income for households, particularly later in life. While these benefits are partly related to rises in potential income as employers shift compensation from taxable income to untaxed fringes, an individual may receive pension and disability insurance payments in excess of his actual pay-in due to the actuarial nature of the payments. Disability rates for men are considerable. One study calculates that among men ages 21 to 46, 10 percent have a disability limiting work. The rate rises to 21 percent among men ages 47 to 64, and 34 percent among men 65 and over.[29] Additionally, the growth in old-age benefits under the Old Age and Survivors Insurance program and in the form of private pension programs appears to be a key factor in the greatly reduced participation of older men – down from 45.8 percent for men 65 and over in 1950 to 19.0 percent by 1980.[30]

Trends in hours worked

As another cause of rising participation rates, we also need to consider whether there has been a substantial drop in average hours worked. For instance, a drop in hours worked per man could have led to an increased need for women workers. It is theoretically possible that the rise in female participation could have led to no change in total hours worked.

TABLE 4.8 Mean weekly hours worked by employed persons, by sex, 1955 to 1996

	Women	*Men*
1955–59	36.4	42.6
1960–64	35.3	42.5
1965–69	36.2	42.7
1970–74	34.2	41.8
1975–79	34.2	41.6
1980–84	34.3	41.0
1985–89	35.5	42.0
1990–94	35.7	42.0
1995–96	35.7	42.2

Sources: 1955–58 – *Current Population Reports Series P-50*, nos. 63 (Table 3), 72 (Table 18), 85 (Table 18), 89 (Table 24); 1959–64 – *Special Labor Force Reports*, nos. 4, 14, 23, 31, 43, 52 (Table D-7 in each issue); 1965–96 – *Employment and Earnings*, January issues. Data are for nonagricultural industries, persons ages 16 and over.

TABLE 4.9 Percentage distribution of hours worked by employed persons, by sex, 1940 to 1995

	Women				*Men*			
	<15	*<35*	*35–40*	*>40*	*<15*	*<35*	*35–40*	*>40*
1940	2.9	18.2	39.3	42.5	1.6	11.0	38.1	50.1
1950	4.6	20.5	52.9	26.6	2.0	10.1	44.3	45.6
1960	9.8	27.6	54.3	18.1	4.4	12.1	46.1	41.8
1970	9.3	31.5	56.4	12.1	4.5	15.3	48.0	36.7
1980	7.4	30.8	56.4	12.8	3.4	13.5	51.7	34.8
1990	—	26.8	53.4	19.8	—	12.0	48.8	39.2
1995	8.2	35.1	43.9	21.0	3.9	18.3	41.3	40.4

Sources: 1940 – Sixteenth Census of the United States: 1940, "The Labor Force," part 1: 259 (Table 86); 1950 – U.S. Census of Population 1950, "Special Reports," part 1, chapter A (Table 13); 1960 – U.S. Census of Population 1960, "Employment Status and Work Experience" (Table 12); 1970 – U.S. Census of Population 1970, "Employment Status and Work Experience" (Table 17); 1980 – 1980 Census of Population, "Characteristics of the Population" (Table 288); 1990 – *Employment and Earnings* 37, no. 4 (April 1992): 35 (Table A-30); 1995 – calculated by the author using data from the Current Population Survey, March 1995. 1940–70 data are for persons ages 14 and over; 1980–95 data are for persons ages 16 and over.

Table 4.8 shows mean weekly hours worked since 1955. For both sexes, there was little change from 1955 to 1970, followed by a slight downward trend through the early 1980s, and an upturn to the present. The averages have declined slightly since 1955 for both women and men. These data do not support the idea that the rise in female participation was mainly in response to a decline in average hours worked by men.

Data on the distribution of hours worked, as shown in Table 4.9, indicate that people tend to cluster in the 35 to 40 hour range, rather than being evenly distributed. In particular, few people work fewer than 15 hours a week. Also, the percentage of persons working long hours – over 40 a week – is rising. The existence of *quasi-fixed costs* for both employers and potential workers can explain these phenomena. Quasi-fixed costs are costs

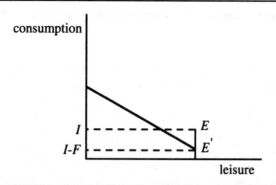

FIGURE 4.12   Effect of quasi-fixed costs of working on the budget constraint

TABLE 4.10   Percentage of women who work less than 35 hours per week, by marital status and age of youngest child in the household, 1995

Age of child	All	Currently married	Never married
No child under 18	23.9	23.2	25.0
Child 6–17	34.2	30.8	49.8
Child 3–5	33.4	34.0	29.9
Child under 3	33.9	33.8	34.4

Source: calculated by the author using data from the Current Population Survey, March 1995.

that are incurred if a person is hired, but that do not vary with hours worked. Many fringe benefits are of this type. For instance, an employer may pay a health-insurance premium for an employee that does not vary with time worked. Employers with substantial and/or rising quasi-fixed costs have incentive to avoid hiring part-time workers or to make them exempt from fringes. On the employee side, examples of quasi-fixed costs include purchase of a monthly parking permit or bus pass for use in commuting and child care costs, if they take the form of paying a weekly fee regardless of hours actually used.

Figure 4.12 shows the effects on the individual's budget constraint of quasi-fixed costs of amount F. The budget constraint consists of the point E, and then becomes a line starting at point E'. Persons faced by this constraint are unlikely to work only a handful of hours, generally preferring either to not work at all or to work a fuller schedule.

However, as Table 4.10 shows, employed women with children are more likely to work part-time than women on average. This implies that their time spent in nonmarket work is relatively more valuable. However, there appears to be a trade-off, with availability of nonearned income determining whether or not a woman works only part-time: as shown in Table 4.10, married women are more likely to work part-time than are never-married women, who do not have access to additional nonearned income in the form of husband's earnings. Among the currently-married, there is little variation by age of youngest child under 18, implying fairly constant valuation of nonmarket work by age of child for this group.

Conclusions about economic factors affecting labor force participation

Which of the above factors are most important in explaining changes in labor force participation? In particular, have labor demand or supply shifts been more important?

While it is clear that both have been important, many analysts have emphasized demand shifts over supply shifts as the main force behind the increase in female rates up until 1970.[31] This is equivalent to arguing that real wage growth explains most of the increase in female labor supply. Since 1970, the combination of rising divorce rates, continued growth of female wages, although at a slower pace, and falling male real incomes appears to explain most of the rise.[32] Male rates have declined – particularly for older men – mainly due to the rise in various sources of nonearned income, implying that supply has shifted more than demand for older men.

Extensions of the simple economic model

In general, economists attempt to explain changes in individual labor supply by looking at changes in wages and income. But clearly many other factors that we have either not considered explicitly or not mentioned at all influence labor participation rates. In an influential 1958 study of female labor force participation, economist Clarence Long included a long list of factors that are still relevant for helping to explain more recent trends:[33]

- changing community attitudes (which would include the feminist movement since Long's time)
- differences in social class
- changing conditions of work
- changing required intensity of work effort
- increases in fringe benefits
- changes in unionization
- social life becoming more dependent on work
- changes in the distribution of income
- changing burdens of credit
- changes in wealth and liquid assets
- changes in leisure-time activities (including an increase in the variety of activities)

There are also other wider social shifts that Long did not explicitly mention, such as the trend towards increasing urbanization and suburbanization.

While it is hard to incorporate some of these changes into the simple economic model of labor supply, others can be incorporated as causing shifts in people's preferences between market and nonmarket output. In general, economists prefer to assume that tastes are relatively stable and that changes in observed behavior are therefore caused by changes in the constraints persons face. If economists can explain changes in behavior using this simple model, then the general scientific principle that simple models are preferable to complex models supports this practice. But this approach leaves economists open to the charge that they are ignoring the very factors that are the most important in explaining what has happened.

Some economists have proposed hypotheses that provide contrasts to the simple economic model of labor participation. The economist and demographer Richard Easterlin has suggested that increases in cohort size since World War II have created economic pressures on young couples to the extent that they are unable to continue the upward trend in the standard of living that their parents enjoyed.[34] These pressures have caused changes in attitudes and behavior relating to work and childbearing. Another economist, Clair Brown, has argued that simple economic models underpredict the actual change in female participation rates, especially between 1970 and 1980, and that there is important evidence that is not reconciled with the simple model.[35] She argues that (1) the composition of family expenditures depends on family market income rather than on full potential market and imputed nonmarket income; (2) families use the same "production techniques" at home, whether or not the wife is employed; and (3) as wives work more, their true leisure drops as their wage rises. She suggests an alternative model in which time and money are not interchangeable and in which social norms and the mature nature of the market economy cause changes in the composition of consumption, which causes rises in married women's participation rates as the household increases its demand for market commodities.

Some objections to the simple economic model can be overcome by extending the model to allow three inputs into the utility function instead of two, so that Utility = f(market goods, nonmarket goods, pure leisure).[36] In drawing both the individual's budget constraint and the household production frontier, we have collapsed nonmarket goods and pure leisure together into the category of nonmarket output. Clearly the components of nonmarket goods and pure leisure can change in relative proportions within the broader category of nonmarket output. Indeed, between 1965 and 1985, total hours spent in productive activity (market and nonmarket) declined by 7 hours for employed women and by 4 hours for employed men, implying that pure leisure has risen for both groups.[37]

The study of allocation of time among more than two types of activities is a new area for economists. One problem is in developing modeling techniques for incorporating constraints on activities. For instance, one study finds that higher wages reduce sleep among men but increase their waking nonmarket time by an equal amount, while among women, the wage effect on sleep is negative but very small.[38] Another study looks at workers who were constrained to take off time without pay from their regular schedules to see how they allocated this freed-up time. Women were both more likely than men to approve of the program and to use the "free" time in production of nonmarket goods rather than pure leisure.[39]

TABLE 4.11 Percentage reporting volunteer work, all and by sex, 1965, 1974, and 1989

	1965	1974	1989
All persons	18	24	20
Women	21	26	22
Men	15	20	19

Sources: Americans Volunteer 1974 (Washington, DC: ACTION, 1975); Howard V. Hayghe, "Volunteers in the U.S.: Who Donates the Time?" *Monthly Labor Review* 114, no. 2 (February 1991): 17–23.

FOCUS

The decline of volunteerism

Many human activities that appear to be unanalyzable by economics, such as the altruistic act of performing volunteer work, are actually prime subjects for economic analysis. Volunteering can be considered as one way of using nonmarket time. Therefore, there should be a decline in overall volunteering as women's labor force participation increases. We can also predict that the rate of volunteering should be higher among women than men because women are more likely to have a lower value of time as their wages are lower than men's. However, over time, as labor force participation and wages converge, we would expect the gender rates of volunteering to converge.

National surveys by the Census Bureau asking persons if they had performed unpaid volunteer work at some point during the previous year were conducted in 1965, 1974, and 1989.[40] As shown in Table 4.11, the numbers indicate a rise in volunteering from 1965 to 1974, followed by a decline in volunteering from 1974 to 1989. However, the 1965 figures are problematic in that the surveyors did not specifically tell people to include church-related volunteering, although many mentioned it voluntarily. This omission may be hiding an actual decline in volunteerism since 1965.

The women's rate shows a greater decline than the men's rate from 1974 to 1989. The men's rate is always lower than the women's rate, as predicted above, but the rates appear to be converging over this time period.

However, those who appear to have the highest value of time are more likely to volunteer. Volunteerism rates are higher for employed persons (23 percent in 1989) than for those who are unemployed (14 percent) or not in the labor force (17 percent), and they are higher for middle-age persons than for young and old people. The stereotypical volunteer in all three years is a middle-age married woman with children, who works at least part-time. These patterns can be reconciled with economic theory. If volunteering has a low cost in terms of time and a high value in utility per unit of time, then busy persons will choose volunteer work over more costly forms of leisure activities. Another explanation is that these persons may be the best able to create consumption value for the family from volunteering. After all, some types of volunteering may involve nonmarket production, such as exploiting economies of scale in childraising by taking turns with other mothers in supervising children (e.g., being den mother for the Scouts) and helping out the PTA so as to improve the value of educational experiences for one's family. However, the high – though falling (from 25 percent in 1974) – volunteerism rate among employed persons implies that the forces of changing demographics (e.g., more retired persons, and overall increases in the wage rate) may be more responsible for the changing rate of volunteering than the rise in women's labor force participation.

Predicting changes in the labor market

The elasticities of the labor supply and demand curves are important in helping us to predict further changes and to predict the possible effects of various labor market policies. (The appendix to this chapter contains a discussion of elasticity.) For example, if the female labor supply curve is relatively steep (inelastic), a given shift in labor demand will have a larger effect on wages and a smaller effect on participation than if the curve were relatively flat (elastic). We may also want to calculate elasticities with respect to other variables that enter into labor supply and demand functions; this will help us to predict the size of demand and supply curve shifts when these variables change.

National demand curves for labor in developed countries appear to be relatively inelastic, with elasticity estimates in the range of -0.15 to -0.50,[41] implying that large shifts in labor supply curves will have noticeable effects on wages. Separate elasticity estimates for the broad classes of white- and blue-collar workers also fall into this range. The elasticity of demand for adult men, particularly white men, appears to be lower than that for other demographic groups.[42]

Some studies have also estimated cross-price elasticities, in which changes in the quantity demanded of one form of labor are related to changes in the wage of other forms of labor or the price of other inputs (in particular, capital). There is a reasonable degree of consensus among labor economists that skilled labor and capital are complements, unskilled labor and capital are substitutes, and that women are substitutes for younger men. However, there is little consensus on the absolute value of these elasticities across studies, and it is not clear whether skilled and unskilled labor are generally substitutes or complements.[43]

Labor economists have particularly focused on the elasticities of labor supply with respect to wages and nonearned income, and they find them generally inelastic. Measures of men's elasticity of labor supply with respect to wages appear to be quite small. A survey of 22 U.S. studies published between 1966 and 1984 found a median labor supply curve elasticity of -0.09, with a range of -0.29 to 0.21.[44] Measures of women's elasticity of labor supply with respect to wages have a wider range and are more likely to be positive: a survey of 44 U.S. studies published between 1976 and 1985 found a median labor supply curve elasticity of 0.77, with a range of -0.89 to 15.24.[45] All of these studies measure wages in cents and hours of work annually, so at the median values for the elasticities, a rise of one dollar in the hourly wage would reduce men's annual hours of work by 9 hours and raise women's annual hours by 77 hours. The studies of men find a median value for total income elasticity of -0.125, with a range of -0.70 to 0.08,[46] while the studies of women find a median value for total income elasticity of -0.08, with a range of -0.89 to 0.48.[47] This implies that an increase in yearly nonearned income of $1000 would lead to a decrease in earned income (due to fewer hours worked at the given wage) of only $125 for men and $80 for women. While these studies bear out the general assumption made by economists and policymakers that women's labor supply is more wage elastic than men's, recent estimates that carefully control for various sources of error in calculating elasticities have found that their supply curves are more similarly sloped than previously thought, implying that the negative range of the female wage elasticities above may be the more relevant range.[48]

Empirical estimation of female labor supply has generally involved two steps, first estimating the probability of working, and then estimating hours worked for those women who do any work at all. More elaborate models jointly estimate labor supply, fertility, and the wage as endogenous variables and as life-cycle decisions, so that sequencing of children and work is determined, as well as the number of children to be had (where the wage may be affected as well by the number of children).[49] Then researchers have to look for truly exogenous factors, including shifts in *wage profiles* (e.g., the whole lifetime sequence of wages, which may rise if labor demand increases). One study finds that birth cohort, education (which may also be endogenous), and wealth have little effect on either lifetime labor supply or fertility, but shifts in the level of the lifetime wage profile are associated with shifts in the lifetime profiles of fertility and employment rates.[50] Another study, using a sample of young women, finds that neither birth order nor childhood family size significantly affect the level or growth rate of women's wages, but family size affects women's employment status: women from small families work less than women from large families when they are young (14 to 22), but work more when they are more mature (22 to 30).[51] This appears to occur due to the effect of family size on childbearing behavior (controlling for education): women from larger families have more children. In general, estimates of the effect of children on labor force participation vary across a wide positive to negative range and are very dependent on the way in which fertility is measured.[52]

One could also incorporate marital status as an endogenous variable (one way is to treat the marriage market as a market for household labor), so the marriage and labor markets are interrelated.[53] One study "dynamically" models labor supply at each point in time as affected by lifetime variables such as wage profiles and by changes in family relationships.[54] The researchers find that these equations are very similar for men and women. Children have little impact in these equations, while changes in marital status strongly affect female labor supply, perhaps because these changes are not perfectly anticipated. Another change which may not be perfectly anticipated, a rise in the unemployment rate, causes a drop in work by unmarried women but a rise in work by married women. The researchers develop an "inertia model" of labor supply, which focuses on assessing the probability that workers will stop working and the probability that nonworkers will start working, as well as considering changes in hours among workers. They reach some conclusions that are generally not obtained using static labor supply models: the presence of children under age 18 appears to slightly reduce male labor supply, and there is some evidence supporting a mutual husband-wife retirement effect. While dynamic models have not come into wide use by policymakers in modeling labor supply responses to policy changes, they are becoming more commonplace in the economics profession.

*P*olicy Application: Subsidized child care

Child care costs can be modeled either as a drop in the net wage after paying for child care per hour worked or as a quasi-fixed cost associated with working (as many day care centers charge a fixed rate per week, regardless of the number of hours the child attends). In either case, the predicted change is a decrease in paid hours worked.

Researchers have looked for this decrease by considering differences among women in the child care costs they face. Relatively expensive child care can reduce mothers' labor force participation in several measurable ways. First, women who are currently not working will continue to stay out of the labor force so as to provide child care themselves. Second, women may work part-time instead of full-time so as to spend more time providing child care themselves. Third, women who are currently working may stop working completely.

Several studies have found this negative relationship between the cost of child care and female labor force participation. One study found that geographic variation in the effects of children on married women's labor force participation was negatively related to both the cost and availability of child care.[55] Another study found child care costs are positively related to higher rates of married mothers' leaving employment and lower rates of their entering employment.[56] The same researchers have estimated the elasticity of labor supply with respect to child care costs as −0.38, or relatively inelastic. They found that if child care were available at zero cost (e.g., fully subsidized), 87 percent of mothers would work, while if it cost $40 per week (in 1980 dollars), only 19 percent would work.[57]

The fact that not all mothers would use nonfamily child care even if it were free implies that they do not view the two types of care as being of equal quality. One 1990 survey of 74 "career-oriented" married mothers, ages 27 to 47 and with at least one year of college,

TABLE 4.12 Child care arrangements of employed women, 1988 and 1995

	1988, for youngest child, women aged:		1995, for children under 6, mother works ≥ 35 hours/week
	23–31	29–39	
Care by relative other than mother	41.2	40.7	33
father	11.3	14.1	—
siblings of child	1.1	8.8	—
other relative	28.8	18.0	—
Care by unrelated person	22.3	24.0	32
Child care center	18.1	10.6	31
Mother care for child at work	3.0	4.2	—
Child cares for self	1.9	24.6	—
Other	13.5	12.1	—
No nonparental arrangement	—	—	12
Weekly expenditures, 1988 ($)	61.51	44.46	—
Average hours per week	39.38	24.69	—
Expenditure per hour ($)	1.56	1.80	—

Sources: Columns 1 and 2 – Jonathan R. Veum and Philip M. Gleason, "Child Care: Arrangements and Costs," *Monthly Labor Review* 114, no. 10 (October 1991): 11 (Table 1), 15 (Table 5). Women's ages at the time of the survey are shown. The second column totals to more than 100 because respondents were allowed to choose more than one type of arrangement. Column 3 – *Statistical Abstract of the United States* (1996): 386 (Table 607).

found that the availability of quality child care was the main factor influencing those who quit their jobs.[58] However, family income was also an important factor in the decision of whether or not to quit: women who left their jobs had husbands who earned between $25,000 and $49,000 annually, while the husbands of those who continued to work earned between $15,000 and $25,000. This implies that there is a trade-off between family income and willingness to provide family child care. However, many women job quitters may be quitting a specific job not to stay home but to find a job that is either more accommodating of their home life or that pays more so that they can afford quality child care. Additionally, not all women who quit jobs do so for family-related reasons. A survey of women who had recently left a job found that 73 percent had quit to work for other companies, 13 percent to start their own businesses, and only 7 percent to take care of their children full-time.[59]

As shown in Table 4.12, employed women are much more likely to use relative care than to use child care in either a child care center or a home situation by a nonrelative. We cannot infer from these data alone whether people choose care by relatives because it is of higher quality or because it is cheaper. But it is clear that for those families paying for child care, child care cost comprises a large proportion of costs associated with working – generally over 50 percent.

Child care subsidies and benefits are currently provided in a variety of ways in the United States by both the public and private sectors. This piecemeal delivery system has been widely criticized as being inequitable and insufficient to provide work incentives for low-income mothers. There is a wide range of governmental child-care programs available with widely varying levels of coverage. Head Start is perhaps the best-known federal program, with a budget of 2.4 billion dollars in 1991.[60] Most states use some of their Title XX Social Services Block Grant, which provides federal funds to states to cover a wide range of social services, in order to fund child care services (to the tune of 2 billion dollars in 1991).[61] State and local governments also provide additional spending on child care services.

Government programs can be classified as either supply-side or demand-side subsidies. The basic effect of lowering the user's child care costs is the same. Supply-side programs include Head Start, some forms of Title XX block grant spending on child care, and the child care center food subsidy program. Demand-side programs include child care voucher programs run under Title XX; the AFDC and food stamp programs' work-expense disregard; and programs run through the tax system, in particular, the Child and Dependent Care Tax Credit and the Flexible Spending Account (FSA), which allows for payment of child care expenses out of pretax income.

The largest child care program run by the federal government is Head Start. However, the largest component of federal government spending on child care is the lost tax revenue due to the use of the tax credit and flexible spending accounts.[62] In 1991, the federal government estimated its "expenditure" on the tax credit alone at 2.3 billion dollars.[63] In addition, workers can pay for up to $5000 of child care using pretax dollars with an FSA if their firm offers this option as an employee benefit and still use the credit to cover child care spending above the FSA cap up to the tax credit cap. Although only about 800 firms offered FSAs in 1985, they have become more prevalent since then; in a 1993 survey of establishments with at least 100 workers, about 12 percent reported offering such accounts.[64]

Businesses have had limited involvement in reducing child care costs for their employees. A minority of establishments provide any child care-related services at all, let alone any services other than counseling and referral. A majority of establishments do report that they offer some type of flexibility in work scheduling. However, these policies may not cover all workers in an establishment.

Assuming that we would like to see more aid for child care, how could the current subsidy system be improved? The federal government has no program with the sole purpose of providing direct assistance to help lower-income families (other than those receiving welfare benefits) pay for child care. Since the current tax credit is nonrefundable, it is of limited usefulness to those families with low or zero tax liability. In order to target benefits at the lower-income families, economist Philip Robins suggests a two-tiered system: a progressive refundable tax credit and a "safety net" of publicly funded child care centers for needs of special groups, located in areas accessible to low-income families.[65] Another factor to consider is whether the existing level of regulation of child-care facilities, which occurs mainly at the state level, is leading to a reduced supply. While regulation is generally perceived as maintaining quality, a less charitable view of such regulation is that it serves as a barrier to entry for possible low-cost child care providers.[66]

Summary

Women have, in general, increased their labor force participation, while men have reduced theirs. Both demand and supply curve shifts have led to these changes. In particular, the increase in available income during late middle age has led men to retire earlier, and the increased demand for clerical and service labor has led to an increase in women's working, even during prime childraising years. Female and male work patterns over the life span have become more similar; their responses to wage and income changes appear to have become more similar as well.

Endnotes

1. Separated persons are included with divorced persons throughout this analysis.
2. Two influential early studies are Clarence D. Long, *The Labor Force Under Changing Income and Employment* (Princeton, N.J.: Princeton University, 1958); and Glen G. Cain, *Married Women in the Labor Force: An Economic Analysis* (Chicago, Ill.: University of Chicago, 1966).
3. James P. Smith and Michael Ward, "Time-Series Growth in the Female Labor Force," *Journal of Labor Economics* 3, no. 1, supplement (January 1985): S59–S90.
4. Valerie Kincade Oppenheimer, *The Female Labor Force in the United States: Demographic and Economic Factors Governing its Growth and Changing Composition* (Westport, Conn.: Greenwood, 1976).
5. Joann Vanek, "Household Technology and Social Status: Rising Living Standards and Status and Residence Differences in Housework," *Technology and Culture* 19, no. 3 (July 1978): 363.
6. John P. Robinson and Melissa Milkie, "Dances with Dust Bunnies," *American Demographics* 19, no. 1 (January 1997): 37–59.
7. There was also a 1981–82 follow-up survey of a subset of the households sampled in 1975–76, but the low response rate and consequent lack of representativeness of the sample has made it less widely used. See F. Thomas Juster and Frank P. Stafford (eds.), *Time, Goods, and Well-Being* (Ann Arbor, Mich.: University of Michigan, 1985), for a set of essays thoroughly detailing the findings from the surveys before the 1985–86 one. Results from a 1993–96 time diary survey are available only in preliminary form and show little change from the 1985–86 patterns, according to John P. Robinson and Geoffrey Godbey, *Time for Life: The Surprising Ways Americans Use Their Time* (University Park, Penn.: Pennsylvania State University, 1997).
8. This increase in housework by men had been widely noted by the popular press and by advertisers, starting in the early 1980s; cf. "Man of the House: More Working Wives Expose Their Hubbies to the Joy of Cooking," *Wall Street Journal* (October 16, 1980): A1; "More Food Advertisers Woo the Male Shopper as He Shares the Load," *Wall Street Journal* (August 26, 1980): A1.
9. Joann Vanek, "Time Spent in Housework," *Scientific American* 231, no. 5 (November 1974): 116–120.
10. Maxine L. Margolis, *Mothers and Such: Views of American Women and Why They Changed* (Berkeley, Calif.: University of California, 1984). She also concludes that there is a somewhat opposing tendency for the prescriptive literature on mothering and housekeeping practices to support the increased demand for female labor.
11. Maxine Margolis "In Hartford, Hannibal, and (New) Hampshire, Heloise is Hardly Helpful," *MS* 4, no. 12 (June 1976): 28–36.
12. Of the remaining hints, two percent were safety-related and the rest fell into miscellaneous categories.
13. Bonnie J. Fox, "Selling the Mechanized Household: 70 Years of Ads in *Ladies Home Journal*," *Gender and Society* 4, no. 1 (March 1990): 25–40.
14. Fox, *op. cit.*: 25 (abstract).
15. Oppenheimer, *loc. cit.*
16. See Shoshana Grossbard-Shechtman and Clive W. J. Granger, "The Baby-Boom and Time Trends in Women's Labor Force Participation," Center for Public Economics, San Diego State University working paper (March 1994) and "Women's Jobs and Marriage – Baby-Boom Versus Baby-Bust," University of California, San Diego Discussion Paper 96–03 (February 1996). The Explorations section of *Feminist Economics* 1, no. 1 (Spring 1995) contains an interesting debate regarding this hypothesis between Grossbard-Shechtman and feminist economist Myra Strober.
17. *Statistical Abstract of the United States* (1996): 105 (Table 150).
18. Robert T. Michael, "Consequences of the Rise in Female Labor Force Participation Rates: Questions and Probes," *Journal of Labor Economics* 3, no. 1, supplement (January 1985): S117–S146.

19. William R. Johnson and Jonathan Skinner, "Labor Supply and Marital Separation," *American Economic Review* 76, no. 3 (June 1986): 455–469.

20. H. Elizabeth Peters, "Marriage and Divorce: Informational Constraints and Private Contracting," *American Economic Review* 76, no. 3 (June 1986): 437–454; Allen M. Parkman, "Unilateral Divorce and the Labor-Force Participation Rate of Married Women, Revisited," *American Economic Review* 82, no. 3 (June 1992): 671–678.

21. Johnson and Skinner, *loc. cit.*

22. Francine D. Blau and Adam J. Grossberg, "Real Wage and Employment Uncertainty and the Labor Force Participation Decisions of Married Women," *Economic Inquiry* 29, no. 4 (October 1991): 679 (Table 1).

23. Blau and Grossberg, *op. cit.*: 678–695; June O'Neill, "A Time-Series Analysis of Women's Labor Force Participation," *American Economic Review* 71, no. 2 (May 1981): 76–80.

24. Blau and Grossberg, *loc. cit.*

25. Augustin Kwasi Fosu, "Labor Force Participation by Married Women: Recent Intercity Evidence," *Eastern Economic Journal* 16, no. 3 (July-September 1990): 229–238.

26. Daniel S. Hamermesh, "The Demand for Labor in the Long Run," *Handbook of Labor Economics* 1, eds. Orley Ashenfelter and Richard Layard (Amsterdam: North-Holland, 1986): 463.

27. Chinhui Juhn, "Decline of Male Labor Force Participation: The Role of Declining Market Opportunities," *Quarterly Journal of Economics* 107, no. 1 (February 1992): 79–121.

28. *Ibid.*

29. Alice Nakamura and Maseo Nakamura, *The Second Paycheck: A Socioeconomic Analysis of Earnings* (Orlando, Fla.: Academic Press, 1985): 50 (Table 2.7.8). Disability rates for women are not inconsiderable either, but a smaller absolute number of women under the age of 60, and a smaller proportion of women than of men in any age group, cite a work-limiting disability as their reason for not working; see *Employment and Earnings* 39, no. 1 (January 1992): 204 (Table 35).

30. Donald O. Parsons, "Male Retirement Behavior in the United States," *Journal of Economic History* 51, no. 3 (September 1991): 657–674. These data are from the Bureau of Labor Statistics; decennial Census data show a drop over this period from 41.4 percent to 19.3 percent.

31. Oppenheimer, *loc. cit.*

32. O'Neill, *loc. cit.*

33. Long, *op. cit.*: 20–29.

34. Richard A. Easterlin, *Birth and Fortune: The Impact of Numbers on Personal Welfare, Second Edition* (Chicago, Ill.: University of Chicago, 1987).

35. Clair Brown, "An Institutional Model of Wives' Work Decisions," *Industrial Relations* 24, no. 2 (Spring 1985): 182–204.

36. This allows for possible complementarity between the inputs as well as substitutability. For example, as market goods decrease in price, a person may substitute them for nonmarket goods and reduce time spent in nonmarket production, but increase time spent in leisure. See Pierre-André Chiappori, "Introducing Household Production in Collective Models of Labor Supply," *Journal of Political Economy* 105, no. 1 (February 1997): 191–209, for a model of this type which also allows for different decision processes for determining household labor supply.

37. Robinson and Godbey, *op. cit.*: 108. Juliet B. Schor, *The Overworked American: The Unexpected Decline of Leisure* (New York: Basic Books, 1991), argues that total hours worked in both market work plus housework have been rising, not falling, for women as well as men, from 1969 to 1987. This conclusion has not been widely accepted in the economics profession due to questions about her measurements of hours worked (see the book review by Frank Stafford in *Journal of Economic Literature* 30, no. 3 (September 1992): 1528–1529), and she did not have access to the 1985–86 time use survey numbers at the time her book was written.

38. Jeff E. Biddle and Daniel S. Hamermesh, "Sleep and the Allocation of Time," *Journal of Political Economy* 98, no. 5, part 1 (October 1990): 928.

39. Victor R. Fuchs and Joyce P. Jacobsen, "Employee Response to Compulsory Short-Time Work," *Industrial Relations* 30, no. 3 (Fall 1991): 501–513.

40. *Americans Volunteer 1974* (Washington, D.C.: ACTION, 1975); Howard V. Hayghe, "Volunteers in the U.S.: Who Donates the Time?" *Monthly Labor Review* 114, no. 2 (February 1991): 17–23.

41. Hamermesh, *op. cit.*: 453.

42. Hamermesh, *op. cit.*: 463.

43. *Ibid.*

44. John Pencavel, "Labor Supply of Men: A Survey," *Handbook of Labor Economics* 1, eds. Orley Ashenfelter and Richard Layard (Amsterdam: North-Holland, 1986): 69, 80. Eight of these studies use data generated experimentally from negative income tax experiments run in several locations from 1968 to 1978. They yield a median of 0.06, with three studies reporting negative elasticities.

45. Mark R. Killingsworth and James J. Heckman, "Female Labor Supply: A Survey," *Handbook of Labor Economics* 1, eds. Orley Ashenfelter and Richard Layard (Amsterdam: North-Holland, 1986): 189–192.

46. Pencavel, *op. cit.*: 57.

47. Killingsworth and Heckman, *loc. cit.*

48. Thomas A. Mroz, "The Sensitivity of an Empirical Model of Married Women's Hours of Work to Economic and Statistical Assumptions," *Econometrica* 55, no. 4 (July 1987): 765–799. Mroz finds a much smaller range of plausible values, with a maximum effect of 150 hours from a $1 wage increase.

49. For example, Victor R. Fuchs, *Women's Quest for Economic Equality* (Cambridge, Mass.: Harvard University, 1988): 62 (Figure 4.2), finds that hourly earnings drop steadily with the number of children ever born.

50. Robert Moffitt, "Profiles of Fertility, Labor Supply and Wages of Married Women: A Complete Life-Cycle Model," *Review of Economic Studies* 51, no. 165 (April 1984): 263–278.

51. Daniel Kessler, "Birth Order, Family Size, and Achievement: Family Structure and Wage Determination," *Journal of Labor Economics* 9, no. 4 (October 1991): 413–426. This sample is taken from the National Longitudinal Survey, 1979–87 waves.

52. See Richard Frank and Rebecca Wong, "Empirical Considerations for Models of Female Labor Supply and Fertility in Developed Countries," *Research in Human Capital and Development* 6 (1990): 3–16, for a survey of studies measuring this relationship.

53. Amyra Grossbard-Shechtman, "A Theory of Allocation of Time in Markets for Labour and Marriage," *Economic Journal* 94, no. 376 (December 1984): 863–882, making the assumption that women have comparative advantage in nonmarket work, derives the result that as the male/female ratio increases, there will be an increased proportion of women who marry and therefore a decrease in female hours worked outside the house.

54. Alice Nakamura and Maseo Nakamura, *The Second Paycheck: A Socioeconomic Analysis of Earnings* (Orlando, Fla.: Academic Press, 1985). They use Panel Study of Income Dynamics data, 1970–79 waves, for individuals who were continuously in the sample with fully reported data on all variables of interest.

55. Ross M. Stolzenberg and Linda J. Waite, "Local Labor Markets, Children and Labor Force Participation of Wives," *Demography* 21, no. 2 (May 1984): 157–170.

56. David M. Blau and Philip K. Robins, "Fertility, Employment, and Child-Care Costs," *Demography* 26, no. 2 (May 1989): 287–310. This study, as well as the study cited below by the same authors, uses 1980 data from a survey of Employment Opportunity Pilot Projects, which oversampled low-income households, but the authors feel that the sample of women does not appear to have unique characteristics that would make these results less general.

57. David M. Blau and Philip K. Robins, "Child-Care Costs and Family Labor Supply," *Review of Economics and Statistics* 70, no. 3 (August 1988): 374–381. Rachel Connelly, "The Effect of Child Care Costs on Married Women's Labor Force Participation," *Review of Economics and*

Statistics 74, no. 1 (February 1992): 83–90, finds a somewhat less sensitive, but still significant effect, so that 69 percent of women would be employed if child care were free.

58. Carol Kleiman, "Child Care a Key Cause of Women Leaving Jobs," *Chicago Tribune* (January 14, 1991), Section 4: 3.
59. *Ibid.*
60. Barbara R. Bergmann, *Saving Our Children From Poverty: What the United States Can Learn From France* (New York: Russell Sage Foundation, 1996): 93 (Table 6.1).
61. *Ibid.*
62. Philip K. Robins, "Federal Support for Child Care: Current Policies and a Proposed New System," *Focus* 11, no. 2 (University of Wisconsin-Madison: Institute for Research on Poverty, Summer 1988): 4.
63. Bergmann, *loc. cit..*
64. Robins, *op. cit.*: 6; *Statistical Abstract of the United States* (1996): 431 (Table 671). Not all firms reporting flexible spending accounts in the survey may have had them for child care, as they are also available for medical expenses.
65. Robins, *op. cit.*: 9.
66. For a study that concludes this is the case, see Anton D. Lowenberg and Thomas D. Tinnin, "Professional versus Consumer Interests in Regulation: The Case of the US Child Care Industry," *Applied Economics* 24, no. 6 (June 1992): 571–580.

*F*urther reading

Ashenfelter, Orley, and Richard Layard (eds.) (1986). *Handbook of Labor Economics, Volume I.* Amsterdam: North-Holland. Definitive collection of theoretical and empirical review essays by eminent labor economists; parts 1 and 2 discuss labor supply and demand, respectively.

Blau, David M. (ed.) (1991). *The Economics of Child Care.* New York: Russell Sage. Collection of papers on child care policy and research.

Booth, Alan (ed.) (1992). *Child Care in the 1990s: Trends and Consequences.* Hillsdale, N.J.: Lawrence Erlbaum Associates. Collection of papers on child care, including sections on child care supply and demand, and quality issues.

Ferber, Marianne (1987). *Women and Work, Paid and Unpaid: A Selected, Annotated Bibliography.* New York: Garland. Comprehensive listing, including abstracts, of papers and books in the general area of economics of gender up through the mid-1980s, including articles on female labor supply and on household production.

Fine, Ben (1992). *Women's Employment and the Capitalist Family: Towards a Political Economy of Gender and Labour Markets.* London: Routledge. Written from a Marxist-feminist perspective, provides a critical assessment of the literature that examines the changing labor market participation of women, exploring such issues as the domestic labor debate, the role of patriarchy theory, gender and labor market theory, the capitalist family, and the position of working women in the economy.

Hayes, Cheryl D., John L. Palmer, and Martha J. Zaslow (eds.) (1990). *Who Cares for America's Children? Child Care Policy for the 1990s.* Washington, D.C.: National Academy Press. Wide-ranging report from the National Research Council, Panel on Child Care Policy.

Jenson, Jane, Elizabeth Hagen, and Ceallaigh Reddy (eds.) (1988). *Feminization of the Labor Force.* Oxford: Oxford University. Collection of scholarly papers considering aspects of the rise in female participation.

Journal of Family and Economic Issues (1996). Vol. 17, nos. 3 and 4 (Winter). Special issue on household time use.

Journal of Human Resources (1994). Vol. 29, no. 2 (Spring). Special issue on "Women's Work, Wages, and Well-Being." Contains a number of important empirical studies in this broad topic area by U.S. and Canadian researchers.

—— (1992). Vol. 27, no. 1 (Winter). Special issue on child care.

Keeley, Michael C. (1981). *Labor Supply and Public Policy: A Critical Review*. New York: Academic Press. Thorough presentation of neoclassical labor supply theory and discussion of both experimental and nonexperimental studies in the 1960s and 1970s.

Discussion questions

1. List the reasons given in the simple economic model for why men have falling and women have rising labor force participation rates and indicate which ones you think are the most important in explaining these trends. Which of the additional factors listed in the section, "Extensions of the simple economic model," do you think are also particularly important in explaining these trends?

2. Why would different birth cohorts have different participation rates at the same age level – e.g., 30 to 34 years old?

3. Consider Table 4.3. The labor force participation of married mothers was below that of single mothers in 1975, but above in 1995. What might have caused this change?

4. Draw an individual's budget constraint for the following cases, assuming some positive amount of nonearned income I:

   (a) a wage rate that rises to one and a half times the base wage for hours worked over 40 hours a week;

   (b) a wage rate that drops to half the base wage for hours worked over 40;

   (c) a wage rate that doubles if the person works at least 40 hours a week;

   (d) a fixed cost F (where $I > F$) associated with working, which is halved if the person works at least 40 hours a week,

   (e) a child care subsidy that is the same amount C per week, regardless of number of hours worked.

5. For each of the constraints in question (3), consider how a change to this constraint from the basic constraint shown in Figure 4.9 would affect:

   (a) a person who is currently working 40 hours a week.

   (b) a person who is currently not working.

6. Consider the Focus on housework and quality. How could you tell whether housework is of higher quality or not? Is there an objective measure?

7. Consider Table 4.7. Why does the probability of getting divorced drop with the length of marriage? Why does it drop at varying rates from year to year in marriage length?

8. Consider Table 4.9. What do you think accounts for the changes in percentage for both sexes who work more than 40 hours a week?

9. Consider the Focus on volunteerism. As women become more likely to participate in paid work, how are organizations that have relied on volunteer labor likely to adjust?

10. Why would a rise in wages have a different effect on men's and women's hours of sleep?

11. How would the increasing availability of substitutes for in-home child care likely affect women's decision as to whether or not to work?

12. Is it economically efficient for the government to subsidize child care costs? Why or why not?

13. When the government estimates its "expenditure" on child care through use of the child care tax credit and flexible spending accounts as foregone tax collected, why is this likely to be an overestimate?

Appendix
Labor supply

This appendix provides the economic tools needed to discuss an individual's decision as to whether or not to work and, if he/she is going to work, how many hours to work. The concept of utility, which has already been used in the appendixes to Chapters 1 and 3, will be used here as well, along with a budget constraint, to describe a person's *labor supply* decision. Related concepts that economists use to discuss forces affecting a person's decision, such as *income* and *substitution* effects, and *elasticity*, will also be discussed.

The decision to work

In order to model the *labor supply* decision of whether and how much to work, we assume that an individual, Jill, has a utility function U containing two arguments, *consumption* (C) and *leisure* (L), so $U = f(C,L)$. Consumption is the composite of all market goods and services that Jill uses. It is measured in monetary units. Leisure is measured in hours and includes time spent on all nonmarket activities, including sleeping. Leisure includes three types of activities: (1) recreational, or *true leisure* activities, such as playing golf and watching television, where time spent in the activity directly generates utility; (2) activities that produce goods and services that are not traded, such as cleaning the house and preparing meals, where time spent in the activity indirectly generates utility through the eventual consumption of these nonmarket products; and (3) activities that are combinations of the previous two types, such as shopping and child care.[1]

Jill tries to create as much utility as possible, subject to constraints on available time and money. Her problem can be formally stated as follows:

Jill maximizes $U = f(C,L)$, by choosing H, where

(i) $C = wH + I$

(ii) $L = L^* - H,$

and

I = nonearned income available to Jill,
L^* = total time available to Jill (= 168 hours, if measured on a weekly basis),
H = hours spent working, and
w = wage rate per hour spent working.

Rearranging (ii) to read $H = L^* - L$, and substituting (ii) into (i) for H, we derive Jill's budget constraint:

$$C = w(L^* - L) + I$$
$$= wL^* + I - wL.$$

The budget constraint shows that total consumption cannot exceed the total value of Jill's time, which we will also refer to as her *potential earned income* (wL^*), plus her nonearned income (I), minus the value of her time spent in leisure (wL). This means that the opportunity cost of an hour of leisure is equal to the wage rate.

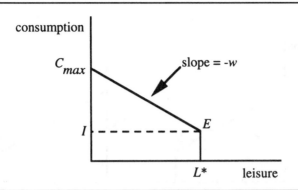

FIGURE 4A.1 Jill's budget constraint

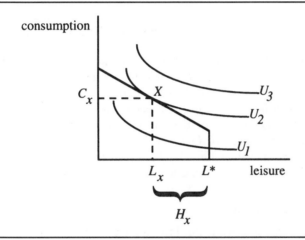

FIGURE 4A.2 Jill's choice of consumption and leisure

Figure 4A.1 shows Jill's budget constraint, where consumption is measured in dollars on the vertical axis and leisure is measured in hours on the horizontal axis. A vertical section of height I appears at point L^* along the horizontal axis, and point E is Jill's *endowment point*, which has the coordinates (L^*, I), showing the total time L^* available to Jill to allocate between leisure and work and her nonearned income I (derived from all other sources other than wages, such as interest, dividends, gifts, and pensions). From point E, the budget constraint rises to the left until it meets the vertical axis at C_{max}. This is the amount of consumption Jill could have if she worked every available hour (so $L = 0$): $C_{max} = wL^* + I$. The slope of the budget constraint along this section is equal to minus the wage rate w: for every hour Jill decides to work, she increases her consumption by amount w and decreases her leisure by one hour.

In Figure 4A.2, three representative indifference curves from Jill's utility function are added to the graph of the budget constraint. Jill's utility is maximized, subject to her budget constraint, at point X, where she consumes C_x and spends L_x hours in leisure. Note

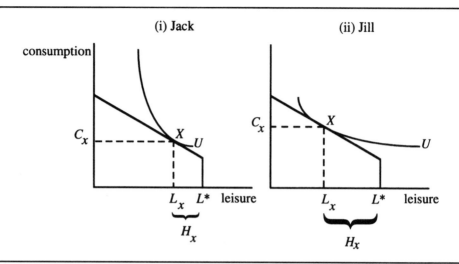

FIGURE 4A.3   Different preferences lead to different choices for Jack and Jill

that $C_x = w(L^* - L_x) + I$. We can also read the number of hours that Jill works on the horizontal axis: $H_x = L^* - L_x$. So $C_x = wH_x + I$, where wH_x is *earned income*, so consumption equals the sum of earned and nonearned income.

Different people will have different preferences for consumption vs. leisure, which will be reflected in the different slopes of their indifference curves. Figure 4A.3 shows some representative indifference curves for Jack and Jill, where Jack gets more utility from leisure relative to consumption than does Jill at any point in the graph. Therefore, given the same budget constraint, Jack chooses to work fewer hours than Jill.

Income and substitution effects

Now consider what happens when conditions change for Jill. We first need to consider how leisure and consumption respond to changes in income, where income is the sum of nonearned income and potential earned income. Good X is a *normal good* if:

$$\frac{\Delta Q_x}{\Delta M} \geq 0$$

where Q_x is the quantity demanded of X and M is income. In the case of a normal good, if income rises, more units of X are demanded; if income falls, fewer units of X are demanded. X is an *inferior good* if:

$$\frac{\Delta Q_x}{\Delta M} < 0$$

In this case, changes in income and changes in quantity demanded of X are negatively correlated.

We will assume that both leisure and consumption are normal goods. Therefore, an increase in nonearned income I will lead to Jill's demanding both more leisure and more consumption. Figure 4A.4 illustrates the two possible results. If Jill is not working, then she will be at her new endowment point E'. Although in this case (i), Jill would like to have

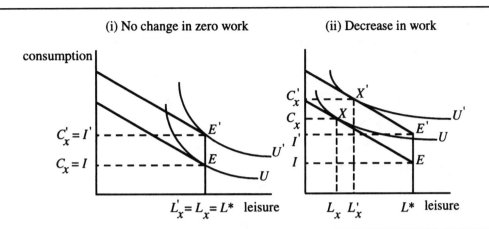

FIGURE 4A.4 Possible effects of an increase in unearned income for Jill

more leisure than L^*, she is constrained by the total amount of time available (in other words, there is no way to buy more hours in a week), so she remains at the constraint. If Jill is working (case (ii)), she will reduce her hours of work so as to increase her leisure, and may even decide not to work at all.[2] A decrease in nonearned income will lead to Jill's tending to reduce both leisure and consumption. If she is currently not working, she may or may not start to work, depending on whether her new optimal amount of leisure (if she were not constrained with respect to total leisure time available) is greater or less than L^*. If she is currently working, she will increase her hours of work.

A change in nonearned income has what economists call a *pure income effect* on the quantities demanded of consumption and leisure, because it does not change the opportunity cost of leisure. It generally causes a change in Jill's behavior. In contrast, when we observe a change in Jill's earned income, it is the result of either a change in nonearned income or a change in Jill's wage.

If Jill is currently not working, a change in her wage has a *pure substitution effect*, because it changes the opportunity cost of leisure but has no effect on her earned income, because she has none. If the wage decreases, she would like to have more leisure, but is already getting L^*, the maximum available amount of leisure, so she stays at E. This is illustrated in Figure 4A.5 (i), where the wage falls from w to w'. If the wage increases, she may stay at E, as in Figure 4A.5 (i) (if the wage returns from w' to w), or be induced to start working, as in Figure 4A.5 (ii), where the wage rises from w to w'. For a given change in w, the flatter Jill's indifference curve at E (i.e., the less consumption she is willing to give up for an additional hour of leisure), the more likely she is to start working.

If Jill is currently working, a change in her wage has both an *income effect* and a *substitution effect* on the quantities demanded of consumption and leisure (because both effects occur, the "pure" is dropped). If the wage increases, the opportunity cost of leisure rises, causing Jill to demand less leisure and more consumption (the substitution effect), and potential earned income rises, causing Jill to demand more of both consumption and leisure (the income effect). Therefore, Jill will unambiguously increase consumption, but leisure may increase or decrease, depending on the relative sizes of the income and substitution effects. The two cases are shown in Figure 4A.6. In each case, the income effect

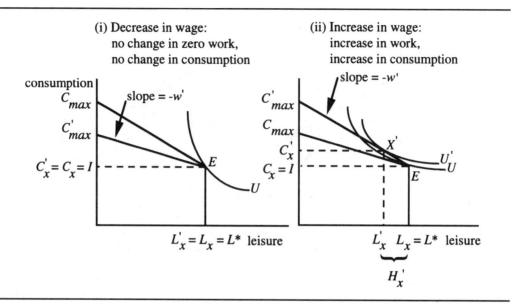

FIGURE 4A.5 Possible effects of a change in the wage rate if Jill is initially not working

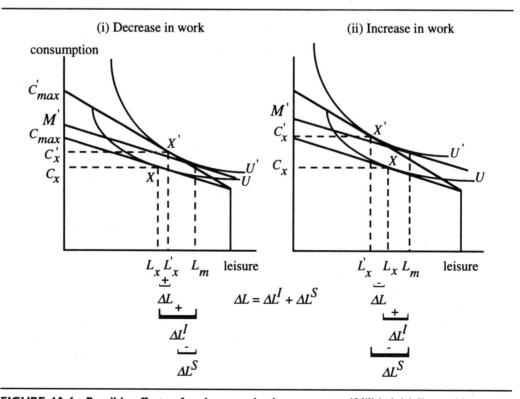

FIGURE 4A.6 Possible effects of an increase in the wage rate if Jill is initially working

can be found by considering the hypothetical case of keeping the wage constant but increasing Jill's nonearned income until her utility equals U', the amount of utility she achieves under the higher wage rate. This would require a total income of M'. The income effect on leisure ΔL^I is measured as the distance from L_x to L_m, where L_x is the initial amount of leisure desired, and L_m is the amount of leisure desired if total income equaled M'. Then the substitution effect on leisure ΔL^S is equal to the distance from L_m to L'_x, which is equivalent to the change in leisure under the hypothetical situation of holding utility constant at the new level U', while the wage is increased to the new level. The actual change in leisure, ΔL, is the sum of the positive income effect, ΔL^I and the negative substitution effect, ΔL^S.

If the wage decreases, the opportunity cost of leisure falls, causing Jill to demand more leisure and less consumption (the substitution effect), and potential earned income falls, causing Jill to demand less of both consumption and leisure (the income effect). Therefore, Jill will unambiguously reduce consumption, but leisure again may increase or decrease. If the substitution effect is so much greater than the income effect that desired leisure is greater than or equal to L^*, then Jill will stop working completely. The three cases of (i) increasing work, (ii) decreasing work but staying employed, and (iii) stopping work completely are shown in Figure 4A.7.

The labor supply curve

For different hypothetical wages, we can trace out Jill's hours of work, as well as show the point where she stops working completely. The relationship between the wage and hours worked is Jill's *labor supply curve*. The wage at which Jill is just indifferent between working and not working is her *reservation wage*.

Figure 4A.8 contains two possible shapes for Jill's labor supply curve. In case (i), the labor supply curve is upward-sloping at all wages above w^*, the reservation wage. At wages below w^*, Jill does not work at all. In case (ii), the labor supply curve bends backward, beginning at w' (where the income effect exactly equals the substitution effect). At wages above w', the income effect exceeds the substitution effect and leisure increases (so hours of work decrease). At wages between w^* and w', the substitution effect exceeds the income effect and leisure decreases.

Along a labor supply curve, the upward-sloping part has positive slope, so $\dfrac{\Delta H}{\Delta w} > 0$. The backward-bending part has negative slope, so $\dfrac{\Delta H}{\Delta w} < 0$. At w', $\dfrac{\Delta H}{\Delta w} = 0$.

Elasticity

Economists are often interested in the relative steepness or flatness of the labor supply curve. To further describe the slope in a particular section of the curve, and to free our estimation of the slope from the measurement units used to create the graph, we can calculate the *elasticity of labor supply* with respect to the wage:

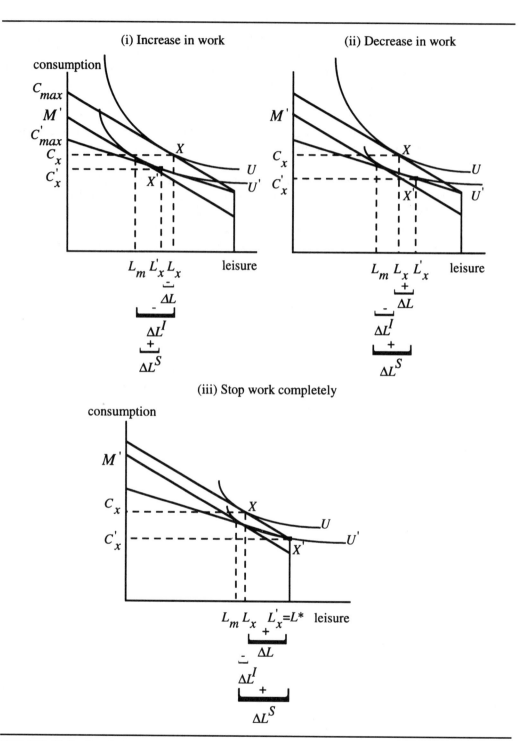

FIGURE 4A.7 Possible effects of a decrease in the wage rate if Jill is initially working

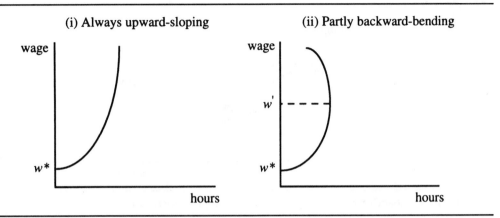

FIGURE 4A.8 Possible labor supply curves for Jill

$$e_s = \frac{\Delta H}{\Delta w}\frac{w}{H}$$

$$= \frac{\dfrac{\Delta H}{H}}{\dfrac{\Delta w}{w}}$$

$$= \frac{\%\Delta H}{\%\Delta w}$$

The elasticity of labor supply is the percentage change in hours worked, divided by the percentage change in the wage.[3] It can be positive or negative, depending on whether we are taking a measurement on the upward-sloping or backward-bending portion of the labor supply curve. If $|e_s| > 1$, the labor supply curve is relatively flat at that point, and labor supply is said to be *elastic*. If $0 \le |e_s| < 1$, the labor supply curve is relatively steep at that point, and labor supply is *inelastic*. If $|e_s| = 1$, labor supply is *unit elastic*, so a percentage wage change causes an equal percentage change in hours worked.

Elasticities can be calculated for any function – including demand and supply curves in all factor and product markets – and for the dependent variable of a function with respect to any independent variable in the function. For instance, economists are often interested in the *income elasticity of labor supply*:

$$e_s^I = \frac{\Delta H}{\Delta I}\frac{I}{H}$$

If leisure is a normal good, the income elasticity of labor supply will be negative. The same ranges apply as above for the absolute value of e_s^I in determining whether labor supply is elastic or inelastic with respect to nonearned income.

Economists are also often interested in the *total income elasticity*, which is defined as:

$$e_s^{TI} = \frac{wH}{I}e_s^I = \frac{wH}{I}\frac{\Delta H}{\Delta I}\frac{I}{H} = w\frac{\Delta H}{\Delta I}$$

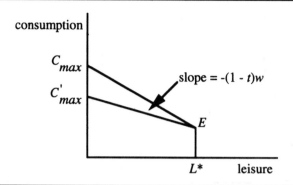

FIGURE 4A.9 Effect of an earnings tax on the budget constraint

This is the ratio of earned to nonearned income, multiplied by the income elasticity of labor supply.

Policy Application: An earnings tax

The framework outlined in this appendix is useful for illustrating how various labor policies affect the labor supply decision. Consider the effect on the budget constraint of the government's putting a proportional tax on Jill's earnings of amount t, where $0 < t < 1$. This will change the slope of Jill's budget constraint from $-w$ to $-(1 - t)w$, as shown below. As shown in Figure 4A.9, the tax causes the budget constraint to rotate downwards from the endowment point E, so that the new maximum amount that Jill can consume if she worked every available hour is reduced from $C_{max} = wL^* + I$ to $C'_{max} = (1 - t)wL^* + I$. Leisure is now relatively cheaper, which, through the substitution effect, will lead her to want to have more of it. However, her total income is reduced at every level of H except for $H = 0$, so this income effect will cause her to reduce her leisure time (again, assuming that leisure is a normal good).

Depending on Jill's position along the budget constraint before the tax is passed, and depending on the relative size of the income and substitution effects, three possibilities can occur, as illustrated in Figure 4A.10. In Figure 4A.10 (i), if Jill did not work before the tax, then she will not work now either, because working would reduce her utility, while her utility will stay the same if she remains at E. If Jill did work, she experiences both a substitution effect, which makes leisure relatively cheaper and induces her to demand more of it relative to consumption, and an income effect, which induces her to demand less of both consumption and leisure. As shown in Figure 4A.10 (ii) and (iii), she may either increase or decrease her total hours of work (where the decrease in work could lead her to stop working completely if the substitution effect is relatively large compared with the income effect).

If there is an earnings tax, the labor supply curve should be drawn with the after-tax wage, $w' = (1 - t)w$, on the vertical axis. Assuming that Jill works at all, she will now move

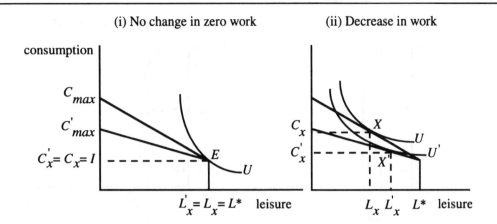

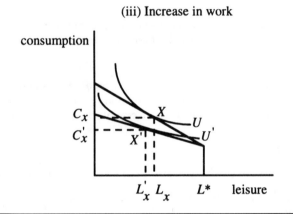

FIGURE 4A.10   Possible effects of an earnings tax

down along the labor supply curve in response to the decline in her after-tax wage. Figure 4A.11 (i) shows movement along the positively sloped portion of Jill's labor supply curve (corresponding to the change in leisure shown in Figure 4A.10 (ii)), while Figure 4A.11 (ii) shows movement along the backward-bending portion of Jill's labor supply curve (corresponding to the change in leisure shown in Figure 4A.10 (iii)).

Endnotes

1. The word *leisure* is used to correspond to the prevailing terminology in economics, not to imply that all nonmarket activities are of type (1).
2. Again, Jill might like not only to quit work but also to have more leisure than L^*, but she is unable to move further to the right than L^*.

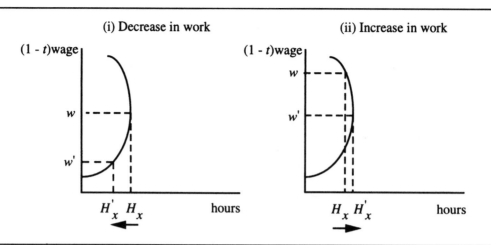

FIGURE 4A.11 Possible effects of an earnings tax on Jill's hours of work

3. Using calculus, the slope at a particular point on the labor supply curve, and therefore the elasticity at a point, can be precisely calculated. Hours worked can be written as a function of w and I:

$$H = f(w, I)$$

The form of the hours function depends on the form of the utility function. Then the elasticity of labor supply with respect to the wage is written using the partial derivative of the hours worked function with respect to w, which is the inverse of the slope of the labor supply curve:

$$e_s = \frac{\partial H}{\partial w} \frac{w}{H}$$

In general, derivatives or partial derivatives can be substituted into all formulas in the text where the ratio of the changes in two variables is used; e.g., e.g., $\frac{dY}{dX}$ for $\frac{\Delta Y}{\Delta X}$, where $Y = f(X)$, or $\frac{\partial Y}{\partial X}$ for $\frac{\Delta Y}{\Delta X}$, and $\frac{\partial Y}{\partial Z}$ for $\frac{\Delta Y}{\Delta Z}$, where $Y = f(X, \ldots, Z)$.

4. See Edward J. McCaffery, *Taxing Women* (Chicago, Ill.: University of Chicago, 1997): Chs. 7 and 8 for a full discussion of this idea.

Discussion questions

1. Assume that Jill is currently not working and that her nonearned income drops.
    (a) Illustrate the case in which she continues not working.
    (b) Illustrate the case in which she now performs some work.

2. If Jill is currently working and her wage rate rises, would she stop working completely?

3. Assume that leisure is an inferior good for Jill.
    (a) If Jill is currently working and suddenly receives an inheritance, will she work more or less?
    (b) If the wage tax increases, what are the substitution and income effects on Jill's leisure?
    (c) If leisure is an inferior good, can Jill's labor supply curve bend backwards?

4. Assume that Jill has no nonearned income.

   (a) Draw her budget constraint and mark her endowment point E.

   (b) Now assume that the government implements a welfare program where anyone who does not work in a given week receives P dollars. In a given week, as soon as a person works for any amount of time, they lose P. What does Jill's budget constraint look like now, and where is her new endowment point E'?

5. How does an income tax, as opposed to an earnings tax, affect the budget constraint?

6. It appears that men have an inelastic response to wage, and therefore earnings tax, changes – in other words, they work about the same number of hours if taxes are increased on their earnings. On the other hand women have a relatively elastic response to wage changes, so an increase in an earnings tax would reduce their hours worked. Optimal taxation theory says it is better to levy taxes on goods with inelastic supply so as to minimize deadweight loss.

   (a) Draw two labor upward-sloping supply graphs, one steep (inelastic) and one flat (elastic).

   (b) Starting at the same wage in both cases, show what happens to hours if a tax of the same amount is levied on each person. In which case is the hours change greater?

   (c) This implies that in order to generate the most tax revenue with the least effect on people's behavior, taxes should be raised on the person with inelastic supply (i.e., men) and lowered on the person with elastic supply (i.e., women). Comment on this proposal.[4]

Labor Force Participation: Consequences for Family Structure

This chapter considers the interaction between changes in women's labor force participation and various changes in U.S. society since World War II, in particular, changes in birth, marriage, and divorce rates and changes in family structure and well-being. We consider how to evaluate whether persons are better or worse off given these changes. The chapter closes with an analysis of policies affecting birth rates.

Demographic trends

Table 5.1 contains basic demographic data for the U.S. since 1947: the median age at first marriage for men and women; annual marriage rates (per thousand persons in the whole

TABLE 5.1 Median age at first marriage by sex and marriage, divorce, and birth rates, all and for subgroups of women, 1947 to 1995

	Age at first marriage		Marriage rates		Divorce rates		Birth rates	
	Men	Women	All	Unmarried W	All	Married W	All	W 15–44
1947–51	23.1	20.4	11.7	93.6	2.8	11.1	25.0	109.1
1952–61	22.7	20.2	9.1	77.9	2.3	9.4	24.6	118.4
1962–71	23.0	20.6	9.7	75.8	2.8	11.8	19.2	94.3
1972–81	23.9	21.5	10.4	67.2	4.9	20.7	15.2	67.6
1982–91	25.8	23.4	10.0	58.3	4.9	21.4	15.9	67.0
1992–95	26.6	24.5	9.1	52.0	4.6	20.5	14.6	65.3

Sources: Age at first marriage: *Current Population Reports Series P-20*, no. 450 (Table A); 484 (Table A-2). Marriage, divorce, and birth rates: 1947–70 – *Historical Statistics of the United States*: 49 (Series B5 and B8); 64 (Series B214 and B216); 1971–87 (marriage and divorce rates, and birth rates through 1980) – *Vital Statistics of the United States* (1988) 1: 1 (Table 1-1); (1987) 3: 1–5 (Table 1-1), 1–6 (Table 1-3), 2–5 (Table 2-1); 1988–94 (marriage and divorce rates) – *Statistical Abstract of the United States* (1996): (Table 146); 1995 (marriage and divorce rates) – *Monthly Vital Statistics Report* 44, no. 12 (July 24, 1996); 1981–95 (birth rates) – *Monthly Vital Statistics Report* 45, no. 11(S) (June 10, 1997): 25 (Table 1).

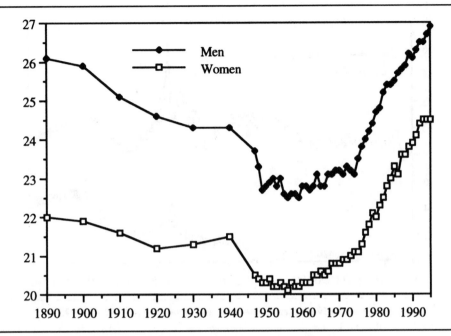

FIGURE 5.1   Median age at first marriage by sex, 1890 to 1995
Source: Current Population Reports Series P-20, nos. 450 (Table A), 484 (Table A-2).

population and per thousand unmarried women); divorce rates (per thousand persons and per thousand married women); and birth rates (per thousand persons and per thousand women ages 15 to 44).

These data display several interesting trends. While the median age at first marriage dipped for both sexes in the 1950s, it has subsequently risen substantially. Marriage rates have fallen since the immediate post-War years, more notably when measured for unmarried women. Divorce rates rose sharply in the 1970s and have since declined slightly, while birth rates dropped sharply in the 1960s and 1970s, leveling in the 1980s. The birth rates for the population and for women ages 15 to 44, also known as the *fertility rate*, have continued to drop in the 1990s.

Demographic data are available on a yearly basis further back in time than labor force data; and, for some series, they are available even further back on a decennial basis. Figures 5.1 through 5.3 use these longer time series to show trends in median age at first marriage, marriage, divorce, and birth. This longer view puts the post-World War II period into perspective, making clearer which changes are particularly anomalous, given past experience. However, the pre-World War II period will be discussed in Chapter 14 rather than in this chapter.

Figure 5.1 shows median age at first marriage by sex back to 1890. It is notable that the recent rise in age at first marriage has surpassed the 1890 highs. It is certainly possible that the 1890 numbers do not represent an earlier peak, so the 1995 ages of 26.9 for men and 24.5 for women may be lower than ages in the nineteenth century. However, the large rise since the early 1970s is striking, compared with the long downward trend from 1890 to the late 1940s and the relatively low ages experienced in the 1950s and 1960s. The

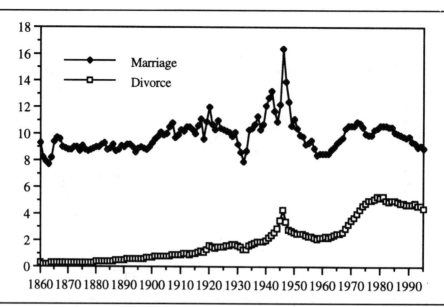

FIGURE 5.2   Marriage and divorce rates per thousand persons, 1860 to 1995

Sources: 1860–1919 – Paul H. Jacobson, *American Marriage and Divorce* (New York: Rinehart and Company, 1959): 21 (Table 2), 90 (Table 42); 1920–70 – *Historical Statistics of the United States*: 64 (Series B214 and B216); 1971–87 – *Vital Statistics of the United States* (1987) 3: 1–5 (Table 1–1); 1–6 (Table 1–3); 2–5 (Table 2–1); 1988–94 – *Statistical Abstract of the United States* (1996): (Table 146); 1995 – *Monthly Vital Statistics Report* 44, no. 12 (July 24, 1996).

lowest median ages for both men and women are for 1956: 22.5 for men and 20.1 for women.

Yearly marriage and divorce rates are available back to 1860. Figure 5.2 plots the marriage and divorce rates per thousand persons from 1860 through 1995 (plots of the marriage rate per thousand unmarried women and the divorce rate per thousand married women yield patterns of peaks and dips practically identical to the ones shown, except for a more notable downturn in marriages measured per unmarried women). The marriage rate, after reaching historical lows during the Civil War, fluctuated slightly around 9 per thousand for the rest of the nineteenth century, but has fluctuated more widely around a mean of 10 per thousand in the twentieth century. The divorce rate has risen steadily since 1860, when it stood at 2 per 10,000 persons. After World War I, the marriage and divorce rates both reached a low in 1932 (during the Great Depression) and peaked in 1946 (the first full year following World War II), showing that periods of great social and economic upheaval tend to affect both series. Since the period immediately following World War II, the marriage rate has exhibited a slight downward trend which has steepened recently, while the divorce rate has risen steadily until recently, when it has appeared to flatten out and even turn down slightly. The 1995 divorce rate of 4.4 per thousand is 2.75 times the 1920 rate of 1.6 per thousand, while the 1995 marriage rate of 8.9 per thousand is 74 percent of the 1920 rate of 12 per thousand.

These changing marriage and divorce rates have had large effects on the population's marital status composition. Table 5.2 shows the distribution of women and men by marital status for all persons over 15, for selected 5-year age groups from ages 20 to 34 (the main

TABLE 5.2 Percentage distribution of marital status by sex, 1950 to 1995

	Women					Men				
	1950	*1970*	*1980*	*1990*	*1995*	*1950*	*1970*	*1980*	*1990*	*1995*
15 and over										
never married	18.5	20.6	22.4	22.8	23.5	24.9	26.4	29.3	29.9	31.0
married	67.0	62.8	59.0	56.8	56.1	68.9	67.7	63.4	60.7	59.1
widowed	12.0	12.7	11.9	11.5	10.6	4.2	3.1	2.5	2.5	2.3
divorced	2.4	4.0	6.6	8.9	9.8	2.0	2.8	4.8	6.8	7.6
20–24										
never married	32.3	36.3	50.2	62.8	66.7	59.0	55.5	68.6	79.3	80.7
married	65.6	60.5	45.9	34.3	30.4	39.9	42.9	29.8	19.7	18.2
widowed	0.4	0.7	0.2	0.1	0.2	0.2	0.2	0.0	0.0	0.0
divorced	1.6	2.5	3.6	2.8	2.7	0.9	1.4	1.6	1.1	1.1
25–29										
never married	13.3	12.2	20.8	31.1	35.3	23.8	19.1	32.4	45.2	51.0
married	83.3	82.5	70.4	61.4	57.5	74.2	77.1	62.2	50.1	44.7
widowed	0.9	1.0	0.4	0.4	0.2	0.3	0.3	0.1	0.1	0.1
divorced	2.5	4.3	8.5	7.1	7.1	1.7	3.0	5.3	4.7	4.1
30–34										
never married	9.3	7.4	9.5	16.4	19.0	13.2	10.7	15.7	27.0	28.2
married	86.2	86.1	78.2	72.3	70.0	84.3	85.6	76.3	65.0	63.2
widowed	1.6	1.5	1.2	0.8	0.6	0.4	0.3	0.1	0.2	0.1
divorced	3.0	5.0	11.1	10.5	10.4	2.1	3.3	7.9	7.9	8.5
65 and over										
never married	8.9	8.1	5.9	4.9	4.2	8.4	7.5	5.1	4.2	4.2
married	35.7	36.5	39.7	41.4	42.5	65.7	72.4	77.6	76.5	77.0
widowed	54.3	52.2	51.0	48.6	47.3	24.1	17.1	13.6	14.2	13.5
divorced	1.1	3.2	3.4	5.1	6.0	1.9	3.0	3.7	5.0	5.2

Sources: 1950–80 – Suzanne M. Bianchi and Daphne Spain, *American Women: Three Decades of Change* (Washington, DC: U.S. Government Printing Office, 1983) (Appendix Table 1); 1990–95 – *Current Population Reports Series P-20*, nos. 450 (Table 1); 491 (Table 1). Married includes both those living with and separately from their spouse.

years for first marrying), and for persons over 65. There are many interesting patterns in these data. In every year, the number of people never married drops sharply from the 20–24 group to the 25–29 group, and drops again moving into the 30–34 group. However, the percentage of people who have not married in the 30–34 group is substantially higher in 1995 than in 1950 – in particular, over one-quarter of the men, which is more than double the rate in 1950. This rate has increased notably since 1970, and for men has had an especially impressive jump since 1980. Meanwhile, the percentage divorced in the 30–34 group has more than tripled for both sexes since 1950.

On the other end of the age spectrum, few people are never married by age 65. Among those currently in their late 60s and older, less than 5 percent have never been married. The percentages by sex of never-married persons were approximately twice as high among those who are 65 and older in 1950. Older persons are more likely to be married or divorced in 1995 than in 1950, but are less likely to be widowed, indicating improved survival rates for

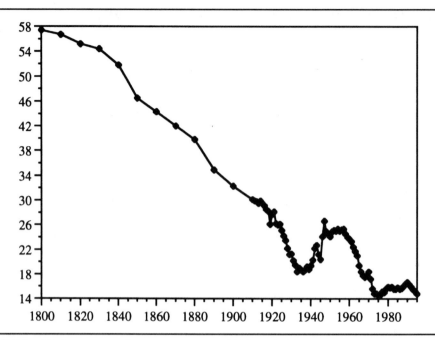

FIGURE 5.3   Birth rate per thousand persons, 1800 to 1995

Sources: 1800–1970 – *Historical Statistics of the United States:* 49 (Series B5 and B6); 1971–80 – *Vital Statistics of the United States* 1 (1988) 1: 1 (Table 1–1); 1981–95 – *Monthly Vital Statistics Report*, 45 no. 11 (June 10, 1997): 25 (Table 1). Data for 1800, 1810, 1830, 1850, 1870, and 1890 are data for whites adjusted to match the overall series that covers 1820, 1840, 1860, 1880, 1900, and is annual starting in 1910.

both sexes. Many persons remarry, leading to lower percentages of divorced persons in this age group than among the 30–34 age group.

The rise in the percentage of never-married persons among younger age groups has received particular notice by both academics and the popular press. Much debate ensued in the 1980s and early 1990s over whether people will tend to remain single throughout their lives or postpone marriage until their late thirties and early forties.[1] In the latter case, the percentage of older never-married persons would remain fairly stable over time, while in the former case, the percentage would drop, indicating a real change from the recent past but perhaps indicating a return to the older pattern of approximately 9 percent remaining unmarried. Various factors, such as the rise in education among women, appear to indicate a movement towards later marriage (i.e., more educated women tend to marry later); however, these trends can also be interpreted as signaling the possibility of a drop in the ever-married rate, as educated women also have lower ever-married rates. Notably, transition rates out of the never-married state slow down substantially among people in their late thirties: 12.5 percent of the 35–39 age group were never-married in 1990; five years later in 1995 11.3 percent of the cohort (now 40–44) were still never-married.[2]

Birth rates are available even farther back in time: Figure 5.3 plots the birth rate per thousand persons from 1800 to 1995. A plot of the fertility rate would yield a practically identical pattern of peaks and dips to the one shown. Over this almost two-century period, the birth rate declined steadily from 57 per thousand persons in 1800 to 18.4 in both 1933 and 1936 (both Great Depression years), rose again after the Great Depression, dipped slightly during World War II, and reached the recent history peak of 26.6 in 1947. Since then, it declined to a low of 14.6 in 1975–76, rose to 16.7 in 1990, and has since declined, down to 14.8 in 1995. The fertility rate, after peaking in 1957 at 122.9 births per thousand women age 15 to 44, had declined to a low of 65.0 in 1976. From 1986 to 1990 it rose, reaching 70.9 in 1990, but subsequently has declined each year, down to 65.6 in 1995. The birth rate had been expected to rise in the late 1980s due to the larger proportion of women age 15 to 44 in the population, but many demographers had not foreseen such a notable increase in the fertility rate. It appears that the rise was a short-term increase in the form of delayed births among women in their 30s and 40s. The birth rate, as well as the marriage and divorce rates, fluctuates from year to year, and it is clearly influenced by longer-term economic and political events such as wars and business cycle downturns. However, the birth rate shows a clear downward trend since the beginning of the nineteenth century (which may extend even further back in time).

The question of causality

We now turn to the task of explaining both long-term and short-term demographic trends. We will consider what economic, social, and political forces affect the marriage, divorce, and birth rates. In particular, we will turn our attention to the relationship between the rise in female labor force participation and trends in birth, marriage, and divorce rates. We will consider theories and evidence pertaining to influences on marriage, divorce, and childbearing separately, and then consider how to integrate both theory and evidence into a general framework incorporating all the important factors that both influence, and are influenced by, these basic demographic rates.

Marriage

Why has the marriage rate been dropping? There are several hypotheses that have economic aspects: (1) higher market work productivity for women; (2) lower relative income for men; (3) fewer men relative to women; (4) reduction of the benefits from family formation; (5) lower cost of substitutes for marriage.[3]

1. **Higher market work productivity for women:** Marriage partners can increase total production and consumption through division of household labor. As women have increased market production capabilities, however, comparative advantage patterns have become more similar and the relative benefits of marriage have decreased. Since there are costs to marriage as well, some persons (particularly women) decide not to marry.

2. **Lower relative income for men:** If relative income is falling for men, but men still wish to have a certain level of assured income before marrying (perhaps so as to guarantee that they will have more power in the household relative to their spouse), they will postpone marriage.

3. **Fewer men relative to women:** While this circumstance can lead directly to fewer marriages because there are fewer men to marry, the argument can be made that the rate will fall even more. If the male/female ratio is falling, men may "get away" with more, including not having to marry women in order to have sexual relations with them. Conversely, some women adapt to this situation so that they do not "need" men.

TABLE 5.3 Number of men per hundred women, all and ages 25 to 44, 1940 to 1995

	1940	1950	1960	1970	1980	1990	1995
All ages	100.7	98.6	97.1	94.8	94.5	95.1	95.4
25–44	98.5	96.4	95.7	95.5	97.4	98.9	99.2

Source: 1940 – *Statistical Abstract of the United States* (1992): 20 (Table 20); 1950–95 – *Statistical Abstract of the United States* (1996): 16 (Table 15).

4. **Reductions in the benefits of family formation:** Over time, many societal functions formerly centered in the family, have shifted to being centered in other social institutions. In particular, economic, religious, and educational functions have shifted outside the family, although families are still useful for reproduction and socialization. Again, the benefits of marriage have decreased, leading to less marriage.

5. **Lower cost of substitutes:** Societal disapproval of both same-sex and opposite-sex cohabitation has apparently lessened significantly, leading to a rise in both forms of households.

All of these hypotheses argue that exogenous economic and social changes have affected the probability of marriage. The first hypothesis, in particular, implies that a rise in the female labor force participation rate causes a fall in the marriage rate. For each of these hypotheses, however, there are opposing tendencies as well which would lead to the prediction of stable or even increased marriage rates – in particular, that the rise in female labor force participation makes marriage more likely, rather than less.

First, the benefits associated with marrying may rise and costs may fall for couples in which both persons are employed. For instance, they may have more similar choices of consumption bundles, given their similar time constraints.

Second, while income for many men may be falling, joint income for couples who both work can be substantial, so a couple who wants to marry need not wait until the husband earns enough to "support" a wife; the woman will now also be able to contribute income. If there are large fixed costs involved in marrying and setting up a household (e.g., if large, costly weddings become more expected), then this should make them able to marry sooner rather than later.

Third, if women as a group receive relatively more benefits from marriage than men, they may be willing to negotiate with men if the number of men drops, so as to maintain a high marriage rate, so that men begin to receive relatively more from marriage, inducing them to continue to marry, or even marry at an increased rate. As shown in Table 5.3, it appears that the number of men per woman in the United States, while declining from 1940 through the 1970s, has since risen. In particular, during the prime marrying and childbearing ages of 25 to 44, the number of men per woman is actually higher now than in 1940. The fact that the proportion of never-married men has continued to rise from 1980 to 1990 implies either that the aggregate sex ratio is not a primary factor in determining the rate of marriage or that the relationship between this ratio and the marriage rate is not stable over time. However, it may still be the case that if marriage markets are defined more narrowly by region, racial/ethnic categories, and possibly other variables (e.g., religious affiliation), that sex ratios are skewed across markets (i.e., many more men than women in one, many more women than men in another), and that this can be the cause of declines in marriage. This issue has been of particular interest in considering the decline in marriage rates among African Americans.[4]

Early marriage as an element of Utopia

The behavioral psychologist B.F. Skinner, in his 1948 utopian fantasy, *Walden Two*, envisions the opportunity for persons to enter into early marriage and childbearing as a desirable element of an ideal society. In this excerpt, Frazier, the leader of Walden Two, an experimental communal society, describes to the narrator, a professor visiting the community, how the separation of production from consumption opportunities enables couples to marry and raise children earlier:[5]

"No doubt the thought of a girl getting married a year or two after she is ready for childbearing strikes you as something characteristic of primitive cultures or, worse still, backward communities in our own country," [Frazier] said. "Early marriages are regarded as inadvisable. The figures show they tend to be less successful in the long run, and they are often plainly impossible from an economic point of view. I need scarcely point out, however, that there's no economic obstacle to marriage at any age in Walden Two. The young couple will live quite as well whether married or unmarried. Children are cared for in the same way regardless of the age, experience, or earning power of their parents."

"... We like to ridicule 'puppy love.' We say it won't last, and judge its depth accordingly. Well, of course it doesn't last! A thousand forces conspire against it. And they are not the forces of nature, either, but of a badly organized society. The boy and girl are ready for love. They will never have the same capacity for love again. And they are ready for marriage and childbearing. It's all part of the same thing. But society never lets them prove it."

"Instead, society makes it into a sex problem," I said.

"Of course!" said Frazier. "Sex is no problem in itself. Here the adolescent finds an immediate and satisfactory expression of his natural impulses. It's a solution which is productive, honorable, and viewed by the community with admiration and pride. How very different from the secrecy and shame which most of us recall in connection with sex at some time or other!"

Another problem with this "marriage squeeze" hypothesis is that it would not necessarily lead to a rise in married women's labor force participation rates. While more women would have to do market work because more women would remain single, the women who did get married, if their comparative advantage lay in nonmarket work, would continue to work in the home. In order to explain this rise, the assumption would have to be made that those women who were "lucky" enough to get married would have to work more in both the market and home in order to maintain their marriage.

Two economists have proposed an alternative causal link between the sex ratio and the female labor force participation rate. While the marriage squeeze hypothesis argues that a drop in the male/female ratio leads to a rise in female labor force participation, they suggest that a rise in female labor force participation leads to a drop in the male/female ratio because the survival rate for women increases (because they have access to more survival-related resources through their increased earned income).[6] Their empirical cross-country analysis supports this causal direction, although they point out that the marriage squeeze hypothesis may still affect female participation indirectly through other variables included in their analysis.

Fourth, as fewer societal functions remain fully in the hands of the family, the costs of marriage for those women who wish to maintain a career in market work may actually be reduced. While entering into marriage used to mean taking on a full set of family respons-ibilities, involving many hours of nonmarket work, now its main purpose has switched to being procreative and recreative. This may make women, in particular, more willing to marry, knowing that they are not being locked into a set of lifelong responsibilities. Sim-ilarly, men no longer need to choose marriage partners based partly on their potential ability to provide nonmarket production, but may choose more compatible partners for true leisure activities. Both sexes may find that having a built-in "date" is more convenient than having to match up with new partners for social activities, particularly if they are engaged in many hours of market work.

Another socioeconomic hypothesis regarding the declining marriage rate is that the marriage market is working less effectively: people are having more trouble making matches, either because they meet fewer potential partners or because the people they meet have less potential. In particular, the rising labor force participation of women may indicate that they have less time available to seek partners, and women may have rising standards for mates linked to their higher education and earning power.[7]

Fifth, it is not clear yet to what degree heterosexual cohabitation merely substitutes for late stages of courtship and/or early stages of marriage, thereby leading to the same marriage rate in a steady state.[8] However, it is likely that some significant proportion of persons who cohabitate will never marry, either because they are in a stable cohabiting relationship or because they break up with one person and do not find a suitable spouse upon reentering the "relationship market." In the case of homosexual cohabitation, little is known about numbers and trends of such households, although it seems reasonable to assume that an increased level of same-sex cohabitation would lead to a decline in the marriage rate (the way marriages are currently legally defined).

Divorce

Why has the divorce rate been rising? Again, economists and other social scientists have looked for forces that increase the costs and decrease the benefits associated with remaining married. Four forces have been suggested as explanations of the rise in divorce: (1) changes in the rules governing divorce; (2) increased ability of women to support themselves and their children instead of remaining in an unsatisfactory marriage; (3) adjustment to a variety of new social norms, including the rise in female labor force participation; and (4) improved access to reliable contraception.

1. Changes in the rules governing divorce: As discussed in Chapters 3 and 4, the availability of no-fault divorce, starting in the 1970s, has been studied as a possible cause of the rise in divorce, with mixed evidence regarding whether these legal changes were more a reaction to the increased demand for divorce or whether they led to many couples decid-ing to divorce who would otherwise have remained married.

2. Increased ability of women to support families alone: Increased market work pro-ductivity for women may lead to divorce. Women no longer have to stay in marriages solely for financial security, even if there are children to be supported. Additionally, altern-ative sources of nonearned income, namely government support, have become increasingly available, again making it easier for unmarried women to raise families.

3. Adjustment to new social norms: Spouses who expected to remain in a traditional division of labor for the duration of their marriage may have trouble adjusting to a change in this division. This may reflect dissatisfaction with an altered power structure within the family as it relates to the shares of family income provided by various family members.

Two-earner families may also experience greater ongoing role conflicts and shortages of time available for nonmarket activities, including shared leisure activities. These conflicts may be at least partially resolved over time as the technology of nonmarket production continues to change to accommodate the greater number of two-earner families.

In general, times of greater uncertainty, regarding either availability of resources for the family or the roles of family members, may lead to divorce. For instance, if a business cycle downturn results in the husband losing his job and therefore at least temporarily ceding his role as primary provider, the friction created in the family may result in divorce.[9]

4. Improved access to reliable contraception (and abortion): If people are less likely to dissolve a marriage when there are children involved, for both social and economic reasons, then reducing the number of married couples that have children – particularly, early in the marriage – will tend to raise the divorce rate.[10]

Again, for all these forces there are opposing tendencies that would lead to the prediction of stable or even reduced divorce rates:

First, to the extent that divorce law changes have resulted in more divorces than would have otherwise occurred, the rate should level off after the "backlog" of bad marriages has been dissolved.

Second, higher family incomes due to the wife's greater market work may tend to reduce conflicts over allocating scarce monetary resources among the family members, thereby reducing the probability of divorce. The potential difficulty in dividing the greater volume of illiquid assets owned by higher-income families may also reduce the probability of divorce.[11]

Third, now that the status quo has changed and many persons, particularly young men and women, are used to the idea that wives will continue to work full-time even after childbirth, fewer divorces may occur. Also, persons who relatively prefer market to nonmarket good consumption (i.e., who prefer the new status quo) will be happier now than in a system where women were less likely to work in the market. In fact, even without assuming prior matching by tastes for market vs. nonmarket good consumption, two-earner families may have more possibilities for joint consumption, as the preferences of family members regarding activities become more similar as both earners have less nonmarket time available.

Additionally, dual-earner families may experience less family income fluctuation across the business cycle. The rising proportion of dual-earner families and consequent reduced variance in family income relative to one-earner families should mean reduced divorce rates.

Fourth, with more access to contraception and abortion, fewer unplanned pregnancies are carried to term, leading to a reduced rate of marriage among younger persons, in particular. Since people who marry young are more likely to divorce, this reduction in "shotgun" marriages would tend to reduce the divorce rate.

Certainly there are people who are influenced in opposite ways by these tendencies. The net effect for many of them is still in debate, although the net effect of all the social changes taken together has been to increase the divorce rate. For instance, a recent comprehensive review of divorce studies done during the 1980s finds that different studies provide evidence for either a positive or a negative link between female labor force participation and divorce.[12]

It is clearly difficult to quantify various aspects of these hypotheses about the causes of divorce, such as stability, but there are variables available that may serve as stand-ins. For example, one study attempts to explain changes in the yearly divorce rate from 1920 to 1974 as a function of several other variables measured yearly:[13]

$$\text{Divorce rate} = f(Y, AGE, MD, U, GI, DF, PA);$$

$$Y = \text{personal disposable income per capita}$$

$$AGE = \frac{\text{population ages } 20\text{--}24}{\text{population ages } 20\text{--}49}$$

$$MD = \frac{\text{marriages currently less than 3 years in duration}}{\text{marriages currently less than 15 years in duration}}$$

$$U = \text{unemployment rate}$$

$$GI = \text{percentage of population in military}$$

$$DF = \text{a contraceptive technology diffusion index}$$

$$PA = \text{monthly public assistance (AFDC) payment per capita}$$

The expectation is that a rise in any one of these variables would cause an increase in the divorce rate. Various statistical specifications of this equation can explain 89 to 95 percent of the variation in the divorce rate in this time period, and the variables enter positively as predicted. The study also uses data on women's wages and men's income to try to explain the divorce rate during 1950 to 1974. Four factors appear to be of primary importance in explaining the rise in the divorce rate: (1) the rise in women's wages, (2) the increased level of public assistance payments, (3) improvements in contraceptive technology during the 1960s, and (4) increased aging in the demographic structure. This last factor means that as the baby boom cohort has entered its marrying years, it has lowered the median duration of marriage, so a greater proportion of married couples face the high probabilities of divorce associated with having married more recently. These last two factors are of particular importance in explaining the 1960–74 acceleration in the divorce rate rather than in explaining the longer-run steady upward trend.

Birth

Why has the birth rate been dropping? Many social and economic forces have been cited as possible contributors to declining fertility rates:[14]

- the shift from an agrarian to an industrial (and increasingly service) economy, and the coincident decline of the rural way of life
- the shift in the economic status of children in the household from producer to consumer
- the spread of universal education
- the substitution of the ethos of rationality for one of traditional values from more religious times[15]
- the declining functions of the traditional family
- the changing status of women
- the development of contraception

These factors can be divided into those that influence tastes and those that influence constraints. Economists tend to try to explain changes in fertility-related behavior by assuming that tastes are relatively constant over time, while the relevant constraints that affect childbearing and raising have been changing. In particular, they have considered the effects of wage and income changes on the number of children born per family, as well as the effects of changing prices that would tend to make families have fewer children but invest more resources in each child.

If childraising is treated as a form of nonmarket production for a family that involves large inputs of time in order to produce "child-based consumption," then rising wages will have both income and substitution effects on time spent in childraising. If child-based consumption is a normal good (which seems a reasonable assumption to make), then we would expect rising wages to lead families to desire more of this good. However, the relative price of child-based consumption rises along with the wage (i.e., the opportunity cost of having children rises), leading families to substitute other market commodities for child-based consumption.

Rising wages will also lead families to attempt to substitute market goods and services for nonmarket goods and services as inputs in the production of child-based consumption. Additionally, if it is cheaper to increase child-based consumption through using more market goods and services in combination with an existing child than it is to increase child-based consumption through having another child, then fewer children will be born, but larger amounts of expenditures will be devoted to each child. A countervailing force exists to the extent that there are economies of scale in production of child-based consumption. This would tend to encourage families to have additional children, as the per capita cost of some inputs (e.g., clothes, toys) into providing a particular level of quality per child declines with the number of children. This may tend to affect the timing of births as well as the number of children if the economies of scale are greater when the children are closer in age. At any rate, it is possible that the total amount of child-based consumption has stayed constant – or even risen – for families, even as family size has fallen.

How much do people tend to spend to raise a child? Estimates for a child born in 1995 of direct cash outlay alone up through age 18 ranged from $107,000 for low-income families and $145,000 for middle-income families to $212,000 for high-income families.[16] Estimates from 1981 of direct cash outlay plus opportunity costs ranged from $168,000 for low-income families to $234,000 for middle-income families (in 1995 dollars), where opportunity costs take the form particularly of foregone market income.[17] Expenditures appear to be rising slightly over time in real purchasing power terms: data from 1960–61 and 1972–73 surveys yield figures of $134,000 and $138,000 (in 1995 dollars), respectively, for middle-income families.[18] However, this is an average over all children; comparison of expenditure data for households with different numbers of children shows that the increase in expenditure from adding additional children to the household decreases with the number of children. It appears that, for most families, adding a second and third child results in only slightly more additional expenditure than that involved in having the first child.[19]

A discussion of how families might rationally decide how many children to have and when to have them presupposes that they have the ability to engage in family planning. In other words, it assumes that they must have contraceptive technology available, including abortions for some. The availability of reliable contraception in the form of the birth control pill, and, for persons who have completed their planned childbearing, increasing reliance on surgical sterilization, has been a crucial factor in allowing families to reduce their fertility if they so desire.

Table 5.4 shows that contraceptive method usage patterns have changed notably in recent years. There has been a large shift away from less reliable traditional methods

TABLE 5.4 Percentage distribution of contraceptive use among married women ages 15 to 44 who report using contraception, 1965 to 1995

	1965	1976	1982	1995
Traditional methods*	63	30	32	27
Birth control pill	24	33	20	20
Female sterilization	7	14	26	31
Male sterilization	5	13	15	18
IUD	1	10	7	1
Implants and injections	—	—	—	3

* This category includes barrier methods, periodic abstinence, and other less-common methods.
Sources: 1965 and 1976 – National Center for Health Statistics, "Trends in Contraceptive Practice: United States, 1965–76," *Vital and Health Statistics* series 23, no. 10 (1982) (Table 7); 1982 – William F. Pratt, William D. Mosher, Christine A. Bachrach, and Marjorie C. Horn, "Understanding U.S. Fertility: Findings from the National Survey of Family Growth, Cycle III," *Population Bulletin* 39, no. 5 (1984) (Table 8); 1995 – Linda Peterson, "Fertility, Family Planning, and Women's Health: New Data from the 1995 National Survey of Family Growth," *Vital and Health Statistics* series 23, no. 19 (May 1997) (Table 42).

(barrier and timing methods) towards more reliable methods – in particular, birth control pill usage and, more recently, sterilization. Sterilization is now the most popular method for married couples. While younger women continue to rely on reversible methods, older women have moved away from use of the pill as more information has become available regarding negative side effects.[20]

Another important assumption concerning the "technology" of childraising is that families are interested in how many children survive to adulthood, not how many children are conceived or born. As the probability of survival has greatly increased over the last century, women can now have fewer births in order to achieve a given number of adult offspring. This factor alone can explain a large portion of the decrease in the birth rate. An increased survival rate also allows parents to practice an "all eggs in one basket (or two)" strategy. While parents may have always preferred having fewer children, with more resources invested per child, a high child mortality rate would make this a risky strategy.

What is the source of utility that parents get from having children? Over time, in developed countries with social security systems, children appear to have evolved into a current consumption good rather than an investment to provide future income for parents. The reduced use of children as investments would tend to reduce birth rates and modify the forms of human capital that parents invest in children from those that tend to be income-producing to those that produce more current consumption value for parents.[21]

How strongly do births respond to wage, income, and employment changes? Births appear to have relatively elastic responses to wage changes. One study for the United States found an elasticity of –1.73 with respect to female wages and 1.31 with respect to male wages (a pure income effect from the woman's point of view).[22] Another study using European data found similar values of –1.34 with respect to female wages and 1.26 with respect to male wages in the more prosperous regions, but –0.76 for female wages and 1.03 for male wages in less prosperous regions.[23] These estimates imply that a 10 percent increase in female wages would reduce births by 8 to 17 percent, while a 10 percent increase in male wages would increase births by 10 to 13 percent. But the timing of the different effects is important to sort out. For instance, one study found that fertility affects employment in the short run, but employment affects fertility in the long run.[24] In other words, having a child tends to make a woman stop working (reflecting her increased value of time spent in nonmarket production), but a woman's working tends to reduce her total number of children. Another study, using Swedish data, finds that rising female wages both delay childbearing and reduce total conceptions.[25]

Another question is how much public policies that affect the constraints faced by the family, either by changing the wage rate or the availability of nonearned income, affect fertility. For instance, income tax rates affect net wages, leading to income and substitution effects on child-based consumption. One study looked for responses to changes in the federal income tax code from 1977 to 1983.[26] In 1979 the personal exemption increased, which tends to increase family income (by the amount of the exemption times the marginal tax rate), while in 1982 the top marginal tax rate was reduced. There appeared to be a positive income effect on the number of children as family income rose (note that the tax break had a larger effect on men's incomes, since they were the higher earners), but the substitution effect of increasing the take-home wage for women overcame the positive income effect and tended to reduce additional births.

While it is hard to evaluate the net effect of all government policies on the fertility rate, many commentators would argue that much could be done both to lower the costs of raising children and to redistribute the costs away from women onto men, or away from families onto society at large. Economist Nancy Folbre has commented that the "unequal distribution of costs of children between men and women has been reinforced by public policies that have served the interest of men as fathers as well as the interests of those employers and taxpayers who are not also mothers."[27] Folbre takes a longer view of the economic processes behind the declining fertility rate, arguing that patriarchy, in general, has made it possible for men to shift the cost of raising children onto individual mothers.[28] However, the transition in many societies to capitalistic structures has diminished patriarchal authority over adult children, thereby reducing the economic benefits for men of having large families. Therefore, men have become more willing to accede to women's demands for increased control over reproduction.[29]

Which causes what?

It is not obvious that causality must run from changes in female labor force participation to changes in demographic variables. For each variable mentioned above, an argument can be made in the opposite direction as well (as was done in Chapter 4), so that declining marriage rates, rising divorce rates, and declining fertility all lead to higher women's labor force participation. While there are no doubt effects in both directions and exogenous forces that are truly the underlying causes of these changes, it is still interesting to ask which change happened first.

One study considers annual data from 1950 to 1980 on female labor force participation (using the rate for married women with a child under age 6), median age at first marriage for women, birth rates, and divorce rates.[30] Changes in each series are related to lagged values of the other series. Lagged values of the rise in female participation help explain the fall in fertility and the rise in median age at first marriage. In the other direction, the drop in cumulative fertility helps explain the rise in female participation.

What is missing from most economic theories of why demographic variables change is a fully developed model of how preferences, or tastes, may be altered through economic

TABLE 5.5 Total number of households, average household size, and percentage distribution of households by type, 1960 to 1995

	1960	1970	1980	1990	1995
Total number of households (in millions)	53.0	63.4	80.8	93.3	99.0
Average household size (number of persons)	3.3	3.1	2.8	2.6	2.6
Family households	85.3	81.2	73.7	70.8	70.0
married couples with children	44.2	40.3	30.9	26.2	25.6
married couples without children	30.3	30.3	29.9	29.8	28.9
other families with children	4.4	5.0	7.5	8.4	9.2
other families without children	6.4	5.6	5.4	6.4	6.4
Nonfamily households	14.7	18.8	26.2	29.2	30.0
women living alone	8.7	11.5	14.0	14.9	14.7
men living alone	4.3	5.6	8.6	9.7	10.3
other nonfamily households	1.7	1.7	3.6	4.6	5.0

Sources: 1960 – *Current Population Reports Series P-23*, no. 163 (August 1989): 10 (Figure 8); *Statistical Abstract of the United States* (1962): 41 (Table 37); 1970–95 – *Current Population Reports Series P-20*, no. 458 (February 1992): A-1 (Table A-1); no. 483 (September 1995): vii (Table A); no. 488 (October 1996): 2 (Table A). Children refers to own children under age 18.

processes. Some economists have considered how lifestyle aspirations may be influenced by relative economic status. Institutionalist economists, notably Clair Brown, have considered how social norms and consumption norms have changed, particularly over the course of the twentieth century as economic growth has occurred.[31] Demographer and economist Richard Easterlin has emphasized shifts in generation size since World War II as creating economic pressures on young couples.[32] These exogenous shifts lead to changes in attitudes and behavior relating in particular to work and childbearing. Such attempts to explain changes in tastes as well as in constraints appear to be promising ways to develop a comprehensive framework for explaining demographic changes.

New household and family patterns

Not only have demographic changes been reflected in changing birth, marriage, and divorce rates, but household and family structures have been altered as well. While data on household and family composition are not available as far back in time, we can still see substantial changes over the period for which data are available. Table 5.5 shows changes in household structure since 1960. The number of households has increased and the proportion of nonfamily households has increased substantially. These data reflect the changes in birth, marriage, and divorce rates: many more persons live alone, average household size has been decreasing, and the percentage of households that are families containing children dropped from 48.6 percent in 1960 to 34.8 percent in 1995.

There has been a notable increase in nonfamily households; in particular, the number of heterosexual unmarried-couple households has risen from 523,000 in 1970 to 3,668,000 by 1995, an increase of over 600 percent.[33] Another notable trend is the rise in single-parent

TABLE 5.6 Percentage distribution of families by family type and labor force status of members, 1960 and 1995

	1960	1995
Married-couple families	87.3	77.7
husband in labor force, not the wife	53.0	17.0
husband and wife in labor force	24.8	43.3
wife in labor force, not the husband	1.8	4.4
neither spouse in labor force	7.7	13.0
Families maintained by women	10.0	17.6
householder in labor force	5.0	11.5
householder not in labor force	5.0	6.1
Families maintained by men	2.7	4.7
householder in labor force	2.0	3.6
householder not in labor force	0.7	1.1

Sources: 1960 – *Working Women: A Chartbook*, U.S. Department of Labor, Bureau of Labor Statistics, Bulletin no. 2385 (August 1991): 49 (Table A-17); 1995 – *Current Population Reports Series P-20*, no. 488 (October 1996): 2 (Table A); 133 (Table 15). Proportions of families maintained by single persons in the labor force are for 1996, from unpublished data.

households. Table 5.6 shows the changing distribution of families by whether or not they contain a married couple and by the labor force participation of the householder(s). Married-couple families represent a declining share of all families, while families maintained by a single woman have risen substantially. Families are more likely to contain a working mother now than in 1960.

The increase in female-headed households has received a great deal of attention over the last thirty years. The increased formation of female-headed households with children is related to both the drop in marriage rates and the rise in divorce rates.[34] It appears that the first factor has been of greater importance for blacks, while the second has been more important for whites. The percentage of births occurring outside marriage in 1993 was 31 percent overall; whites had a rate of 24 percent and blacks had a rate of 69 percent![35] Observers worry both about concrete factors, such as the low average incomes for female-headed households, and about less concrete factors such as whether fathers have become superfluous in modern society.[36]

Changes in well-being of households and families

If rising female labor force participation has caused particular demographic changes, what is the net change in economic well-being for various persons affected by these changes? It will come as no surprise that it is difficult to evaluate whether or not people are better off.

How to measure changes in well-being

Take the case of a married-couple household where the wife increases her hours spent in market work. Household income for such households that remain intact will rise. But how much better off is this household?

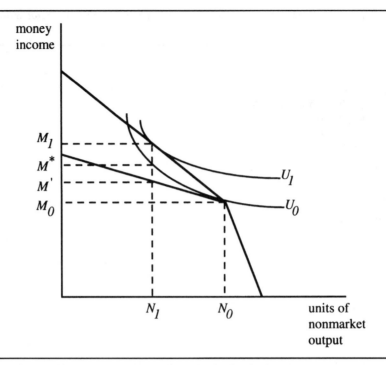

FIGURE 5.4 Measurable and unmeasurable gains in family income

Consider the situation shown in Figure 5.4. When the wife's wage rises, she switches from doing only nonmarket work to doing some market work, reducing her hours spent in nonmarket work. The household moves from (M_0, N_0) to (M_1, N_1) along the new higher budget constraint, representing a clear gain in utility for the household as it moves from indifference curve U_0 to the higher indifference curve U_1. But how can we measure this utility gain in money? While measured income has risen by $(M_1 - M_0)$, nonmarket consumption has dropped by $(N_0 - N_1)$. The value of this reduction in nonmarket consumption must somehow be subtracted from the gain in measured income.

One way to attempt to measure the gain in well-being is to hold market hours worked constant at the new higher level and see how much more money is generated under the higher wage. In Figure 5.4, M' indicates the level of income that the household would previously have earned had the wife worked this number of hours. Therefore $(M_1 - M')$ is the increase in household income, holding nonmarket output constant at the new (lower) level. This will be less than $(M_1 - M_0)$ by the amount $(M' - M_0)$, which represents the opportunity cost of increasing nonmarket hours from N_1 to N_0, measured at the old wage rate. This overestimates the gain to the household, but by less than simply counting the change in money income as the gain.

The real gain to the household can be computed through conducting the thought experiment of taking money away from the household until the utility level is the same as before the wage change. M^* represents the amount of money income, combined with nonmarket goods at level N_1, that would return the household to the original utility indifference curve. Therefore, $(M_1 - M^*)$ is the real gain in well-being for the household measured in money terms. Unfortunately, M^* is unobservable without actually conducting the experiment.[37]

Effects on inequality between households

It is also hard to judge whether increased female labor force participation has tended to reduce differences in consumption between households. As more households contain two working spouses, we might expect to see greater equality of income across households, although this may still not translate into more equal consumption of total nonmarket and market goods.

There will be a tendency for the increase in female labor force participation to lead to increased family earnings variance if there is a positive correlation between the earnings of one spouse and the labor supply of the other, and if there is a positive correlation between the spouses' wage rates. There appears to be a positive correlation between wage rates of spouses for both whites and blacks, along with a positive correlation between earnings of one spouse and the labor supply of the other for blacks, but a negative correlation for whites.[38] Among married-couple families, it appears that the variance in the husband's earnings is greater than the variance in family earnings for whites, though not for blacks.[39]

Additionally, household income variance over the business cycle appears to have been reduced through the increase in two-earner families, as families are better able to maintain some flow of earned income even if one family member becomes unemployed. For instance, in 1991 (a recession year), the unemployment rate for wives was 4.3 percent and for husbands was 4.2 percent, but only 1.6 percent of married-couple families had no employed members and only 2.2 percent had no full-time employed members.[40]

However, the shift in household composition towards an increased proportion of single persons and of female-headed families has led to greater inequality of income between household types. In particular, different types of households have different poverty rates. Additionally, women who have returned to the labor force in the aftermath of divorce appear to have relatively lower living standards than the general population, as well as lower living standards than they had previous to their divorce.[41]

Tradeoffs for working women

Much attention regarding the effects of the increased female participation rate has focused on the effects of working on women's well-being.[42] For women who work full-time and have children, the pressure on their time may be extreme, leaving them with little true leisure. Alternatively, many women who choose to work in particularly demanding jobs may find that having a family is not an option, either through their own choice or through lack of opportunity to marry and/or have children.

Economist Victor Fuchs locates the main group of women experiencing significantly increased earnings in the 1980s as those women under age 40, and argues that the different balance in their lives between career and family is responsible for their increased earnings power. When considering the 1.5 million white women in their 30s who earned more than $25,000 in 1986, he found that over 50 percent of these women are childless, as compared with 24 percent of comparably aged white women who earn less than $25,000 and 9 percent of comparable women who are not working. Among high-earning white men in their 30s, only 28 percent are childless.[43]

Certainly there has been some opinion in the popular press, as well as among academics, that the price of success for women in the labor market is too high.[44] If young women knew that they faced a significantly reduced probability of marrying and eventually having children if they chose a more challenging work life, they would evaluate undertaking such a career path differently than if there were no such trade-offs involved. But the question of timing versus levels is critical here: it is one thing for a woman to believe that she will have to delay having children in order to get a career on track; it is another thing to believe that she will have to forego having children at all. It appears that delaying childbirth and reducing family size have tangible results in terms of women's economic well-being. A study of women ages 60 or over in 1976 has found that later childbearers and those with fewer children (though this factor is less important) appear to be substantially better off financially by this point in their lives, measured by income, living standard, or assets.[45]

FOCUS

The price of success? Higher education and family life

Must women give up marriage and children to achieve career success, and vice-versa? Economist Claudia Goldin studied five cohorts of white college graduate women, tracking their patterns of family and work in order to characterize each group.[46] The first group, graduating college from 1900 to 1919, had a stark choice of either family or career. The second group, graduating from 1920 to 1945, tended to have a job (rather than a career), followed by a family. The third group, graduating from 1946 to 1965, tended to have family, followed by a job. The fourth and fifth groups, graduating respectively from 1966 to 1979 and 1980 to 1995, desired to have a career as well as a family.

While it is too soon to tell whether or not the fifth group has been successful in attaining this desired balance, Goldin studied the fourth group and found that many had not attained both goals. When she defined having a career as having hourly earnings exceeding that of the 25th percentile in the male earnings distribution, she found that about one-third had achieved a career. However, only about 17 percent had both attained a career and had children, while over half had children, but not a career.

On the other hand, consider economist Myra Strober's case study of Stanford University Business School's 1974 MBA class.[47] This class had 34 women, comprising 11 percent of the graduating class, which was the first time a sizable number of women had gone through the program. The class was surveyed in the spring of 1974 before graduation, and again in the spring of 1978. In 1978, their gender ratio of annual earnings was 0.79, substantially above the national average at that time for year-round full-time workers. Among the men, by 1978, 69 percent were married, 28 had never been married, and 3 percent were separated, widowed, or divorced. The distribution among the women was very similar: 65 percent married, 31 percent never-married, and 4 percent separated, widowed, or divorced. 43 percent of the men and 35 percent of the women had already had children; the rate for the women is lower, but not substantially so.

Effects on children

Finally, let us consider the effects on children of the demographic changes outlined in this chapter. We will focus on the economic effects, namely changes in the resources available to children, and socioeconomic indicators that may be linked with children's economic well-being as adults. In particular, the rising number of persons raised for a significant portion of their childhood in single-parent households has been striking.

The percentage of children in households with both parents has fallen from 85 percent in 1970 to 69 percent in 1995.[48] This drop in dual-parent households has had a significant effect on children in that fewer resources are available for their use. The situation is clearly more critical when the absent parent is less tied to the household financially and socially, as in many cases where children are born to unmarried mothers. However, single-parent households that form following divorce also experience reduced resources relative to married-couple households. Less income is available for use by the children, given the additional expense of running two separate households. Additionally, the child's household may not receive adequate child support. Also, due both to the mother's often having to spend more time in market (and often nonmarket) work, and to decreased contact with the father,[49] the amount of time the parents devote to child care is often reduced.

Cases of extreme hardship, namely children in families below the poverty line, are indicative of the worsening relative position of children. While the percentage of children in poverty has dropped substantially since 1960, the incidence of poverty among children is almost twice that of adults: 20.8 percent for children versus 11.3 percent for adults in 1995.[50] This is a significant rise compared with earlier decades: in 1960 and 1970, the rate for children was only one-third above the adult rate (25.9 percent for children and 19.4 percent for adults in 1960; 16.2 percent for children and 12.4 percent for adults in 1970).[51] The average length of time spent in poverty for children who enter poverty is about seven years, more than a third of their childhood.[52] While poverty during any part of a child's life is of concern, part of the concern surrounding the high rate of children raised in poverty stems from the worry that their impoverished situation may continue during their adulthood and be perpetuated for their children, as well.

FOCUS

Teenage mothers and the cycle of poverty

Although the birthrate among teenagers has been dropping recently, it remains higher than a decade ago, and birthrates for black and Hispanic teenagers are almost three times as high as for whites.[53] Researchers have been interested in the question of whether both the mothers and their children are thereafter destined to lower economic outcomes due to their birth circumstances.

Between 1966 and 1968, 404 pregnant Baltimore women younger than 18 who had not had a previous child were interviewed by a team of researchers.[54] They were reinterviewed one, three, five, and seventeen years after the initial interview. Their first-born children were interviewed five, seventeen, and twenty-one years after their mothers' initial interview. The results underline the variability of outcomes experienced: the women interviewed were not all destined to a permanent existence on welfare, nor were their children invariably fated to follow in their mothers' footsteps and become teenage parents themselves. However, the children's rates of teenage parenting were higher than for the general population, and those who became teenage parents appeared to have bleaker futures in store than those their mothers faced.

In discussing the original generation in the study, the researchers report that the women "had generally suffered considerable short-term handicaps as a result of an early first birth, including low levels of education and early employment." But the 17-year follow-up interview provided a picture of greater variability in the consequences of early childbearing. Many of the women had managed to return to school and to leave public assistance and find stable employment; only a small fraction had large families. Only slightly more than one-third were married. The researchers noted that "in comparison with samples from several national surveys, the Baltimore mothers were clearly not as successful as metropolitan-area black women of similar age who had delayed childbearing until their 20s."

Observing the children of the original sample of women, the researchers found that 36 percent of the female children had a live birth before age 19, so almost two-thirds did not become teenage mothers. They interpret this as showing that "daughters do not necessarily, or even usually, 'inherit' early childbearing from their mothers." As 51 percent of the daughters reported becoming pregnant before age 19, it is clear that abortions are significantly reducing the rate of teenage motherhood. Duration of the mother's welfare receipt did not appear to increase the daughter's probability of early childbearing, but a recent welfare history for the mother increased the daughter's probability.

Comparing the group of children who had become teenage parents themselves to their mothers in terms of educational achievement, however, shows that the children were almost twice as likely as their mothers to have failed one or more grades in school. Also, the mothers had achieved more educationally by the same age than had the children, even though the children were less likely to be married than their mothers (assuming marriage as an impediment to further schooling). A much higher proportion of the younger generation is receiving public assistance (60 percent vs. 31 percent of the mothers at the same age). The researchers assess the picture for these persons as bleak, although their general findings give hope that the next generation, as well, will have many members who will escape poverty.

Other indicators of children's well-being besides measurement of financial resources available to them also show declining well-being. Performance on scholastic aptitude tests has exhibited a long downward trend: for example, from a total average score of 975 on the SAT in 1960 to 910 in 1995, a drop of 7 percent.[55] Child obesity rates have been rising steadily for the last three decades, with 22 percent of children ages 6 to 17 overweight as of 1995.[56] Besides indicating that children may not be as well-off as they could be during childhood, these trends are also worrisome because they indicate that children enter adulthood with factors that may lead to less success for them as adults. On the other hand, infant and child mortality rates have fallen drastically – from 41 of every thousand newborns dying before their 20th birthday in 1960, to only 18 in 1993.[57] This gain in well-being is reduced somewhat by the rising suicide and homicide rates for young persons: for persons ages 15 to 19, the suicide rate rose from 3.6 per 100,000 in 1960 to 10.9 in 1993 and the homicide rate rose from 4.0 to 17.1 in 1994 – a rise of between a tripling and a quadrupling for these rates.[58]

Other aspects of children's well-being are often hard to measure. For instance, while there has been much interest in the psychological and social effects of divorce on children, it is difficult to interpret results. Several studies have argued that children are hurt by divorce in both the short-run and the long-run, including having higher rates of depression both in childhood and adulthood and being more likely to subsequently divorce themselves.[59] However, it is not clear if this is a result of their being in troubled families to begin with or of having to go through the divorce process. Other researchers have argued that while the short-run effects may be bad for children, in the long-run it is better to rectify a troubled family situation through separation or divorce than to leave such a family intact.[60]

We cannot ascertain how well off the children would have been had they remained in their intact families.

How to improve well-being

This discussion of the effects of demographic changes on various groups' well-being has yielded mixed results. While many families appear to have higher financial resources due to smaller family sizes and more working women, other families are worse off because they contain fewer high-earning adults.

The causal links between female labor force participation, demographic changes, and changes in well-being are not well-established, and they need not be either stable or reversible. For instance, if the rise in female labor force participation has led to an increase in the divorce rate and a fall in the marriage rate, it does not follow that reducing female labor force participation will lead to a return to previous levels of marriage and divorce rates. Also, even if we all agree, for instance, that a lower divorce rate would be desirable and that this is unlikely to occur without some form of policy intervention or dramatic social change, there are potentially ways to achieve that lower rate that have not yet been observed in the short period that data on human societies have been compiled.

Finally, to the extent that we are concerned with the well-being of particular groups – especially, children – who have little influence on their living situations, these problems are everyone's concern, not just mothers'. For instance, even if the well-being of a child is reduced subsequent to a woman's increasing her hours of market work, the solution is not necessarily that the woman should reduce market work. Other family members may, instead, increase their share of child care, and persons who are not family members may also help out.

*P*olicy Application: Regulation of fertility – access to contraception and abortion

Given that extremely reliable contraceptive methods have been available in the United States for several decades, the high rates of unplanned pregnancy and abortion are remarkable. As shown in Table 5.8, the number of abortions per hundred live births has risen substantially over the past two decades, from 23.9 in 1973 (approximately one out of five conceptions) to a high of 43.6 in 1983, followed by a steady drop to 37.9 by 1992 (one out of 3.6 conceptions).[61] Women who have abortions in the United States are predominantly young, white, and unmarried. However, the rate for nonwhites in 1991 of 54 per thousand women was 2.7 times that of white women, who had a rate of 20 per thousand women.

The U.S. abortion rate is substantially higher than those for many countries with similar political structures and levels of industrial development. Table 5.7 contains recent available legal abortion rates for other countries. Communist and formerly communist countries have rates in general that are much higher than those for noncommunist industrialized countries.[62] These countries appear to rely on abortion as one of their primary means of birth control. The United States, with a rate in 1987 of 27.1 abortions per thousand women ages 15 to 44, is notably higher than the rates for countries in Western Europe, and is over 5 times as high as the Netherlands.

Table 5.8 compares the United States with England and Wales in terms of the legal abortion rate per thousand women ages 15 to 44. Abortion rates for England and Wales

TABLE 5.7 Legal abortion rates per thousand women ages 15 to 44, selected countries, various years

Country (Year is 1987–88 unless otherwise noted)			
former Soviet Union	111.9[†]	Australia	16.6
Romania (1983)	90.9[†]	Israel	16.2[†]
former Yugoslavia (1984)	70.5	Poland	14.9[†]
Bulgaria	64.7	England and Wales	14.2
Cuba	58.0	Tunisia	13.6
former Czechoslovakia	46.7	France	13.3[†]
Brazil (1991)	39.3*	Canada	12.1
China	38.8	Iceland	12.0
Hungary	38.2	Finland	11.7
Columbia (1990)	32.0*	New Zealand	11.4
Singapore	30.1	Italy (1993)	9.8
United States	27.1	Belgium (1985)	7.5
former East Germany (1984)	26.6	former West Germany	7.0[†]
Mexico (1990)	22.0*	Netherlands	5.3
Sweden	19.8	Ireland	4.8[†]
Japan	18.6[†]	Bangladesh (1989)	3.4[†]
Denmark	18.3	India	3.0[†]
Norway	16.8		

* Women ages 15 to 49.
[†] Data are incomplete.
Sources: Italy – Silvana Salvini Bettarini and Silvana Schifini D'Andrea, "Induced Abortion in Italy: Levels, Trends and Characteristics," *Family Planning Perspectives* 28, no. 6 (November/December 1996): 267; United States – *Statistical Abstract of the United States* (1996): 86 (Table 115); Brazil, Colombia, and Mexico – Susheela Singh and Gilda Sedgh, "The Relationship of Abortion to Trends in Contraception and Fertility in Brazil, Colombia and Mexico," *International Family Planning Perspectives* 23, no. 1 (March 1997): 4; all others – Stanley K. Henshaw, "Induced Abortion: A World Review, 1990," *Family Planning Perspectives* 22, no. 2 (March/April 1990): 76 (Table 2).

are substantially lower than U.S. rates and do not show the clear increase in the late 1970s and early 1980s that the U.S. data display; rather, they show a rise in the late 1980s, leveling off at a higher level in the 1990s. Table 5.8 also includes recent data for both countries by age group. Rates are higher in all age groups for the United States, particularly for younger women.

Why are abortion rates so much higher in the United States than in the United Kingdom? Analyst Colin Francome suggests several sources for the difference, as well as general cultural differences: (1) abortions are easier to obtain in the United States; (2) U.S. teenagers have sex earlier on average than U.K. teenagers; (3) U.S. women have less access to contraception, particularly teenage women, while birth control is generally free in the United Kingdom.[63] It is notable that 70 percent of British women ages 15 to 44 were using contraception in 1982–83, as compared with 54 percent of U.S. women.[64] In general, it appears that women in countries economically comparable to the United States both have greater access to contraception and are more likely to use it.[65]

It is interesting to consider how changes in public policies affecting use of contraception and abortion might change these figures. Let us consider two government policies that affect the U.S. abortion rate: (1) subsidizing contraception for poor women and (2) subsidizing abortion for poor women. The first policy tends to reduce the abortion rate,

TABLE 5.8 Legal abortion rates per thousand women ages 15 to 44, United States, 1973 to 1992, and England and Wales, 1973 to 1994, and by age group, 1991–92

	United States	*England and Wales*
1973	16.3	11.5
1975	21.7	11.0
1977	26.5	10.4
1979	28.8	12.0
1981	29.3	12.5
1983	28.5	11.9
1985	28.0	12.9
1987	27.1	14.1
1989	26.8	15.4
1991	26.3	15.0
1992	25.9	14.4
1994	—	14.0
1991–92, by age		
Under 15	7.0	3.2
15–19	37.5	19.4
20–24	56.6	25.9
25–29	33.7	18.4
30–34	19.2	12.5
35–39	10.3	7.8
≥40	1.7	1.6

Sources: U.K.: Great Britain Office of Population Censuses and Surveys, *Abortion Statistics* (1996); U.S., 1973–80 – C. Tietze, *Induced Abortion*, 5th edition (Population Council, 1983): 33; U.S. 1981–92 – *Statistical Abstract of the United States* (1996): 86 (Tables 115, 116). England and Wales rates from 1985 on are estimated based on the rate per 1,000 women 14–49, taken as the ratio in 1983 and 1984 to the rate per 1,000 women 15–44.

while the second increases it. Policies that affect the price and/or availability of contraception and abortion will affect private and public budgets. If female labor supply is reduced by increased fertility, then policies that result in additional births will tend to reduce female labor participation and market hours of work, reducing income and taxes, as well as leading to additional public and private spending related to these additional births.

A study that estimated the amount of public savings from providing contraception found that almost one in four U.S. women who use a reversible contraceptive method rely on public funds to help finance their method, either through use of a publicly funded family clinic or a private physician reimbursed by Medicaid.[66] If these publicly funded services were not available, the study estimates that another 1.2 to 2.1 million unintended pregnancies would occur in a year's time (where the range is generated through assuming various alternative contraceptive use patterns). This is a substantial increase over the approximately 400,000 unintended pregnancies these women currently experience. In the 1987 fiscal year, the federal and state governments combined spent $412 million on contraceptive services for women who otherwise might not have been able to obtain them. The study contrasts this figure to the estimated total additional costs for medical care, welfare, and supplementary nutritional programs during the first two years after a birth for those pregnancies that are not ended, plus the increased costs for publicly funded abortions – a total increase in costs of $1.2 to 2.6 billion. Therefore, the public savings through running these programs represent approximately $4.40 saved for every dollar of public funds spent to provide contraceptive services. This huge differential implies that expanding these programs would yield further cost savings, though at a declining rate per dollar spent.

Several studies have estimated the price and income elasticities of demand for abortions.[67] The author have found that the demand for abortions is responsive to both price and income, although inelastic (with elasticities ranging from −0.35 to −0.81 with respect to price, and 0.79 to 0.84 with respect to income). These figures imply that a ten percent rise (fall) in the price of an abortion will lead to between a 3.5 and 8 percent fall (rise) in the number of abortions performed. One can analyze the effect of outlawing abortion through its effect on raising the price (as persons have to enter the black market or travel abroad to receive one). For instance, an increase in price of 50 percent would have led to a predicted decrease in 1992 of as many as 610,000 abortions. These decreases would have been caused both by an increase in contraceptive use and an increase in pregnancies carried to term.

Such a substantial decrease in abortions, to the extent that it would lead to an increase in births to poorer women, would again entail an increase in public spending. Studies of state medicaid abortion funding bans and restrictions are unanimous in finding that both bans and restrictions have a significant effect on increasing the birth rate among low-income women;[68] a widely-cited conservative estimate is that "20 percent of pregnancies that would have ended in abortion, were it not for Medicaid limitations, instead resulted in birth."[69] One study that looks not only at the public costs in the first two years, but also at the full present discounted future public cost of such a birth, found an estimated public cost of almost one hundred times the cost of fully funding the abortion.[70]

Summary

There are long-term trends of increasing divorce rates, falling birth and fertility rates, and a recent downturn in the marriage rate. These trends have resulted in a rising number of never-married persons, persons living alone, and single-parent families. While the coincidence of rising female labor force participation rates is notable, causal relationships run in both directions, and other forces, such as improved contraceptive technology, are important explanatory variables.

The effects of these trends on well-being are also hard to determine, particularly because the distribution of household types has been affected. While married-couple families generally have more earned income, the net effects on consumption of market and nonmarket goods are smaller, and there are fewer married-couple families. The effects on children of recent trends appear to be generally negative, as the children appear to have less access to family resources in the forms of money and parental time.

Endnotes

1. David E. Bloom and Neil G. Bennett, "Modeling American Marriage Patterns," *Journal of the American Statistical Association* 85, no. 412 (December 1990): 1009–1017.
2. *Current Population Reports Series P–20*, nos. 450 (Table 1); 491 (Table 1).
3. Thomas J. Espenshade, "Marriage Trends in America: Estimates, Implications, and Underlying Causes," *Population and Development Review* 11, no. 2 (June 1985): 193–245, contrasts the first four of these hypotheses.

4. C.f. M. Belinda Tucker and Claudia Mitchell-Kernan (eds.), *The Decline in Marriage Among African Americans: Causes, Consequences, and Policy Implications* (New York: Russell Sage, 1995).

5. B. F. Skinner, *Walden Two* (New York: Macmillan, Revised Edition, 1976): 121–122. Courtesy of the B.F. Skinner Foundation.

6. Marianne A. Ferber and Helen M. Berg, "Labor Force Participation of Women and the Sex Ratio: A Cross-Country Analysis," *Review of Social Economy* 49, no. 1 (Spring 1991): 2–19.

7. Sociologist Linda Waite, quoted in Laurie Goering, "Fewer Walking Down that Aisle," *Boston Globe* (August 9, 1992): 42.

8. Larry L. Bumpass and James A. Sweet, "National Estimates of Cohabitation: Cohort Levels and Union Stability," Center for Demography and Ecology, University of Wisconsin-Madison, National Survey of Families and Households Working Paper no. 2 (June 1989); Larry L. Bumpass, James A. Sweet, and Andrew Cherlin, "The Role of Cohabitation in Declining Rates of Marriage," Center for Demography and Ecology, University of Wisconsin-Madison, National Survey of Families and Households Working Paper no. 5 (August 1989).

9. Peter Jensen and Nina Smith, "Unemployment and Marital Dissolution," *Journal of Population Economics* 3, no. 3 (October 1990): 215–229, find, using Danish data, that unemployment of the husband is a causal factor of marital dissolution, while unemployment of the wife does not matter.

10. Parents are more likely to remain married if they have at least one son than if they have only daughters: see S. Philip Morgan, Diane N. Lye, and Gretchen A. Condran, "Sons, Daughters, and the Risk of Marital Disruption," *American Journal of Sociology* 94, no. 1 (July 1988): 110–129.

11. As more women become well-paid, they may have reduced incentive to divorce, given the (slightly) increased chance that they will end up having to pay alimony or child support; see Jane Bryant Quinn, "Sauce for the Goose," *Newsweek* (January 25, 1993): 64.

12. Lynn K. White, "Determinants of Divorce: A Review of Research in the Eighties," *Journal of Marriage and the Family* 52, no. 4 (November 1990): 904–912.

13. Robert T. Michael, "Why Did the U.S. Divorce Rate Double Within a Decade?" *Research in Population Economics* 6 (1988): 367–399.

14. Charles F. Westoff, "Fertility in the United States," *Science* 234, no. 4776 (October 31, 1986): 554–559.

15. One might consider this a switch to an ethos of individuality, or self-interest.

16. "Expenditures on a Child by Families: 1995 Report," Center for Nutrition Policy and Promotion, U.S. Department of Agriculture, Misc. Publication no. 1528. Figures are for husband-wife families.

17. Thomas J. Espenshade, *Investing in Children: New Estimates of Parental Expenditure* (Washington, D.C.: Urban Institute, 1984).

18. Espenshade, *op. cit.*: 66.

19. Edward P. Lazear and Robert T. Michael, *Allocation of Income Within the Household* (Chicago, Ill.: University of Chicago, 1988), is a detailed study of income allocation among household members; Martin Browning, "Children and Household Economic Behavior," *Journal of Economic Literature* 30, no. 3 (September 1992): 1434–1475, reviews several studies that attempt to calculate adult equivalence scales.

20. Robert A. Hatcher, Felicia Guest, Felicia Stewart, Gary K. Stewart, James Trussell, and Erica Frank, *Contraceptive Technology, 12th Revised Edition* (New York: Irvington, 1984): 56–57.

21. Of course, the parent may derive more utility from having a higher-earning child, therefore leading to the same investment pattern in the child's human capital as before.

22. William P. Butz and Michael P. Ward, "The Emergence of Countercyclical U.S. Fertility," *American Economic Review* 69, no. 3 (June 1979): 318–328. See Diane J. Macunovich, "The Butz-Ward Fertility Model in the Light of More Recent Data," *Journal of Human Resources* 30,

no. 2 (Spring 1995): 229–254 for a critique of these results; however in her study, "Relative Income and Price of Time: Exploring Their Effects on U.S. Fertility and Female Labor Force Participation," *Population and Development Review* 22, Supplement (1996): 223–257, she nonetheless finds a strong negative response of births to female wages, as well as a strong positive response of births to male relative income.

23. C.R. Winegarden, "Women's Fertility, Market Work and Marital Status: A Test of the New Household Economics with International Data," *Economica* 51, no. 204 (November 1984): 447–456.

24. James C. Cramer, "Fertility and Female Employment: Problems of Causal Direction," *American Sociological Review* 45, no. 2 (April 1980): 167–190.

25. James J. Heckman and James R. Walker, "The Relationship Between Wages and Income and the Timing and Spacing of Births: Evidence from Swedish Longitudinal Data," *Econometrica* 58, no. 6 (November 1990): 1411–1441.

26. Leslie A. Whittington, "Taxes and the Family: The Impact of the Tax Exemption for Dependents on Marital Fertility," *Demography* 24, no. 2 (May 1992): 215–226.

27. Nancy Folbre, "The Pauperization of Motherhood: Patriarchy and Public Policy in the United States," *Review of Radical Political Economics* 16, no. 4 (Winter 1984): 72.

28. Nancy Folbre, "Of Patriarchy Born: The Political Economy of Fertility Decisions," *Feminist Studies* 9, no. 2 (Summer 1983): 261–280.

29. Folbre (1983): 263.

30. Robert T. Michael, "Consequences of the Rise in Female Labor Force Participation Rates: Questions and Probes," *Journal of Labor Economics* 3, no. 1, supplement (January 1985): S117–S146.

31. Clair Brown, "Consumption Norms, Work Roles, and Economic Growth, 1918–80," *Gender in the Workplace*, eds. Clair Brown and Joseph A. Pechman (Washington, D.C.: Brookings Institution, 1987): 13–49 (with commentary following); *American Standards of Living* (Cambridge, Mass.: Blackwell, 1994).

32. Richard A. Easterlin, *Birth and Fortune: The Impact of Numbers on Personal Welfare, Second Edition* (Chicago, Ill.: University of Chicago, 1987).

33. *Statistical Abstract of the United States* (1996): 56 (Table 61).

34. Mary Jo Bane and David T. Ellwood, "Single Mothers and Their Living Arrangements," report prepared for U.S. Department of Commerce, no. PB84–196146 (Washington, D.C.: National Technical Information Service, March 1984). See George A. Akerlof, Janet L. Yellen, and Michael Katz, "An Analysis of Out-of-Wedlock Childbearing in the United States," *Quarterly Journal of Economics* 111, no. 2 (May 1996): 277–317, for a novel argument for why out-of-wedlock births have increased, relating the erosion of the shotgun marriage custom to increased availability of contraception and legal abortion.

35. *Statistical Abstract of the United States* (1996): (Table 90).

36. William Raspberry, "The Superfluous Father?" *Commercial Appeal* (January 28, 1992): A7; Jerry W. McCant, "The Cultural Contradiction of Fathers as Nonparents," *Family Law Quarterly* 21, no. 1 (Spring 1987): 127–143, discusses the existence of cultural discrimination against granting fathers full parental status in U.S. society.

37. Recall from Chapter 4 that quasi-fixed costs associated with market work may increase as another household member switches to market work, and that progressive tax systems will reduce the gain in marginal income if the family moves into a higher tax bracket. Edward P. Lazear and Robert T. Michael, "Real Income Equivalence among One-Earner and Two-Earner Families," *American Economic Review* 70, no. 2 (May 1980): 201–208, uses 1972–73 Consumer Expenditure Survey data to show that the after-tax income for married couples without children is only 25 percent higher for couples where both spouses work than for couples where only one spouse works; also total current consumption for the two-earner couples is only 17 percent higher.

38. James P. Smith, "The Distribution of Family Earnings," *Journal of Political Economy* 87, no. 5, part 2 (October 1979): S162–S192, using 1960 and 1970 Census data. See also Maria Cancian, Sheldon Danziger, and Peter Gottschalk, "Working Wives and Family Income Inequality Among Married Couples," *Uneven Tides: Rising Inequality in America*, eds. Sheldon Danziger and Peter Gottschalk (New York: Russell Sage, 1993): 195–221.

39. Smith, *loc. cit.*

40. *Employment and Earnings* 39, no. 1 (January 1992): 172 (Table 8), 216 (Table 49).

41. Leslie A. Morgan, *After Marriage Ends: Economic Consequences for Midlife Women* (Newbury Park, Calif.: Sage, 1991).

42. Analyses of the relative physical and mental health of employed and nonemployed women have yielded the result that employed women are either more or no less healthy and adjusted than nonemployed women. However, the usual problem of sample selection may be operating here: perhaps healthy women are more likely to become employed. See Margaret W. Matlin, *The Psychology of Women* (New York: Harcourt Brace Jovanovich, 1992): 184–188, for a discussion of these findings.

43. Victor R. Fuchs, *Women's Quest for Economic Equality* (Cambridge, Mass. Harvard University, 1988): 67.

44. Cf. Sylvia Ann Hewlett, *A Lesser Life: The Myth of Women's Liberation in America* (New York: William Morrow & Co., 1986).

45. Sandra L. Hofferth, "Long-Term Economic Consequences for Women of Delayed Childbearing and Reduced Family Size," *Demography* 21, no. 2 (May 1984): 141–155.

46. Claudia Goldin, "Career and Family: College Women Look to the Past," National Bureau of Economic Research Working Paper no. 5188 (July 1995).

47. Myra H. Strober, "The MBA: Same Passport to Success for Women and Men?" *Women in the Workplace*, ed. Phyllis A. Wallace (Boston, Mass.: Auburn House, 1982): 25–44.

48. *Statistical Abstract of the United States* (1996): 65 (Table 81).

49. Elizabeth Hervey Stephen, Vicki A. Freedman, and Jennifer Hess, "Near and Far: Contact of Children with Their Non-Residential Fathers," *Journal of Divorce and Remarriage* 20, nos. 3–4 (1993): 171–191, discuss the general infrequency of contact and the declining rate of contact in the years following divorce, particularly for nonresidential parents who do not pay child support.

50. *Current Population Reports Series P–60*, no. 194 (Table 2). Comparing the rates for persons under 18 to persons 18 to 64, the ratio is higher among blacks (1.86) than among Hispanics (1.60) or whites (1.69).

51. Victor R. Fuchs, "Why Are Children Poor?" National Bureau of Economic Research Working Paper no. 1984 (July 1986): 6 (Table 1).

52. Irwin Garfinkel and Sara S. McLanahan, *Single Mothers and Their Children: A New American Dilemma.* (Washington, D.C.: Urban Institute, 1986): 168.

53. "Teen Moms," *U.S. News & World Report* (November 11, 1996): 14.

54. Frank F. Furstenberg, Jr., Judith A. Levine, and Jeanne Brooks-Gunn, "The Children of Teenage Mothers: Patterns of Early Childbearing in Two Generations," *Family Planning Perspectives* 22, no. 2 (March/April 1990): 54–61.

55. This drop may be due at least in part to an expansion of the number of persons taking the test to include a larger percentage of those who are less academically capable; see the Focus on test bias in Chapter 7.

56. C. Everett Koop, *Shape Up America! Annual Report* (1996): 1. Fuchs, *op. cit.*: 110–113, suggests a possible causal chain for these trends: a decline in care and supervision by parents due to the rise in single-parent households and the increase in female participation, leading to a rise in the number of both "latchkey" children (who are self-supervising) and in the number of children who are (perhaps) more loosely supervised by nonparental adults; therefore the children spend more time watching television, which leads to obesity and lowered academic achievement.

57. Victor R. Fuchs and Diane M. Reklis, "America's Children: Economic Perspectives and Policy Options," *Science* 255 (January 3, 1992): 41; *Statistical Abstract of the United States* (1996): 89 (Table 120).

58. Fuchs and Reklis, *op. cit.*: 42 (Table 1); *Statistical Abstract of the United States* (1996): 15 (Table 14); 102 (Table 140); 204 (Table 315).

59. See Judith Wallerstein, *Second Chances: Men, Women, and Children a Decade after Divorce* (New York: Ticknor & Fields, 1989).

60. Researchers cited in Jane E. Brody, "Children of Divorce: Steps to Help Can Hurt," *New York Times* (July 23, 1991): C1, C9.

61. Data in this paragraph are from *Statistical Abstract of the United States* (1996): 86 (Tables 115, 116). Note that there is strong evidence of underreporting of abortions, with an estimate that only 40 to 60 percent of actual abortions are being reported in U.S. household surveys; see Elise F. Jones and Jacqueline Darroch Forrest, "Underreporting of Abortion in Surveys of U.S. Women: 1976 to 1986," *Demography* 29, no. 1 (February 1992): 113–126.

62. More recent data confirm this continued pattern; see United Nations Economic Commission for Europe, *Women and Men in Europe and North America 1995* (1995): 14.

63. Colin Francome, *Abortion Practice in Britain and the United States* (London: Allen & Unwin, 1986).

64. Jane Silverman and Elise F. Jones, "The Delivery of Family Planning and Health Services in Great Britain," *Family Planning Perspectives* 20, no. 2 (March/April 1988): 68–74.

65. Elise F. Jones, Jacqueline Darroch Forrest, Stanley K. Henshaw, Jane Silverman, and Aida Torres, "Unintended Pregnancy, Contraceptive Practices and Family Planning Services in Developed Countries," *Family Planning Perspectives* 20, no. 2 (March/April 1988): 53–67.

66. Jacqueline Darroch Forrest and Susheela Singh, "Public-Sector Savings Resulting from Expenditures for Contraceptive Services," *Family Planning Perspectives* 22, no. 1 (January/February 1990): 6–15.

67. Donna S. Rothstein, "An Economic Approach to Abortion Demand," *American Economist* 36, no. 1 (Spring 1992): 53–64; Christopher Garbacz, "Abortion Demand," *Population Research and Policy Review* 9, no. 2 (May 1990): 151–160; Marshall H. Medoff, "An Economic Analysis of the Demand for Abortions," *Economic Inquiry* 26, no. 2 (April 1988): 353–359.

68. See James Trussell, Jane Menken, Barbara L. Lindheim, and Barbara Vaughan, "The Impact of Restricting Medicaid Financing for Abortion," *Family Planning Perspectives* 12, no. 3 (May/June 1980): 120–130; Willard Cates, Jr., "The Hyde Amendment in Action: How Did the Restriction of Federal Funds for Abortion Affect Low-Income Women?" *Journal of the American Medical Association* 246, no. 10 (September 4, 1981): 1109–1112; Carol C. Korenbrot, Claire Brindis, and Fran Priddy, "Trends in Rates of Live Births and Abortions Following State Restrictions on Public Funding of Abortion," *Public Health Reports* 105, no. 6 (November-December 1990): 555–562; Deborah Haas-Wilson, "The Economic Impact of State Restrictions on Abortion: Parental Consent and Notification Laws and Medicaid Funding Restrictions," *Journal of Policy Analysis and Management* 12, no. 3 (Summer 1993): 498–511; Mark I. Evans, Elizabeth Gleicher, Eugene Feingold, Mark Paul Johnson, and Robert J. Sokol, "The Fiscal Impact of the Medicaid Abortion Funding Ban in Michigan," *Obstetrics and Gynecology* 82, no. 4, part 1 (October 1993): 555–560; Rebecca M. Blank, Christine C. George, and Rebecca A. London, "State Abortion Rates: The Impact of Policies, Providers, Politics, Demographics, and Economic Environment," *Journal of Health Economics* 15, no. 5 (October 1996): 513–553.

69. Evans *et al.*, *op. cit.*: 556.

70. Paul M. Sommers and Laura S. Thomas, "Restricting Federal Funds for Abortion: Another Look," *Social Science Quarterly* 64, no. 2 (June 1983): 340–346.

71. See Theodore C. Bergstrom and Mark Bagnoli, "Courtship as a Waiting Game," *Journal of Political Economy* 101, no. 1 (February 1993): 185–202, for data on mean ages of marriage by gender for a large number of countries and for an intriguing attempt to explain this phenomenon.

72. Folbre (1983): 279.

Further reading and statistical sources

Alan Guttmacher Institute. *Family Planning Perspectives*. Bimonthly issues, containing research articles utilizing data collected by Institute surveys of health practitioners on abortion and contraceptive use. The Institute operates a useful website (www.agi-usa.org).

——. *International Family Planning Perspectives*. Similar to the above publication, but with a focus on data from developing countries.

Browning, Martin (1992). "Children and Household Economic Behavior," *Journal of Economic Literature* 30, no. 3 (September): 1434–1475. Useful survey article covering the recent literature on estimating the demand for children and the effects of children on labor supply.

Fuchs, Victor R. (1988). *Women's Quest for Economic Equality*. Cambridge, Mass.: Harvard University. Highly readable discussion of women, work, and family issues in the United States since 1960, stressing how the task of childrearing shapes womens' lives.

National Center for Health Statistics. *Monthly Vital Statistics Reports*. Monthly issues providing more recent vital statistical data prior to publication in *Vital Statistics of the United States*. The NCHS operates a useful website (www.cdc.gov/nchswww/nchshome.htm).

——. *Vital Statistics of the United States*. Annual publication in three volumes containing statistics on birth, marriage, divorce, and death. Published with about a three-year lag, so statistics for 1988 were available starting in 1992.

Weitzman, Lenore, J., and Mavis Maclean (eds.) (1992). *Economic Consequences of Divorce: The International Perspective*. Oxford: Oxford University. Twenty-four papers, mostly by lawyers and sociologists, discuss divorce in different countries and focus on world changes in divorce laws and patterns.

Willis, Robert J. (1987). "What Have We Learned from the Economics of the Family?" *American Economic Review* 77, no. 2 (May): 68–81. Useful review article summarizing the major developments and listing important publications up through 1986 in family economics.

Discussion questions

1. Who do you believe receives more benefits on average from marriage, women or men?

2. Consider the Focus on early marriage. Do you think that a large proportion of people would choose to marry early if it were financially feasible to do so?

3. As is shown in Figure 5.1, the median age of first marriage for men is at all points in time above the median age for women. A direct implication of this, which is in fact generally true across societies and eras, is that women tend on average to marry men who are older than themselves.[71] Can you give an economic explanation for why this occurs?

4. What causes are mentioned herein regarding the fall in the marriage rate, rise in the divorce rate, and fall in the birth rate? Which causes would you consider more economic, and which more sociological? What other causes can you think of that are not discussed in this chapter?

5. For the five changes considered at length in this chapter (female labor force participation, median age at first marriage, marriage, divorce, and births), mention for each pair of variables an influence that would lead from one to the other in each causal direction – e.g., explain how the rising female participation rate could lead to the rising divorce rate, and explain how the rising divorce rate could lead to the rising female participation rate.

6. Do economic factors tend to affect timing rather than levels of demographic events? For example, do women who work tend to put off births until they are older, but still have as many children? Do women who work marry later, but still marry eventually?

7. Can the invention and improvement of contraceptive methods be considered truly exogenous? For instance, could changes in contraceptive technology have been caused by the increased female labor force participation rate?

8. Consider the Focus on higher education and family life. Do you think that gender differences are more or less likely to appear in more recent groups of MBA graduates? Do you think that gender differences are more or less likely to appear in more recent groups of college graduates?

9. Consider the following quote: "Childrearing in the United States today stands out as an activity that is conducted despite, rather than because of, economic self-interest."[72] Can you cite some evidence supporting this claim?

10. Consider the Focus on teenage mothers and the cycle of poverty. What kinds of public policies might help an even greater number of these daughters of teenage mothers to escape poverty, even after becoming teenage unwed mothers themselves?

11. If two households have identical opportunities for production of both market and nonmarket goods (i.e., identical productivity rates and the same number of persons), yet one household has two members doing market work, while the other has only one member doing market work, what can we conclude, if anything, about their relative well-being?

12. What effects would you predict of making more contraceptive methods (e.g., the pill) available on an over-the-counter basis rather than by prescription only?

13. Why would expanding government-subsidized contraception programs yield cost savings at a declining rate per dollar spent?

14. Taking into account the income elasticities of abortion reported in the text, what is the predicted effect of rising wages on the abortion rate, all else equal?

15. How would the short-run and long-run effects of outlawing abortion differ?

Part II
Policy application: Welfare Reform

Many government policies affect the decision whether or not to work and many government policies affect families, but few are as controversial as welfare. This discussion of welfare draws upon material from the preceding three chapters and shows how it is a necessary component for evaluating comprehensive social programs. We first outline the dimensions of poverty in the United States, and then discuss the possible effects of welfare programs on labor force participation, family formation and dissolution, and poverty. Then a variety of recently-implemented and alternative approaches to reforming welfare are considered, particularly with respect to whether they will reduce work disincentives relative to current programs, reduce female-headed family formation, and reduce poverty.

What is welfare?

In the United States, "welfare" is a combination of programs. Welfare programs include Aid to Families with Dependent Children (recently retitled Temporary Assistance for Needy Families – TANF, but I will still refer to it by its better-known acronym, AFDC), food subsidies – in the form of food stamps, WIC (Special Supplemental Food Program for Women, Infants and Children), and subsidized school lunches, health care provision under Medicaid, and housing assistance – either in the form of subsidies for privately provided housing, or in the form of public housing provided at below-market rental rates. These are all forms of *means-tested assistance*, where a person must have low income in order to qualify for the benefits. Table IIP.1 shows the percentages of both all persons and poor persons who receive means-tested assistance, for those in all forms of living arrangements and for those in female-headed families.[1] Over one in four persons live in households that receive some form of means-tested assistance. The rates of reliance on these forms of assistance are much higher for persons in female-headed families.

Who is poor?

What percentage of the population is poor, and who is more likely to experience poverty? Poverty is defined relative to an income threshold, or poverty line, which varies by family size and number of adults in the family. In 1995, families with two adults and two children with income below $15,455 were considered poor; the line for families with one adult and two children was $12,278.[2] Using U.S. poverty line definitions, almost one out of seven persons is poor. The probability by race varies noticeably: almost one out of three blacks is poor, and about two out of every seven persons of Hispanic origin. Over time, the percentage of persons in poverty has decreased, but it has risen from its low point in recent years. Also, different demographic groups experience very different poverty rates. Table IIP.2 shows that the percentage of persons in poverty has declined overall since 1959, but has actually risen since 1970. And even though poverty rates have fallen substantially for blacks, they are still substantially higher than the overall poverty rate; rates for Hispanics are higher than for whites and are rising.

TABLE IIP.1   Percentage of persons living in households receiving means-tested assistance, 1995

	Any such assistance	Assistance, excluding school lunches	Medicaid	Food stamps	Cash assistance	Public or subsidized housing
All persons	27.0	21.4	17.9	10.6	10.3	4.5
Poor persons	74.0	65.6	56.7	48.9	39.1	18.8
In families with female head	60.5	51.4	45.1	35.4	32.8	15.6
In poor families with female head	92.0	84.8	76.5	71.8	61.4	32.2

Source: U.S. Census Bureau, unpublished data from the March 1996 Current Population Survey.

TABLE IIP.2   Percentage of persons in poverty by family type, all and by race and Hispanic origin, 1959 to 1995

	1959	1970	1980	1990	1995
All persons	22.4	12.6	13.0	13.5	13.8
in families – female householder	49.4	38.1	36.7	37.2	36.5
in families – other	18.2	7.6	7.4	7.1	7.2
unrelated individuals	46.1	32.9	22.9	20.7	20.9
White	18.1	9.9	10.2	10.7	11.2
in families – female householder	40.2	28.4	28.0	29.8	29.7
in families – other	14.7	6.3	6.4	6.2	6.6
unrelated individuals	44.1	30.8	20.4	18.6	19.0
Black	55.1	33.5	32.5	31.9	29.3
in families – female householder	70.6	58.7	53.4	50.6	48.2
in families – other	50.8	20.9	16.0	14.9	10.8
unrelated individuals	57.0	48.3	41.0	35.1	32.6
Hispanic origin	—	24.3	25.7	28.1	30.3
in families – female householder	—	51.5	54.5	53.0	52.8
in families – other	—	19.0	18.0	19.9	22.1
unrelated individuals	—	30.0	32.2	34.3	37.0

Source: Current Population Reports Series P-60, no. 194 (Table C-1); 1970 Hispanics: no. 81 (Table 7).

A crucial determinant of the overall poverty rate is the relative proportion of families who are female-headed. As shown in Table IIP.2, persons in these families are more likely to experience poverty than are other persons; and, as shown in Table IIP.3, the proportion of such families has been rising over time.

Even though the percentage of persons in female-headed families who are poor has dropped, they comprise a higher proportion of the poor. Persons in female-headed families have risen from less than one out of five persons in poverty to almost two out of five. Among poor blacks, persons in female-headed families comprise two-thirds of the poor, up from less than one-quarter in 1959.[3]

TABLE IIP.3   Female-headed families as a percentage of families, all and by race and Hispanic origin, 1960 to 1995

	1960	1970	1980	1990	1995
All families	10.0	10.8	15.1	16.5	17.6
white	8.7	9.6	11.9	12.9	13.7
black	22.4	28.3	41.7	43.8	45.9
Hispanic origin	—	16.7*	21.8	23.1	24.0

* Figure is for 1972.
Sources: 1960–80 – *Current Population Reports Series P-60*, nos. 68, 81 (Table E), 91 (Table 45), 133 (Tables 18, 39); 1990–95 – *Current Population Reports Series P-20*, nos. 447, 488 (Table 17).

Family recomposition has had a striking effect on children's living arrangements. Well over twice as great a percentage of children live in female-headed families now as in 1959: up from 9 percent in 1959 to 23.6 percent in 1995. For blacks, the percentage has risen to over one out of two children. Not surprisingly, the percentage of poor children who live in female-headed families has had a corresponding rise: from 24.1 percent in 1959 to 57 percent in 1995.[4] This increase was fueled mainly by the increase in the percentage of poor black children in female-headed households.

In conclusion, while a majority of persons in poverty are white (over two-thirds in 1995) and do not live in female-headed households, the incidence rates of poverty are much higher for female-headed and minority households. Therefore, poverty analysts recently have focused on the needs of these households in trying to devise methods for reducing the proportion of them in poverty.

*E*ffects of welfare programs

Welfare programs can have both good and bad effects on participants. Possible good effects include increasing the well-being (and often the income) of poor families. Welfare reduces insecurity for families concerning future income flow. It allows people to avoid "settling" for bad jobs, which is also an argument in support of unemployment compensation (although one might still want to set a time limit on payments, as with unemployment compensation). Some analysts have argued that the existence of welfare programs leads to better mental health and better school achievement among recipients, perhaps due to less fluctuation of income for these households. And welfare can allow persons to escape bad living situations, such as a bad marriage, which they otherwise would have to stay in out of need for the income provided by their spouse.

Possible bad effects include the stigma that recipients experience (although this can provide an incentive for people to get off welfare); poor mental health; reduction of work and, therefore, earned income for these households; and effects on family formation and dissolution. Some marriages that would have actually increased well-being for recipients in the long run may dissolve, or not occur at all.

In measuring welfare program effects, analysts are once again faced with the sample selection problem. For instance, in noting that persons on welfare may have low motivation and poor mental health, one must ask whether these phenomena are caused by welfare or are the reasons why people are on welfare.

Analysts agree that the existence of welfare reduces the amount of work done by recipients. While it is true that households receive benefits from participating in welfare, in the form of both nonearned income and additional time that can be spent in nonmarket activities, there are three reasons why the long-run costs of work reduction may outweigh the short-term benefits for welfare recipients. First, persons may have reduced incentive to invest in education and training that would improve their future earnings potential. Second, work skills that recipients currently possess may depreciate due to disuse. Third, a cycle of low motivation and consequent dependency on government aid may start, in which persons become less desirable workers through inactivity and reduce their probability of achieving future employment.

Social benefits and costs associated with welfare programs involve different considerations than individual recipient benefits and costs. Welfare programs are costly, in terms of both monetary outlay and the foregone output that could have been produced by persons on welfare. Mothers, however, may create more social benefit by staying home with their children than going out to work. The primary government consideration behind welfare reform may be to reduce the costs of running welfare programs, but generally consideration is given as well to whether welfare recipients would be made better off by being required to work more or to enter into training programs.

In analyzing welfare program effects, economists have concentrated on examining the nature and extent of work disincentives and discussing the effects of welfare on family formation and dissolution. We now consider these two areas in more detail.

Welfare and the labor-leisure tradeoff

Figure IIP.1 illustrates two possible forms that a welfare program might take. In each case, the existence of a welfare program affects an individual's budget constraint and, therefore, the choice of consumption (C) and leisure (L). Recall that "leisure" includes all nonmarket activities, including recreation, housework, and child care. In each case, if a person does not work at all, he/she is guaranteed a level of nonearned income W. In case (i), this income is available until a person's total income (earned income plus W) equals P. After this point, W is taken away at the rate of a dollar for every dollar of earned income, for an effective tax rate on earned income of 100 percent. In case (ii), the amount of nonearned income is immediately reduced for every dollar of earned income at an effective tax rate of t, so that net earned income per hour of work equals $(1 - t)w$, where w is the wage rate. By the time the person's total income equals P, all the nonearned income has been taken away.

We can now compare a person's choice of consumption and leisure under the situations of no welfare available and welfare available. Figure IIP.2 shows the three possible choices under a welfare program of the type shown in Figure IIP.1 (i). Consider a person who is earning income exactly equal to the designated poverty level before this welfare program is enacted. In each case, the person has increased utility through participating in the program, and reduces hours of work. The choice of how much to reduce time spent in market work depends on the person's relative preferences for consumption versus leisure. In case (i), the person can maintain the same level of consumption as before, but can reduce work and increase leisure from L_x to L'_x. In case (ii), a person with a relatively great preference for leisure reduces work even more, resulting in a level of income and consumption below the poverty level. In case (iii), the person has an even greater relative preference for leisure, and stops doing market work entirely; in this case, all income is nonearned income in the form of welfare payments.

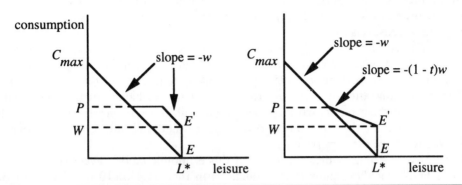

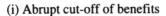

FIGURE IIP.1   Effects of welfare on the budget constraint

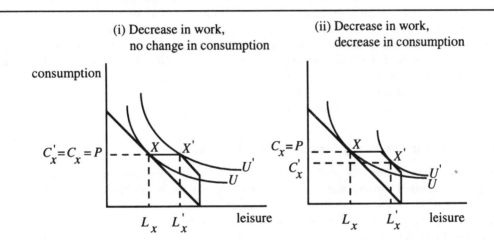

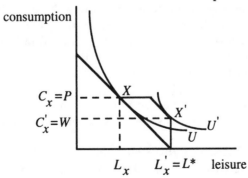

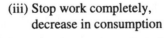

FIGURE IIP.2   Possible effects of welfare

Figure IIP.2 illustrates the work disincentives involved in welfare programs. This is a standard result for any program that causes people to experience an increase in potential nonearned income. Even persons who are earning income above the poverty level before the welfare program is instituted may decide to reduce earned income so as to qualify for welfare and increase leisure.

This analysis does not imply that persons on welfare will necessarily stop working completely. In fact, workers comprise a relatively high proportion of the poor: 41 percent of the poor reported working in 1995, and it is likely that many of the rest have earnings or other income that they are reluctant to report for fear of having their benefits reduced. However, few of them report working year-round, full-time: 10 percent in 1995.[5] This is not surprising, because those persons who work year-round, full-time, generally earn enough money to rise above the poverty line.

There is very strong evidence in favor of this economic model. Every study of welfare programs finds that they cause work reductions in the range of 10 to 50 percent of the number of hours of work that would be supplied if welfare were not available.[6] However, not many people appear to reduce their work so as to become eligible for welfare; some 95 percent would still be eligible if they continued working at their pre-welfare levels.[7]

This analysis of welfare programs and work incentives has two implications for why we might expect rates of welfare recipiency to vary by sex. First, if women have relatively greater preferences for time spent in nonmarket activities, they are more likely to be on welfare. This can occur because they have greater responsibilities for child care, which tend to increase the value of their nonmarket time. Second, if women face a lower potential wage than men, they will be less likely to work. So any factor that lowers their wage relative to men will tend to increase their relative proportion on welfare.

Effects of welfare on family formation and dissolution

The question of whether U.S. welfare policy has caused a sharp reduction in the number of two-parent families among the poor has generated a raging debate. In particular, the question of whether the precipitous rise in female-headed families that began in the 1960s was caused mainly by the development of AFDC has been answered both affirmatively and negatively by different commentators.[8] One view is that welfare policy has no effect on the formation of female-headed families, but that a generous welfare policy would lead to no more poor female-headed families. The opposite view is that overly generous welfare policies multiply the number of female-headed families and make children worse off. The truth appears to lie somewhere in between. Two welfare analysts, after reviewing the results of a range of studies, argue that welfare (in particular, AFDC) accounted for between 9 and 14 percent of the increase in female-headed families in the 1960s and early 1970s.[9] But AFDC does not seem to account for the continued increase in female-headed families, because real benefits from AFDC and food stamps have been dropping: average welfare benefits were 22 percent lower in value in 1981 than in 1970.[10] The analysts instead consider the rise in female-headed families to be more attributable to the fact that women now earn more, which reduces the costs of being single and increases the likelihood of marital disruption.

Additionally, for blacks, analysts argue that the high unemployment rates of black males appear to preclude their becoming stable marriage partners. In the 1970s and 1980s, the ratio of employed black men to young black women dropped considerably as black male unemployment, discouraged worker, and incarceration rates rose. Some analysts consider that this ratio is a key determinant of black poverty rates through its effect of reducing black marriage rates.[11] A problem with this explanation, however, is that the marriage rate has declined for both unemployed and employed black men. One study has found that while both work and earnings are strong predictors of marriage, they do not explain the difference in marriage rates between blacks and whites: blacks have become increasingly less likely to marry, but, from 1970 to 1980, only a small fraction of the change in marriage rates can be explained by changes in economic performance.[12]

Another source of information on the effect of AFDC on family formation beside the historical record is the variation in AFDC levels across states. Since states individually set benefit levels, a large range of benefits has developed across states; this range appears to exceed interstate differences in living costs and wage levels.[13] Nonetheless, studies have found no obvious relationship between the percentage of children not living in two-parent families and AFDC benefit levels; the same is true for other measures of family structure, such as divorce rates and out-of-wedlock birth rates, even when other socioeconomic characteristics that differ across states are statistically controlled.[14]

Most economists who have surveyed the welfare literature would agree with the statement that "virtually all careful studies of the effects of the current welfare system suggest that even relatively large variations in welfare benefits across states or over time can account for only small differences in family structure."[15] In addition, those studies that find some effect do not conclude that these effects are necessarily bad. For instance, one study points out that an increase in AFDC benefits would theoretically reduce the probability that women would bother to search for a husband and would tend to increase the duration of search for those who continue to look, as they can afford to be picky. Therefore, the probability of marriage is reduced over a fixed time period. While the researcher finds this to be the case, he argues that this may be good because people will end up making better matches when they do marry.[16] Economists, therefore, tend to consider the work disincentive effects to be the most clearly proven negative effect of current welfare programs, and their suggestions for welfare reform have tended to focus on reduction of work disincentives and ways to build actual work incentives into welfare. However, welfare reform suggestions often address the problem of family dissolution as well.

Approaches to welfare reform

Approaches to welfare reform have taken several very different tacks. Some propose to reduce the effective tax rate on earned income. Others involve increasing the level of non-earned income made available to households, while others involve decreasing the level. Finally, there are programs that switch to a greater proportion of cash benefits, versus those that move away from provision of cash benefits. We will now consider several types of proposals, ranging from completely discontinuing welfare to switching to a more holistic service provision system. Generally the more comprehensive proposals involve spending more on services for the poor in the short run, with the goal of reducing the number of recipients and the amount of money devoted to welfare programs in the long run. We will conclude by outlining the 1996 welfare reform act and considering some of its potential effects.

Welfare benefit reduction

The simplest proposal is to either greatly reduce benefits or do away with the welfare system completely. Benefit reduction has the income effect of increasing work; however, people will clearly be worse off in the short run, and may continue to be worse off in the long run, as well, if their earnings fail to pull them out of poverty. Exemptions would be granted for disabled persons and, under some proposals, for single mothers. However, the existence of such exemptions would lead to incentives for persons to attempt to be classified as exempt. Some level of minimal charitable help, such as soup kitchens and homeless shelters, would no doubt continue to be provided by both private and public agencies and would probably need to be expanded. While such proposals seem heartless to many, others argue that this "cold turkey" approach is the best way to cut the perceived cycle of work motivation reduction and increasing dependency that welfare may breed.

A somewhat less drastic proposal is to put a time limit on benefits, perhaps reducing them gradually as time on welfare lengthens. This would encourage people to treat welfare as a temporary benefit, as unemployment compensation is intended to be. Currently the pool of welfare recipients is skewed towards long-term dependency: while 30 percent of recipients are on welfare for two years or less, 40 percent spend three to seven years on welfare, and 30 percent spend eight or more years on welfare. This final group comprises 65 percent of the monthly caseload, so their situation is the most noticeable.[17] If these long-term recipients comprise an important part of a self-perpetuating underclass, limiting benefit recipiency may be the only way to break this cycle.[18]

Expansion of universal benefits

Conversely, some analysts argue that expansion of universal benefits (non-means-tested) will obviate the need for specific welfare programs. Such expansion will have the income effect of potentially decreasing work, but will actually improve work incentives relative to welfare for those currently not working. This occurs because universal benefits have no implicit tax. For instance, a study using data for Great Britain from 1973 to 1982, when the welfare program had a 100 percent implicit tax, finds that higher nonearned income (other than welfare) increases the probability of single mothers' working, while a higher guaranteed welfare benefit reduces it.[19] Such universal benefits could include a refundable tax credit that would serve as a "safety net," guaranteeing one-half to two-thirds of the poverty line,[20] or child and adult allowances, in which each person receives a certain amount of income whether or not they file a tax return.

A slightly less than universal benefit that might still have a substantial work incentive effect is to have the government guarantee provision of fringe benefits supporting work effort, such as child care and health insurance, even at very low levels of work. One study finds that single mothers' labor supply is reponsive to child care subsidies: a 50-percent subsidy increases the probability that a black single mother is employed from 25 percent to 28 percent, and free care raises the probability to 33 percent. A much larger effect is found for whites, where a 50-percent subsidy increases the probability that a white single mother is employed from 30 percent to 50 percent, and free care raises the probability to 70 percent.[21] Another study finds that a woman's health affects her work effort and potential earnings, and that children's health affects the hours a woman has available to work. This suggests that policies that directly affect the budget constraint, such as those that reduce the

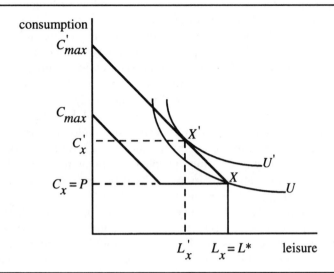

FIGURE IIP.3 Effects of substituting child support payments for welfare for currently nonworking parent

effective tax rate, are unlikely to increase labor force participation for single mothers in poor health or with disabled children. The researchers find that extending health insurance coverage to all children of single mothers without respect to AFDC status would induce a large percentage of these mothers to seek and accept employment, as would a plan that covers all workers who work over 15 hours a week.[22]

Increasing child support

A potential source of nonearned income for female-headed households that does not have the work disincentive effects of welfare programs is child support. This source has come under increased scrutiny by policymakers, both because it has the potential of reducing the use of governmental funds and because it has widespread public appeal.[23] In 1991, of women raising children with absent fathers, 56 percent were awarded child support; 76 percent of these women actually received support, and it comprised 17 percent of their total income. Of these women, 39 percent of those below the poverty level were awarded child support; 70 percent actually received it, and it comprised 34 percent of their total income.[24] It is clear that an increased level of support for these women would be helpful for improving their well-being.

Figure IIP.3 demonstrates that not only will women be better off receiving child support in place of welfare payments, but their work effort will tend to increase. Child support provides nonearned income but steepens the slope of the budget constraint for low-income persons because, unlike welfare, it is not taken away if income is earned. If we assume the amount of child support to be equal to the amount of welfare payment P, so that the person becomes ineligible for welfare, the unambiguous result is an increase in well-being and an increase in work, shown as a movement from X to X'.

Several studies support this prediction. One recent study finds that young mothers who receive child support are more likely to work than nonrecipients.[25] Another study finds that women with child support tend to have higher earnings and work longer hours than women who do not, even after controlling for differences in education and work experience.[26]

Another study ran simulations to estimate how much improving child support payment amount and delivery would reduce the poverty rate for female-headed households.[27] The authors found that improved enforcement of current child support awards would not greatly reduce welfare expenditures or the proportion of poor single mothers. If, however, more women were awarded child support and were faithfully paid either by the father or the government, their poverty incidence would be reduced by one-fourth. To eliminate poverty among single mothers through this mechanism, child support would have to be delivered at levels two to three times the current amounts. The authors point out: "At these levels the father's ability to pay becomes problematic in many cases. Thus better child support, even if strictly administered, cannot by itself be realistically expected to solve the problem of poverty for single mothers and their children."[28]

Given that many fathers lack the ability to pay child support at a level that would lift their children out of poverty, many policymakers are considering the feasibility of setting up child support assurance systems. Such a system would attempt to hold noncustodial parents to their child support obligations while, at the same time, guaranteeing a minimum assured benefit to single-parent families.[29]

Another reason why improved child support collection is an appealing avenue of reform is the possibility that incentives for men both to father children out of wedlock and to divorce would be reduced. Conversely, incentives for women in these circumstances are increased! One study which attempts to see which of these two effects prevails finds that stronger child support enforcement appears to reduce marital breakup.[30] However, along with wielding the "stick" of increased child support payments to change men's incentives, it also may be profitable to add a "carrot" to change incentives for both sexes to make having children while one is young less appealing. One welfare analyst has proposed offering a voucher to teenagers (both men and women) in impoverished families in "underclass" areas, conditional on their remaining childless and finishing high school with a reasonable academic record. This voucher could then be used to pay for college, vocational training, or on-the-job training in a community service job.[31]

FOCUS

Making noncustodial parents pay

Almost one child in five in Massachusetts is covered by a child support order. By 1992, the Massachusetts State Revenue Department had spent five years combing through records to create a revealing financial dossier on 72,000 divorced, noncustodial parents (of whom over 90 percent are fathers).[32] The Revenue Department has developed a set of computer programs that match computer data files containing child support orders with files containing state tax returns, bank reports on accountholders' interest income, lottery winners, and recipients of workers' compensation. This comparison enables Revenue Department officials to attach bank accounts, real estate, workers' compensation payments, and even lottery winnings in order to meet child support obligations. For instance, the Revenue Department has increased child support payments from workers' compensation from $5 million to $20 million annually.

The analysis found that many absent fathers conceal wealth, or otherwise avoid paying a level of child support they could afford. For example, there were 1300 cases in which the Revenue Department discovered that missing fathers own investment real estate, while their former wives are collecting AFDC payments. This led Revenue Commissioner Mitchell Adams to comment that the department was "collecting probably only one-quarter of the child support that could be fairly collected." Another state official commented that the data supported the idea that "the average child support order should be much higher than it is, perhaps 50 to 100 percent higher," arguing that as a result, the state "could make a big dent in the welfare population."

Less optimistic analysts such as Stuart Miller, senior legislative analyst for the American Fathers Coalition, point out that a significant number of nonpaying fathers are imprisoned, often because of child support noncompliance.[33] Additionally, Miller states that many other delinquent fathers are "addicts, alcoholics, disabled, mentally incapacitated, unemployed," or even dead (with a 1992 General Accounting Office report estimating that this is the case in as many as 14 percent of delinquency cases).

Workfare

Another possibility is to convert welfare to a work-relief or guaranteed jobs program – i.e., "workfare." The call has been increasing over time for enforcement of mandatory work requirements for all able-bodied people on welfare, including mothers of young children, particularly as the overall rate of labor force participation has been rising for these mothers. The notion of entitlement has fallen out of favor in the United States. However, workfare is popular not just because it is felt that the poor "owe it" to society to help support themselves but because it may benefit recipients as well. For instance, it has been suggested that workfare will improve social behavior and social and psychological standing for participants,[34] and that it can open a door on a wider world for poor persons, particularly mothers who before had been confined mainly to their homes and to the social circle of their immediate family.[35] Participants in current state-run programs generally do experience increased earnings. However, welfare programs involving a substantial work requirement actually cost more to run than basic welfare.

Holistic approach – the case-based method

A worry of many social service professionals is that welfare reform proposals that focus on improving work incentives without addressing other needs of poor families are superficial solutions to the deeper problems of poverty. They often advocate a switch to a service-delivery method of administering welfare that would combine social service provision with cash payments and attempt to reduce the amount of cash support received by poor families, while continuing to provide social services. This approach generally takes the form of empowering case workers to arrange for delivery of a wide range of services to their clients, including psychological counseling for individuals and families, child care of an educational nature, job training and placement, and educational support for children. The payoff from such programs may be more from keeping the children from following in their parents' footsteps than from getting the parents themselves off welfare.

While such programs are appealing in their intent to recognize the complicated dynamics of poverty, economists are generally skeptical of their ability to realize their lofty goals. Economists have generally taken the view that the best way to reduce poverty is either to provide enough money for families to rise above the poverty line or to provide families with a level of work skills that will enable them to rise above the line by themselves. Families with higher income would then be able to provide services directly for their children. This direct approach appears to be more cost-effective in the short run, but is open to the criticism that it perpetuates dependency in the long run. However, publicly funded programs with long-run goals that have high costs in the short run appear doomed to failure by the short evaluation horizons of federal, state, and local governments.

FOCUS

The Free the Children antipoverty program

The city of Memphis, located in Shelby County, Tennessee, has a large poor black population and is one of the poorest cities in the United States. In 1987 the Memphis area was reported to have a 20 percent poverty rate, the highest rate of the 100 largest metropolitan areas in the country.[36] In 1986 a Culture of Poverty Think Tank was appointed by County Mayor Bill Morris to consider how to improve this situation. The think tank's 1987 report, "Free the Children: Breaking the Cycle of Poverty," advocated a joint city-county government 10-year program to reduce the county's welfare rolls by at least 74 percent by December 31, 1997 "by providing jobs, job training, affordable housing, improved education and the self-motivating incentive of hope."[37] The program would begin with a year-long demonstration project that would target a low-income neighborhood and work with a group of families in the neighborhood to attempt to improve their well-being.

In April 1988 the Free the Children Program was launched. An office was opened in the designated Free the Children neighborhood, which consisted of four census tracts containing about 11,000 people in 1980. This was clearly a highly segregated neighborhood in severe trouble: over 96 percent of the residents were black, 59 percent qualified for welfare programs, and 80 percent of the births to residents were illegitimate. A total of 125 families were chosen to participate in the pilot program through an application process aimed at enrolling a variety of family types. The pilot program consisted of assigned caseworkers who were to "help clients finish school and get job training, jobs, day care for children, and decent housing."[38] Funds were shifted from other antipoverty programs run by the county.

The local newspaper, The Commercial Appeal, continued to report on Free the Children at regular intervals during the first year, creating a regular column. One of the first activities associated with the program was to take a census of the area, which showed that the population had declined to less than 6000 residents since 1980, and that 895 homes and other buildings had been demolished in the area since 1980.[39] Additional stories highlighted grants received by the program and private charitable agencies and local businesses that offered services and jobs to program participants.

When the one-year anniversary of the Program rolled around, however, a lack of progress was apparent. Although the enrolled families were supposed to have committed to formal plans to get out of poverty, the plans had not yet even been created.[40] The Commercial Appeal ran a supportive article on the program, optimistically titled "Poverty Battlers Learning Lessons: Old Mistakes Shunned,"[41] and then began to phase out its coverage, so that by the following year, the program had almost completely disappeared from public notice. While some activity continued in the area – notably, the building of several new low-cost single-family homes by the local chapter of the national charity Habitat for Humanity – the Free the Children Program had effectively become yet another government social service agency, rather than the comprehensive program it had strived to become. No formal evaluation of the first year was performed, the original lofty goal of welfare roll reduction of 74 percent by 1997 was never mentioned, and Mayor Bill Morris never mentioned the program in public at all.

Recent welfare reform in the U.S.

Recent changes in the U.S. have led to the dismantling of the federal system in favor of a system wherein states are given federal welfare funds to spend essentially as they please. The 1996 Personal Responsibility and Work Opportunity Reconciliation Act, which fulfilled President Clinton's campaign pledge to "end welfare as we know it," can be viewed as the culmination of a series of events that began when several pieces of Reagan-era federal legislation encouraged development of state-run workfare programs. In 1981 OBRA (Omnibus Budget Reconciliation Act) gave states power and flexibility in designing workfare programs; CWEP (Community Work Experience Program) allowed states to require AFDC recipients to work in public or nonprofit agencies. Additionally, states were allowed to divert welfare grants to use as wage subsidies for private employers. The Family Support Act of 1988 required mothers on AFDC with children over age three (or over age one at state option) to participate in job training, education, job search, or job placement. Transitional support services, including child care, were to be provided for one year following AFDC ineligibility due to increased earnings.

States operate under several constraints if they want to continue to receive federal support for their welfare recipients. Adults cannot receive more than two consecutive years of benefits, and no more than five years worth in their lifetime. States must cut benefits of mothers who refuse to cooperate in locating fathers who are in child support arrears. Federal aid is unavailable for unmarried teen parents who are not living at home or under adult supervision, and teen parents must attend school. States will be penalized by losing part of their lump-sum grant if they do not get a significant percentage of recipients to work. Finally, the five states showing the largest percentage reductions in out-of-wedlock births by October 1998 receive bonuses.

Most states have responded to these challenges by implementing a wide range of plans, some of which had already been operating as experiments under federal regulation waivers implemented before the 1996 law took effect. Some of the most striking are Wisconsin (stringent work requirements in order to receive cash assistance, which appear to have caused a drop in the caseload even before 1996), Connecticut (single mothers can receive full welfare benefits up to earnings of $13,000 annually), and Oregon (which will use some of its funds for wage subsidies).[42] The plans combine elements of all the reform approaches outlined above. From a social scientist standpoint, this has created a fascinating social experiment as 50 different plans are implemented simultaneously, and welfare researchers will be busy for the next few years assesssing what works and what does not.

Concerns of plan opponents have in large part focused on the fear that welfare recipients will remain impoverished once their benefits are cut and will not receive adequate training to ever escape poverty through their own work efforts. It is quite plausible that many current recipients have such a low potential wage and such high potential quasi-fixed costs (e.g., child care and transportation), that even if they worked long hours they would not be able to escape poverty. Studies of the literacy and basic skill attainment of AFDC recipients show that a majority have very low levels, making it difficult for them to obtain employment, let alone well-paying employment.[43]

Strikingly, the one policy that has apparently has had an effect on poverty reduction is the Earned Income Tax Credit, which allows low-income persons to claim a refundable (i.e., payable, rather than merely offsetting tax liabilities) tax credit of up to 40 percent of earnings.[44] This program has been around since 1975, but was expanded significantly in 1993, notably by making welfare recipients eligible. Approximately 14 million families received the credit as of 1995. While this policy has not been considered a welfare program due to its focus on the working poor, it restores work incentive, does not carry stigma, and is closest in form to the negative income tax proposals (wherein both taxes and transfers are handled through the income tax system) which many economists have advocated for decades as an alternative to the complicated tax and transfer system that has developed in the U.S.

Endnotes

1. Many people who are not technically in poverty receive these forms of assistance. However, all poor persons do not receive government assistance. While the coverage rate has risen over time, there are people who either choose not to participate in these programs or are not aware that they are eligible for them.

2. *Current Population Reports Series P-60*, no. 194 (Table 1). The poverty lines are based roughly on calculations of the amount of money needed to purchase food for a basic nutritious diet and then increased by a factor related to the proportion of a household budget devoted to food. The definitions are then increased each year to adjust for inflation. The use of income to determine poverty status has been criticized because it ignores various noncash benefits (such as housing subsidies and food stamps) that increase consumption levels for poor households; cf. "Measuring the Effect of Benefits and Taxes on Income and Poverty: 1979 to 1991," *Current Population Reports Series P-60*, no. 182-RD. Another problem with arriving at an accurate head count for those in poverty is income underreporting; people may underreport in order to be eligible for various benefit programs. Corrections for these factors would reduce the number of persons in poverty.

3. *Current Population Reports Series P-60*, no. 194 (Table C-1).

4. *Current Population Reports Series P-60*, no. 194 (Table 2).

5. *Current Population Reports Series P-60*, no. 194 (Table 3).

6. Robert Moffitt, "Incentive Effects of the U.S. Welfare System: A Review," *Journal of Economic Literature* 30, no. 1 (March 1992): 16.

7. Moffitt, *op. cit.*: 17.

8. Charles Murray, *Losing Ground: American Social Policy, 1950–1980* (New York: Basic Books, 1984), is the book best known for fueling this debate. James Patterson, *America's Struggle Against Poverty, 1900–1980* (Cambridge, Mass. Harvard University, 1981), is a comprehensive history of U.S. twentieth century social policy through 1980.

9. Irwin Garfinkel and Sara S. McLanahan, *Single Mothers and Their Children* (Washington, D.C.: Urban Institute, 1986): 167. Note that this is a different assertion than saying that AFDC does not have a large influence on the creation of female-headed households; AFDC does increase the number of such households, because single mothers are more likely to become household heads. (Otherwise, they might have lived with their parents or other relatives.)

10. David T. Ellwood and David T. Rodda, "The Hazards of Work and Marriage: The Influence of Male Employment on Marriage Rates," Malcolm Wiener Center for Social Policy, Kennedy School of Government Paper no. H-90–5 (March 1991): 2. Benefit levels, unlike the poverty level, are not indexed to inflation but are raised at the will of state legislatures.

11. William Julius Wilson and Katherine M. Neckerman, "Poverty and Family Structure: The Widening Gap Between Evidence and Public Policy Issues," *Fighting Poverty: What Works and What Doesn't*, eds. Sheldon Danziger and Daniel Weinberg (Cambridge, Mass.: Harvard University, 1986): 232–259.

12. Ellwood and Rodda, *op. cit.*: 22.

13. Paul E. Peterson and Mark C. Rom, *Welfare Magnets: A New Case for a National Standard* (Washington, D.C.: Brookings, 1990).
14. David T. Ellwood and Lawrence H. Summers, "Is Welfare Really the Problem?" *The Public Interest* 83 (Spring 1986): 57–78.
15. Ellwood and Rodda, *op. cit.*: 1.
16. Robert M. Hutchens, "Welfare, Remarriage, and Marital Search," *American Economic Review* 69, no. 3 (June 1979): 369–379.
17. Garfinkel and McLanahan, *op. cit.*: 169–170.
18. Christopher Jencks and Paul E. Peterson (eds.), *The Urban Underclass* (Washington, D.C.: Brookings, 1991). Ken Auletta, *The Underclass* (New York: Random House, 1982), provides a general treatment of the subject.
19. John F. Ermisch and Robert E. Wright, "Welfare Benefits and Lone Parents' Employment in Great Britain," *Journal of Human Resources* 26, no. 3 (Summer 1991): 424–456.
20. Robert H. Haveman, "New Policy for the New Poverty," *Challenge* 31, no. 5 (September–October 1988): 33–34.
21. Jean Kimmel, "The Effectiveness of Child-Care Subsidies in Encouraging the Welfare-to-Work Transition of Low-Income Single Mothers," *American Economic Review* 85, no. 2 (May 1995): 271–275.
22. Barbara L. Wolfe and Steven C. Hill, "The Effect of Health on the Work Effort of Low-Income Single Mothers," *Journal of Human Resources* 30, no. 1 (Winter 1995): 42–62. They find that extending such a benefit only to workers who work over 35 hours a week or only guaranteeing catastrophic health insurance would have little effect on work incentives for these women.
23. Andrea H. Beller and John W. Graham, *Small Change: The Economics of Child Support* (New Haven, Conn.: Yale University, 1993).
24. *Statistical Abstract of the United States* (1996): 385 (Table 605).
25. Jonathan R. Veum, "Interrelation of Child Support, Visitation, and Hours of Work," *Monthly Labor Review* 115, no. 6 (June 1992): 40–47, uses National Longitudinal Youth Survey data from 1988.
26. John W. Graham and Andrea H. Beller, "The Effect of Child Support Payments on the Labor Supply of Female Family Heads: An Econometric Analysis," *Journal of Human Resources* 24, no. 4 (Fall 1989): 664–688.
27. Barbara R. Bergmann and Mark D. Roberts, "Income for the Single Parent: Child Support, Work, and Welfare," *Gender in the Workplace*, eds. Clair Brown and Joseph A. Pechman (Washington, D.C.: Brookings, 1987): 247–270.
28. Bergmann and Roberts, *op. cit.*: 262–263.
29. The state of Wisconsin has recently developed such a child support assurance system; see the discussion in Irwin Garfinkel, Sara McLanahan, and Philip K. Robins, *Child Support Assurance: Design Issues, Expected Impacts, and Political Barriers as Seen from Wisconsin* (Washington, D.C.: Urban Institute, 1992).
30. Lucia A. Nixon, "The Effect on Child Support Enforcement on Marital Dissolution," *Journal of Human Resources* 32, no. 1 (Winter 1997): 159–181.
31. Isabel V. Sawhill, "The Underclass: An Overview," *The Public Interest* 96 (Summer 1989): 14.
32. Peter J. Howe, "Mass. Gets Data on Fathers: Child Support to Be Harder to Dodge," *Boston Globe* (July 1, 1992): 25, 29.
33. Stuart A. Miller, "The Myth of Deadbeat Dads," *Wall Street Journal* (March 2, 1995): A14.
34. Lawrence M. Mead, *Beyond Entitlement: The Social Obligations of Citizenship* (New York: Free Press, 1986).
35. Lawrence M. Mead, *The New Politics of Poverty: The Nonworking Poor in America* (New York: Basic Books, 1992): 176.
36. Peggy McCollough, "Think Tank Offers Plan for Breaking Bonds of Poverty," *Commercial Appeal* (August 18, 1987): A4.
37. Editorial, *Commercial Appeal* (August 20, 1987).

38. Peggy McKenzie, "CSA Funds, Workers Shift to Poverty Plan," *Commercial Appeal* (April 25, 1988): A9.
39. Peggy McKenzie, "Census Giving Form to Faces of Poverty," *Commercial Appeal* (May 23, 1988): A1.
40. Peggy McKenzie, "Op-Act Aims at Renewal of Dreams," *Commercial Appeal* (April 17, 1989): A4.
41. Deborah M. Clubb, "Poverty Battlers Learning Lessons: WOP Mistakes Shunned," *Commercial Appeal* (May 7, 1989): B1–B2.
42. Dana Milbank, "Welfare Overhaul, Shifting Power and Money To the Individual States, Gets Under Way Today," *Wall Street Journal* (October 1, 1996): A24; Robert Rector, "Wisconsin Beats the Feds on Welfare Reform," *Wall Street Journal* (March 6, 1997): A14; John Harwood, "The Bumpy Road From Welfare to Work," *Wall Street Journal* (May 13, 1997): B1, B6.
43. Alec R. Levenson, Elaine Reardon, and Stefanie R. Schmidt, "Welfare Reform and the Employment Prospects of AFDC Recipients," *Jobs & Capital* (Summer 1997).
44. Joel F. Handler, *The Poverty of Welfare Reform* (New Haven, Conn.: Yale University, 1995): 139–144.

*F*urther reading and statistical sources

Abramovitz, Mimi (1996). *Regulating the Lives of Women: Social Welfare Policy from Colonial Times to the Present, Revised Edition*. Boston, Mass.: South End. Historical overview and perspective on the U.S. social work profession and social welfare policies.

Bane, Mary Jo and David T. Ellwood (1994). *Welfare Realities: From Rhetoric to Reform*. Cambridge, Mass.: Harvard University. Collection of empirical essays on welfare patterns and trends along with policy recommendations.

Blank, Rebecca M. (1997). *It Takes a Nation: A New Agenda For Fighting Poverty*. Princeton, N.J.: Princeton University. Highly readable, comprehensive coverage of what is known about poverty, along with policy recommendations from a leading economist expert on welfare issues.

Cottingham, Phoebe H., and David T. Ellwood (eds.) (1989). *Welfare Policy for the 1990s*. Cambridge, Mass.: Harvard University. A set of essays by social scientists on issues in the debate over welfare reform, including targeting of long-term welfare recipients, child support reform, and the costs of welfare programs.

Danziger, Sheldon H., and Daniel H. Weinberg (eds.) (1986). *Fighting Poverty: What Works and What Doesn't*. Cambridge, Mass.: Harvard University. Comprehensive collection of papers from a 1984 conference on poverty, focusing on effects of welfare, welfare reform, and other methods of reducing poverty, such as job creation and training.

Ellwood, David T. (1988). *Poor Support: Poverty in the American Family*. New York: Basic Books. Written for general public by an economist; good layout of issues in area of welfare reform.

Feminist Economics (1995). Vol. 1, no. 2 (Summer). Contains an Explorations section: "The Welfare Reform Debate You Wish Would Happen," with a reform proposal by economists Barbara Bergmann and Heidi Hartmann, the Help for Working Parents Plan, and reactions to the proposal from four leading welfare researchers.

The Future of Children. journal put out by thinktank with the same name; recent issues on "Welfare to Work" (Spring 1997) and "Children and Poverty" (Summer/Fall 1997) can be found at its website (www.futureofchildren.org).

Garfinkel, Irwin, and Sara S. McLanahan (1986). *Single Mothers and Their Children: A New American Dilemma*. Washington, D.C.: Urban Institute. Discusses growth in number of mother-only families and problems faced by these families.

Gueron, Judith M., and Edward Pauly (1991). *From Welfare to Work*. New York: Russell Sage. Discusses workfare and evaluation of workfare programs from the 1980s.

Institute for Women's Policy Research. This economic policy thinktank has a large ongoing project evaluating welfare reform across the states; reports from this project and other gender-economics relevant articles can be found at its website (www.iwpr.org).

Moffitt, Robert (1992). "Incentive Effects of the U.S. Welfare System: A Review," *Journal of Economic Literature* 30, no. 1 (March): 1–61. A thorough review of the economic literature on the various effects of welfare programs, including measurement of the degree of work reduction and evaluation of workfare programs.

Quarterly Review of Economics and Finance (1997). Vol. 37, no. 2 (Summer). Contains a Focus section: "Before the Welfare States: Learning from Early Experiments with Public Relief in the Nineteenth Century," with four interesting papers by economic historians.

Rodgers, Harrell R., Jr. (1996). *Poor Women, Poor Families: The Economic Plight of America's Female-Headed Households, Third Edition.* Armonk, N.Y.: M.E. Sharpe. Overview of the dimensions of poverty for female-headed households, with reform suggestions.

Rose, Nancy E. (1995). *Workfare or Fair Work: Women, Welfare, and Government Work Programs.* New Brunswick, N.J.: Rutgers University. Historical account of work programs in the U.S., and a good overview of more recent workfare attempts.

Schram, Sanford F. (1995). *Words of Welfare: The Poverty of Social Science and the Social Science of Poverty.* Minneapolis, Minn.: University of Minnesota. Thought-provoking collection of essays at the intersection of postmodernism and political economy.

Seavey, Dorothy K. (1996). *Back to Basics: Women's Poverty and Welfare Reform.* Wellesley, Mass.: Wellesley College Center for Research on Women. Comprehensive discussion of statistics, research, and recent policy debates and reforms.

Urban Institute. Numerous papers on welfare and related issues available at this thinktank's website (www.urban.org).

Wilson, William Julius (1996). *When Work Disappears: The World of the New Urban Poor.* New York: Alfred A. Knopf. Influential book on the causes and effects of job loss in central cities.

Discussion questions

1. Draw the two possible outcomes in terms of consumption and leisure, for a person who is currently earning income equal to the poverty level, after a welfare program of the type shown in Figure IIP.1 (ii) is enacted.

2. What does the existence of welfare do to a person's reservation wage?

3. What are the pros and cons of capping welfare benefits so that families with two or more children receive no more money than families with one child?

4. Why might better delivery of child support payments reduce the incentive for single parents to remarry (or marry in the first place)?

5. Consider the Focus on tracking down income of noncustodial parents. Can you think of ways that this approach could be extended to identify even more income? Do you believe that support awards could be greatly increased in many cases?

6. Which of the proposed welfare reforms, if any, are likely to reduce the rate of formation of female-headed households? If none appears to have this effect, can you think of a policy that would reduce it?

7. Consider the pros and cons of enforcing a strict and short time limit on AFDC recipiency – say two years. How would such a policy deal with repeated use of AFDC, interspersed with periods of nonrecipiency?

8. Consider the Focus on Free the Children. Are comprehensive antipoverty programs doomed to failure? If so, why? If not, what would it take to make them work? Could they be cost-effective?

9. The Earned Income Tax Credit allows a person to receive a refundable tax credit for about 40 percent of the person's earnings.

    (a) Show how this changes an individual's budget constraint who has no nonearned income (including no welfare as an option). Is the individual better or worse off? Does the person work more, less, or the same number of hours?

    (b) Show how this changes an individual's budget constraint who could have welfare (i.e., show how this modifies either or both panels of Figure IIP.1).

    (c) Illustrate a case where a person currently on welfare will switch into work after the EITC policy is passed. (Hint: how might you modify a panel of Figure IIP.2?) Illustrate a case where a person currently on welfare will not change behavior.

10. A negative income tax takes money away from persons with income over a certain level and gives money to persons with income below that level. Assume for simplicity that the tax rate is constant t and the guaranteed base income for someone with no earnings is W, the same as in Figures IIP.1 and IIP.2.

    (a) Show how this changes an individual's budget constraint who currently has no nonearned income (including welfare as an option) and pays no taxes. Is the individual better or worse off? Does the person work more, less, or the same number of hours?

    (b) How is this different than Figure IIP.1(ii)?

    (c) Illustrate what happens to a person currently on welfare after the negative income tax policy is passed as a replacement to welfare. (Hint: how might you modify a panel of Figure IIP.2?)

    (d) What would have to be changed about the levels of t and/or W for persons to be better off under the negative income tax policy than they were under welfare?

11. Economists and other analysts are interested in the question of whether states with more generous benefits become "welfare magnets," attracting recipients from other states. Why might you expect this to happen, given the neoclassical model of how persons make decisions? Why might you not expect this to happen, given the same model?

The Earnings Puzzle: Why Do Women Earn Less than Men?

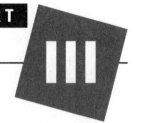

*T*his middle part of the book turns to the central question facing economists interested in gender issues: why do women earn less than men? Here we explore the different causes of the gender earnings gap. In particular, we want to abstract from the facts about labor force participation – such as the facts that many women do not do any market work and that many women work fewer hours than most men – and directly address the question of why women who do choose to work in the market make lower *hourly earnings* on average than do men.

Chapters 6 through 9 address the question of what theories can account for gender earnings differences, both within and between jobs. Chapter 6 explores the links between the jobs that men and women hold and the pay that each group receives in those jobs. Differences in the distribution of men and women across jobs are discussed in detail, and the gender-related earnings patterns within and between jobs are discussed as well. The exclusion and crowding models, which link gender pay differences to segregation practices, are discussed.

Chapters 7 through 9 take up, in turn, three groups of arguments for possible variance in pay within and between jobs. Chapter 7 develops the human capital model, which implies that differences in education, experience, and training can account for differences in pay between persons. Chapter 8 examines the model of compensating differentials, which implies that differences in preferences for aspects of work other than pay can account for differences in pay between persons. Chapter 9 considers several models of discrimination, all of which attribute differences in pay to differences in persons' treatment by employers. However, the discrimination models differ in whether they attribute prejudice to employers, employees, or customers, and in whether or not prejudice is assumed at all.

Part III concludes with a policy application that draws on material from all four chapters: the study of the rationales for and possible effects of comparable worth policies.

Gender Segregation in the Workplace

Gender segregation in the labor force is a pervasive phenomenon with deep roots in the gender division of labor in both modern and historical societies. Segregation occurs within and between firms, occupations, and industries. This chapter characterizes the current and past nature of gender segregation of workers, explores theories of why segregation occurs and persists, examines the link between segregation and the gender earnings differential, and considers how various policies might affect segregation patterns.

The situation in various occupations

As the proportion of women in the labor force has increased, women have entered both traditionally female and traditionally male occupations. Let us discuss a variety of different occupations to illustrate the range of different patterns found in terms of sex composition. General trends for blue-collar, pink-collar, professional, and managerial occupations are considered. The special cases of apparently stable, highly segregated occupations are considered in terms of how the minority group within them fares. Then different occupations that have had a sharp rise in percentage of females are considered.

Blue-collar occupations

Blue-collar occupations remain the most heavily male area of the occupations. These include production jobs, craft jobs such as carpenters and electricians, and transportation-related jobs, as well as less-skilled jobs such as garbage collectors and construction laborers. Most of the occupations in which women posted disproportionately small gains in employment are in this area.[1]

For example, truck driving has seen a large increase in women, but the percentage is still low, rising only to over 4 percent today compared with under 2 percent in 1978.[2] Female drivers indicate that besides facing male hostility and being treated as sex objects, they have had to overcome strong doubts about their capabilities from prospective employers.[3] One woman related that when she walked up to the loading dock:[4]

TABLE 6.1 Percentage of bachelor's and master's degrees awarded to women, selected fields, 1974, 1984, and 1994

Field	Bachelor's			Master's		
	1974	1984	1994	1974	1984	1994
Accounting	13.7	47.0	55.1	10.5	36.6	45.7
Architecture	6.6	23.5	29.6	10.1	25.8	32.3
Business management	9.8	41.5	47.2	3.2	29.5	35.2
Computer science	16.4	37.1	28.4	12.9	29.3	25.8
Economics	14.6	34.1	29.5	14.2	23.5	32.7
Education	73.5	76.0	77.3	59.9	72.0	76.7
Engineering	1.6	14.1	16.4	2.3	10.4	15.4
Journalism	45.7	62.5	63.6	38.0	56.1	63.9
Pharmacy	25.9	49.4	63.0	18.3	35.4	44.9

Source: U.S. National Center for Education Statistics, *Digest of Education Statistics* (1976) (Table 112), (1987) (Table 152), (1996) (Table 244). Year refers to end of academic year, e.g., 1972–73.

All the guys would glare, as if to say, "What is *she* doing here?" They gave me four 55-gallon drums and said, "If you can load 'em, you can haul 'em." So I got the dolly while they stood back and watched. I had to climb up to push that thing over, but I passed the test. I knew that I couldn't break down or quit, because I was representing any other women who would come along.

Pink-collar occupations

Women continue to enter the clerical and service occupations in large numbers. While these occupations were already feminized by 1970, they continued their feminization process throughout the 1970s and 1980s.[5] Meanwhile men continued to shun these jobs. Only three service occupations had noticeable gains in male representation: cooks, kitchen workers, and house servants.[6] Notably, many of the men entering these areas are members of minorities, and many are recent immigrants.

The professions

In the professions as a whole, there has been a noticeable trend of rising female participation rates. In fact, it is startling how many of the younger members of the various professions are women now, compared with 20 years ago. Table 6.1 compares percentages of bachelor's and master's degrees awarded in various professions to women in the 1974, 1984, and 1994 school years. In all these cases save for education, there was a sharp rise from 1974 to 1984 and a continuing rise from 1984 to 1994 at both levels (except for bachelor's and master's degrees in computer science, and bachelor's degrees in economics), but women were still less likely than men to receive the master's degree in all these fields except education and journalism; also the percentage of women drops in all years in going from bachelor's to master's degrees except for architecture (also engineering in 1974 and journalism in 1994).

In 1956 only 3 percent of law degrees were awarded to women. By 1994 the percentage had risen to 43 percent.[7] This is sizable feminization of a prestigious profession. Women, however, are overrepresented among the less-well-paying jobs in law, such as jobs in legal clinics, and appear not to rise to the top even in the most lucrative area of large law firms.[8] In 1994, the percentage of law firm associates who were female was 39 percent, and the percentage of law firm partners who were female was 13 percent.[9]

Female lawyers may, however, be having their biggest impact on the law profession, as well on the working world as a whole, through the efforts of some of them to "redraw the landscape of a legal world by replacing the 'male' value system of rights, rules, and hierarchies with 'female' values based on relationships, responsibility and caring."[10] Women lawyers are found in large numbers in government, the nonprofit sector, and in family law, and about 15 percent of judges were women in 1996,[11] implying that there may be more sympathetic ears for hearing a recasting of the law to embody more "female" values.

In 1950 10 percent of medical degrees were awarded to women. By 1994 the percentage had risen to 38 percent.[12] While women earn less than men in the profession, as shown in Table 6.10, it is still an extremely attractive option in terms of the pay and employment possibilities. To older women in the profession, in particular, the increased openness of the profession is an impressive change. One 42-year-old, who went to medical school at age 34, commented: "I always wanted to be a doctor, but I was always told to do something more 'acceptable.' Women of my generation had to make conscious choices between career and family. But since then, the trail has been blazed by many women, and today you can be a doctor and have a family."[13]

Managers

A 1990 survey of 4012 senior managers in 800 major corporations found that only 19 were women – under 0.5 percent.[14] Meanwhile, women filled over a third of all management positions, compared with 19 percent of such positions in 1972.[15] Studies by Columbia and Stanford Universities of women MBAs show that starting salaries are similar between the sexes, but that seven years out the door, the women are 40 percent behind the men.[16] This difference cannot be explained by arguments that women overall do not yet have the experience to rise high in the pay and responsibility structure. The term "glass ceiling" has been coined to describe the phenomenon that while it now appears possible for women to rise to the top, few actually make it. The term has been used to describe the situations found in law firms and academic medicine, as well as in corporations. It appears to many that a relatively impenetrable wall, built from covert discriminatory practices on the part of top-level managers, exists. An alternative explanation is that few women, compared with men, are willing to make the sacrifices in terms of time and effort necessary to rise to the top of a major corporation.[17]

Various programs have been suggested for trying to help women "crack the glass ceiling." They include reducing workloads for women after they give birth, and offering training sessions to promote leadership development.[18] The implications of such programs will be considered at length in Chapter 7.

Tokens: Women in predominantly male occupations

In 1975 the percentage of women in U.S. Congress was 4 percent; in 1997 it was 11 percent. A similar small rise is found in other corridors of power, such as major corporations and the top echelons in professions. A small number of women in an occupation may be "tolerated" in the sense of not leading to notice on anyone's part that the occupation is becoming female-dominated or even integrated.[19] In fact, they may be viewed as an asset in the sense of receiving disparate attention, thereby drawing attention away from the lack of rank-and-file members and/or the failure of a proportionate number of women to make the rise from the rank-and-file. About medicine, one female psychiatrist said: "Right now, women doctors in positions of power are window dressing, with one scattered here and one scattered there – without enough votes to make a change in academia, hospital administration or professional associations."[20] Nevertheless, it appears that women in male-dominated occupations make substantially less relative to the men in the occupation, even though they make more than most members of female-dominated occupations.

FOCUS

Directors and officers at Fortune 500 companies

Women are not yet proportionately represented at middle management, but they are clearly underrepresented among top management, even in consumer industries that sell mainly to women. In 1992, *Fortune* magazine surveyed 201 chief executives of companies (CEOs) in the Fortune 500 and found that only 2 percent considered it very likely and 14 percent somewhat likely that the company would have a female CEO in the next ten years.[21] Table 6.2 contains some recent data illustrating the small numbers of women at the highest levels of corporate America.

Top dogs: Men in predominantly female occupations

At colleges that I visit in the course of lecturing, I often bet students that the librarians in charge at the college library are men. By "in charge" I mean the head librarian, the head of reference, and the heads of most of the special collections – in particular, any that are particularly valuable and/or prestigious. I am rarely proved wrong. Librarians as a whole are over 80 percent female. However, a disproportionate percentage of the most prestigious and influential positions, which are generally also the best-paying, are held by men. In fact, any position that involves supervisory capacities is disproportionately male.

One female-dominated profession where this tendency of men to rise to the "top dog" positions has met with particular dismay from the rank-and-file is nursing. Many nurses actively resent men who enter nursing because they are viewed – probably accurately – as tending to rise to supervisory positions more often than women. Similarly, men in clerical positions are often considered by themselves and their peers to be just "stopping through" on their way up to management; this impression is generally validated by their later career paths.[22] Sociologist Christine Williams uses the phrase "glass escalator" to describe men's apparently accelerated progress to the top in female-dominated occupations.[23]

TABLE 6.2 Number of men and women directors and officers at Fortune 500 companies by industry, 1990

	Directors			Officers		
	Women	Men	%Female	Women	Men	%Female
Aerospace	8	213	3.6	7	272	2.5
Apparel	6	84	6.7	10	89	10.1
Chemicals	17	609	2.7	14	629	2.2
Computers	12	221	5.2	15	461	3.2
Electronics	23	434	5.0	7	564	1.2
Food	26	522	4.7	12	698	1.7
Industrial and farm equipment	9	329	2.7	7	372	1.8
Metals	6	267	2.2	8	269	2.9
Pharmaceuticals	18	203	8.1	11	270	3.9
Publishing and printing	18	235	7.1	13	244	5.1
Soaps and cosmetics	17	84	16.8	8	185	4.1
Textiles	4	103	3.7	4	127	3.1
Transportation equipment	0	51	0.0	1	66	1.5
Total*	254	5,384	4.5	175	6,502	2.6

* For all Fortune 500 companies.
Source: Joann S. Lublin, "Rights Law to Spur Shifts in Promotions," *Wall Street Journal* (December 30, 1991): B1. Figures provided by Mary Ann Von Glinow, University of Southern California. Reprinted by permission of *Wall Street Journal,* © 1991 Dow Jones & Company, Inc. All rights reserved worldwide.

Interpretation of large changes in the proportion of women in some occupations

Studies of occupations that have shown recent rises in percentage of females have concluded that these rises in female participation may be accompanied by increased intraoccupational segregation and by job *de-skilling*. The general pattern for intraoccupational segregation is that men tend to become more and more concentrated in the higher-paying jobs within the occupation or within the higher-paying firms.[24] De-skilling is the process by which jobs in an occupation become more routinized and generally involve less responsibility. This may or may not be a situation in which persons in the occupation have either less formal education or less on-the-job training. De-skilling may be a primary reason why wages fall as these occupations become more female-dominated.

It appears that the question upon seeing a rise in percentage of females in a traditionally male occupation is: is *resegregation*, *ghettoization*, or integration occurring? Observed rises in percentage of females may be an intermediate step in the process of *tipping*, which is the eventual abandonment by men of male-dominated occupations that are entered by a critical mass of women, leading to the creation of a newly female-dominated occupation. (In the opposite case, a male-dominated occupation is created.)[25] The final outcome of the tipping process is resegregation of the occupation. Alternatively, the percentage of females may eventually stabilize at a higher level, but the women may be predominantly in particular jobs within the occupation, specifically the lower-paying, less prestigious jobs – i.e., ghettoization. The other possibility, an occupation with a stable, integrated population, appears to be the rarest outcome. Specific occupations are discussed below to illustrate these various phenomena.

The tipping phenomenon

Examples of job tipping abound. Although there were almost no women bank tellers before World War II, over 90 percent of tellers were female in 1980. Meanwhile, salaries and career-advancement possibilities dropped precipitously.[26] Clerical professions, in general, were predominantly male when they first came into existence in large numbers as the industrial revolution generated more need for paper processors; all of these occupations are now female-dominated and generally considered to be the female ghetto of jobs.[27]

It is rare to find an occupation that tips from predominantly female to predominantly male. The most interesting example may be the occupation of baby-delivering, once performed almost exclusively by female midwives, then performed almost exclusively by male doctors, and only recently becoming a more heavily female subspecialty within the medical profession. In Britain, the invention and use of forceps by a particular set of related male doctors in the seventeenth century led in part to this development.[28] Forceps deliveries had a high success rate, and women were soon demanding this new technology to aid their births. In the United States as well as in Britain, the male-dominated medical profession was instrumental in urging that women turn away from use of midwives for home deliveries in favor of hospital deliveries performed by doctors. Whereas in 1910, about 50 percent of babies were delivered by midwives, fewer than 1 percent were by 1970.[29]

De-skilling

Insurance adjustment appears to be a clear case of de-skilling accompanying the feminization of the occupation. This occupation changed from being 30 percent female in 1970 to 72 percent by 1988.[30] A case study of this occupation concluded that the feminization was a direct result of the routinization and automation of the work process, primarily through the introduction of computerized claims-processing. Claims processing has become more of an indoor office job, instead of one that entails traveling to claim sites and exercising individual judgment. Men abandoned these jobs, and firms hired women to replace them. Concurrently, the pay associated with this occupation declined.[31]

Different skills, but not necessarily lesser skills?

Contrast the previous case illustrating de-skilling to the case of court reporting. Modern court reporting involves the use of a 22-key stenotype machine. One needs to be able to record in excess of 200 words per minute to become a court reporter. Previous to development of the stenotype, shorthand systems were developed for pen and paper and are still in use in many situations. However, as the percentage of pen writers has declined, the percentage of females has been rising. In 1942 the profession was 74 percent male, and only

10 percent of the members used a stenotype machine.[32] By 1975 the profession was only 45 percent male,[33] and 87 percent of the members used a stenotype machine.[34] Additionally, a survey of schools teaching the subject in 1975 indicated that the student body was only 10 percent male.[35]

By 1990 there were practically no pen writers left in the courts, and the profession was moving toward the increased use of computer systems to aid the cumbersome process of transcribing the paper tape record produced by the stenotype machine into a finished transcript of court or deposition proceedings. A 1990 survey of Tennessee court reporters found that 81 percent were women, 7 percent were pen writers, and 84 percent reported using a computer-aided transcription system at least part of the time.[36] It appears that the skills required to enter this profession are actually greater now than in the past and/or that they are so different from those in the pen-writing days – including the demand for greater manual dexterity – that a smaller percentage of the male population than of the female population is capable of doing the work.

Meanwhile, it appears that salaries continue to be high for this occupation, despite compositional changes. Court reporting requires only a high school degree, plus the necessary training to develop speed and accuracy in reporting.[37] Yet court reporters' average earnings were greater than those for many professionals requiring a B.S. or B.A. degree, including teachers, engineers, and pharmacists.[38] It is impossible to answer the question of how high earnings would have been had the profession remained male-dominated. It is notable that in states with higher proportions of female court reporters, the wages appear to be lower. However, these also tend to be the states such as Arkansas and Mississippi where wages are lower in general.[39]

Ghettoization

Examples were given above of occupations in which women are found in the less prestigious jobs. In some occupations, the differential placement of men and women is less obvious to the outsider. For instance, in baking, which would appear to be a relatively undifferentiated occupation in terms of jobs and pay, the percentage of female bakers has risen from 25.4 percent in 1970 to 47.8 percent in 1988.[40] However, men continue to dominate production baking, meaning that they are more likely to be found in automated factories, where the jobs are higher-paying. The absolute number of men has declined due to automation; meanwhile, women continue to be found in the roles of finishing and packaging baked goods, in the lower-paying retail sector. The evidence suggests that technological innovations in preserving dough has allowed for more "bake-off" bakeries, where prepared dough is delivered for baking rather than dough being prepared from scratch on the spot. The expansion of the baking workforce in these retail outlets has accommodated the rising female employment.[41]

Integration

It is notably difficult to find an example of a truly integrated occupation, where the proportion of women closely matches their representation in the workforce, where the rate of change in the sex ratio is small, and where women are not ghettoized. Bartending appears to be such a case. Female bartenders were 21 percent of the total in 1970, rising sharply to 44 percent in 1980, but leveling off at 50 percent by 1988. The unique characteristics of the profession are worth noting. Exclusionary laws that existed prior to 1970 at both the state level and within the bartenders' union were struck down. There is no job ladder in bartending to allow for segregation by rank and no range of industries for bartenders to separate into. (Four-fifths of bartenders work in the single industry of food and beverage service.) Finally, since only one or two bartenders work per shift, there is little or no opportunity for division of labor or for the distinction of a "managing" bartender. However, one might well expect to find traditions of only men or only women being hired into particular bars or shifts.[42]

Segregation index values

For many purposes, it is useful to create a summary measure that characterizes the overall level of segregation, such as a *segregation index*. This allows us to compare changes over time in the degree of segregation and differences between countries and between demographic groups and sectors within a country. The most commonly calculated index, used to measure segregation for two types of people (e.g., men and women, or whites and nonwhites) between any number of different classifications (e.g., occupations), is the *Duncan index of dissimilarity*.[43] This index number is calculated as:

$$100 * \sum_{i=1}^{N} \frac{\left| \dfrac{X_i}{X} - \dfrac{Y_i}{Y} \right|}{2}$$

where there are N occupations and X_i is the number of persons of a group in occupation i, X is the total number of persons in this group, Y_i is the number of persons in a comparison group in occupation i, and Y is the total number of persons in the comparison group. The index sums up the absolute value of the differences between the proportions of each group (measured relative to each group's total employment) for each occupation. The index ranges from 0 (complete integration) to 100 (complete segregation). Notice that this index uses the implicit definition of integration as a situation where the *proportional representation* of each group is the same in all occupations as for the national workforce. For instance, if 30 percent of the national workforce is female, then the index would measure 0, or complete integration, only if each occupation were 30 percent female. An interpretation of the index is that it shows what percentage of either group would have to switch occupations in order to achieve complete integration. If the index equals 40, either 40 percent of men would have to switch into relatively female-dominated occupations or 40 percent of women would have to switch into male-dominated occupations. While other indexes can also be used to characterize segregation, the Duncan index has been widely used and has thereby become a standard of comparison across different researchers' efforts.[44]

To see how this index is calculated, consider the following set of hypothetical cases. Assume that there are only two occupations in the country, blue-collar and pink-collar. Table 6.3 illustrates four cases for the distribution of employed men and women between these two occupations. Note that we do not need to know how many women and men there are *in toto* in the workforce; we only need to know the percentage distributions of

TABLE 6.3 Examples of calculating the Duncan dissimilarity index

Blue-collar	Pink-collar	Index values	Outcome
Extreme cases:			
(a) 100% of all employed men	100% of all employed women	$D = \dfrac{\|100-0\|}{2} + \dfrac{\|0-100\|}{2} = 100$	complete segregation
(b) 40% of men, 40% of women	60% of men, 60% of women	$D = \dfrac{\|40-40\|}{2} + \dfrac{\|60-60\|}{2} = 0$	complete integration
Intermediate cases:			
(c) 60% of men, 40% of women	40% of men, 60% of women	$D = \dfrac{\|60-40\|}{2} + \dfrac{\|40-60\|}{2} = 20$	low segregation
(d) 80% of men, 20% of women	20% of men, 80% of women	$D = \dfrac{\|80-20\|}{2} + \dfrac{\|20-80\|}{2} = 60$	high segregation

TABLE 6.4 Occupational sex segregation indexes, all and by race, 1960 to 1990

	1960	*1970*	*1980*	*1990*
All	64	66	59	53
Whites	63	66	59	55
Nonwhites	70	64	56	50

Sources: Calculated by the author using data from Census of Population and Housing, 1960, Public-Use Microdata 1/100 Sample; Census of Population and Housing, 1970, Public-Use Microdata 1/100 B States Sample; Census of Population and Housing 1980, Public-Use Microdata 1/100 C Sample; Census of Population and Housing 1990, Public-Use Microdata 1/100 Sample.

men and women across occupations. At one extreme, if all men are blue-collar workers and all women are pink-collar workers, there is complete occupational segregation. At the other end of the spectrum, if the same percentage of employed men as employed women are found in each occupation, there is complete integration. Two intermediate cases are illustrated as well, which show that the index increases as the percentages of women and men diverge more extensively across occupations.

Turning now to actual numbers for the U.S. workforce, Table 6.4 shows occupational segregation indexes for 1960 to 1990. Sex segregation indexes are calculated for the whole workforce, as well as separately for whites and nonwhites. There has been a notable downward trend in segregation since 1960.[45] While in 1960, 64 percent of either men or women would have had to change jobs to drive the overall index down to 0, by 1990 only 53 percent would have had to switch. The patterns for whites and nonwhites are similar, but with a more notable decline among nonwhites.

The rise from 1960 to 1970 both overall and for whites may be explained by the fact that the number of occupational categories available in the data rose sharply between 1960

TABLE 6.5 Sex segregation indexes by level of disaggregation, 1990

Number of job categories:	6	16	83	503	36,669
Index value:	33	37	48	53	59

Source: Calculated by the author using data from the Census of Population and Housing 1990, Public-Use Microdata 1/100 Sample.

TABLE 6.6 Occupational sex segregation indexes by age, education, and sector, 1990

Age group:	*25–34*	*35–44*	*45–54*	*55–64*	
Index value:	53	54	57	59	
Years of school:	*0–8*	*9–11*	*12–15*	*16*	*>16*
Index value:	56	56	58	46	43
Sector:	*Private*	*Public*			
Index value:	54	51			
Private/Public:	*Goods*	*Services*	*Federal*	*State*	*Local*
Index value:	52	52	43	48	56

Source: Calculated by the author using data from the Census of Population and Housing 1990, Public-Use Microdata 1/100 Sample.

and 1970, from 291 occupations to 438. The number of categories rose again in 1980, to 503, but the classification system did not change between 1980 and 1990. Increasing the number of categories over time imparts an upward bias to the index calculations. Opinion is divided as to whether it is better to attempt to standardize over time by using a smaller number of matched, more inclusive categories or whether the increasing number of classifications is a legitimate reflection of segregation.[46]

Using 1990 Census data, one can clearly see the effect on the index of increasing the number of occupational categories. Census data contain several levels of detail for describing occupational and industrial categories. As shown in Table 6.5, using six very broad occupational classes, the index value is 33.[47] It climbs to a level of 59 if the fullest possible job class detail – 503 occupations within 224 different industries – is used, which yields a total of 36,669 occupied job classifications (because most occupations are not represented in all industries).[48] The biggest jump in the index is found in moving from 16 to 83 occupational categories, when the index climbs from 37 to 48. So, even at a very nondetailed level of occupational classification, segregation is quite high.

Another way to look at the data is to calculate the index for subsets of the labor force. Using 1990 Census data, Table 6.6 presents segregation indexes for four age groups, five schooling groups, the public and private sectors separately, the private sector broken down between goods-producing and service-oriented industries, and the public sector broken down between federal, state, and local governments. Index values rise slightly with age. By educational attainment, values drop off greatly for the top two educational groups. Differences between the public and private sectors in occupational segregation are small, although the public sector is slightly lower overall. No difference is found in the private sector between the goods-producing and service industries, but segregation declines as the level of government rises from local to federal. Table 6.6 demonstrates that segregation

TABLE 6.7 Occupational race segregation indexes by sex, 1960 to 1990

	1960	1970	1980	1990
Men	45	38	28	24
Women	50	36	26	22

Sources: Same as Table 6.4.

is remarkably consistent across subsectors of the economy. This consistency implies that sectoral and demographic shifts cannot be counted on to create much downward movement in the segregation index calculated for the entire labor force.

As a contrast to these trends in occupational sex segregation, consider the patterns for race segregation over this time period. Table 6.7 contains occupational race segregation indexes calculated separately by sex. These indexes show a marked decline in race segregation since 1960 for both women and men. Additionally the race segregation series of indexes both start and end at lower levels than the sex segregation series. By 1990 only 24 percent of either white or nonwhite men and 22 percent of white or nonwhite women would have had to switch jobs in order to achieve racial integration within each gender group.

How much sex segregation are we overlooking by concentrating on the occupational detail available in Census data? Case studies of particular occupations often show a great deal of intraoccupational segregation, and it appears that men tend to be concentrated in the higher-paying subspecialties in both highly male and highly female occupations. For instance, among economists – a predominantly male occupation – there are large sex differences in research specialties, with most of the women in the more applied fields such as labor economics, and few women working on the theoretical side of the discipline.[49] Among librarians – a predominantly female occupation – men are proportionately overrepresented in administrative positions in research libraries.[50]

There is scant evidence regarding segregation index values at more detailed levels of job classification than simply occupations, but research in this area is quite unanimous in finding high levels of segregation. When individual firms or establishments[51] are studied and attention paid to segregation by job classes, intrafirm values of the Duncan index commonly rise to 90. In one study of 373 establishments, men and women in 60 percent of the establishments were completely segregated by job title, i.e., there was no job type in which both men and women were found.[52]

It appears that without drastic social change, no more than a slow downward trend in sex segregation is likely for the foreseeable future. Factors that could maintain the currently observed high levels of sex segregation include the growth of jobs in occupations that are presently quite segregated, such as clerical jobs, and the possible slowdown of further rises in female participation in occupations such as those that have experienced an influx of women in the recent past. One should not, however, look only at new positions as providing the possibility of reallocation of women and men across occupations. Mobility between occupations and jobs is quite high, and desegregation could conceivably be brought about primarily by job changers rather than by new entrants and exits from the labor market.[53] It appears, however, that there is little possibility in the near future of achieving levels of occupational sex segregation as low as those currently found for race segregation.

"Okay...Heads, I hunt animals and you raise the kids. Tails..."

© 1994: Reprinted courtesy of Bunny Hoest and *Parade Magazine*

Cross-cultural segregation data

How representative is the modern U.S. experience of sex segregation patterns in general? This section sketches some general patterns found in collected ethnographic data on a wide variety of societies, some historical and some contemporary.[54]

Research on both other industrialized nations and preindustrial cultures provides interesting similarities and contrasts. Industrialized countries that have been studied extensively include the larger Western European nations, Japan, Israel, and Russia.[55] In these societies, which can be considered roughly comparable to the United States in terms of occupational distribution and female labor force participation, it is clear that despite substantial variability in age patterns of labor-force participation and in the extent to which women engage in market work, there is substantial similarity across cultures in the high level of sex segregation. Moreover, the same occupations tend to be dominated by men or women in all these countries.

This pattern of an occupation's being dominated by the same sex in different industrial societies does not carry over as a good description across nonindustrial societies. In examining evidence derived from ethnographic reports on societies from different time periods and from all parts of the world, it is striking both how few activities are integrated within any culture and how activities vary in their assignment to one or the other sex, depending on the culture.[56]

Table 6.8 Percentage distribution of societies by activity group segregation

	Societies in which the activity is performed by:			
Activity	*Only or mostly men*	*Both men and women*	*Only or mostly women*	*No. of societies in sample*
Hunting	100	0	0	738
Metal working	100	0	0	360
Boat building	96	3	1	215
Fishing	79	15	6	562
House building	75	10	15	457
Animal husbandry	64	22	14	412
Leather working	46	5	49	280
Weaving	30	12	58	265
Pottery making	9	5	86	328
Gathering	8	14	78	396
Agriculture	32	32	36	639

Source: Calculated by the author using data from George P. Murdock, *Ethnographic Atlas* (Pittsburgh, Penn.: University of Pittsburgh, 1967).

Illustrating these points, Table 6.8 uses data from these 863 societies to create a simple breakdown for 11 activity groups by whether only or mostly men, both sexes equally, or only or mostly women perform chores in the activity group. Only metal working and hunting are exclusively male activities; no activities are exclusively female; and few societies assign any of the activities to both sexes equally. Additionally, this tabulation conceals sex segregation that may take place within any activity group. For example, in agriculture, women may handle only certain crops or animals, while men tend to others.

To demonstrate this point and underline the earlier point about the lack of exclusively female economic activities, Table 6.9 contains data from 224 nonindustrial societies for which detailed descriptions of work activities are available. Activities are classified for each society by whether they are done exclusively or predominantly by one sex or the other. The first column (*M*) gives the number of tribes for which the particular activity is only performed by males. The second column (*M-*) gives the number of tribes in which women engage in the occupation only relatively infrequently or in a subordinate capacity. The third column (=) counts those tribes in which the occupation is either carried on indifferently by either sex or cooperatively by both (which still implies that complete sex segregation of the activity may be occurring at any point in time). The fourth column (*F-*) counts those tribes where women predominate, and the fifth column (*F*) counts those tribes where women exclusively perform the activity. The sixth column (*Percent*) gives a rough index of the degree of masculine involvement in the occupation, where the first five columns are scored 100, 75, 50, 25, and 0, respectively, and the scores averaged for each activity.

Even activities that are predominantly female, such as water carrying, are undertaken exclusively by men in some societies. Still, Table 6.9 conceals the fact that specific subactivities within an activity group may be regarded as exclusively performed by males or females. For example, in the course of building a house, men may raise the timbers, while women prepare and affix the roofing material.

TABLE 6.9 Number and percentage of societies in which a particular activity is strongly or weakly gender-typed

Activity	M	M-	=	F-	F	Percent
Metal working	78	0	0	0	0	100.0
Weapon making	121	1	0	0	0	99.8
Pursuit of sea mammals	34	1	0	0	0	99.3
Hunting	166	13	0	0	0	98.2
Manufacture of musical instruments	45	2	0	0	1	96.9
Boat building	91	4	4	0	1	96.0
Mining and quarrying	35	1	1	0	1	95.4
Work in wood and bark	113	9	5	1	1	95.0
Work in stone	68	3	2	0	2	95.0
Trapping or catching of small animals	128	13	4	1	2	94.9
Work in bone, horn and shell	67	4	3	0	3	93.0
Lumbering	104	4	3	1	6	92.2
Fishing	98	34	19	3	4	85.6
Manufacture of ceremonial objects	37	1	13	0	1	85.2
Herding	38	8	4	0	5	83.6
House building	86	32	25	3	14	77.0
Clearing of land for agriculture	73	22	17	5	13	76.3
Net making	44	6	4	2	11	74.1
Trade	51	28	20	8	7	73.7
Dairy operations	17	4	3	1	13	57.8
Manufacture of ornaments	24	3	40	6	18	52.5
Agriculture – soil preparation and planting	31	23	33	20	37	48.4
Manufacture of leather products	29	3	9	3	32	48.0
Body mutilation, e.g., tattooing	16	14	44	22	20	46.6
Erection and dismantling of shelter	14	2	5	6	22	39.8
Hide preparation	31	2	4	4	49	39.4
Tending of fowls and small animals	21	4	8	1	39	38.7
Agriculture – crop tending and harvesting	10	15	35	39	44	33.9
Gathering of shellfish	9	4	8	7	25	33.5
Manufacture of non-textile fabrics	14	0	9	2	32	33.3
Fire making and tending	18	6	25	22	62	30.5
Burden bearing	12	6	33	20	57	29.9
Preparation of drinks and narcotics	20	1	13	8	57	29.5
Manufacture of thread and cordage	23	2	11	30	73	27.3
Basket making	25	3	10	6	82	24.4
Mat making	16	2	6	4	61	24.2
Weaving	19	2	2	6	67	23.9
Gathering of fruits, berries and nuts	12	3	15	13	63	23.6
Fuel gathering	22	1	10	19	89	23.0
Pottery making	13	2	6	8	77	18.4
Preservation of meat and fish	8	2	10	14	74	16.7
Manufacture and repair of clothing	12	3	8	9	95	16.1
Gathering of herbs, roots and seeds	8	1	11	7	74	15.8
Cooking	5	1	9	28	158	8.6
Water carrying	7	0	5	7	10	8.2
Grain grinding	2	4	5	13	114	7.8

Source: George P. Murdock, "Comparative Data on the Division of Labor by Sex," *Social Forces* 15, no. 4 (May 1937): 551–553. Reprinted with permission. Copyright © The University of North Carolina Press.

The economic type of society – whether foraging (hunter-gatherer), horticultural (simple agriculture), pastoral (herding), or agrarian (advanced agriculture) – does not appear to influence this pattern of the relative scarcity of integrated activities, although exceptions can be found at the foraging level, as discussed in Chapter 12.[57] Segregation in tribal societies is much more prevalent than integration, and it is so extreme in some societies that almost all work activities are defined as either male or female, with the result that the sexes congregate in "sexual ghettos" while carrying out their daily work routines.[58] Widespread sex segregation, rather than the prevalence of sex-dominance of particular activities, is the tie bridging these preindustrial cultures' segregational practices to the industrial societies discussed above.

Theories of why segregation occurs and persists

The above data make a convincing case for the view that sex segregation is widespread. This section of the chapter will examine different explanations of why this phenomenon occurs and persists: (1) gender differences in tastes for work activities, (2) gender differences in abilities for work activities, leading to the exploitation of comparative advantage through division of market labor, (3) efficiency in separating the sexes so as to reduce work disruptions related to sexual tensions, (4) needs to balance market with nonmarket labor and other familial concerns, (5) imperfect information about relative abilities between the sexes on the part of employers, and (6) exploitation of most women by men or by another subset of society.

Gender-linked differences in tastes and/or abilities

Given the prevalence of segregation, it is natural to look for factors common to all human societies to explain this phenomenon. The first factors to consider are differences in tastes and abilities between the genders, regardless of the type of society examined, that lead to different job choices for men and women.

Considering differences in abilities first, a piece of evidence supporting the idea that differences in abilities alone cannot be the cause of segregation is found in the data presented above on preindustrial societies. As noted, there are only a few cases among those that have been studied (such as hunting) where men predominate in all societies, and no activities are ascribed solely to women. This implies also that sex-linked differences in tastes between people, while a possible cause of sex segregation, must be generally society-specific. It appears that differences between the genders in tastes for various job characteristics are a strong determinant of the labor supplies to different occupations.[59] Still, the very fact that tastes do appear to differ among societies (for work as well as for other things, e.g., food) casts doubt on whether they can be considered as exogenous, sex-linked forces leading to occupational segregation.

The importance of efficient allocation of human resources

If women are, indeed, predisposed to be more efficient at some tasks and men at others, then any imposed decline in segregation that caused certain tasks to be performed by the less apt parties would be inefficient. If this is true, then in an ideal state, men and women would be free to choose whatever job best suited them, given their tastes and abilities upon entering (and subsequently relocating within) the labor market. There would be no justification for imposing an outcome of integration on such a system, or for permitting attitudes and practices that impose segregation.

Even if men and women have similar distributions of similar tastes and abilities, a highly segregated situation could be more efficient than an integrated one. One argument, which has appeared frequently in the popular press, is that any situation in which men and women work together has sexual ramifications that may not be conducive to maintaining an efficient workplace. Concern is expressed that sexual harassment, disruptive office romances, and nepotism accompany the increase of women in the workplace.[60] However, this is an argument for segregating worksites, not for segregating by job class within a worksite. These problems arise with or without the existence of men and women in the same job class. While men and women are currently highly segregated by occupation, they frequently come into contact during the workday. The stereotypical female secretary-male boss situation has been in existence for decades, with the accompanying closeness sometimes leading to unpleasant situations, but also often leading to mutually pleasant and productive situations. In addition, some writers cite positive aspects of increased workplace contact between men and women to be reaped by both employers and employees, such as increased loyalty to the firm and more cooperation between workers.[61]

Finally, the different structures of occupations, in conjunction with market-nonmarket work divisions, may motivate segregation. In societies that maintain a division between market and nonmarket activities, such as the United States today, whichever sex has primary responsibility for the nonmarket activities, such as childrearing or household chores, may take on market tasks that are compatible with the demands these nonmarket activities create.[62] This may involve choosing occupations in which part-time employment is more likely[63] or in which intermittent labor force participation is not heavily penalized.[64] However, if no difference in tastes or abilities is postulated, it is still indeterminate which sex will be the one to choose nonmarket over market activities.

Segregation as a response to market imperfections

Alternatively, could sex segregation arise because of labor market imperfections, such as the situation in which employers have imperfect information about an individual's abilities? Employers may hire women only for female-dominated jobs if individual ability is unobservable. If women are not observed in nontraditional jobs, then there is no reason to update the belief that they are not found in those positions because they cannot do such jobs effectively. In this situation, no individual employer may have incentive to change, and there would be room for intervention which would improve overall efficiency. Increasing female representation in male-dominated jobs (and vice-versa) would enable employers to revise their beliefs based on actual experience. With more information, workers could be better allocated among jobs. This approach suggests placing persons in jobs nontraditional for their sex for the purpose of allowing people to see how they do in such positions, rather than of having a large effect on the relative earnings of the sexes in the short run. This might well be a useful approach for those dissatisfied with the current state of sexual integration to take. Since we do not have a large sample of integrated occupations, let alone integrated societies, it might be worth running a large social experiment to see what happens in an integrated society. Any possible loss in efficiency during the trial period might be offset by the value of running such an experiment in order to observe how an integrated society operates.

The importance of distributional considerations

The preceding two sections were concerned with allocative efficiency, defined as the distribution of men and women in the workforce so as to maximize total output of goods and services without regard to the distribution of output. But both the distribution of output in a society and the total output produced matter in evaluating overall social welfare. Does segregation serve the needs of both sexes, or does it favor one sex over the other? Or is some other subset of the society, not necessarily divided along sex lines, favored by this system?

The idea that men are the ones who benefit from sex segregation has been advanced by many writers.[65] Empirical evidence that female-dominated occupations pay less than male-dominated ones is often cited to show that there are effects of sex segregation on earnings that benefit men over women. This may be the most forceful argument for changing the system, but it also implies that sex segregation will be difficult to change using policies that focus primarily on the workplace. If segregation is a symptom of underlying discrimination, then concentrating on it rather than modifying the underlying taste for discrimination is not a long-run solution.

Another idea is that for a social system to persist, the majority of the society must find some benefits in it, though different benefits depend on one's social situation. For example, while women may not reap huge direct monetary rewards in the workplace under a system that relegates them to lower-paying jobs, given an income-sharing system such as marriage, they may find that other rewards are available, such as the possibility to engage solely in nonmarket labor during certain periods in their lifespan. At any point in time, this system would benefit married women more than unmarried women. However, at a point in society in which conditions are rapidly changing – as is the case now with high divorce rates and lower marriage rates – enough dissatisfaction may occur for people to question the system.

Immutability vs. changeability

A theme running through the previous sections is the contrast between the viewpoint that segregation is basically an immutable state versus the view that change is possible. If there are strong forces pushing a society towards segregation, there is a high probability that policies designed to lessen segregation will be adapted to in ways that preserve the prevalence of segregation, with segregation perhaps re-emerging in forms less noticeable, given our present ways of measuring its extent. We have already seen evidence on the consistency of segregation patterns across cultures. The previous section of this chapter also provided evidence on changes within occupations that support this statement.

At the same time, public policies affecting other social practices appear to have had substantial effects, which argues that some social practices can be changed through active intervention. One example is the apparently large effect of antidiscrimination laws on non-white hiring and earnings patterns. However, gender differences in both earnings and hiring have proved to be more resistant to change. Some observers use this contrast between eroding race differences and more constant gender differences as evidence that gender differences are immutable – i.e., essential. Others reject this view and argue that gender and race differences are essentially different phenomena and that appropriate remedies differ as well.

Theoretical structures used by those seeking to justify desegregation will be inherently unsatisfying if they do not build in an avenue for change in underlying motivations. If segregation reflects learned feelings, in contrast to being the reflection of a set of immutable basic feelings, then it may be possible to change those feelings. An empirically plausible model, in which employers and employees become progressively more gender-blind in their work behavior as they are exposed to more men and women working in nontraditional jobs, is needed before a good case can be made that desegregational policies can really have long-term effects in the workplace. A normative decision that gender-blindness is desirable, either because discrimination is undesirable in itself or because the outcomes under discrimination (such as women receiving lower wages) are unsatisfactory, is still required before one should attempt to modify underlying tastes. These two aspects would comprise a coherent position: gender-blind behavior is desirable, and integration in all aspects of society leads to gender-blind behavior as tastes and beliefs are changed through seeing men and women perform capably in a wide variety of roles.

FOCUS

Blind selection processes

One might expect that use of a truly gender-blind selection process in selecting new hires might result in more women in various occupations. Recently, economists Claudia Goldin and Cecilia Rouse documented the effects of the increased implementation of blind auditions in selecting symphony orchestra members.[66] Potential hires for major orchestras now play their audition while sitting behind a screen; some orchestras even roll out a carpet to muffle footsteps or ask players to remove their shoes while walking onto the stage so as not to have them reveal their sex. Meanwhile, female musicians have increased their share of top positions notably, comprising less than five percent of players in the top five symphony orchestras in 1970, but 25 percent as of 1996. Goldin and Rouse demonstrate that use of a screen significantly increases the probability that a woman will win the opening, accounting for as much as 46 percent of the increase in percentage female since 1970.

An interesting contrast is provided to this strong result by the findings from a study of double-blind versus single-blind refereeing processes in journal article selection.[67] *The American Economic Review* carried out a two-year experiment in which every other submitted paper was sent to referees with the authors' names removed. Economist Rebecca Blank found that acceptance rates were lower and referees more critical under double-blind reviewing, but the patterns were not significantly different by sex.[68] Interestingly, Blank found that the reviewers of the supposedly anonymous papers were able to correctly identify at least one author on a paper 46 percent of the time.[69] Nevertheless, *The American Economic Review* has instituted double-blind refereeing on all submitted papers.

The relationship between segregation and earnings

Let us now explore the relationship between segregation and the gender earnings gap. It has been noted by many researchers that jobs with a high percentage of women generally pay less than jobs with a low percentage of women. Does this imply that there is a causal relationship linking the two phenomena and, if so, what form does it take?

TABLE 6.10 Percentage female, gender earnings ratio, and median weekly earnings for selected occupations, 1996

Occupation	Female (%)	Gender earnings ratio	Median weekly earnings
Engineers	9	0.82	949
Police and detectives	15	0.84	606
Computer programmers	30	0.93	772
Doctors	31	0.58	1,133
Lawyers and judges	34	0.77	1,150
Marketing managers	36	0.65	912
College teachers	38	0.82	870
Sales jobs	43	0.60	474
Editors and reporters	50	0.80	688
Waiters and waitresses	70	0.82	271
Elementary teachers	83	0.90	662
Nursing aides	86	0.84	292
Registered nurses	91	0.95	697
Secretarial jobs	98	1.04	404

Source: Employment and Earnings 44, no. 1 (January 1997) (Table 39).

To illustrate this phenomenon, Table 6.10 presents data on percentage of females, female-male median weekly earnings ratios, and median weekly earnings for a variety of occupations. Three empirical regularities can be noted. The first is that there does appear to be a negative correlation between percentage of females and median weekly earnings for this set of occupations. In fact, the simple correlation coefficient for this table is −0.62.[70] Second, the female-male earnings ratio is positively correlated with the percentage of females (the simple correlation coefficient for the table is 0.52); that is, men still make more than women in every occupation, but the gap is narrower in the more female-dominated ones. Finally, the male-dominated occupations in the table include some of the most prestigious ones: medicine, law, and college teaching. Meanwhile, the female-dominated occupations include the traditional service-oriented professions, such as nursing and elementary school teaching.

In measuring the overall effect of segregation on the gender earnings gap, one can decompose the earnings gap into portions due to within-occupation (or firm, establishment, or job) gender differences and between-occupation gender differences. One such study found that the gender earnings gap caused by occupational segregation ranges from 11 percent in manufacturing to 26 percent in services (that is, the gender earnings ratio would still be 0.89 in manufacturing if women were paid the same as men within each occupation but maintained their different occupational distribution), while the earnings gaps caused by establishment and job segregation are both about 6 percent across industries.[71] Another study estimates that interfirm segregation is extremely prevalent, and that it can account for up to 50 percent of the gap.[72]

As shown above, there are several explanations of why gender segregation occurs and persists in societies, and it is not necessary to conclude that segregation is a bad thing. If people are free to choose positions based on their tastes and abilities, including their desire for monetary compensation, then a variety of patterns can result, ranging from complete segregation to complete integration. However, if segregation is the outcome of a process in which people are not free to choose a position because some jobs are closed to persons of a given group, then this is disturbing, particularly if this process generates lower wages for one group and higher wages for another. This link between segregation and lower earnings for women has led to much support for comparable worth policies, which will be discussed in detail in the policy application that concludes Part III.

The actual process that generates lower wages for women, even if women and men are equally skilled, could take one (or both) of two forms. One, the *exclusion model*, is that women are systematically excluded from higher-paying jobs and hired only to fill lower-paying ones. This model assumes that pay is not linked to availability of labor – i.e., that pay rates are not determined by market forces. The second form, the *crowding model*, is that women are systematically excluded from more desirable jobs and crowded into less desirable ones. However, desirability need *not* be related *ex ante* to the pay, but might, for instance, involve status considerations. This model assumes that wage rates are ultimately determined by market forces, but that female labor supply is artificially reduced in the more desirable jobs. This practice leads to an increased supply of female labor to the less desirable jobs and depresses wages in the less desirable jobs below what they would be if crowding were not occurring.[73] Simultaneously, wages are increased in the more desirable jobs due to the decreased labor supply.

Figure 6.1 represents the crowding model, using two occupations – blue-collar and pink-collar. Before women are excluded from the blue-collar occupation and therefore crowd into the pink-collar occupation, wages are the same in the two occupations. After the supply of labor increases to the pink-collar occupation, its wage falls and employment increases. Meanwhile, the supply of labor to the blue-collar occupation is decreased, causing its wage to rise and employment to decrease.

This discussion assumes that men and women have equal abilities in both occupations and that the occupations have similar structures in terms of the type of work performed. However, one argument against a causal interpretation for the negative relationship between percentage female and pay in occupations is that this correlation is picking up other factors that vary systematically between male-dominated and female-dominated jobs. For instance, if female-dominated occupations offer more part-time work opportunities, women may be attracted into them for the ability to better maintain both market and nonmarket work. Alternatively, men may be attracted into occupations that allow for more overtime work, once they have determined that they should specialize in market work. This assumes that comparative advantage patterns dictate that women are more likely than men to do at least some nonmarket work.

Table 6.11 shows that women and men do tend to be found in occupations with different hours structures. This evidence takes two forms. One, which can be seen in reading across the rows, shows that within a given set of occupations (classified by percentage female), women are more likely than men to be found working part-time, and men are more likely than women to be working full-time. Reading down the columns, we see that there is a positive correlation for both sexes between the type of occupation, in terms of degree of percentage female, and the percentage of workers who work part-time, and that there is also a negative correlation between percentage female and the percentage of workers who work overtime.

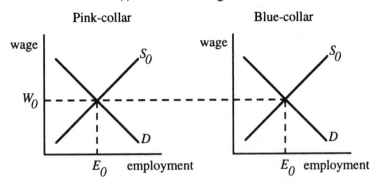

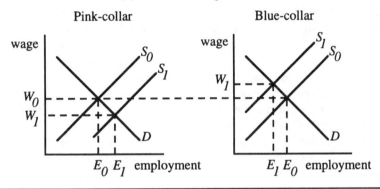

FIGURE 6.1 Effects of crowding

TABLE 6.11 Part-time and overtime work, employed persons, ages 25 to 64, 1990

% of occupation that is female	Usual hours under 30 (%)		Usual hours over 40 (%)	
	Women	Men	Women	Men
0–24.9	12.4	3.8	24.6	38.8
25–49.9	12.7	3.8	22.9	43.9
50–74.9	18.1	5.6	16.1	36.2
75–100	20.5	7.8	11.9	26.9

Source: Calculated by the author using data from the Census of Population and Housing 1990, Public-Use Microdata 1/100 Sample.

To the extent that wages vary systematically with hours worked, this pattern provides a partial explanation for the observed negative correlation between percentage female and hourly earnings. It is clear that many part-time jobs pay lower hourly rates than comparable full-time jobs; this can occur for reasons unrelated to discriminatory behavior on the part of employers. On the cost side, part-time workers may be less productive than full-time workers per hour worked, or the costs of using part-time workers may be higher than of using full-time workers. On the labor supply side, as stated above, workers (particularly women) may be willing to take these jobs at a lower rate as a trade-off for having more flexibility between market and nonmarket work; a large number of such persons would drive down the wage in these jobs relative to jobs that have few part-time work possibilities. It is even clearer that jobs requiring overtime must pay higher average rates because higher overtime pay rates are fixed by law for many jobs.

So, one explanation for the observed correlation between percentage female and earnings levels is that other variables that are also positively correlated with percentage female are the ones responsible for the observed negative correlation with earnings. These variables could include other factors about jobs besides the hours structure, such as riskiness or pleasantness of the work, an idea explored in more detail in Chapter 8. Another explanation is that there are systematic differences in the types of jobs that women and men tend to take in terms of the skills needed for the jobs and/or the abilities that the people in those jobs have. Studies of the relationship between earnings and percentage female generally control for factors such as the average educational level required in the job (or the average education held by persons in the job) and the amount of experience people who hold each job tend to have.[74] However, there are many factors that are generally not measurable by researchers – given time, money, and/or current measurement techniques – that can have an effect on earnings, including physical characteristics such as height, weight, and agility, as well as psychological characteristics such as leadership and motivation. Since no researcher can ever hope to account for all possible earnings-linked characteristics that persons may have, the objection that the researcher has left out some crucial factor and therefore spuriously linked percentage female with lower earnings for a job classification is unavoidable. Nevertheless, as we have seen above, evidence can be gleaned from a variety of sources to better help us understand the mechanisms that lead to particular occupations' becoming male- or female-dominated and, thereby, allow us to isolate factors that have changed over time to see if we can explain the relationship between percentage female and earnings.

While there are exceptions, the evidence is clear that there is a strong correlation between lower pay and higher percentage female across most occupations. Also, women are more likely to be found on the lower rungs in any occupation. The question is, why do these patterns occur? Here the evidence is mixed. While some occupations show evidence of routinization and de-skilling concurrent with women entering them, others – such as many of the professions – appear to be becoming more demanding. Also, while some of the pay gap may be attributable to differences in training and experience, women who have decided to enter the most demanding occupations in terms of training and yearly hours (e.g., doctors and lawyers) face some of the largest gaps in earnings relative to men.

The crucial question, which will be examined in the following three chapters, is how much of this pattern is attributable to discriminatory behavior on the part of employers, leading to exclusion and crowding, and how much of it is attributable to freely made choices on the part of women.

FOCUS

University coaches' salaries

Both *The Chronicle of Higher Education* and the National Collegiate Athletic Association recently conducted studies that drew attention to the large disparity in salaries paid to men's and women's teams coaches at universities.[75] *The Chronicle* found that "at the median Division I institution in 1995–96, the average salary paid to the head coach of a men's team was 44 per cent higher than that paid to the head coach of a women's team."[76] The biggest percentage difference between the average for men's coaches and the average for women's coaches was found at the University of Dayton: $57,050 and $16,470 respectively, for a difference of 246 percent more paid to the men's coaches. This translates into a pay disparity by gender of coach as well, as few women are found coaching men's teams – although about 52 percent of women's team coaches are men.

*E*ffects of workforce policies on segregation

This section considers how segregation patterns might be influenced by various current and proposed workforce policies aimed at improving women's well-being, including anti-discrimination policies, comparable worth, and job training programs. These policies are not generally implemented because of their effects on segregation, but they have such effects nonetheless.

Policies are categorized according to their primary focus: (1) those designed to affect wages, (2) those that attempt to modify employer behavior concerning hiring and promotion, (3) those aimed at workers rather than employers, namely training and other educational programs, (4) programs such as child care subsidies that affect decisions about whether or not and to what extent to participate in the labor force, and (5) those that target sex integration as a specific desired outcome.

Policies affecting wages

Some policies advocate adjusting the wages that come out of present-day market solutions. The most topical such policy is comparable worth, which essentially involves raising the wages in female-dominated jobs to equal the wages in male-dominated jobs that are deemed to be "comparable." Comparable worth has been implemented in some settings, mainly state and local governments, and has been advocated for wider use. Proponents and opponents are divided as to what the effects of a broad-based implementation of comparable worth would be on occupational segregation. In fact, it turns out that there is no way to prove that comparable worth will lead to either increased or decreased segregation.

There is a clear contrast between supporters and opponents of comparable worth in terms of what they generally think the effects on segregation will be. Supporters think it will decrease segregation because higher wages in traditionally female jobs will encourage men to move in. Opponents think it will increase segregation because higher wages in traditionally female jobs will discourage women from moving out.[77] The logic on both sides is correct in direction for supply-side effects, but neither allows for changes in labor demand, nor does existing research allow one to determine the relative magnitudes of these effects. Generally, both women and men will find a job more appealing if it pays more. The ratio of women to men depends upon who on the margin finds it most appealing – the new men attracted to the job or the new women – and also upon whom employers choose to hire.

One study, which created a computer simulation of an economy-wide comparable worth system, found that under a comparable worth policy in which wages were raised in female-dominated jobs, women increased their labor supply relative to men in jobs throughout the economy.[78] When wages were raised in female-dominated occupations, many women found it worthwhile to work more, while many married men benefited from their spouse's higher income and therefore found it optimal to work less. This outcome is consistent with the discussion of substitution and income effects of wage and nonearned income changes as discussed in Chapter 4. Although in this model labor force participation is couched in terms of total hours worked rather than by a head count and unemployment shows up as worksharing rather than loss of jobs, it still has implications for segregation as it is usually measured in that the women ended up comprising a larger proportion of hours worked in both female- and male-dominated occupations. Note that in such a real-life situation, the segregation index might therefore show no change.

In general, policies that affect wages in one or more jobs have an indeterminate effect on segregation. Wage increases make a job more desirable to both sexes, and wage decreases have the opposite effect, but the net change in segregation is impossible to determine unless a complete specification of the relative changes in female and male supply and the hiring decisions of employers is made. There is no *a priori* reason to assume that hiring patterns either respond to changes in the sex ratio of prospective employees or stay constant.

There is, however, the possibility that hiring patterns can be affected by legal restrictions forcing employers to consider the make-up of the applicant pool and hire in proportion to the sex and race proportions found therein. If this rule is enacted, as is the case in strong applications of antidiscrimination laws, then supply-side decisions will determine occupational make-up, given a particular job structure. Under strong applications of affirmative action, an employer may even be required to hire proportionately more women and minorities than their representation in the applicant pool. If this were the case, then the hiring rule can, in fact, determine the gender make-up of occupations. One might expect vacancy rates to rise in such a situation, as employers compete for the few female applicants.

There is still opportunity for an employer to reclassify jobs in such a way as to resegregate the workforce, but this becomes much harder to do if one is required to list all individual openings in a firm and consider the applicant pool for each job separately. Before listing rules came into widespread use, people generally applied to a firm for whatever position might be available and employers were free to decide where to place such persons. This can still be done to some extent, but records are often kept as to who has applied for a particular job. In addition, open advertisement of internal labor market positions within firms also creates a record of the applicant pool for each promotional possibility that can be monitored for evidence of gender bias in intrafirm mobility. The possibility of a discrimination lawsuit should serve as a restraining factor if employers attempt to promote men over women.

Policies affecting training

If rules such as affirmative action and antidiscrimination policies – which call for hiring and promotion in proportion to applicant pools – are binding, then observed outcomes are indicative of the relative supplies of men and women for particular jobs. If the outcomes in this case still reflect a large degree of sex segregation, then attempts to influence relative supplies must be undertaken if segregation is to be reduced.

One such policy is the attempt, using government-sponsored training programs, to prepare women for employment in traditionally male-dominated occupations. The actual effect of these programs on sex segregation appears to have been minimal, although individual participants may have benefited from receiving higher wages in these occupations than they would have in other areas. Training these women did not ensure that they would find an opportunity to apply their skills, as they were still subject to the decisions of employers regarding specific positions and the general availability of positions.[79]

A more fundamental policy is to increase awareness of work options among the young at a stage when they are able to adjust their secondary education so as to take advantage of a chosen option. This means both informing children about different occupations and telling them what background is required in order to enter these occupations, so that they can train appropriately for a chosen field. There is little argument to be made against increasing the information available to young people; the question is how much to devote to stressing particular occupations, such as engineering to women or teaching to men, in an attempt to influence the sex ratios in such fields. Still, it appears that gender differences in educational attainment, in both the decision of what type, if any, of postsecondary training to get and the choice of college major among college attendees, have large influences on subsequent differences in occupational choice.[80]

Policies affecting labor force participation decisions

Many other policies beside basic education and training affect women's and men's decisions about what type and amount of labor force participation to seek. This decision may indirectly affect the level of segregation. For example, availability of cheap, high-quality child care would affect many women's decisions as to whether and how much to participate in the labor market. Other policies of current interest include the availability of on-site child care, maternity leave, and flex-time. However, policies that either increase or decrease labor force participation need have little or no effect on segregation. To the extent that women on the margin are more likely to enter female-dominated occupations, an increase in their employment will increase workforce segregation. If, however, women are more likely to enter male-dominated occupations under these circumstances, then such policies would have the opposite effect.

Other workforce policies

Other policies that do not fall under the categories considered above include directly rewarding employers who act to reduce segregation. For instance, instead of concentrating on penalizing firms that discriminate, one could provide subsidies to firms that show marked improvement in integrating women into traditionally male jobs and/or in improving women's pay relative to men's. Such subsidies could provide a market advantage to these firms and make them relatively more profitable than firms who make no such efforts, or at least counter any costs incurred from implementing these changes.

Still other policies can augment existing workplace institutions, creating new employment possibilities without directly utilizing existing firms. One such policy is to increase the number of self-employed persons by small business funding through loans, subsidies, or outright grants. For this policy to affect segregation, women (and/or men) have to enter nontraditional lines of business, such as plumbing and home improvement, rather than setting up shop in more traditional fields such as beauty care and catering. To the extent that the distribution of independent retailers and service providers is affected by differing costs of capitalizing such businesses, making the costs of entering, say, plumbing and catering equivalent on the margin would tip more women into the former than are presently found. Still, basic tastes and training would affect the number of persons suited to enter each trade.

Conclusions about the effects of various policies

From the empirical evidence to date, it appears that current policies have had a limited effect on segregation. While there have been some shifts in the relative numbers of men and women to certain occupations (as reflected in changes in the percentage female for those occupations), it is difficult to attribute these changes to any particular policy.

The main point to be gained from the arguments made above is that one should be wary of any claims that a particular policy will definitely either increase or decrease sex segregation. The answer in each case depends crucially on the particular assumptions made about labor supply and demand responses to the policy. To the extent that hiring preferences of employers are suppressed through imposition of hiring rules, the relative supply of male and female workers effectively determines the level of segregation. Many policy analysts, however, assume the former point and concentrate on supply responses.

If achieving a greater degree of integration in the workplace is desired, then clearly new strategies need to be tried if the rate of integration is to be accelerated. One point to be considered in advocating particular strategies is whether the time frame for desired change is short or long. Some strategies, such as stepping up efforts to create a sex-blind educational environment, will take longer for their effects to be felt in the workplace, but they may have more lasting and widespread effect than "quick fixes" such as retraining women already in the labor force to enter nontraditional occupations. Additionally, policies need to be undertaken simultaneously if the probability of success in achieving integration is to be increased substantially. In light of the discussion above, a combination of policies designed to affect both hiring practices and the relative supplies of women and men to different jobs is required so that pressure on both the demand and the supply side of the labor market is tuned towards integration.

Policy Application: Affirmative action

The implementation of affirmative action policies provides an interesting case study in the contrast between such policies' sizable effect on minority employment – particularly for blacks and Hispanics – and the small effect on white female employment. It appears that workforce sex segregation in the form of distribution of workers between the covered and uncovered sectors, where the sector covered by affirmative action is currently more male-dominated (and appears to contain relatively better-paying jobs), has not been greatly influenced by these policies.

Affirmative action policy originally focused on improving employment possibilities for blacks. Starting in 1941 with Franklin Roosevelt's Executive Order 8002, a series of executive orders has barred race discrimination by federal contractors. In 1961 John Kennedy's Executive Order 10925 required contractors to implement affirmative action and established sanctions, including contract termination, against noncompliers. Lyndon Johnson's Executive Order 11246 beefed up enforcement, and his Executive Order 11375 in 1967 expanded affirmative action to include women. However, effective regulations enforcing this expansion did not reach full stride until after the Equal Employment Act of 1972. Since 1972, all federal contractors and first-tier subcontractors with 50 or more employees (or a contract worth $50,000 or more) must agree to "take affirmative action to ensure that applicants are employed and that employees are treated during employment without regard to their race, color, religion, sex, or national origin." These actions include maintaining written affirmative action plans containing goals and timetables for correcting deficiencies in equal employment opportunity. In addition, many organizations that are not required to have an affirmative action plan nonetheless have them, in varying degrees of formality.

It is not clear that affirmative action policies have been particularly successful in increasing the representation of women in better-paying positions, nor do researchers agree as to how much of the increase that has occurred can be attributed to such policies. Enforcement of affirmative action regulations has been sketchy.[81] The Equal Employment Opportunity Commission is limited to responding to discrimination complaints, while the Office of Federal Contract Compliance Programs, the main government agency concerned with affirmative action in the workplace as the overseer agency for federal contractors, is understaffed to the point where it would take 38 years for it to investigate each contractor workplace once.[82] Out of the employers it checked in 1994–95, 75 percent were in substantial noncompliance.[83]

How might one measure the impact of affirmative action on women's employment patterns? One way is to compare changes in female employment in the covered sector with changes in the uncovered sector. For instance, several studies compare federal contractors, who are covered by affirmative action, with similar employers who are not covered.[84] While studies concentrating on the effects of affirmative action on women's employment in the early 1970s found little effect – or even net employment losses – for white women,[85] by the late 1970s black women appear to have benefited substantially, and white women somewhat. Table 6.12 shows that in 1974, 27.6 percent of the average federal contractor workforce were white women, compared with 39.4 percent among noncontractor employees.[86] Because federal contractors are more likely than noncontractors to be in the manufacturing sector and less likely to be in the service or retail trade sector, we would expect women's employment share to be lower among contractors. However, women's employment growth in the contractor sector outstripped growth in the noncontractor sector. By 1980 employment of white women had increased by 1.2 percent among contractors, but only by 0.6 percent among noncontractors. The author of this study concludes that affirmative action has had a modest effect in increasing white women's employment: "If white female employment share among contractors had grown only at the slower noncontractor rate, roughly 2 percent fewer white females would have been employed among federal contractors in 1980." Black

TABLE 6.12 Female employment share (percentage) by federal contract status, 1974 and 1980

Contractor?	White female		Black female		Other female	
	Yes	*No*	*Yes*	*No*	*Yes*	*No*
1980	28.8	40.0	4.5	5.9	2.8	3.6
1974	27.6	39.4	3.0	4.7	1.6	2.4
Change	1.2	0.6	1.5	1.2	1.2	1.2

Source: Jonathan S. Leonard, "Women and Affirmative Action," *Journal of Economic Perspectives* 3, no. 1 (Winter 1989): 63. Reprinted with permission.

women have made more sizable employment gains overall, but less of a difference in growth rates appears between sectors.

Studying the effect of affirmative action on federal contractors overstates the impact of implementing affirmative action throughout the economy to the extent that contractor gains represent a reshuffling from noncontractors that could not occur if there were no uncovered sector. It could also understate the effect if there are spillover effects on noncontractors that raises their female employment as well, but this appears unlikely.[87] This methodology also misses the effects on the uncovered sector of voluntary affirmative action or affirmative action mandated as a remedy following litigation under Title VII of the Civil Rights Act of 1964, which applies to all private employers with 15 or more employees and bars employment discrimination on the basis of race, color, religion, sex, or national origin.

A recent paper critiques this methodology, pointing out that there are no specific statistical controls for wage and technology differences between the sectors.[88] Economic theory predicts that firms subject to affirmative action will have higher costs than firms who are not if they find hiring restrictions binding in the sense of limiting their ability to substitute between inputs (e.g., between black workers and machinery). The paper finds that constraints were binding in 1980 and that "the cost of complying with affirmative action averaged 6.5 percent of total costs for constrained firms."[89] This indicates that such restrictions may cause supply to contract in the covered sector, thereby reducing the sector's demand for labor. One could interpret this as a social cost of enforcing integration.

Summary

As the female labor force grows, women are entering many occupations where they were underrepresented in the recent past, particularly the professions. However, they also continue to cluster in the service and clerical sectors and are making slower inroads into blue-collar occupations. As the percentage of females rises in different occupations, these occupations become resegregated, ghettoized, or integrated.

Sex segregation indexes have been dropping since 1960, but the rate of change is much less than for race segregation indexes, and the levels are much higher. Segregation is prevalent in all societies. Across industrialized societies, men and women are found in similar occupations; across nonindustrialized societies, occupations vary in their assignment to men or women. Six explanations are offered for the prevalence of sex segregation, ranging from choice-based arguments to discrimination. These explanations are not mutually exclusive.

The interpretation of the relationship between pay and percentage female for a job is problematic. While there is a negative correlation between the two, it may be due to factors about the different jobs in which men and women are found or to discrimination on the part of employers that leads women to be barred from entering particular jobs without difficulty.

The effects of particular workplace policies on segregation are generally unpredictable and hard to discern. Affirmative action policies appear to have had little effect on sex segregation, particularly for white women.

Endnotes

1. Barbara F. Reskin and Patricia A. Roos, *Job Queues, Gender Queues: Explaining Women's Inroads into Male Occupations* (Philadelphia, Pa.: Temple University, 1990): 19.
2. Hank Whittemore, "I Want Respect, That's All," *Parade* (July 10, 1988): 4–5.
3. See Jean R. Schroedel, *Alone in a Crowd: Women in the Trades Tell Their Stories* (Philadelphia, Pa.: Temple University, 1985), for a collection of interviews with women working in predominantly male occupations.
4. Whittemore, *op. cit.*: 4.
5. See Louise Kapp Howe, *Pink Collar Workers* (New York: Putnam, 1977), for a collection of interviews with women working in these occupations during the mid-1970s.
6. Reskin and Roos, *op. cit.*: 18.
7. *Digest of Education Statistics* (1996): 281 (Table 254).
8. Cynthia Fuchs Epstein, *Women in Law, Second Edition* (Urbana, Ill.: University of Illinois Press, 1993). See also American Bar Association Commission on Women in the Profession, *Unfinished Business: Overcoming the Sisyphus Factor* (1996).
9. American Bar Association Commission on Women in the Profession, *op. cit.* Accounting, another profession in which large partnership firms are dominant, shows similar patterns by sex; see Shari H. Wescott and Robert E. Seiler, *Women in the Accounting Profession* (New York: Markus Wiener, 1986).
10. Ted Gest, "Feminizing the Law: The New Meaning of Equality," *U.S. News & World Report* (June 17, 1991): 48.
11. *Employment and Earnings* 44, no. 1 (January 1997): (Table 39).
12. *Digest of Education Statistics* (1996): 281 (Table 254).
13. Carol Kleiman, "Number of Women Doctors No Longer So Anemic," *Chicago Tribune* (May 20, 1991), Section 4: 5.
14. Carol Kleiman, "3 Firms Serve as Catalysts for Women," *Chicago Tribune* (January 23, 1991), Section 3: 3.
15. "Women Make Slow Progress up the Corporate Ladder," *The Economist* (March 14, 1987): 61–62. See also Rochelle Sharpe, "The Waiting Game," *Wall Street Journal* (March 28, 1994): A1, A10, and related articles in the same issue, for information from a 1992 study of firms reporting to the U.S. Equal Employment Opportunity Commission.
16. Kleiman (January 23, 1991).
17. Those women who do rise to the top receive great attention from the press. Cf. Joseph B. White and Carol Hymowitz, "Watershed Generation of Women Executives is Rising to the Top," *Wall Street Journal* (February 10, 1997): A1, A8.
18. Kleiman (January 23, 1991).
19. For the classic discussion of the tokenism phenomenon, see Rosabeth Moss Kanter, *Men and Women of the Corporation* (New York: Basic Books, 1977).
20. Kleiman (May 20, 1991), quoting Dr. Michelle Harrison.
21. Anne B. Fisher, "When Will Women Get To the Top?" *Fortune* 126, no. 6 (September 21, 1992): 44–56. On a brighter note, see Joseph B. White and Carol Hymowitz, "Broken Glass: Watershed

Generation of Women Executives Is Rising To the Top," *Wall Street Journal* (February 10, 1997): A1, A8.

22. Carl Hoffman and John Shelton Reed, "Sex Discrimination? The XYZ Affair," *Public Interest* 62 (Winter 1981): 21–39.

23. Christine Williams, *Still a Man's World: Men Who Do "Women's Work"* (Berkeley, Calif.: University of California, 1995).

24. Francine D. Blau, *Equal Pay in the Office* (Lexington, Mass.: Heath, 1977).

25. Barbara F. Reskin and Patricia A. Roos, "Status Hierarchies and Sex Segregation," *Ingredients for Women's Employment Policy*, eds. Christina Bose and Glenna Spitze (Albany, N.Y.: State University of New York, 1987): 3–21.

26. Myra H. Strober and Carolyn L. Arnold, "The Dynamics of Occupational Segregation among Bank Tellers," *Gender in the Workplace*, eds. Clair Brown and Joseph A. Pechman (Washington, D.C.: Brookings, 1987): 107–148.

27. The clerical labor situation in Great Britain is described in Samuel Cohn, *The Process of Occupational Sex-Typing: The Feminization of Clerical Labor in Great Britain* (Philadelphia, Pa.: Temple University, 1985).

28. Diane Mason, "Facts About Forceps," *American Baby* (October 1990): 48–51.

29. Barbara Ehrenreich and Deirdre English, "Witches, Midwives, and Nurses: A History of Women Healers" (Detroit, Mich.: Black and Red, 1973): 33.

30. Reskin and Roos (1990): 18.

31. Polly A. Phipps, "Occupational Resegregation among Insurance Adjusters and Examiners," *Job Queues, Gender Queues: Explaining Women's Inroads into Male Occupations*, eds. Barbara F. Reskin and Patricia A. Roos (Philadelphia, Pa.: Temple University, 1990): 225–240.

32. Mary Louise Gilman, "Changing Times," *National Shorthand Reporter* (December 1976): 26–27.

33. Wesley V. Gales, "?Men Wanted?" *National Shorthand Reporter* (May 1976): 26–27.

34. Gilman, *loc. cit.*

35. Sandra W. McFate, "Men Wanted," *National Shorthand Reporter* (February 1976): 13–15.

36. Hollie W. Sharpe and Vincent W. Smith, "A Profile of the Tennessee Shorthand Reporter," *Journal of Court Reporting*, 52, no. 10 (August 1976): 30–32.

37. Gary M. Cramer, "How Long Does it Take?" *Caligrams* 17 (July 1989): 12–13.

38. McFate, *loc. cit.*

39. *Ibid.*

40. Reskin and Roos (1990): 18.

41. Thomas Steiger and Barbara F. Reskin, "Baking and Baking Off: Deskilling and the Changing Sex Makeup of Bakers," *Job Queues, Gender Queues: Explaining Women's Inroads into Male Occupations*, eds. Barbara F. Reskin and Patricia A. Roos (Philadelphia, Pa.: Temple University, 1990): 257–274.

42. Linda A. Detman, "Women behind Bars: The Feminization of Bartending," *Job Queues, Gender Queues: Explaining Women's Inroads into Male Occupations*, eds. Barbara F. Reskin and Patricia A. Roos (Philadelphia, Pa.: Temple University, 1990): 241–255.

43. Otis Dudley Duncan and Beverly Duncan, "A Methodological Analysis of Segregation Indexes," *American Sociological Review* 20, no. 1 (1955): 210–217.

44. For a discussion of other useful measures, see Christina Jonung, "Patterns of Occupational Segregation by Sex in the Labor Market," *Sex Discrimination and Equal Opportunity*, eds. Gunther Schmid and Renate Weitzel (New York: St. Martin's, 1988): 44–68; and Victor R. Fuchs, "A Note on Sex Segregation in Professional Occupations," *Explorations in Economic Research* 2, no. 1 (Winter 1975): 105–111.

45. These patterns are corroborated and discussed in several papers, including Judith Fields and Edward N. Wolff, "The Decline of Sex Segregation and the Wage Gap, 1970–80," *Journal of Human Resources* 26, no. 4 (Fall 1991): 608–622; and Mary C. King, "Occupational Segregation by Race and Sex, 1940–88," *Monthly Labor Review* 115, no. 4 (April 1992): 30–36.

46. For a discussion of this point, see Jerry Alan Jacobs, *The Sex-Segregation of Occupations and the Career Patterns of Women* (Ann Arbor, Mich.: University Microfilms International, 1983).

47. The classes are: Managerial and Professional; Technical, Sales, and Administrative Support; Service; Farming, Forestry, and Fishing; Precision Production, Craft, and Repair; and Operators, Fabricators, and Laborers.

48. There are only 500 inhabited occupations as the three military occupation codes are excluded.

49. Myra H. Strober and Barbara B. Reagan, "Sex Differences in Economists' Fields of Specialization," *Women and the Workplace*, eds. Martha Blaxall and Barbara Reagan (Chicago, Ill.: University of Chicago, 1976): 292–307.

50. Betty Jo Irvine, *Sex Segregation in Librarianship* (Westport, Conn.: Greenwood, 1985).

51. A firm consists of one or more establishments, which are physical locations where the firm operates. For instance, a chain of restaurants is a firm, while each individual restaurant is an establishment.

52. William T. Bielby and James N. Baron, "A Woman's Place Is with Other Women: Sex Segregation Within Organizations," *Sex Segregation in the Workplace: Trends, Explanations, Remedies*, ed. Barbara F. Reskin (Washington, D.C.: National Academy, 1984): 27–55.

53. Rachel A. Rosenfeld, "Job Changing and Occupational Sex Segregation: Sex and Race Comparisons," *Sex Segregation in the Workplace: Trends, Explanations, Remedies*, ed. Barbara F. Reskin (Washington, D.C.: National Academy, 1984): 56–86. Jerry A. Jacobs, *Revolving Doors: Sex Segregation and Women's Careers* (Stanford, Calif.: Stanford University, 1989), documents high mobility between male-dominated, neutral, and female-dominated fields on the part of individual women and a slow net rate of accumulation of women in male-dominated areas.

54. This theme will be developed further in Parts IV and V.

55. Patricia A. Roos, *Gender and Work: A Comparative Analysis of Industrial Societies* (Albany, N.Y.: State University of New York, 1985), considers Japan, Israel, the United States, and nine countries in Western Europe. The situation in Russia (the Soviet Union) is examined by Gail Warshofsky Lapidus, "Occupational Segregation and Public Policy: A Comparative Analysis of American and Soviet Patterns," *Women and the Workplace*, eds. Martha Blaxall and Barbara Reagan (Chicago, Ill.: University of Chicago, 1976): 119–136. Sweden is examined in Christina Jonung, *loc. cit.*

56. These data are derived from the cross-cultural files maintained at the University of Pittsburgh, as reported by George Murdock, *Ethnographic Atlas* (Pittsburgh, Pa.: University of Pittsburgh, 1967); and George P. Murdock and Douglas R. White, "Standard Cross-Cultural Sample," *Ethnology* 8, no. 4 (October 1969): 329–369. A study of these data in terms of sexual division of labor is George P. Murdock and Caterina Provost, "Factors in the Division of Labor by Sex: A Cross-Cultural Analysis," *Ethnology* 12, no. 2 (1973): 203–225.

57. See Charlotte G. O'Kelly and Larry S. Carney, *Women and Men in Society, Second Edition* (Belmont, Calif.: Wadsworth, 1986).

58. Peggy Sanday, *Female Power and Male Dominance: On the Origins of Sexual Inequality* (Cambridge, United Kingdom: Cambridge University, 1981).

59. Mary Corcoran and Paul Courant, "Sex Role Socialization and Labor Market Outcomes," *American Economic Review* 75, no. 2 (May 1985): 275–278; Randall K. Filer, "The Role of Personality and Tastes in Determining Occupational Structure," *Industrial and Labor Relations Review* 39, no. 3 (April 1986): 412–424.

60. For discussion of sexual harassment and sexuality in organizations, see Barbara A. Gutek, *Sex and the Workplace: The Impact of Sexual Behavior and Harassment on Women, Men, and Organizations* (San Francisco, Calif.: Jossey-Bass, 1985); Jeff Hearn, Deborah L. Sheppard, Peta Tancred-Sheriff, and Gibson Burrell (eds.), *The Sexuality of Organization* (London: Sage, 1989).

61. Barbara Kantrowitz, "Love in the Office," *Newsweek* (February 15, 1988): 48–52.

62. This was discussed in Chapter 3; see Gary Becker, "Human Capital, Effort, and the Sexual Division of Labor," *Journal of Labor Economics* 3, no. 1 (January 1985): 33–58.

63. This argument is advanced by Victor R. Fuchs, "Women's Quest for Economic Equality," *Journal of Economic Perspectives* 3, no. 1 (Winter 1989): 25–41.

64. For a lively debate on this last hypothesis, see Solomon Polachek, "Occupational Self-Selection: A Human Capital Approach to Sex Differences in Occupational Structure," *Review of Economics and Statistics* 63, no. 1 (February 1981): 60–69; Paula England, "Wage Appreciation and Depreciation: A Test of Neoclassical Explanations of Occupational Sex Segregation," *Social Forces* 62, no. 3 (March 1984): 726–749; Solomon Polachek, "Occupational Segregation: A Defense of Human Capital Predictions," *Journal of Human Resources* 20, no. 3 (Summer 1985): 437–439; Paula England "Occupational Segregation: Rejoinder to Polachek," *Journal of Human Resources* 20, no. 3 (Summer 1985): 441–443; and Solomon Polachek, "Occupational Segregation: Reply to England," *Journal of Human Resources* 20, no. 3 (Summer 1985): 444. This issue is discussed in more detail in Chapter 7.

65. Cf. Barbara R. Bergmann, "Occupational Segregation, Wages and Profits When Employers Discriminate by Race or Sex," *Eastern Economic Journal* 1, no. 2 (April-July 1974): 103–110; Heidi Hartmann, "Capitalism, Patriarchy, and Job Segregation by Sex," *Women and the Workplace*, eds. Martha Blaxall and Barbara Reagan (Chicago, Ill.: University of Chicago, 1976): 137–169; Jean Lipman-Bluman, "Toward a Homosocial Theory of Sex Roles: An Explanation of the Sex Segregation of Social Institutions," *Women and the Workplace*, eds. Martha Blaxall and Barbara Reagan (Chicago, Ill.: University of Chicago, 1976): 15–31; Myra H. Strober, "Toward a General Theory of Occupational Sex Segregation: The Case of Public School Teaching," *Sex Segregation in the Workplace: Trends, Explanations, Remedies*, ed. Barbara F. Reskin (Washington, D.C.: National Academy, 1984): 144–156.

66. Claudia Goldin and Cecilia Rouse, "Orchestrating Impartiality: The Impact of 'Blind' Auditions on Female Musicians," National Bureau of Economic Research Working Paper no. 5903 (January 1997).

67. In double-blind processes, neither the author nor the reviewer knows each other's identity. In single-blind processes, the reviewer knows the author's identity. Journals vary in their policy both within and between academic disciplines, with natural science and medical journals tending to be single-blind, political science and sociology journals tending to be double-blind, and economics journals split, with a higher proportion using single-blind. A few journals use a nonblind process (in economics only *Review of Radical Political Economy*, to the best of my knowledge), where the referee signs the report given to the author.

68. Rebecca M. Blank, "The Effects of Double-Blind versus Single-Blind Reviewing: Experimental Evidence from *The American Economic Review*," *American Economic Review* 81, no. 5 (December 1991): 1041–1067.

69. Blank, *op. cit.*: 1051.

70. A *correlation coefficient* for variables X and Y is defined as:

$$r_{xy} = \frac{V_{xy}}{\sqrt{V_{xx}V_{yy}}}$$

where

$$V_{xy} = \frac{1}{n}\sum_{i=1}^{n}(X_i - \overline{X})(Y_i - \overline{Y}),$$

the *covariance* of X and Y,

$$V_{xx} = \frac{1}{n}\sum_{i=1}^{n}(X_i - \overline{X})^2 \text{ and } V_{yy} = \frac{1}{n}\sum_{i=1}^{n}(Y_i - \overline{Y})^2,$$

are the *variances* of X and Y respectively, and

$$\overline{X} = \frac{1}{n}\sum_{i=1}^{n} X_i \text{ and } \overline{Y} = \frac{1}{n}\sum_{i=1}^{n} Y_i$$

are the means of X and Y respectively.

A correlation coefficient ranges from -1 to 1, where 1 indicates perfect positive correlation between the two variables (i.e., when one variable increases in value, the other also increases), 0 indicates no correlation between the two variables, and -1 indicates perfect negative correlation between the two variables (i.e., when one variable increases in value, the other decreases).

71. Erica L. Groshen, "The Structure of the Female/Male Wage Differential: Is It Who You Are, What You Do, or Where You Work?" *Journal of Human Resources* 26, no. 3 (Summer 1991): 457–472.

72. William J. Carrington and Kenneth R. Troske, "Gender Segregation in Small Firms," *Journal of Human Resources* 30, no. 3 (November 1992): 503–533.

73. This model was first developed by Bergmann, *loc. cit.*

74. Cf. David A. Macpherson and Barry T. Hirsch, "Wages and Gender Composition: Why Do Women's Jobs Pay Less?" *Journal of Labor Economics* 13, no. 3 (July 1995): 426–471, who control for a large number of skill-related occupational characteristics and are able to reduce the measured effect of gender composition on earnings substantially, but not completely. Notably, Barry Gerhart and Nabil El Cheikh, "Earnings and Percentage Female: A Longitudinal Study," *Industrial Relations* 30, no. 1 (Winter 1991): 62–78, find use of longitudinal data to estimate earnings equations drives the percentage female penalty effect down substantially for women, but does not reduce the penalty for men.

75. Jim Naughton, "A New Debate Over Disparities in Coaches' Salaries," *Chronicle of Higher Education* 43, no. 36 (May 16, 1997): A35–A36.

76. Naughton, *op. cit.*: A35.

77. Henry J. Aaron and Cameran M. Lougy, *The Comparable Worth Controversy* (Washington, D.C.: Brookings, 1986).

78. Perry C. Beider, B. Douglas Bernheim, Victor R. Fuchs, and John B. Shoven, "Comparable Worth in a General Equilibrium Model of the U.S. Economy," *Research in Labor Economics* 9 (Greenwich, Conn.: JAI, 1988).

79. See Linda J. Waite and Sue E. Berryman, "Occupational Desegregation in CETA Programs," *Sex Segregation in the Workplace: Trends, Explanations, Remedies*, ed. Barbara F. Reskin (Washington, D.C.: National Academy, 1984): 292–307; Irmtraud Seeborg, Michael C. Seeborg, and Abera Zegeye, "The Impact of Nontraditional Training on the Occupational Attainment of Women," *Journal of Human Resources* 19, no. 4 (Fall 1984): 452–471.

80. Arthur E. Blakemore and Stuart A. Low, "Sex Differences in Occupational Selection: The Case of College Majors," *Review of Economics and Statistics* 66, no. 1 (February 1984): 157–163.

81. Barbara R. Bergmann, *In Defense of Affirmative Action* (New York: BasicBooks, 1996): 8.

82. Bergmann, *op. cit.*: 53–54.

83. Bergmann, *op. cit.*: 44.

84. Morley Gunderson, "Male-Female Wage Differentials and Policy Studies," *Journal of Economic Literature* 27, no. 1 (March 1989): 62 (Table 3), summarizes studies.

85. Morris Goldstein and Robert S. Smith, "The Estimated Impact of the Anti-discrimination Program Aimed at Federal Contractors," *Industrial and Labor Relations Review* 29, no. 4 (July 1976): 523–543; James J. Heckman and Kenneth I. Wolpin, "Does the Contract Compliance Program Work? An Analysis of Chicago Data," *Industrial and Labor Relations Review*, 29, no. 4 (July 1976): 544–564.

86. Jonathan S. Leonard, "Women and Affirmative Action," *Journal of Economic Perspectives* 3, no. 1 (Winter 1989): 61–75.

87. *Ibid.*

88. Peter Griffin, "The Impact of Affirmative Action on Labor Demand: A Test of Some Implications of the Le Chatelier Principle," *Review of Economics and Statistics* 74, no. 2 (May 1992): 251–260.

89. Griffin, *op. cit.*: 259.

90. This puzzle was posed by a correspondent in the "Ask Marilyn" column, *Parade* (April 28, 1996): 6. It is an example of what is referred to in probability and statistics texts as Simpson's Paradox.

*F*urther reading

Blaxall, Martha, and Barbara B. Reagan (eds.) (1976). *Women and the Workplace: The Implications of Occupational Segregation*. Chicago, Ill.: University of Chicago. Older book containing some classic articles on sex segregation, particularly of a more discursive theoretical nature.

Brown, Clair, and Joseph A. Pechman (eds.) (1987). *Gender in the Workplace*. Washington, D.C.: Brookings. Collection of scholarly papers on various gender issues, including part-time work, and women and unionism.

Federal Glass Ceiling Commission (1995). *Good for Business: Making Full Use of the Nation's Human Capital: The Environmental Scan*. Washington, D.C.: U.S. Government Printing Office. Fact-finding report from the Glass Ceiling Commission, 1991–96, which conducted studies and issued recommendations concerning the advancement of women and minorities, particularly into management positions. Lists all commissioned reports in an appendix. All the reports are available for downloading at the School of Industrial & Labor Relations, Cornell University website (www.ilr.cornell.edu).

Jacobs, Jerry A. (1989). *Revolving Doors: Sex Segregation and Women's Careers*. Stanford, Calif.: Stanford University. Study using national data of women's entrance and exit patterns into occupations.

Michael, Robert T., Heidi I. Hartmann, and Brigid O'Farrell (eds.) (1989). *Pay Equity: Empirical Inquiries*. Washington, D.C.: National Academy. Collection of scholarly papers on various issues related to occupational segregation and its link with pay.

O'Kelly, Charlotte G., and Larry S. Carney (1986). *Women and Men in Society: Cross-Cultural Perspectives on Gender Stratification, Second Edition*. Belmont, Calif.: Wadsworth. Very useful textbook discussing gender roles in a wide variety of modern and premodern societies. Provides valuable world view of sex segregation patterns and gives a picture of how anthropologists and sociologists approach the puzzle of sex segregation.

Reskin, Barbara F. (ed.) (1984). *Sex Segregation in the Workplace: Trends, Explanations, Remedies*. Washington, D.C.: National Research Council. Committee report summarizing findings from a major research initiative; clearly lays out issues and patterns.

Reskin, Barbara F., and Heidi I. Hartmann (eds.) (1986). *Women's Work, Men's Work: Sex Segregation on the Job*. Washington, D.C.: National Research Council. Collected articles on sex segregation that accompany and provide background for preceding committee report.

Reskin, Barbara F., and Patricia A. Roos (1990). *Job Queues, Gender Queues: Explaining Women's Inroads into Male Occupations*. Philadelphia, Pa.: Temple University. Contains many useful chapter-length case studies of particular occupations that have experienced gender recomposition.

Roos, Patricia A. (1985). *Gender and Work: A Comparative Analysis of Industrial Societies*. Albany, N.Y.: State University of New York. Useful empirical comparison of developed countries, mainly European data, on a number of labor force measures, including percentage female by occupation.

Scott, Alison MacEwen (ed.) (1994). *Gender Segregation and Social Change: Men and Women in Changing Labour Markets*. Oxford, United Kingdom: Oxford University. Interesting set of related studies of labor market patterns in six cities in the United Kingdom carried out by an interdisciplinary research team.

Tomaskovic-Devey, Donald (1993). *Gender & Racial Inequality at Work: The Sources & Conse-quences of Job Segregation*. Ithaca, N.Y.: ILR. Describes original survey of North Carolina adults; forceful discussion of shortcomings of neoclassical economic theory and advocacy of social closure and status explanations for segregation patterns.

Wilkinson, Carroll Wetzel (1991). *Women Working in Nontraditional Fields: References and Resources 1963–1988*. Boston, Mass.: G.K. Hall & Co. Bibliography for works, mainly historical and case study, on women in male-dominated occupations.

Williams, Christine (1989). *Gender Differences at Work: Women and Men in Nontraditional Occu-pations*. Berkeley, Calif.: University of California. Examines empirical data on nontraditional occupations; no particular theoretical underpinning.

Discussion questions

1. Consider a job that you currently hold or held in the past. Describe the segregation patterns that you found within the firm, the occupation, and the industry. What do you think the causes of these patterns were?

2. Table 6.1 shows that the percentage of bachelor degrees awarded to women in computer science and economics has declined since 1984. What might have caused these declines? Why might the two fields diverge in their pattern when it comes to master's degrees (still rising in economics, falling in computer science)?

3. Consider the Focus on directors and officers at Fortune 500 companies. Do you think that company policies would change if a higher proportion of these persons were women?

4. Consider two countries, A and B. In each country there are only two occupations: white-collar and blue-collar. White-collar jobs pay twice as much as blue-collar jobs. In Country A, 30 percent of the working women and 70 percent of the working men are in white-collar jobs. In Country B, 35 percent of the working women and 90 percent of the working men are in white-collar jobs.

   (a) What is the Duncan index for each country?
   (b) What is the female-male earnings ratio for each country (assuming that everyone works the same number of hours)?
   (c) In your opinion, in which country are women better off?

5. In the country of X, men and women can work in any of three occupations (farmer, cook, or hunter). The distribution of men and women across the occupations and their wage rates are listed below:

Occupation	Distribution (%)		Wages ($)	
	Women	Men	Women	Men
Farmer	40	40	10	8
Cooker	50	20	15	10
Hunter	10	40	20	12

   (a) Compute the Duncan index.
   (b) What is the average wage of women? Of men? What is the ratio? What is the gap?
   (c) What would women earn if they had men's jobs (i.e., if their distribution across the occupations was the same as men's)? Now what is the ratio? In this case, how much of the gap is explained by occupational differences?

(d) What would men earn if they had women's jobs? Now what is the ratio? In this case, how much of the gap is explained by occupational differences?

6. Consider the Focus on blind selection processes. Why might the study of refereeing have found less of a gender effect than the study of orchestral auditions? Can you think of other selection processes that could be turned into gender-blind selection processes? In your example, would it likely increase the proportion of women selected?

7. Using the data in Table 6.9, discuss which activities are likely to contain a high degree of sexual segregation by subactivity and which activities are likely to also involve physical separation for the sexes during the workday.

8. Some of the occupations in Table 6.10 appear to be "outliers;" in other words, they do not conform well to the overall pattern. For example, computer programmers are predominantly male, yet women are paid very nearly equally with men in this occupation. Why might this be the case? Are there other apparent outliers?

9. If an occupation is completely segregated, could it appear in Table 6.10? Why or why not? Is this a problem in studying the link between segregation and earnings?

10. Consider the Focus on coaching salaries. Give some potential explanations for why men's team coaches are paid more. If salaries are raised for women's team coaches relative to men's team coaches, what might happen to the percentage of women coaching each type of team?

11. Draw diagrams similar in style to Figure 6.1 to show what would happen to the labor markets for nurses and doctors if women were at first barred from attending medical school and then the bar was dropped.

12. Which explanations of society-wide sex segregation do you find least plausible? Which do you find most plausible? Can you think of particular areas of the U.S. workscene that appear to lend evidence for each explanation?

13. Consider the effects on segregation of expanding the use of the employment policies of provision of on-site child care and maternity leave and availability of flex-time. In what ways would the increased use of these policies tend to increase or decrease sex segregation of the labor force?

14. Consider Table 6.12: can you think of reasons other than affirmative action for the rise of female employment in the covered sector from 1974 to 1980?

15. A company decides to expand, so it opens a factory, creating 455 new openings.[90] For the 70 white collar positions, 200 men and 200 women applied, of which 30 men and 40 women were hired. For the 385 blue collar positions, 400 men and 100 women applied, of which 300 men and 85 women were hired. A federal Equal Employment enforcement official notes that many more men were hired than women and decides to investigate. The company president denies discrimination, arguing that in both the white collar and blue collar fields, the percentage of female applicants hired was greater than the percentage of male applicants hired. But the government official argues that a woman applying for a position at the firm was less likely to be hired than a man applying for a position at the firm. As the current law is written, if women have a greater chance of being denied employment, then this is a violation.

(a) Calculate the relevant percentages to check each side's assertions.
(b) Can both sides be right? Explain what causes this apparent paradox.

Causes of Earnings Differences: Human Capital

CHAPTER 7

*T*his chapter considers the effects of gender differences in formal education, work experience, and on-the-job training on earnings. First, a theory of how education, experience, and training affect earnings through the creation of human capital is developed. Then, systematic differences between the sexes in the quantity and type of this form of investment are explored. Empirical studies that measure the effects of gender differences in human capital on the gender earnings gap are examined to see how much of the gap can be accounted for by these differences. Finally, policies affecting human capital investment are considered with regard to how they might affect the gender earnings gap.

What is human capital?

Investment in abilities linked to productive capability can take many forms. While investment is often thought of as the process of increasing one's stock of machines that can replace labor or make labor more productive, another way to invest is to increase an employee's knowledge and skill, thereby turning unskilled labor into skilled labor. Skilled labor embodies human capital.[1] Learning to read and write is an investment in human capital. So is learning to drive a car, to type, or to speak effectively in public. As we will see below, many other forms of human behavior embody some human capital investment aspects. Any activity that has an educational component may be an investment in human capital. Therefore, many jobs that utilize human capital can also involve investment in human capital.

An employee "rents" the use of human capital to an employer. A wage is not only compensation for the time that a person spends working but also compensation for the firm's use of the person's capital stock during the time spent working. Wages provide the measurable return on human capital. This fact implies one reason why women make less than men: they may have less human capital.

A broad conception of human capital would include any form of investment that increases a person's well-being. An increase in well-being could stem from either (1) an increase in a person's productivity in market or nonmarket work or (2) an increase in a person's satisfaction with time spent in market work, nonmarket work, or leisure. This conception can account for why a person who has no plans to do market work might still go to college or why a person takes classes in college that are not linked to future work productivity. An art history course can enhance enjoyment of time spent in art museums, but generally it increases future income for only those persons planning to work in the field of art.

Systematic differences in type of human capital is a second explanation for the gender earnings gap. Women may be more likely to invest in human capital that has high nonmarket return, while men tend to invest in human capital with high market return. Also, women may be more likely to invest in human capital that increases satisfaction with time spent in market work, nonmarket work, or leisure, while men tend to invest in human capital with a high return in wages but little increase in satisfaction.

The general vs. specific human capital distinction

While computers are used in many different firms, particular software programs (such as a surgery room scheduling or a videotape rental program) are useful only in particular firms. Similarly, some forms of human capital are useful only in particular firms or jobs, while other forms are useful in a broad range of situations. This distinction leads to two broad categories of human capital: *general* and *specific* human capital. For instance, the ability to read would be considered to be general human capital, while the ability to play the cello generates monetary return only if one is involved in the music industry. Human capital may be even more specific for a particular industry, such as knowledge of a particular firm's operating procedures. We will see below why women and men might be expected to have different mixes of general and specific human capital and why these different mixes could generate different rates of return on their stocks of human capital.

*H*ow human capital investments affect earnings

Consider the decision of whether or not to make an investment of time or money. The return on the investment must be higher than the next best alternative use of the time or money. More specifically, the *present value* of the stream of payments generated by the investment must be larger than the present value of the next best alternative.

For example, suppose that you are deciding whether to spend another year in school; the alternative use of your time is to work. It will cost you a year's tuition and fees to attend school. The benefit of attending school for another year is that your earnings for every subsequent year will be higher than otherwise.

The present value (PV) of this year of school is

$$PV = -C_0 - E_0 + \frac{B_1 - E_1}{(1 + r)} + \frac{B_2 - E_2}{(1 + r)^2} + \frac{B_3 - E_3}{(1 + r)^3} + \ldots + \frac{B_n - E_n}{(1 + r)^n}$$

$$= -C_0 + \sum_{i=0}^{n} \frac{B_i - E_i}{(1 + r)^i}$$

where

n = number of years until retirement; i indexes time from the current point 0 up through year n,

C_0 = costs associated with attending school (incurred only while attending school, therefore only in year 0),

B_i = earnings in year i with an additional year of school (where $B_0 = 0$; i.e., the person does not work while attending school),

E_i = earnings in year i if no additional schooling is obtained, and

r = the interest rate.

Each year's earnings must be divided by $(1 + r)^i$ so as to generate the value in current dollars of money received in the future. (A dollar earned today can be put in the bank and will earn interest over the next year. At a rate of 5 percent, it will be worth $1.05 in a year's time. Therefore, $1.05 received a year from now is worth $1.00 today; that is, it has a present value of $1.00.) If PV is greater than zero, the investment is considered to be worthwhile. Therefore, a rational individual would make the investment, because it will increase satisfaction.

There are several strong assumptions embedded in this simple model. First, it assumes that the future interest rate is known and constant over the individual's lifetime. This is a big assumption; however, someone trying to decide whether or not to attend school could see if this calculation is positive using a plausible range of interest rates. Alternatively, one could calculate the interest rate which would make PV equal zero – i.e., the *internal rate of return*. If the internal rate of return is high, then it is probable that the investment will be profitable to undertake. It appears that the rate of return on education is high: for secondary schooling, an average of about 11 percent in a developed country and 15 to 18 percent in a less-developed country; for higher education, about 9 percent in a developed country and 13 to 16 percent in a less-developed country.[2] These rates are higher than the rates for other investments available to most individuals.

Second, the model assumes that the future path of earnings for the individual is known under either educational alternative. Again, a plausible range of earnings under each alternative can be used to make a rough calculation. For instance, in comparing the earnings of college-educated and high-school educated persons, it is clear that average earnings for college-educated persons are higher. One could use the average difference from the past in order to calculate one's probable future return on a college education.

Education

Consider the effects of an investment in formal education. Formal education includes attendance at elementary school, junior high, high school, junior college, and college, as well as at a trade school, technical institute, or other off-the-job training program. To illustrate graphically the effects of an additional investment in formal education on earnings, Figure 7.1 compares a hypothetical individual's earnings path with a high school education to the path with a college education. The earnings path, or *age-earnings profile*, for the typical high-school-educated worker is fairly flat. By contrast, the profile for the typical college-educated worker is rising with age, and crosses the profile for the high school worker shortly after college graduation.

The shaded area in Figure 7.1 represents the outlays for tuition, books, and fees associated with attending college for four years. The profile during college is negative for most persons, even if a part-time job is held. In Figure 7.1, the person does not work during

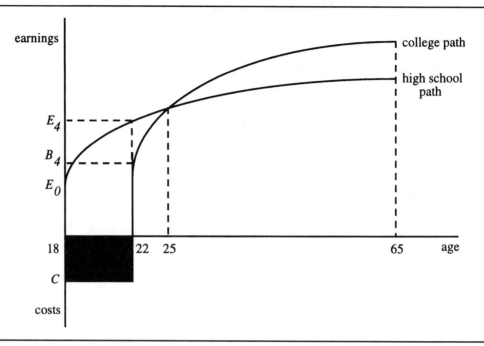

FIGURE 7.1   Alternative age-earnings profiles for an individual by educational level

college, so C is the total cost per year of attending college. He/she foregoes a starting yearly salary of E_0 to attend college. Upon graduation, he/she receives a starting yearly salary of B_4, which is higher than the starting salary that would have been received upon graduating high school but lower than the salary that would have been earned had he/she worked continuously since high school, E_4. Because the profile for a college graduate is steeper than for a high school graduate, however, he/she will soon overtake and pass the high school graduate. The difference between these profiles, appropriately discounted using the present-value method, represents the net benefit of receiving a college education relative to a high school education.

Table 7.1 supports the hypothesis that a college education "pays off" in terms of higher earnings, and does so soon after graduation. Both male and female college graduates make substantially higher yearly incomes than do high school graduates of the same age, although women receive a greater relative premium than do men at all points in time. However, these differences may be attributable in part to differences in innate productivity between the two groups. Also, the rate of return on college apparently varies over time, due to relative demand and supply of the two types of workers, with the rate rising substantially in the 1990s.

Human capital theory is not the only way to explain the positive relationship between education and earnings. An alternative theory, the *screening* theory, is that people get higher education to signal that they are intrinsically more productive workers, but that education in itself adds nothing to the productivity of workers. While this theory is interesting and evidence can be found to support this view, it has the same implications for comparisons between persons – namely, that receiving more education leads to higher earnings.[3]

TABLE 7.1   Median income ratios, college graduates to high school graduates, by sex, ages 25 to 34, 1967 to 1995

	Men	*Women*
1967	1.26	1.38
1970	1.30	1.39
1975	1.15	1.25
1978	1.11	1.22
1980	1.18	1.26
1985	1.36	1.40
1990	1.41	1.60
1995	1.51	1.59

Sources: 1967–90 – *Current Population Reports Series P-60*, nos. 75 (Table 4), 80 (Table 49), 105 (Table 47), 123 (Table 50), 132 (Table 51), 156 (Table 35), 174 (Table 29). 1995 – U.S. Census Bureau, unpublished data. Data are for year-round, full-time workers. Up through 1990, college graduates are those who have received no more than four years of college, and high school graduates are those who have completed four years of high school.

On-the-job training

An alternative way to acquire human capital is to receive on-the-job training, which can consist of a formal apprenticeship program or a less formal situation provided by an employer. The prediction is that jobs that provide training will pay less than jobs that do not, all else equal, because part of the value of the job is the value of the human capital which accrues to the worker. Thus, many apprenticeship programs pay a minimal wage, but generally require no monetary outlay on the part of the worker other than perhaps purchase of the tools necessary to enter the trade. Figure 7.2 compares two jobs, one of which has a training component, while the other offers no training. As in Figure 7.1, the job with the training component initially has a lower wage, but it has a higher wage upon completion of the training portion of the job and puts the person on a steeper earnings profile.

In Figure 7.2, the job with a training component pays a minimum yearly salary of B_0 for the first four years, while training occurs. Meanwhile, the comparable job with no training component has a starting yearly salary of E_0 and rises steadily, achieving a salary of E_4 after four years. After the four years of training end, the job with the training component experiences a rise in salary to B_4, and the earnings profile rises more steeply from that point than does the profile for the job which provided no training.

Experience

In Figures 7.1 and 7.2, all the age-earnings profiles rise with age. What causes this rise? According to human capital theory, increases in work experience can also entail increased human capital investment and can cause these rising profiles. A job in which experience makes one more productive should therefore pay more over time; alternatively, a job in which one becomes no more productive with experience should have a flat profile. Part-time workers accumulate less human capital simply because fewer hours are worked and, therefore, less work experience is obtained. This difference can explain why wages are generally lower and earnings profiles flatter for part-time workers than for full-time workers.

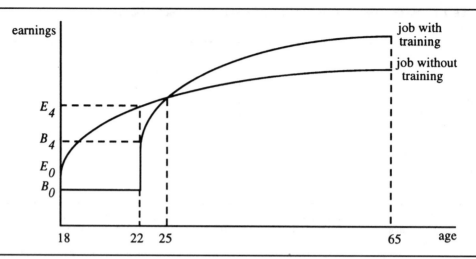

FIGURE 7.2 Alternative age-earnings profiles for an individual by amount of on-the-job training

Receiving formal education or on-the-job training may make you better able to turn on-the-job experience into human capital or may cause you to enter into jobs with more possibility for accruing additional human capital through experience, accounting for the steeper slope of those profiles.

Another reason why earnings profiles would be steeper for jobs involving training is that employers may wish to bind workers to their firm in order to make sure that the employer receives the return on the investment in human capital. Here, the distinction between general and specific human capital becomes important. Employers are generally unwilling to provide workers with general human capital investments, such as remedial education, because they are concerned that the workers they train will leave the firm soon after training and the firm will receive no return on this training investment. This fact leads to two predictions: (1) most general human capital will be provided through formal education rather than through on-the-job training or work experience and (2) workers who are receiving on-the-job training or work experience of a general nature will be paid wages below their marginal product during the training period and wages above their marginal product after the training period. This allows the employer to average wage costs over a longer period but actually make a profit on workers who leave right after training concludes. Additionally, it gives the workers incentive to stay on after training, as other firms would pay them no more than their marginal product if they switched jobs. While the worker's marginal productivity is rising over time, the pay rate is actually rising at a steeper level, at least in the years directly following training. Figure 7.3 illustrates this case. The worker completes a seven-year apprenticeship period during which wages are less than marginal product, after which point the wage rises above marginal product. Here the rule for the firm to follow in setting earnings is to set the present value of the earnings stream equal to the present value of the stream of marginal product of the worker.

Firms may also be hesitant to make specific human capital investments in persons who they think will be leaving the firm. A trade-off as shown in Figure 7.3 may exist in terms of earnings versus productivity for specific capital. Workers will not, however, be willing to

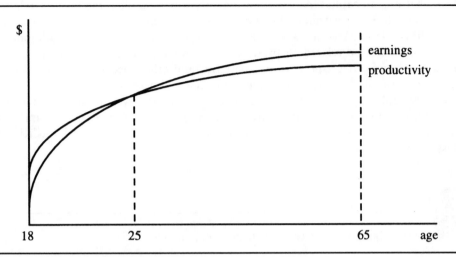

FIGURE 7.3 **Earnings and actual productivity for an individual**

make specific capital investments without guarantee of future employment that will provide a return on these investments. This leads to the prediction that little specific capital will be provided in formal educational settings, instead being developed on the job through training and experience. No one would want to spend the time learning how a particular company does its accounting, for instance, without first being guaranteed employment in that company.

Why do all the earnings profiles in Figures 7.1 through 7.3 exhibit flattening slope after a certain age? One explanation is based on the value of work experience: the worker learns the most about work in the first few years on the job; after that, additional valuable work experience may not be obtained, leading to this slowdown in the earnings growth rate.

Alternatively, the worker may continue to learn useful skills and facts that augment the store of human capital, while other portions of his/her human capital depreciate. Just as with machinery – such as automobiles, which lose value as they age – a worker's skills can decline in value over time. Some skills that took a worker much time to learn may become useless in a very short period of time (e.g., learning to use a slide rule shortly before electronic calculators became widely used). Earnings profiles will become downward-sloping if depreciation occurs with no offsetting accumulation of new human capital.[4] The value of a formal education will generally decrease, the longer ago it occurred. This is particularly true in fields where knowledge is accruing rapidly and work techniques are modified constantly, such as computer programming.

The idea that human capital can depreciate underscores the importance of continuity in work history. To the extent that women have more work interruptions than do men, they are more likely to be on a lower earnings profile with a flatter slope. This is both because they do not accumulate as much human capital through work experience and because their existing stock of human capital is depreciating. In fact, in contrast to other forms of capital, the depreciation rate of human capital may increase if it is not used. While women may develop different forms of human capital while doing nonmarket work, their market-work-related human capital may still depreciate.

Note that human capital theory is not the only way to explain the positive relationship between experience and earnings. Institutionalists, including economists and sociologists, argue that this relationship can be caused by legal, other contractual, or traditional agreements that need not be related to productivity. Similar institutionalist arguments can be provided to explain other aspects of pay patterns, and other theories are advanced as well that explain parts of the earnings puzzle. Covering all these theories is both outside the scope of this book and outside the scope of economics. However, human capital theory is a coherent theory that accounts for many of the pay patterns observed in the data. Over the past few decades, it has become more and more a part of the received knowledge of the neoclassical economics tradition.

FOCUS

The "mommy track" controversy

In 1989 Felice Schwartz, the president and founder of Catalyst, a nonprofit organization that works with corporations to foster the career and leadership development of women, published an article in *Harvard Business Review*.[5] "Management Women and the New Facts of Life" both stirred up a huge debate and led to a new catch phrase in the national media (one that she did not coin). Schwartz differentiated between two types of managerial women, the "career-primary" woman and the "career-and-family" woman, and argued that the two types should be treated differently by corporations. The following are some excerpts from her article and other people's reactions to the "mommy track" concept:

> "The cost of employing women in management is greater than the cost of employing men. This is a jarring statement, partly because it is true, but mostly because it is something people are reluctant to talk about." (Felice Schwartz)

> "Many people who support women's rights don't want to look at this issue because they would prefer to believe women don't leave their jobs after they give birth. It is very disconcerting to see women who received extensive training in their twenties leave in their thirties when they become mothers." (Jane Bryant Quinn, columnist)[6]

> "Businessmen hear that women cost corporations more and instantly, many of them grab on to that and say, 'We don't have to pay women as much, since women obviously cost us more and they're more trouble'." (Pat Schroeder, congresswoman)[7]

> "Some women put their careers first. . . . The secret to dealing with such women is to recognize them early, accept them, and clear artificial barriers from their path to the top." (Schwartz)

> "There are more than two groups of women. There's no practical way to divide them." (Fran Rodgers, President of Work/Family Directions, a consulting firm)[8]

> "I'm not sure we should honor lack of family as a criterion and value women who are willing to put it aside." (Faith Wohl, director of employee relations at Du Pont Co.)[9]

> "The career-and-family woman . . . can give you a significant business advantage as the competition for able people escalates. Sometimes . . . she will switch gears in mid-life and re-enter the competition for the top." (Schwartz)

"If you go part-time, you're signaling to your employer you're on the B-team." (Richard Belous, economist at the National Planning Association)[10]

"The more employers make special provisions for women, the more they find reasons not to hire them." (Ann Leibowitz, legal counsel for Polaroid Corp.)[11]

"If the Mommy Track becomes a slower track for certain periods in your career, well, I am willing to accept that. What I am not willing to accept is that it totally turns off my options later to get back on track." (Jayne Day, partner, Peat Marwick)[12]

"If special tracks are offered only to women and not men, it guarantees that women will be stuck as the primary parent, [and that is] precisely what needs to change." (Diane Ehrensaft, psychologist)[13]

"'Mommy Track' is one of those devastating journalistic catch phrases that come along now and then and overwhelm all rational discussion of some serious topic.... *Mommy Track* smacks of derision toward child rearing and carries a heavy implication of a semipermanent caste system intended to hold women back. So any worthwhile plan that would allow workers to take time off or reduce their office duties to take care of children will be subject to recurrent spasms of Mommy Track bashing." (John Leo, columnist)[14]

The significance of human capital theory for occupational choice

The amount and type of human capital needed to enter and succeed in various occupations varies greatly. Occupations vary in terms of the general vs. specific capital mix, including the mix between capital that is specific to the occupation, capital that is specific to an industry that utilizes the occupation, and capital that is specific to a firm that hires workers of that occupation. Occupations also vary in terms of the expected depreciation rate of capital specific to that occupation. For these two reasons, a person's plan for future work interruptions will theoretically influence choice of occupation.

Another point that must be considered is that persons vary in their ability and desire to create various forms of human capital. All persons are not equally good at producing all forms of human capital, so a skill that takes one person a year to learn may take another person two years (e.g., reaching a particular typing speed). Therefore, we expect the person who is better at learning typing than at creating other forms of human capital with similar payoffs to spend more time learning to type.[15] Noneconomic considerations, however, can influence both the amount and the mix of human capital. For instance, a creationist might be a rapid learner in the area of evolutionary biology, but would prefer not to spend time learning material that is in conflict with his/her religious beliefs. If ability and/or desire to acquire various forms of human capital vary systematically by sex, this variation can lead to differences in occupational distribution and earnings by sex.

Until now, this discussion has implicitly assumed that people have free choice as to what forms of human capital to create. However, there may be barriers to entry for particular types of investment, such as restricted entry into professional schools. If there is differential access by sex to various forms of human capital, the clear implication is that such discrimination reduces earnings for women.

Is occupational choice influenced by the type of human capital required?

Consider the two types of human capital: general and specific. In order to receive payback on specific capital, a worker must stay in the occupation where the payback will be received. In order for the employee to receive payback on training, the firm must have steeper profiles, with lower starting salaries for jobs requiring specific capital than for jobs requiring general capital, all else being equal. Therefore, people who plan to work fewer years and or to work intermittently are more likely to be found in occupations requiring general capital.

Now, consider variation in occupations by length of training period. Occupations that require long training periods must have higher earnings after training ends than occupations that require shorter training periods, all else being equal. Otherwise, people would get a higher rate of return in the occupation with the shorter training period and would choose not to enter the one with the long training period. People who plan to work fewer years are accordingly, more likely to be found in occupations with shorter training periods and, therefore, lower earnings.

For both of these reasons, systematic differences in planned worklife by sex are predicted to affect the gender earnings ratio. Below we will see evidence that women both plan shorter worklives and actually have shorter worklives than do men.

Is occupational choice influenced by the depreciation rate of human capital?

A straightforward implication of human capital theory is that persons will make their human capital investments so as to maximize return. Therefore, occupational variations in the cost of labor force intermittency will cause an individual to choose the occupation that imposes the smallest penalty, given their desired lifetime participation, all else being equal.[16]

Consider occupations where the depreciation rate of specific occupational capital is so great that re-entrants to the occupation are treated as if they were new entrants. If the age-earnings profile is very steep in these occupations, exiting the occupation and re-entering would put re-entrants at a significant earnings disadvantage relative to those who stay in continuously. In fact, we would expect that the profile would be steep in these occupations in order to induce people to stay in continuously; otherwise people would choose other occupations with less penalty for withdrawal.

Therefore, we would expect to see people choose between occupations based on their expected length of stay and intermittency patterns, and that this sorting of workers is reflected in lower earnings for occupations where there is less of a link between experience and productivity. We will see evidence below that many women plan to take time off during their career, and that most women, in fact, do not work continuously.

Is there feedback from societal discrimination into occupational choice?

If women and men are equally productive, yet men are paid more than women, then women are receiving a lower return on human capital than men. If women anticipate this pay discrimination, they will invest less in market-work-related human capital relative to other forms of investment than they would otherwise. Therefore wages will be lower for women than for men, not only directly because of workplace discrimination, but also indirectly due to discrimination, because they have less human capital.

If occupations differ in terms of the wage differential paid to women and men of equal productivity, women will be more likely to invest in specific human capital for the less discriminatory occupations. This creates a different occupational choice process for women than for men. In particular, occupations that are lower-earning but less discriminatory are relatively more attractive to women than they would be in a world with no discrimination.

FOCUS

Is there gender bias in educational testing?

Researcher Phyllis Rosser argued in a 1987 report that the main ability/college admission tests given to high schoolers in the United States – the SAT, PSAT, and ACT – systematically underpredict the abilities of girls.[17] She reports that in 1986, girls scored 61 points lower on the SAT than boys – 50 points lower in math and 11 points lower in verbal – and that the gap had been widening since 1972, particularly in the verbal section.[18] On the PSAT, which is used to identify potential National Merit Scholars, in the 1986–87 school year, girls scored 54 points lower than boys – 41 points lower in math and 13 points lower in verbal.[19] And on the ACT, girls averaged 6.0 units lower overall – 2.8 units lower in math, 2.5 lower in natural science, 1.7 lower in social studies, and 1 unit higher in English.[20] Yet girls have higher average grades than boys in both high school and college.[21]

This gender gap in scores implies that girls' chances are then reduced relative to boys' for (1) gaining admission to the college of their choice; (2) obtaining college tuition aid awarded by National Merit Scholarship Corp. and other companies, government agencies, and foundations; and (3) entering special education programs for gifted students. While many colleges compensate for lower female scores in both their admissions and scholarship procedures, girls may not be aware of this procedure, and they may pass up applying to particular colleges because they consider their chances of getting in low, based on their scores. The National Merit Scholar procedure (undertaken in order to improve the gender mix in the candidate pool) is to choose potential scholarship recipients based on the math score plus two times the verbal score, but this does not lead to equal numbers of female and male recipients: in 1995–96, 39 percent of National Merit Scholars were female, even though 55 percent of students taking the PSAT (the first step in qualifying for the scholarships) were female.[22]

The Educational Testing Service (ETS), creator of the PSAT and SAT tests, has suggested that the gender gap arises because more girls than boys take the test, and that this larger pool of girls includes many girls with low ability. Two factors cast doubt upon this explanation. First, boys appear in much greater numbers among the high scorers: two times as many boys as girls score over 650.[23] Second, a sex gap in scores is found for all racial and ethnic groups, regardless of whether the mean group score is high or low, ranging from a difference in 1985 in average SAT scores of 43 points for African-Americans, up to 76 points for Puerto Ricans.[24] More Asian-American boys than girls take the test, with a sex gap of 49 points, and equal numbers of Mexican-American boys and girls take the test, with a sex gap of 70 points.[25]

What are the potential sources of gender bias on these tests? Rosser suggests four possible sources:[26]

1. The rushed nature of the test, along with the multiple-choice format. Girls are less likely to guess, so while they answer more questions correctly of the ones they complete, they complete fewer questions.
2. Men are featured more often in test questions than are women. ETS researchers have found that this directly affects girls' scores.

3. Boys are better on questions about objects, girls on questions about human relations; tests may focus on male interests and activities.
4. A shift in test content over time towards math and science, away from arts, humanities, reading comprehension, and writing.

More recent data continue to show a gender gap in scores, although the gap has narrowed substantially since 1986. For the 1994–95 school year, girls scored 43 points lower on the SAT (40 points lower in math and 3 points lower in verbal skills), and they received a 20.7 composite score on the ACT, while boys scored 21.0.[27] As of late 1996, the Department of Education had decided to change the format of the PSAT by adding a test of writing skills, an area in which girls tend to do better than boys.[28] ETS continues to parry claims of bias against girls in its tests, recently releasing a report that states that the gap between boy and girl performance on tests is narrower than is commonly believed and that boys lag far behind girls on tests of writing ability.[29]

TABLE 7.2 Percentage female in selected educational categories, 1961 to 1994

Category	1961	1970	1980	1990	1994
Graduating seniors, high school	48.6	50.5	51.0	—	—
College students	37.6	41.2	51.4	54.5	55.4[†]
Graduating seniors, bachelor's degree	38.2	43.1	49.0	53.2	54.5
Graduating with master's degree	32.3	39.7	49.4	52.6	54.5
Graduating with professional degree	2.7	5.2	24.8	38.1	40.7
Graduating with doctoral degree	10.5	13.3	29.7	36.4	38.5

[†] preliminary data.
Source: U.S. National Center for Education Statistics, *Digest of Education Statistics* (1996): 108 (Table 98), 176 (Table 169), 253 (Table 239).

*E*vidence of effects of human capital differences on gender earnings differences

Let us now consider evidence on the nature of human capital differences by sex, the relationship between occupational choice and depreciation, and the link between human capital differences and the overall gender earnings gap. The various predictions of human capital theory regarding sex differences are considered one by one. First, are there systematic differences in the amount of education, on-the-job training, and work experience by sex?

Table 7.2 contains some statistics on enrollment rates by sex. Educational differences by sex have narrowed over time to the point where women are more likely to attend and graduate from college than men, although men are more likely to receive professional or doctoral training than women. Overall, there is little difference in total years of formal schooling between the sexes.

Turning to differences between the sexes in terms of on-the-job training, several studies have found that men are more likely to receive such training than are women.[30] One study estimates that at least two-thirds of the relative wage differential between men and women *within* occupations is accounted for by sex differences in turnover and training.[31]

TABLE 7.3 Work preferences for age 35 of young women compared with actual employment status of mature women, by race

	Education			
	12 years	*13 to 15 years*	*16+ years*	*All Educational levels*
Whites				
% young women who prefer to work at age 35	26.8	18.1	32.7	28.6
% mature women in labor force	45.1	43.6	54.7	45.9
Blacks				
% young women who prefer to work at age 35	62.1	60.6	57.7	59.3
% mature women in labor force	67.1	79.0	95.1	67.1

Source: Steven H. Sandell and David Shapiro, "Work Expectations, Human Capital Accumulation, and the Wages of Young Women," *Journal of Human Resources* 15, no. 3 (Summer 1982): 350. Reprinted with permission of the University of Wisconsin Press. Data for young women are from the National Longitudinal Survey of Women ages 14 to 24 in 1968. Data for mature women are from the National Longitudinal Survey of Women ages 30 to 44 in 1967; respondents over age 40 are excluded.

Another study finds that acquisition of on-the-job training for young women is positively related to their expectations of future labor force participation. However, comparison of the actual labor force attachment of mature women with young women's preferences for future labor force participation, as shown in Table 7.3, indicates that many young women underestimate the amount of future labor force attachment and therefore underinvest in on-the-job training.[32]

More evidence is available on the differences by sex in terms of total work experience and continuity of work experience. Table 7.4 contains some relevant statistics. Men are more likely than women to work continuously and to have more *tenure* – i.e., to stay on a particular job for a longer time. Men have more years of work experience and work a larger percentage of their total potential work years. This is strong evidence that women acquire less human capital in the form of work experience. However, one study has found no significant difference by gender in the probability of leaving one's first employer.[33] Additionally, a study comparing young women and men finds that switching jobs is associated with significantly higher wage growth for young men than for young women, implying different relationships between tenure and earnings by sex.[34]

Several studies find evidence of a depreciation effect on wages caused by gaps in work experience.[35] One study finds that women who have a worklife gap subsequently have a partial rebound in earnings, but never catch up with those women who work continuously.[36]

Several researchers have addressed the question of whether women choose occupations where human capital depreciates less rapidly. One researcher finds that the wage penalty for work gaps is no less in these occupations than in predominantly male occupations, and that women whose employment was more continuous are no more apt to choose predominantly male occupations.[37] Another researcher, using the same data set but a different

TABLE 7.4 Differences in work history by sex, workers ages 21 to 64, 1984

	Men	*Women*
Percentage of workers with one or more work interruptions	13.2	47.0
Percentage of potential work-years spent away from work	1.6	14.7
Percentage distribution of workers by years of work experience		
less than 5 years	8.8	14.3
5 to 9 years	18.5	27.9
10 to 19 years	32.3	35.1
20 years or more	40.4	22.8
Percentage distribution of workers by tenure on current job		
less than 2 years	22.0	25.6
2 to 4 years	22.7	29.1
5 to 9 years	19.4	22.5
10 years or more	35.8	22.8

Source: Current Population Reports Series P-70, no. 10 (Tables A, C, E). Potential work-years is defined as age minus years of schooling minus 6 years.

TABLE 7.5 Percentage reductions in value of career-related knowledge after a career interruption of 1 to 3 years, selected academic disciplines

Field	*1 year*	*2 years*	*3 years*
Physics	16.72	30.65	42.30
Chemistry	13.50	25.17	35.27
Sociology	10.26	19.46	26.72
Psychology	9.67	17.39	26.27
Biology	8.31	15.94	22.93
History	3.78	7.41	10.91
English	2.63	5.20	7.70

Source: John M. McDowell, "Obsolescence of Knowledge and Career Publication Profiles: Some Evidence of Differences among Fields in Costs of Interrupted Careers," American Economic Review 72, no. 4 (September 1982): 752–768. Reprinted with permission.

statistical model, finds the opposite.[38] This prediction of human capital theory has not been satisfactorily resolved.

The amount of on-the-job training and experience does appear to differ by sex, with women amassing less of these forms of human capital. What about the mix between general and specific capital? One study finds that women who take less nonmarket time choose occupations that require more human capital and, in particular, more specific human capital.[39] This finding is in line with human capital theory predictions.

Turning to the question of how the type of human capital investment varies by sex, both high school and college course choices (including major in college) vary systematically by sex.[40] Part of this difference appears to be linked to the relative depreciation rates of different kinds of human capital. Table 7.5 contains depreciation rates calculated for various types of academic knowledge by measuring the rates of literature decay in terms of number of citations per year for leading scholarly journals. A study using data from the

TABLE 7.6 Percentage distribution of scores on the SAT and GRE quantitative tests by sex and percentage female by score range

| Score range | Frequencies by Sex | | % Female GRE-Q | % Female SAT-Math |
	Male GRE-Q	Female GRE-Q		
200–300	3.6	7.8	71.6	66.1
301–350	3.3	7.2	71.6	63.4
351–400	5.5	11.1	70.0	60.3
401–450	7.2	13.2	67.9	56.8
451–500	10.7	15.7	62.9	52.7
501–550	12.8	14.8	57.2	48.7
551–600	14.6	12.6	49.9	43.6
601–650	13.0	8.2	42.2	38.6
651–700	12.8	5.5	33.4	32.3
701–750	10.2	2.8	24.0	25.2
751–800	6.2	1.0	15.9	16.4

Source: Morton Paglin and Anthony M. Rufolo, "Heterogeneous Human Capital, Occupational Choice, and Male-Female Earnings Differences," *Journal of Labor Economics* 8, no. 1, part 1 (January 1990): 137. Reprinted with permission of the University of Chicago Press, © 1990. GRE data are from a tape of 1981–82 test takers. SAT data are for 1983 from the College Entrance Examination Board.

National Longitudinal Survey of High School Seniors in 1972 and data of the type shown in Table 7.5 found that women with higher expected fertility tend to select majors that are "progressively less subject to atrophy and obsolescence; and that expected fertility explains a sizable amount of the male-female differences in college majors."[41]

However, gender differences in college major could be generated by gender differences in ability to create different types of human capital. Compare the distributions of mathematical ability on SAT and GRE tests by sex, as shown in Table 7.6. Mathematical ability is an important determinant of field choice of major for college students, and differences in earnings across fields are largely explained as a return to the use of scarce quantitative abilities in the production of human capital. This also can account partially for the observed male-female differences in earnings and occupational choices of recent college graduates.[42] However, data on college majors, as shown for example in Table 6.1, indicate that there was a large shift between the 1970s and 1980s among women towards relatively well-paying (which would be, by implication of human capital theory, higher-skilled) fields, which appears to have contributed to a decline in the gender earnings gap among college graduates.[43]

Net effect on the gender earnings gap

We have seen evidence that there are systematic differences in the type and quantity of human capital investment by sex. How much do these differences contribute towards explaining the gender earnings gap?

Work experience appears to have the most notable effect. Several studies have found that between one-fourth to one-half of the sex difference in earnings between men and women is attributable to differences in work experience histories.[44] Reducing women's higher turnover rate would probably have a substantial effect on their earnings. For instance, one study finds that use of a three-year rather than a six-year rotation policy on military postings reduces military wives' earnings by 40 percent.[45]

However, after accounting for differences in human capital, not all of the difference in earnings between men and women is explained. One researcher, after conducting a particularly sophisticated statistical study, concludes:[46]

> If men were to quit the labor force at the same rate as women, with the same experience, tenure, and occupational structure as women, they would have jobs substantially inferior (in terms of training) to those they actually hold, with consequently much lower wages. However, if women were to reduce their quit rate, increase their labor force experience and tenure, and change their occupational composition, they would obtain only marginally better jobs, and the wage gap would not narrow appreciably.... Only if women's labor force experience and tenure assured them of the same kind of jobs as men would women have an incentive to change their participation behavior and reduce their quit rates.

While the findings of many studies concur with the basic predictions of human capital theory regarding relative amounts and types of investments by men and women, the human capital model cannot explain all of the gender earnings gap. Differences in the amount of work experience and in specific forms of human capital are more important in explaining the gap than are differences in amount of education. But even these causes cannot explain more than 50 percent of the gap. We must turn to other explanatory factors to finish accounting for the gap.

Unmeasured factors

How much goes unmeasured in statistical studies of earnings? The appendix to this chapter contains a simple graphical/numerical example to illustrate how such studies are done. The average human-capital-based statistical study of earnings equations for a national sample of workers generally accounts for between 10 and 35 percent of the total variation in earnings. These studies generally include: (1) a range of human capital-related variables, such as years of education and work experience; (2) demographic variables, such as age, number of children, and marital status; and (3) locational variables, such as urban or rural residence, and state or region of residence. Studies are generally more successful at explaining the variation in worker earnings within an occupation, but they still leave a vast amount of the variation in workers' earnings unexplained. What could account for the rest of the variation? Let us consider some of the categories of factors generally omitted from statistical studies of earnings:

- *Ability*: For any job you have had or have observed, think of the different people you worked with. You probably noticed the wide range of speed, accuracy, politeness, and other abilities that affect productivity. Some of those people will end up earning more, some less, and part of that earnings difference is related to these differences in abilities.
- *Motivation*: People also vary in their interest and commitment to a job, a factor that can directly affect their productivity.
- *Physical characteristics*: Height, weight, voice timbre, hair color; these characteristics may affect your earnings either as legitimate qualifications for a job or as factors leading to discrimination.[47]

- *Luck*: After accounting for all systematic factors, there will still always be unexplained variation in earnings among workers that must be attributed to random unforeseeable events (e.g., meeting a person on the bus who ends up hiring you or losing a job because the office burns down). No statistical study can ever hope to account for "kismet."

Also, there are factors whose effect on earnings can be measured only indirectly through their effects on included variables. For instance, if a person is discouraged from obtaining higher education and other forms of human capital, this discouragement will show up in their lower levels of human capital, but it cannot be measured directly. Similarly, ability to create productive human capital will be correlated with the level of human capital obtained, but it is difficult to measure directly.

In fact, people's motivation to invest in human capital can be altered by experiences that discount their abilities, such as negative evaluations from a parent or teacher. Alternatively, some people appear to achieve more than their initial expectations for training because they have received warm encouragement from parents, teachers, or friends. There is strong evidence that women are more likely than men to be discouraged from attempting academic achievement, and that much of this discouragement is related to their sex rather than to their actual ability.

FOCUS

Is the classroom climate chilly for women?

A number of schools have conducted surveys and other research in order to determine how women and men are treated differently in classrooms on their campuses. The results were summarized in a 1982 paper by Roberta Hall that has circulated widely among faculty.[48] The following are excerpts listing the types of behaviors that can have a negative impact on women's academic and career development, the reactions women may have to these behaviors, and some quotes from surveyed students and faculty:

"A chilling classroom climate puts women students at a significant educational disadvantage. Overtly disparaging remarks about women, as well as more subtle differential behaviors, can have a critical and lasting effect. When they occur frequently – especially when they involve 'gatekeepers' who teach required courses, act as advisors, or serve as chairs of departments – such behaviors can have a profound negative impact on women's academic and career development by:

- discouraging classroom participation;
- preventing students from seeking help outside of class;
- causing students to drop or avoid certain classes, to switch majors or subspecialties within majors, and in some instances even to leave a given institution;
- minimizing the development of the individual collegial relationships with faculty which are crucial for future professional development;
- dampening career aspirations; and
- undermining confidence."

"Instead of sharpening their intellectual abilities, women may begin to believe and act as though:

- their presence in a given class, department, program, or institution is, at best, peripheral or, at worst, an unwelcome intrusion;
- their participation in class discussion is not expected, and their contributions are not important;
- their capacity for full intellectual development and professional success is limited; and
- their academic and career goals are not matters for serious attention or concern."

"While women students may be most directly harmed by an inhospitable climate, men students are also affected. If limited views of women are overtly or subtly communicated by faculty, some men students may experience reinforcement of their own negative views about women, especially because such views are confirmed by persons of knowledge and status. This bias may make it more difficult for men to perceive women students as full peers, to work with them in collaborative learning situations, and to offer them informal support as colleagues in the undergraduate or graduate school setting. Moreover, it may hamper men's ability to relate to women as equals in the larger world of work and family beyond the institution."

"Students in one of my classes did a tally and found that male professors called on men more often than on women students. What male students have to say or contribute is viewed as having more importance than what female students have to contribute in class."

"Every time I tell my advisor about my dissertation, he says, 'Oh, that's a very important issue for women.' My thesis involved issues that are important for both men and women, but he persists in relating to me as a woman rather than as a serious student, as if the two were incompatible."

"When I volunteered the fact that I was a politics major, [the professor] expressed surprise and asked, 'Now why would you want to do that?' when he had commended the same information just minutes before to one of the men."

"I told my advisor I wanted to continue working towards a Ph.D. He said, 'A pretty girl like you will certainly get married. Why don't you stop with an M.A.?'"

Policy implications of human capital theory for the gender earnings gap

The implications of this evidence for the human capital theory for those seeking to reduce the gender earnings gap are obvious: increase the amount and alter the mix of human capital that women have in order to increase their earnings. As women continue to enter graduate programs in greater numbers, their increased human capital in the form of formal education will pay off in terms of higher earnings. However, women also need to alter the mix of human capital received through formal education, choosing those forms with higher payoff rates. This mainly involves their entering nontraditional majors that develop skills in high demand in the labor market. Educational programs, including orientations, scholarships, and loan paybacks, can serve as incentives for women to enter these areas. The major effort launched by engineering departments to recruit women in the 1970s, was rewarded with a rise in percentage female in engineering programs from about 1 percent of enrollments in the early 1970s to over 12 percent by the early 1980s.

The issue of how to deal with discontinuous work histories is more difficult. Women have less incentive to invest in human capital if they are planning to exit from the labor force, and many women feel it is important to exit from the labor force if they are responsible for childraising. Convincing women not to exit the labor force without changing the traditional balance of family responsibility requires incentives, monetary and nonmonetary, to make it possible for them to balance career and family responsibilities. Alternatively, the balance of responsibility for child care in particular, but other nonmarket work as well, must be changed if women are to be able to work a larger percentage of their lives in market work. If this can be done, then women will have the incentive to invest in more specific human capital and enter on-the-job training programs in greater numbers.

Policy Application: Nontraditional job training programs

One way to influence the amount and type of human capital received by women is to enroll them in government-subsidized training programs to prepare them to enter male-dominated occupations. One method of evaluating the success of such programs is to compare the wages received by male and female graduates of the programs. A better, but more difficult way, would be to calculate how much more the women earn after receiving this type of training than they would have earned after receiving training for female-dominated occupations.

Training programs that were administered at many locations nationally during the 1970s under the Comprehensive Employment and Training Act (CETA) have provided evidence on this issue. One study took a national sample of persons enrolling in CETA programs, including both people who trained to enter traditional female occupations and others who trained for traditional male occupations.[49] Trainees for integrated occupations (between 49.5 and 74.5 percent male) were excluded from the study; 391 men and 397 women were compared in terms of the percentage holding jobs, the type of job held, and their wages.

The study found that women who received nontraditional training did not experience the same degree of success as the men who trained for similar occupations, even after controlling for a number of human capital factors. Although the women did increase their probability of being employed in nontraditional jobs by training for them, the women were less likely than the men to be employed in male-dominated occupations, which suggests that discrimination in hiring was still a problem. The study also found that nontraditional training did not improve the economic position of women more than traditional training. Women in the study who received nontraditional training were not more likely to be employed than women who received traditional training, and they did not receive significantly higher wages.

These results are limited in their generality, as the sample comprised relatively disadvantaged individuals who had relatively little formal education when they entered the CETA training programs. However, one implication is that better linkages need to be developed between training institutions and employers, so as to increase the probability that those women who train for male-dominated occupations subsequently receive employment in them.

In general, job training programs for disadvantaged persons that target women appear more effective than those that target men, perhaps because the traditionally female less-skilled jobs that the women are trained for are currently in greater demand than traditionally male less-skilled jobs.[50] Therefore nontraditional job training may currently actually be needed for men given the current state of the low-skill labor market.

Summary

Human capital theory leads to several predictions regarding gender differences in hourly earnings: (1) If women have less human capital than men, they will make less; (2) women may be more likely to invest in human capital that has high nonmarket return; (3) women may be more likely to invest in human capital that increases satisfaction with time spent in market work, nonmarket work, or leisure, while men may invest in human capital with a high return in wages but little increase in satisfaction; and (4) women are less likely to invest in specific human capital.

The empirical evidence on the accuracy of these predictions is strong. In particular, women and men have large differences in work experience. There are also systematic differences by sex in amounts of specific capital and on-the-job training. These differences can account for up to 50 percent of the gender earnings gap. However, much of the variation in earnings, both among women and men and between women and men, remains unexplained.

The implications of this evidence for creating policies to close the gender gap are clear: increase the amount and alter the mix of human capital that women have in order to increase their earnings. However, the issue of how to deal with discontinuous work histories is difficult. Women have less incentive to invest in human capital if they are planning to exit from the labor force.

Endnotes

1. This theory was developed by several economists associated with the University of Chicago, including Gary S. Becker, Jacob Mincer, and Theodore W. Schultz. By now it has become part of the basic neoclassical model of economics. The classic reference in this area is Gary S. Becker, *Human Capital: A Theoretical and Empirical Analysis, with Special Reference to Education, Third Edition* (Chicago, Ill.: University of Chicago, 1993).

2. George Psacharopoulos, "Returns to Education: A Further International Update and Implications," *Journal of Human Resources* 20, no. 4 (Fall 1985): 583–604.

3. Michael Spence, "Job Market Signaling," *Quarterly Journal of Economics* 87, no. 3 (August 1973): 355–374.

4. Geoffrey Carliner, "The Wages of Older Men," *Journal of Human Resources* 17, no. 1 (Winter 1982): 25–38, looks at depreciation rates in a sample of men age 45 to 64 in the late 1960s. He finds a decline in wage rates due to human capital depreciation of about 1 percent annually in the early fifties, rising to about 2 percent annually after age 60. However, this decrease in wages was offset by the general increase in wage levels over this period, so the earnings profiles for these men did not decline.

5. Felice N. Schwartz, "Management Women and the New Facts of Life," *Harvard Business Review* 67, no. 1 (January-February 1989): 65–76.

6. Sharon Johnson, "Opinions on the Mommy Track," *Woman* (October 1989): 38–41.

7. Neil Chesanow, "The Mommy Track: What It Means to Women," *Woman* (October 1989): 38–41.

8. Barbara Kantrowitz, "Advocating a 'Mommy Track'," *Newsweek* (March 13, 1989): 45.

9. Elizabeth Ehrlich, "The Mommy Track: Juggling Kids and Careers in Corporate America Takes a Controversial Turn," *Business Week* (March 20, 1989): 126–134.

10. Ehrlich, *op. cit.*: 132.

11. Kantrowitz, *loc. cit.*

12. Janice Castro, "Rolling Along the Mommy Track," *Time* (March 27, 1989): 72.

13. Chesanow, *op. cit.*: 41.

14. John Leo, "Reality Check for Harassed Parents," *U.S. News & World Report* (April 3, 1989): 64.

15. A person's pattern of comparative advantage in producing return on human capital matters, not his/her absolute advantage. A person may pick up typing very rapidly, but learn lessons slowly in medical school. Nevertheless, if the payoff to becoming a doctor is very high, the person will train to become a doctor instead of a secretary. Some doctors may type better than their secretaries, but that does not mean they should work as secretaries. And we have all had the experience of dealing with people who appear to be completely inept in carrying out their job, and we wonder why they are doing it; but they may be even worse at alternative forms of employment. Some people are good at creating many forms of human capital rapidly; others are slow at creating many forms of human capital. However, since the more talented people cannot do everything in their limited time, less talented people find work as well.

16. Solomon Polachek, "Occupational Self-Selection: A Human Capital Approach to Sex Differences in Occupational Structure," *Review of Economics and Statistics* 63, no. 1 (February 1981): 60–69.

17. Phyllis Rosser, *Sex Bias in College Admissions Tests: Why Women Lose Out, 2nd Edition* (Cambridge, Mass.: FairTest, 1987).

18. Rosser, *op. cit.*: 2.

19. Rosser, *op. cit.*: 3. These score differences are given in SAT terms, which involves multiplying the PSAT score by ten.

20. Rosser, *op. cit.*: 4.

21. Rosser, *op. cit.*: 2.

22. "Closing the Gender Gap on PSATs," *US News & World Report* (October 14, 1996): 28.

23. Rosser, *op. cit.*: 17.

24. Rosser, *op. cit.*: 16.

25. Rosser, *op. cit.*: 17.

26. Rosser, *op. cit.*: Appendix V.

27. *Statistical Abstract of the United States* (1996): 177 (Tables 274 and 275).

28. *US News & World Report, loc. cit.*

29. Kim Strosnider, "A Controversial Study of Testing Finds the Gap Between Boys and Girls is Shrinking," *Chronicle of Higher Education* 43, no. 36 (May 16, 1997): A34, reporting on *Gender and Fair Assessment* (Mahwah, N.J.: Lawrence Erlbaum Associates, 1997).

30. Cf. Lisa M. Lynch, "Private-Sector Training and the Earnings of Young Workers," *American Economic Review* 82, no. 1 (March 1992): 299–312; Anne Beeson Royalty, "The Effects of Job Turnover on the Training of Men and Women," *Industrial and Labor Relations Review* 49, no. 3 (April 1996): 506–521.

31. Elizabeth M. Landes, "A Test of the Specific Capital Hypothesis," *Economic Inquiry* 15, no. 4 (October 1977): 523–538, using the 1967 Survey of Economic Opportunity.

32. Steven H. Sandell and David Shapiro, "Work Expectations, Human Capital Accumulation, and the Wages of Young Women," *Journal of Human Resources* 15, no. 3 (Summer 1982): 335–353, using data from the National Longitudinal Surveys of Young Women, ages 14 to 24 in 1968.

33. Lisa M. Lynch, "Differential Effects of Post-School Training on Early Career Mobility," National Bureau of Economic Research Working Paper no. 4034 (March 1992).

34. Pamela J. Loprest, "Gender Differences in Wage Growth and Job Mobility," *American Economic Review* 82, no. 2 (May 1992): 526–532.

35. Jacob Mincer and Haim Ofek, "Interrupted Work Careers: Depreciation and Restoration of Human Capital," *Journal of Human Resources* 17, no. 1 (Winter 1982): 3–24; Donald Cox, "Panel Estimates of the Effects of Career Interruptions on the Earnings of Women," *Economic Inquiry* 22, no. 3 (July 1984): 386–403; Leslie S. Stratton, "The Effect Interruptions in Work Experience Have on Wages," *Southern Economic Journal* 61, no. 4 (April 1995): 955–970.

36. Joyce P. Jacobsen and Laurence M. Levin, "Effects of Intermittent Labor Force Attachment on Women's Earnings," *Monthly Labor Review* 118, no. 9 (September 1995): 14–19, using Survey of Income and Program Participation data from 1983 to 1986.

37. See Paula England, "The Failure of Human Capital Theory to Explain Occupational Sex Segregation," *Journal of Human Resources* 17, no. 3 (Summer 1982): 358–370; "Wage Appreciation and Depreciation: A Test of Neoclassical Explanations of Occupational Sex Segregation," *Social Forces* 62, no. 3 (March 1984): 726–749; and "Occupational Segregation: Rejoinder to Polachek," *Journal of Human Resources* 20, no. 3 (Summer 1985): 441–443. Data are from 1967.

38. Solomon Polachek, "Occupational Segregation Among Women: Theory, Evidence, and a Prognosis," *Women in the Labor Market*, eds. Cynthia Lloyd, Emily Andrews, and Curtis Gilroy (New York: Columbia University, 1979): 137–167; "Occupational Segregation: A Defense of Human Capital Predictions," *Journal of Human Resources* 20, no. 3 (Summer 1985): 437–439; and "Occupational Segregation: Reply to England," *Journal of Human Resources* 20, no. 3 (Summer 1985): 444. See also Moon-Kak Kim and Solomon W. Polachek, "Panel Estimates of Male-Female Earnings Functions," *Journal of Human Resources* 29, no. 2 (Spring 1994): 406–428, for a newer approach to this question.

39. Nadja Zalokar, "Male-Female Differences in Occupational Choice and the Demand for General and Occupation-Specific Human Capital," *Economic Inquiry* 26, no. 1 (January 1988): 59–74, using data from the National Longitudinal Survey of Mature Women for 1972.

40. Charles Brown and Mary Corcoran, "Sex-Based Differences in School Content and the Male Female Wage Gap," *Journal of Labor Economics* 15, no. 3, part 1 (July 1997): 431–465.

41. Arthur E. Blakemore and Stuart A. Low, "Sex Differences in Occupational Selection: The Case of College Majors," *Review of Economics and Statistics* 66, no. 1 (February 1984): 157–163.

42. Morton Paglin and Anthony M. Rufolo, "Heterogeneous Human Capital, Occupational Choice, and Male-Female Earnings Differences," *Journal of Labor Economics* 8, no. 1, part 1 (January 1990): 123–144.

43. Eric Eide, "College Major Choice and Changes in the Gender Wage Gap," *Contemporary Economic Policy* 12, no. 2 (April 1994): 55–63.

44. Steven H. Sandell and David Shapiro, "The Theory of Human Capital and the Earnings of Women: A Reexamination of the Evidence," *Journal of Human Resources* 13, no. 1 (Winter 1978): 103–117, estimates about one fourth. Jacob Mincer and Solomon Polachek, "Family Investments in Human Capital: Earnings of Women," *Journal of Political Economy* 82, Supplement (March/April 1974): S76–S108, estimates one-half. Jacob Mincer and Solomon Polachek, "Women's Earnings Reexamined," *Journal of Human Resources* 13, no. 1 (Winter 1978): 119–134, estimates between 19 and 49 percent.

45. Deborah M. Payne, John T. Warner, and Roger D. Little, "Tied Migration and Returns to Human Capital: The Case of Military Wives," *Social Science Quarterly* 73, no. 2 (June 1992): 324–339.

46. Reuben Gronau, "Sex-related Wage Differentials and Women's Interrupted Labor Careers–the Chicken or the Egg," *Journal of Labor Economics* 6, no. 3 (July 1988): 277–301.

47. Susan Averett and Sanders Korenman, "The Economic Reality of The Beauty Myth," *Journal of Human Resources* 31, no. 2 (Spring 1996): 304–330, using 1988 NLSY data, find some evidence of labor market discrimination against obese women, although they find little evidence that obese African American women suffer an economic penalty relative to other African American women. Daniel S. Hamermesh and Jeff E. Biddle, "Beauty and the Labor Market," *American Economic Review* 84, no. 5 (December 1994): 1174–1194, using an three-category rating system on data from the late 1970s, find an earnings penalty of 5–10 percent for plain people and a slightly smaller earnings premium for attractive people of both sexes.

48. Roberta M. Hall, "The Classroom Climate: A Chilly One for Women?" (Washington, D.C.: Association of American Colleges, 1982). Reprinted with permission. See also Bernice Resnick Sandler, Lisa A. Silverberg, and Roberta M. Hall, *The Chilly Classroom Climate: A Guide to Improve the Education of Women* (Washington, D.C.: National Association for Women in Education, 1996).

49. Irmtraud Streker-Seeborg, Michael C. Seeborg, and Abera Zegeye, "The Impact of Nontraditional Training on the Occupational Attainment of Women," *Journal of Human Resources* 19, no. 4 (Fall 1984): 452–471.

50. Rebecca M. Blank, *It Takes a Nation: A New Agenda For Fighting Poverty* (Princeton, N.J.: Princeton University, 1997): 176–177.

51. Larry V. Hedges and Amy Nowell, "Sex Differences in Mental Test Scores, Variability, and Numbers of High-Scoring Individuals," *Science* 269 (July 7, 1995): 41–45.

*F*urther reading and statistical sources

Becker, Gary S. (1993). *Human Capital: A Theoretical and Empirical Analysis, with Special Reference to Education, Third Edition*. Chicago, Ill.: University of Chicago. The classic work in this area in an updated edition; still relevant and readable.

Ehrenberg, Ronald G., and Robert S. Smith (1997). *Modern Labor Economics: Theory and Public Policy, 6th Edition*. New York: HarperCollins. An undergraduate labor economics textbook; clearly lays out theory of human capital, along with its many applications.

Filer, Randall K., Daniel S. Hamermesh, and Albert Rees (1996). *The Economics of Work and Pay, Sixth Edition*. New York: HarperCollins. An undergraduate labor economics textbook; provides a clear discussion of human capital theory and applications.

Harlan, Sharon, and Ronnie Steinberg (1989). *Job Training for Women: The Promise and Limits of Public Policies*. Philadelphia, Pa.: Temple University. Thorough discussion of empirical findings from government training program evaluations.

Manski, Charles F., and David A. Wise (1983). *College Choice in America*. Cambridge, Mass.: Harvard University. Comprehensive discussion of the choice of higher education institution type; has the theoretical underpinning of human capital theory.

Mincer, Jacob (1974). *Schooling, Experience and Earnings*. New York: National Bureau of Economic Research. Classic monograph exploring human capital theory and applications.

Polachek, Solomon W., and W. Stanley Siebert (1993). *The Economics of Earnings*. Cambridge, United Kingdom: Cambridge University. Handbook/textbook; lays out human capital theory clearly and shows applications.

Schultz, Theodore (1963). *The Economic Value of Education*. New York: Columbia University. Classic work; clear exposition of human capital theory, though somewhat dated findings.

National Center for Education Statistics. *Digest of Education Statistics*. Published annually; contains statistics about education, including enrollment and degrees granted. The entire volume is available on-line at the NCES website (www.ed.gov/NCES/).

*D*iscussion questions

1. For the following forms of human capital, indicate subareas that are general or specific, whether you think the rate of investment in the subareas varies by sex, and, if so, why the rate of investment in them varies by sex:

    (a) Typing/word processing
    (b) Driving
    (c) Computer programming
    (d) Russian translation
    (e) Childraising

2. Consider the Focus on the Mommy Track. Do you agree or disagree with each response to Felice Schwartz's quotes? Can you think of other factors in favor of or against the development of a two-track system for women in management?

3. If possible, find out the distribution of students by major and by sex at your school. What do you think accounts for gender differences in major among the students at your school? Do you see patterns by sex that show systematic differences by expected depreciation rate, corresponding to the data on depreciation rates in Table 7.5?

4. Interview at least six and at most ten friends at your school, with equal numbers of each sex, who have a declared major. Ask them the following questions:
    (a) How did you decide whether or not to attend college?
    (b) How did you decide which college to attend?
    (c) How did you decide what major to pursue?
    (d) What are your career plans, including possible graduate training?
    (e) What are your family plans – i.e., are you planning to have children and, if yes, do you plan to quit or reduce paid work when they are young?
    (f) Ask them directly, if they haven't already discussed this, whether their choice of major was influenced by their family plans.

    Summarize your findings and discuss whether they lend support to the human capital model. Also discuss whether you think your results are similar to what a survey of all U.S. college students would find.

5. Consider the Focus on gender bias in testing. Does the fact that women receive higher grades than men in high school and college imply that they are of higher ability? What else could account for this pattern?

6. Girls appear to have smaller variance in their test scores than boys do. This is true for a wide range of "IQ" tests.[51] Explain how this might explain girls' underrepresentation among Merit Scholars. Does this mean there is no sex discrimination in testing? What about the schooling process might cause this smaller variance?

7. Are there other skills besides the ability to do math that are in short supply in the country and therefore command a high wage? Does the ownership of these abilities vary by sex?

8. Can you list additional factors that you think would have an effect in determining hourly earnings that were not mentioned in the section on "Unmeasured factors?" For these factors, explain how you would measure them – i.e., what questions would you ask people to determine the importance of these factors, and how could you include them in an equation?

9. What are the pros and cons of requiring firms to make available professional-level part-time positions for parents?

10. Consider the Focus on classroom climate. Is the classroom climate on your campus "chilly" for women? Do you think that men and women are susceptible to gender attitudes conveyed by professors? Does the classroom climate affect motivation for students (either positively or negatively)? Does the classroom climate affect motivation differently for men and women?

11. In what ways might the structure of the formal education system hinder women's achievement of economic equality?

12. What are the pros and cons of requiring all vocational training programs to admit numbers of women and men proportional to their representation in the labor force?

Appendix
Regression analysis

The main statistical tool that economists use to analyze the relationship between earnings and various possible influences on earnings is called regression analysis. This technique is used for much more than merely analyzing this particular relationship, both within economics and in many other scientific fields. This appendix covers the basics of regression analysis for readers who have not been exposed to this topic, developing a specific example rather than presenting a theoretical exposition. For those who are familiar with the technique, this appendix may be skipped or read quickly for a review of the topic.

Consider the possible determinants of earnings. A researcher collects data on 12 workers, as shown in Table 7A.1. Being familiar with the human capital model, the researcher hypothesizes that earnings is positively related to both education and age. The researcher first plots the points for earnings and education, as shown in Figure 7A.1.

While there appears to be a positive relationship between earnings and education, the researcher would like a quantitative estimate of this relationship, as well as a feeling for how accurate this estimate is. One simple way to do this is to draw a straight line on the graph that is as close as possible to each point. An estimate of the relationship between earnings and education can then be determined by measuring the slope of the line. Additionally, a measure of the accuracy of this relationship can be determined by seeing how far from this line the data points tend to lie.

Regression analysis is a way of drawing such a line and measuring its accuracy. Regression analysis consists of fitting a line to the data by minimizing the sum of the squared vertical distances for each point from the line. Then the equation for the line can be determined (its intercept and slope), and a statistic based on the number of data points and their average squared distance from the line can be calculated to determine the accuracy of the line equation. This is generally done using a statistical program on a computer.[1]

TABLE 7A.1 Data for twelve workers on earnings, education, and age

Person	Weekly earnings	Years of schooling	Age
1	100	8	21
2	150	6	24
3	210	7	22
4	300	9	30
5	350	12	25
6	400	12	30
7	425	15	33
8	500	14	23
9	650	13	60
10	760	12	56
11	990	16	38
12	1,000	16	40

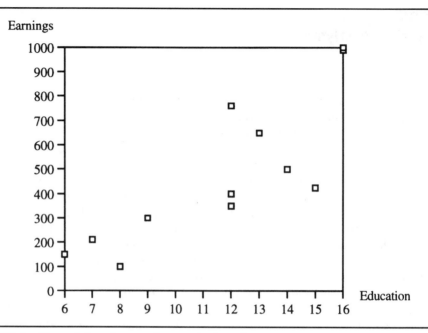

FIGURE 7A.1   Plotted data for earnings and education

Using such a program,[2] the researcher fits a linear equation to the data, as shown in Figure 7A.2. The equation shows both the vertical intercept of the fitted line, −369, and the slope of the line, 73. This indicates that for these 12 workers, an additional year of schooling is associated with an additional 73 dollars in weekly earnings. The number in parentheses under the slope is the *t*-statistic for the slope. This number indicates whether the estimated slope is significantly different from zero. A rule of thumb is that a *t*-statistic of absolute value 2 or more means that the estimate is different from zero. The notation R^2 = .66 indicates the "goodness of fit" of the line to the data points. It is a summary measure based on the sum of squared distances of the points from the line. The *R*-squared statistic ranges from 0 to 1, where 1 would indicate a perfect fit – i.e., the case where all the points lie exactly on the line.

Now the researcher decides to investigate the relationship between age and earnings, first plotting the data and fitting a line to the data, as shown in Figure 7A.3. Noticing that the line does not appear to fit the data points very well, as measured by the *R*-squared statistic and from just looking at the data, the researcher decides to try to fit a curve to the data instead. Hypothesizing that earnings at first rise with age and then begin to fall, the researcher tests the idea that earnings are related to both age and age squared. This relationship is consistent with the idea that human capital depreciates over time. This hypothesis can easily be incorporated into the regression framework as shown in Figure 7A.4; regression lines can be curved, as long as the equation relating the variables can be expressed in additive form.

This regression has a higher *R*-squared statistic,[3] indicating improved fit for the equation as well as *t*-statistics greater than 2 for both age and age-squared; these facts indicate that this regression is preferable to the one containing only age.

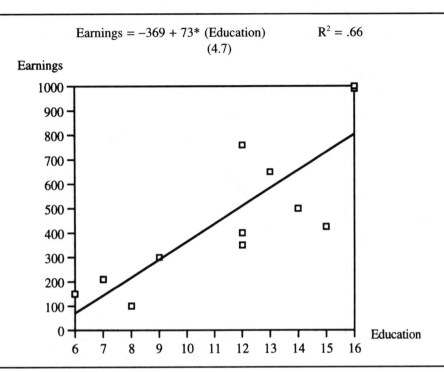

FIGURE 7A.2 Data and earnings regression using education

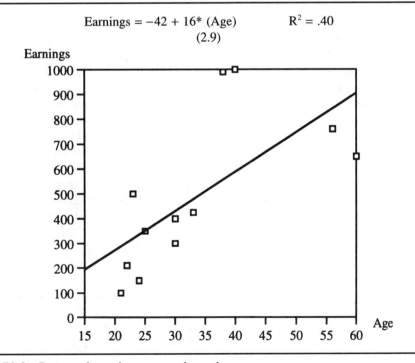

FIGURE 7A.3 Data and earnings regression using age

$$\text{Earnings} = -1560 + 102* \,(\text{Age}) - 1.1* \,(\text{Age})^2 \qquad R^2 = 0.63$$
$$(3.2) \qquad\qquad (2.7)$$

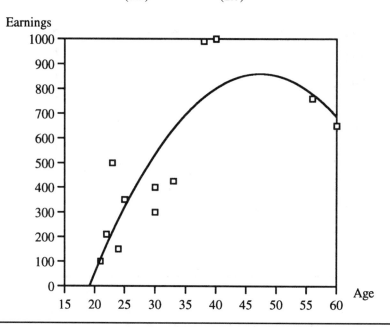

FIGURE 7A.4 Data and earnings regression using age and age-squared

Finally, the researcher decides to combine age, age-squared, and education into one regression in an attempt to explain earnings differences between these individuals more thoroughly than either age or education alone can explain. At this point, it becomes impossible to continue to graphically depict the regression line in two dimensions.[4] Therefore, the researcher must make decisions about goodness of fit of the equation based solely on the statistics. The results for this regression are shown in Table 7A.2, along with the results from the earlier regressions treating education, and age and age-squared separately.

A dilemma now arises in comparing Equations (d) and (e) in Table 7A.2. While the R-squared statistic rises slightly upon moving from Equation (d) to Equation (e) (upon adding age-squared to the regression), the coefficients of age and age-squared are not significantly different from zero as measured by the t-statistics! Since the determination of significance of coefficients and the determination of goodness of fit are both dependent on the number of workers in the sample, if the researcher could add additional workers to the data set, Equation (e) might become clearly preferable to (d). However, in this situation, the researcher must choose between a slight rise in overall goodness of fit of the equation and a situation in which all the variables can be said to have significant (different from zero) effect on earnings. Generally the latter case will be preferable.

Note that the coefficients on education and age vary, depending on whether they are considered separately or together. Compare the coefficient on education from equation (a) to the coefficient in (d). Here, when age is excluded from the regression, education appears to have a greater effect on earnings than it really does have. Because age and education

TABLE 7A.2   Earnings regressions using education, age, and age-squared

(a) Earnings = −369 + 73*(Education)	$R^2 = .66$
(4.7)	
(b) Earnings = −42 + 16* (Age)	$R^2 = .40$
(2.9)	
(c) Earnings = −1560 + 102* (Age) − 1.1* (Age)^2	$R^2 = .63$
(3.2) (2.7)	
(d) Earnings = −488 + 58* (Education) + 9* (Age)	$R^2 = .75$
(3.9) (2.2)	
(e) Earnings = −1039 + 45* (Education) + 48* (Age) − 0.5* (Age)^2	$R^2 = .76$
(2.4) (1.4) (1.1)	

are related in this sample of workers, part of the effect of increasing age on earnings is incorrectly attributed to education. Similarly, age becomes less important in equation (d) than in (b), where education is excluded. It is always important to try to think of what variables are being excluded from a given regression equation that may be affecting the coefficients on included variables and to try to think of what effect their inclusion would have on the size of the coefficients on included variables.

For those wishing to know more about the regression technique, including refinements, alternatives, and additional diagnostic statistics, there are many textbooks in econometrics available, all of which cover these topics.[5]

*E*ndnotes

1. Many such programs that run on both mainframe and personal computers are available. Popular ones among economists include EViews, SAS, SPSS-X, Statview, Systat, and TSP.
2. The graphs in this appendix are drawn using Cricket Graph on a Macintosh; the regression equations are calculated using Statview on a Macintosh.
3. The R-squared statistics reported herein are adjusted for the number of right-hand side variables.
4. There are statistical software packages available that can create a three-dimensional depiction of relationships between three variables, including MacSpin on the Macintosh.
5. I recommend G. S. Maddala, *Econometrics* (New York: McGraw-Hill, 1977).

*D*iscussion questions

1. In Table 7A.2, the intercept for each equation is negative. What is the interpretation of the intercept? Is it plausible to have negative intercepts?

2. In Figure 7A.4, it the curve were continued down to the right, it appears that very old people would have zero earnings. Is this plausible? How can this regression be correct?

3. Using a statistical software package, input the following data on 12 workers' weekly earnings, years of education, and age:

Earnings	Education	Age
950	15	38
1000	16	40
300	8	21
500	9	30
350	12	25
500	12	30
525	6	33
600	14	23
400	7	24
325	6	22
860	12	56
750	13	60

(a) Graph the data as in Figure 7A.1.

(b) Using regression analysis, fit equations to the data graphically as in Figures 7A.2–7A.4.

(c) Write out the earnings equations as in Table 7.1.

(d) Which equation appears to describe the data best?

(e) What happens to the equations containing education if you add a squared term for education?

(f) If you had to pick only one variable in order to predict earnings for this sample, would you pick earnings or age?

4. Collect data from a sample of twelve employed persons as in question (3).

(a) Run earnings equations on your sample as in question (3).

(b) If you have persons of both sexes in your sample, add a *dummy variable* for sex (i.e., a variable that takes the value "0" for men and "1" for women, or vice versa) in your earnings equations. Is there evidence in your sample that women make less than men?

(c) How was your sample selected? Could your sample collection method have influenced your results? If so, how?

5. What other variables besides age, education, and sex might you want to include in an earnings equation? How would you ask people the right questions to ascertain those variables, and how would you code them for inclusion in an earnings equation?

6. Suppose you wanted to test whether or not the payoff to an additional year of education was the same for men as for women. How would you set up your regression analysis in this case?

Causes of Earnings Differences: Compensating Differentials

CHAPTER

8

*T*his chapter elaborates on the following famous quotation and shows its relevance to the issue of why women earn less than men:

> The five following are the principal circumstances which, so far as I have been able to observe, make up for a small pecuniary gain in some employments, and counterbalance a great one in others: first, the agreeableness or disagreeableness of the employments themselves; secondly, the easiness and cheapness, or the difficulty and expence of learning them; thirdly, the constancy or inconstancy of employment in them; fourthly, the small or great trust which must be reposed in those who exercise them; and fifthly, the probability or improbability of success in them. (Adam Smith, *Wealth of Nations*, 1776, Book 1, Chapter X, Part 1)

While the second above-mentioned "principal circumstance" for why jobs pay differently has already been discussed in Chapter 7, the other four remain to be explored. This chapter first contains a discussion of *compensating differentials* and their predicted effects on both the distribution of men and women across jobs and the relative pay of men and women in jobs. Second, evidence on whether or not compensating differentials contribute sizably to the gender earnings gap is examined. The chapter closes with a discussion of the implications of the theory of compensating differentials for gender-related policy issues.

What is a compensating differential?

> The wages of labour vary with the ease or hardship, the cleanliness or dirtiness, the honourableness or dishonourableness of the employment. (Adam Smith, *Wealth of Nations*, Book 1, Chapter X, Part 1)

Adam Smith made this statement both as an empirical observation and as a hypothesis about how labor markets work. Subsequent economists have found it consistent with the general economic methodology of focusing on equilibrium situations in all types of markets, including markets for labor. The basic idea is that the wages paid to various types of labor must, in general, equalize total advantages, both pecuniary and nonpecuniary, among them.[1] If this were not the case, so that one job both paid more and was more pleasant, then workers would flock to hold that job, thereby driving down its wage through a rightward shift of the labor supply curve for that job. Meanwhile, wages in the spurned jobs would rise, due to the leftward shift of the labor supply curves for those jobs. The process of migration between jobs would cease when the wage in the pleasant job was sufficiently depressed and wages in other jobs were sufficiently high to make workers indifferent between the various jobs. The difference between the now higher wage in the spurned jobs and the lower wage in the pleasant job is the *compensating differential*. Alternatively, if one job is more unpleasant than others, the wage in it would rise, while wages in other jobs would fall, so that again a compensating differential would arise in labor market equilibrium.

How do compensating differentials affect earnings?

> A journeyman blacksmith, though an artificer, seldom earns so much in twelve hours as a collier, who is only a labourer, does in eight. His work is not quite so dirty, is less dangerous, and is carried on in day-light and above ground. (Adam Smith, *Wealth of Nations*, Book 1, Chapter X, Part 1)

Following this reasoning on how labor markets equilibrate, jobs that are less desirable should have higher wages than average, while jobs that are more desirable should have lower wages than average. However, as the quote from Adam Smith shows, there are complicating factors to be considered while looking for such wage patterns. One is that jobs generally contain mixes of factors, some of which may be positive and some negative; the two may cancel each other out and therefore no compensating differential would arise. Secondly, jobs often appear to be both high-paying and pleasant, or both low-paying and unpleasant. These wage patterns can often be explained by checking to see if they satisfy the condition of "all else being equal." For instance, many jobs require a college education, which under human capital theory would require that they pay higher wages than jobs with lower educational requirements. The strong correlation between desirability and level of skills required can obscure patterns of compensating differentials.

Alternatively, as in the quote from Adam Smith, a job may be at a higher skill level but still pay less than a lower-skill, less-pleasant job. Measuring the wage difference between the two jobs would lead to an underestimate of the compensating differential for relative pleasantness. Again, it is necessary to control for differences in skill level (and therefore productivity differences reflected in wages) in order to measure correctly compensating differentials.

Good jobs

> Honour makes a great part of the reward of all honourable professions. In point of pecuniary gain, all things considered, they are generally under-recompensed. (Adam Smith, *Wealth of Nations*, Book 1, Chapter X, Part 1)

In Smith's thinking, jobs ranked high in terms of status have to be paid less on average to compensate for this status gain. To the extent that status is related to pay, this effect may be hard to untangle. However, in surveys asking people their opinions about the relative status of occupations, there is not a perfect correlation between status and pay. One researcher has constructed a prestige index, the Bose index, scaled from 0 to 100; values for selected occupations are shown in Table 8.1.[2] Clearly the positive correlation between pay and

TABLE 8.1 Median income, median education, and the Bose index, selected occupations, 1960

Occupation	Median income	Median education	Bose index
College presidents and deans	6,988	17.4	96
Civil engineers	6,861	16.2	88
Secondary school teachers	5,122	16.8	83
Economists	5,180	15.9	79
Librarians	4,146	16.2	75
Dentists	3,975	16.0	73
Elementary school teachers	1,795	16.1	63
Accountants	4,532	12.8	58
Nurses	3,830	13.2	57
Policemen and detectives	3,041	12.1	47
Clergymen	2,219	12.8	47
Piano tuners and repairers	3,373	11.5	46
Bakers	2,441	9.7	31
Plasterers	3,333	8.5	29
Fishers	2,250	8.7	25
Farm laborers	899	7.5	11
Midwives	1,250	5.9	4

Source: Christine E. Bose, *Jobs and Gender: A Study of Occupational Prestige* (New York: Praeger, 1985): 152–165. An imprint of Greenwood Publishing Group, Inc., Westport, Conn. Reprinted with permission.

prestige is not perfect; for instance, accountants rank higher in pay but lower in prestige than librarians.

Other factors that make jobs relatively good include pleasant working conditions, such as clean facilities and roomy offices; a high level of fringe benefits, such as free or subsidized food and athletic facilities; cooperative coworkers; and low supervision of hours (such as not having to take timed breaks). All these factors should therefore lead to a *negative compensating differential.*

The implications for the gender earnings difference are thus: if women are more likely than men to choose jobs with relatively pleasant working conditions, their earnings will be lower, all else being equal.

Bad jobs

Disgrace has the contrary effect. The trade of a butcher is a brutal and odious business; but it is in most places more profitable than the greater part of common trades. The most detestable of all employments, that of public executioner, is, in proportion to the quantity of work done, better paid than any common trade whatever. (Adam Smith, *Wealth of Nations*, Book 1, Chapter X, Part 1)

By analogy to the status argument, jobs that have related stigmas should pay relatively well. In fact, stigma may be more obvious to the onlooker than status. For instance, garbage collection may pay better in many locales than other forms of relatively unskilled labor. The comparable worth case of *Lemons* v. *City of Denver* pointed out that nurses hired by Denver municipal hospitals were paid less per hour than Denver garbage collectors.

Stigma is not the only reason why a job might be bad. Other factors predicted to lead to relatively higher wages, or a *positive compensating differential*, include riskiness, dirtiness, and difficulty in getting and keeping a job. If men are more prone than women to choose jobs with relatively unpleasant working conditions, their earnings will be higher, all else being equal.

Most studies of compensating differentials have, in fact, focused on whether or not relatively bad jobs have higher wages. This may be, in part, because there are some more easily quantified ways to measure badness of a job. In particular, the risk of injury is quantifiable, and statistics on workplace injuries and work-related illness are routinely collected by government agencies.

The risk of entering unemployment and the average duration of unemployment can be readily measured for different industries and occupations. Again, the prediction would be that workers require higher wages in jobs with a greater probability of layoff, all else being equal, in order to compensate them for the risk of losing earnings.

Carrying the argument concerning probability of unemployment further, some high prestige occupations, such as acting, have an unbalanced wage structure in that the top members of the occupation make extremely high wages, while the vast majority of the members make very low wages, often not enough to subsist on without taking a second job. This job could be considered bad in the sense that the probability of success in acting is low; on the other hand, the payoff to success is phenomenal. Under the theory of compensating differentials, this payoff structure can be an equilibrium if the average payoff is somewhat higher than that found in other occupations.[3]

FOCUS

Death on the job

While the two most dangerous jobs in the United States are astronaut and U.S. President, they (luckily) do not account for many total casualties.[4] However, about 23 people die every workday in the United States while on the job. Farming/forestry, mining, construction, and transportation are the most dangerous industries; vehicle accidents caused the most job-related deaths. This does not include the much more numerous group of people who suffer crippling injuries on the job, or who die of job-related illnesses. For instance, while there are fewer deaths on-the-job in manufacturing, exposure to toxic materials may make manufacturing the most risky sector by raising workers' fatal illness rates.

For working women, murder is the greatest cause of on-the-job deaths, accounting in 1992 (when the first census of work-related fatalities was taken) for 170, or 40 percent, of the 426 women who died at work. This statistic received much attention in the national press.[5]

However, men are much more likely to be murdered on the job. Overall, men account for 93 percent of job-related deaths. Out of the 5,657 men who died on the job in 1992, 15 percent, or 849, were murdered. So five times as many men were murdered as women while on the job. As one reader of the *New York Times* commented in his letter complaining about the paper's take on the statistics: "the reason that a greater proportion of female deaths in the workplace are murders is not that women are murdered at a higher rate than men, because they are not. It is rather that men are killed at a higher rate by other causes."[6]

Table 8.2 contains some recent statistics on occupational fatality rates.

TABLE 8.2 Selected occupations in order of risk of death, 1995

Occupation	Fatal occupational injuries per 100,000 workers
Sailors and deckhands	115
Fishers	104
Timber-cutters and loggers	101
Airplane pilots	97
Mining machine operators	78
Garbage collectors	60
Taxicab drivers and chauffeurs	46
Construction laborers	39
Bulldozer operators	31
Farm workers	30
Roofers	29
Electric power installers and repairers	28
Truck drivers	26
Police and detectives	17
News vendors	16
Firefighters	13
Guards	11
Cashiers	4
Managers	3
Clerical workers	1
Professions	1

Source: Bureau of Labor Statistics, Census of Fatal Occupational Statistics, 1995 (Table 2).

Sorting of workers across firms and industries

The preceding discussion of compensating differentials needs to be qualified in two ways. One is that jobs are generally not easily separated into good and bad groups; rather, they fall along a continuum. Indeed, the nonpecuniary compensation associated with a job may be of a rather ambiguous form, such as particular workplace features that some people like and others are indifferent to or actually dislike. (For example, some people consider working closely with others to be a good thing, while others prefer to work alone). This fact leads to the second qualification: people have different preferences for job characteristics.

This second qualification can lead to an overturning of the basic theory of compensating differentials discussed above, in that compensating differentials need not arise even when jobs vary significantly in nonpecuniary characteristics.[7] Consider Adam Smith's evaluation of the wages of butchers, in which above-average compensation is necessary to induce persons to enter a "brutal and odious business." More recent writers have noted that this condition may have been related to the cultural homogeneity of eighteenth-century Britain. In fact, if enough individuals have no strong feelings about butchering, then it would be possible to fill all available butchering positions without generating any compensating differential.[8]

Consider Adam Smith's other example of a bad job: public executioner. Currently the number of executions in the United States is very low. Certainly no two executions ever occur simultaneously in the same state, and not all states allow capital punishment. Therefore, the maximum number of executioners currently needed is less than 50. Is it not likely that there are 50 individuals in a country of over 200 million who would actually be willing to do the job free, let alone not require above-average pay to do this job? For jobs that are in relatively low demand, it seems highly likely that enough people can be found to fill the job, especially in a large, heterogeneous society, without generating any compensating differential.

Now consider the various nonpecuniary job characteristics mentioned above. Regarding working conditions, one expects workers to choose between firms based on pay rates and on the working conditions available. Some workers are willing to trade earnings for additional hours flexibility, such as part-time work or flex-time schedules. Other workers are interested in working overtime and might well be willing to work additional hours at their primary job for less than the government mandated time-and-a-half rate. (In fact, many people hold more than one job, often working a second job at a lower hourly rate than on their first job.) In the same industry, one firm could hire part-time employees and another firm full-time employees, and in equilibrium the two firms would be equally profitable. Wages might or might not differ between the firms, depending on the relative productivity of part-time and full-time workers, the relative costs (and therefore relative labor demand) of managing the two types of workers, and the relative supply of the two types of workers.

Consider the provision of fringe benefits across firms. Again, we expect to see workers choose between firms partly on the basis of different mixtures of fringe benefits. Unmarried workers would be relatively uninterested in life insurance, workers without children would be less interested in child care benefits, and married workers whose spouse already had family health coverage through his/her job would be uninterested in health insurance. In particular, single childless workers would probably prefer higher earnings and lower fringe benefits, and would be attracted to firms offering that particular compensation mix.

Turning to relative risk tolerance, it is not inconceivable that some persons might actually seek out jobs offering relatively high risk levels and that the wages in these jobs might actually be lower than average as a result of the high labor supply – for instance, the position of ski instructor. While many persons would consider such jobs undesirable due to the high rate of injury, the relatively low demand for such jobs may again be easily met by the supply of risk-seeking persons.

Interest in or lack of interest in "honour" may also vary in the population. Taking the psychological categories of "introvert" and "extrovert" as an example, introverts may be less concerned than extroverts with how others view their lives and, therefore, not be dissuaded from entering relatively low-prestige occupations that interest them for other reasons. The relative numbers of introverts and extroverts in a population will influence the patterns of compensating differentials related to prestige.

In each of these cases, differences in the distribution of preferences between the male and female populations can lead to sex segregation, with or without accompanying compensating differentials. For instance, if 10 percent of the male population but only 1 percent of the female population is risk-seeking, then we would expect on average that only 1 of 11 persons in a risky occupation would be female.

Gender differences in preferences for job characteristics

What evidence is there that women and men differ systematically in their preferences for various job characteristics? Additionally, do gender-related differences in preferences translate into differences in earnings?

Evidence of preference patterns can be obtained in several ways. Researchers can ask men and women to rate various job characteristics in terms of their desirability. However, even if men and women rate job characteristics equally in terms of desirability, they can still end up choosing different jobs due to constraints on their preferences, such as the need to accommodate nonmarket work, including child care. Additionally, data can be collected to see how the jobs that men and women actually take differ.

There are clear differences in work and pay patterns between the sexes. Men are more likely than women to work swing shifts (both evening and night) and these shifts pay more than day shifts. Data were presented in Chapter 6 on the relationship between part-time work, overtime work, and percentage female for various occupations, showing women are less likely to work overtime and men are less likely to work part-time. Also, women appear to receive a smaller portion of their earnings as pay contingent on job performance.[9]

While preferences can be unrelated to one's current work status, data of this type are usually collected from workers who are asked to consider the characteristics of their current job. For example, Table 8.3 lists job characteristics that men and women were asked to rate in the 1977 Quality of Employment Survey. The job characteristics are a mix of objective and subjective concepts.

Table 8.4 shows which of the job characteristics in Table 8.3 were actually rated differently on average by the sexes, where the difference was statistically significant. Men rated their jobs higher in terms of variety, autonomy, challenge, and applicability of their skills. They also considered their jobs to be more hazardous than did the women in the sample and had longer commutes and a higher rate of job-related illness. Women rated their jobs higher in terms of role clarity. They also held jobs requiring more physical effort, had more supervision, had better relations with coworkers, and had more freedom to take time off from work. Note that for many of the job characteristics listed in Table 8.3, men and women did not differ in their rating of their jobs, including comfort, security, prospects for promotion, and provision of fringe benefits.

Another study, which compared work attitudes by gender using a sample of production workers, retail sales workers, and mid-level clerical workers drawn from Massachusetts, West Germany, and Israel, found that the women had a higher concern for work hygiene and for attaining direct satisfaction from work, while men were more concerned about the content of work, had a higher commitment and attachment to their employment and occupation, reported higher work satisfaction, had a more instrumental orientation towards work, and were more interested in advancement at work.[10]

However, worker heterogeneity within gender group may dwarf the heterogeneity related to gender. For instance, a study of women's attitudes towards the use of video display terminals in their jobs found that they varied systematically with education, social class, race and ethnic status, age and life situation, economic needs, attitude towards "women's issues," and experiences with sex discrimination.[11] Indeed, there appears to be little evidence that men and women differ in their overall, or "global" job satisfaction.[12]

TABLE 8.3 Measures of job characteristics

Job Characteristic	Value range*	Concept
Variety	6–24	Number of different tasks done on the job and creativity required to accomplish them
Autonomy	6–24	Freedom to define pace and method of work
Task identification	3–12	Completion of entire task rather than a small component of it
Task significance	3–12	Perception of the importance of one's job
Feedback	2–8	Extent of feedback regarding job performance
Responsibility	3–12	Degree to which the job affects project outcome and to which one will receive credit
Role conflict	4–16	Extent to which job requirements cannot be satisfied
Role clarity	4–16	Extent to which job requirements are clearly stated and understood
Effort	3–12	Degree to which job requires rapid and sustained pace or physical effort
Moral	2–8	Degree to which job does not require the worker to compromise personal values
Comfort	7–28	Comfort of the physical work environment
Challenge	6–24	Intrinsic challenge contained in the job
Security	1–4	Belief of unlikelihood of layoff or discharge
Relations with coworkers	3–12	Degree to which worker enjoys on-the-job relations with coworkers
Promotion	3–12	Prospects for promotion
Supervision	5–20	Worker's assessment of quality of supervision and how well worker gets along with supervisor
Resource adequacy	6–24	Adequacy of physical and environmental resources provided to accomplish job
Fringe benefits	0–100	Percentage of possible fringe benefits (out of 18) provided
Number of hazards	0–14	Number of hazardous working conditions (chemicals, extreme noise, etc.)
Bad physical condition	0–3	Worker's perception to the extent of problems caused by physical conditions in the workplace
Commute	(hours)	Time spent commuting from home to work
Freedom to take time off	1–4	Ease with which worker can take time off for personal reasons
Use of skills	1–4	Extent to which job fully uses worker's skills and training
Ease of change	1–4	Ease with which worker could change work schedule
Uncertainty	1–4	Likelihood of permanently losing job within the next few years although worker would like to retain it
Job-related illness	0 or 1	Whether worker reports physical illness caused or aggravated by the job
Satisfactory days	0 or 1	Whether worker reports satisfaction with the days he or she works
Satisfactory hours	0 or 1	Whether worker reports satisfaction with the hours he or she works

* Different questions were scaled differently, but a lower number always indicates that the job has less of that quality.
Source: Randall K. Filer, "Male-Female Wage Differences: The Importance of Compensating Differentials," *Industrial and Labor Relations Review* 38, no. 3 (April 1985): 426–437. © Cornell University. Reprinted with permission of the *Industrial and Labor Relations Review*. Data are from the 1977 Quality of Employment Survey.

TABLE 8.4 Job characteristics on which the sexes differ significantly in their ratings

Job Characteristic	Men	Women
Variety	20.20	18.76
Autonomy	18.79	17.37
Role clarity	14.60	15.08
Effort	9.65	10.81
Challenge	16.84	16.11
Relations with coworkers	9.28	9.66
Supervision	15.02	15.57
Number of hazards	4.78	2.28
Commute	0.39	0.28
Freedom to take time off	2.00	2.31
Use of skills	3.36	3.13
Job-related illness	0.07	0.04

Source: Randall K. Filer, "Male-Female Wage Differences: The Importance of Compensating Differentials," *Industrial and Labor Relations Review* 38, no. 3 (April 1985): 426–437. © Cornell University. Reprinted with permission of the *Industrial and Labor Relations Review.*

FOCUS

Gender differences in "selling out"

Economist Robert Frank posed a series of hypothetical choices to a group of Cornell University seniors to see how much more they would have to be paid to work for less "socially responsible" organizations relative to more "socially conscious" ones.[13] Not surprisingly, they did report requiring what he called "a moral reservation premium" in order to work for the less desirable choices. The report I read did not say if there were gender differences in the survey, so I tried out the choices on my Spring 1997 Economics of Gender students to see if there would be gender differences in "selling out." Below are the five choices I posed to my students, along with the percentage of each sex who said they would prefer the latter job and how much more those persons said they would have to be paid in order to take the former job:

- lawer for the National Rifle Association vs. lawyer for the Sierra Club
  91% of the women – $892,000; 92% of the men – $388,000
- ad copywriter for Camel cigarettes vs. ad copywriter for the American Cancer Society
  91% of the women – $310,000; 92% of the men – $281,000
- language teacher for the CIA vs. language teacher in high school
  50% of the women – $117,000; 42% of the men – $55,000 (note there was reversal of the Cornell view of which was the desirable choice)
- accountant for a large petrochemical company vs. accountant for a large art museum
  91% of the women – $106,000; 58% of the men – $27,000
- recruiter for Exxon vs. recruiter for the Peace Corps
  86% of the women – $146,000; 50% of the men – $39,000

So in this sample, women say they require more money in order to sell out than do men.

Evidence on compensating differentials from wage regressions

Researchers have used several different methods to look for the effects of job characteristics on earnings. All the methods rely on the statistical technique of regression analysis (discussed in the appendix to Chapter 7), but differ in focus and sampling structure. The first method is to take two sectors (e.g., profit and nonprofit, or union and nonunion), control for differences in the workers between the sectors, see how much wage difference remains, and argue that this differences is related to differences in working conditions and/or fringe benefits between the two sectors.

A second method is to take a group of workers dispersed among a set of industries or occupations, again control for differences between the workers, and include variables relating to working conditions across industries and occupations (e.g., differences in overtime requirements) to see how much of the remaining variance in earnings between workers can be explained. The coefficients on these variables provide measures of how much each individual working condition affects earnings.

A third method is to examine a single industry or occupation and consider workers in different firms to look for firm-level differences in working conditions and fringes. Again, the attempt is made to control for differences between the workers. One example of this method is a study of school teachers that looked at variations in fringe benefits and working conditions across school districts and found that there were compensating differentials in wages to offset these variations.[14]

In all these cases, if a compensating differential is found and if men and women are distributed differently across sectors, industries, occupations, and firms (as we know they are from Chapter 6), then their different distribution and their subsequently different pay can be partially explained by their relative interest in different nonpecuniary aspects of the job. This assumes free choice of jobs on the part of workers; otherwise the distribution of workers across jobs reflects discrimination as well.

Because many studies looking for compensating differentials have used only males in the samples of workers, they cannot shed light on the gender earnings gap.[15] Many of these studies find only limited support for the existence of compensating differentials, and in some cases where support is found, it is not clear that the possibility of important omitted worker characteristics can be reasonably ruled out. The strongest effect is generally found by studies looking for higher wages in comparatively risky jobs. There is also evidence that industries with a relatively high probability of lengthy layoffs pay higher wages.[16]

The relationship between unionization and higher wages has been examined extensively by economists.[17] While many studies consider higher wages to be caused by either monopoly power on the part of unions or higher productivity on the part of unionized workers, some studies have concentrated on the negative factors associated with unionized industries. Industries with higher strike propensities and higher fatality rates appear to pay higher wages.[18] This can help explain the union-nonunion wage differential. Unionized industries also appear to pay higher wages partly because union jobs have less desirable working conditions than nonunion jobs particularly regarding the pace and scheduling of work.[19] To the extent that women are underrepresented in the unionized sector, compensating differentials account for part of the gender wage difference. One study using data for women only found *positive* compensating differentials in hazardous union jobs but *negative* compensating differentials in hazardous nonunion jobs, leading the authors to speculate that women in those jobs have poor access to information concerning job hazards.[20]

A study that compares earnings for white-collar workers in nonprofit firms with earnings in for-profit firms finds lower wages in the nonprofit sector. This finding can be interpreted as a compensating differential for the opportunity a nonprofit firm provides to create products with positive externalities. If people care about others and want to feel responsible for improvement in the well-being of others, these jobs will be viewed as more desirable. To the extent that women are overrepresented in the nonprofit sector, compensating differentials can again account for part of the gender wage difference.

An alternative explanation for wage differences that is always difficult to rule out, however, is that lower-quality workers are found in the lower-paid positions, and that controls in wage regressions for human capital are not picking up all of this quality effect. Perhaps nonunion firms hire lower-quality workers. Similarly, the lower pay that nonprofit firms can afford to offer may attract mostly lower-quality workers.[21] One study that tries to explain the well-known regularity that small firms pay less than big firms finds that small-firm workers have more unstable work histories, as well as lower human capital endowments, than large-firm workers.[22] Small firms also employ a disproportionate number of women.

Some studies have concentrated on the hours structure of jobs to look for higher wages in inflexible establishments and lower wages in relatively flexible establishments. One study, in comparing establishments with mandatory overtime provisions to those without, found no evidence of compensatingly higher straight-time wages.[23]

Finally, differences in preferences for work characteristics may account for earnings differences both directly due to job choice and indirectly through their effect on investment in particular types of human capital. A study of young people that collected data on college major as well as on job preferences found that the sexes differed significantly in both areas, as shown in Table 8.5.[24] Job preferences alone accounted for between 6 and 27 percent of the gender earnings gap for this group of young college graduates, but differences in college major accounted for an additional 28 to 43 percent of the gap.[25] In terms of explaining which major a person was likely to choose, persons who were relatively interested in making money were more likely to choose a business major, while those who were not interested in making money were more likely to choose careers in science. Persons interested in being a leader but less interested in opportunities to work with people were more likely to major in business or health-related fields. Persons who were more interested in helping others were more likely to major in the humanities.

Gender differences in returns to job characteristics

Other studies have considered the possibility of different returns to various job characteristics by sex. For instance, a job involving high worker autonomy might pay all workers more than jobs with low autonomy, but still pay men more than women. This could be related either to discrimination or to the relative supplies of men and women to these jobs. However, this latter point requires the assumption that men and women performing an identical job are nevertheless not considered to be perfect substitutes by the employer. These studies may, in fact, provide the most incontrovertible evidence that discrimination is occurring in the workplace. The only way to avoid this conclusion is to argue that the study did not adequately control for productivity differences between men and women, or that the jobs that women held in the study were not really comparable to the jobs that the men held.

TABLE 8.5 Percentage distribution of job preferences and college majors by sex

	Men	*Women*
Preferences		
Making money not important	15	22
Making money somewhat important	63	67
Making money very important	22	11
Helping others not important	8	2
Helping others somewhat important	45	26
Helping others very important	47	72
Being a leader not important	20	42
Being a leader somewhat important	50	46
Being a leader very important	22	13
Working with people not important	20	6
Working with people somewhat important	40	25
Working with people very important	40	68
College major		
Business	26	13
Computer science	2	2
Education	9	27
Engineering	10	1
Humanities	7	11
Health or biology	5	14
Science or math	3	2
Social sciences	11	11
Professional	13	7
Other	13	12

Source: Thomas N. Daymont and Paul J. Andrisani, "Job Preferences, College Major, and the Gender Gap in Earnings," *Journal of Human Resources* 19, no. 3 (Summer 1984): 412–413. Reprinted with permission of the University of Wisconsin Press. Data are from the National Longitudinal Studies of the High School Class of 1972. All means are significantly different by sex except for the percentages of respondents choosing computer science, the social sciences, and "other," as a major.

A study using the data reported in Tables 8.2 and 8.3 has found that, not only do significant differences exist between the working conditions typical of jobs held by women and those held by men, but men and women are rewarded differently for certain job characteristics. The conclusion of this study is that these differences suggest a need to pay higher wages in order to attract employees to the jobs held by men.[26] Another study finds that monetary control – i.e., control over funds at the firm – is positively associated with higher earnings for both sexes, but is associated with higher monetary rewards for men than for women.[27]

Finally, the study using the data discussed in Table 8.5 also finds that men and women experience different relative returns to their job preference variables. Men who indicated a strong desire to help others and to work with people earned less than other men. Women who indicated a strong desire to help others did not experience as much of a wage cut relative to other women, and women who indicated a strong desire to work with people earned the same as the average woman.

Relative importance of job characteristics in determining wages

While it appears that various job characteristics are associated with higher or lower wages across jobs, how much of a combined effect do they have in determining wages? In particular, how important are these variables, as compared with other factors such as variations in human capital?

One study compares the effect on occupational wage differentials of conventional economic variables (e.g., years of education and experience) with the effect of job characteristics and finds that job characteristics explain few of the differentials and that their effects are dwarfed by the amount attributable to conventional (i.e., human capital) variables.[28] Another study calculates that working conditions can account for approximately 10 percent of the gender earnings gap, while about 30 percent can be accounted for by differences in personal characteristics.[29] Ten percent seems a reasonable upper bound of the effect of working conditions on the overall gender earnings gap.

However, the effect attributed to the particular variable of percentage female in a job, which is included in many wage equations, may be diminished considerably by the inclusion of variables measuring job characteristics. One researcher, using 1980 data on occupational characteristics, including pay, concludes: "Once compensating differentials for a job's effort, responsibility, fringe benefits, and working conditions are taken into account, there *is no significant relationship between an occupation's gender composition and its wages* for either men or women. What appears to be an effect in the combined equation results from lower wages for women within each occupation."[30]

Policy implications of compensating differentials for the gender earnings gap

The main policy implication from the theory of compensating differentials is that labor markets should be essentially unregulated with respect to the mix of job characteristics offered by different firms, occupations, and industries. So long as workers have full information about job characteristics, including riskiness, and so long as entry into particular jobs is not restricted, workers will make utility-maximizing choices on their own which, assuming heterogeneous preferences, will involve different mixes of pecuniary and nonpecuniary characteristics.

Throughout the entire chapter, however, the implicit assumption has been that non-pecuniary differences between jobs are essentially immutable – an intrinsic part of the job. But this need not be the case. For instance, different firms within an industry can vary widely in their workplace practices. This is certainly noticeable in the variation in accident rates among firms – a difference that leads to each firm's having its own accident rating for the purposes of determining its worker compensation premium level. Therefore, one question to ask in evaluating the legitimacy of work practices that exclude a group of potential workers is whether those characteristics were established to exclude this group or to meet the requirements necessary for the job to be performed efficiently. For instance, a firm that has only full-time jobs will effectively reduce the number of women seeking work in that firm. Is it not possible to reorganize these jobs to allow for some part-time work? Restrictions relating to physical features become more suspect as labor-assisting machinery becomes more and more widespread. In the case of occupations such as flight attendant,

height, weight, sex, and age restrictions clearly are of no relevance to the ability of potential applicants to perform the job; witness the current group of flight attendants, which
includes many men and older women, as contrasted to the almost exclusively young female
group found on airplanes in earlier years. No loss of life has ever been ascribed to the
changed demographics of flight attendants.

Policy Application: Workplace regulations

Firms that have production procedures entailing a particular level of risk for a given group
of people may decide to ban those people from the firm, or from particular jobs within the
firm. The following paragraphs are excerpted from a study of how to manage risk while
maintaining an acceptable level of free choice on the part of workers.[31] The writer, economist W. Kip Viscusi, takes the view that in most circumstances, labor markets should be
allowed to operate freely, without regulation by agencies such as the Occupational Safety
and Health Administration (OSHA), in order to allow individuals to match up with jobs
that will vary in riskiness and in pay. However, he allows for the possibility of government
intervention in cases where risk levels are hard to determine and where worker choices may
impose costs on others.

> The risk posed by a particular job varies widely for different individuals. Many
> particularly controversial instances involve risks strongly correlated with one's sex
> or race. Blacks with the gene for sickle-cell anemia may incur a greater risk of
> harm from the low-oxygen conditions faced by a pilot, and female mail sorters
> have a greater frequency of back injuries when moving the standard seventy-pound
> mail sacks.
>
> The employer and the worker's fellow employees also may have a stake in the
> allocation of workers to jobs. Worker injuries and illnesses disrupt production,
> lead to additional training costs, boost workers' compensation benefits, and affect
> the firm's reputation, which in turn alters wage rates. A worker's careless behavior
> may also result in injuries to other workers.
>
> For many jobs involving strength, dexterity, and other risk-related physical
> characteristics, employers are very selective in filling positions. Sometimes this
> selectivity is related quite explicitly to the risk. Smokers are not permitted to work
> at the Johns-Manville asbestos plant because they face a risk of lung cancer almost
> a hundred times greater than nonsmokers. Similarly, no women are permitted to
> work in the pigment paint division of the American Cyanamid Corporation be-
> cause lead exposures pose considerably larger risks to pregnant women. Distinc-
> tions based on sex have been widely condemned, in part because the women
> previously working in the division agreed to become sterilized to keep their jobs. In
> contrast, the ban on smoking received widespread publicity and, unlike the lead
> case, did not lead to a critical OSHA review. Society may feel more strongly about
> distinctions based on unalterable personal characteristics than about individual
> choices that have increased one's riskiness in a job.
>
> A mechanism by which markets might reduce the costs imposed on others
> from this heterogeneity is by altering the worker's wage rate. Accident-prone work-
> ers who impose greater losses on others should be paid a lower wage to reflect
> these expected costs. This wage flexibility is often limited in practice by wage floors

(such as the minimum wage), limitations on the variation of wage rates if the source of the heterogeneity in riskiness is highly correlated with personal characteristics (particularly race, sex, and age), and institutional rigidities that prevent variation of the wage structure on an individual basis. Financial mechanisms also may have inherent limitations since there can be no adequate *ex post* compensation for a worker who is killed as a result of hazardous behavior by his coworkers.

Once the costs are imposed on parties beyond the labor market transaction, market processes become even more inadequate. The imposition on taxpayers of social insurance costs for injured workers has traditionally been the most pressing concern of this type. Much more disturbing problems have arisen in the past few decades as we have begun to learn more about the possibly catastrophic implications of workplace exposures for fetuses subjected to radiation, lead, and other carcinogens. Although the mother may take the baby's interests into account in selecting a job, there is no assurance that the preferences of the unborn will be fully reflected in her decision. Moreover, the mother may not have complete information regarding the risk to the fetus, or she may be unable to alter the risk. For example, a woman with high lead levels in her blood before becoming pregnant will continue to have possibly hazardous lead levels even if she leaves the job associated with the exposure.

Situations such as these may pose major difficulties for the employer as well. If he prevents such exposures by excluding all women from the job, he may exclude a substantial number of workers who would not have had a baby exposed to the risk. Alternatively, failure to discriminate in this fashion may increase his liability and the pressure to incur the costs of preventing possible adverse outcomes. In such a case government regulations that define the employer's obligations precisely may benefit the employer by sharing some of the responsibility for his decisions.

Summary

The theory of compensating differentials predicts that unpleasant jobs will pay more than pleasant jobs, all else being equal, where relative pleasantness can include low risk of injury, low risk of unemployment, good fringe benefits, and many other working conditions. The theory is qualified in the case of heterogeneous worker preferences, so that supply and demand for particular jobs must be taken into account and no compensating differential may arise even though jobs vary in their working conditions.

Women and men as groups express different preferences for some working conditions, and they are found in different types of jobs, classified by working conditions. Their different preferences for job characteristics influence their human capital investment choices as well. Additionally, the relative payoff to different job characteristics varies by sex.

Differences in job characteristics explain part of the gender earnings gap, but they cannot explain as much as do differences in human capital investment by sex. Working conditions may be set by the firm so as to screen out men or women implicitly or explicitly.

Endnotes

1. Sherwin Rosen, "The Theory of Equalizing Differences," *Handbook of Labor Economics* 1, eds. Orley Ashenfelter and Richard Layard (Amsterdam: North-Holland, 1986): 641–692.

2. Christine E. Bose, *Jobs and Gender: A Study of Occupational Prestige* (New York: Praeger, 1985). The index is based on measures of prestige calculated for 108 occupations in the National Longitudinal Survey. These measures are related to female median earnings and education through calculation of a regression equation, and the equation is used to predict index scores for the occupations in the 1960 Census, based on their median earnings and education. The relationship between femaleness and prestige is not taken into account separately from the earnings and education differences. This index is less satisfactory than a measure of prestige collected independently.

3. Readers who have studied uncertainty in a microeconomics class will recognize that this statement depends on the relative risk aversion of persons entering the acting profession. The average payoff must be higher in acting than in other professions with less income variation if persons are risk-averse; if they are risk-neutral, the average payoff must be equal, and if they are risk-loving, it will be lower.

4. J. Paul Leigh, *Causes of Death in the Workplace* (Westport, Conn.: Quorum, 1995): 8. Measured per astronaut years (3400 deaths per 100,000) and years of democracy (2304 deaths per 100,000) respectively, these rates are notably higher than the highest numbers in Table 8.2.

5. Cf. "High Murder Rate for Women on Job," *New York Times* (October 3, 1993) Section 1: 29.

6. Kingsley R. Browne, "On Not Misreading Murder Statistics," *New York Times* (October 10, 1993) Section 4: 14.

7. Mark R. Killingsworth, "A Simple Structural Model of Heterogeneous Preferences and Compensating Wage Differentials," *Unemployment, Search and Labour Supply*, eds. Richard Blundell and Ian Walker (Cambridge, United Kingdom: Cambridge University, 1986): 303–317.

8. Albert Rees, "Compensating Wage Differentials," *Essays on Adam Smith*, eds. Andrew S. Skinner and Thomas Wilson (Oxford: Clarendon, 1976): 336–349.

9. Keith W. Chauvin and Ronald A. Ash, "Gender Earnings Differentials in Total Pay, Base Pay, and Contingent Pay," *Industrial and Labor Relations Review* 47, no. 4 (July 1994): 634–649.

10. Judith Buber Agassi, *Comparing the Work Attitudes of Women and Men* (Lexington, Mass.: Lexington Books, 1982): 244 (Table 14–3).

11. Alan F. Westin, "Employer Policies to Enhance the Application of Office System Technology to Clerical Work," *Computer Chips and Paper Clips: Technology and Women's Employment, Volume 2: Case Studies and Policy Perspectives* (Washington, D.C.: National Academy, 1987): 313–342.

12. Paul Spector, *Industrial and Organizational Psychology: Research and Practice* (New York: Wiley & Sons, 1996): 229, reviews a number of studies, several of which are themselves meta-studies, and reports no evidence of significant gender differences in global job satisfaction.

13. Richard Morin, "Unconventional Wisdom: The High Price of Selling Out," *The Washington Post* (February 9, 1997): C5.

14. Randall W. Eberts and Joseph A. Stone, "Wages, Fringe Benefits, and Working Conditions: An Analysis of Compensating Differentials," *Southern Economic Journal* 52, no. 1 (July 1985): 274–280.

15. For a survey of early studies see Charles Brown, "Equalizing Differences in the Labor Market," *Quarterly Journal of Economics* 94, no. 1 (February 1980): 113–134.

16. Daniel S. Hamermesh and John R. Wolfe, "Compensating Wage Differentials and the Duration of Wage Loss," *Journal of Labor Economics* 8, no. 1 part 2 (January 1990): S175–S197.

17. See H. Gregg Lewis, *Union Relative Wage Effects: A Survey* (Chicago, Ill.: University of Chicago, 1986) and Richard Freeman and James Medoff, *What Do Unions Do?* (New York: Basic Books, 1984) for surveys of this literature.

18. J. Paul Leigh, "Do Union Members Receive Compensating Wages for Accepting Employment in Strike-prone or Hazardous Industries?" *Social Science Quarterly* 65, no. 1 (March 1984): 87–99.

19. Greg Duncan and Frank Stafford, "Do Union Members Receive Compensating Wages?" *American Economic Review* 70, no. 3 (June 1980): 355–371.

20. J. Paul Leigh and Andrew M. Gill, "Do Women Receive Compensating Wages for Risks of Dying on the Job?" *Social Science Quarterly* 72, no. 4 (December 1991): 727–737, uses data from Texas for 1975–84.
21. Anne E. Preston, "The Nonprofit Worker in a For-Profit World," *Journal of Labor Economics* 7, no. 4 (October 1989): 438–463.
22. David S. Evans and Linda S. Leighton, "Why Do Smaller Firms Pay Less?" *Journal of Human Resources* 24, no. 2 (Spring 1989): 299–318.
23. Ronald G. Ehrenberg and Paul L. Schmann, "Compensating Wage Differentials for Mandatory Overtime?" *Economic Inquiry* 22, no. 4 (October 1984): 460–478.
24. Thomas N. Daymont and Paul J. Andrisani, "Job Preferences, College Major, and the Gender Gap in Earnings," *Journal of Human Resources* 19, no. 3 (Summer 1984): 408–428.
25. Charles Brown and Mary Corcoran, "Sex-Based Differences in School Content and the Male/Female Wage Gap," *Journal of Labor Economics* 15, no. 3, part 1 (July 1997): 431–465, also find that college major accounts for a large percentage of the gender earnings gap, but do not find that high school course selection is important.
26. Randall K. Filer, "Male-Female Wage Differences: The Importance of Compensating Differentials," *Industrial and Labor Relations Review* 38, no. 3 (April 1985): 426–437.
27. Marianne A. Ferber and Joe L. Spaeth, "Work Characteristics and the Male-Female Earnings Gap," *American Economic Review* 74, no. 2 (May 1984): 260–264.
28. Robert C. Dauffenbach and Charles R. Greer, "A Comparison of Job Analytic and Conventional Economic Variables as Explanations of Occupational Earnings Differentials," *Journal of Economics and Business* 36, no. 1 (February 1984): 43–64, using survey data from 1970.
29. Filer, *op. cit.*: 433.
30. Randall K. Filer, "Occupational Segregation, Compensating Differentials, and Comparable Worth," *Pay Equity: Empirical Inquiries,* eds. Robert T. Michael, Heidi I. Hartmann, and Brigid O'Farrell (Washington, D.C.: National Academy, 1989): 153–170.
31. W. Kip Viscusi, *Risk by Choice* (Cambridge, Mass.: Harvard University, 1983): 132–135. Reprinted by permission of the publisher from *Risk by Choice* by W. Kip Viscusi, Cambridge, Mass.: Harvard University Press, Copyright © 1983 by the President and Fellows of Harvard College.

*F*urther reading

Bose, Christine E. (1985). *Jobs and Gender: A Study of Occupational Prestige.* New York: Praeger. Study by a sociologist of the relationships between status, pay, and occupational segregation.

Dorman, Peter (1996). *Markets and Mortality: Economics, Dangerous Work, and the Value of Human Life.* Cambridge: Cambridge University. Provocative and important critique of the neoclassical theory of compensating differentials; very effective to read as a counterpoint to Viscusi (1983).

Ehrenberg, Ronald G., and Robert S. Smith (1997). *Modern Labor Economics: Theory and Public Policy, 6th Edition.* New York: HarperCollins. Labor economics textbook containing a clear discussion of the theory of compensating differentials.

Frank, Robert (1985). *Choosing the Right Pond: Human Behavior and the Quest for Status.* New York: Oxford University. Provocative book concerning relationship between status, productivity, and pay.

Polachek, Solomon W., and W. Stanley Siebert (1993). *The Economics of Earnings.* Cambridge, United Kingdom: Cambridge University. Handbook/textbook, contains chapter on compensating differentials.

Viscusi, W. Kip (1983). *Risk by Choice.* Cambridge, Mass.: Harvard University. Readable discussion of the application of the theory of compensating differentials to the evaluation of riskiness of work; brings up many important policy implications.

Discussion questions

1. Give examples of jobs in which you would most expect to see positive or negative compensating differentials. Then explain why, in fact, no such differential might occur, or why a compensating differential might actually arise, but in the opposite direction.

2. Consider the data in Table 8.1. Do you think the correlation between income and prestige is higher or lower than the correlation between education and prestige? Do you think that these relationships have changed since 1960? Do you think that women or men value job prestige more highly?

3. Why are men more likely than women to work swing shifts? What might make women more likely than men to work swing shifts?

4. Do women tend more than men to avoid occupations where the probability of success is low, even though the payoff for succeeding is high? If yes, does this mean they are more risk-averse in general?

5. Consider the data in Table 8.2. Are they likely to correlate with percentage female by occupation? Why might women be found in less risky occupations and men in more risky occupations? Do you consider this a factor that is viewed differently by sex?

6. Is there a job you would not do, no matter how much it paid? Do you think that most other people would agree with you? Do you think that people of the same sex as you would be more likely to agree with you than people of the opposite sex?

7. Consider the Focus on selling out. Do you think students at your school would agree with the choices as to which is the more desirable job? Do you think you would find gender differences in the answers at your school? What are the problems with this methodology of uncovering compensating differentials? Do you think the less desirable jobs do pay more?

8. Consider friends at your school for a variety of majors. How much of their selection of major do you think is related to their job preferences?

9. Why might compensating differentials related to various job preferences differ by sex?

10. Consider a firm that refuses to hire women to work in its plant, handling lead, unless they are sterilized. Is this a reasonable requirement? What alternatives are available?

11. If firms have labor market power (e.g., can act as monopsonists), would you expect compensating differentials to arise? Can you construct a scenario in which men receive compensating differentials, but women do not?

Causes of Earnings Differences: Discrimination

How can the effects of discrimination on the gender earnings gap be measured? This chapter takes a different approach than Chapters 7 and 8, in that first the evidence on discrimination is presented, then various theories of discrimination are considered. This approach is taken because in examining the effects of discrimination on the gender earnings difference, the links between theory and evidence are not clear-cut, and it is most useful to consider the difficulty of strengthening those links after seeing the evidence that leads most people to conclude that discrimination is widespread. The final section discusses the various policy approaches to combating discrimination that have been attempted and evaluates their success.

How economists define discrimination

Theories considered in this chapter stress labor market demand-side factors in generating different outcomes for two groups that are otherwise considered to be alike in all taste and productivity-related factors. We have already considered (in Chapters 7 and 8), theories that rely on differences in labor supply between the two groups. *Workplace discrimination* occurs when two persons who have equal productivity and tastes for work conditions, but who are members of different groups, receive different outcomes in the workplace in terms of the wages they are paid and/or of their access to jobs.

For economists, discrimination is not synonymous with prejudice. As we will see below, some theories of discrimination hinge on the existence of monopsony power or imperfect information on the part of employers. Also, labor market discrimination is not necessarily attributable to employers. In some discrimination theories, the employer is acting as the agent for the prejudices of customers or employees. These two distinctions are not generally made by noneconomists.

While many bases are used for discrimination, such as sex, race, class, height, weight, sexual preferences, religious beliefs, and ethnic background, discrimination theories do not fit all of these cases equally well. In particular, theories that were developed to discuss race discrimination may not describe sex discrimination well. In race discrimination, interaction between the two groups is often limited both within and without the workplace; in contrast, the two sexes are generally not separated in private life. A male employer who discriminates against women in the workplace has a mother, is often married, and often has daughters. Sex discrimination does not necessarily entail an aversion to mixing with persons of the opposite sex in all daily settings the way race discrimination often does (although examples of cultures exist where the sexes are highly segregated in all aspects of life).

Economists tend to limit their discussion of discrimination to discrimination in pay, hiring, and promotion practices. Their goal is to identify how much these discriminatory practices contribute to the gender earnings gap. Discussion will occur later in the chapter as to how appropriate or possible it is to attempt to narrow the field of inquiry so much. Focusing on workplace discrimination may lead to economists' missing more important ways in which discrimination affects society, as well as overlooking the ways in which discrimination outside the workplace affects workplace outcomes.

Overview of evidence of workplace discrimination

Evidence of workplace discrimination is often indirect. Particularly as penalties for discrimination increase, discrimination may occur in more subtle ways that require more sophisticated analyses to uncover. However, as the sophistication of the detection method increases, the number of qualifications that can be brought up concerning the detection method increases as well. Evidence in discrimination lawsuits usually takes the form of both direct testimony and statistical studies of earnings and employment patterns. Economists who want to measure the economy-wide effects of discrimination generally rely on statistical studies alone. However, the newer technique of auditing has been used in particular applicable situations to estimate the amount of discrimination; it incorporates elements of direct observation with statistical sampling techniques.

Direct testimony

It is very easy to find people who have been discriminated against. Anecdotal evidence of discrimination is widely found in the popular press, in legal testimony, and in scholarly studies. Employers go on record during trials saying that women are less capable than men and that they have acted on this belief in making employment decisions. The sheer volume of complaints is unassailable evidence that sex discrimination is pervasive and therefore likely to have measurable effects on women's earnings.

The fundamental problem with anecdotal evidence for economists, no matter how reliable the source, is the difficulty in using it to analyze exactly how much of the gender earnings gap is attributable to discrimination. We do not know how many cases go unreported, sometimes because potential plaintiffs do not realize that they have been subject to discrimination, other times because they do not want to undergo the monetary and psychic costs associated with lodging a complaint. Also, the sample of companies that undergo investigation during or prior to discrimination suits may or may not be representative of general workplace practices.

FOCUS

The difficulties of filing discrimination charges

Law professor Eleanor Swift writes about her discrimination grievance:[1]

> I filed a sex discrimination grievance against my employer, the University of California at Berkeley and its School of Law (Boalt Hall), in February 1988. This was eight months after I had been denied tenure and had left the university.... In December 1988 my grievance was settled. Under the agreement, I received what I had asked for. A committee of five distinguished academics wholly outside Boalt was appointed to consider the question of my tenure. This committee was given the tenure files of the six men tenured at Boalt in the 1980s and was instructed to derive Boalt's tenure standard from these files. Then, this standard was to be applied to me. This carefully designed process of comparative review was, to my knowledge, an unprecedented resolution of a discrimination case.... The committee made a unanimous recommendation that I be promoted to tenure.
>
> While my case had a happy ending, most women who share my experience are not so fortunate.... What makes the odds against a successful outcome so high? My case plainly illustrates what I think are the major obstacles: proof, cost, and motivation.

Proof of bias

Some evidence of discriminatory intent, some fact giving rise to the inference that gender was an improper consideration, is a necessary element of a discrimination case alleging disparate treatment. Such proof is very hard to find, particularly since the academic personnel system is shrouded in secrecy.... The evidence that I relied on in my grievance . . . came from two sources. First were the statistics.... In 1988 there were only three tenured women and approximately 45 tenured men on Boalt's faculty. Between 1974 (the last time a woman had been promoted to tenure) and 1987, only two tenure-track women were hires: Marjorie Shultz and me. Marjorie was denied tenure in 1985; I was denied tenure in 1987. But during the 1980s, six males had been considered for promotion to tenure at Boalt and all six had been promoted.

These are powerful statistics, but they may not have made the case.... Each individual [tenure] case, viewed in isolation, can be made to seem reasonable to a neutral outside reviewer. Only if cases are lined up next to each other . . . can the fairness and equality of standards be tested.

This comparison was done by two top-level administrators at UC Berkeley, both of whom are women.... These two women analyzed the pattern of tenure decisions at Boalt [using confidential files] and concluded that "detailed examination of the records . . . suggests the existence of a pattern of discrimination against . . . women."

Both sources of proof persuaded the Committee on Privilege and Tenure that I had established a *prima facie* case, meaning there was sufficient reason to believe that my rights and privileges had been violated to justify a full-scale evidentiary hearing on my grievance.

Staggering costs

Waging a legal battle involves staggering costs. Financing the case, finding a lawyer who will take the case on a reduced fee arrangement, and supporting yourself while working on the case are problems that sometimes simply cannot be solved.... I saved money by contributing many hours of legal services myself.... I also received offers of support from my family, and obtained a sizable award for attorneys' fees when the grievance was settled in December 1988; yet the case still cost me more than $50,000 without even going to the full hearing.

If the financial costs are staggering, the personal costs are incalculable. . . . The case takes over your life. Even when I was not actively working on it, I was thinking about it. It was impossible to concentrate on anything else. Thus there was no real option for me to do other "real work". . . . When the grievance was settled, it was even worse. Tasks related to implementing the settlement . . . took months to complete before the tenure committee could be launched in April 1989.

Psychological obstacles

Perhaps the hardest decision of all was the initial decision to file the discrimination grievance. . . . I faced a psychological obstacle that prevents many women, and many members of racial and ethnic minorities, from using antidiscrimination laws to fight back. . . . To employ these laws, one has to identify oneself publicly in the degrading role of victim and wage the battle on an individual basis, charging other individuals with acts of illegal discrimination.

But I never would have filed the grievance simply to get my job back. What persuaded me was that I had the chance to vindicate the principles of equality and fairness that I . . . believed were being violated on the campus. After all, as one friend put it, if victims don't speak out, the system doesn't have the chance to correct itself. . . . The identification of my case with public goals enabled me to overcome both the role of victim and the isolation of proceeding as an individual.

Auditing

The auditing technique, which appears to date back to use in England in 1966,[2] has been used most successfully in uncovering banking, housing market, and hiring discrimination.[3] In the hiring case, matched pairs of testers are sent out to contact employers. The testers are as identical as possible in all relevant characteristics such as experience and education, but they differ by race or sex. The testers approach the employers independently within a short period of time, and their different rates of receiving initial shows of interest, job interviews, and job offers are calculated. This method provides both direct evidence of hiring discrimination by particular employers that can bolster a lawsuit and a measure of hiring discrimination in general for a particular geographic area or industry. It is not useful in determining the extent of pay and promotion discrimination, since testers do not actually take jobs in the examined companies, although starting pay offers could be compared across testers.

Indirect evidence from earnings regressions

By far the most widely used method by economists for attempting to measure discrimination, either nationwide or in a more limited sphere, is statistical analysis of wage patterns. The problem is that wages – and employment – are determined by both labor supply and labor demand, so differences between persons are caused by a combination of factors, while discrimination is considered to operate through the demand side of the labor market. Researchers attempting to measure the amount of the wage differential attributable to demand-side discrimination try to control for supply-side factors through use of regression analysis. The

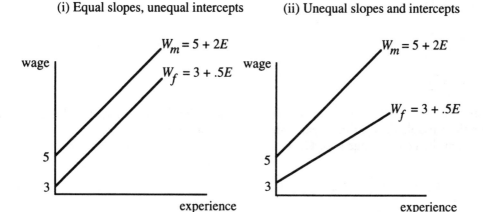

FIGURE 9.1 Alternative assumptions about experience–wage profiles for men and women

unexplained amount of the wage differential is then attributed to discrimination. However, as it is difficult or even impossible to account for all supply-side factors, the unexplained portion of the wage differential can never be absolutely certified to have been caused by discrimination.

Once a particular wage equation is estimated, how is it used to discuss earnings and employment differentials? The simplest way of discussing earnings differentials is to assume that discrimination takes the form of paying men a constant amount more than women, regardless of their level of qualifications. This is equivalent to specifying that wage equations for men and women differ only in intercept, not in slope, as in Figure 9.1(i). This assumption makes the gender differential easy to calculate but has the disadvantage of not allowing the returns to various factors such as education and experience to vary by sex. A more general model of the way in which discrimination may operate requires estimation of separate equations by sex, which allows both the intercept and the slope of the wage equations to vary by sex, as in Figure 9.1(ii). Then differences between, say, the coefficients on experience between the two equations can be discussed.

However, pair-by-pair comparisons of coefficients are unsatisfying, as they do not allow calculation of a summary measure with which to discuss the full effects of group differences on earnings. A common method for calculating wage differentials that controls for measurable productivity-related characteristics is to use wage regressions to create adjustments of relative earnings based on worker characteristics.[4]

There are several ways in which to make such adjustments. In comparing female and male earnings, we may want to calculate how much men would earn if they were to receive payment based on the female relationship between personal characteristics and earnings. Conversely, we may want to see how the average woman would fare relative to the average man if she were subject to the male earnings relationship.

A regression of wage W on personal characteristics can be estimated of the form $W = \sum_{}^{n} \beta X$, where X is a set of n characteristics and β is the corresponding set of n coefficients for a set of persons. Regressions have the characteristic that evaluating them at the mean for all independent variables yields the mean wage for the group. So, if separate equations are estimated for men and women, the mean wages for men and women can be calculated as:

$$\overline{W}_m = \sum^n \beta_m \overline{X}_m$$

$$\overline{W}_f = \sum^n \beta_f \overline{X}_f$$

where the subscript m denotes male values, the subscript f denotes female values, and a bar over the variable denotes the mean value for that variable.

Then the gender wage gap, G, is

$$G = \overline{W}_m - \overline{W}_f = \sum^n \beta_m \overline{X}_m - \sum^n \beta_f \overline{X}_f$$

and the unadjusted gender wage ratio, U, is

$$U = \frac{\overline{W}_f}{\overline{W}_m} = \frac{\sum^n \beta_f \overline{X}_f}{\sum^n \beta_m \overline{X}_m}$$

We can normalize the gap relative to the male wage so that it will range from 0 to 1:

$$g = \frac{G}{\overline{W}_m} = 1 - U$$

An adjusted wage ratio can be calculated in one of two ways, using either the male mean characteristics (A) or the female mean characteristics (A')

$$A = \frac{\sum^n \beta_f \overline{X}_m}{\sum^n \beta_m \overline{X}_m}$$

$$A' = \frac{\sum^n \beta_f \overline{X}_f}{\sum^n \beta_m \overline{X}_f}$$

In A, the numerator is increased relative to the unadjusted wage ratio, while in A', the denominator is reduced relative to the unadjusted wage ratio. Theoretically, there is no way to predict which will produce a larger adjustment. Also, neither method is constrained to yield a ratio less than 1; even if U is less than 1, A and/or A' may end up greater than 1, which would imply discrimination in favor of the group in the numerator of U.

Then the unexplained proportion of the gap can be defined in one of several ways, either using A, as in the equation for d below; using A', as in the equation for d' below, or using a different numerator than for d, as in the equation for d^* below:

TABLE 9.1 Actual and adjusted mean hourly earnings ratios by race and sex, 1994

	Nonwhite men	Nonwhite women	White women	Nonwhite women
	White men	White men	White men	Nonwhite men
Actual	0.72	0.84	0.71	0.83
Adjusted	0.88	0.98	0.75	0.85
Gap	0.28	0.16	0.29	0.17
Unexplained proportion of gap	0.43	0.13	0.86	0.88

Source: Calculations by the author. The sample consists of year-round full-time workers ages 25 to 64, working in the private sector. Adjusted earnings are calculated using regressions of log hourly earnings, controlling for age, age squared, education, education squared, region, degree of urbanization, veteran status (for men), number of children ever born (for women), and marital status. These variables are all statistically significant and account for between 20 and 23 percent of the total variation in earnings within each race-sex group, as measured by the adjusted R-squared statistic. Data are from the Current Population Survey, March 1995.

$$d = \frac{1 - A}{1 - U} = \frac{\sum\limits^{n}(\beta_m - \beta_f)\overline{X}_m}{G}$$

$$d' = \frac{1 - A'}{1 - U}$$

$$d^* = \frac{\sum\limits^{n}(\beta_m - \beta_f)\overline{X}_f}{G}$$

Inasmuch as we cannot tell whether A or A' will be larger, we cannot predict whether d or d' will be larger. However, if $\overline{X}_m > \overline{X}_f$ and $\beta_m > \beta_f$ for all n characteristics, then $d > d^*$.

Consider the earnings ratios and gap calculations in Table 9.1. The adjusted ratios incorporate differences between the groups in terms of education, age, geographical distribution, and other factors that are generally considered to reflect taste and productivity differences. The adjusted ratios are the average of A and A'.[5] Accounting for differences in these variables in constructing earnings ratios narrows the gender earnings gap but does not close it. For example, white women make 71 percent as much as white men, but if men and women had similar characteristics, then white women would make 75 percent as much as white men. The gap is 29 cents on the dollar ($100 - 71$), of which 4 cents (or 14 percent of the gap), is explainable by differences in characteristics between white women and men; that leaves 25 cents (or 86 percent of the gap) unexplained after the adjustment process. Here I am calculating the unexplained proportion as

$$d^{**} = \frac{1 - \dfrac{A + A'}{2}}{1 - U}$$

Earlier results paint a similar picture, underscoring both the robustness of the result and the lack of change in the adjusted gender earnings ratio in the recent past. A survey of 22 studies done between 1964 and 1981 found an average unadjusted gender earnings ratio of 0.58 and an adjusted ratio on average of 0.71, yielding an average unexplained gap of 69 percent. In the 8 studies with no controls for occupation and experience, the average unexplained gap percentage was 87; in the 6 studies with both types of controls, the average unexplained percentage was 51.[6] Another survey of 41 studies done between 1973 and 1994 found an average adjusted ratio of 0.75.[7] This study also found that results were dependent on the particular worker characteristics used by researchers and the definition of earnings used, with estimates based on hourly wages yielding a smaller gap than estimates based on annual or weekly earnings.

Note that the gap by race between men and between women is narrower. In general, as is true in Table 9.1, studies of race differences using these adjustment methods manage to close a larger proportion of the gap.[8]

Note also that the methods of adjusting wages above do not tell us what the world would look like if there were no discrimination. In such a case, male wages would likely be lower and female wages higher, and the wage equation relating wages to characteristics would have different coefficients, where the coefficient on any one variable would likely be between $ß_m$ and $ß_f$.[9]

While many studies take an economy-wide view of the gender earnings gap, others limit their focus to a particular part of the economy or use a particular partitioning of the economy. By doing this, they control factors such as differences between sectors of the economy for their effects on wages. This is commonly done either by looking only at people in a subset of industries or a subset of occupations, or by incorporating industry or occupational-level data into regressions. However, the level of detail can be set even finer. For instance, smaller subsets of the economy that have been the focus of studies of gender wage differentials include: a set of occupations within a set of industries;[10] one occupation[11] or a set of occupations in one industry;[12] or a set of occupations in one geographic labor market,[13] in one firm,[14] or in a set of firms.[15] In general, studies focusing on increasingly narrow segments of the labor market are able to explain greater and greater proportions of the wage differential between groups of workers, but the gender wage gap still remains after these adjustments are made. In a study of one insurance firm, over 90 percent of the observed sex differential is explained by included variables, some of which (e.g., manager evaluations of workers) may already incorporate discrimination.[16]

Generally, individual-level data are used to perform these analyses, with one observation per worker. While the general statistical method used has been ordinary least squares regression (as illustrated in the appendix to Chapter 7), various complaints have been brought against this technique in the more recent literature, leading to use of more sophisticated versions of regression analysis to attempt to counter these problems. One potential problem is sample selection bias if employment discrimination leads to many workers not receiving jobs at all. For instance, observed wages may understate the amount of discrimination if reservation wages are not allowed to vary by group; i.e., fewer minority workers may take jobs because they receive fewer high wage offers.[17] Another problem is that omitted variables may be correlated with included variables; i.e., unmeasured (and generally unobservable) performance-related ability may be correlated with sex and therefore lead to a biased estimate of the coefficients on included variables such as education and experience.

One approach to the omitted variables problem is to limit the sample to particular groups of workers to try to control for unobservable differences. In one study, for instance, the researchers reason that comparing never-married women and men would yield a cleaner measurement of workplace discrimination by avoiding the effects of marriage on product-ivity and by using only those women who are less likely to have traditional beliefs about sex roles. Upon calculating adjusted earnings, they conclude that employers discriminate in favor of women![18] Another study compares the wages of male and female displaced workers before and after they became displaced to test for discrimination. (The displacement was caused by workplaces closing or permanent layoffs due to slack demand. The researcher argues that, in these cases, the employer did not discriminate in choosing who to fire.) If there is widespread discrimination, displaced women would be more likely to have a greater wage loss than displaced men because they have a smaller set of jobs to pick from. On the other hand, if the gender earnings gap occurs because women are less likely to invest in specific human capital than men, the men would have a greater wage loss from displace-ment. The researcher finds that women suffer a greater wage loss,[19] a finding corroborated by other researchers who also find that fewer women than men become re-employed after displacement.[20]

A novel approach to measuring discrimination is to compare pay changes for particular jobs when the gender of the jobholder changes. A study of over 20,000 high-level admin-istrators in 821 colleges and universities finds the usual result that female administrators make less than male administrators, even after controlling for individual, institutional, and positional (e.g., president or dean) characteristics. In addition, positions that change over time from being held by a man to being held by a woman tend to have a drop in pay, while positions that change from women to men tend to have a large pay increase.[21]

Indirect evidence from employment patterns

Gender employment differences between sectors of the economy have been focused on less than gender earnings differences in empirical work, although some of the discrimination theories presented below make their strongest predictions about employment patterns and their relationship to earnings. However, many court cases involve statistical evidence of promotion/mobility differences, and several academic studies of this type have been under-taken as well. Again, these studies provide interesting evidence of gender differences, but they are subject to varying interpretation of why these differences exist. The basic problem, as with gender earnings differences, is whether supply-side causes of employment differ-ences have been adequately controlled.

One study considers a division within a large company that had no obviously discrim-inatory institutional features.[22] Promotion was from within, so people at the top levels had worked their way up from entry-level jobs. This promotional structure is called an *internal job ladder*. The division had 6000 employees, 5500 of whom were at the entry level; 82 percent of entry-level jobs were held by women. However, in 1978, only 74 percent of the promotions from the entry level were women, and in earlier years the average had been 64 percent. This looked like strong evidence of discrimination in the firm's promotion practices. On closer examination, however, it turned out that men and women were pro-moted in proportion to the expressed interest of each sex in being promoted. If the pool of prospective promotees was limited to the group expressing interest, then the company appeared to be nondiscriminatory with respect to promotions from that pool.

Another study of a large insurance firm having internal job ladders finds that while women workers comprise 73 percent of the firm, only 9 percent of the employees in the highest work grades of the firm are women (grades 20 through 28 of 28 levels).[23] Upon analysis of the determinants of promotion, it appears that the different occupations men and women hold within the firm are important determinants of their different promotion possibilities. The researcher concludes that discrimination in this firm – if it is discrimination – takes the form of putting women into particular occupations.

Another study, using national data, points out that concentrating on measurement of wage gaps alone does not completely describe the impact on workers of discrimination, since pay discrimination will lead to employment reductions by discriminated-against workers as well if their labor supply is upward-sloping.[24] The authors calculate for 1984 that over 5 million women who did not work would have worked in a nondiscriminatory world.

Conclusions from earnings and employment patterns

Employment and earnings patterns lay out a consistent picture of women predominantly occupying lower-paid jobs and making less than men even after adjustment for differences in tastes and productivity-related characteristics. These patterns have been viewed as evidence of discrimination, but they are not incontrovertible proof. As discussed above, promotion differences may still be explainable by employee choice. Wage differences may be related to productivity-related variables that are not included in the regression analysis. And, as we will see below, these patterns do not help us much in sorting between the various sources and reasons for discrimination. Without a better idea of the underlying causes of these phenomena, it is not clear what the best approach is to effectively combat discrimination.

Even after the obvious objections are taken into account, however, statistical analyses of employment and earnings patterns (including wage regressions of the type discussed above) have become admissible evidence of discrimination in lawsuits. In fact, somewhat to economists' surprise, they have "become the standard form by which the litigation of disputes over allegations of race and sex discrimination proceeds,"[25] even as debate continues both within and without the courtroom on how to interpret them.[26]

FOCUS

The Sears case

In 1973 the Equal Employment Opportunity Commission (EEOC) began to investigate Sears, Roebuck & Company for systematic sex discrimination. At that point, the giant retailing company was the nation's largest private employer of women, and the EEOC had received hundreds of sex discrimination complaints about Sears.[27] In 1979 the EEOC brought 42 major claims against Sears for discrimination in hiring, promotion, and pay. On February 3, 1986, the Federal District Court in Chicago ruled against the last remaining claims. This case stirred up much acrimony in the academic feminist community, as one of the witnesses for Sears, Professor Rosalind Rosenberg, was accused by other professors (particularly women historians) of serving as a pawn for Sears, effectively letting down the feminist cause.[28]

Professor Rosenberg went on public record in an editorial in the *New York Times* following the conclusion of the case:[29]

There is, for a start, no basis to the claim that this decision has discredited the use of statistics – evidence of numerical differences between men and women in certain jobs – to demonstrate discrimination. Courts have long recognized the relevance of statistics in such cases, and they will continue to do so. What made the commission's claim unusual was that it was based entirely on statistical evidence – without supporting testimony by witnesses, or other evidence.

Indeed, after a six-year investigation, the commission's lawyers were unable to identify a single victim of discrimination at Sears or even anyone who had witnessed discrimination. Judge John A. Nordberg's opinion does not reject statistical evidence in itself; it merely recognizes that numerical disparities alone are not enough to prove discrimination except in extraordinary circumstances.

Judge Nordberg also found that the commission's statistics were "replete with flaws." The "most egregious" flaw was the assumption that men and women were equally interested in and qualified for jobs in commission sales. Sears showed, through evidence from its own workforce and the nation at large, that this assumption was false, and Judge Nordberg concluded that Sears' record of hiring women in such jobs "met all reasonable estimates of the proportion of qualified and interested women."

Rosenberg concludes by obliquely attacking her critiics:

Feminists who take the position that employer discrimination is the only significant factor explaining women's economic disadvantages actually contribute to society's reluctance to explore a whole range of social policies that must be developed if women are to achieve equality. Consideration of such policies cannot possibly proceed so long as talk of differences remains taboo.

Actually, as reporter Susan Faludi subsequently discovered and recounted in her best-selling 1991 book *Backlash*, the EEOC *did* put women witnesses on the stand, although they were not a central part of the case:[30]

During the trial, Sears attorneys kept alluding to the vast numbers of female job applicants who weren't interested in commission sales work. The EEOC attorneys pressed them to produce some names from this reputedly voluminous list. After much stalling, Sears offered only three. Through social security records, the EEOC's attorneys were able to track down two of them. And both agreed to testify – for the EEOC.

Both women had done commission work in the past, and had applied to Sears hoping for commission work there as well, only to be turned down.[31] Faludi also reports:[32]

As soon as Sears found out that it was the subject of an EEOC probe, the retailer's personnel office had managed to find plenty of interested women in a hurry – enough to double the proportion of women in commission sales by the following year, and even triple and quadruple the ranks of women in such "male" departments as auto parts, plumbing, heating, and fencing.

Faludi observes that by the time the case came to trial, the political climate at the EEOC had changed: Reagan-appointed EEOC chairman (later Bush-appointed Supreme Court Justice) Clarence Thomas maintained that the gender inequities in the Sears case could be easily explained by such factors as education and commuting patterns. Additionally, Reagan-appointed Judge Nordberg was skeptical of the existence of employment discrimination against women: at one point during the trial, he demanded that EEOC attorneys demonstrate that American women had ever faced employment discrimination.[33]

How do discrimination theories explain gender workplace differences?

One economist, in reviewing the discrimination literature, complains that "the first thing to note is how little economic theory is actually used in the empirical work."[34] Indeed, many analyses of earnings and employment patterns have been done without reference to any particular discrimination theory. However, human capital theory clearly dominates this body of work. It is almost impossible to find a paper in this area which does not either implicitly or explicitly rely on the human capital paradigm in explaining how earnings are determined.

Many economists consider that extending regression analysis to include all productivity-related characteristics would lead to a disappearance of the unexplained portion of the gender earnings gap. Therefore, they often do not bother to refer to a discrimination theory in their work, because in their view, discrimination cannot be proved to exist. However, many other economists believe it critical to develop theories of how discrimination operates and to develop tests that could differentiate between different discrimination theories. In this section of the chapter, we will review various discrimination models and consider some studies that have attempted to test the validity of particular models. The first test a model must pass is to be consistent with the evidence presented so far in this book; namely, it must generate both a gender earnings gap and sex segregation. Secondly, in the view of many economists a plausible theory must give rise to a long-run equilibrium state for the economy in which discrimination persists, a condition consistent with the lasting nature of gender earnings and segregation patterns. These points will be discussed further below.

We will consider two broad classes of discrimination models: (1) models involving a taste for discrimination, derived from prejudice, and (2) models involving no prejudice, but rather a market imperfection – some departure from the basic neoclassical model of fully competitive markets – that leads to discriminatory behavior on the part of employers. These departures involve either the existence of market power on the part of a group in the society or imperfect information about worker productivity.

Models involving tastes for discrimination

The earliest writer who makes a serious attempt to model labor market discrimination is Bronfenbrenner (writing in 1939), who develops models of union bargaining that include discrimination considerations.[35] However, interest in discrimination is usually considered as dating from 1957, when Gary Becker published his dissertation.[36] In his monograph, Becker proposes three models of discrimination that vary crucially in the source of the prejudice. The prejudiced parties are employers, who will only hire from disliked groups of workers if they can pay them a lower wage than members of the preferred group; employees, who require higher wages to work with certain types of persons than with others; or customers, who will patronize firms who hire certain types of workers. In these models involving prejudice, no actual or perceived differences in productive ability of individuals is necessary in order to generate a wage differential. In each case, the discriminating party is said to have a "taste for discrimination" that can be measured in monetary terms.

Employer discrimination

In the employer discrimination model, employers are posited to have a utility function in which profits enter positively and number of undesired employees enter negatively. This contrasts with the usual assumption in economics that the only thing that firms care about is profits. Employers are willing to trade off profits for higher wages to desired employees in order to avoid contact with undesired employees. This preference gives rise to a wage differential between the employer's psychic wage W' for the group and the money wage W for the group,

$$W' = W (1 + D_i)$$

where D_i is the *discrimination coefficient* for employer i. D_i measures the percentage difference of psychic cost from money cost for the prejudiced person. The larger D_i is, the more prejudiced the person.

The employer discrimination model can be reworked as an employer nepotism model instead, in which favored employees are paid "more" rather than disfavored employees being paid "less" than in the absence of preferential behavior.[37] This is clear from the equation above: if disliked employees cost more to the employer in psychic terms than the money wage, the employer will be willing to pay favored employees up to W' in order to avoid hiring disliked employees. The prediction in either formulation is clear: lower wages for members of the disliked group, higher wages for the preferred group.

This model has been the most widely cited and tested of Becker's three models to this date. When they speak of discrimination, many people implicitly are referring to this model. However, the model has a serious problem in that it does not appear to support a long-run competitive market equilibrium. If there are employers who do not have a taste for discrimination, they can concentrate on maximizing profits. They will hire members of the disliked group at their lower wages, giving them lower production costs than discriminating employers. Therefore, the assumption of zero profit in long-run equilibrium in competitive markets implies that competition from nondiscriminating firms will drive discriminating firms out of business.

Becker realized this, but argued that all sectors of the economy are not competitive. In fact, he argued, one would expect to see more discrimination in less competitive areas of the economy. Monopoly power in the product market would allow employers to expend some of their economic profit in the form of higher wages for the preferred group, and we would expect to see more members of the preferred group in monopolistic industries – hence, segregation as well as a gender earnings gap.

Many studies have tried to evaluate this argument, often by looking for a positive relationship between profits and the gender earnings gap. One difficulty in testing this theory is that monopoly power is not perfectly measured by profits. If, in fact, discriminating monopolists are paying higher wages out of profits, this will decrease profits and lead to a negative relationship between profits and the gender earnings gap. A better method is to look for industry structural elements that can lead to monopoly power, such as exercise of patents or exclusive control over critical production inputs. One study that looks for a negative relationship between industry concentration ratios (which measure the percentage of sales accounted for by the top four firms in the industry – a measure of market power under particular assumptions about firm interaction) and gender employment and earnings ratios finds that some industries fit the predicted pattern, while others do not.[38]

Employee discrimination

If an employee has a taste for discrimination, then the psychic wage W' he gets if he has to work with members of the disliked group is

$$W' = W (1 - D_j)$$

where W is the money wage and D_j is the discrimination coefficient for employee j.

This model leads to several predictions regarding gender differences. First, men who work in integrated firms will require higher wages than men who work in all-male firms. This leads employers to prefer to run segregated firms, even though they themselves are not prejudiced, so as to avoid having to pay men higher wages. If women are cheaper, then employers prefer to have an all-female firm rather than an all-male firm. Therefore, an equilibrium condition is to have complete segregation, but no wage differential. Also, in firms where managers are not also owners, this model can explain why hiring can be discriminatory even if the owners are not prejudiced.[39]

This model can be modified to refer to occupational proximity rather than physical proximity. If employees require higher wages only in order to work with women in the same occupation but are indifferent to the presence of women in the firm in other occupations, then a firm may be integrated, but be segregated by occupation within the firm. Note that this does not require that a particular occupation must be female or male in all firms, and it therefore does not necessarily lead to national occupational segregation.

This model can also be modified to have an interesting feedback property. If prejudiced men cannot work as efficiently in integrated firms as in segregated firms, then female marginal productivity is lowered – i.e., adding a woman to an all-male firm results in less increase in revenue than adding another man. So, even though women need be no different than men in human capital endowment and employers pay wages equal to marginal product, firms will pay women less than men.

Much anecdotal evidence, particularly from women who have worked in blue-collar occupations, supports the view that employees have a taste for discrimination.[40] Additionally, several formal tests of the employee model of discrimination have been conducted, generally using employment rather than earnings data. One study finds support for the employee model using national manufacturing data and looking at the correlation in gender employment ratios between job types that were hypothesized to be in relatively closer or more distant contact in the workplace.[41] In another study, where the researchers initially hypothesized that presence in a nontraditional job would lead to a higher probability of turnover for young workers (due supposedly to pressures from both coworkers and other persons to quit), the women in nontraditional areas did not have a higher rate of turnover than average, and men in occupations that were predominantly female actually had lower turnover rates.[42] A third study notes that the employee model, with minor additional assumptions, leads to the prediction that one should see the greatest gender wage difference within geographic areas where segregation is most costly to achieve; thus, as the size of the labor market and/or the proportion of women in it increases, it becomes easier to maintain segregated workplaces for any given wage level.[43] If employers instead hire randomly, segregation decreases, holding wages constant. Using establishment-level data for 159 counties in the state of Georgia, the researchers find support of the random hiring hypothesis rather than evidence of employee discrimination.

Customer discrimination

If a customer has a taste for discrimination, then the psychic price P' of a good provided by the member of a disliked group is

$$P' = P (1 + D_k)$$

where P is the money price and D_k is the discrimination coefficient for customer k. In this case, customers seek to purchase services from firms that do not employ members of the disliked group. In order to remain profitable, firms must either pay the disliked group members less (to make up for the lowered revenue associated with their employment) or avoid hiring them completely.

It is possible that customers find members of the disliked group objectionable only in particular jobs. For instance, it has been noted that servers in coffee shops tend to be female, while servers in expensive restaurants tend to be male. Additionally, customers may only find face-to-face contact with an employee of the disliked group objectionable. This leads to the prediction that women may be more likely to be found doing "behind the scene" jobs.

If there are enough jobs considered "appropriate" or "nonobjectionable" that women can take, there will be complete sex segregation, but no gender wage gap. In fact, if a gap persisted, employers would have incentive to substitute "female-appropriate" jobs for "female-inappropriate" jobs as much as possible, because they would reduce labor costs. This behavior on the part of employers would increase demand for women, thereby eroding the wage gap.

Again, much anecdotal evidence supports the view that customers have tastes for discrimination in certain situations. Formal tests of the theory are harder to find, although the theory has been tested as an explanation of racial earnings and employment patterns and has found support in that arena.

Reconciliation of taste-based discrimination with the crowding model

Can the evidence of widespread workplace sex segregation existing alongside a pattern of lower wages in female-dominated jobs be reconciled with a model of tastes for discrimination? Note that workforce segregation is predicted, either in addition to or as an alternative to a wage differential, by all three of Becker's models. In the employer discrimination model, nondiscriminating employers use only women because they are cheaper. However, no segregation is predicted in the long run, as discriminating employers do not exist in long-run equilibrium. In the employee and customer discrimination models, if women and men are completely segregated by job (or by firm), then no wage differential need arise to compensate persons with tastes for discrimination. However, in the customer discrimination model, segregation and a wage differential can coexist if women are placed in lower-paying jobs.

In models where tastes drive discrimination, segregation need not lead to lower wages for women unless there is less capital for them to work with (so capital must be assumed not to be perfectly mobile) and/or fewer jobs are open to women – i.e., they are crowded into a limited number of occupations. Employers may or may not have to explicitly bar women in order to create segregated occupations. If the discrimination coefficient is very large for particular jobs, then the wage that women would have to accept in order to work in those areas would be so low that it would generally fall below their reservation wage. However, if wage discrimination is prohibited by law, employers would have to resort to hiring restrictions. Systematic exclusion of women from particular jobs will lead to lower wages in unrestricted jobs and higher wages in restricted jobs than in the case where no exclusion exists (i.e., the crowding model discussed in Chapter 6). The result is a pattern of segregation where women are found in lower-paying jobs. Note that offsetting labor demand curve shifts may occur in response to this wage difference. If female-dominated jobs are at all substitutable for male-dominated jobs, and if employers are not adverse to hiring women who work in female-dominated occupations, replacing expensive male workers (e.g., managers) with cheap female workers (e.g., clerical workers) will improve profits. The existence of long-run wage differentials in the crowding model assumes that these forces are not sufficient to eradicate the wage gap between female- and male-dominated occupations.

As we will see below, segregation that leads to lower wages in female-dominated jobs is also predicted by other models that do not hinge on prejudice, particularly rent-seeking and two-sector models. Crowding is a phenomenon caused by underlying discriminatory forces, which may or may not be caused by prejudice. Also, discrimination need not automatically lead to crowding.

Models of discrimination that do not involve prejudice

Many economists are dissatisfied with assuming prejudicial tastes as the basis for discrimination. In these models, discrimination cannot be fully explained because the source of discrimination is exogenous to the model. Additionally, the fundamental tenet of neoclassical economics, that firms maximize profit, is not upheld in the employer discrimination model. In contrast, in many of the models presented below, profit-maximizing behavior leads to discrimination. In the rest of the models in this section, utility-maximizing behavior on the part of individuals leads to discrimination, but prejudice does not appear as an additional variable in the utility function. Instead, individuals are driven primarily by the desire to gain more income (and, sometimes, higher status as well).

Monopsony models

A demand-side theory that does not require nonprofit-maximizing behavior (i.e., exercise of prejudice) on the part of employers to generate discriminatory behavior is that employers band together and act as a purchasing consortium. While there is not literally just one employer, the group of employers is said to have monopsony power.[44] For instance, in a famous court case (*Lemons* v. *City of Denver*), a group of nurses claimed that hospitals in Denver were conspiring to pay nurses below-market wages. The existence of monopsony power leads to a situation in which workers are paid less and fewer are hired than in a competitive labor market (see the appendix to Chapter 1). If monopsony power is more likely to operate in occupational labor markets in which women predominate, this will lead to a gender pay differential.

Unlike a firm operating in a competitive market which, by assumption, is a small part of the total demand for labor and which sees a perfectly elastic supply of labor at the given market wage, a monopsonist faces the actual upward-sloping supply curve for the market because the monopsonist is the only buyer in the market. A monopsonist knows that the

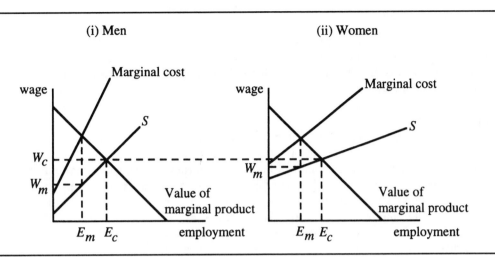

FIGURE 9.2 Monopsony labor market effects for men and women where women have more elastic supply

marginal cost of hiring another employee is that the market wage will rise, so more will have to be paid to all previously hired employees as well as paying the new employee's wage. Therefore, the profit-maximizing choice for a monopsonist is to offer a lower wage than the market level, which leads to fewer workers wanting to take this job than in a competitive market. Figure 9.2 shows that the difference between the competitive market outcome and the monopsony outcome depends on the elasticity of labor supply. If workers have relatively elastic labor supply, the wage will not be depressed by as much as if the supply curve is relatively inelastic.

One model combines the monopsony model with prejudice on the part of male employees, employers have monopsony power, and men dislike working with women; additionally, women have more inelastic labor supply than do men.[45] This situation will lead to both sex segregation and lower pay for women, in contrast to the pure employee discrimination model, which can lead to segregation but not lower pay if men and women are equally productive.

The usual arguments economists make against the prevalence of monopsony power has been made in this case as well: namely, that it is unlikely that monopsony power could operate on a nation-wide level over long periods of time and that, over time, labor mobility has been increasing. Additionally, both cross-sectional and time-series evidence using national data demonstrate that women have more elastic labor supply than do men.[46] This would lead to the opposite conclusion from the above model: namely, that male wages would be more likely to be reduced by the existence of monopsony power than would female wages. However, a counterargument is that married women are less mobile than men because they tend to accompany their husbands to a geographical area and look for a job only within this area. Therefore, the assumption of relatively inelastic female labor supply is realistic if labor markets are geographically localized.[47] Another counterargument is that if firms care about other costs related to labor besides wages, such as recruitment costs, then they have wage-setting ability that can lead to the monopsony outcome of pay discrimination against the group with more inelastic labor supply.[48]

Rent-seeking models

The standard monopsony model presented above is one of a broader set of models that argue that one group in the economy can band together to improve their well-being at the expense of the rest of the society. Often this rent-seeking behavior takes the form of offering persons excluded from the group wages below their marginal product. It can also take the form of imposing regulations that have the effect of transferring societal resources to the group.

Economist Anne Krueger argues that one can conceptualize the black and white communities as trading partners and apply optimum tariff theory from international trade.[49] If the white community is large enough to have some market power, it can make itself better off by imposing a tariff on the hiring of black labor. Such tariffs will support long-run wage differentials. The problem with this model is that it requires some mechanism for forcing all white employers to enforce the tariff arrangement. In the absence of such an enforcement mechanism, white employers could profit by "smuggling" black labor without paying the tariff.

Economist George Akerlof's model of status-based wages provides the tariff enforcement mechanism that Krueger's model requires but does not provide.[50] Akerlof argues that in small markets in which every participant is a potential trader, a social custom regulating hiring of various groups can be stable. A nondiscriminating employer will lose profits because the discriminating majority will boycott his business. Since markets are small by assumption, the loss of even a few traders will be costly in foregone profits.

The usefulness of this model, as with Becker's consumer discrimination model, is limited to situations that conform to its assumptions. This model may apply best to rural communities in which a small group of people can monitor each other's behavior.

Another important feature of Akerlof's model is that the rules governing intergroup trading must already be established, known, and accepted by nearly everyone. However, there are many instances of societies in which opinions vary as to appropriate behavior. For instance, customs concerning race relations change over time, even in societies that once appeared to have consensus.

Economist Jennifer Roback argues that individuals have preferences for the behavior of other people. The level of conformity to social norms is a public good (e.g., hire only men, in which case the price of conforming to the norm is the wage differential). A person accepts the norm if the price of conforming is less than the marginal rate of substitution between market goods and conformity.[51] Again, the social norm must hold only within certain communities that the person feels bound to, such as members of a group of employers. Such groups will attempt to force the society as a whole to provide as much as possible of this public good so that they can enjoy its benefits without fully bearing its costs, hence the rent-seeking aspect of this model. Roback's model provides a way of conceptualizing psychic cost that implies that prejudice may be shaped by forces external to the individual, but – as in Akerlof's model – does not explain where prejudice comes from in the first place.

These rent-seeking models have been applied more to racial discrimination than to sexual discrimination because it is easier to conceive of racial groups as being separable in the society. Since men and women come together in family units that generally share income and status, the gains and losses caused by actions meant to benefit men are not so clearly divided between men and women as these models assume. Mainly for this reason, these models have not received much notice and have undergone little formal testing.

Two-sector models

Two-sector models of discrimination are distinguished by the idea that initial differences unrelated to initial productivity between either types of jobs or groups of workers can lead to situations in which initially equally productive workers end up making different wages. However, as the driving force leading to discrimination, they may require either rent-seeking, such as the theories discussed above, or imperfect information, such as the statistical discrimination theories discussed below. Two-sector models attempt to explain the widespread existence of sex segregation and the relationship between percentage female and the gender earnings gap.

Why are women excluded from some jobs but not others? In Becker's models, this occurs because the taste for discrimination on the part of employers, employees, or customers varies from job to job. An alternative view is that of rent-seeking, combined with the possibility that some utility is derived from status: if men call the shots, they can reserve the higher-status jobs for themselves and derive additional utility from occupying high-status jobs as well as from attaining higher pay.[52] Status must be partially determined by job factors other than pay for this model to work, which is not a stringent requirement.

In the classic dual labor market model, there are primary and secondary labor markets, and the very nature of the type of employment alters worker characteristics.[53] The primary labor market consists of high-paying jobs of long duration and dependable internal job ladders leading to better positions; the secondary market consists of low-paying jobs with high turnover, low training requirements, and no opportunity for advancement. Even if workers have no productivity differences upon taking their first job, those who initially work in the secondary market have difficulty switching into the primary market. For instance, their pattern of switching jobs due to the type of work available in the secondary sector may make them undesirable to primary-sector employers.

Other models also focus on the labor market entry point as the crucial place where labor market discrimination occurs. Firms with seniority systems (including those created by unions) and internal job ladders make it hard for employment composition to become more heavily female if few females are hired to begin with, particularly if women have higher turnover than men (even if turnover is unrelated to productivity). As in the case of dual labor markets, limiting access at the entry point for women will lead to few women further up the job ladder or seniority system, even without any additional discriminatory behavior. However, these theories are not useful in explaining why the initial hiring rates should differ by group.

One model extends the idea of dual labor markets to include the concept of *efficiency wages*, where worker productivity is increased by increases in pay, in order to generate gender hiring differences as part of the model.[54] However, this model hinges on the assumption that women and men differ both in quit rates and in manageability, though not in their potential productivity. Assume also that detection of shirkers is more difficult in the primary sector – i.e., there is imperfect information about worker productivity. Then, the wage premium of the primary sector over the secondary sector must be larger for workers who are less likely to be caught shirking (in order to keep them from shirking by raising their potential loss if they are caught), and higher quit rates lead to higher wage premiums (because the future stream of expected earnings is lower for those who are more likely to quit). If women have lower labor force attachment, they will require larger wage premiums than men in the primary sector jobs. Additionally, if women are more docile and easier to manage than males, the cost of supervision is higher for men than for women, and the wage premiums offered to men will be higher. Women receive more supervision and lower wage premiums for the same work intensity, which is difficult for firms to achieve if men and women work side by side, so two occupations are needed: one with high supervision and low wage premiums, and a second with low supervision and high premiums. Therefore, employers attempting to minimize wage costs and supervisory costs will prefer to place men in primary sector jobs and women in secondary sector jobs, leading to both occupational segregation and wage differentials.

In this model, there are differences between and men and women, but they are not productivity differences, and the wage differential is rooted in the way in which employers extract labor power from workers, not in the differences themselves. A study that tests this model shows both that the depressing effect of female employment on wages in an industry occurs most strongly in large plants (the researchers assume that monitoring costs increase with plant size and that the percentage female indicates the percentage of secondary jobs) and that for men there is a larger trade-off between supervision costs and wages than for women.[55]

Statistical discrimination models

A final branch of demand-side theory that does not rely on prejudice to generate differential outcomes is the set of statistical discrimination models.[56] Statistical discrimination is consistent with pure profit-maximization on the part of firms and is consistent with long-run equilibrium. These models require imperfect information on individual productivity and, in some cases, different distributions of unobserved productivity-related characteristics between groups. In general, as the individual is unable to perfectly signal actual productive ability to the employer, group averages enter into the employer's decision as to what to pay him/her. On average, the employer makes a correct assessment of ability, but this can lead, in some models, to different incentives as to how much human capital to attain and can, therefore, lead to lower average productivity for some groups.[57]

Consider first a simple model that will generate identical group mean wages and therefore might be considered nondiscriminatory. However, individuals in general are not paid for their actual productivity. Assume two groups of workers, subscripted by i and j, who have identically distributed marginal productivities, MP_i and MP_j. While the group means are known to employers, workers cannot directly signal their individual productivity. Instead, employers know their scores on a test that attempts to measure productivity, and employers know the group variances on the test. Each individual's test score is equal to his/her marginal productivity, plus a randomly distributed error term ε that has a mean value of zero for both groups:

$$T_i = MP_i + \varepsilon_i^m$$

$$T_j = MP_j + \varepsilon_j^f$$

By assumption, the test score (T) is a more reliable indicator of productivity for i workers (men) than for j workers (women), so that the variances of ε_i^m and ε_j^f have the relationship

$$\sigma^2_{\varepsilon^f} = \sigma^2_{\varepsilon^m}$$

Then, as shown in Figure 9.3, wages will be a weighted average of group average marginal product and test score, where test score will be weighted more lightly for women than for

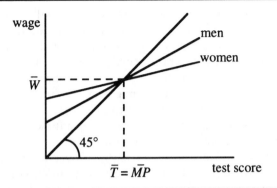

FIGURE 9.3   Statistical discrimination where group averages are equal

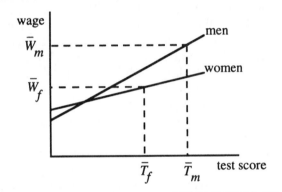

FIGURE 9.4   Statistical discrimination where group averages are different

men in determining wages. The group averages of both wages and test scores are equal, but high-scoring women will be paid less than high-scoring men, while the opposite holds true for low-scoring women and men.

In this case, the groups have equal average wages, so this model cannot explain the gender earnings gap without some modification. However, assume that one group has both relatively heterogeneous innate work-related ability and relatively homogeneous testing ability, so that its test scores are more reliable indicators of productivity (perhaps because personnel managers are all of this group and are better able to assess their own group's productivity). Then this group becomes the high-wage/high-training group because their marginal return to human capital is higher than for the other group. This leads to a situation (as pictured in Figure 9.4) where the average wage for each group is equal to the group's average marginal product, but productivity is endogenous, and differences in group average productivities are a direct result of the incentives provided by employers, which are embodied in the different wage schedules. Different average wages are paid to groups whose average levels of "premarket" (in this case innate) abilities are the same. In this case, a policy banning separate wage schedules actually increases efficiency.[58]

In statistical discrimination models, both high-ability workers (particularly of the lower-paid group) and employers would benefit by employers' being better able to identify their actual ability. However, low-ability workers have incentive to conceal their ability so that the group mean, which is above their actual ability level, will have a larger influence on their earnings. Employers would generally like to elicit additional information about workers that they can use in determining the likelihood of their being highly productive. For instance, if married men are generally more productive than unmarried men, it is to the benefit of married men to let employers know their marital status, while single men would prefer to keep their status secret (or might even want to wear a wedding ring so as to pretend they are married without having to lie).

Another factor besides ability differences leading to statistical discrimination is reliability differences. Persons often point to the higher turnover rates of women relative to men in arguing that employers are justified in preferring men over women as employees. If there are nonnegligible costs involved in hiring and training employees, then this will lead to higher costs associated with women on average, and an employer will prefer men over women as employees.

Other reliability factors include absenteeism from work and performing below ability due to illness or consumption of drugs or alcohol. Women are more likely to be absent from work than men, both for illness and other reasons. Calculated in terms of the number of absentees per 100 full-time employed persons in the gender group, women had a rate of 3.3 absentees due to illness and 3.0 due to other reasons, while men had a rate of 2.2 absentees due to illness and 1.7 due to other reasons. Notably, married women with children under the age of six had an overall rate of 10.7 absentees, while married men with children under six had a below-average rate for men of 3.5 absentees. Even unmarried women who had no children under 18, who have the lowest absentee rate among women of 5.6 absentees, had a higher rate than men.[59] Men, however, are more likely than women to report using drugs and alcohol. A survey of young workers ages 19 to 27 in 1984 found that 9.5 percent of the men and 4.2 percent of the women reported using drugs at work; 11.6 percent of the men and 6 percent of the women reported drinking alcohol at work to the point where it interfered with the work; 4.4 percent of the men and 1.6 percent of the women reported getting drunk on the job; and 3.4 percent of the men and 2.4 percent of the women missed work due to a hangover.[60]

FOCUS

Job interviewers' techniques

In 1989 management professor Arthur Berkeley published an editorial in the *Wall Street Journal* detailing interviewing stratagems that some employers use to elicit information that they are prohibited by law from asking for directly.[61] The following are some excerpts from his article:

> It's the law: Interviews for such employment-related decisions as hiring, transfer and promotion are supposed to be conducted in an objective fashion with no personal inquiries that aren't clearly job-related.... All personnel administrators and most, if not all, managers know the law. Yet what actually occurs in an interview frequently deviates dramatically from the legally permissible. For years the actual substance of interviews has been a dirty little secret with no one willing to own up to the sorts of illegal inquiries frequently made of candidates.

In numerous conversations with personnel specialists, interviewers, and employees a clear pattern emerges of illegal inquiries and methodologies used to obtain unlawful information about candidates. . . . Most impermissible areas of inquiry appear to be directed at women.

• Sneaky stratagems: One large manufacturing firm uses the simple expedient of having a low-level personnel clerk ask the candidate about her choice of health-insurance plans. . . . For example, one woman told the clerk she definitely wanted a program that would cover her three young children, one of whom always seemed to be ill. Given this information, the company decided not to hire her.

Another effective technique is used by a large financial-services firm, which takes the job candidate to lunch at a nice restaurant. Given the informal atmosphere, the applicant is more easily caught off guard by a personal inquiry. Typically the prospective supervisor and his assistant eat lunch with the candidate and begin to discuss their children. One of the firm's supervisors says, "I'll say something like: 'Our car-pool arrangements got messed up this morning and I was almost late for work.' Then I ask the applicant if anything like that ever happens to her. And almost always, the information I want will just come pouring out."

• The direct approach: Most starkly, some employers – often in an informal lunch or cocktail setting – will ask flat out about a woman's family situation, putting the candidate in an extremely delicate position. If the female applicant refuses to answer the question, citing its illegality, she runs a very real risk of alienating the interviewer and wrecking her chances of being hired. If she answers the question truthfully, the information may prove fatal to her candidacy.

• Sneaky responses: In what was the most startling revelation in this area, I learned that many women respond falsely to these illegal inquiries, rationalizing that since the questions are unlawful, they are morally entitled to offer untrue responses. Said one woman, the divorced mother of two children, one of whom is severely handicapped: "Even though I'm a very reliable worker, I knew if I told the truth, I wouldn't get the job, and I needed this job badly. So I said I wasn't married – which was true – and I had no intention of having children – which is sort of true because certainly I don't plan to have any more children . . . I got the job."

Can discrimination exist in equilibrium?

A major critique of the employer discrimination model is that it is incompatible with long-run profit maximization. So long as some employer (or potential employer) derives no utility from discriminatory behavior but is profit-maximizing, that employer will be able to undercut the prices of the discriminating employers and capture the entire market. Also, models that rely on market power for a group in the society (i.e., monopsony models) hinge on the ability of that group to maintain such power. Cartel arrangements are subject to cheating, as there is always incentive to cheat so long as the cartel does not fall apart completely. The employee, customer, and statistical discrimination models are compatible with maintaining a long-run equilibrium state.

However, existence of an equilibrium does not imply that an alternative and preferable equilibrium could not be achieved for the economy. For instance, in the model of dual labor markets with efficiency wages, taxing male employment and subsidizing female employment in the primary sector would improve total welfare; quotas for female employment would yield the same result. In the statistical discrimination model where women underinvest in human capital, outlawing use of group averages in determining wages would lead to an increase in human capital for women and a corresponding increase in total production.

In models where discrimination is caused by prejudice, however, requiring integrated firms and no pay differences leads to a utility loss for the prejudiced group. Society may decide to discount utility derived from prejudice in calculating societal gains and losses, perhaps hoping that the long-run effect of antidiscrimination policies will be a reduction in tastes for prejudice and a corresponding reduction in the utility loss from not being able to exercise them.

Feedback effects from labor market discrimination

Many economists and noneconomists have complained about the discipline's focus on labor market outcomes to the exclusion of considering other economic effects of discrimination. In part this is because the feedback effects in both directions may be quite substantial. As one economist has remarked:[62]

> The labor market does not stand alone, insulated from the society at large. Rather, these markets are nestled into society, processing and filtering the prevailing customs and political and social arrangements and translating these into particular, tangible economic outcomes. . . . Market outcomes reflect social relations and feed back on them, and nowhere is the importance of this interaction more pronounced than in the dynamics of discrimination.

In general, the models of discrimination discussed above are compatible with incorporation of feedback effects. However, the methods used to measure the effects of workplace discrimination are not satisfactory for measuring feedback effects. If women realize that they will be undercompensated relative to their actual marginal productivity in the workplace, then they have less incentive to invest in human capital. Therefore they will receive lower wages than men not only because of the direct effect of discrimination but because of this indirect effect that the existence of discrimination has caused them to underinvest in human capital relative to what they would have done in a nondiscriminatory society. This means that estimating the effect of discrimination by calculating wage ratios that adjust for differences in male and female characteristics will lead to an underestimate of the full effect of discrimination on earnings.

Another problem is that discrimination in other sectors of the economy may affect productivity and, thereby, affect earnings. For example, if women are excluded from particular forms of human capital investment that offer high rates of return, they will end up earning less than in a society where all areas of investment are open to persons regardless of gender. Again, the adjusted wage ratio method of measuring discrimination will lead to an underestimate of the actual effect of discrimination on the gender earnings gap.

One recent study that attempts to measure a portion of the feedback effect through seeing if working women who report labor market discrimination behave differently subsequently, finds mixed support for the feedback hypothesis.[63] While women who report discrimination are subsequently more likely to switch employers, have children, and marry, they do not accumulate less work experience, nor do they have lower wage growth relative to women who do not report discrimination.

Devices for combating discrimination

In this section, both explicit policies and other efforts to reduce discrimination in the workplace are discussed. Other policies aimed at reducing discrimination in other spheres, such as education, are discussed in other chapters.

Explicit policies

The U.S. federal government, governments in many other countries, and many state and local governments have equal pay laws. Enforcement may be weak, but at least the legislation is in place to ban such practices. There are both equity and efficiency rationales for government intervention. First, we have seen the argument made above in several of our theoretical models that discriminatory practices reduce national output by discouraging proper matching of workers to jobs for which they are best suited, reducing overall employment of women who might be more productive in the market than in the nonmarket sector, and reducing incentives for some workers, both male and female, to get additional training that will lead to increases in productivity. Since discrimination does not appear to be disappearing speedily of its own accord and not all sectors of the economy are competitive, waiting for competition to stamp out discrimination is too long-run a solution to be politically acceptable.

Surprisingly, employers may actually welcome antidiscrimination rules that remove their discretion in pay and hiring. If the main source of discrimination is employees, such rules enable nondiscriminatory employers to form an effective cartel against the employees, allowing them both to integrate workplaces and to avoid paying higher wages.

There are, however, problems with antidiscriminatory policies as well. Policies requiring equality of result may be antithetical to the goal of equality of opportunity, leading to the problem of reverse discrimination. For instance, if a company is required to promote in proportion to the gender distribution in its entry-level job pool, it may have to overlook a higher proportion of men who express interest in promotion if fewer women are interested in promotion.

A different problem is that policies may not be comprehensive enough to wipe out subtle forms of discrimination. For instance, employers still have flexibility in setting requirements and determining pay levels for jobs; thus, they are free to follow the letter of the law, but not the intent. This situation leads to questions. For instance, are the requirements for a job actually needed, or are they used as barriers? Do firms hire the best worker for an opening regardless of sex, or do they decide in advance which sex they wish to attract and thereby determine the level of pay to advertise?

Unions

Many analysts look to unions as a positive force in the battle against sex discrimination. Unions may contribute to this cause both by increasing the number of women in their ranks, which tends to increase women's access to higher-paying jobs, and by serving as a political mechanism for equal pay laws, collective bargaining agreements that aid women, and other negotiated outcomes. The government employee union, AFSCME, has been notably active in lobbying on these issues. But unions also may serve as a barrier to entry for women into particular professions. Historically, it indeed appears that unions have more often made things worse for women by not opening their ranks to them.

Also, even if unions help both male and female members, they may end up helping men more than women and thereby make the sex gap worse. For instance, one study compares wages and mobility for state employees in New York, which has statewide collective bargaining, to Maryland, which does not have statewide collective bargaining.[64] The wage gap is wider in New York than in Maryland, but there is more upward mobility for both sexes in New York than in Maryland. Unions create seniority systems in place of "merit" systems or other employer-determined systems; however, seniority systems are gender-neutral only when female unionism rates and seniority distributions equal men's.

Even as unions become more open to women, they may be able to go only so far in improving women's wages and employment.[65] Since unionism has the effect of reducing employment in the unionized sector and creating longer job queues for unionized jobs, unionized employers may be able to be choosier in selecting employees from the labor pool. One study's findings for the 1970s and early 1980s suggest that union employers are willing to hire the least productive white males from the available pool and are only willing to hire the best qualified of the black and female workers.[66]

Political methods and networking

Other semiformal and informal methods exist for combating workplace discrimination. Consumers can boycott discriminating firms. Women who have attained a position in a firm where they can influence hiring decisions can lobby for additional women to be hired and promoted. Business and professional women have formed informal groups with the intent of referring business to one another and of recommending group members for positions. To the extent that group membership in such business networks improves professional visibility, individual productivity may be more easily observed by potential employers, which implies that statistical discrimination could become a less important force.[67] However, while these methods should not be underestimated, it is not clear that they are either quick or reliable, and they cannot fully replace more formal antidiscrimination approaches.

*P*olicy Application: Anti-discrimination legislation

In the United States, two legislative acts, the Equal Pay Act of 1963 and Title VII of the Civil Rights Act of 1964, have provided the basis for antidiscrimination actions by the federal government. The Equal Pay Act requires equal pay for work of equal skill, effort, responsibility, and working conditions:

> No employer having employees subject to any provisions of this section shall discriminate, within any establishment in which such employees are employed, between employees on the basis of sex by paying wages to employees in such establishment at a rate less than the rate at which he pays wages to employees of the opposite sex in such establishment for equal work on jobs the performance of which requires equal skill, effort and responsibility, and which are performed under similar working conditions, except where such payment is made pursuant to (i) a seniority system; (ii) a merit system; (iii) a system which measures earnings by

quantity or quality of production; or (iv) a differential based on any other factor other than sex: Provided, That an employer who is paying a wage rate differential in violation of this subsection shall not, in order to comply with the provisions of this subsection, reduce the wage rate of any employee. (29 U.S. Code 206 (d) (1) (1970))

Title VII, also known as the Equal Employment Opportunity provisions, forbids wage and employment discrimination on the basis of race, color, religion, national origin, and sex:

It shall be an unlawful employment practice for an employer – (1) to fail or refuse to hire or to discharge any individual, or otherwise to discriminate against any individual with respect to his compensation, terms, conditions, or privileges of employment, because of such individual's race, color, religion, sex, or national origin; or (2) to limit, segregate, or classify his employees or applicants for employment in any way which would deprive or tend to deprive any individual of employment opportunities or otherwise adversely affect his status as an employee, because of such individual's race, color, religion, sex, or national origin. (42 U.S. Code 2000e, et seq.)

Compliance with both acts is upheld through complaints and routine investigations, which may or may not be effective in eliminating most violations, depending on the willingness of plaintiffs to come forward, the probability of being investigated, and the probability that a sizable penalty will be awarded.[68] Both individual and class action suits may be brought under these acts. The Civil Rights Act created an agency, the Equal Employment Opportunity Commission, to receive and investigate complaints and attempt conciliation. A 1972 amendment of Title VII provided for more effective enforcement by expanding coverage (covering private employers with 15 or more employees, labor unions, and employment agencies) and giving the Equal Employment Opportunity Commission the right to sue employers.[69]

The expected combined effect of these two acts should be to raise women's earnings. The effect on women's employment, both overall and in particular occupations, could be either positive (due to reduction of barriers to entry) or negative (if employers attempt to reduce hiring of women while still paying those who are hired equal wages).

Several studies have tried to gauge the effect of these antidiscrimination acts.[70] The general methodology for looking for effects on women's earnings is to measure the gender earnings ratio before and after these acts began to be enforced, while controlling for other forces that may have had an effect on the ratio. One study, using aggregated Current Population Survey data from 1955 through 1971 and Census data for 1960 and 1970, finds no statistically significant effect on the gender earnings gap over this period.[71] A series of three studies by economist Andrea Beller uses individual data from the Current Population Survey from 1967–68 and 1974–75 to compare the gender earnings ratio before and after the 1972 Amendment.[72] Her studies all find that the stricter enforcement leads to larger effects, and that increasing the probability of an investigation is more effective than increasing the probability of a settlement. She finds that the gender earnings ratio rose by 7 to 10 percent over this period due to Title VII enforcement. However, much of the rise in the earnings ratio occurred due to a decrease in men's earnings rather than from a rise in women's earnings.

A fourth study by Beller uses the same time frame to look at the probability of women entering male-dominated occupations.[73] She finds a reduced gender difference in the probability of being employed in a male-dominated occupation, both because the female probability increases and because the male probability decreases. Increasing the probability of a settlement is more effective than increasing the probability of an investigation for reducing employment differences. Finally, Jonathan Leonard, using manufacturing industry data by state, regresses the change between 1966 and 1978 in percentage of workers who are female on the number of Title VII class action suits per employer to gauge the overall effect on employment.[74] He finds generally little effect on employment, with some evidence of a slight negative effect.

Summary

Evidence of workplace discrimination takes three forms: anecdotal evidence from personal testimony, auditing surveys, and statistical analyses of earnings and employment. All three show evidence of widespread discrimination, although statistical analyses are subject to qualifications.

Two main types of economic theories have been developed to explain discrimination: those based on prejudice and those based on departures from the model of perfect competition. The source of prejudice can be employers, employees, or customers. Departures from the model of perfect competition can involve market power on the part of a group in the society or imperfect information about worker productivity. These theories are grouped by their primary characteristic into monopsony models, rent-seeking models, two-sector models, and statistical discrimination models.

A comprehensive model would have to explain the gender earnings and employment patterns, including segregation, observed in societies. Each model explains some situations well and is less applicable to others. Models vary in their ability to justify discrimination existing in a long-run equilibrium. Most models can incorporate feedback effects to and from behavior outside the workplace, particularly in considering investment in human capital.

Policies to combat discrimination include equal pay laws and laws prohibiting discrimination in hiring and promotion. These policies appear to have had some effect narrowing the gender earnings gap.

Endnotes

1. Eleanor Swift, "The Battle for Tenure: How One Professor Challenged the System and Won," *Radcliffe Quarterly* 76, no. 4 (December 1990): 22–27. Reprinted with permission.
2. Peter A. Riach and Judith Rich, "Measuring Discrimination by Direct Experimental Methods: Seeking Gunsmoke," *Journal of Post Keynesian Economics* 14, no. 2 (Winter 1991–92): 143–150. The study derived from this project, *Report on Racial Discrimination* (London: Political and Economic Planning, 1967), looked at racial discrimination in the housing market, the labor market (both employment agencies and employers), and services (car insurance providers, car rental firms, and hotels).
3. In the case of banking discrimination, the testers (here matched in terms of credit history and current financial position) approach loan offices to see if the rates of being offered credit vary. In the housing market case, as well as investigating the probability that members of different groups are offered a mortgage, real estate agents can be tested to see if they show members of different groups property in different neighborhoods (a practice known as "steering"), and

landlords can be tested to see if they refuse to rent to the testers. These practices have been investigated more in relation to race discrimination than sex discrimination. For a detailed description of the auditing technique and discussion of its applications, see Michael Fix and Raymond J. Struyk (eds.), *Clear and Convincing Evidence: Measurement of Discrimination in America* (Washington, D.C.: Urban Institute, 1992). For an interesting account of how to implement a student-staffed project of this type, see David Neumark, with the Assistance of Roy J. Bank and Kyle D. Van Nort, "Sex Discrimination in Restaurant Hiring: An Audit Study," *Quarterly Journal of Economics* 111, no. 3 (August 1996): 915–941.

4. This method was first used in the early 1970s to analyze racial and union vs. nonunion wage differences, as well as gender wage differences. See Orley Ashenfelter, "Racial Discrimination and Trade Unionism," *Journal of Political Economy* 80, no. 3, part 1 (May/June 1972): 435–464; Alan Blinder, "Wage Discrimination: Reduced Form and Structural Estimates," *Journal of Human Resources* 8, no. 4 (Fall 1973): 436–455; Ronald Oaxaca, "Male-Female Differentials in Urban Labor Markets," *International Economic Review* 14, no. 3 (October 1973): 693–710; and Ronald Oaxaca, "Sex Discrimination in Wages," *Discrimination in Labor Markets*, eds. Orley Ashenfelter and Albert Rees (Princeton, N.J.: Princeton University, 1973): 124–154.

5. For a discussion of alternative weighting schemes, see David Neumark, "Employers' Discriminatory Behavior and the Estimation of Wage Discrimination" *Journal of Human Resources* 23, no. 3 (Summer 1988): 279–295.

6. Francine D. Blau and Marianne A. Ferber, "Discrimination: Empirical Evidence from the United States," *American Economic Review* 77, no. 2 (May 1987): 316–320.

7. T.D. Stanley and Stephen B. Jarrell, "Gender Bias in Gender Studies? A Meta-Regression Analysis," working paper, Department of Economics and Business, Hendrix College and Department of Economics and Finance, Western Carolina University (March 1996).

8. See Glen G. Cain, "The Economics of Labor Market Discrimination: A Survey," *Handbook of Labor Economics* 2, eds. Orley Ashenfelter and Richard Layard (Amsterdam, New York: North-Holland, 1986): 760.

9. There are alternative ways of measuring the effect of discrimination on earnings. For instance, we might define the amount of discrimination as the difference between actual pay and the amount that women would earn if their pay were based on their actual marginal productivity, which is how factors should be paid in an efficiently operating labor market. One study that uses this definition, Michael D. Robinson and Phanindra V. Wunnava, "Measuring Direct Discrimination in Labor Markets Using a Frontier Approach: Evidence from CPS Female Earnings Data," *Southern Economic Journal* 56, no. 1 (July 1989): 212–218, estimates that discrimination lowers the average hourly earnings of women by about 26 percent relative to what they would earn if they were paid according to their marginal productivity. This method leads to the implication that 50 to 75 percent of the *unexplained* gender earnings gap is due to discrimination, while the rest would be attributed to unmeasured differences between women and men. This method does not require assuming that men and women are identical in order to measure the unexplained differential. However, this method does rely on a particular distributional assumption about earnings, namely, that discrimination can be measured by adding a truncated half-normal error term to a traditional log earnings equation (in addition to the usual normally distributed error term) and seeing if the estimated value of this term is negative. This rather technical modification to basic regression analysis has not been widely adopted.

Another commonly used presentation method is to estimate a "discrimination coefficient" D. We would like to calculate:

$$D = \frac{\dfrac{W_m}{W_f} - \left(\dfrac{W_m}{W_f}\right)^{\circ}}{\left(\dfrac{W_m}{W_f}\right)^{\circ}}$$

where $\left(\dfrac{W_m}{W_f}\right)^{\circ}$ is the wage ratio that would be observed in the absence of discrimination; and $\dfrac{W_m}{W_f}$ is the actual wage ratio. The larger D is, the greater the amount of discrimination. Note that there is no upper bound on this measure. Given the impossibility of measuring $\left(\dfrac{W_m}{W_f}\right)^{\circ}$ directly, a decision similar to that made in the text in choosing an adjustment method must be made. Using the coefficients from either the male or the female wage equation, one can estimate $\left(\dfrac{W_m}{W_f}\right)^{\circ}$ as either

$$\frac{\sum \beta_m \overline{X}_f}{\sum \beta_m \overline{X}_m} \quad \text{or} \quad \frac{\sum \beta_f \overline{X}_f}{\sum \beta_f \overline{X}_m}$$

Or, one can take an average of the two as our measure of what the wage ratio would look like in the absence of discrimination.

10. For example, Myra H. Strober and Carolyn L. Arnold, "Integrated Circuits/Segregated Labor: Women in Computer-Related Occupations and High-Tech Industries," *Computer Chips and Paper Clips: Technology and Women's Employment; Vol. II: Case Studies and Policy Perspectives* (Washington, D.C.: National Academy, 1987): 136–182.
11. Myra H. Strober and Carolyn L. Arnold, "The Dynamics of Occupational Segregation among Bank Tellers," *Gender in the Workplace*, eds. Clair Brown and Joseph A. Pechman (Washington, D.C.: Brookings, 1987): 107–148.
12. Barbara Baran, "The Technological Transformation of White-collar Work: A Case Study of the Insurance Industry," *Computer Chips and Paper Clips: Technology and Women's Employment; Vol. II: Case Studies and Policy Perspectives* (Washington, D.C.: National Academy, 1987): 25–62.
13. Francine D. Blau, *Equal Pay in the Office* (Lexington, Mass.: Lexington Books, 1977), studies clerical occupations in the Boston area.
14. Barry A. Gerhart, "Salaries, Salary Growth, and Promotions of Men and Women in a Large, Private Firm," *Pay Equity: Empirical Inquiries*, eds. Robert T. Michael, Heidi I. Hartmann, and Brigid O'Farrell (Washington, D.C.: National Academy, 1989): 23–43.
15. Robert Cabral, Marianne A. Ferber, and Carole A. Greene, "Men and Women in Fiduciary Institutions: A Study of Sex Differences in Career Development," *Review of Economics and Statistics* 63, no. 4 (November 1981): 573–580.
16. Heidi I. Hartmann, "Internal Labor Markets and Gender: A Case Study of Promotion," *Gender in the Workplace*, eds. Clair Brown and Joseph A. Pechman (Washington, D.C.: Brookings, 1987): 59–92. See Veronica F. Nieva and Barbara A. Gutek, *Women and Work: A Psychological Perspective* (New York: Praeger, 1981): Chapter 6, for a discussion of evaluation bias, both pro-male and pro-female.
17. Steven B. Isbell and Lewis H. Smith, "Simultaneous Measurement of Race and Gender Discrimination: A Special Application to Black Females," revised version of paper presented at 1988 Southern Economic Association Meetings (November 1989).
18. Price V. Fishback and Joseph V. Terza, "Are Estimates of Sex Discrimination by Employers Robust? The Use of Never-Marrieds," *Economic Inquiry* 27, no. 2 (April 1989): 271–285.
19. Janice Fanning Madden, "Gender Differences in the Cost of Displacement: An Empirical Test of Discrimination in the Labor Market," *American Economic Review* 77, no. 2 (May 1987): 246–251.
20. Nan L. Maxwell and Ronald J. D'Amico, "Employment and Wage Effects of Involuntary Job Separation: Male-Female Differences," *American Economic Review* 76, no. 2 (May 1986): 373–377.

21. Jeffrey Pfeffer and Jerry Ross, "Gender-Based Wage Differences: The Effects of Organizational Context," *Work and Occupations* 17, no. 1 (February 1990): 55–78.

22. Carl Hoffman and John Shelton Reed, "Sex Discrimination? The XYZ Affair," *Public Interest* 62 (Winter 1981): 21–39.

23. Hartmann, *loc. cit.*

24. Marjorie Baldwin and William G. Johnson, "Estimating the Employment Effects of Wage Discrimination," *Review of Economics and Statistics* 74, no. 3 (August 1992): 446–455.

25. Orley Ashenfelter and Ronald Oaxaca, "The Economics of Discrimination: Economists Enter the Courtroom," *American Economic Review* 77, no. 2 (May 1987): 325.

26. See Mark R. Killingsworth, "Analyzing Employment Discrimination: From the Seminar Room to the Courtroom," *American Economic Review* 83, no. 2 (May 1993): 67–72; and Robert S. Follett, Michael P. Ward, and Finis Welch, "Problems in Assessing Employment Discrimination," *American Economic Review* 83, no. 2 (May 1993): 73–78.

27. Susan Faludi, *Backlash: The Undeclared War Against American Women* (New York: Crown Publishers, 1991): 378. For a fascinating description of the Sears case, see pp. 378–388.

28. For writings on the case by some of Rosenberg's critics, see Ruth Milkman, "Women's History and the Sears Case," *Feminist Studies* 12, no. 2 (Summer 1986): 374–400; and Alice Kessler-Harris, "Academic Freedom and Expert Witnessing," *Texas Law Review* 67, no. 2 (December 1988): 429–440.

29. Rosalind Rosenberg, "What Harms Women in the Workplace," *New York Times* (February 27, 1986): A23. Reprinted with permission.

30. Faludi, *op. cit.*: 385.

31. Faludi, *op. cit.*: 385–386.

32. Faludi, *op. cit.*: 379–380.

33. Faludi, *op. cit.*: 384.

34. Saul D. Hoffman, "Comment on Chapters by Blau and Datcher," *Labor Economics: Modern Views*, ed. William Darity Jr. (Boston, Mass. Kluwer-Nijhoff, 1984): 243.

35. M. Bronfenbrenner, "The Economics of Collective Bargaining," *Quarterly Journal of Economics* 53, no. 4 (August 1939): 535–561.

36. Gary S. Becker, *The Economics of Discrimination, Revised Edition* (Chicago, Ill.: University of Chicago, 1971).

37. Matthew S. Goldberg, "Discrimination, Nepotism, and Long-Run Wage Differentials," *Quarterly Journal of Economics* 97, no. 2 (May 1982): 307–319. One can construct an employer taste continuum from pure nepotism to pure discrimination and, under different assumptions concerning position on the continuum, prefer one decomposition of the wage gap over another, in terms of interpreting the male wage as a premium or the female wage as a discount; see David Neumark, "Employers' Discriminatory Behavior and the Estimation of Wage Discrimination," *Journal of Human Resources* 23, no. 3 (Summer 1988): 277–295.

38. Walter Haessel and John Palmer, "Market Power and Employment Discrimination," *Journal of Human Resources* 13, no. 4 (Fall 1978): 545–560.

39. There is some evidence that manager-controlled large firms discriminate more than owner-controlled large firms. See William G. Shepherd and Sharon G. Levin, "Managerial Discrimination in Large Firms," *Review of Economics and Statistics* 55, no. 4 (November 1973): 412–422; and Sharon G. Levin and Stanford L. Levin, "Profit Maximization and Discrimination," *Industrial Organization Review* 4, no. 1 (1976): 108–116.

40. See Jean Reith Schroedel, *Alone in a Crowd: Women in the Trades Tell Their Stories* (Philadelphia, Penn.: Temple University, 1985).

41. Sharon M. Oster, "Industry Differences in the Level of Discrimination Against Women," *Quarterly Journal of Economics* 89, no. 2 (May 1975): 215–229.

42. Linda J. Waite and Sue E. Berryman, "Women in Nontraditional Occupations: Choice and Turnover," Rand Report no. R-3106-FF (Santa Monica, Calif.: Rand, 1985), using NLS data on both civilian and military persons.

43. Cotton M. Lindsay and Michael T. Maloney, "A Model and Some Evidence Concerning the Influence of Discrimination on Wages," *Economic Inquiry* 26, no. 4 (October 1988): 645–660.

44. Janice Fanning Madden, *The Economics of Sex Discrimination* (Lexington, Mass.: Lexington Books, 1973).

45. Nancy M. Gordon and Thomas E. Morton, "A Low Mobility Model of Wage Discrimination – With Special Reference to Sex Differentials," *Journal of Economic Theory* 7, no. 3 (March 1974): 241–253.

46. Ronald G. Ehrenberg and Robert S. Smith, *Modern Labor Economics: Theory and Public Policy, 4th Edition* (New York: HarperCollins, 1991): 199–202.

47. Janice Fanning Madden, "A Spatial Theory of Sex Discrimination," *Journal of Regional Science* 17, no. 3 (December 1977): 369–380. Haim Ofek and Yesook Merrill, "Labor Immobility and the Formation of Gender Wage Gaps in Local Markets," *Economic Inquiry* 35, no. 1 (January 1997): 28–47, support this immobility argument by finding that the wage gap between married men and women is smaller in larger urban labor markets.

48. Michael Sattinger, "Discriminatory Monopsony Outcomes Without Monopsony Market Power," Department of Economics, State University of New York at Albany Discussion Paper no. 96–3 (January 1996).

49. Anne Krueger, "The Economics of Discrimination," *Journal of Political Economy* 71, no. 5 (October 1963): 481–486.

50. See George Akerlof, "The Economics of Caste and of the Rat Race and Other Woeful Tales," *Quarterly Journal of Economics* 90, no. 4 (November 1976): 599–617; "A Theory of Social Custom, of Which Unemployment May Be One Consequence," *Quarterly Journal of Economics* 94, no. 4 (June 1980): 749–775; and "Discriminatory, Status-Based Wages among Tradition-Oriented, Stochastically Trading Coconut Producers," *Journal of Political Economy* 93, no. 2 (April 1985): 265–276.

51. Jennifer Roback, "Racism as Rent Seeking," *Economic Inquiry* 27, no. 4 (October 1989): 661–681.

52. Barbara F. Reskin and Patricia A. Roos, "Status Hierarchies and Sex Segregation," *Ingredients for Women's Employment Policy*, eds. Christina Bose and Glenna Spitze (Albany, N.Y.: State University of New York, 1985): 3–21.

53. Samuel R. Friedman, "Structure, Process, and the Labor Market," *Labor Economics: Modern Views*, ed. William Darity, Jr. (Boston, Mass.: Kluwer-Nijhoff, 1984): 175–217.

54. Jeremy I. Bulow and Lawrence H. Summers, "A Theory of Dual Labor Markets with Application to Industrial Policy, Discrimination and Keynesian Unemployment," *Journal of Labor Economics* 4, no. 3 (July 1986): 376–414.

55. Michael D. Robinson and Phanindra V. Wunnava, "Discrimination and Efficiency Wages: Estimates of the Role in Male-Female Wage Differentials," *New Approaches to Economic and Social Analyses of Discrimination*, eds. Richard R. Cornwall and Phanindra V. Wunnava (New York: Praeger, 1991): 55–64.

56. See Dennis J. Aigner and Glen G. Cain, "Statistical Theories of Discrimination in Labor Markets," *Industrial and Labor Relations Review* 30, no. 2 (January 1977): 175–187, for a discussion of this type of theory.

57. Cf. Amy Farmer and Dek Terrell, "Discrimination, Bayesian Updating of Employer Beliefs, and Human Capital Accumulation," *Economic Inquiry* 34, no. 2 (April 1996): 204–219.

58. Shelly J. Lundberg and Richard Startz, "Private Discrimination and Social Intervention in Competitive Labor Markets," *American Economic Review* 73, no. 3 (June 1983): 340–347.

59. *Employment and Earnings* 41, no. 1 (January 1994): 252 (Table 61).

60. Philip M. Gleason, Jonathan R. Veum, and Michael R. Pergamit, "Drug and Alcohol Use at Work: A Survey of Young Workers," *Monthly Labor Review* 114, no. 8 (August 1991): 3–7.

61. Arthur Eliot Berkeley, "Job Interviewers' Dirty Little Secret," *Wall Street Journal* (March 20, 1989): A14. Reprinted with permission.

62. Thomas F. D'Amico, "The Conceit of Labor Market Discrimination," *American Economic Review* 77, no. 2 (May 1987): 313.
63. David Neumark and Michele McLennan, "Sex Discrimination and Women's Labor Market Outcomes," *Journal of Human Resources* 30, no. 4 (Fall 1995): 713–740.
64. Deborah M. Figart, "Gender, Unions, and Internal Labor Markets: Evidence from the Public Sector in Two States," *American Economic Review* 77, no. 2 (May 1987): 252–256.
65. See Dorothy Sue Cobble (ed.), *Women and Unions: Forging a Partnership* (Ithaca, N.Y.: ILR, 1993), for a set of papers on intraunion policy directions regarding women.
66. Dwight W. Adamson, "Differences in Union Relative Wage Effects Across Gender and Race: A Longitudinal Analysis," *Journal of Economics* 19, no. 2 (Fall 1993): 79–91.
67. Paul Milgrom and Sharon Oster, "Job Discrimination, Market Forces, and the Invisibility Hypothesis," *Quarterly Journal of Economics* 102, no. 3 (August 1987): 453–476.
68. See Barbara R. Bergmann, *The Economic Emergence of Women* (New York: Basic Books, 1986): Chapter 7, for a discussion of the application of Title VII to: the use of sex as a predictor of performance; pension plans; discrimination on grounds of customer preferences; protective legislation; tests or requirements for employment; seniority systems; employers who countenance sexual harassment; and treatment of pregnant employees.
69. See Thomas G. Abram, "The Law, Its Interpretation, Levels of Enforcement Activity, and Effect on Employer Behavior," *American Economic Review* 83, no. 2 (May 1993): 62–66, for a discussion of trends in the numbers and types of discrimination cases and actions filed.
70. These studies are summarized in Morley Gunderson, "Male-Female Wage Differentials and Policy Responses," *Journal of Economic Literature* 27, no. 1 (March 1989): 46–72.
71. Ronald Oaxaca, "The Persistence of Male-Female Earnings Differentials," *The Distribution of Economic Well-Being*, ed. F. Thomas Juster (Cambridge, Mass.: Ballinger, 1977): 303–354.
72. Andrea Beller, "EEO Laws and the Earnings of Women," *Industrial Relations Research Association Proceedings* (Madison, Wis.: University of Wisconsin, 1976): 190–198; "The Impact of Equal Employment Opportunity Laws on the Male-Female Earnings Differential," *Women in the Labor Market*, eds. Cynthia Lloyd, Emily Andrews, and Curtis Gilroy (New York: Columbia University, 1979): 304–330; and "The Effect of Economic Conditions on the Success of Equal Employment Opportunity Laws: An Application to the Sex Differential in Earnings," *Review of Economics and Statistics* 62, no. 3 (August 1980): 370–387.
73. Andrea Beller, "Occupational Segregation by Sex: Determinants and Changes," *Journal of Human Resources* 20, no. 2 (Spring 1985): 235–250.
74. Jonathan Leonard, "Antidiscrimination or Reverse Discrimination: The Impact of Changing Demographics, Title VII, and Affirmative Action on Productivity," *Journal of Human Resources* 19, no. 2 (Spring 1984): 145–174.

*F*urther reading

Albelda, Randy, Robert Drago, and Steven Shulman (1997). *Unlevel Playing Fields: Understanding Wage Inequality and Discrimination*. New York: McGraw Hill. Contrasts neoclassical and political economy (radical) approaches to discrimination.

Becker, Gary S. (1971). *The Economics of Discrimination, Revised Edition*. Chicago, Ill.: University of Chicago Press. The classic work in the field, first published in 1959; attempts to define the field of study and clearly lays out the three Becker models of discrimination.

Bergmann, Barbara R. (1986). *The Economic Emergence of Women*. New York: Basic Books. Contains many good references to antidiscrimination court cases, as well as useful material on other gender policy issues.

Blau, Francine D. (1984). "Discrimination against Women: Theory and Evidence," *Labor Economics: Modern Views*, William Darity Jr. (ed.) Boston, Mass.: Kluwer-Nijhoff: 53–89. Excellent layout of economic models of discrimination, along with evaluation of evidence concerning discrimination.

Cain, Glen G. (1986). "The Economic Analysis of Labor Market Discrimination: A Survey," *Handbook of Labor Economics*, 2, Orley Ashenfelter and Richard Layard (eds.) Amsterdam, N.Y.: North-Holland, 693–785. Thorough outline of basic theory for a wide range of economic models of discrimination. Comprehensive bibliography.

Cherry, Robert D. (1989). *Discrimination: Its Economic Impact on Blacks, Women, and Jews.* Lexington, Mass.: Lexington Books. Handbook/textbook; contrasts conservative, liberal, and radical economic views on the causes and effects of discrimination.

Polachek, Solomon W., and W. Stanley Siebert (1993). *The Economics of Earnings.* Cambridge, United Kingdom: Cambridge University. Handbook/textbook; contains chapter on gender in the labor market, focusing on discrimination vs. human capital theories, particularly intermittent participation.

Sloane, Peter J. (1985). "Discrimination in the Labour Market," *Labour Economics*, Derek Carline *et al.* (eds.) London: Longman: 78–158. Another thorough review of economic theory of discrimination, along with the standard statistical evidence.

Discussion questions

1. What methods are used to provide evidence of sex discrimination in the workplace? What are their relative advantages and drawbacks?

2. Consider the Focus on the difficulties of filing discrimination charges. What are the social costs and benefits of making it easier for people to bring discrimination charges?

3. Investigators went to car dealerships in Chicago with instructions to follow a standardized bidding technique in negotiating new car purchase prices. They found that salespersons tended to accept lower final offers from men than from women. Is this evidence of discrimination against women by car dealerships?

4. Consider the Focus on the Sears case. Have you observed gender differences in the sales force by type of product sold when you have gone shopping? If you have, what are your views on what generates these differences?

5. If one group knows that it is being discriminated against by another group, is it best for them to discriminate back?

6. An employer says that he really hates immigrants, but that he is not willing to pay a premium to hire a native-born worker instead. Does this employer have a "taste for discrimination" as Becker defines it?

7. Assume that men have 20 years of experience on average and women have 10 years of experience.
    (a) Assume that both male and female wages (W) are determined by $W = 15 + .25E$, where E is years of experience. What will the pay gap be? Does this gap indicate discrimination?
    (b) Now assume that male and female wages are determined differently:

    Men: $W_m = 20 + .25E$

    Women: $W_f = 10 + .25E$

    Now calculate the pay gap. How much can be attributed to differences in experience? How much is unexplained? Does the residual depend on average experience of men or women?
    (c) Now assume two new equations:

$$W_m = 20 + .5E$$
$$W_f = 18 + .25E$$

Now calculate the pay gap. How much can be attributed to differences in experience (calculated both ways)? How much is unexplained? Does the residual depend on average experience of men or women? How?

8. Assume that women and men are perfect substitutes in production, but both male employers and male employees have a taste for discrimination against women.

   (a) What will the labor market look like in terms of the gender earnings ratio and the segregation of men and women?

   (b) Now assume that the government passes and enforces a law making it illegal to pay women less than men for the same type of job. Will this law affect the segregation pattern? What about the unemployment rates of men and women?

9. Describe the different discrimination theories and indicate for each how applicable you think it is to explaining the gender earnings gap.

10. Will discrimination by employers increase or decrease their profits?

11. Would you expect to find more or less discrimination in owner-operated businesses than in manager-run businesses?

12. Would you expect to find more or less discrimination in nonprofit firms than in for-profit firms?

13. Would you expect to find more or less discrimination in the governmental sector than in the private sector?

14. Consider the Focus on job interviewers' techniques. If an employee is subsequently discovered to have lied so as to sidestep these strategems, is the employer justified in firing the employee?

15. Some unions will admit anyone who pays dues. Other unions ration membership based on criteria such as completion of a training program. Is one type of union more likely to discriminate than the other?

16. Why might subsidizing the wage of new hires reduce pay discrimination? Discuss the pros and cons of this policy and the underlying rationale for it.

Part III
Policy application: Comparable Worth

As has been amply shown so far, women make less than men, and the gender earnings gap is not closing rapidly over time. Additionally, the differential distribution of women and men between job types appears to be linked to the gender earnings gap. Both because of the slow rate of change and because of the observed link between pay and occupational gender distribution, comparable worth policies have been proposed as a radical but necessary measure in order to close the gender earnings gap.

A discussion of comparable worth policies provides an opportunity to consider the materials presented in Chapters 6 to 9 in a unified setting. The two explanations for the gender wage differential presented in Chapters 7 and 8, human capital differences and compensating differentials, are contrasted to the explanation presented in Chapter 9: discrimination. Whether implementation of a comparable worth policy is a good idea or not depends on which explanations are right. Additionally, the importance and fairness of market forces in determining wages are attacked head-on, for comparable worth is an alternative method for determining wages.

What is comparable worth?

Compensation of employees according to "comparable worth" is one of the most sweeping changes ever proposed for the U.S. economy. Its advocates argue for nothing less than a complete overhauling of the manner in which pay is presently determined by firms and governments. Even if only some sectors in the economy institute comparable worth policies, these limited programs could have wide-ranging effects on wages, employment, labor force participation, production, and income distribution. Comparable worth has a compelling sound of fairness and, therefore, political acceptability. Even without an economy-wide federal mandate, this fact may lead to its widespread adoption through an accretion of court cases, state-level lobbying, and collective bargaining agreements.

Throughout this section, a distinction is maintained between comparable worth as a criterion and comparable worth policies, which are specific proposals for how to apply this criterion. Comparable worth is the premise that job characteristics should receive equal returns, regardless of what job they are embodied in or who performs the job. A comparable worth policy attempts to impose this criterion in some form in some compensation-setting environment. Because some writers use "comparable worth" to refer directly to a policy, the distinction has become blurred in practice.

While comparable worth became widely known in the 1980s, this is not to say that the often-used catchphrases for it – "equal pay for equal value" and "pay equity" – had not been heard earlier. In the mid–1940s, comparable worth was discussed when various national equal-pay acts were proposed and rejected.[1] Comparable worth was again discussed during the debates over formulation and passage of the Equal Pay Act in 1963,[2] but it was not explicitly included in the Equal Pay Act.[3] Some states passed comparable worth laws in the 1960s and 1970s that covered state employees, but – much as with earlier state laws (passed in the 1940s and 1950s) – these statutes were generally unenforced.[4] In 1977 comparable worth again came to national attention as a Carter administration platform.

NOW and other women's rights organizations endorsed it, as did the major unions (especially those involved in organizing public employees).

Generally, the type of comparable worth policy proposed is to raise wages for all holders of a job that is found to have equivalent job points, under some chosen rating system, as another higher-paying job. In theory, this criterion need have nothing to do with the maleness or femaleness of the job. While other implementations could occur, such as lowering wages for some jobs or re-equilibrating comparable jobs to a central point, it is clear that, at least in the first round of wage-change, only the former strategy would be politically feasible (though downward adjustment could occur later through limiting wage increases).

What kinds of data lead advocates to call for wage adjustments, and what data are needed in order to implement comparable worth? Table IIIP.1 contains evaluations of six job titles from the comparable worth study done for Washington State employees. Four "compensable factors" were designated and the level of skill embodied in each job was described by a set of stock phrases, each of which implies a range of points. Points can then be summed up to arrive at a point total for each job. Totals are then compared across jobs, along with actual salaries for evidence of discrepancies in salary per point.

Secretary and nurse, the two female-dominated jobs from this list, make less than do male-dominated jobs with fewer total points. This type of pattern turns up over and over again when rating studies are performed on organizations, and is taken as *prima facie* evidence of widespread institutionalized discrimination against women. These rating studies can then be used to remove pay differences between jobs with similar point totals.

The pros and cons of comparable worth

Opponents of comparable worth attack on four grounds:

1. Advocates of comparable worth are committing the intrinsic value fallacy; there is no way to determine *a priori* the value of a job.
2. Wage-setting systems are economically inefficient; they create labor shortages in some markets and an oversupply of labor in others, they lead to a nonoptimal factor mix throughout the economy by affecting the relative prices of capital and types of labor, and they do not correct the fundamental inefficiency in the labor market: barriers to entry for higher-paying occupations.
3. The administrative costs of setting up and maintaining a wage-setting system would be high.
4. Comparable worth would actually hurt some of those it is meant to help by increasing unemployment in female-dominated occupations.

Proponents counter these assertions in the following ways:

1. Job valuation systems already exist and are widely used by institutions to set wages.
2. Rather than making the system more inefficient, an existing inefficiency – discrimination – will have been corrected. There will be negligible unemployment effects.
3. The costs of reworking the system will not be high, given existing job valuation systems and personnel management methods.
4. Not changing the system is also unfair to particular groups of individuals; the gains to those who are helped will more than offset the losses to those who are hurt.

Let us now consider these points more carefully.

TABLE IIIP.I Evaluations of job titles from the Washington State employees comparable worth study

Job title	Knowledge and skills	Mental demands	Accountability	Work conditions	Total points	Salary as of 1/85
Delivery truck driver	No previous experience required. Brief on-the-job learning period required. (61)	Standardized work routines. Recall rather than analysis required. (10)	Duties routine, work closely controlled. (13)	Moderate lifting, some danger. Conditions occasionally undesirable. (13)	97	$382
Auto mechanic	Mechanical skill required. (106)	Similar procedures and methods, analysis of recurring nature. (26)	Methods clearly defined, work frequently reviewed. (30)	Moderate lifting, some danger. Conditions occasionally undesirable. (13)	175	$465
Secretary (Grade III)	Activities require vocational competence and/or adeptness. Capability in dealing with others required. (122)	Similar procedures and methods, analysis of recurring nature. (35)	Methods clearly defined, work frequently reviewed. Actions influence results. (40)	Job at a desk. Little lifting, danger minimal. (0)	197	$306
Civil engineer	Comprehension of complex principles and practices. Capability in dealing with others required. (160)	Varying or complex procedures. Routine analysis. (53)	Activities generally defined, review after the fact. Actions influence results. (61)	Moderate lifting, some danger. Conditions occasionally undesirable. (13)	287	$513
Registered nurse	Comprehension of complex principles and practices. Requires capability to persuade and motivate. (184)	Varying or complex procedures. Nonroutine analysis. (70)	Activities generally defined, review after the fact. Actions influence results. (70)	Moderate lifting, some danger. Disagreeable conditions much of the time. (17)	341	$411
Senior computer systems analyst	Comprehension of complex principles and practices. Capability in dealing with others required. (212)	Varying or complex procedures. Nonroutine analysis. (80)	Activities generally defined, review after the fact. Actions influence results. Moderate fiscal impact. (80)	Job at a desk. Little lifting, danger minimal. (0)	372	$553

Source: Barbara R. Bergmann, "Does the Market for Women's Labor Need Fixing?" *Journal of Economic Perspectives* 3, no. 1 (Winter 1989): 56. Reprinted with permission. Characterizations of job requirements are taken from "State of Washington, Comparable Worth Study, September 1974," prepared by Norman D. Willis in consultation with Ann O. Worcester (Norman D. Willis & Associates, Management Consultants). Salaries and point scores are from an unpublished tabulation made for Bergmann by Helen Remick, Director, Office of Affirmative Action, University of Washington.

The intrinsic value paradox revisited

The first problem with comparable worth for opponents is that it sounds like an argument for "just pricing" of labor. Comparable worth proponents often illustrate their case by using an unjust-sounding fact such as that the nurses hired by Denver received less on an hourly wage basis than the city's tree trimmers.[5] This type of argument is an inviting target for economists, who in general agree with the idea that "the only reliable indicator of the value of a job is the wage an employer is willing to pay a person to fill it."[6] One economist has written:[7]

> At least as far back as the Middle Ages, the concept of "just price" has had some appeal. Practical considerations, however, have won out over philosophical musings. Most people recognize how inefficient it would be to use an evaluation system independent of the market to set wages or prices of consumer goods. So, for example, we accept a higher price for diamonds than for water, even though water is undoubtedly more important to our survival, and a higher wage for lawyers or engineers than for clergymen or bricklayers, even though they may be equally important to our well-being.

The idea of breaking a job down into its component skills and valuing them separately runs into the same problem, as well as the problem that skills need not have identical worth in different jobs. Comparable worth opponents would, in general, agree with the statement that "there is no scientific way and therefore no objective way to quantify an abstract attribute such as skill."[8]

Comparable worth proponents concede that there are many conceptual and methodological problems involved in job evaluation and classification, including innate sex-related biases, lack of agreement among evaluators as to job ratings, and argument over which job factors should be compensated.[9] There are several types of sex-related biases. One is that both men and women may rate jobs that are typically performed by women lower than jobs typically performed by men if they have consciously or unconsciously identified women's work as less valuable (perhaps because they know that it is lower-paid). Indeed, notwithstanding the examples in Table IIIP.1, it is not automatically the case that the system used to rate jobs will lead to an improvement in women's wages. An examination of the Factor Evaluation System used by the federal government since 1973 showed that no weighting scheme for the nine factors used would yield higher average job worth scores for female-dominated jobs as compared with male-dominated jobs, for on no factor did women score higher than men.[10] Another source of bias is that women and men have apparently internalized different standards of what constitutes a fair wage, at least with respect to some jobs.[11]

These problems with achieving consensus mean that for a national policy to achieve full comparability, wage differentials could only be identified and eradicated using one national job-rating system. Otherwise, the different methods used by different organizations, as well as the different values individual raters would calculate, would lead to different results in different companies and regions. One study that compares three states' job-rating studies (Kansas, Michigan, and Iowa) shows that they differ significantly in the number of factors considered, relative weights, and ratings.[12]

There are actually two approaches to job evaluation: the "a priori" and "policy-capturing" approaches.[13] The former involves using point systems that assign predetermined values to skills and then rating jobs by the sum of the point values attached to the amounts of each skill they require. The latter approach is to run a regression of wages on job characteristics for current jobs in a firm, adjusted for percentage female, and use the coefficients on job characteristics as the values of those characteristics for the organization.[14] This latter methodology has been favored over the former by many advocates, as the former method appears to suffer more from its "resistance to modification, general lack of flexibility or responsiveness to firm-specific factors, and probable [sex] bias."[15] However, both methods still suffer from the arbitrariness inherent in deciding which job factors should be included in the analysis, as well as from the assumption that jobs can be broken down into discrete components that should be valued equally across jobs.

Still, proponents argue that one method, or a combination, could be made reputable enough to receive consensus. Additionally, they point out that most large organizations, both governmental and private, already use job-rating systems, and that unions also use them in negotiating pay agreements. They are a widely accepted personnel practice, as job descriptions are already used to advertise positions, and job ratings can be used to justify pay levels so that they appear nonarbitrary (or, at least, less arbitrary than alternative systems), regardless of the built-in arbitrary nature of the rating systems. Proponents argue that it is unrealistic to think that wages move freely with fluctuations in labor supply and demand. Opponents point out, however, that current job rating systems often build in labor market considerations, such as having a compensation factor for labor scarcity, and therefore are subject to market forces.

Could comparable worth make things worse?

Opponents argue that comparable worth, while designed to improve women's earnings by combating labor market discrimination, would actually make things worse, both by making labor markets work less efficiently for the economy as a whole and by actually hurting some of the women it is meant to help. By overriding wage differentials that arise through the compensating differential mechanism and by subverting market forces, labor surpluses will arise in some markets, shortages in others. Labor will not be channeled correctly into its most efficient uses, and the economy will suffer a loss of output. Even in the case where wage differentials are caused by discrimination, comparable worth is not preferable to other policies that attack discrimination directly.

Consider the case of an economy for which the following four assumptions hold: (1) differences in productivity across individuals are attributable to different investments in human capital; (2) no one discriminates; (3) all factor and product markets are perfectly competitive; and (4) everyone is in complete agreement as to which job attributes are good or bad. In this model, wage differences among individuals within a job are attributable to the different amounts of human capital embodied in those individuals; across jobs, wage differences for any given skill level are attributable to society's decision about which jobs are more or less disagreeable. Any group differences in wages and occupational distribution are traceable to underlying differences in productive ability. Indeed, the term "job" ceases to have much meaning here, as all work could be described using one regression equation in which all forms of human capital and job characteristics enter and each person's wage rate is thereby perfectly explained. Any attempt to impose a higher wage for a particular job leads to a situation like the case of imposing a minimum wage (as discussed in the appendix to Chapter 1): fewer people are hired to perform the job even though more people want to do it, leading to unemployment and a loss of output.

Now, allow discrimination to enter the model and assume that it leads to the crowding phenomenon discussed in Chapter 6, in which women are systematically barred from certain jobs and/or firms and are forced into the segments of the economy willing to hire them, albeit at a lower wage. In this situation, a wage realignment would again lead to an efficiency loss. The problem is that employers' tastes for discrimination are not automatically eradicated by the onset of a new wage policy. Discriminating employers would still consider women to be more costly than men, and nothing prevents a demand shift away from jobs that are female-intensive, so long as male-intensive occupations can be substituted somewhat for female-intensive occupations. This can lead to a loss of employment for women and a rise in the wage for the male occupations, leading to another round of wage-raising for the female occupations.

Figure IIIP.1 illustrates this case. For two occupations, A and B, assume that in the absence of barriers to entry into either occupation, the wage and number of persons would be the same in both (i). Now assume that a barrier prevents women from entering occupation A. The labor supply curve, driven by the movement of women, shifts left in A and right in B (ii), causing the wage to rise and employment fall in occupation A, while the wage falls and employment rises in occupation B. Then, imposition of a wage in B equal to the wage in A without eradicating the barrier leads to a drop in employment and a rise in unemployment in occupation B (iii): those who still have their jobs are better off, while those who are now unemployed are worse off.

As in the case of a minimum wage, however, there is another instance in which raising wages may clearly improve allocative efficiency. Let us modify the third assumption above to allow for monopsony power in the female-dominated jobs. If all the other assumptions hold, then raising wages to competitive levels in monopsonistic labor markets is an optimal solution, though not the only solution; one could, instead, directly attack the buyer cartels and attempt to restore the labor market to a competitive structure. An alternative is to consider application or expansion of the antitrust laws to address such wage-fixing.[16] However, the plausibility of widespread monopsonistic power is questionable; if only isolated cases are found, it is difficult to see why economy-wide imposition of a comparable worth policy would be necessary to counteract them.

Now let us modify the fourth assumption, that tastes are homogeneous, and include sex-linked differences in tastes in our model. Assume that women and men have completely different preferences for job attributes, but that all men have the same preferences, as do all women. Then men and women have nonidentical distributions across job types, but we cannot predict the relative wages or actual distributions across job types, as they depend on the relative supplies of male and female labor and demands for different jobs.

Upon expansion of this case to the more general case of heterogeneous preferences, in which both men and women are distributed along continua of tastes for certain job characteristics, the theory of compensating differentials breaks down.[17] Since people now disagree about what constitutes desirable job characteristics, there is no reason to expect that job characteristics will have any discernible relation to wages. In the case where the second assumption, nonexistence of discrimination, is violated as well, we are now unable to tell whether the unexplained portion in wage regressions is attributable to job characteristics or to discrimination. Here, it is unclear whether a comparable worth policy would lead to a smaller loss in efficiency than in the case where the entire unexplained portion is attributable to discrimination; the relative result depends on the sizes of the various labor supply and demand responses.

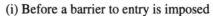

(i) Before a barrier to entry is imposed

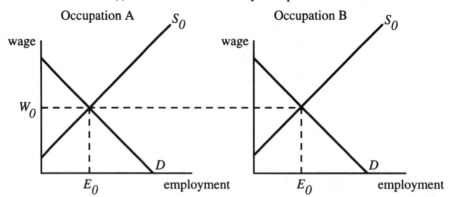

(ii) After a barrier to entry is imposed on Occupation A

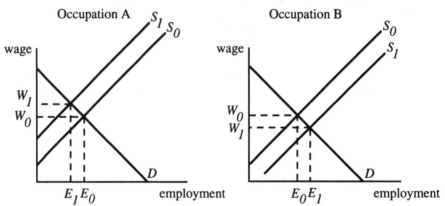

(iii) After comparable worth is imposed

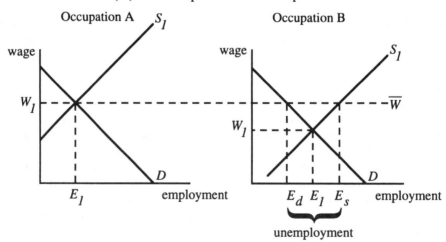

FIGURE IIIP.I   Comparable worth in the case of crowding

Finally, consider that it is difficult to calculate the actual gains and losses for individual women and men if they are making decisions in a joint decision framework such as marriage. The labor market participation of both spouses may be altered by relative wage changes, and consumption decisions within a marriage may be dependent on relative contributions to family income.

How much do all these possible departures from the simple model matter? In the simplest economic model, interfering with wages is undesirable on efficiency grounds; in departures from the simple model, a trade-off exists between efficiency and equity, and we must decide both what the dimensions of the trade-off are and whether or not it is acceptable.

FOCUS

Comparable worth for professors

Currently, salaries vary greatly for professors in different academic disciplines. Additionally, women professors earn less on average than male professors at all rank levels. For the 1996–97 academic year, the average salary for male full professors was $68,884, while that for female full professors was $60,702 (88% as much); for assistant professors the average for men was $42,256, for women $39,643 (94% as much).[18] While part of this difference can be accounted for by discrimination within departments and by the different distributions of men and women by institution,[19] part is related to the different distributions of women and men across departments. Therefore, comparable worth appears to be a useful way to close these salary differences.

Consider the two jobs of English professor and economics professor in the same liberal arts college. The two jobs look very similar on paper. In both cases, the training involves receiving a Ph.D. Both involve teaching and advising students, with the same number of hours in the classroom and (we will assume) similar class sizes and numbers of advisees. Both involve a research component, which is generally measured by the quantity and quality of publications, and both involve administrative duties, including serving on college committees and helping out with departmental duties. The two types of professors appear to be equal in quality and, therefore, should receive equal wages under the concept of comparable worth. Assume that this is, in fact, initially an equilibrium position, as shown in Figure IIIP.2 (i). What happens now under this policy if the demand for economics courses increases and the demand for English courses decreases? At the current wage, there is excess demand for economics professors and an excess supply of English professors, as shown in Figure IIIP.2 (ii).

In order to meet these enrollment shifts, colleges can either lower hiring standards for economics professors (e.g., stop requiring a Ph.D.) and raise them for English professors (e.g., require postdoctoral training), or allow wages to reequilibrate the labor markets, which will lead to higher pay for economics professors and lower pay for English professors. Or they can refuse to change their hiring patterns, leading to larger economics course sizes and smaller English course sizes (or long waiting lists for economics courses, if class sizes are capped). Under the first option, while wages are held equal across occupations, the quality of the two groups of professors is now unequal, violating the principle of comparable worth. Under the second option, comparable worth is also violated as the wages are no longer equal. Under the third option, the quality of the service provided is diminished, which also violates the comparable worth principle.

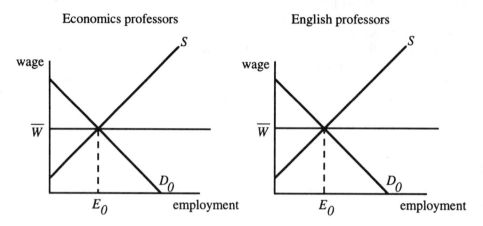

(i) Initial equilibrium positions for economics and English

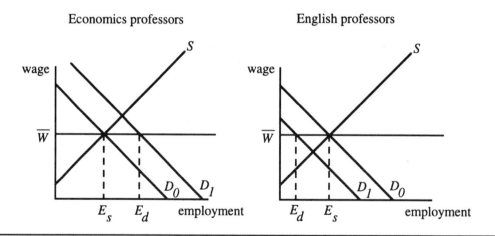

(ii) After demand increases for economics and decreases for English

FIGURE IIIP.2   Effects of comparable worth on markets for professors

*H*ow would comparable worth be implemented nationally?

The section above implicitly considers a comparable worth policy that covers all firms and adjusted wages nationally for particular occupations, so that an occupation would have the same wage no matter what firm it is in – a much broader policy than is generally proposed. There are, however, numerous ways in which a national comparable worth policy might be implemented. In this section, we consider four factors: (1) existence of an uncovered sector, (2) realignment of wages within, but not between, firms, (3) specification of a dynamic policy, and (4) implementation costs.

How might the case in which covered and uncovered sectors exist differ from the total coverage case?[20] This is an interesting question, as the most likely development for comparable worth is its widespread acceptance by governmental bodies. In general, labor will flow out of the covered sector into the uncovered sector. Indeed, even in systems where all wages in the formal work sector are under a comparable worth agreement, we might expect the underground and home production economies to increase in size. One model finds that the efficiency losses are greater if an uncovered sector exists than they would be with full coverage.[21] An important consideration in these models is how to characterize the governmental budget constraint. Employment need not drop at all in the government sector, but in this case the whole economy would have to shrink to cover the increased governmental wage bill through increased taxes. If there is a binding constraint on taxes, one would expect to see an immediate reduction in employment and eventual downward adjustment of wages in the government sector.[22] Public sector employment in both female-dominated occupations and the sector as a whole is likely to drop, assuming any binding budget constraint and any possibilities for substitution between labor types within the sector.

Another case is the situation in which wages are only realigned within firms.[23] Here it is especially important to model explicitly the dynamics of the situation. One might well find firms with fewer job categories over time. For example, any firm that hires both clerks and truck drivers might contract out most of its clerical work in order to avoid having to pay clerical workers the same amount as their drivers. This is similar to the partial coverage case in that the effect of reducing the wage gap will be diminished. Correcting only intrafirm gender differentials may be ineffective, as it can lead to further segregation and allow gender wage differentials to continue.

Perhaps the most important dimension of any proposed comparable worth scheme would be to address formally the dynamics of the policy as the system goes through adjustment phases. To do this, one would need to model explicitly the economy's reactions over time. For labor markets to clear, real wages would need to fall. In the longer run, technological change and changes in the capital stock would lead to the need for periodic re-evaluation of the values to be attached to different job skills, because labor productivity is dependent upon how labor combines with capital and other inputs in production processes. Administrators would need to adapt comparable worth calculations to changing labor market conditions. Another consideration is the hiring rules to be formulated to accompany the wage changes. Hiring rules can have a major effect on how people move across occupations after a comparable worth policy is enacted. Also, just as advocates of affirmative action do not press for its continuing unchanged forever, comparable worth proposals must explicitly define the future of comparable worth, including the possibility of phasing it out.

Finally, it is clear that the implementational problems and potential costs involved in setting up and administering any comparable worth policy are numerous. However, no solid figures have been estimated yet, and it is hard to debate the particulars of a policy unless one knows how much of the economy it will cover, how detailed the job descriptions will be, how much allowance will be built in for individual firms' special features, and what kind of hiring rules will be enforced. The costs of implementing a comparable worth policy include the costs of establishing job classifications, prosecuting wrongdoers, and discussing exceptions, as well as updating rankings and dealing with new jobs. These costs might be absorbed by a national rating bureau, or left for individual organizations to bear as they work out their own job rating systems.

TABLE IIIP.2   The estimated impact of implementing comparable worth in five jurisdictions

Jurisdiction	Percentage gain for women	Gender earnings ratio		Cost as percentage of payroll
		Before	*After*	
Iowa	12	0.74	0.82	6
Manitoba	15	0.82	0.87	3
Michigan	14	0.79	0.88	7
Minnesota	21	0.74	0.88	9
Washington	21	0.77	0.90	10

Sources: Elaine Sorensen, "Implementing Comparable Worth: A Survey of Recent Job Evaluation Studies," *American Economic Review* 76, no. 2 (May 1986): 366; Morley Gunderson, *Comparable Worth and Gender Discrimination: An International Perspective* (Geneva: ILO, 1994): 79.

*E*stimation of potential comparable worth benefits and costs

Several authors have attempted to estimate the costs of implementing a comparable worth policy.[24] One study uses the "a priori" job evaluation studies undertaken by four states in preparation for implementing comparable worth for state employees and calculates the estimated percentage gain for women, the effect on the gender earnings ratio among these employees, and the cost of implementing comparable worth as a percentage of payroll for state government employees.[25] Another study uses actual data from provincial government employees in Manitoba.[26] These figures are shown in Table IIIP.2. The estimated cost of implementing comparable worth ranges from 3 to 10 percent of total payroll, and the earnings gain for women ranges from 12 to 21 percent. Earnings for women and men are still not equalized, but the ratio rises as high as 90 cents on the dollar for the state of Washington.

Another study, using the "policy capturing" method on national data to estimate the effect of a national comparable worth policy that would equalize wages for occupations only within industries, comes up with smaller effects in terms of the percentage gain for women and, therefore, on the earnings ratio: a rise in female earnings from 66 percent of male earnings before the policy to between 69 and 72 percent afterwards; and, in the case of partial coverage (the government sector and large firms), a rise to between 67 and 68 percent.[27] A more recent study estimates that women's earnings would rise to 80.5 percent of male earnings if national comparable worth were implemented and that the male-female poverty rate gap would be virtually eliminated.[28]

An alternative – and, from the economists' viewpoint, preferable way of figuring the cost of implementing a national comparable worth policy – is to calculate the deadweight loss associated with such a policy – i.e., how much of potential national output is sacrificed in the redistributional effort. One study calculates a loss of about 1 percent of national output per year that the policy is in effect.[29]

Finally, what about calculations of the distributional impact of a comparable worth policy? One study looks at the intrafemale redistribution of income, using the assumptions that only women employed in jobs that are at least 60 percent female, in public sector jobs (excluding teachers, for lack of private sector comparability) or private sector jobs in firms with 500 or more employees, would receive wage adjustments. It concludes that only 23 percent of female workers would be covered and that they would tend to be the higher-paid women.[30] Another study concludes, after taking into account intrafamily labor supply substitution, that single women and married men would be helped. Married women would end up working more hours and contributing a greater share to family income, while married men would reduce work effort.[31]

*E*valuation of actual comparable worth policies

Discussion of comparable worth policy effects need not be conducted on a purely theoretical level. There are currently several state and local governments that have implemented comparable worth policies, as well as several jurisdictions in Canada, and the national wage-setting policy in Australia has comparable-worth-like features. These cases allow us to develop some ideas about how such policies are implemented, as well as to see if the policies succeed in raising wages for women, with or without reductions in employment.

One drawback to using these cases to extrapolate to what would happen if comparable worth policies become more widespread is that these cases, save for Australia, involve governmental bodies rather than firms. Governments are not subject to profit-making considerations, and they may be able to pass along the cost of wage increases by reducing services or by increasing their budget. Only if some form of budgetary and/or service-provision constraint is imposed on governments would we expect to automatically see a reduction of employment or a wage reduction for some occupations in order to keep the wage bill constant. The usefulness of these exercises for predicting private sector results depends on how strongly market forces affect governments.[32]

Several U.S. cities, including Denver[33] and San Jose, have been involved in comparable worth lawsuits or union negotiations. The San Jose case, which involved a strike by union workers, has yielded conflicting interpretations of the effects of comparable worth. One study concludes that the pay adjustments raised wages approximately 5.7 percent in female jobs and reduced employment in female jobs by about 6.6 percent relative to what it would have been (actual employment rose); no measurable effect on wages or employment was found for male jobs. This author concludes that the real losers were "persons (particularly women) in the private sector or not in the labor force who were seeking public-sector jobs."[34] Another study, in comparing San Jose's wage and employment growth with the growth in neighboring cities, finds that there was significantly greater wage growth in affected jobs and that employment growth was still higher than in surrounding cities; interestingly, the targeted jobs actually experienced an increase in their proportion of female employment, implying either that the higher wages did not attract male applicants or that hiring policies favored female applicants.[35]

Many U.S. states have performed job evaluation studies to lay the groundwork for implementation or as feasibility studies, and twenty states have implemented some form of comparable worth policy for their employees, although activity on this front has lessened noticeably since the late 1980s.[36] Four states that have been studied extensively subsequent to implementation of comparable worth policies are Minnesota,[37] Iowa,[38] Oregon,[39] and Washington.[40] Minnesota is the first state to have implemented a comparable worth policy. From 1981 to 1986, when implementation was completed, the gender wage ratio rose from 0.74 to 0.82 (somewhat less than predicted in Table IIIP.2).[41] Relative to what would have occurred in the absence of wage adjustments, employment in female jobs fell (actual employment rose).[42] In the cases of Iowa and Oregon, large gains for women in the original proposal were reduced as the process evolved. (In Iowa, the plan had been to raise the gender earnings ratio to 0.86 rather than 0.82.) Some of the planned gains for women in Iowa were redistributed to union members and supervisors. However, it appears that in both states, low-wage earners and workers with the least education and experience gained the most, with the policy mutating operationally into a poverty relief program in Oregon.[43] In Washington, the gender wage ratio rose from 0.80 in 1983 to 0.86 in 1987 (again, less than predicted in Table IIIP.2), following an earlier narrowing of the wage ratio from 1980 to 1983 (rising from 0.76 in 1980) that may have reflected earlier upward adjustments in pay before the comparable worth policy was formally implemented. As in Iowa, returns to work experience and schooling declined under comparable worth. Unemployment effects have not been calculated for these two states.

Canada has implemented various forms of comparable worth for federal workers and in all but two of its twelve provinces and territories.[44] The case of Ontario's comparable worth policy is the most interesting, because it covers private sector employers as well as civil servants and is proactive, requiring employers to implement pay equity whether or not there has been a complaint. All employers with 100 or more employees were required to implement policies as of January 1992. Preliminary evidence on the mean pay equity wage adjustment scheduled by firms implies that the male-female wage gap could be reduced by as much as forty-five percent if compliance is widespread.[45]

The Australian case is particularly interesting as it is the only case prior to Ontario in which a comparable worth policy has been applied to both public and private sectors.[46] In Australia, minimum wage rates are set nationally for many occupations and/or industries by wage tribunals. Prior to the 1968 "equal pay for equal work" decision, women's wages were set below men's wages within occupations. Then, in 1972, the Conciliation and Arbitration Commission extended the equality concept to include "equal pay for work of equal value." This was fully implemented by 1975, although some groups – notably nurses – were not covered by this decision, and were forced into further legal action in 1986 in Victoria and South Australia to win wage increases.[47]

The increase in the gender earnings ratio was immediate and notable. Whereas in 1973 the ratio was 0.76, by 1975 it had risen to 0.82; it rose to 0.84 by 1978. However, one economist has suggested that economic forces would have led to the ratio rising to such levels eventually, anyway, bringing up the point that comparable worth may be a faster way to arrive at an eventual wage raise rather than a solution to a problem that would otherwise never be resolved.[48] This does not mean that speedier wage gains are not important to those people receiving them, nor that efficiency losses (as measured in unemployment and/or lost national output) during the transition period are negligible.

As in the San Jose case, there has been disagreement over the actual effects of this policy on employment. While the data show continuing increases in female employment since 1972, the need to correct for employment growth that would have occurred regardless of this policy is again apparent. The 1970s, in particular, were a period of female labor force growth in developed countries. Again, the question is whether growth was reduced relative to what it would have been in the absence of this comparable worth policy. One study concludes that shortly after this policy took effect, the relative growth rate of female employment was reduced from 4.5 percent to 3 percent annually.[49] A second study, which considers both the immediate employment effects and the longer employment trend, finds a reduction in the female-to-male employment ratio in November 1975 of 5 percent, but negligible effects on this ratio by the end of 1977, implying – as with the wage gains – that comparable worth policies may have no permanent effects on the economy but merely speed up changes that are occurring anyway.[50]

Conclusions from case studies

From these case studies, it appears that comparable worth policies can, indeed, achieve notable gains in earnings for members of female-dominated occupations, and can lead to a quick jump in the gender earnings ratio in covered sectors. While the gap cannot be driven to zero, these policies lead to a much larger gain in wages in a much shorter time than has been achieved under other policies aimed at raising female wages. This is convincing evidence that these policies can be efficacious in raising female wages.

It is harder to ascertain directly the effects on female employment, or on employment in general, from these limited applications of comparable worth. In particular, implementation only in the public sector makes it harder to observe the predicted employment effects. It is therefore impossible to predict, based on these studies, what the employment effects would be in a fully covered economy. Additionally, the "what would have happened otherwise" case is obscured by general growth in public sector employment over this period. However, economic analyses that attempt to control for the underlying growth in employment generally do find that employment growth is slowed slightly by the implementation of comparable worth policies. The existence of these unemployment effects in Minnesota and in Australia reminds us that female earnings gains are not costless, either to women as a whole or to economies.

The need for policies to correct discrimination

Where does this discussion of comparable worth lead? If differences in wages between men and women are due to differing productivities or tastes, then no interference in labor market operation is required. Rather, if we wish to see improvement in women's incomes without direct subsidy, it should be undertaken by either improving their productivity or changing their tastes. Almost all members of society would agree, however, that if differences are due to sex discrimination, coming about either through crowding or through systematic underpaying of women made easier by segregating them (so as to get around antidiscrimination laws), these differences should be eradicated. In this case, action needs to be taken.

Alternatives to comparable worth

Comparable worth policies need not be considered in a vacuum. As discussed in previous chapters, there are alternative policies that could lead to higher wages for women, reduced job segregation, and higher wages in presently female-dominated occupations – three goals often mentioned in discussions of comparable worth policies. Two alternatives are increased enforcement of antidiscrimination laws and more active affirmative action. Some economists argue that the appropriate response to discrimination is to attack barriers to entry for certain occupations, since they are the source of economic inefficiency, rather than raise wages in the free-entry occupation.[51] Therefore any policy that attempts to lower entry barriers directly is preferable in their view to comparable worth. Comparable worth proponents argue that these methods have been tried and have not worked, so it is time to try a more radical approach.

However, beefing up existing types of policies does not exhaust our list of alternatives. Another possibility is direct income transfers from men to some or all women.[52] Another novel possibility is to give firms that raise pay for disadvantaged occupations special tax incentives or tax credits for capital equipment that will raise the productivity of these workers.[53]

Finally, let us consider two extensions of the basic goal that a comparable worth policy is expected to attain – namely, that of raising women's pay relative to men's. We may care more about certain groups of women and wish to target them directly. One policy goal is to recompense older women who are victims of past discrimination and who lack the ability to change jobs. Then any policy that raises their income will be useful in achieving this goal. If we rule out both retraining subsidies and direct income transfers, the remaining choice is to change their wages. If female wages are low due to crowding, then any policy that alleviates crowding will be helpful. But a comparable worth policy does not alleviate crowding, although it does raise wages. However, vigorous enforcement of antidiscrimination statutes and affirmative action hiring will channel younger women into less populous, male-dominated occupations, thereby lowering the supply of labor to the female-dominated crowded occupations and raising the wages over what they would otherwise be. Removal of barriers to entry thus appears to be the better policy.

Another goal is to raise the income levels of women and their families, especially if those women are family heads raising children. Certainly poverty, especially among female-headed households with dependents, is a pressing issue. Under comparable worth policies, some families and individuals are hurt and some are helped. It is hard to see why this is a better policy for alleviating low incomes than direct income transfers to poor people or better access to higher-paying jobs in male-dominated fields.

*E*ndnotes

1. Mark Aldrich and Robert Buchele, *The Economics of Comparable Worth* (Cambridge, Mass. Ballinger, 1986): 24.
2. Elaine Johansen, *Comparable Worth: The Myth and the Movement* (Boulder, Colo.: Westview, 1984): 43.
3. However, cases have since been brought under the Equal Pay Act that argue for its applicability in such situations, as discussed in Walter Fogel, *The Equal Pay Act: Implications for Comparable Worth* (New York: Praeger, 1984).
4. Ronald G. Ehrenberg and Robert S. Smith, "Comparable Worth in the Public Sector," *Public Sector Payrolls*, ed. David A. Wise (Cambridge, Mass.: National Bureau of Economic Research, 1987): 244.
5. Nancy Barrett, "Poverty, Welfare, and Comparable Worth," *Equal Pay for UNequal Work*, ed. Phyllis Schlafly (Washington, D.C.: Eagle Forum Education and Legal Defense Fund, 1984): 32.
6. Henry J. Aaron and Cameran M. Lougy, *The Comparable Worth Controversy* (Washington, D.C.: Brookings, 1986): 4.
7. June O'Neill, "The Comparable Worth Trap," *Wall Street Journal* (January 20, 1984); reprinted in *Equal Pay for UNequal Work*, ed. Phyllis Schlafly (Washington, D.C.: Eagle Forum Education and Legal Defense Fund, 1984): 263–266. See the Focus in Chapter 1 for discussion of this paradox.
8. John Raisian, Michael P. Ward, and Finis Welch, "Pay Equity and Comparable Worth," *Contemporary Policy Issues* 4, no. 2 (April 1986): 8.

9. Donald Treiman, *Job Evaluation: An Analytic Review* (Washington, D.C.: National Academy of Science, 1979), is a general discussion of the problems involved in job evaluation, rating, and classification. Eliot R. Hammer, *Pay Inequity: A Guide to Research on Social Influences* (New York: Garland, 1986), is another comprehensive work on job evaluation systems. For a discussion of gender bias in the evaluation process, see Leslie Zebrowitz McArthur, "Social Judgment Biases in Comparable Worth Analysis," *Comparable Worth: New Directions for Research*, ed. Heidi I. Hartmann (Washington, D.C.: National Research Council, 1985): 53–70; for specific discussion of gender bias in the widely-used Hay system see Ronnie J. Steinberg, "Gendered Instructions: Cultural Lag and Gender Bias in the Hay System of Job Evaluation," *Work and Occupations* 19, no. 4 (November 1992): 387–423. For a discussion of the lack of agreement among evaluators as to job ratings, see Donald J. Schwab, "Job Evaluation Research and Research Needs," *Comparable Worth: New Directions for Research*, ed. Heidi I. Hartmann (Washington, D.C.: National Research Council, 1985): 37–52. For a discussion of the arguments among evaluators over which job factors should be compensated, see Danielle P. Jaussad, "Can Job Evaluation Systems Help Determine the Comparable Worth of Male and Female Occupations?" *Journal of Economic Issues* 18, no. 2 (June 1984): 473–482.

10. Doris M. Werwie, *Sex and Pay in the Federal Government: Using Job Evaluation Systems to Implement Comparable Worth* (New York: Greenwood, 1987).

11. Elaine Sorensen, "Equal Pay for Comparable Worth: A Policy for Eliminating the Undervaluation of Women's Work," *Journal of Economic Issues* 18, no. 2 (June 1984): 465–472.

12. Richard E. Burr, "Are Comparable Worth Systems Truly Comparable?" Center for the Study of American Business Formal Publication no. 75 (St. Louis, Mo.: July 1986).

13. Ronnie Steinberg and Lois Haignere, "Separate but Equivalent: Equal Pay for Work of Comparable Worth," *Gender at Work: Perspectives on Occupational Segregation and Comparable Worth*, ed. Barbara Reskin (Washington, D.C.: Women's Research and Education Institute of Congressional Concerns on Women's Issues, 1984): 24–26.

14. Aldrich and Buchele, *op. cit.*, Chapter 4, offer a thorough discussion of the policy-capturing method, advocating the use of the percentage female in the job as the basis for the femaleness correction factor. One alternative correction method is to run the wage equation using only men (if possible, given that many jobs may contain no men).

15. Steinberg and Haignere, *op. cit.*: 25.

16. Mark R. Killingsworth, "Economic Analysis of Comparable Worth and its Consequences," *Proceedings of the Thirty-Sixth Annual Meeting*, ed. Barbara Dennes (Madison, Wis.: Industrial Relations Research Association, 1985): 189.

17. Mark R. Killingsworth, "Heterogeneous Preferences, Compensating Wage Differentials, and Comparable Worth," *Quarterly Journal of Economics* 102, no. 4 (November 1987): 727–741.

18. Denise K. Magner, "Increases in Faculty Salaries Fail to Keep Pace With Inflation," *Chronicle of Higher Education* 43, no. 43 (July 3, 1997): A9. Data are from a survey conducted annually by the American Association of University Professors.

19. According to the American Association of University Professors survey, independent private institutions pay more at all rank levels than do public institutions, while private church-related institutions pay less.

20. The case in which the federal government becomes the covered sector is discussed in Ehrenberg and Smith, *op. cit.* Perry C. Beider, B. Douglas Bernheim, Victor R. Fuchs, and John B. Shoven, "Comparable Worth in a General Equilibrium Model of the U.S. Economy," *Research in Labor Economics* 9 (Greenwich, Conn. JAI, 1988): 1–52, consider the case in which part of the private sector converts along with the government.

21. Beider *et al.*, *loc. cit.*

22. Sharon Bernstein Megdal, "Comparable Worth: Some Issues for Consideration," *Contemporary Policy Issues* 4, no. 2 (April 1986): 40–51.

23. George Johnson and Gary Solon, "Estimates of the Direct Effects of Comparable Worth Policy," *American Economic Review* 76, no. 5 (December 1986): 1117–1125.

24. For a survey of such studies, see Ronald G. Ehrenberg, "Empirical Consequences of Comparable Worth," *Comparable Worth: Analyses and Evidence*, eds. M. Anne Hill and Mark R. Killingsworth (Ithaca, N.Y.: ILR, 1989): 90–106.

25. Elaine Sorensen, "Implementing Comparable Worth: A Survey of Recent Job Evaluation Studies," *American Economic Review* 76, no. 2 (May 1986): 364–367.

26. Morley Gunderson, *Comparable Worth and Gender Discrimination: An International Perspective* (Geneva: International Labour Office, 1994): 79.

27. Johnson and Solon, *loc. cit.*

28. Deborah M. Figart and June Lapidus, "A Gender Analysis of U.S. Labor Market Policies for the Working Poor," *Feminist Economics* 1, no. 3 (Fall 1995): 60–81.

29. Beider *et al.*, *loc. cit.*

30. Robert S. Smith, "Comparable Worth: Limited Coverage and the Exacerbation of Inequality," *Industrial and Labor Relations Review* 41, no. 2 (January 1988): 227–239, using data from the May 1979 Current Population Survey.

31. Beider *et al.*, *loc. cit.*

32. For a discussion of how to interpret job characteristics and wage data derived from the public sector, see Jerry A. Jacobs and Ronnie J. Steinberg, "Compensating Differentials and the Male-Female Wage Gap: Evidence from the New York State Comparable Worth Study," *Social Forces* 69, no. 2 (December 1990): 439–468, and the comment directly following their article by Randall K. Filer, "Compensating Differentials and the Male-Female Wage Gap: A Comment," *Social Forces* 69, no. 2 (December 1990): 469–473.

33. Frances C. Huttner, *Equal Pay for Comparable Worth: The Working Woman's Issue of the Eighties* (New York: Praeger, 1986).

34. Mark Killingsworth, *The Economics of Comparable Worth* (Kalamazoo, Mich.: W.E. Upjohn Institute, 1990): 212–213.

35. Shulamit Kahn, "The Economic Implications of Public-Sector Comparable Worth: The Case of San Jose, California," *Industrial Relations* 31, no. 2 (Spring 1992): 270–291.

36. Elaine Sorensen, *Comparable Worth: Is It a Worthy Policy?* (Princeton, N.J.: Princeton University, 1994): 87.

37. For a thorough discussion of the Minnesota implementation at the state and local levels, see Sarah M. Evans and Barbara J. Nelson, *Wage Justice: Comparable Worth and the Paradox of Technocratic Reform* (Chicago, Ill.: University of Chicago, 1989). Killingsworth (1990), Sorensen (1994), and Rhoads (1993) devote sections to the Minnesota case, with some contrasting interpretations.

38. For a discussion of the implementation of comparable worth by the Iowa State government, see Peter F. Orazem and J. Peter Mattila, "The Implementation Process of Comparable Worth: Winners and Losers," *Journal of Political Economy* 98, no. 1 (February 1990): 134–152, or "Comparable Worth and the Structure of Earnings: The Iowa Case," *Pay Equity: Empirical Inquiries*, eds. Robert T. Michael, Heidi I. Hartmann, and Brigid O'Farrell (Washington, D.C.: National Academy, 1989): 179–199.

39. Joan Acker, *Doing Comparable Worth: Gender, Class, and Pay Equity* (Philadelphia, Penn.: Temple University, 1989).

40. June O'Neill, Michael Brien, and James Cunningham, "Effects of Comparable Worth Policy: Evidence from Washington State," *American Economic Review* 79, no. 2 (May 1989): 305–309.

41. Sarah M. Evans and Barbara J. Nelson, "The Impact of Pay Equity on Public Employees: State of Minnesota Employees' Attitudes Toward Wage Policy Innovation," *Pay Equity: Empirical Inquiries*, eds. Robert T. Michael, Heidi I. Hartmann, and Brigid O'Farrell (Washington, D.C.: National Academy, 1989): 200–221.

42. Killingsworth (1990): 135.

43. Orazem and Mattila (1989): 197; Acker (1989): 26.

44. Gunderson, *op. cit.*: 61.

45. Marjorie L. Baldwin, "Pay Equity in Ontario: Is It Closing the Wage Gap?" mimeo (February 1994).
46. See R.G. Gregory and V. Ho, "Equal Pay and Comparable Worth: What Can the U.S. Learn from the Australian Experience?" Australian National University, Centre for Economic Policy Research, Discussion Paper no. 123 (July 1985); Robert G. Gregory and Ronald C. Duncan, "The Relevance of Segmented Labor Market Theories: The Australian Experience of the Achievement of Equal Pay for Women," *Journal of Post-Keynesian Economics* 3, no. 3 (Spring 1981): 403–428; and Killingsworth (1990).
47. Killingsworth (1990): 238.
48. Killingsworth (1990): 260.
49. Gregory and Duncan, *op. cit.*: 420–421.
50. Killingsworth (1990): 263.
51. Daniel Fischel and Edward Lazear, "Comparable Worth and Discrimination in Labor Markets," *University of Chicago Law Review* 53, no. 3 (Summer 1986): 903–904.
52. Fischel and Lazear, *op. cit.*: 909–910.
53. Barrett, *loc. cit.*

Further reading

Aaron, Henry J., and Cameran M. Lougy (1986). *The Comparable Worth Controversy*. Washington, D.C.: Brookings. Short, readable layout of the views of proponents and opponents of comparable worth; writers come down on the opposing side.

Aldrich, Mark, and Robert Buchele (1986). *The Economics of Comparable Worth*. Cambridge, Mass.: Ballinger. Longer work, laying out the basic issues and advocating a policy-capturing approach to implementation of comparable worth.

England, Paula (1992). *Comparable Worth: Theories and Evidence*. New York: Aldine de Gruyter. Comprehensive work, providing thorough overview of topic, particularly of various theoretical approaches to comparable worth.

Gunderson, Morley (1994). *Comparable Worth and Gender Discrimination: An International Perspective*. Geneva: International Labour Office. Another useful primer on the topic.

Hartmann, Heidi I. (ed.) (1985). *Comparable Worth: New Directions for Research*. Washington, D.C.: National Research Council. Collection of essays, including discussion of relationship of compensating differentials to comparable worth and discussion of job evaluation methods.

Hill, M. Anne, and Mark R. Killingsworth (eds.) (1989). *Comparable Worth: Analyses and Evidence*. Ithaca, N.Y.: ILR. Collection of essays, including explanation of why economics cannot be used to justify comparable worth, and discussion of probable effects of implementing comparable worth.

Killingsworth, Mark R. (1990). *The Economics of Comparable Worth*. Kalamazoo, Mich.: W.E. Upjohn. Scholarly work laying out economic critiques of comparable work and attempting to evaluate the effects of comparable worth policies in several implementations, including Minnesota, Australia, and San Jose.

Michael, Robert T., Heidi I. Hartmann, and Brigid O'Farrell (eds.) (1989). *Pay Equity: Empirical Inquiries*. Washington, D.C.: National Academy. Collection of scholarly papers on various facets of comparable worth and evidence of pay inequities.

Paul, Ellen Frankel (1989). *Equity and Gender: The Comparable Worth Debate*. New Brunswick, N.J.: Transaction Publishers. Clear, concise introduction to the issue of comparable worth by a political scientist, laying out the issues and explaining why the author is against implementation of comparable worth policies. Also provides a history of comparable worth legislation up to the publication year.

Rhoads, Steven E. (1993). *Incomparable Worth: Pay Equity Meets the Market*. Cambridge, United Kingdom: Cambridge University. Discusses Minnesota, Australia, and equal pay legislation in the United Kingdom and European Community generally.

Roback, Jennifer (1986). *A Matter of Choice: A Critique of Comparable Worth by a Skeptical Feminist.* New York: 20th Century Fund. Short book; lays out the basic arguments against comparable worth by an economist with feminist sympathies.

Sorensen, Elaine (1994). *Comparable Worth: Is It a Worthy Policy?* Princeton, N.J.: Princeton University. Thoughtful study critiquing results in the empirical literature from the 1980s, including Killingsworth's results for Minnesota.

Wilborn, Steven L. (1986). *A Comparable Worth Primer.* Lexington, Mass.: Lexington Books. Another competent introduction to the topic of comparable worth.

——. (1989). *A Secretary and a Cook: Challenging Women's Wages in the Courts of the United States and Great Britain.* Ithaca, N.Y.: ILR. Illustrates concepts underlying comparable worth through a discussion of two actual court cases.

Discussion questions

1. Consider an employer who runs a translation firm. He has only two types of employees: French-English translators and Spanish-English translators. If the French translators, who are predominantly male, are better paid than the Spanish translators, who are predominantly female, is that convincing evidence of discrimination? If not, what could cause this difference?

2. Do the four "compensable factors" used in Table IIIP.1 correspond to human capital and/or compensating differential concepts? Is the method used in Table IIIP.1 a valid way to compare jobs? Is it a valid way to determine pay?

3. Consider the estimates in Table IIIP.2 regarding estimated costs and effects on the gender earnings gap of comparable worth policies. Do these amounts seem large or small to you? Would you consider the costs an appropriate price to pay to reduce the earnings gap? Are payroll costs the appropriate way to measure the costs of the policies?

4. Consider the Focus on comparable worth for professors. Do you think that there are large differences in quality between departments at your school? If yes, what do you think causes them? Are there large differences in pay between departments at your school? If yes, what do you think causes them?

5. If the entire public sector implemented comparable worth, how do you think that would affect the private sector?

6. Consider the following comparable worth plan:
   - all firms with 100 or more employees must set up a job valuation system, consisting of an index by which all the jobs in the firm will be ranked. Factors to be considered in assigning points must include the four points included in Table IIIP.1. Other factors may also be included, so long as they do not make direct reference to gender, race, ethnicity, religion, or age. Firms may develop their own weighting schemes in creating an overall index incorporating these various factors (e.g., Table IIIP.1 weights points associated with each factor equally).
   - jobs that have equal index values must pay the same wage rate; however, no employee's wage can be reduced in order to achieve this goal. The number of years an employee has been doing a job is still allowed to affect pay, but the system linking seniority to pay must be the same across jobs with equal index values.

   Consider the potential benefits and costs of this plan to society. Consider also how firms and individuals would react to implementation of this policy in both the short run and the long run. Would you vote for or against it? What types of amendments might you want to make, if any?

Cross-Societal Comparisons: Are Gender Differences the Same Everywhere?

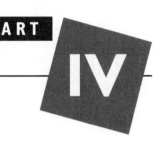

*T*his part attempts to answer the compelling question: are gender differences the same everywhere? So far this book has essentially been a lengthy case study of post-World War II U.S. society. Now we consider to what extent the conclusions generated from studying the United States are generalizable, and what additional lessons can be learned from studying other societies.

Chapters 10 through 13 provide a framework for addressing these questions. Chapters 10 through 12 take up, in turn, three sets of societies, grouped roughly by the level and nature of their economic and social development. Chapter 10 considers those countries most similar to the United States in terms of level of economic development. Similarities and differences in gender-related work patterns are considered, and social policies are contrasted across these countries. Chapter 11 considers various examples of socialist and cooperative societies, some of which comprise an entire country and some of which comprise subsets within a country (e.g., Israeli kibbutzim). The tension between state-imposed gender equality norms and ongoing gender differences is outlined and discussed. Chapter 12 considers nonindustrialized societies that have tended to remain traditional in social structure. Patterns across broad geographic groups are contrasted, and the relationship between gender inequality and type of economic organization is discussed.

Chapter 13 addresses the question of how social and economic development processes affect gender differences within developing societies. The related questions of whether or not development leads to greater or lesser gender equality and how different approaches to development may increase or reduce gender inequality are also considered.

Industrialized Capitalist Societies

*I*n comparing gender differences across societies, a natural place to start a comparison with the detailed U.S. experience presented so far is countries that have attained a similar level of economic and social development and have roughly similar political structures. This chapter first provides summary evidence on employment and earnings patterns for this group of countries; then, examples of recent changes in particular countries are presented. The chapter concludes with a survey of relevant social policies across these countries.

Overview of levels and trends in these countries

What group of societies are generally regarded as being the most developed? In this chapter *society* is taken as being essentially synonymous with *country*, although there are social groups within each country that may differ greatly from the majority of the population in terms of various social and economic indicators (e.g., indigenous peoples in the United States and Canada tend to have much lower measures on the various development indicators mentioned below). For the purposes of this chapter, the comparison group of 25 countries (often referred to as the advanced industrialized countries) is taken as the 29 members (as of 1997) of the Organisation for Economic Cooperation and Development (OECD), excluding the Czech Republic, Hungary, Mexico, Poland, and Turkey, and adding Israel. This grouping is partly data-driven, as these countries have roughly comparable data collection and presentation methods and are basically the same group as those that rank highest on the United Nations' human development index; Israel's high ranking on this scale (number 24) leads to its inclusion, and the other OECD countries' lower rankings (ranging from number 37 for the Czech Republic to number 84 for Turkey) lead to their exclusion.[1] This group of countries is characterized as of 1994 by high gross national product (GNP) per capita (with a cross-country mean of $21,000), high rates of primary and secondary education for both sexes, high life expectancy at birth (77 years), low infant mortality rates (7 per 1000 live births), a highly urbanized population (75 percent), and low fertility rates (1.7 total live births per woman).[2] Whenever data are available for this group of countries, comparisons will be drawn in the following section between their employment

TABLE 10.1 Labor force participation rates by sex and proportion of labor force that is female

	% Labor force/population		
Country	Women	Men	Women/labor force
Iceland	80.6	89.5	0.47
Sweden	74.4	78.1	0.48
Denmark	73.8	84.2	0.45
Norway	71.1	82.2	0.46
United States	70.5	85.3	0.46
Finland	69.9	77.1	0.47
Canada	67.8	82.6	0.45
Switzerland	67.5	97.5	0.39
United Kingdom	66.2	84.0	0.44
New Zealand	64.9	83.9	0.44
Australia	63.4	85.2	0.43
Austria	62.1	81.0	0.43
Japan	62.1	90.6	0.41
Portugal	62.0	80.8	0.45
Germany	61.8	80.8	0.43
France	59.6	74.4	0.45
Netherlands	57.4	79.1	0.42
Luxembourg	56.5	97.2	0.36
Belgium	55.1	72.4	0.42
South Korea	52.7	76.4	0.40
Israel	51.6	69.0	0.43
Ireland	47.2	78.5	0.38
Greece	44.6	74.6	0.38
Spain	44.1	74.0	0.38
Italy	42.9	73.9	0.37

Sources: Labor force participation rates – OECD, *Labour Force Statistics 1974–94*, Part 2 (Country Tables). Data are from 1994 for persons ages 15 to 64. Women as percentage of economically active population and all data for Israel – ILO, *Yearbook of Labour Statistics* (1992–1996) (Table 1). Data are from 1994 or 1995 for persons ages 15 to 64 except Norway, Sweden, Spain, and the United States (16 to 64); South Korea (15 to 59); Denmark (1996); United Kingdom (1993); Belgium (1992); Luxembourg (1991); and Switzerland (1990).

and earnings patterns, including labor force participation rates, part-time rates, gender earnings ratios, and unionism rates.

Labor force participation

Table 10.1 displays labor force participation rates, along with the percentage of the "economically active" population that is female, for countries where data are available. Countries are listed in decreasing order of female labor force participation rate. These data generally refer only to the middle-age range of the population (generally, ages 15 to 64). The term "economically active" used by the International Labour Office (ILO) is a broader term than "labor force," reflecting differences in labor force definitions and data collection

TABLE 10.2 Percentage of employment that is part-time by sex

Country	Women	Men
Netherlands	66.1	16.1
Switzerland	52.2	8.3
Iceland	47.4	11.0
Norway	45.7	10.1
United Kingdom	42.7	5.6
Australia	42.6	11.7
Sweden	39.0	9.3
New Zealand	37.3	10.4
Japan	36.0	11.5
Denmark	34.5	10.8
Germany	33.8	3.6
Belgium	30.5	3.0
France	29.5	5.3
Canada	28.9	10.7
Austria	28.8	4.2
United States	26.9	10.9
Ireland	22.1	5.0
Luxembourg	18.4	1.7
Spain	17.0	3.1
Portugal	13.0	5.1
Italy	12.7	3.1
Finland	10.9	5.3
Greece	8.4	2.8

Source: OECD, *Employment Outlook* (July 1997): 177 (Table E). Data are from 1996 except Germany and Greece (1995).

across countries. The cross-country mean ratio of economically active women to total economically active is 0.43. The 1994 cross-country mean labor force participation rates are 81.3 percent for men and 61.2 percent for women. These rates have followed a general trend of dropping rates for men and rising rates for women: the 1969 cross-country means were 90.6 percent for men and 44.8 percent for women. The correlation coefficient over time between the male and female rates has risen sharply from essentially no correlation in 1969 (0.03) to a positive correlation in 1994 of 0.51, so countries with a high rate of male labor force participation generally also have a high rate of female labor force participation.[3] The correlation between 1969 and 1994 rates by sex is 0.46 for men and 0.81 for women, showing that countries with high participation rates in 1969 were more likely to have high rates in 1994.

Table 10.2 compares part-time rates by sex across countries, with countries listed by decreasing value of female part-time rate. There is a wide variation in part-time rates around the cross-country means of 31.5 percent for women and 7.3 percent for men, and a strong correlation of 0.74 between the male and female part-time rates. However, in all countries, the part-time rate for women is significantly higher than the rate for men, indicating that hours-worked percentages would be more heavily male than the proportion of the labor force that is male.[4] Finally, countries with high labor force participation rates for women also tend to have high part-time rates for women, with a correlation of 0.50. (The same pattern holds for men, with a correlation of 0.31.)

Turning to additional cross-country comparisons of employment patterns, women and men in Western Europe appear to display similar gender patterns of attitudes towards work schedules as do U.S. respondents. A 1983 survey of European Community members found that among persons employed full-time, 11 percent of the men and 22 percent of the women would prefer to hold part-time jobs for less money; among persons employed part-time, 40 percent of the men and 18 percent of the women would prefer full-time employment. However, motivation levels for work were similar for men and women: 63 percent of men and 60 percent of women responded that they would continue to work even if they had enough money to live in whatever style they liked.[5]

In some employment-related areas, the United States remains an outlier. For instance, the number of businesses created by women is growing in nearly all developed countries, often at a rate greater than for men, but the greatest increase has occurred in the United States. Women average 25 percent of self-employed persons, with the highest percentages in the United States and Canada.[6]

Convergence in rates of economic activity and female participation appears to be occurring in developed countries, with similar relationships appearing between social and demographic factors.[7] Women's participation rates rose mainly due to the growth of participation among married women. Common declines in fertility and rises in divorce in the 1970s appear to be related to these labor force growth rates, with the usual concerns about causal direction.[8] A notable exception is Ireland, where from 1961 to 1981, Irish female labor force participation rates remained low even as significant structural shifts occurred. (Employment shifted out of agriculture into industry, and services as Ireland followed an export-led development strategy.) One analyst attributes this variance to blatant sex discrimination by the state.[9]

While unemployment rates are hard to compare across countries because there is no standard definition of unemployment, one can compare nonemployment rates, since the definition of employment displays less variation. These rates appear to be rising for men and dropping for women across OECD countries – the same pattern as seen in the United States.[10] Again, the underlying relationships of structural changes in developed economies – the shift from manufacturing to services – and the availability of nonearned income for men in the form of rising earnings of women, appear to explain the commonness of this pattern across these countries.

These labor market trends will become even easier to follow in the future. As data collection and definitions become increasingly standardized (often, as part of multi-country economic arrangements), data are becoming available on a more regular and consistent basis. For instance, each European Community member state is supposed to conduct an annual survey of its labor force and send the data file to the Statistical Office of the European Community.[11] The area of cross-country comparisons will become more and more important as a subfield within the economics of gender in following years.

Occupational segregation

Data limitations become more severe in the comparison of segregation patterns across countries. Strictly comparable data on occupational distribution by sex are generally available

TABLE 10.3 Occupational sex segregation indexes using seven occupational categories

Country	Index	Country	Index
Austria	45	Germany	38
Luxembourg	45	Canada	37
Ireland	44	New Zealand	37
Finland	43	United Kingdom	37
Denmark	42	Netherlands	36
Norway	42	Switzerland	35
Israel	41	United States	34
Australia	41	Greece	25
Spain	40	Japan	23
Sweden	39	South Korea	22
Belgium	38	Portugal	21
France	38		

Source: ILO, *Yearbook of Labour Statistics* (1992–1996) (Table 2B). Data are from 1993 or 1994, except Greece (1992), Germany, Ireland and Luxembourg (1991), France (1982), and Belgium (1981).

only for a very aggregated set of occupational categories. Table 10.3 displays sex segregation index calculations using seven broad categories.[12] Countries are listed in order of decreasing index value, where lower values imply less sex segregation.

The occupational sex segregation level, even at this very aggregated level of data, is substantial in most of these countries, but it is actually higher in Western Europe, as well as in other English-speaking countries, than in the United States. Why is segregation so low in Greece, Japan, South Korea, and Portugal? Some analysts have speculated that a stronger tradition of participation in physical work on farms for women in these countries leads to their high representation in both farm and manufacturing sectors (production workers).[13]

While there have been case studies that attempt to ascertain the extent of sex segregation within firms,[14] index sensitivity to level of aggregation and sex segregation trends have not been as highly scrutinized for other countries as for the United States. However, the basic patterns of sex segregation appear to be quite similar across developed countries.

Earnings differentials

Table 10.4 displays gender earnings ratios by country, with countries listed in order of decreasing earnings ratio value. For countries with available data, the cross-country mean nonagricultural earnings ratio is 0.73; the manufacturing earnings ratio mean is 0.76. Japan has the lowest ratios for both nonagricultural and manufacturing earnings (0.51 and 0.44); Australia has the highest nonagricultural ratio, Sweden the highest ratio in manufacturing.

It is notable that half of these countries display higher ratios than does the United States, even though occupational sex segregation is higher in many of these countries. In fact, the correlation between the segregation index and the gender earnings ratio is substantial and positive (0.60)! This raises the question of whether it is necessary to reduce segregation in order to increase the gender earnings ratio.

TABLE 10.4 Nonagricultural hourly earnings ratios, women to men

Country	Women/men	Country	Women/men
Australia	0.90	United States	0.76
Sweden	0.90*	Belgium	0.75
Norway	0.87*	Germany	0.74
Denmark	0.83	Ireland	0.71*
Iceland	0.82	Luxembourg	0.71
France	0.81	United Kingdom	0.71
New Zealand	0.81	Portugal	0.68
Greece	0.80*	Switzerland	0.67
Netherlands	0.79	South Korea	0.57
Finland	0.78*	Japan	0.51

* For manufacturing only.
Sources: all countries except United States – ILO, *Yearbook of Labour Statistics* (1992–1996) (Table 16). Data are from 1993 or 1994, except Denmark and Japan (1991). Germany refers to the former GDR (West Germany). United States – 1994 median weekly earnings for year-round full-time workers, *Employment and Earnings* 42, no. 1 (January 1995): 207 (Table 37).

How have these ratios changed over time? In general, they reached their relatively high levels (relative to the United States, that is) only recently, after being at similar or lower levels than the U.S. ratio through the early 1970s. However, as we will see below in the examples of Australia and the United Kingdom, responses to equal pay initiatives in the 1970s appear to have been much stronger in these countries than the United States experienced from its equal pay legislation.

One factor in many of these countries that is very different from the U.S. experience is the strength of organized labor.[15] Indeed, the experiences in some of these countries provide evidence to support the idea that women do better in general, across-the-board bargaining situations than in individualized wage-setting situations. Table 10.5 shows unionism rates by sex and proportion of female union members, with countries listed by decreasing female union membership rate. The Scandinavian countries stand out as having very high unionism rates, as well as high rates of female representation among union members. Overall the correlation between high female unionism (measured by the first column in Table 10.5) and the gender earnings ratio is 0.47 (0.45 using the third column in Table 10.5).

Case studies can shed additional light on the significance of bargaining structures in determining the gender earnings ratio. For instance, a study of the gender wage gap in Swedish banks found that the difference increased in 1983 after declining prior to 1983 – the author attributed this change to increased discretionary wage decisions by management.[16]

However, examples from the recent past, where collective bargaining has led to institutionalized sex discrimination, are not hard to find. Prior to the mid–1970s, explicit sex-based wage differentials were commonly found in collective agreements in Denmark, Ireland, New Zealand, and Australia.[17] In Ireland, wage differentials based on marital status were also common, and a woman was often required to resign her job upon marriage.[18] The existence of widespread collective bargaining does not automatically lead to favorable outcomes for women.

TABLE 10.5 Union membership rates by sex and proportion of union membership that is female

Country	Union members		Women/Unions
	Women	Men	
Sweden	88.3	82.4	0.50
Finland	74.9	68.6	0.51
Denmark	71.6	78.0	0.46
Ireland	47.3	59.9	0.32
Australia	41.5*	53.2*	0.35
Austria	36.7	56.8	0.31
United Kingdom	33.3	44.0	0.38
Canada	30.2	39.4	0.37
West Germany	21.6	46.7	0.25
Japan	18.9	29.9	0.28
Netherlands	13.0	35.2	0.18
Switzerland	12.7	34.2	0.19
United States	12.6	19.7	0.36
France	7.0	13.0	0.30

* Average of estimates from membership records and household survey.
Source: OECD, *Employment Outlook* (1991): 116 (Table 4.8). Data are from 1985, 1986, 1987, 1988, or 1989 except Ireland, which are from 1981.

FOCUS

Institutionalized pay discrimination in New Zealand

In New Zealand, as in Australia, wages are mainly set on a national level through national negotiation between unions and employers.[19] This situation was not particularly beneficial for women, as it formally perpetuated lower women's wages for the same work that men were performing. This formal system began with the Arbitration Court's 1903 Christchurch Tailoring Trades Awards, which prescribed a female rate at about 50 percent of the male rate. This prescription received statutory sanction in the 1936 Industrial Conciliation and Arbitration Amendment Act, which specified that the Arbitration Court should fix the male basic wage rate at a sufficient level to enable a man to support a family of five in a reasonable standard of comfort. In 1954, this statute was revised to omit the family support criterion, but the custom of setting sex-based wage rates continued.

Shortly after World War II, the Arbitration Court raised the women's rate to 70 percent of the male rate, mirroring changes in Australia. However, unlike the situation in Australia, the New Zealand Arbitration Court continued to resist abolishing the sex-based wage differential "on the grounds that such an important social and economic issue was a matter for Parliament, a matter which was not considered by Parliament until 1972."[20]

What caused the movement towards equal pay and also, in some countries, towards equal opportunity? The United States and the United Kingdom were influential through their examples in determining the shape that laws in various countries took. Additionally, two supranational instruments have greatly influenced the debate over equal pay. ILO Convention No. 100, drafted in 1951, states that signatory nations shall "ensure the application to all workers of the principle of equal remuneration for men and women workers for work of equal value."[21] Then, in 1957, six nations in Western Europe signed the Treaty of Rome, establishing the European Economic Community (EC). Article 119 of the Treaty of Rome sets out the EC's equal pay guarantee, stating that: "Each Member State shall during the first stage ensure and subsequently maintain the application of the principle that men and women should receive equal pay for equal work."[22] However, various deadlines for the implementation of Article 119 were missed and, throughout the 1960s, successive reports of the European Commission on the progress of the member states' implementation of the equal pay guarantee indicated that very little progress had been made.[23]

Table 10.6 shows when various developed countries joined the group of countries having an equal pay act in effect. Notes in the table indicate where formal legislative action was preceded by collective agreement actions that embodied equal pay. The United States, along with Ontario, is a clear front-runner in this table, while Japan is a notable laggard. European countries tend to cluster in the mid- to late 1970s, due to pressure from the EC on member nations during this period to comply with Article 119.

Movement towards comparable worth laws has been slow, although collective bargaining agreements in some countries – notably, Australia – embody comparable worth principles. The Netherlands is the only European country that at one time had a national job evaluation system used to determine government pay policy. Although this is no longer the case, most firms in the Netherlands still use some job evaluation system when determining wages.[24]

Besides legislative initiatives and their effect in reducing discrimination, one would also (based on the human capital theory) expect that countries where women and men had relatively similar productivity-related characteristics would tend to have more equal pay. As a very rough measure of this tendency, Table 10.7 displays data on percentage female rates among persons receiving bachelor and graduate degrees by country. There is a very strong correlation of 0.85 between percentage female among bachelor degree recipients and the gender earnings ratio, and also a strong correlation of 0.42 between percentage female among graduate degree recipients and the gender earnings ratio. While many of these countries have attained parity in bachelor degree recipiency, or have notably higher percentages than would indicate parity, women continue to receive a smaller share of graduate degrees. Japan is a notable outlier in having much lower rates for both bachelor and graduate degree attainment for women. The United States is notable for having the highest proportion of women among graduate degree recipients. It should be noted that college attendance rates are much lower in other developed countries than in the United States, so data for them reflect a smaller body of persons. Additionally, vocational training, which is more common in other countries, may continue to lead to high levels of sex segregation by tracking young persons into occupations considered sex-appropriate.

Studies have been performed for other countries, similar to those using U.S. data, that attempt to ascertain how much of the gender earnings gap is attributable to differences in human capital and whether changes in the gap over time are attributable to decreased discrimination or relative increases in women's human capital. For instance, a study using Danish

TABLE 10.6 First full year an equal pay act was in effect, selected countries

Country	Year	Notes
Canada		Legislation relating to labor relations and civil rights under provincial jurisdiction; 1956 federal statute for covered employees.
Ontario	1951	First province to enact equal pay statute.
Quebec	1976	Last province to enact equal pay statute.
United States	1964	
France	1974	1946 constitution guarantees equality; 1950 law covering collective agreements.
Australia	1975	National wage-setting agreements; 1972 ruling by national commission to take full effect by 1975.
Luxembourg	1975	1965 law covering collective agreements.
Belgium	1976	1975 national collective agreement.
Netherlands	1976	
Ireland	1976	
United Kingdom	1976	Enacted 1970 to take effect by 1976.
Denmark	1977	1973 national collective agreement.
Italy	1978	
New Zealand	1979	Equal pay implemented in public sector by 1965; national statute enacted 1972 to take full effect by 1979.
Austria	1980	
Germany	1980	1949 constitution guarantees equality; interpreted to mean equal pay in 1955.
Sweden	1980	1960 widespread collective agreement to take full effect by 1965; 1979 act concerns equal access as well as pay.
Japan	1987	1947 labor standards law prohibited discrimination in pay; 1985 act concerns equal access as well as pay.

Sources: Janice Bellace, "A Foreign Perspective," *Comparable Worth: Issues and Alternatives, 2nd Edition*, ed. E. Robert Livernash (Washington, D.C.: Equal Employment Advisory Council, 1984): 139–172; Alice H. Cook, "International Comparisons: Problems and Research in the Industrialized World," *Working Women: Past, Present, Future*, eds. Karen Shallcross Koziara, Michael H. Moskow, and Lucretia Dewey Tanner (Washington, D.C.: Bureau of National Affairs, 1987): 346–349; Linda N. Edwards, "Equal Employment Opportunity in Japan: A View from the West," *Industrial and Labor Relations Review* 41, no. 2 (January 1988): 240.

data from 1976 to 1984 finds that the gap narrowed over this period due to improved productivity-related characteristics of women, but that men still received a higher return to such characteristics.[25] Wage structures for women and men appear to continue to differ in developed countries, as well as women's still having less human capital, but the relative contribution of these factors to the gap varies across countries. In an influential series of papers, economists Francine Blau and Lawrence Kahn have demonstrated that the contribution to the gender earnings gap of the wage structure, including the lack of decentralized wage-setting and the greater level of wage inequality, is greater in the United States than in the other countries.[26] They conclude that the U.S. gender earnings gap would be similar to that in Sweden and Australia, the countries with the smallest gaps, if the U.S. had their lower level of pay inequality.[27] Therefore, even though U.S. women's work qualifications are high relative to those of men, they fare worse relative to men than women in other countries.

TABLE 10.7   Percentage of bachelor's and graduate degrees awarded to women, 1988

Country	Bachelor's degree	Graduate (master's, doctorates, professional) degrees
Norway	64.5	33.6
Sweden	56.6	23.4
Canada	54.9	44.4
United States	52.6	48.0
Spain	52.5	25.9
Greece	52.3	32.4
Australia	50.5	32.3
Finland	49.0	31.5
Italy	47.4	34.5
New Zealand	46.7	35.9
United Kingdom	45.3	39.2
France	45.0	40.1
Austria	42.6	21.0
Ireland	42.6	32.3
Belgium	40.2	30.5
former West Germany	37.9	26.3
Switzerland	32.3	25.9
Japan	26.3	13.3

Source: U.S. National Center for Education Statistics, *Digest of Education Statistics* (1993): 421 (Table 397). Data for New Zealand and Spain are from 1987.

FOCUS

Swedish hiring quotas

In 1974, Sweden implemented a rule requiring that firms utilizing the national location assistance program, which includes loans, grants, and training subsidies, make available for each sex at least 40 percent of the total number of new positions in aided establishments. This approach to increasing female labor force participation is an alternative to the U.S. affirmative action program and, as such, has been studied to see if it has resulted in changes in total female employment and in sex segregation.[28] This program may be characterized as a net hire quota system, as compared with the U.S. new hire quota system.

Due partly to the limited scope of covered firms and the widespread use of exemptions, the program affected only a small portion of the labor market – approximately 0.05 percent of employment in 1983–84. However, it appears that the program is directly responsible for part of the rise in female employment since 1974. The impact can be judged by looking at how many firms in the program were right at the female quota level (assuming that these firms would have preferred to have hired fewer women). However, firms have no incentive under the program to increase female employment beyond 40 percent of new employment, so the effect of this program in further increasing female employment may diminish over time. Finally, since placing women in nontraditional jobs was not required for firms to be in compliance, the program appears to have had little effect on occupational segregation.

Examples from particular countries

Having surveyed some relevant data for advanced industrialized countries, we now turn to a more detailed discussion of recent trends in some of these countries. First, it is instructive to compare recent experiences in three culturally similar countries, the United States, the United Kingdom, and Australia, so the U.K. and Australian cases will be developed at greater length. Next, Japan provides an interesting example of a country that has a very high level of human development, but some low values of economic indicators for women. Finally, Sweden is an interesting and much-studied country because of its position at the forefront of changing social policy and the corresponding radical change in its socioeconomic variables over a short period of time.

The United Kingdom

The United Kingdom is the only country in the EC that passed an equal pay act before it was formally required to do so.[29] Although fewer cases than were expected have arisen, the United Kingdom has experienced by far the most equal-pay suits of any EC country,[30] which may indicate particularly egregious cases of discrimination or a greater willingness to report suspected discrimination.

In contrast to the U.S. experience, the U.K. equal pay legislation appears to have had a quick and notable effect on the gender earnings gap. Several studies of the U.K. experience have come to the conclusion that women's relative pay rose by about 15 percent as a result of this legislation, leading to a narrowing of the wage gap by between 30 and 50 percent.[31] The largest rise occurred in the year directly before the pay legislation took effect (there was a long gap between passage of the Equal Pay Act in 1970 and implementation of the legislation in December 1975); after passage, the earnings ratio actually dropped slightly before leveling off around 0.65 for full-time workers by the early 1980s. This strong positive relationship between equal pay legislation and women's pay increases is not found in any of the other countries in Europe. In general, in the rest of the EC the gender earnings ratio increased before equal pay legislation was enacted.[32] Relative pay increases do not appear to have occurred at the expense of increased unemployment among either sex.[33]

Passage of the Equal Pay Act has apparently not completely eradicated discrimination. A study using 1980 data calculates that women's pay would then have been about 20 percent higher in the absence of discrimination.[34] However, this is a much smaller difference than is found in earlier years. Another study has found that women's pay would have been about 51 percent higher in 1972 without discrimination; this difference had dropped to 32 percent by 1977.[35]

While the U.K. gender earnings ratio had risen and stayed above the U.S. ratio during the late 1970s and early 1980s, by the end of the 1980s the U.S. ratio had risen to surpass the U.K. ratio. This latter rise appears to be related to differences in female work patterns between the two countries. The United Kingdom has continued to display a low labor force participation rate for women with a young child: among women with a child under 5 years of age, only 9 percent work full-time, while 23 percent work part-time.[36] The female part-time rate, as shown in Table 10.2, is much higher in the United Kingdom.

Women have lower rates of representation in the higher-paying occupations.[37] Finally, life cycle work patterns differ: while women tend to enter the labor force at younger ages in the United Kingdom than in the United States, they are far more likely to experience a subsequent interruption in their workyears, and their interruptions are generally of longer duration.[38]

Australia

As in the other industrialized countries, Australian female labor force participation rates – for married women, in particular – have been rising rapidly. While only 6.5 percent of married women were in the labor force in 1947, by 1961 this figure had risen to 17 percent, by 1966 to 27 percent, by 1971 to 33 percent, and by 1987 to 49 percent.[39] A prominent element in explaining this rise appears to be rises in female wages.

In Australia, minimum wage rates are set nationally for many occupations and/or industries by state or federal wage tribunals. By 1975, the concept of "equal pay for work of equal value" had been fully implemented for this wage-setting process.[40] While many workers are paid wages above the minimum levels, apparently more women were at minimum levels than were men, and occupational sex segregation was high. The gender earnings ratio, which had been rising steadily anyway due in part to the gradual abolition of differential minimum wages by sex,[41] rose sharply in the mid-1970s, jumping by six points from 1973 to 1975.

As in the case of the United Kingdom, this is not to say that pay discrimination is not still widespread in Australia today. Two recent studies, both of which use advanced statistical methods to control for alternative sources of earnings differences, still find evidence of pay discrimination.[42] Another Australian study, which considers 12 different models of pay differences, decides that the monopsony model and neo-Marxist theories (where internal labor markets and occupational stratification are artificial devices – i.e., not related to productivity differences – used by employers to gain control), both of which assume employer power in the labor market, are the only two not contradicted by the data.[43]

Other forces have been operating to close the Australian earnings gap over time without the support of equal pay legislation, but differences in work patterns by sex remain. For example, women have been rapidly closing the gender gap in job tenure. Whereas in 1972 mean tenure was 38.4 months for men and 29.5 months for women, by 1986 mean tenures were 38.3 and 32.9 months for men and women, respectively.[44]

In comparing the U.S., U.K., and Australia experiences, the different earnings patterns in the 1970s are intriguing. While the U.S. gender earnings ratio stayed relatively constant throughout the 1970s, earnings ratios in the United Kingdom and Australia took large jumps in the mid-70s. Since human capital levels for women and men and labor force participation trends were quite similar across these countries, it appears that the institutional changes in the form of equal pay initiatives were responsible for these jumps.[45] In the 1980s, however, the U.S. ratio began to move upwards, while in Australia and the United Kingdom, the ratios leveled off. It has not yet been adequately resolved by researchers whether this is due to greatly improved levels of female human capital in the United States relative to the other countries, a decrease in discrimination in the United States, institutionalized wage rigidity in Australia and the United Kingdom brought about by the higher level of collective wage-setting, or some other set of reasons.

Japan

Japan is an interesting example to contrast to the set of English-speaking countries discussed above. While Japan is ranked No. 3 on the United Nation's Human Development Index, it has the lowest gender earnings ratio in Table 10.4, the lowest percentage of female bachelor and graduate degree recipients in Table 10.7, and a lower female labor force participation rate than the Scandinavian and English-speaking countries in Table 10.1. It has, however, the lowest segregation index value in Table 10.3, and its female part-time rate is neither exceptionally high nor exceptionally low. Inasmuch as Japan is the only Asian country in this group of countries, it is natural to consider how cultural differences can lead to such divergent patterns. But it is also the case that institutions combating sex discrimination have developed much later in Japan than in the other countries; its equal pay and access law dates only from 1986. Therefore, it will be interesting to see how Japan progresses in the near future, now that its official status on discrimination is more in line with that of other industrialized nations.

Even after passage of equal employment opportunity legislation, there are strong forces in Japanese society against both higher female labor force participation rates and a higher earnings ratio.[46] First, although a woman is no longer required to quit her job when she marries or bears her first child, there is still strong social pressure on women to stop working while raising children. This pressure is reinforced by government policies: the income tax system supports the provision of nonmarket work by providing a high deduction for a nonworking spouse, while dual-earner families must file separate returns.[47] This pressure is manifested in the relatively low labor force participation rates among women ages 25 to 34 (52 percent in 1984), even among more educated women. Secondly, the internal job ladders and lifetime employment system found in large Japanese firms (where the better-paying jobs are) make it hard for women to find relatively well-paying work when they re-enter the labor force after taking time out for childraising. Japanese women are much more likely than Japanese men to experience downward mobility with age. While they are equally likely to start work in large firms as are men (although not in the same jobs), their probability of leaving large firms is much higher.[48] Also, part-time work rates for older women are much higher than in the United States. But while Japanese women appear to bear a disproportionate amount of the employment adjustment burden to macroeconomic shocks, they still enjoy greater employment security than U.S. workers of either sex.[49]

One would expect little increase in the near future in the Japanese gender earnings ratio due to the continuing large gender differences in human capital acquisition. Differences in higher education graduate rates have already been noted, and differences in job experience are large as well. As an additional piece of evidence, Table 10.8 contains data on employer-provided on- or off-the-job training rates by sex from the small number of developed countries where such data are available. While training rates are much higher in Japan for both sexes, the sex differential in rates is much greater there as well. This differential tends to lead to relatively high wages for both sexes compared with other countries, but to a greater gender earnings gap than in these other countries, which is exactly what is found.

Analysts of Japanese society are in general agreement that Japanese women experience more extreme forms of discrimination than their Western counterparts but that pressure for more opportunities for women has been increasing.[50] These pressures are both social and economic in nature. As Japan has chronic labor shortages due to extremely limited

TABLE 10.8 Incidence of training among employees by sex

Country	Women	Men
Japan		
any training	60.6	80.2
within last two years	25.8	40.4
Norway	32.8	33.3
France	22.8	28.8
Netherlands	18.0	28.0

Source: OECD, *Employment Outlook* (1991): 144 (Table 5.1b). Data are from 1986, 1988, or 1989. Exact definition of training varies across surveys.

immigration and as younger Japanese resist the social pressure to work long hours, women will have to increase their market work if Japanese economic growth is to continue at a high rate. Given the relatively inelastic female labor supply caused by cultural pressures, the predictions are that both upward pressure on female wages and social pressure to reduce nonmarket obligations for women in order to increase the elasticity of supply are inevitable.

Sweden

Let us turn now to a much-studied country, Sweden, which is notable for having the highest female labor force participation rate in Table 10.1, the highest gender earnings ratio in Table 10.4, and the highest unionism rates for both sexes in Table 10.5. The Swedish industrial relations system is notable not only for these high unionism rates but also because the unions are highly federated and negotiations are generally at the sector level between national employers' associations and national unions. Most important labor market changes in Sweden, including equal pay implementation, take place through collective bargaining agreements rather than through legislative action. This accounts for the relatively late passage of equal opportunity legislation, since the general feeling in Sweden is that collective bargaining agreements are the best way to create and implement changes.

The Swedish government has, however, taken a lead in enacting social policies.[51] This has been done through a two-pronged approach of creating policies that affect both work and family. Table 10.9 lists some of the critical legislative initiatives, most of which were the first of their kind in any country.

While many of these programs have noteworthy aspects, probably the most famous Swedish policy is parental leave. It is the most generous such program, although the other Scandinavian nations also allow fathers to take paid leave.[52] The program is financed through payroll taxes and is paid out directly through social insurance offices. As of 1997, parents could share 15 months of paid leave per child, of which each parent has 30 nontransferable days (leading to the dubbing "father's month"). The first 12 months are paid at 75 to 85 percent of regular pay; the last 3 months are compensated at a minimum level of 60 Krone (about $7.50) a day.[53]

The program is not viewed as a complete success in terms of breaking down traditional gender roles. The percentage of eligible fathers who took parental leave has risen from 3 percent in 1974 to 78 percent by 1994; however, the percentage of total leave days

TABLE 10.9 Swedish work-family policy

Year	Policy
1937	Maternity benefits.
1939	Worker discrimination on the basis of pregnancy abolished.
1947	Child allowance.
1971	Separate income tax assessments for husband and wife.
1974	Paid parental leave for infants, unpaid leave for sick children.
1975	Preschool programs.
1978	Paid parental leave extended to 270 days.
1979	Parents of infants entitled to six-hour workdays.
1980	Paid parental leave extended to 360 days, leave for sick children increased to 60 days.
1994	Paid parental leave extended to 450 days, leave for sick children increased to 120 days.
1995	"Father's month" instituted, nonparents eligible for sick children leave.

Sources: Statistics Sweden (March 1985); "General Facts on Sweden" and "Child Care in Sweden," *Fact Sheets on Sweden* (Stockholm, Sweden: Svenska Institutet, 1997).

accounted for by fathers is only about 11 percent.[54] Also, fathers seldom take leave during the first six months of the child's life.[55] While fathers who take parental leave generally like it and are more likely to report significant involvement in subsequent child care than fathers who do not take leave, still only 40 percent report sharing equally in child care (as compared with 20 percent of fathers who do not take leave).[56]

Two Swedish social trends have been widely noted: the high percentage of people who are cohabiting, with a corresponding high percentage of births to unmarried women; and the below-replacement birth rate. Swedish fertility rates, after reaching a low of 1.6 births per woman in 1981, have risen somewhat since then to a rate of 1.7 in 1996 – still below replacement. These trends, particularly the latter, are viewed with some measure of concern in Sweden.[57] While only 1 percent of Swedish couples were in consensual unions in 1960, by the 1980s, about 25 percent of couples were in consensual unions, as contrasted to about 5 percent in the United States at the same time.[58] In the 1980s, over half of Swedish births were out of wedlock, as contrasted to about 20 percent of American births.[59] Additionally, it appears that the high cohabitation rate does not lead to a significantly lower divorce rate. 45 percent of Swedish marriages end in divorce, as compared with slightly over 40 percent of U.S. marriages.[60] Additionally, women who marry subsequent to cohabitation have about an 80 percent higher subsequent divorce rate than those who do not cohabit.[61] The interesting question is whether or not these trends would have occurred without Sweden's social policies. Many observers have argued that they would not have occurred – or, at least, not with such force.

Has Sweden reached a state of equality between the sexes? The answer is clearly no, although the progress towards gender equality from a society with clearly defined gender roles is striking. Swedish women do not yet appear satisfied with the trade-offs they face. In a series of surveys in 1968, 1974, and 1981, Swedish mothers consistently reported lower levels of well-being and higher levels of fatigue and psychological distress in comparison with other demographic groups.[62] In some ways, it is amazing how little has changed: a 1975 survey found that women did much more of the housework among both married and cohabiting couples.[63]

FOCUS

Comparing tax system effects for Sweden and Germany

While Sweden has had a system of compulsory separate taxation, with high progressivity since 1971, Germany has "split" income taxation, with a substantial "marriage gain." The two systems can be compared in terms of the different after-tax incomes that one-earner and two-earner couples receive in each system (assuming that men are the earners in one-earner couples for notational simplicity):

Germany:
two-earner couple's after-tax income $= w_m h_m + w_f h_f - t^G(w_m h_m + w_f h_f - 2b^G)$
one-earner couple's after-tax income $= w_m h_m - t^G(w_m h_m - 2b^G)$

Sweden:
two-earner couple's after-tax income $= w_m h_m + w_f h_f - t_m^S(w_m h_m - b^S) - t_f^S(w_f h_f - b^S)$
one-earner couple's after-tax income $= w_m h_m - t_m^S(w_m h_m - b^S)$

where

i $= m$ (male) or f (female),
j $= G$ (Germany) or S (Sweden),
$w_i =$ hourly wage for spouse i,
$h_i =$ number of hours worked by spouse i,
$t_i^j =$ tax rate faced by spouse i in country j,
$b^j =$ standard personal deduction in country j,

and $t_m^S > t^G > t_f^S$ (assuming $w_m h_m > w_f h_f$); that is, the tax rate for the higher earner in Sweden (here assuming it is the male's earnings that are higher) is above the tax rate in Germany, which in turn is above the tax rate for the lower earner in Sweden.

If potential before-tax income were roughly equal by sex across the countries, we would predict that a greater percentage of spouses would be in two-earner families in Sweden. This would be the case because the second earner's after-tax income would be larger as a percentage of before-tax income in Sweden than in Germany, and one-earner families both receive a larger deduction and face a lower marginal tax rate in Germany than in Sweden, leading to a larger percentage of after-tax income in Germany.

Economist Siv Gustafsson has studied the relative effects of tax systems on women's labor supply across these two countries.[64] In the mid-1980s, real before-tax family income (corrected for purchasing power parity) was very similar in the two countries. However, there was a higher percentage of two-earner married couples in Sweden, which is reflected in the different trends and levels in married women's labor force participation rates. As shown in Table 10.10, while they have risen in both countries, the rise has been much more pronounced in Sweden. Additionally, Gustafsson finds that the effect of children on female labor supply is strongly negative in Germany but has no effect in Sweden. She estimates that labor force participation by German women would increase from 50 to 60 percent if they were in the Swedish tax system, and would decrease for Swedish women from 80 to 60 percent if they were in the German system.[65]

Another tax system effect is reflected in the different participation rates for unmarried women, as seen in Table 10.10. Germany's system provides a marriage incentive, while Sweden's system is neutral. Thus, in Sweden, younger women comprise a larger percentage of this participation category and create a higher (and rising) participation rate than in Germany, where the unmarried category has a larger percentage of older women (particularly widows), with a correspondingly lower labor force participation rate.

TABLE 10.10 Female labor force participation rates by marital status, Germany and Sweden

	Married	*Unmarried*
Germany:		
1963	35.9	79.1
1984	47.5	58.8
Sweden:		
1963	47.0	69.6
1986	82.9	76.7

Sources: Germany – *Statistische Jahrbücher*, diverse Jahrgänge, Ergebnisse des Microzensus, 1983/1984 EG Arbeitskräftestichprobe; Sweden – *Statistics Sweden*.

Social policies across advanced industrialized countries

This section first outlines demographic trends in advanced industrialized countries. The interrelationships of these demographic trends with the labor market trends outlined at the beginning of this chapter involve the usual causality questions; e.g., does increased female labor force participation lead to declining birth rates and increased divorce rates – or vice-versa? Then two important sets of social policies that address certain of these trends are considered: policies with pronatalist implications, and antipoverty policies.

Common demographic trends

It is clear that certain trends are shared across the advanced industrialized countries.[66] For instance, fertility rates have been declining for a long time, to the point where they are well below the replacement level (of 2.1 births per woman) in most industrialized countries. These birth rate declines have led to smaller household and family sizes in these countries, as well as a declining proportion of young and an increasing proportion of old people. Marriage rates have declined and median ages at first marriage have risen, although in the United States the marriage rate is still at a much higher level and the median age at first marriage at a lower level than in comparable countries. This difference is related to the higher incidence in Western Europe of consensual union, which in some families is increasingly viewed as an alternative rather than a prelude to marriage (e.g., in Sweden, where the average length of cohabitation is increasing).

All these countries have experienced increased divorce rates, although the United States continues to have a much higher dissolution rate (one of every two marriages) than Western Europe (one of every three or four marriages). Due to both decreased marriage rates and increased divorce rates, the share of households that contain married couples is decreasing everywhere except in Japan, mainly in the category of married couples with children (which has also declined in Japan). The big increase has come in one-person households, a trend related to increased urbanization rates (as people in rural areas generally do not live alone). The percentage of the population 65 and over who live alone is over 30 percent in most of these countries, although Japan is again an exception, with a lower but rising rate. Finally, births to unmarried women are increasing everywhere, which is an additional factor leading to smaller household and family sizes. Because of this trend, along with the increased divorce rates, single-parent households as a percentage of households with children are increasing everywhere, with the greatest percentage by far in the United States.

The United States and Japan are notably out of step with the other countries: Japan because it continues to have more traditional demographic patterns, the United States because it is traditional in some ways (e.g., high marriage rate, high rate of children cared for privately) but untraditional in others (e.g., high divorce rate, large percentage of female-headed households). The countries (such as Sweden and other Scandinavian countries) that seem the least traditional appear to have higher social safety nets and more comprehensive work-family policies, including pronatalist policies.

Pronatalist policies

Policies that have pronatalist effects are widespread, and they are quite common in Western Europe.[67] This is not surprising, given the below- or near-replacement birth rates currently found in most of these countries. While pronatalist policies can include a wide range of measures, including such radical ones as banning abortion and contraception, Western European emphases have been on reducing the costs involved with raising children. These policies basically fall into three categories: (1) family/child allowances, (2) family/infant care leaves, and (3) subsidization and/or public provision of child care. Let us briefly consider each category in terms of provision differences across advanced industrialized countries and effects on female labor supply and the quantity/quality trade-off in children.

1. Family allowances theoretically have the effect of reducing labor supply for all family members by increasing nonearned income. However, they will tend to reduce female labor supply more than male labor supply if women continue to bear responsibility for childraising and other nonmarket activities. In particular, family allowances that increase with family size may tend to reduce female labor supply as increasing demand for child care services leads women to value their nonmarket time more highly. However, while child allowances are very common (67 countries had them by the early 1980s, including all of the advanced industrialized countries except the United States[68]), it is not apparent that they have had much effect on either female labor supply or fertility rates.

2. Family leaves, whether paid or unpaid, are more likely to lead to sustained or increased female labor supply in the life cycle sense of allowing women to avoid having to quit work and subsequently find a new job after caring for an infant. Their effect on the birth rate is ambiguous. On the one hand, they may raise the birth rate through causing more working women to have children. On the other hand, they may lower the birth rate by causing more women to work than would have otherwise, as working women tend to have fewer children. National family leave policies are extremely common in industrialized countries, and appear to have come into widespread use with little dissatisfaction voiced by employers. The United States is the last to join this group, with an unpaid leave policy effective in 1993. One study compares family leave policies for Sweden, West Germany, and France, finding no effect on the birth rate, a slight effect of increasing female labor supply, and a widespread view that such policies improve working conditions for women.[69] Another study of nine European countries from 1969 to 1993 also finds that paid parental leave policies cause small increases in female labor supply, and that lengthier leave policies have had some effect in lowering women's wages relative to men.[70]

3. Subsidized child care, by lowering the price at which child-based consumption can be produced, should tend to increase this form of consumption for families. Since consumption can be taken in the form of increased investment per child rather than in an increased number of children, however, the effect on the birth rate is ambiguous. To the extent that women must work to take advantage of child care, this policy would tend to increase female labor supply. However, an Australian study found that many nonemployed women utilized child care services (particularly preschool) as well.[71] Publicly provided child care service levels vary across countries, with the highest levels found in Scandinavia and France,[72] and low rates in the United Kingdom and the Netherlands. For instance, in Sweden, about 62 percent of children under age seven are cared for in government-sponsored child care facilities.[73] All countries report a shortage of publicly funded child care, so queues abound for available care at existing prices (where sometimes the price is zero).[74]

Have these various pronatalist policies been effective in increasing births? There is little evidence that they have been successful. For instance, in France, which has perhaps the most explicitly pronatalist policy stance, the fertility rate has been declining since 1961. Although it has leveled off recently, it is still below replacement level. The rest of Western Europe also continues to have fertility below replacement level, although it is certainly possible that rates might be even lower, were it not for these policies.

Finally, have these policies led to reduced female labor supply? The net effect also depends on the form of interactions between policies and between policies and the existing structure of labor markets. One study compares the British and French experiences, using household survey data from 1980–81. In France, government policies and the labor market structure appear to exert both stronger negative and stronger positive effects on female labor supply than in Britain. The negative effect comes from family allowance policies; the positive effects come from higher female wages in France and less part-time employment. Additionally, French child care and education policies have reduced the negative effect on female labor supply of having a young child. French women are, however, more polarized between continuously working or not working at all, while British women are more likely to work at some point during their lives.[75]

Antipoverty programs

While poverty rates have generally fallen in industrialized countries, particularly among older people, demographic groups remain who experience higher than average poverty rates. In particular, an increasingly common problem in industrialized countries is the number of poor female-headed households.[76] This may actually be a relatively worse problem in developed countries than in undeveloped countries because of a lack of extended household structures. The rates vary across these countries: while female-headed families comprise about 25 percent of Swedish families, they make up only about 4 percent of Israeli families (and these families are mostly headed by widows).[77] Sweden is also notable for being especially generous to such families, raising the question of whether public income support is a significant factor leading to the formation of single-parent households.

In surveying antipoverty policies across developed countries, the generalization can be made that countries with universal benefits tend to provide higher income for poor families, particularly female-headed families, than countries with means-tested benefits. such as the U.S.[78] It also appears that it is possible, through use of universal benefits and/or non-means-tested benefits conditioned on other variables (e.g., child allowances and child support assurance), to reduce welfare use while both providing female-headed families with higher living standards and avoiding creation of work disincentives and long-term dependency. The larger question of whether more extensive social safety nets have been costly to Western European countries in terms of reduced economic growth (given that they are financed through highly progressive income tax systems) is important. The lower growth rates experienced in these countries in the 1980s – notable when compared with U.S. and Japanese growth rates – have led even rich countries such as Sweden and the Netherlands to feel some economic pressure to scale back their safety net, although wholesale reductions have not yet occurred.

Policy Application: Child allowances

Countries have instituted child allowance programs in a variety of forms. Some countries, such as France, supplement a basic child allowance with a means-tested benefit for certain low-income families. Allowances can vary with the age of the child as well, and may be decreased or increased for each additional child, or each child over a certain threshold (e.g., two).

The 1997 U.S. tax bill instituted child allowances in the form of a refundable tax credit. The refundability means that its benefits are not limited to those families with tax liability, the way the dependent care allowance is. The child allowance is in addition to the current nonrefundable dependent care allowance. Parents receive $400 for each child 16 and under in 1998, rising to $500 per child in 1999. Phase-out of the credit begins for couples with income of $110,000, and for singles with income of $75,000.

While most countries allow persons to receive apportioned payment of allowances at regular intervals, use of the tax system to provide child allowances means that most people will receive a lump sum once a year if they receive any actual cash at all. This factor, combined with the low level of the benefit, means that the program is unlikely to stimulate many persons to increase initial births in response to this program, but may conceivably provide stimulus for second and higher-order births. The French pronatalist system, in providing a larger benefit for third children, considered that the most likely persons to be affected in their birth decisions were those families with two children already, and focused resources on those families.

Summary

Industrialized capitalist societies – or advanced industrialized countries – share basic trends, including increasing female labor force participation, declining fertility and marriage rates, rising gender earnings ratios, and increasing rates of divorce and single-adult households. However, there are also important variations among these countries. While Western European countries have fairly homogenous trends and policies, the United States and Japan appear as outliers on many measures, and the Scandinavian countries (particularly Sweden) appear to have undergone faster rates of change. Equal pay and opportunity legislation and work-family policies appear to be becoming more similar across countries, through processes of conscious imitation and common underlying social trends.

*E*ndnotes

1. See United Nations Development Programme, Human Development Report 1995 (Oxford, United Kingdom: Oxford University): 130–133, for how the index is calculated. The OECD countries included in the tables in this chapter include the top 21 countries by this index, plus Luxembourg (number 27), South Korea (number 29), and Portugal (number 35). Canada is ranked no. 1, followed in order by the United States, Japan, the Netherlands, Norway, Finland, France, Iceland, Sweden, and Spain.
2. World Bank, World Development Report 1996 (Tables 1, 6, 9, 28, 29).
3. See endnote 70 in Chapter 6 for the correlation coefficient formula and discussion of its range.
4. Unfortunately, a similar systematic comparison of overtime rates by sex is not possible.
5. *European Women and Men in 1983* (Brussels, Belgium: Commission of the European Communities, 1983): 68; 71. The representative survey of persons 15 years and older covered 9790 people in the ten countries comprising the European Community in 1983: Belgium, Denmark, France, FRG, Greece, Ireland, Italy, Luxembourg, the Netherlands, and the United Kingdom.
6. Candida G. Brush, "Women Business Owners: An International Perspective," Boston University, School of Management, Entrepreneurial Management Institute Working Paper no. 90–1–1 (January 4, 1990): 2.
7. See Marjorie Galenson, *Women and Work: An International Comparison* (Ithaca, N.Y.: Cornell University School of Industrial and Labor Relations, 1973), as a source of older data.
8. See Jacob Mincer, "Intercountry Comparisons of Labor Force Trends and of Related Developments: An Overview," *Journal of Labor Economics*, 3, no. 1, supplement (January 1985): S1–S32, for a discussion of trends from 1960 to 1980 for many of the countries covered in this chapter. The rest of this journal supplement is devoted to in-depth studies of 12 developed countries, including the former USSR, Japan, Israel, the United States, Australia, and seven Western European countries, the results from which are summarized in the Mincer article.
9. Jean Larson Pyle, *The State and Women in the Economy: Lessons from Sex Discrimination in the Republic of Ireland* (Albany, N.Y.: State University of New York, 1990).
10. Edward Balls, "Working Women and the Rise of the House-Husband," *Financial Times* (July 27, 1992): 4.
11. Angela Dale and Judith Glover, "An Analysis of Women's Employment Patterns in the United Kingdom, France, and the United States: The Value of Survey-Based Comparisons," U.K. Department of Employment Research Paper no. 75 (1990): 1. These are household-based surveys using a sample of about 60,000 to 100,000 households for larger countries, 30,000 to 50,000 for medium-size countries, and 10,000 in Luxembourg.
12. See Chapter 6 for the segregation index formula and discussion of its range. The worker categories used are: (1) professional, technical, and kindred; (2) administrative, executive, and managerial; (3) clerical; (4) sales; (5) farmers, fishers, loggers, and related; (6) crafts, production process, and laborers not elsewhere classified; (7) service, sports, and recreation.
13. Francine D. Blau and Marianne A. Ferber, "Women's Work, Women's Lives: A Comparative Economic Perspective," *Women's Work and Women's Lives: The Continuing Struggle Worldwide*, eds. Hilda Kahne and Janet Z. Giele (Boulder, Colorado: Westview, 1992): 28–44.
14. Cf. Catherine Dutoya and Annie Gauvin, "Assignment of Women Workers to Jobs and Company Strategies in France," *Flexibility in Labour Markets*, ed. Roger Tarling (London: Academic Press, 1987): 127–144.
15. See Alice H. Cook, Val R. Lorwin, and Arlene Kaplan Daniels, *Women and Trade Unions in Eleven Industrialized Countries* (Philadelphia, Pa.: Temple University, 1984), for a set of country studies regarding unions and women.
16. Joan Acker, "Thinking About Wages: The Gendered Wage Gap in Swedish Banks," *Gender and Society* 5, no. 3 (September 1991): 390–407.

17. Janice Bellace, "A Foreign Perspective," *Comparable Worth: Issues and Alternatives, 2nd Edition,* ed. E. Robert Livernash (Washington, D.C.: Equal Employment Advisory Council, 1984): 153.
18. Bellace, *op. cit.*: 150.
19. This section draws on Bellace, *op. cit.*: 167.
20. *Ibid.*
21. Bellace, *op. cit.*: 140.
22. Bellace, *op. cit.*: 141–42.
23. Bellace, *op. cit.*: 142.
24. Bellace, *op. cit.*: 155. For a general discussion of the Netherlands situation, see Marga Bruyn-Hundt, "Economic Independence of Women in the Netherlands," *Women's Work in the World Economy, Issues in Contemporary Economics* 4, proceedings of the Ninth World Congress of the International Economic Association, Athens, Greece, eds. Nancy Folbre, Barbara Bergmann, Bina Agarwal, and Maria Floro (New York: New York University, 1992): 120–131.
25. N. Smith and N. Westergaanrd-Nielsen, "Wage Differentials Due to Gender," *Journal of Population Economics* 11, no. 2 (October 1988): 115–130.
26. Francine D. Blau and Lawrence M. Kahn, "The Gender Earnings Gap: Learning from International Comparisons," *American Economic Review* 82, no. 2 (May 1992): 533–538; "Wage Structure and Gender Earnings Differentials: An International Comparison," *Economica* 63, Supplement (May 1996): S29–S62.
27. Blau and Kahn (1996): S29.
28. Charles Brown and Shirley J. Wilcher, "Sex-Based Employment Quotas in Sweden," *Gender in the Workplace*, eds. Clair Brown and Joseph A. Pechman (Washington, D.C.: Brookings, 1987): 271–298.
29. Bellace, *op. cit.*: 145.
30. Bellace, *op. cit.*: 147.
31. See A. Zabalza and Z. Tzannatos, "The Effect of Britain's Antidiscriminatory Legislation on Relative Pay and Employment," *Economic Journal* 95, no. 379 (September 1985): 679–699; A. Zabalza and Z. Tzannatos, *Women and Equal Pay: The Effects of Legislation on Female Employment and Wages in Britain* (Cambridge, United Kingdom: Cambridge University, 1985); and Zafiris Tzannatos, "The Economics of Discrimination: Theory and British Evidence," *Current Issues in Labour Economics*, eds. David Sapsford and Zafiris Tzannatos (New York: St. Martin's, 1989): 177–207.
32. Peter J. Sloane, "The Male/Female Earnings Differential in Britain and Europe: Are There Lessons for the United States?" *Family and Work: Bridging the Gap*, eds. Sylvia Ann Hewlett, Alice S. Ilchman, and John J. Sweeney (Cambridge, Mass.: Ballinger, 1986): 139–160.
33. Heather E. Joshi, Richard Layard, and Susan J. Owen, "Why Are More Women Working in Britain?" *Journal of Labor Economics* 3, no. 1, supplement (January 1985): S147–S176, find no decline in the relative demand for women workers after the wage rise; Tzannatos, *loc. cit.*, finds that the overall wage bill increased at the expense of profits.
34. Robert E. Wright and John F. Ermisch, "Gender Discrimination in the British Labour Market," *Economic Journal* 101, no. 406 (May 1991): 508–522.
35. H.E. Joshi and M. Newell, "Pay Differences Between Men and Women: Longitudinal Evidence from the 1946 Birth Cohort," University of London Centre for Economic Policy Research Discussion Paper no. 156 (1987).
36. Sara Arber and Nigel Gilbert, "Re-assessing Women's Working Lives: An Introductory Essay," *Women and Working Lives: Divisions and Change*, eds. Sara Arber and Nigel Gilbert (London: Macmillan, 1992): 4 (Table 1.1).
37. Patricia A. Roos, *Gender and Work: A Comparative Analysis of Industrial Societies* (Albany, N.Y.: State University of New York, 1985): 50–51 (Table 3.3).
38. Mark B. Stewart and Christine A. Greenhalgh, "Work History Patterns and the Occupational Attainment of Women," *Economic Journal* 94, no. 2 (September 1984): 493–517.

39. Karen Mumford, *Women Working: Economics and Reality* (Sydney, Australia: Allen & Unwin, 1989): 6 (Table 2.1). See also A. Edwards and S. Magarey (eds.), *Women in a Restructuring Australia: Work and Welfare* (Sydney: Allen and Unwin, 1995), for more recent background on economic gender issues in Australia.

40. See Jocelyn Clarke and Kate White, *Women in Australian Politics* (Victoria, Australia: Dominion, 1983); and Sophi Watson (ed.), *Playing the State* (New York: Verso, 1990) for discussions of how the Australian women's movement, through its emphasis on economic rights, particularly the right to equal pay, was an important political force in pushing for equal pay as well as for subsequent antidiscrimination and affirmative action legislation.

41. According to Bellace, *op. cit.*: 165–166, the female minimum wage rate had been increased to 75 percent of the male rate by 1950, and it remained at this level until 1969, at which point the female rate was increased in stages to 100 percent of the male base rate; however, in 1973 the Commonwealth Commission stated that only men would be guaranteed a wage above the minimum, a decision that was then reversed in 1974.

42. See Michael P. Kidd and Rosalie Viney, "Sex Discrimination and Non-random Sampling in the Australian Labour Market," *Australian Economic Papers* 30, no. 56 (June 1991): 28–49; and Paul Miller and Sarah Rummery, "Male-Female Wage Differentials in Australia: A Reassessment," *Australian Economic Papers* 30, no. 56 (June 1991): 50–69.

43. Mumford, *op. cit.*

44. Mumford, *op. cit.* (Table 5.1).

45. Robert G. Gregory, Roslyn Anstie, Anne Daly, and Vivian Ho, "Women's Pay in Australia, Great Britain, and the United States: The Role of Laws, Regulations, and Human Capital," *Pay Equity: Empirical Inquiries*, eds. Robert T. Michael and Heidi I. Hartmann (Washington, D.C.: National Academy, 1989): 222–246 (including commentary).

46. See Linda N. Edwards, "Equal Employment Opportunity in Japan: A View from the West," *Industrial and Labor Relations Review* 41, no. 2 (January 1988): 240–250.

47. Aiko Shibata, "The Effects of Japanese Income Tax Provisions on Women's Labour Force Participation," in *Women's Work in the World Economy, Issues in Contemporary Economics* 4, proceedings of the Ninth World Congress of the International Economic Association, Athens, Greece, eds. Nancy Folbre, Barbara Bergmann, Bina Agarwal, and Maria Floro (New York: New York University, 1992): 169–179.

48. Mary C. Brinton, Hang-Yue Ngo, and Kumiko Shibuya, "Gendered Mobility Patterns in Industrial Economies: The Case of Japan," *Social Science Quarterly* 72, no. 4 (December 1991): 807–816.

49. Susan N. Houseman and Katharine G. Abraham, "Female Workers as a Buffer in the Japanese Economy," *American Economic Review* 83, no. 2 (May 1993): 45–51.

50. See Alice C.L. Lam, *Women and Japanese Management: Discrimination and Reform* (London: Routledge, 1992); and Janet E. Hunter (ed.), *Japanese Women Working* (London: Routledge, 1993).

51. See Phyllis Moen, *Working Parents: Transformation in Gender Roles and Public Policies in Sweden* (Madison, Wis.: University of Wisconsin, 1989).

52. Linda Haas, *Equal Parenthood and Social Policy: A Study of Parental Leave in Sweden* (Albany, N.Y.: State University of New York, 1992): 13–14.

53. "General Facts on Sweden" and "Child Care in Sweden," *Fact Sheets on Sweden* (Stockholm, Sweden: Svenska Institutet, 1997).

54. Haas, *op. cit.*: 61 (Table 3.1); "Child Care in Sweden," *Fact Sheets on Sweden* (Stockholm, Sweden: Svenska Institutet, 1997).

55. Haas, *op. cit.*: 64.

56. Haas, *op. cit.*: 139, 158.

57. See Britta Hoem and Jan M. Hoem, *One Child Is Not Enough: Who Has a Second and a Third Child in Modern Sweden?* (Stockholm, Sweden: University of Stockholm, 1986).

58. David Popenoe, "Family Decline in the Swedish Welfare State," *Public Interest* no. 102 (Winter 1991): 66.

59. *Ibid.*

60. Popenoe, *op. cit.*: 67; "Child Care in Sweden," *Fact Sheets on Sweden* (Stockholm, Sweden: Svenska Institutet, 1997).

61. Neil G. Bennett, Ann Klimas Blanc, and David E. Bloom, "Commitment and the Modern Union: Assessing the Link Between Premarital Cohabitation and Subsequent Marital Stability," *American Sociological Review* 53, no. 1 (February 1988): 127–138, using data from the 1981 Women in Sweden Survey.

62. Moen, *op. cit.*: 136.

63. Moen, *op. cit.*: 21.

64. Siv Gustafsson, "Separate Taxation and Married Women's Labor Supply," *Journal of Population Economics 5*, no. 1 (February 1992): 61–85; "Public Policies and Women's Labor Force Participation: A Comparison of Sweden, Germany, and the Netherlands," *Investment in Women's Human Capital*, ed. T. Paul Schultz (Chicago, Ill.: University of Chicago, 1995): 91–112.

65. Gustafsson (1995): 112.

66. This section draws on Constance Sorrentino, "The Changing Family in International Perspective," *Monthly Labor Review* 113, no. 3 (March 1990): 41–58, which compares 10 countries: Canada, Denmark, France, West Germany, Italy, Japan, the Netherlands, Sweden, the United Kingdom, and the United States. All statements about trends are based on this subset of countries but are likely to have more general application to the advanced industrialized countries. See also Karen Oppenheim Mason and An-Magritt Jensen (eds.), *Gender and Family Change in Industrialized Countries* (Oxford: Clarendon, 1995).

67. C. Alison McIntosh, *Population Policy in Western Europe* (New York and London: M.E. Sharpe, 1983).

68. Sheila B. Kamerman, "Women, Children, and Poverty: Public Policies and Female-headed Families in Industrialized Countries," *Women and Poverty*, eds. Barbara C. Gelpi, Nancy C. M. Hartsock, Clare C. Novak, and Myra H. Strober (Chicago, Ill.: University of Chicago, 1986): 55.

69. Joseph P. Allen, "European Infant Care Leaves: Foreign Perspectives on the Integration of Work and Family Roles," *The Parental Leave Crisis: Toward a National Policy*, eds. Edward F. Zigler and Meryl Frank (New Haven, Conn.: Yale University, 1988): 245–275.

70. Christopher J. Ruhm "The Economic Consequences of Parental Leave Mandates: Lessons from Europe," working paper, University of North Carolina Greensboro (February 1997).

71. Francis Teal, "The Use and Cost of Child Care in Australia," *Australian Economic Review* no. 97 (January/March 1992): 3–14.

72. See Barbara R. Bergmann, *Saving Our Children from Poverty: What the United States Can Learn From France* (New York: Russell Sage Foundation, 1996), for a thorough discussion of the French child care system.

73. "Child Care in Sweden," *Fact Sheets on Sweden* (Stockholm, Sweden: Svenska Institutet, 1997).

74. Sorrentino, *op. cit.*: 54.

75. Shirley Dex and Patricia Walters, "Franco-British Comparisons of Women's Labour Supply and the Effects of Social Policies," *Oxford Economic Papers* 44, no. 1 (January 1992): 89–112.

76. Kamerman, *op. cit.*: 41–63, surveys Australia, Canada, France, West Germany, Israel, Sweden, the United Kingdom, and the United States. For a pair of recent papers drawing U.S.-Canada comparisons, see Maria J. Hanratty and Rebecca M. Blank, "Down and Out in North America: Recent Trends in Poverty Rates in the U.S. and Canada," *Quarterly Journal of Economics* 107, no. 1 (February 1992): 233–254; and Rebecca M. Blank and Maria J. Hanratty, "Responding to Need: A Comparison of Social Safety Nets in the United States and Canada," mimeo (January 1991).

77. This figure for Sweden is not inconsistent with data presented above; the United States has a higher rate of female-headed households.

78. Kamerman, *op. cit.*: 50 (Table 4).
79. Richard V. Burkhauser, Greg J. Duncan, Richard Hauser, and Roland Berntsen, "Wife or Frau, Women Do Worse: A Comparison of Men and Women in the United States and Germany After Marital Dissolution," *Demography* 28, no. 3 (August 1991): 353–360.

*F*urther reading and statistical sources

Farley, Jennie (ed.) (1985). *Women Workers in Fifteen Countries*. Ithaca, N.Y.: Industrial and Labor Relations Press. Informative essays on Great Britain, France, West Germany, Sweden, Switzerland, Italy, Japan, Israel, and the United States, as well as the former USSR, China, the former Yugoslavia, Bangladesh, Egypt, and India.

International Labour Office. *Bulletin of Labour Statistics*. Published quarterly, updates figures as available for countries included in the *Yearbook of Labour Statistics*. The ILO maintains a publications list but no data as of yet at its website (www.ilo.org).

—— (1995). *Women Workers: An Annotated Bibliography, 1983–94*. Covers English-language publications issued by the International Labour Office during this period; derived from the LABORDOC database maintained by the ILO.

——. *Yearbook of Labour Statistics*. Published annually, a compendium of data from national surveys, updated continually. Labor force by age and sex, employment and earnings statistics by sex for all countries where data are available. 1989 edition covers census data for the years 1945 to 1989.

Kahne, Hilda, and Janet Z. Giele (1992). *Women's Work and Women's Lives: The Continuing Struggle Worldwide*. Boulder, Colo. Westview. Overview essays and spotlights on particular countries, including Great Britain, Japan, and the Nordic Countries.

Organisation for Economic Cooperation and Development. *Employment Outlook*. Published annually, contains statistics on labor markets along with good analysis of labor market conditions. The OECD maintains a publications list but no data as of yet at its website (www.oecd.org).

—— (1985). *The Integration of Women into the Economy*. Useful report on women, including discussion of their industrial and occupational distribution, with data on OECD countries up through 1982.

——. *Labour Force Statistics*. Published annually, contains statistics on labor force participation, employment, unemployment, etc. for the countries that are members of the OECD.

——. *Quarterly Labour Force Statistics*. Published quarterly, contains quarterly statistics on labor force participation, employment, unemployment, etc. for the countries in the OECD that collect quarterly or monthly labor force data. Also has annual data and quarterly data from the preceding two years.

Roos, Patricia A. (1985). *Gender and Work: A Comparative Analysis of Industrial Societies*. Albany, N.Y.: State University of New York. Looks for similarities and differences in gender patterns across a subset of advanced industrialized countries.

United Nations. *Demographic Yearbook*. Published annually, contains vital statistics (population size and composition and birth, marriage, divorce, and death rates) for countries where data are available (which includes most OECD countries). The UN maintains a publications list and some data at its website (www.un.org).

—— (1995). *Women and Men in Europe and North America 1995*. Joint publication of the United Nations Economic Commission for Europe with Eurostat, the Statistical Office of the European Communities. Very helpful collection of statistics on many of the countries in this chapter as well as some Eastern European countries; very good graphics.

U.S. Department of Commerce, Bureau of the Census. The Census Bureau operates a useful international database at its website (www.census.gov/ipc/www/idbnew.html).

Willborn, Steven L. (ed.) (1991). "Women's Wages: Stability and Change in Six Industrialized Countries," special issue of *International Review of Comparative Public Policy*, Vol. 3. Greenwich, Conn.: JAI. Discusses situations in Australia, Canada, Great Britain, Japan, Sweden, and the United States.

Discussion questions

1. Order the countries in Table 10.1 in decreasing order of male labor force participation rate. Does this ranking provide any insights about cross-country similarities and differences?

2. Order the countries in Table 10.2 in decreasing order of male part-time employment rate. Does this ranking provide any insights about cross-country similarities and differences?

3. Order the countries in Table 10.7 in decreasing order of graduate degree percentage female. Does this ranking provide any insights about cross-country similarities and differences?

4. Consider the Focus on pay discrimination in New Zealand. Can you think of circumstances in which a pay system that provides a "male basic wage rate at a sufficient level to enable a man to support a family of five in a reasonable standard of comfort," with a correspondingly lower female basic wage rate, would be justified?

5. Consider the Focus on Swedish hiring quotas. Under what circumstances will a new hire quota system be more effective in increasing female employment than a net hire quota system? If the turnover rate of men is higher than that of women, which is more effective? Which is more effective in reducing sex segregation?

6. What are the problems with interpreting the effects of Swedish family leave as increasing fathers' subsequent likelihood of sharing equally in child care?

7. The study of Swedish cohabitation mentioned in the chapter found that women who cohabited for 3 years or more had about a 50 percent higher dissolution rate than women who cohabited for shorter durations; also, after about 8 years of marriage, the dissolution rates are identical across cohabiters and noncohabiters. What forces might generate these patterns?

8. Consider the Focus on tax system effects in Sweden and West Germany. How do you think your country's income tax system compares with these two systems in terms of whether or not it tends to discourage the formation of two-earner couples, both through disincentives relative to one-earner couples and through disincentives to marry?

9. German social policy creates a much more secure safety net (set at about 40 percent of the population's average net income) than U.S. social policy. But a study comparing outcomes after separation/divorce in the United States and West Germany found that women in West Germany experience even sharper drops in economic status after marital dissolution than do U.S. women, while men in the two countries fare about the same.[79] What could cause this pattern?

10. One can consider child allowances as one way of replacing the traditional insuring function that childbearing once was. In advanced industrialized countries, now that children do not provide a return on the investment parents make in them by supporting their parents when they are old, the state will provide the return on this form of investment. Should the state do this? Is there an economic justification for such an action?

11. Do you think that the institution of the U.S. child allowance program is a good idea? If so, should the program be expanded beyond its current form? If so, in what ways?

Socialist and Cooperative Societies

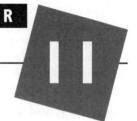

*T*his chapter discusses a set of societies united more by a similar ideological outlook regarding gender roles than by level of economic development. These societies include the currently communist countries of Cuba and China, both of which have relatively low human development indicators; the formerly communist countries of Eastern Europe, which have relatively high human development indicators; and various commune-based societies that operate on a subnational level. While separate human development indicators are not calculated for subnational societies, they are, nonetheless, of considerable interest with regard to whether such societies display significantly different gender patterns than the larger countries in which they operate. The case of Israeli kibbutzim, which has been studied most extensively, will be considered as an example of this phenomenon. In the case of Eastern Europe, where these countries have recently undergone wrenching political and economic change and are on course towards becoming capitalist systems, the discussion focuses both on patterns during their previous incarnation and on the effects that transition has on gender differences.

The chapter opens with a discussion of why we might expect to find more gender equality in these societies. Then data are surveyed to attempt to determine whether this is, in fact, the case during socialist regimes. Some individual countries are considered at greater length, with the aim of comparing them both with each other and with the set of industrialized capitalist societies discussed in Chapter 10.

Why these societies might be expected to display more gender equality

Starting with Marx and Engels, socialist theorists have considered gender inequality, or "the woman question," as eminently solvable by the adoption of a socialist system.[1] Marx and Engels were both influenced by a book by American anthropologist Lewis H. Morgan that outlined a matrilineal theory of original human society.[2] This work led Engels to spell out the route to solution of "the woman question" in his 1884 monograph, *The Origin of the Family, Private Property, and the State.*

Engels viewed the end of private property as the key to overthrowing the social structure that caused marriages of convenience rather than love to be made and that perpetuated both sexual and economic inequality between the sexes:[3]

> With the passage of the means of production into common property, the individual family ceases to be the economic unit of society. Private housekeeping is transformed into a social industry. The care and education of the children becomes a public matter. Society takes care of all children equally, irrespective of whether they are born in wedlock or not. Thus, the anxiety about the "consequences," which is today the most important social factor – both moral and economic – that hinders a girl from giving herself freely to the man she loves, disappears. . . . Here a new factor comes into operation, a factor that, at most, existed in embryo at the time when monogamy developed, namely individual sex love.

Engels' ideas were taken up by other socialist theorists and activists, but the basic plan and perceived outcomes remained unchanged. Hilda Scott, who has analyzed women's conditions in Eastern Europe, explains: "*The Origin of the Family* provided a program for the socialist women's movement which has remained virtually unmodified down to the present. First the complete equality of man and woman before the law; then women's economic independence through employment outside the home, this to be made possible through the assumption of household duties by society."[4] These goals have all been proclaimed by the former or current leaders of Eastern European nations, China, and Cuba.[5] This explicit commitment to gender equality on the part of the state is not found in nonsocialist countries.

However, this top-down approach to gender equality may fail for many reasons. First, equality directives may not be carried out by those managers actually responsible for hiring, pay, and promotion. Second, education and training programs may continue to be sex-segregated. Third, women may resist doing more paid work in place of unpaid work, particularly if they prefer to provide their own child care, and men may resist women giving up traditional roles as well. Therefore, presocialist employment patterns may be perpetuated, whether generated by discrimination or by freely chosen differences in human capital and work characteristics by sex.

While, as we will see, this program as actually attempted within socialist countries cannot be viewed as an unqualified success, important ideas from it continue to fuel feminism, both inside and outside socialist countries. These include the views that property relations are dehumanizing for both women and men, that it is liberating for women to work for pay, that housework is exploitative of women, and that small children can be well-tended by nonfamily members.[6]

*E*valuation of actual practices

In evaluating how successful socialist societies have been in achieving the goal of gender equality, researchers have been hampered by data unavailability. While some countries, such as China, are hindered by the sheer size of the task of undertaking, for example, a regular national census, other countries have felt it better to suppress routine data collection so as to control the information made available about living and working conditions during what may have been viewed as a transitional period before full communism (and full equality) was achieved.

TABLE 11.1 Labor force participation rates by sex, East Europe and OECD averages, 1960 and 1989

	Women		Men	
	1960	*1989*	*1960*	*1989*
East Europe average	67	71	97	80
OECD average	46	58	94	83

Sources: OECD, *Employment Outlook* (1991) (Tables A.1, A.2); Soviet Union 1960: Gur Ofer and Aaron Vinokur, "Work and Family Roles of Soviet Women: Historical Trends and Cross-Section Analysis," *Journal of Labor Economics* 3, no. 1, supplement (January 1985): S332 (Table 1); labor force participation rate for women in East Germany 1989: Hedwig Rudolph, Eileen Appelbaum, and Friederike Maier, "After German Unity: A Cloudier Outlook for Women," *Challenge* 33, no. 6 (November–December 1990): 33. Data are from 1960–61 in the earlier period for persons ages 15 to 64 except: Bulgaria (for 1956), Romania (for 1956 and covers 14 to 64 year olds in that year), and Soviet Union (1960 only for women ages 20 to 54).

The United Nations, the World Bank, and other extranational agencies have managed to track basic demographic indicators for most of these countries. On the United Nations' Human Development Index, these countries range from a rank of 37 for the Czech Republic down to 108 for China. GNP per capita is calculated at $2100 in 1994. As of 1994 all these countries have very high rates of primary and secondary education for both sexes, fairly high life expectancy at birth (a mean of 70 years), fairly low infant mortality rates (18 per 1000 live births), a fairly urbanized population (61 percent), and below-replacement fertility rates (1.8 total live births per woman).[7] These indicator values lie between those found for the industrialized capitalist countries covered in Chapter 10 and the nonindustrialized countries studied in Chapter 12.

While labor market data are not as readily available for these countries as for the industrialized capitalist countries, it is possible to draw some quantitative comparisons both among these countries and among countries with similar cultural backgrounds. Table 11.1 presents average labor force participation rates for 1960 and 1989 for the six Eastern European countries that have separate data by sex available for this period, and compares these averages to the Organisation for Economic Cooperation and Development (OECD) averages. The trends across these countries mirror the trends of dropping male participation and rising female participation found in the industrialized capitalist countries. Romania is an exception in that the female participation fell from 78 percent in 1956 to 68 percent by 1989. Eastern European labor force participation rates for both men and women were already quite high in the early 1960s. The upward trend for women is much smaller and the downward trend for men more pronounced, falling below the OECD average in 1989.

Table 11.2 presents recent labor force participation rates by sex and the proportion of the economically active population when available for Eastern European countries, as well as Cuba and China. Table 11.2 contains numbers for both 1989 and 1995 where available, allowing us to see the effects of the transition to market systems on these indicators for some countries. For the four countries in the top of the table (Bulgaria, Hungary, Poland and Romania) where the cleanest comparison can be made, it is quite clear that transition has led to a large reduction in the measured labor force participation rates for both women and men, with varying effects on the proportion of women in the labor force. In the Czech Republic and Slovakia, it again appears that female labor force participation has fallen, and men's participation has clearly fallen in Slovakia, with a greater effect on women leading

TABLE 11.2 Labor force participation rates by sex and proportion of labor force that is female, 1989 and 1995

| | *%labor force/population* | | | | *Women/labor force* | |
| | *Women* | | *Men* | | | |
Country	*1989*	*1995*	*1989*	*1995*	*1989*	*1995*
Bulgaria	74.0	66.2	81.0	71.3	0.50	0.48
Hungary	62.0	50.2	75.0	67.4	0.46	0.44
Poland	64.1	60.4	79.1	73.6	0.45	0.46
Romania	68.0	66.1	83.0	78.7	0.45	0.46
Czechoslovakia	77.0	—	82.0	—	0.47	—
Czech Republic	—	65.6	—	82.2	—	0.46
Slovakia	—	61.4	—	76.6	—	0.45
East Germany	80.0	73.8	—	79.1	0.51	0.44
West Germany	55.5	60.0	82.2	81.8	0.40	0.41
Soviet Union	70.7	—	81.3	—	0.48	—
Russian Federation	—	51.6	—	69.6	—	0.47
Belarus	75.2	—	82.6	—	0.49	—
Kazakhstan	70.0	—	82.2	—	0.47	—
Moldova	70.6	—	81.3	—	0.49	—
Ukraine	75.2	—	86.8	—	0.49	—
Estonia	76.4	66.0	83.2	77.8	0.50	0.48
Latvia	76.3	—	84.0	—	0.50	—
Lithuania	70.8	—	81.5	—	0.48	—
Azerbaijan	—	46.8	—	78.7	—	0.38
Yugoslavia	—	—	—	—	0.40	—
Slovenia	—	62.6	—	73.4	—	0.46
Albania	—	36.5	—	48.6	—	0.43
China	—	—	—	—	—	0.38
Cuba	41.2	—	72.6	—	0.36	—
OECD average	58.3	61.6	82.9	81.8	0.41	0.43

Sources: ILO, Yearbook of Labour Statistics (1991–96) (Tables 1, 3-A); earlier labor force participation rates for Bulgaria, Czechoslovakia, Hungary, and Romania and percentage employed for Bulgaria: OECD, *Employment Outlook* (1991) (Tables A.1, A.2); earlier labor force participation rate for women in East Germany: Hedwig Rudolph, Eileen Appelbaum, and Friederike Maier, "After German Unity: A Cloudier Outlook for Women," *Challenge* 33, no. 6 (November–December 1990): 33. Earlier data are from 1988–90 and later data are from 1994–95, for persons ages 15 to 64 except: Albania and Azerbaijan (all persons, for 1993), Latvia (for 1993); Bulgaria (earlier data for 1985, later data for 1992); Cuba (all persons 15 and over), East Germany (for women 15–60), and Ukraine (ages 20 to 64). Proportion of employed is used in place of economically active population for Belarus, Bulgaria, Czechoslovakia, East Germany, Latvia, Yugoslavia, and Romania.

to a slight decline in their labor force representation. In Germany, labor market statistics continue to be collected separately for the two parts of the country, allowing for interesting comparisons. East German women have significantly reduced their proportion in the labor force over a period in which, conversely, West German women have increased theirs (in

TABLE 11.3 Occupational sex segregation indexes using seven occupational categories

Country	Index	Year
Bulgaria	41	1985
Slovakia	35	1993
Slovenia	33	1991
Hungary	32	1990
Poland	31	1994
Romania	29	1992
Macedonia	25	1991
China	10	1982
East Germany	47	1991
West Germany	36	1991

Source: ILO, *Yearbook of Labour Statistics* (1985–1996) (Table 2B).

keeping with trends in Western Europe); however, they still have a significantly higher participation rate than their West German counterparts. The net result of transition has been to bring down the higher female labor force participation rates in Eastern Europe to a level on par with the OECD countries (where their averages are shown in the bottom row).

Table 11.3 displays sex segregation index calculations where available using the seven broad categories as in Chapter 10. These index values are comparable to the OECD range, although more similar to the less industrialized countries in the OECD; although China is notably more integrated. A larger percentage of workers of both sexes are in the agricultural sector in the socialist and formerly socialist countries than in the OECD, and a higher percentage of women in Eastern Europe (as in the OECD) work in the service sector than in either manufacturing or industry (except in Romania, which has a particularly large agricultural sector). The occupational concentration of women in education, retailing, health and welfare, and light industry is similar to that found in the OECD.

It would be particularly interesting to compare levels and changes in gender earnings ratios in Eastern Europe to those for the OECD. However reliable historical wage data have been very difficult to come by. The Soviet Union ratio appears to have remained constant at about 0.70 from 1960 through 1980,[8] and 1989 data show the full-time earnings ratio to be between 0.68 and 0.75.[9] Poland also appears to have a ratio around 0.70.[10] More recently, data for the Czech Republic indicate an overall earnings ratio of 0.71 in 1991 and 0.68 in the manufacturing sector in 1994.[11] East Germany continues to show a higher ratio than West Germany (0.77 versus 0.74 in 1994), along with lower wages for both women and men. An educated guess would be that the earnings ratios in these countries would tend to fall in the middle of the OECD range.

Finally, a comparison of particular interest, given the explicit socialist goal that women be freed from the yoke of housework, is time use patterns by sex across socialist and capitalist countries. A set of time-use studies done in a coordinated fashion across twelve countries in 1965–66 has provided invaluable, if somewhat out-of-date, evidence on this topic.[12] Both women and men in the Eastern European countries included in this sample (Poland, Yugoslavia, Bulgaria, Czechoslovakia, Hungary, East Germany, and the Soviet Union) averaged a higher percentage of their time in paid work than people in the OECD countries (Belgium, France,

West Germany, and the United States): 24 percent of their time as opposed to 19 percent. Meanwhile, women spent the same average percentage of time in household care in both the Eastern European and OECD countries: 21 percent.[13] Eastern Europeans also worked more total hours (paid plus unpaid) than persons in the OECD countries.

More recent data from the 1970s and 1980s on time allocation are available for several Eastern European and OECD countries.[14] The Eastern European countries continued to show people working more hours than in developed capitalist countries, although they experienced declines in both paid and unpaid work time along with the other countries. In addition, women's workload relative to men's tended to increase in the socialist countries, while it decreased in the OECD countries.

What conclusions can be drawn from these sketchy sources of evidence on work patterns? While women (and men) clearly have higher rates of paid work in socialist countries than in comparable nonsocialist countries, this has not meant that their unpaid work has been substantially reduced or that their relative earnings are substantially higher. However, the lower dispersion of both earnings and income in socialist countries compared with that in capitalist countries, combined with a social safety net of universal benefits, means that women are less likely to be substantially worse off than men, even though they are still overrepresented among the poor in these countries.

It is the virtual consensus of authorities on Eastern Europe that the high female labor force participation rates experienced throughout the postwar period have been driven not by ideology or by better unpaid work support but by the high demand for female labor due to chronic labor shortages.[15] Labor markets in these countries were constrained both by limits on labor mobility between regions as well as between occupations and industries, as well as by limited immigration.

FOCUS

Causes of the progress of women in the Soviet Union

Economist Barbara Bergmann reminisces about a discussion of women in the Soviet economy during an academic conference:[16]

> The expert on the Soviet economy who was present explained rather plaintively that the penetration of women into the ranks of the professions and the skilled crafts had occurred in the USSR only because of the wholesale slaughter of the male population – in the revolution, in two world wars, and in the Stalinist purges. In short he characterized female progress in Russia as the dismal side effect of a series of historic atrocities. I was unable to resist remarking that I hoped it would not require such an extreme sequence of events to bring about sex equality in America.

Studies of the Soviet system have generally judged official policy regarding gender equality to have failed. One study for 1939 to 1975 that compares the Soviet gender earnings ratio to the ratio in Western Europe (the two were approximately equal in the 1970s) decides that occupational segregation rather than wage discrimination is the key to explaining the Soviet Union earnings gap.[17] The occupational segregation was caused by several forces, including:

1. women's need to accommodate their role as primary provider of unpaid work,
2. sex-typed training in the education system,
3. protective legislation restricting women from entering some occupations, and
4. discrimination by authorities in charge of hiring and promotion decisions.

The Soviet Union also experienced a fair amount of social and demographic change, where many of the trends mirrored those occurring in OECD countries. For example, the divorce rate had risen to about one of every three marriages as of the mid-1980s,[18] and remains significantly higher than Western European rates. The median age at first marriage, however, had dropped by about three years from 1966 to 1986 (in part due to the increase in the nonRussian population, particularly among Muslims), and about one-fourth of women were married by age 18.[19] Russian birth rates were low and falling, but nonRussian birth rates remained high, leading to an overall population increase. While the percentage of births to unmarried women was high – about 14 percent of all births in 1987 (up from around 6 percent in the 1970s)[20] – this was not viewed (at least officially) as a problem, partly because it kept the Russian birth rate from falling still lower.

Other Eastern European countries, particularly those closest to Western Europe both geographically and culturally, provide elements of both contrast and similarity to these findings.[21] For instance, Poland also has restrictive protective legislation, noticeable sex segregation with a strong negative link between wages and percentage female, and few women in the professions (save the health and teaching professions).[22] The countries generally display high and rising divorce rates and, among the urban population, low and falling birth rates. The governments appear to be undecided as to whether it is better to support pronatalist policies or to continue to maintain policies that encourage high labor force participation.[23] As shown in Chapter 5, East European countries are notable for having high abortion rates. Policies such as family leave and child care provision, however, have pronatalist elements, although (as was discussed in Chapter 10) they may not end up having much effect on birth rates.

One might still ask whether women (and men) in socialist societies respond to economic incentives in the same ways as we would predict for market societies, or whether distortions are introduced in planned economic systems (e.g., the practice of channeling persons into occupations based more on ability and need than on personal preference). For instance, if wages were relatively high for women relative to their ability to generate nonmarket output, then it would be natural to expect them to have relatively high labor force participation rates relative to women in other countries. One study contrasting historical female labor force patterns in the Soviet Union to patterns in the OECD concluded that women in the Soviet Union responded to the same economic incentives, and in the same directions, as did OECD women.[24]

Examples from particular countries

While the preceding discussion has focused mainly on the Eastern European countries – particularly the former Soviet Union, for which the most data are available – much can be learned as well from considering facets of life in other socialist systems. This section focuses on aspects of life in different societies that have received particular notice from commentators. First, China, the most populous of the socialist countries, will be considered. Then, Cuba, an example of an ongoing socialist country under stable leadership, will be examined.

The kibbutz system of Israel will then be considered as an example of communal life, with some view towards drawing a contrast between gender differences in the kibbutzim and the rest of Israel.[25] Finally, the effects of the ongoing transition in Eastern Europe, from socialism to democratic capitalism, will be discussed in terms of its effects on economic gender differences.

China

China provides an interesting counterpoint to the now-retired socialist regimes of Eastern Europe in its massive size, its different cultural background, and its leadership's attempt to move to a market economy while maintaining a socialist political structure and strict social control.[26] The presocialist mass culture, which involved a blend of official and social Confucianism overlaid on a background of folk beliefs and Buddhism, was a very different precondition than that found in the more educated (and certainly more Westernized) Eastern European countries. In particular, women inhabited a much more subjugated position in China than in Eastern Europe. They essentially became slaves to the families they married into, often at a very young age in arranged marriages. Consequently, female children were regarded as relatively worthless, since they would leave their family upon marriage and cease contributing any production to the family. Women were generally not educated and were expected to take responsibility for housework, child care, and some agricultural production.

Major social reorganization began in China after 1949. The population, largely rural peasants, was subjected to a series of economic and social changes, including political indoctrination, collectivization of farming, and the development of more industry, both large- and small-scale, depending on the era.

Collectivization was of mixed blessing to women. One researcher argues that the degree of collectivization in the rural area correlates with the degree of visibility and the scale of rewards distributed to women. Collectivization, however, by its institutionalized demands on women for increased, intensified agricultural labor, exacerbated the conflict for women between their productive and reproductive roles.[27]

On the social front, policies were almost immediately undertaken by the Chinese Communist Party to better the conditions of women.[28] Regulations instituted in 1951 gave women paid maternity leave and allowed pregnant women to switch to lighter work in the seventh month of pregnancy. Midwives were retained by the party in order to reduce the high rates of maternal and infant death during childbirth. Rural health and education of women increased considerably.

The best-known and most-discussed Chinese social policy is the single-child family policy, started in 1979. Under this policy, undertaken as a draconian measure to lower China's birthrate, women are strongly encouraged to abort any subsequent fetus. It is, of course, in direct contrast to the orthodox Marxian view that overpopulation is a capitalist myth. The Chinese Communists have been pragmatic in this regard, arguing that planning is difficult in a nation that is large and growing rapidly. The policy has probably had a greater effect in freeing women from household duties than any other socialist country's policies. In addition, the relatively widespread availability of child care (less in rural areas), both in the form of factory and "street" nurseries, and in the informal form of older women working for mutual-aid teams, has enabled women to maintain high labor force participation. Nevertheless, Chinese women continue to express dissatisfaction with collective child care, partly because they doubt the quality of the low-paid child care workers.

It would be hard to argue that women in China are worse off than before the Communist regime came into power. The traditional system was extremely male-biased, and women were treated as chattel. However, traditional gender inequality persists among Chinese peasants, including rumors of high female infanticide rates, and it is considered an ongoing problem by the government.[29] Note that the bias toward male births in China need not be explained as a purely cultural factor: because women leave the household upon marriage, they are not a good investment, while sons bring daughters-in-law into the household. Therefore, private benefit-cost analysis on the part of many peasant households can lead to a surplus of sons over daughters.[30]

FOCUS

How many "missing girls" are there in China?

Demographers Sten Johansson and Ola Nygren have attempted to calculate the size of the supposed shortfall of female children in China.[31] Using Swedish data on sex ratios at birth, which has been continuously collected since 1749, they estimate that the "natural" sex ratio at birth is between 105 and 106 males per hundred females, and that it oscillates randomly within a narrow range. Over time, this ratio has risen from 104 males per hundred females in 1751–1760 to 106 males per hundred females in the 1980s, as a result of reduced rates of stillbirths and miscarriages, which are more likely to affect male babies. In China, however, the sex ratio at birth rose from 104.5 males per hundred females in 1969 to 107.4 by 1980, and to 111.0 in 1987. Therefore, they calculate that there are about half a million "missing girls" in 1987.

While disturbing, this statistic does not imply that all of these girls were aborted or killed shortly after birth. Some of them are reported as stillbirths and then given away for adoption, while other female births are not reported at all. A look at adoption statistics shows that adoptions of girls far outnumber those of boys: in 1987 the sex ratio of adoptees was 27 males per hundred females.

Another factor indicative of differential treatment of male and female children in China is the infant death sex ratio. Using data from both developed and undeveloped countries, Johansson and Nygren estimate the "normal" infant death ratio at about 130 males per hundred females. However, China had an infant death ratio from 1985 to 1987 of about 115 males per hundred females. While this statistic does not explain birth rate differences, it does help explain the overall skewed sex ratio in China.

While the skewed sex ratio in China has often been attributed to the one-child rule, another demographer, Ansley Coale, argues that this is not as important a factor as is the continuing bias in Chinese society in favor of males. Ethnic minority areas where the policy is not enforced have female shortages, while Shanghai and Beijing, where the rule is enforced, have no shortages.[32] It will be interesting to see how China deals with the "marriage gap" that is coming in the near future, with researchers projecting that "by the year 2020, one million men a year in China will reach marriageable age, but will not be able to find a bride."[33]

Recently, the Chinese government's "iron rice bowl" policy of guaranteeing able-bodied persons a job that would feed them for life has been dropped in favor of allowing factories to adjust their labor forces, particularly in older industries such as coal and steel. This move towards a market economy has led to a disproportionate number of women among the laid-off workers. One observer reports: "Factory managers regard women as burdensome because of the need to pay maternity benefits, and so women often are last hired and first fired. In addition, women are less likely than men to protest if they are dismissed."[34] This trend may lead to a decreased birth rate, as women forego births or even undergo sterilization so as to keep their jobs. Also, open debate is occurring over whether so many women should be working, even though (as shown in Table 11.2) women's proportion of the labor force is below that in most industrialized countries.[35] And, ironically, movement towards decollectivization of the agricultural system has reinforced traditional gender roles in rural households, thereby potentially reducing women's entitlements even as rural incomes rise.[36]

Cuba

Cuba is also an interesting case for contrast, since it is the only Latin American socialist country we are considering in this chapter and, therefore, comes from a different tradition of gender roles. As shown in Table 11.2, the female labor force participation rate is much lower in Cuba than in the other socialist countries, but it has risen substantially since the revolution. The legacy of "machismo" has been difficult, but not impossible, to counteract through political and social change.

Since Fidel Castro came to power in Cuba in 1959, he has spoken of "the need to free women from domestic slavery so that they could participate widely in production to the benefit of women themselves and the Revolution."[37] In the mid-1970s, Cuba went a step beyond other socialist countries by implementing the Cuban Family Code, which explicitly makes husband and wife equally responsible for housework and child care.[38] This is a strikingly different approach from attempting to provide communal housework and child care services, as other countries have done in the hope that families would make use of them in order to ease the domestic burden. Material constraints on Cuban society have made it difficult for Castro to attempt the latter course. While public child care facilities have been built, they are a considered lower priority by government planners than investment in directly productive capital.

This political initiative followed the attempt in the late 1960s to mobilize women in great numbers to enter the labor force in both manufacturing and agricultural capacities. This effort proved problematic, as over three-quarters of the women who entered the labor force in 1969 left work before the year ended.[39] This turnover appeared to be directly related to the pressure women felt from having to maintain housework and child care duties as well as paid labor.

Today, the main obstacle to women's achieving equality in terms of pay and occupational distribution is employers' tendency to treat them as a reserve labor force. The Cuban principle of guaranteed employment applies only to men and to female household heads. Therefore, many women experience high job turnover, and their employment is reduced in times of economic pressure when it is hard to employ all men. While Cuba has an equal pay law, women are overrepresented in the lower-paying jobs. There is also evidence that managers refuse to hire women, partly because firms are responsible for paying the full cost of the mandated 18-week paid maternity leave (six weeks before and twelve weeks after childbirth). Given the relatively high birthrate in Cuba, this can be a substantial cost consideration for employers. Since subsidies and other material support from the Soviet Union were reduced considerably following its reorganization, economic pressures on Cuba have increased, reducing the probability of additional radical change regarding the roles of women in the labor market.[40]

Israeli kibbutzim

The kibbutz system dates back to 1909, when the first kibbutz was founded by Jewish settlers of Palestine. The system experienced a large population increase in the 1940s, absorbing European war refugees. Many of these refugees were young people who had radical socialist leanings, in sharp contrast to the Orthodox Judaism practiced by their parents.[41] They brought along socialist ideas concerning gender equality and attempted to implement them in the kibbutzim. By 1983, 3.4 percent of the Jewish population of Israel, or about 115,000 persons, lived in 267 settlements.[42]

What are the possibilities for gender inequality to develop in this system? Property and income are owned by the kibbutz, which is run as a collective. All kibbutz members receive the same food, clothing, housing, and health services, and no salaries are paid. Inequality would have to take the form of differences in privilege, power, and prestige in terms of the roles each sex takes within the community.[43]

Women appear to be viewed as supplementary to the extent that the main aim of the kibbutz is to maintain agricultural production. Women are less likely to work in agriculture due to physical strength considerations and tradition, and more likely to work in child care, education, and food preparation. All of these are considered secondary functions that support the agricultural function of the kibbutz.[44]

One study compares occupational segregation index values for the kibbutzim population to the entire Israeli population.[45] A comparison of 1961 and 1983 finds that the kibbutz system had higher index values at both points and appeared to be stable in its sex segregation pattern, with an index value of 69 for both years when calculated at the two-digit level of occupational aggregation. (The same basic patterns result when the indexes are calculated at the one-digit or the three-digit coding level for occupations.) Meanwhile, the index for all of Israel rose from 54 in 1961 to 59 in 1983, still well below the level in the kibbutzim. The range of occupations open to kibbutzim women was much more limited than for the general Israeli population.[46] Additionally, women were much less likely to be found in kibbutzim leadership ranks.[47]

Studies concur that sexual division of labor was less evident in the past (there were also fewer women as a percentage of kibbutzniks). When the kibbutz system was first founded, the majority of members spent most of their time in agricultural production. It was only after achieving a certain financial size and level of stability that additional stratification developed.[48]

Women who remain on the kibbutz do not generally appear to be unhappy with the division of labor or the resulting division of nonpecuniary benefits.[49] However, they are more likely to leave the kibbutz than are men, both after arriving there as adults and after being born there. This factor has been of ongoing concern to kibbutzim; while the current high rate of immigration serves to keep their population up, they want to maintain at least replacement-level birth rates so as to have future generations to draw upon. Clearly, dissatisfied individuals among both sexes leave, skewing the sample of people on kibbutzim towards the satisfied ones. Female subordination may appear more natural to both second and third generation kibbutzniks and to recent immigrants, most of whom hail from the Orthodox Jewish traditions of Eastern Europe, so this problem may be diminishing. Additionally, one of the major sources of dissatisfaction for women in the past, the attempt to raise children communally rather than in family units within the kibbutzim, has been essentially discontinued.[50] However, while kibbutzim may provide a stable communal way of life, this is not a system in which gender equality is greater than in the surrounding society.

Transition in Eastern Europe

The biggest news story of the 1990s has been the fall of the Soviet empire and the subsequent attempts of the Soviet Union and its satellites to transform themselves into viable market-oriented economies and democratically governed nations. As this process began, various Eastern European countries were at different points on the road to achieving systems more along the lines of those found in Western Europe. While Hungary had already developed some aspects of a capitalist economy, it had retained central planning features and political aspects of socialism that required revision.[51] East Germany had the unique situation of being essentially absorbed by its capitalist twin, West Germany. However, all these countries were in the situation of having to revise their existing social policy structure, partly by necessity, as their economic status became shakier after dissolution of the empire, and partly due to philosophical changes brought about by the changing political structure.

One of the most notable aspects of this transition has been its strong labor market effects. Unemployment, which had not existed officially, has become a reality. Although much employment may have been in the form of underemployment, where people were not working a full day, and unproductive employment, where people were producing at a level below that predicted by their pay, it is also the case that the opening of markets to foreign entry and the dismantling of parts of the bureaucratic structure led to widespread worker displacement through factory and office closings. This trend has been reflected in dropping labor force participation rates for both sexes across these countries (as shown in Table 11.2), along with rising unemployment rates.[52]

While it is clear that economic circumstances have generally worsened for people in these countries, the question remains as to whether women or men are affected more by these changes. The answer varies in degree across countries by the pre-transition distribution of women and men across different sectors of the economy, the degree to which multiple-earner families can absorb unemployment and underemployment of one or more family members, and the degree to which social services that affect women and men differently are maintained or rolled back. But the basic characterization that emerges from studies of the various countries is that a disproportionate number of women lost their jobs relative to men and have had more trouble regaining employment.[53]

Another common element across these countries is that there has been a significant reduction in the amount of time spent queuing for scarce commodities, a benefit which does tend to accrue to women. In addition, although time spent shopping has been reduced, this does not mean that total nonmarket work has decreased. As social services have been cut back, women have been more likely to have picked up the slack in areas such as child care and eldercare.

In East Germany, for example, it appears that women are bearing the brunt of the transition, both in terms of increased unemployment and in terms of increased nonmarket work responsibilities. As one East German official noted early in 1993, Eastern German "women in general have lost from unification, but working mothers have lost far more."[54] A striking reflection of the increased pressure on East German women was the large drop in the birth rate following unification, accompanied by a rise in female sterilization.[55]

Several features of women's preunification working conditions in East Germany were unique, compared with those in OECD countries. East German women had the highest female labor force participation rate and were much less likely to work part-time than their OECD counterparts. They had attained high educational levels, with few women lacking either a vocational certificate or a college degree and their participation covered a broad occupational and industrial employment spectrum. These conditions appear to have been enabled, to a large degree, by the heavy use of institutionalized child care and other support services that replaced traditional nonmarket activities, particularly as contrasted to the situation in West Germany.[56] Preunification, in East Germany, over 80 percent of preschool-aged children could be accommodated in preschools and nurseries, even for those under the age of three. In West Germany, only about 4 percent of children under three and 30 percent of children between three and four could be accommodated. East German nursery schools and kindergartens were run by public authorities or by enterprises, with the parents paying only for meals and diapers, and they were open from 6 a.m. to 6 p.m. In contrast, West German kindergartens – run by public authorities, the churches, or private groups, but only rarely by enterprises – can be quite expensive, although sometimes the fees are means-tested, and many are only open half the day. In East Germany, hot meals were generally served in the cafeterias of enterprises and in kindergartens and schools. There were also publicly run service houses attached to many firms, at which, for example, dirty laundry could be dropped off in the morning and clean laundry picked up at the end of the day.[57]

Due both to the unavailability of public funding and to reduced provision of child care by increasingly strapped firms, widespread closing of both public and private child care facilities has occurred, making it more difficult for mothers to work. Demand for female labor has also declined; in the current high unemployment situation, it appears that employers avoid hiring young women, in particular, "wary of potential absenteeism and the state's liberal maternity leaves."[58] Additionally, East German women were overrepresented in those economic sectors that have shrunk the most once transition was underway – e.g., administrative positions related to the operation of central planning. By early 1993, the employment rate for adult women had fallen to almost half its 1988 level.[59]

Summary

While socialist systems have made notable strides towards achieving gender equality, notably high female labor force participation rates and fairly high relative earnings for women, they have been hampered by the continuing problem of how to devolve family household work and child care responsibilities onto the community. In some situations, like the Israeli kibbutzim, women actively objected to giving up child care responsibilities, in particular. In other situations, such as in Cuba, material constraints prevented full realization of the potential of providing such services to all who wished to use them. Additionally, traditional sex role systems, as reflected in continuing occupational sex segregation and continuing greater responsibility of women for nonmarket work, have proved more intractable than theorists had imagined. Nevertheless, as many socialist systems make the transition to capitalism, the effects of reduced communal support for social functions such as childraising have had a noticeable impact on women's ability to continue high levels of participation in paid work.

Endnotes

1. See *The Woman Question: Selections from the Writings of Karl Marx, Frederick Engels, V.I. Lenin, Joseph Stalin* (New York: International Publishers Co., 1951).

2. Lewis H. Morgan, *Ancient Society, or Researches in the Lines of Human Progress from Savagery Through Barbarism to Civilization* (New York: Henry Holt & Co., 1877). This influence is discussed by Robert C. Tucker (ed.), *The Marx-Engels Reader, Second Edition* (New York: W.W. Norton, 1978): 734. Engels drew heavily on notes on Morgan's book made by Marx.

3. Tucker, *op. cit.*: 745–746.

4. Hilda Scott, *Does Socialism Liberate Women? Experiences from Eastern Europe* (Boston, Mass.: Beacon, 1974): 36.

5. Muriel Nazzari, "The 'Woman Question' in Cuba: An Analysis of Material Constraints on its Solution," *Women and Poverty*, eds. Barbara C. Gelpi, Nancy C. M. Hartsock, Clare C. Novak, and Myra H. Strober (Chicago, Ill.: University of Chicago, 1985): 65.

6. Scott, *op. cit.*: 209. For discussion on the issue of how the "woman question" has been dealt with during the early part of the transition in Eastern Europe, see Barbara Einhorn, *Cinderella Goes to Market: Citizenship, Gender and Women's Movements in East Central Europe* (London: Verso, 1993).

7. World Bank, *World Development Report 1996* (Tables 1, 27, 28, 29, 31).

8. Jacob Mincer, "Intercountry Comparisons of Labor Force Trends and of Related Developments: An Overview," *Journal of Labor Economics*, 3, no. 1, supplement (January 1985): S6 (Table 3).

9. Gail W. Lapidus, "The Interaction of Women's Work and Family Roles in the Former USSR," *Women's Work and Women's Lives*, eds. Hilda Kahne and Janet Z. Giele (Boulder, Col.: Westview, 1992): 146–147.

10. Halina Grzymala-Moszczynska, "Women in Poland," *Women in Cross-Cultural Perspective*, ed. Leonore Loeb Adler (New York: Praeger, 1991): 64.

11. ILO, *Yearbook of Labour Statistics* (1992–96) (Tables 16, 17).

12. Alexander Szalai (ed.), *The Use of Time: Daily Activities of Urban and Suburban Populations in Twelve Countries* (The Hague, Netherlands: Mouton, 1972). Peru, the twelfth country in the sample, is not included in the reported results.

13. John P. Robinson, Philip E. Converse, and Alexander Szalai, "Everyday Life in Twelve Countries," *The Use of Time: Daily Activities of Urban and Suburban Populations in Twelve Countries*, ed. Alexander Szalai (The Hague, Netherlands: Mouton, 1972): 114.

14. F. Thomas Juster and Frank P. Stafford, "The Allocation of Time: Empirical Findings, Behavioral Models, and Problems of Measurement," *Journal of Economic Literature* 29, no. 2 (June 1991): 475–477; United Nations Development Programme, *Human Development Report 1995*: 95–96.

15. Scott, *op. cit.*: 212.

16. Barbara R. Bergmann, "Feminism and Economics," *Challenge* 27, no. 4 (July–August 1984): 49.

17. Alastair McAuley, *Women's Work and Wages in the Soviet Union* (London: George Allen & Unwin, 1981). Michael Paul Sacks, *Women's Work in Soviet Russia: Continuity in the Midst of Change* (New York: Praeger, 1976), supports McAuley's findings. For additional discussion of the situation in the Soviet Union from its inception to the 1970s, see Gail Warshofsky Lapidus, "Occupational Segregation and Public Policy: A Comparative Analysis of American and Soviet Patterns," *Women and the Workplace: The Implications of Occupational Segregation*, eds. Martha Blaxall and Barbara B. Reagan (Chicago, Ill.: University of Chicago, 1976): 119–136; Dorothy Atkinson, Alexander Dallin, and Gail Warshofsky Lapidus (eds.), *Women in Russia* (Stanford, Calif.: Stanford University, 1977); Gail Warshofsky Lapidus, *Women in Soviet Society: Equality, Development, and Social Change* (Berkeley, Calif.: University of California, 1978); and Gail Warshofsky Lapidus (ed.), *Women, Work, and Family in the Soviet Union* (Armonk, N.Y.: M.E. Sharpe, 1982).

18. Lena Zhernova, "Women in the USSR," *Women in Cross-Cultural Perspective*, ed. Leonore Loeb Adler (New York: Praeger, 1991): 73.

19. Harold Takooshian, "Soviet Women," *Women in Cross-Cultural Perspective*, ed. Leonore Loeb Adler (New York: Praeger, 1991): 83.

20. Zhernova, *loc. cit.*

21. See Scott, *op. cit.*, as a historical study on Czechoslovakia in particular, where the author had lived.

22. Halina Grzymala-Moszczynska, "Women in Poland," *Women in Cross-Cultural Perspective*, ed. Leonore Loeb Adler (New York: Praeger, 1991): 64–65.

23. Lapidus, *op. cit.* (1982): 42, points out that this reflects a basic contradiction in Marxian socialism, which is pronatalist and anti-Malthusian, valuing maternity as of social as well as private benefit, but it also wishes to extend full economic and social liberation to women.

24. Gur Ofer and Aaron Vinokur, "Work and Family Roles of Soviet Women: Historical Trends and Cross-Section Analysis," *Journal of Labor Economics* 3, no. 1, supplement (January 1985): S328–S354.

25. The economic roles of women and men in religious communities professing gender equality have not been widely studied by economists, but are of interest in considering interpretations of equality and gaps between theory and practice; cf. Priscilla J. Brewer, " 'Tho' of the Weaker Sex': A Reassessment of Gender Equality Among the Shakers," *Signs* 17, no. 3 (Spring 1992): 609–635.

26. For background, see Elisabeth Croll, *Feminism and Socialism in China* (London: Routledge & Kegan Paul, 1978); Elisabeth Croll, *Women and Rural Development in China: Production and Reproduction* (Geneva, Switzerland: International Labour Office, 1985); Lucy C. Yu and Lee Carpenter, "Women in China," *Women in Cross-Cultural Perspective*, ed. Leonore Loeb Adler (New York: Praeger, 1991): 188–203; and Gale Summerfield, "Chinese Women and the Post-Mao Economic Reforms," *Women in the Age of Economic Transformation*, eds. Nahid Aslanbeigui, Steven Pressman, and Gale Summerfield (London and New York: Routledge, 1994): 113–128.

27. See Elisabeth Croll, "Rural Production and Reproduction: Socialist Development Experiences," *Women's Work: Development and the Division of Labor by Gender*, eds. Eleanor Leacock, Helen I. Safa, and contributors (South Hadley, Mass.: Bergin & Garvey, 1986): 224–252, for a discussion of the effects of collectivization on gender relations, using the Soviet Union, China, Cuba, and Tanzania as examples.

28. Carolyn Teich Adams and Kathryn Teich Winston, *Mothers at Work: Public Policies in the United States, Sweden, and China* (New York: Longman, 1980).

29. Delia Davin, "Women, Work and Property in the Chinese Peasant Household of the 1980s," *Male Bias in the Development Process*, ed. Diane Elson (Manchester, United Kingdom: Manchester University, 1991): 29–50.

30. See the Focus on sex ratios in Chapter 12 for more discussion of what causes skewed sex ratios.

31. Sten Johansson and Ola Nygren, "The Missing Girls of China: A New Demographic Account," *Population and Development Review* 17, no. 1 (March 1991): 35–51.

32. Ansley J. Coale, "Excess Female Mortality and the Balance of the Sexes in the Population: An Estimate of the Number of 'Missing Females'," *Population and Development Review* 17, no. 3 (September 1991): 517–523.

33. Janet Basu, "China's Looming 'Marriage Gaps'," *Stanford Observer* 29, no. 3 (Spring 1995): 10.

34. Sheryl WuDunn, "Layoffs Put New Woes on Chinese," New York Times News Service article in *The Commercial Appeal* (May 16, 1993): A16.

35. Gale Summerfield "Effects of the Changing Employment Situation on Urban Chinese Women," *Review of Social Economy* 52, no. 1 (Spring 1994): 40–59.

36. Nahid Aslanbeigui and Gale Summerfield, "Impact of the Responsibility System on Women in Rural China: An Application of Sen's Theory of Entitlements," *World Development* 17, no. 3 (1989): 343–350.

37. Muriel Nazzari, "The 'Woman Question' in Cuba: An Analysis of Material Constraints on its Solution," *Women and Poverty*, eds. Barbara C. Gelpi *et al.* (Chicago, Ill.: University of Chicago, 1985): 65, paraphrasing from Fidel Castro, "Speech to the Women" (Havana, 1959): 9.

38. Marjorie King, "Cuba's Attack on Women's Second Shift, 1974–1976," *Women in Latin America: An Anthology from Latin American Perspectives*, eds. Eleanor Leacock and contributors (Riverside, Calif.: Latin American Perspectives, 1979): 118–131.

39. Nazzari, *op. cit.*: 74.

40. See Sandor Halbebsky and John Kirk, *Transformation and Struggle: Cuba Faces the 1990s* (New York: Praeger, 1990).

41. Charlotte G. O'Kelly and Larry S. Carney, *Women and Men in Society, Second Edition* (Belmont, Calif.: Wadsworth, 1986): 282–283.

42. Shoshana Neuman, "Occupational Sex Segregation in the Kibbutz: Principles and Practice," *Kyklos* 44, Fasc. 2 (1991): 203–219.

43. O'Kelly and Carney, *op. cit.*: 286.

44. Judith Buber Agassi, "Theories of Gender Equality: Lessons from the Israeli Kibbutz," *Gender and Society* 3, no. 2 (June 1989): 160.

45. Neuman, *loc. cit.*

46. O'Kelly and Carney, *op. cit.*: 286.

47. Lionel Tiger and Joseph Shepher, *Women in the Kibbutz* (New York: Harcourt Brace Jovanovich, 1975): 262.

48. *Ibid.*

49. See Aviva Zamir, *Mothers and Daughters: Interviews with Kibbutz Women* (Norwood, Pa.: Jerome S. Weiman, 1986).

50. Clyde Haberman, "Scene: A Purist Kibbutz. Topic: Bringing Up Baby," *New York Times* (October 12, 1994): A4, profiles the one remaining kibbutz with communal childrearing.

51. For a discussion of events in Hungary, see Julia Szalai, "Some Aspects of the Changing Situation of Women in Hungary," *Signs* 17, no. 1 (Autumn 1991): 152–170.

52. Robert W. Bednarzik, "Helping Poland Cope with Unemployment," *Monthly Labor Review* 113, no. 12 (December 1990): 25–33.

53. Cf. Bozena Leven, "Unemployment Among Polish Women," *Comparative Economic Studies* 35, no. 4 (Winter 1993): 135–146; ; Sue Bridger, Rebecca Kay, and Kathryn Pinnick, *No More Heroines? Russia, Women and the Market* (London and New York: Routledge, 1996)

54. "Women of Eastern Germany Under Pressure Not to Have Children," Washington Post/L.A. Times Wire Service article in *Cereal Info* (April 28, 1993): 2, quoting Editha Beier.

55. *Ibid.*

56. See Lynn Duggan, "Restacking the Deck: Family Policy and Women's Fall-Back Position In Germany Before and After Unification," *Feminist Economics* 1, no. 1 (Spring 1995): 175–194, for further discussion of family policy effects in the two Germanies.

57. Hedwig Rudolph, Eileen Appelbaum, and Friederike Maier, "After German Unity: A Cloudier Outlook for Women," *Challenge* 33, no. 6 (November-December 1990): 36.

58. *Cereal Info, loc. cit.*

59. *Ibid.*

60. Tucker, *op. cit.*: 745.

*F*urther reading and statistical sources

Aslanbeigui, Nahid, Steven Pressman and Gale Summerfield (eds.) (1994). *Women in the Age of Economic Transformation: Gender Impact of Reforms in Post-Socialist and Developing Countries*. London and New York: Routledge. Includes case studies of the former East Germany, Poland, Romania, the former Soviet Union, and China.

Funk, Nanette and Magda Mueller (eds.) (1993). *Gender Politics and Post-Communism: Reflections from Eastern Europe and the Former Soviet Union*. London and New York: Routledge. Reflective essays on transition, mostly by female scholars from the treated countries.

Kahne, Hilda, and Janet Z. Giele (1992). *Women's Work and Women's Lives: The Continuing Struggle Worldwide*. Boulder, Colo. Westview. Overview essays and two chapters on socialist economies in transition, plus one contrasting former East and West Germanies.

Moghadam, Valentine M. (ed.) (1993). *Democratic Reform and the Position of Women in Transitional Economies*. Oxford: Clarendon. Overview essays and chapters on socialist economies in transition.

United Nations, Economic Commission for Europe (1995). *Women and Men in Europe and North America 1995*. Joint publication with Eurostat, the Statistical Office of the European Communities. Very helpful collection of statistics on many of the countries in this chapter as well as many countries in Western Europe and the U.S. and Canada; very good graphics.

Discussion questions

1. Why might one believe that the abolition of private property is a necessary condition for real gender equality?

2. Engels believed that monogamy arose from economic causes, but that if private property were abolished, people would be more likely to be monogamous.[60] Do you agree or disagree?

3. Consider the Focus on women's progress in the Soviet Union. What do you think would happen in your country if there were a wholesale loss of men?

4. Consider the Focus on "missing girls" in China. By what types of policies could the Chinese government attempt to reduce the bias towards male children?

5. Can the approach tried in Cuba of mandating equal responsibility for nonmarket work by sex within the family be successful without a corresponding commitment to provision of communal household support services?

6. Women were the main force in the kibbutzim system pushing for children to remain with the family rather than with the community. Does this indicate anything about their relative preferences for traditional family structure and childraising?

7. Consider the gender effects of German reunification. Are the changes that East German women face a clear loss of relative position (relative both to West German women and to German men)? To what extent does the possibility of higher living standards after reunification offset their reduced participation in paid work?

8. How could a transition from socialism to capitalism be made easier for women? How could it be made easier for men? Is redistribution from women to men inevitable in the transition process?

9. How might an economist go about calculating whether a given individual is helped or hurt by economic transition?

10. Does this chapter provide fuel for the view that gender roles are immutable, or for the view that they are changeable?

Nonindustrialized Traditional Societies

CHAPTER

12

*T*his chapter considers a broad group of societies – namely, those with relatively non-industrialized economies. Consequently, we need to consider broader questions than were addressed in Chapters 10 and 11, such as: Do we study societies to look for regularities, or to look for exceptions? Is it useful to develop typologies of societies? These questions have generally lain outside the realm of economics and more within the disciplinary borders of anthropology. However, in developing a broader view of economic patterns by gender, it is necessary to think about how systematic examination of other countries that have very different social structures and economic development levels can provide insights on the forces motivating economic gender differences across societies. In order to begin this process, data, where available, are presented on contemporary labor market behavior for a broad range of countries. Then, the chapter discusses inherent limitations in evaluating labor market data for societies that are not highly industrialized. Next, a typology of societies by level of agricultural development and its ability to generate insights about the sexual division of labor and relative status of women across societies is considered. Then, some individual countries are considered to illustrate particular economic gender dynamics that have occurred as they became industrialized. The chapter closes with an analysis of how the mechanism of rural-urban migration has affected gender differences in many countries.

Overview of levels and trends in these countries

What group of societies are included in this chapter? Again in this chapter, *society* is taken as synonymous with *country*, although there is high variability in social and economic indicators between social groups within many nonindustrialized countries. This group of over 150 countries is characterized as of 1994 by low GNP per capita (with a cross-country mean of $3200, but a population-weighted average of $1100 per capita), low primary and secondary education rates for both sexes, low life expectancy (a mean of 63 years at birth), high infant mortality rates (66 per 1000 live births), a fairly rural population (44 percent urbanized), and high fertility rates (4.7 total live births per woman).[1] Reliable statistical data are collected irregularly in most of these countries, due to limited resources and political restrictions. Where data are available for this group of countries, comparisons are drawn below between their employment and earnings patterns, including labor force participation rates, occupational segregation indexes, and gender earnings ratios.

Labor force participation

Table 12.1 shows labor force participation rates where available for a comparable age range,[2] alphabetically by region and within region in declining order of female participation. There is a great deal of variability in female participation and proportion of the working population that is female, both within and between regions. Not surprisingly, there is less variation in male participation rates, although they range lower than rates for industrialized countries. North Africa and the Middle East are notable for having very low female participation. The widest range of rates is found in Africa. Rates in Central and South America do not rise over 59 percent of the female population in the prime-age range, while several African countries have rates above the majority of European countries. However, as in all the countries we have studied in Chapters 10 and 11, female rates are everywhere (except Burundi!) below male rates, and women almost never comprise the majority of the labor force.

What factors generate such variability across countries? Cultural factors appear to be important; additionally there appear to be strong links between low female labor force participation rates and low female literacy, high fertility, and high income inequality. One study has isolated the last feature as the most notable link.[3]

Analysts have suggested that four basic patterns of female labor force participation are found across countries:[4]

1. *The industrial society pattern:* a high female participation level exists due to high wages, the desire for better living conditions, and a reduced workload in the home. Many young people postpone marriage and remain in the labor force. Notions that women's place is in the home and that economic progress can free women from doing paid labor create an upper limit for female employment.
2. *The Latin American pattern:* female participation varies considerably but participation in nondomestic labor is generally low. Postponement of marriage is uncommon, but is sometimes practiced to permit wage work. Domestic labor is common among young girls from rural areas.
3. *The Caribbean pattern:* female participation rates vary considerably, but generally are higher than those in other areas. Higher female participation results from family instability and the need to be self-sufficient in the event of family disorganization. Domestic labor is infrequent. Trading is the major economic activity for women.
4. *The Muslim Middle Eastern pattern:* female participation is very low because of cultural attitudes and practices that prohibit women from public activities.[5] Inhibiting factors include early marriage and female seclusion. Women in these cultures (including some South Asian women) are expected to concentrate time and effort on their families.

This typology is somewhat problematic in its lack of discussion of African and Australasian labor force participation patterns, although individual countries can be analyzed to determine which of these patterns they express.

TABLE 12.1 Labor force participation rates by sex and proportion of labor force that is female

Region	Country	% Labor force/population		Women/labor force
		Women	Men	
Africa:				
	Burundi	92.0	91.4	0.53
	Burkina Faso	79.4	88.9	0.50
	Malawi	75.3	80.6	0.51
	Central African Republic	69.7	87.7	0.47
	Seychelles	64.5	83.6	0.43
	St. Helena	62.8	95.6	0.41
	Ethiopia	59.5	84.7	0.41
	Benin	59.1	90.6	0.44
	Namibia	51.9	71.4	0.44
	Congo	48.8	69.3	0.44
	Zimbabwe	48.5	79.4	0.40
	Guinea	47.4	82.4	0.40
	Mauritius	47.0	86.6	0.35
	Reunion	46.5	67.4	0.42
	Cape Verde	44.7	87.9	0.38
	Equatorial Guinea	44.1	92.7	0.35
	Botswana	43.6	76.9	0.39
	Ivory Coast	42.7	89.3	0.31
	Nigeria	37.5	80.3	0.34
	Sudan	31.3	85.6	0.28
	Swaziland	28.6	66.1	0.34
	Senegal	24.3	83.1	0.24
Asia:				
	Thailand	65.2	83.8	0.44
	Bangladesh	63.3	90.0	0.40
	Singapore	54.3	82.7	0.39
	Macao	53.5	75.1	0.43
	Indonesia	52.8	83.6	0.39
	Philippines	50.7	83.8	0.37
	Malaysia	37.0	77.3	0.32
	Sri Lanka	35.8	74.8	0.33
	Maldives	20.5	79.1	0.20
	Pakistan	14.6	85.0	0.14
Australasia:				
	Vanuatu	80.2	89.7	0.47
	Guam	62.8	86.3	0.38
	New Caledonia	54.2	86.1	0.37
	French Polynesia	51.0	77.0	0.37
	Cook Islands	46.9	74.8	0.37
	American Samoa	44.0	60.9	0.41
	Western Samoa	40.2	77.3	0.32
	Tonga	37.8	77.5	0.34
	Niue	36.9	86.3	0.38

TABLE 12.1 cont'd

Region	Country	%Labor force/population		Women/labor force
		Women	Men	
Caribbean:				
	Cayman Islands	75.9	87.7	0.48
	Bermuda	74.9	87.2	0.47
	Barbados	74.9	85.4	0.50
	Bahamas	70.4	83.6	0.47
	Jamaica	67.3	76.8	0.48
	Grenada	67.1	82.9	0.49
	U.S. Virgin Islands	64.7	76.3	0.48
	Antigua and Barbuda	61.9	78.1	0.46
	Guadeloupe	61.4	75.4	0.46
	Anguilla	60.7	82.0	0.43
	Netherlands Antilles	59.3	78.8	0.45
	Haiti	49.8	82.0	0.40
	Trinidad and Tobago	49.3	81.1	0.37
	St. Vincent	49.2	85.6	0.36
	Dominica	47.0	79.8	0.42
	Puerto Rico	39.9	70.1	0.41
Central America:				
	El Salvador	43.6	82.2	0.39
	Panama	41.4	80.1	0.34
	Nicaragua	39.7	87.5	0.34
	Mexico	37.0	84.0	0.32
	Costa Rica	36.0	84.0	0.30
	Honduras	34.7	86.4	0.30
	Guatemala	29.4	91.9	0.26
	Belize	21.6	46.8	0.32
North Africa/Middle East:				
	Cyprus	55.7	87.3	0.39
	Kuwait	34.3	53.9	0.24
	Turkey	34.0	80.8	0.30
	Bahrain	30.4	89.8	0.18
	Morocco	25.1	74.9	0.26
	Egypt	23.0	74.0	0.23
	Tunisia	21.7	79.3	0.21
	Jordan	13.2	74.8	0.14
	Iraq	10.5	75.3	0.12
	Iran	9.3	82.7	0.10
	Algeria	8.1	80.2	0.09
South America:				
	Falkland Islands	59.2	91.2	0.36
	Uruguay	57.6	84.7	0.43
	Paraguay	56.4	89.3	0.42
	French Guiana	54.8	78.2	0.38
	Bolivia	52.8	75.8	0.44

TABLE 12.1 cont'd

		%Labor force/population		Women/labor
Region	Country	Women	Men	force
South America:				
	Brazil	52.5	84.9	0.40
	Colombia	51.6	82.3	0.43
	Peru	49.5	79.4	0.40
	Argentina	47.1	82.4	0.37
	Venezuela	43.7	84.1	0.34
	Suriname	39.7	76.8	0.35
	Guyana	39.3	81.2	0.34
	Chile	33.9	75.2	0.32
	Ecuador	29.3	83.3	0.27

Source: ILO, *Yearbook of Labour Statistics* (1991–96) (Table 1). Data are from 1986–96 for persons ages 15 to 64 except Grenada and Suriname (for 15 to 65); Columbia, Costa Rica, Tunisia, and Swaziland (for 15 to 69); Guadeloupe (for 15 to 59); Jamaica and Uruguay (for 14 to 64); Guam and Puerto Rico (for 16 to 64); New Caledonia (for 20 to 64); and Anguilla, Bolivia, Brazil, Burkina Faso, the Caymans, Chile, Egypt, El Salvador, Guyana, Honduras, Iraq, Mexico, Morocco, Nicaragua, Niue, Panama, Senegal, Sri Lanka, Thailand, and Western Samoa (for 15 and over). The Congo data are for 1984; and Equatorial Guinea, Guinea, and the Sudan, for 1983.

Additionally, five patterns of how female labor force participation varies by age have been proposed, the first four of which pertain to countries with medium to high overall female labor force participation rates:[6]

1. central peak or plateau: no drop in female labor force participation during the childrearing years (e.g., Thailand);
2. late peak: women enter the labor force after childrearing (e.g., Ghana);
3. early peak: women work before childrearing, with no re-entry (e.g., Argentina);
4. double peak: participation drops during childrearing (e.g., Korea); and
5. participation rate is low and flat with respect to age (e.g., the Middle East).

Pattern (1) is found in Eastern Europe and Southeast Asia, while (3) is prevalent in Latin America and Western Europe, although there the pattern is moving towards (1). African countries tend to fall under either (1) or (2). Causal relationships are not directly implied by these patterns, although the different effect across cultures of marriage and subsequent childrearing on female labor force participation is apparently the main source generating variability.

Male labor patterns have received less scrutiny due to their lesser variability and their lack of variation in peak patterns. The general pattern is for male participation to rise early in life and to remain high throughout the lifespan. The main variations that enter with higher stages of development are a slightly delayed entry into the labor force, as more men continue to higher levels of education, and an earlier exit from the labor force, reducing rates among the youngest and oldest cohorts of men. However, some countries do have notably lower male participation rates, perhaps reflecting higher numbers of discouraged workers in tighter labor markets.

Occupational segregation

For comparison of segregation patterns across nonindustrialized countries, comparable data on occupational distribution by sex are available only for a very aggregated set of occupational categories, and data are not generally collected frequently. Table 12.2 displays sex segregation index calculations for the most recent available year from 1995 back through 1980 using seven broad categories.[7] Countries are listed in order of decreasing index value within geographic region. It is hard to generalize, except to note that countries with a large agricultural sector (e.g., most of Africa) tend to have low segregation values. Compared with the range of 21 to 45 found in the industrialized countries, much wider ranges are found in Asia and North Africa/Middle East (a range of 8 to 60), and countries in the Australasian, Caribbean, Central American, and Middle Eastern regions all appear to have somewhat higher segregation values on average.

The great variation in occupational segregation both within and across regions casts doubt on those theories of sex segregation that stress sex differences that do not vary by society – e.g., biological differences or preferences by sex that are not culturally specific. Additionally, from country to country, the percentage of workers that is female by occupational category varies greatly. This is in contrast to the pattern found in the developed countries, where the same occupational categories tend to be either female- or male-dominated across countries.

There is evidence that sex segregation is decreasing over time. One study of changes in sex segregation from 1960 to 1980 for 56 countries at various levels of development found a slight decline in the majority of the countries, but no straightforward links between development and the level of segregation.[8] Another study of segregation index changes in 22 Latin American countries from 1980 to 1990 found an average decline of 3 points which was related to rising female labor force participation and falling male labor force participation, as well as overall GDP growth, export growth, and the relative movement towards or away from export orientation.[9]

Earnings differentials

The difficulty in collecting systematic, dependable data at a national level in developing countries is particularly evident in the paucity of data available on earnings rates by sex.[10] Table 12.3 contains data for the fifteen countries in this sample for which the ILO has been able to collect earnings rates by sex. These ratios may strike you as surprisingly high, given that these countries are less developed. Additionally, for countries where data are available both overall and for manufacturing, the ratio is actually higher overall than in manufacturing in Costa Rica, Cyprus, Egypt, Kenya, Singapore, Sri Lanka, Swaziland, and Turkey by about ten percent (which was not found in the developed countries), while it is lower by about five percent in the Cook Islands and Paraguay.

The fact that these ratios are notably higher in these countries than in industrialized countries may reflect the sample selection aspect of female labor force participation in these countries: those women who work in jobs included in the sample earn fairly high wages. Particularly if these ratios reflect earnings for larger, generally better-paying firms, which are more likely to be included in surveys in any country, doubt is cast on their

TABLE 12.2 Occupational sex segregation indexes using seven occupational categories

Region	Country	Index	Year
Africa:			
	Seychelles	46	1981
	South Africa	46	1991
	Cape Verde	35	1990
	Nigeria	35	1986
	Sao Tomé and Principe	32	1981
	Namibia	30	1991
	Zambia	30	1980
	Zimbabwe	24	1987
	Equatorial Guinea	23	1983
	Gambia	22	1983
	Ghana	21	1984
	Sudan	20	1983
	Botswana	19	1991
	Malawi	18	1987
	Comoros	15	1980
	Rwanda	12	1989
	Togo	12	1981
	Mauritius	9	1990
	Ethiopia	5	1995
	Burkina Faso	3	1985
Asia:			
	Bangladesh	60	1986
	Malaysia	49	1993
	Brunei	42	1981
	Philippines	38	1994
	Maldives	25	1990
	Pakistan	25	1992
	Singapore	20	1993
	India	16	1981
	Thailand	15	1994
	Indonesia	13	1990
	Macao	13	1993
	Sri Lanka	8	1994
Australasia:			
	American Samoa	62	1981
	French Polynesia	51	1988
	Niue	50	1986
	New Caledonia	43	1989
	Tonga	43	1990
	Fiji	40	1986
	Cook Islands	38	1991
Caribbean:			
	British Virgin Islands	57	1980
	Turks and Caicos	51	1980
	U.S. Virgin Islands	50	1990
	Dominican Republic	49	1981

TABLE 12.2   cont'd

Region	Country	Index	Year
	Bahamas	45	1989
	Bermuda	42	1980
	Dominica	40	1989
	St. Vincent	39	1980
	Puerto Rico	38	1995
	Caymans	37	1991
	Barbados	36	1993
	Haiti	35	1990
	Trinidad & Tobago	34	1991
	Netherlands Antilles	32	1992
	Grenada	31	1988
Central America:			
	Belize	56	1980
	Panama	55	1991
	Honduras	49	1992
	Guatemala	41	1991
	Costa Rica	41	1994
	Mexico	40	1993
	El Salvador	33	1991
North Africa/Middle East:			
	United Arab Emirates	60	1980
	Algeria	55	1987
	Kuwait	50	1988
	Syria	49	1991
	Bahrain	45	1991
	Turkey	44	1993
	Iraq	40	1987
	Egypt	30	1995
	Iran	30	1986
	Cyprus	21	1989
	Morocco	18	1982
	Tunisia	11	1989
South America:			
	Falkland Islands	57	1991
	Suriname	48	1992
	Chile	47	1994
	Guyana	47	1980
	Venezuela	46	1993
	Paraguay	42	1993
	Ecuador	41	1990
	French Guiana	40	1982
	Uruguay	39	1993
	Bolivia	38	1991
	Brazil	35	1990
	Colombia	30	1992
	Peru	24	1994

Source: ILO, *Yearbook of Labour Statistics* (1985–96) (Table 2B).

TABLE 12.3 Nonagricultural hourly earnings ratios, women to men

Country	Women/men
Sri Lanka	0.97
Myanmar	0.95*
El Salvador	0.94*
Turkey	0.93
Cook Islands	0.89
Egypt	0.85
Kenya	0.85
Costa Rica	0.77
Paraguay	0.74
Singapore	0.73
Thailand	0.68
Macau	0.63*
Cyprus	0.60
Swaziland	0.58
Malaysia	0.54*

* For manufacturing only.
Source: ILO, *Yearbook of Labour Statistics* (1992–96) (Table 16). Data are from 1989–94.

representativeness. Women appear to be much more likely to be employed in lower-paying sectors of nonindustrialized economies. According to the United Nations Development Programme: "Women typically work about 25 percent longer hours than men: up to 15 hours more a week in rural India and 12 hours more in rural Nepal. But their total remuneration is less because of their lower wage rate and their preponderance in agriculture and the urban informal sector, where pay tends to be less than in the rest of the economy. In urban Tanzania 50 percent of the women working are in the informal sector, in urban Indonesia 33 percent and in Peru 33 percent."[11]

There are very few studies yet for undeveloped countries in which an attempt is made to unearth the causes of the earnings gap, and they have led to divergent results. A study of workers in Rawalpindi City, Pakistan, shows that for this sample, in which the gender earnings ratio is 0.60, about 40 percent of the gap is attributable to differences in characteristics between male and female workers;[12] an older study of Cyprus found 38 percent of the gap (with a ratio of 0.55) was attributable to differences in characteristics.[13] These results are roughly in line with results for the United States and other industrialized countries, indicating that employed women in undeveloped countries may not encounter worse discrimination with respect to pay than do women in developed countries. However, for six other countries where such studies have been carried out (Argentina, Colombia, Haiti, Kuwait, Malaysia, and Venezuela), differences in worker characteristics accounted for between 4 and 25 percent of the earnings gap; notably, the gender earnings ratios were higher in these samples, ranging from 0.64 in Kuwait to 0.87 in Haiti.[14] Finally, a study using 1977 data from Tanzania found that the entire gap was attributable to human capital differences![15]

Time use

Time use studies for agricultural societies show more striking gender differences than in industrialized societies. Women in rural Botswana in 1975 averaged 59.4 total hours in market and nonmarket work per week, while men averaged 47.8; women in Nepalese villages in 1981 averaged 75.6 hours in total work, while men averaged 52.6.[16]

The main factor causing women to have such high work levels appears to be the large amounts of housework they perform, particularly for women in rural areas and smaller towns. In one study conducted in Keneba, Gambia, women were spending over seven hours a day in cooking and water fetching out of a total of eleven hours a day spent on housework.[17] In a study from Queretaro, Mexico, women were spending over nine hours each day on housework.[18] Women in cities in developing countries, however, appear to have housework hours in line with women in developed countries; a study in Lima, Peru, found women spending about 5 hours daily on housework, for about 21 percent of their time, the same as in the developed countries.[19]

These time budget studies imply that women could realize large time reductions on certain repetitive tasks for relatively low capital costs on development projects such as provision of wells and fuel-efficient stoves. For instance, in one study of two Mozambican villages that measured time use before and after a water standpipe was installed, the average adult woman reduced time spent fetching water by almost two hours a day, reallocating the saved time almost equally between other forms of work and rest.[20]

Methods for evaluating the extent and value of work

The above data indicate that it is difficult to generalize about work patterns across the nonindustrialized world, but two generalizations can be made about the direction of biases in the data. First, definitions and collection methods for labor force activity will cause a downward bias for female participation and an upward bias for male participation. Second, because of women's greater participation in nonmarket work, measurements of their contribution to national product will be biased downward. While these problems occur in both developed and undeveloped countries, to the extent that the nonmarket and informal labor market sectors are of greater size in undeveloped countries, the mismeasurements are likely to be greater there.

Measurement of labor force activity

Richard Anker of the ILO has been instrumental in developing a reasoned critique of measurement methods.[21] He focuses on the problems both in collecting data and in creating a definition of labor force activity. Various problems can occur in data collection. Answers may be biased towards socially accepted norms (e.g., women not admitting to working outside the home, while men are less likely to admit they are not working for pay), respondents may have difficulty in understanding key words (e.g., work, main activity), informants may be nonrepresentative, and interviewers (who are often male) may bias estimates of female labor force participation downwards due to the way they interpret answers.

FOCUS

Time use in Togo

A study of Togolese rural women was conducted in 1985.[22] The survey analysts derived the following prototypical daily routine for Togolese rural women (75 percent of the women in Togo live in rural areas):[23]

4:00:	get up.
4:00–7:00:	fetch water in a series of trips.
7:00–8:00:	clean, prepare meal.
8:00–1:00:	collect wood, wash clothes, and/or do field work.
1:00–3:00:	cook meal and eat.
3:00–4:30:	grind millet for evening meal.
4:30–5:00:	rest.
5:00–6:00:	fetch water.
6:00–8:00:	cook meal and eat.
8:00:	go to bed.

According to this schedule, on average over ten hours a day are devoted to meal preparation and consumption and water carrying.

A deeper problem is how to define the labor force. Anker considers four possible definitions, each one broader than the previous one:

1. All persons who are paid.
2. All persons whose activities are market-oriented (i.e., whose output/service is sold).
3. All persons engaged in activities that are included in national income accounts (e.g., include unpaid animal tending along with other aspects of food production that currently are counted).
4. All persons producing items that are generally purchased in developing countries but are not necessarily included in national income accounts (e.g., gathering fuel, fetching water).

Anker shows how two surveys in India generate female labor force activity rates ranging from 4.5 percent up to 93.3 percent, depending on how broadly labor force activity was defined, while the current ILO definition generates rates between 53 and 75 percent. (The broader definitions added gathering sticks, making cow dung cakes for fuel, and fetching water.)[24]

Valuation of unpaid work

A problem related to the issue of how to define labor force activity is how to value unpaid work. Anker maintains national income estimates would be increased by 25 to 50 percent on average if unpaid work were taken into account.[25] A large number of studies have attempted to come up with the optimal method for valuing unpaid work.[26] Anker's colleague at the ILO, Luisella Goldschmidt-Clermont, has reviewed over forty such studies and has developed a framework for comparing methodologies.[27] The techniques fall into a two-by-two matrix: input- vs. output-oriented methods; methods measuring volumes vs. methods measuring values. Volumes can be expressed in units appropriate to the particular activity – e.g., number of workers or units of time. Market values are generally used for both inputs and outputs. Value methods, which are more commonly used than volume methods and more compatible with existing national product measures, fall into six input-oriented categories and two output-oriented categories. The input value methods include use of:

1. the wage of a substitute worker who would perform all of the various tasks done by the unpaid worker;
2. the foregone wage, or opportunity cost, of the person performing unpaid work;
3. the wage for market-equivalent functions;
4. the wages of workers performing similar market functions;
5. the average wage, or the legal minimum wage; and
6. the wage in kind (noncash benefits received by the unpaid worker).

The output value methods include use of:

1. the price of a market replacement for the unpaid work, and
2. the price of consumer expenditures related to the unpaid work.

Although input-value methods are more common, Clermont prefers output-related evaluations (as does Anker) as being more in keeping with the way that national product is defined (the sum of output times price per unit of output).

Clearly, adding the value of unpaid work to paid work in calculating national product would lead to a large increase in the estimated value of work done by women in all societies. The United Nations Development Programme estimates that 66 percent of female work and 24 percent of male work in developing countries is uncounted in the current UN System of National Accounts, and that females in these countries account for 53 percent of total time in all economic activities.[28] This has been viewed by many commentators as an important step towards ensuring that the economic importance of women receives full due in the political system. Additionally, economists view this as important, both for accuracy and for the sake of development planning.[29] For instance, development policies that shift many workers from unpaid to paid work can cause an increase in national product as currently measured but actually lead to a decrease in true national product if these workers are actually less productive at paid work than they were at unpaid work. Unfortunately, just as with national income accounting in general, there is not one perfect, easily implemented way in which to measure the value of unpaid work.

Level of gender inequality by type of society

We turn now to a consideration of how gender inequality, measured in both economic and noneconomic terms, may vary by type of society. One stratification method, developed by anthropologists, considers the type of agriculture performed in the society. This theoretical structure cuts across geographical and cultural boundaries, emphasizing, instead, the underlying economic structure developed by the interaction between the environment and the technology used by societies to obtain food from the environment. These structures can involve barter and/or formal or informal sharing of resources and outputs, but they do not necessarily involve exchange of money. Therefore, we will consider them premarket and preindustrial systems, although still economic systems. We will consider four broad types that correspond roughly to higher and higher levels of economic development (but only debatably to higher levels of social development): forager, horticultural, pastoral, and agrarian societies.[30] These societies are discussed mainly with reference to the defining level of technology, the degree of gender division of labor, and the level of male dominance perceived by observers within and without the culture. Central gender-related questions to be addressed by multicultural studies include: (1) Do sexual divisions of labor inevitably result in differences in power (in particular, control over material aspects of life, but also control over ideology), or is it possible to have "separate but equal" roles? (2) Are women universally subordinate? (3) If the answer to (2) is no, what types of societies are egalitarian with regard to gender?[31]

Forager societies

Forager societies are also known as hunter-gatherer societies. Because they have limited technology available with which to increase their agricultural productivity, they tend to be found only in ecological systems where noncultivated food is in plentiful, consistent supply. They are characterized by small, flexible communities, small family size, and little inequality by sex or other factors. Current examples include aboriginal peoples in Australia.

Six main patterns of gender division of labor appear in these societies:

1. Both sexes gather separately, men hunt (e.g., the Hadza of Tanzania).
2. Both sexes gather and hunt communally (e.g., the Mbuti Pygmies of Zaire).
3. Women gather, men hunt (e.g., the Bushmen of the Kalihari; the Washoe Indians of the U.S. Great Basin, who varied between (2) and (3), depending on the season).
4. Men hunt, women process the catch (e.g., Eskimos).
5. Women hunt some animals and gather, men hunt others and fish (e.g., the Tiwi of Australia).
6. Both sexes hunt, fish, and gather separately (e.g., the Agta of the Philippines).

The division of labor is related to the need for strength in hunting and fishing and associated with child care for women, so most societies do not even bother to train young girls to hunt. Meat sharing leads to wider contacts and influence for men, even though the women through their gathering may provide a larger share of daily food.

Forager societies appear to be the most sexually permissive type of society. Male dominance is limited, although in some societies (e.g., Eskimos) men do appear to be quite dominant. Childrearing appears to be less rigid, with many unisex activities for children, and both sexes may be found caring for children. While work may be subject to gender division, daily life is carried on communally, so the sexes intermingle frequently.

FOCUS

Flexible gender roles in American Indian societies

In many American Indian tribes, across several geographic regions, there was an interesting role referred to by some writers as cross-gender persons and by others as members of a third gender.[32] As one anthropologist describes these individuals, they "typically acted, sat, dressed, talked like, and did the work of the other sex." As children, they avoided taking on traditional tasks considered appropriate to their sex, and the adults would teach them the skills associated with the other sex instead. There was often a ceremony around their time of puberty to formally associate this role with them. Homosexual behavior appears to have been inextricably tied to these roles: The cross-gender males, or *berdaches*, took husbands and male lovers, and the cross-gender females, or *amazons*, had wives and female lovers. Lovers of these cross-gender persons were not considered to be cross-gender themselves. Berdaches and amazons were generally not only tolerated in their societies but often considered to be special or more valuable, and families who had one were often honored. Tribes could have one role but not the other, and the berdache role is found in more tribes than the amazon role. These roles met with much disfavor among whites who came in contact with the Indians, and by the end of the nineteenth century, many tribes had either discontinued the practice or practiced it surreptitiously. The role has been somewhat revived among some tribes, including the Lakotas and Navajos. Similar roles are still found in societies in other regions, including the *xanith* in Oman, the *mahu* of Tahiti, and the *hijra* in India.[33]

Horticultural societies

Horticultural societies employ a simple digging-stick and hoe version of agriculture. Their higher agricultural productivity allows them to develop more permanent, larger, and denser settlements than forager societies. Current examples include many tribes in South America, including the Yanamamö Indians in Brazil and Venezuela (who are infamous for their high rates of wife-beating).

Three main patterns of sexual division of labor appear:

1. men clear and cultivate (e.g., the Hopi).
2. men clear, women cultivate (e.g., the Iroquois).
3. men clear, both sexes cultivate, but often different crops; men may cultivate the prestige crops and women the staples (e.g., tribes in highland New Guinea).

In the more advanced horticultural societies, where more interaction occurs between tribes, females often handle the trading. This pattern is particularly common in Africa, where it is also common for both sexes to raise both prestige and staple crops (but, again, often different crops of both types by sex).

These societies display a range of gender relationship patterns, although they tend to be more male-dominated than forager societies. A range of marriage structures is found, including the fairly common practice of polygyny. Children are socialized into appropriate gender roles at an early age, with girls often performing childrearing tasks at a young age. It is not uncommon for men and women to lead almost separate daily lives.

Pastoral societies

In pastoral societies, the primary reliance for sustenance is on livestock herding and use of pasturage. These societies tend to be nomadic to some degree, as they must move herds around to feed and water them; their agricultural productivity is not high enough for them to keep the animals penned and feed them with raised produce. Current examples include many tribes in North Africa, sub-Saharan Africa, and Afghanistan.

These societies are generally viewed as male-dominated and display strong sex segregation patterns. Men do most of the herding, particularly of the larger animals. Women are occasionally involved in dairy activities; they may raise smaller animals, but mainly have household responsibilities, including childraising. Children learn their gender roles early, as boys help with the herding and learn fighting skills, while girls help with household chores. Women tend to have limited rights in relation to their husbands and their extended network of kinsmen. Divorce is common, but women have a harder time obtaining a divorce than do men.

Agrarian societies

Agrarian societies are characterized by the development of larger, immobile settlements. Through the application of more advanced technology, agricultural productivity is high and consistent enough to maintain such settlements. Fields are fertilized, irrigated, and plowed by the use of animals. Current examples include peasant populations in Africa, Asia, and Latin America; historical examples include the great civilizations of ancient Egypt, Greece, Rome, and China. In their most developed, productive form, these civilizations generated enough agricultural surplus to be able to support cities with populations not directly involved in agricultural production.

These societies display a much higher degree of stratification by gender and class than the other three society types. The development of a separate domestic sphere for women is attributable to these societies; it is found in its most extreme form in Muslim societies, where upper-class women, in particular, are secluded. Women were thereby isolated from the means of production and, in some societies, were (and are) treated more as property than as individuals with defensible rights. Children quickly enter the appropriate gender sphere, thereby perpetuating the division of labor where men work outside the home and women maintain the home and raise children.

Unifying principles

One broad study of the relative status of women in preindustrial societies, which defines status more broadly than just with respect to control over material factors, concludes: "Women seem never to fully dominate men in all of social life, but the degree of male dominance ranges from total to minimal."[34] Therefore, comprehensive theories attempting to explain the relative status of women to men must both allow for variation across cultures along the range from total male dominance to egalitarianism and explain why female dominance has not arisen in any circumstances.

What underlying principles can be developed to explain the apparently increasing level of male dominance and sexual division of labor, moving up the ladder, technologically speaking, through these four groups of societies? Analyst Peggy Sanday has developed the theory that peoples in dangerous environments have a higher degree of male dominance, while lush societies have more equality.[35] The gender division of labor is driven by male dominance, as men take the more prestigious tasks.

Another theory ties male dominance and the gender division of labor to the extent of private property and development of tools that can increase production and be owned privately. Only at the lowest technological levels, such as in forager societies, where there is little property, is there the possibility of egalitarianism. Once there is property, some of which is in the form of the means of production, then men are able to control it through their greater mobility (due to not bearing children) and/or physical strength. This theory is somewhat at odds with Sanday's theory, because it may be harder to maintain property in dangerous environments. An alternative view that integrates the two, but subordinates Sanday's theory, is that the most dangerous environments are man-made: as property increases and the means of production are consolidated in a few hands, the level of struggle increases in a society.

Other theories can be developed to explain why the degree of male dominance varies across societies. We have not considered the role of other stratifications such as caste or the question of whether social custom is an exogenous force for the gender division of labor and/or male dominance.[36] Additionally, we have not considered how the relative scarcity or abundance of one or the other sex might affect gender dynamics across societies. Consideration of relative bargaining power in such circumstances, and the need one sex might feel to control the availability of the other, can lead to various theories.

FOCUS

Sex ratios across societies

Sex ratios vary notably from country to country and region to region. In the world as a whole, there are 99 females per 100 males; 50.4 percent of the world population is male.[37] However, the 1990 censuses in India and China counted 93 and 94 females per 100 males respectively; Asia as a whole averages 95 females per 100 males. There are many other countries with highly skewed ratios towards males, including among the most populous: Bangladesh, Egypt, Pakistan, Papua, New Guinea, and Turkey. In East Asia and sub-Saharan Africa, however, there are 101 and 102 females per 100 males respectively. The ratios are also skewed towards females in developed countries.

These sex ratios are affected by net migration and by birth and mortality differences.[38] For instance, the ratios of 95 males per 100 females in the combined United States, Europe, and Japan and 88 per 100 females in the Russian Federation continue to reflect past war losses and past low fertility. In many countries, the skewed ratio may be created in part by social practices, or it may be the result of periods of hardship that tend to favor the survival of one sex (generally females) over the other (e.g., droughts in Africa and wars). However, some analysts have argued that sex ratios are a strong causal factor in creating social practices as well, including female labor force participation, sexual freedom, institutionalized homosexuality, polyandry, polygyny, wifesharing, and exchange of material possessions at the time of marriage.[39]

Alternatively, social practices such as polygamy and status systems may cause male bias. Consider the Trivers-Willard hypothesis: in polygamous societies, parents in good condition who will have strong healthy offspring should have males, parents in poor condition should have females.[40] One can think of this as a competition to have the most grandchildren: "a son in good condition can physically exclude other males from breeding and inseminate more females . . . than his equally fit sister. But a son in poor condition will do worse than his sister because he will probably fail to win any females at all."[41] Different biological mechanisms have been proposed for how this might happen: dominant persons/animals may produce more of certain critical hormones, influencing the likelihood of a particular sex of baby being developed; one sex may better survive maternal stress during gestation. Selective infanticide also can occur.

While male bias is extremely common, some groups favor females.[42] The hypothesis predicts that high-status females will have more of whatever child stays with the group after marriage, because status can only be passed on reliably to children who stay. It appears that the higher the social status of people and the more polygamous, the more likely they favor males. This pattern has emerged in various studies of preindustrial groups such as eighteenth-century German farmers, nineteenth-century Indian castes, and medieval Portuguese and current African pastoralists. This pattern is consistent with the hypothesis in two ways: first, a rich son is more likely to have multiple partners and thereby produce more offspring than a daughter; second, even in many monogamous societies, sons inherit wealth and status, but daughters leave home upon marriage.[43] Meanwhile, farther down the social scale, a poor son may be unlikely to marry at all, but a poor daughter may marry a rich man. Ethnographer Lee Cronk has studied the Mukogodos of Kenya, who are a kind of underclass to the Masai and Samburu, and has found that they are more likely to pay to have a daughter treated by a doctor than a son, and that more daughters than sons survive to the age of four. Many of the daughters marry rich Masai and Samburu men, while many sons fail to marry even one wife.[44]

Note that existence of bias does not imply that the population as a whole will have an imbalanced sex ratio, since imbalances reward parents for having the rarer sex and restore the balance. However, it appears that sexism is worsening in some countries such as India, where male bias appears to have spread to all status levels.[45] Such developments imply that new influences in developing countries are overwhelming fundamental principles of natural selection.

Examples from particular countries

Every country, as well as every society within a country, can provide both counterpoints and supporting points to develop our views of how women and men differ across economic situations. There are many possible inquiries to be developed, and it is left to the curious reader to delve into particular historical or contemporary examples. This section considers contemporary situations in three countries to illustrate ways in which men and women are subject to different economic opportunities and constraints in industrializing countries and ways in which people attempt to cope with economic problems by using various strategies. These situations include the use of homework, or subcontracting systems, in Mexico; changes in the textile industry in India; and changes related to the increasing number of poor female-headed households in Kenya. These situations lead to very different coping mechanisms in undeveloped countries, compared to developed countries, due to the lack of enforceable labor laws and the lack of a social safety net other than one's own kin and friends.

Mexico

The process of subcontracting production from large, often multinational firms to sweatshop and home-based workers is a major and growing source of income for a large percentage of Mexico's working women.[46] This is striking, considering that developed countries such as

Britain and the United States long ago moved away from such a practice. It is interesting to consider whether Mexico, long considered one of the most promising of the developing countries, will follow a similar path to development, or whether development will stall due to use of such work practices.

Subcontracting in Mexico, while generally thought of as mainly occurring in the textile industries (as was the case in Britain and the United States), actually involves a number of production methods that are generally performed in factories in developed countries. For instance, an electrical appliance firm may subcontract for various inputs, such as electronic coils.

Subcontracting is problematic from a social standpoint because its forms are generally resistant to enforcement of labor regulation, such as laws mandating safe working conditions, limited workhours, minimum wages, and avoidance of child labor. Also, workers in these situations generally are paid less than workers in the larger, originating firms. The flip side is that use of such relationships appears to have greatly increased female employment, both through substitution of lower-paid female labor for higher-paid male labor and through expansion of demand for these products due to low labor costs. Women appear to be viewed as more desirable workers than men due to their lower absenteeism rates, greater dexterity, and greater patience. Therefore, while the subcontracting system tends to divide the labor force, reducing worker power, it appears to have benefits for women due to the very unenforceability of labor regulations in this sector.

India

The textile industry in India has existed for centuries, and historically it appears to have provided good opportunities for women workers. The *Arthaśāstra* (circa fourth century B.C.) prescribes equal wages for men and women artisans producing silk in worksheds and lays down measures to protect female artisans from sexual harassment by male supervisors.[47] There were large numbers of independent, skilled women in the spinning industry at the beginning of the colonial period, but starting in the second half of the nineteenth century, these women rapidly disappeared from the industry. Their disappearance coincided with "the colonial period of deindustrialization, the flooding of Indian markets with Lancashire textiles and, eventually, with textiles produced by Indian mills."[48] Spinning continues to be a traditionally female occupation widely practiced by rural households to generate income. In the silk textile sector, women used to rear silkworms, spin, and weave; now they mainly work as unpaid helpers in the households of weavers and rearers.

Why did women disappear from the higher-paid, professionalized parts of the textile industry? Scholars studying this question have offered several hypotheses. First, some have noted that female spinners are concentrated in the sector using the oldest technology. Even if new technology comes along, they continue to use the old, because they do not have the funds to invest in the new capital equipment or are unwilling to dedicate the necessary high proportion of family income to such an investment.[49] Second, concerning the silk industry, one scholar has noted that sericulture (silkworm raising) used to serve as a supplementary source of income for agricultural peasant households. When landholdings shrank and the share of income from sericulture increased, men tended to assume control and women's roles became secondary.[50]

Third, while a large number of women were employed in cotton and jute mills when the modern textile industry emerged in the late nineteenth century, their numbers subsequently

dwindled. This may have been due in large part to protective legislation. Legal restrictions on the employment of women and children were imposed by the colonial government
in 1912 under pressure from Lancashire. These restrictions were followed by protective
labor laws modeled on ILO conventions.[51] These protective tendencies appear to have been
reinforced by middle-class beliefs that factory work by women was bad for children and
family.[52]

Fourth, urban factories face an increased supply of male labor, as workers displaced
from rural areas flow into the cities. In earlier periods, male textile workers tended to be
seasonal migrants from rural areas, whereas a large number of women workers were from
the urban working class. Thus, employers who prefer to hire men instead of women find it
easier to do so. A recent study of the Bombay textile industry indicates both the expansion
of an urbanized male labor pool and a decrease in women's textile employment.[53]

Finally, some scholars argue that changing production methods, rationalization of the
textile industry, technological change, and adoption of a three-shift production system in
textile factories have all tended to reduce women's participation.[54]

Kenya

It is estimated that over 29 percent of the households in Kenya are headed by women.[55]
However, in some low-income areas – particularly rural areas – female-headed households
comprise between 60 and 80 percent of all households. This appears to be much higher
than estimates for other countries. Many of these households are headed by widows, often
with a number of children to raise, given the high birth rate in Kenya. This is in addition
to households where the head is an absentee male, who usually has migrated to a city for
work and who may or may not provide remittances to his rural family.

Several coping mechanisms have developed that are either adaptations of traditional
forms of behavior or are completely new methods. Some women are sending children to be
raised by members of the extended family, (particularly grandmothers living in rural areas),
so that they may also migrate to the city and find work. Household units are also formed
to contain nonrelatives, particularly other women, either in paid boarding relationships
or informal household resource sharing.[56] Women also develop informal social and work
support networks, including informal at-home joint production, such as brewing beer.
Women who remain in rural areas have assumed increased responsibility for traditionally
male agricultural tasks. Additionally, the traditional – though not widespread, – social
practice of "woman marriage" continues, wherein a woman can acquire a wife by paying
a bride price to the bride's kin. One study found 3 percent of the households in one rural
community of Nandi tribespeople were headed by female "husbands."[57]

Policy Application: Rural-urban migration disincentives

While rural-urban migration flows are a widespread phenomenon in the developing world,
the sex composition of the flow of workers varies from region to region and country to
country, depending on the type of worker required in the urban areas. These unbalanced
flows affect sex composition (as well as the age composition) in the rural and urban areas,
leading to sex ratio imbalances within countries between these sectors. Patterns also vary
by whether migration is internal or external to a country. Men tend to migrate longer

distances and are more likely to participate in external migration.[58] Europe and the Middle East have received net "guest worker" flows from less developed countries that are predominantly male, although domestic worker flows are mostly female. In Latin America, internal rural-urban migrants are predominantly women; in Africa and generally across the rest of the developing world, they are predominantly men. This had led to an urban sex imbalance (and a rural imbalance in the opposite direction) of approximately 109 women for every hundred men in Latin American cities, while in African cities there are about 92 women for every hundred men.[59] These patterns vary by age as well: for instance, in Uruguay, men are the majority in the 20 to 24 age group of migrants, and women are the majority among the 15 to 19 age group and older ages.[60] These women mainly become domestic workers in the cities, which is the case in the rest of Latin America as well.[61]

While remittances to rural areas help sustain those remaining in these areas, work burdens may increase for those who remain behind (if migrants do not represent pure surplus labor). In Africa, in particular, women have remained behind, assuming almost full responsibility for agricultural production as well as maintaining households and children. Lesotho is an interesting case. Only men have been allowed to enter South Africa to work, and many men leave Lesotho to work in the South African gold mines.[62] In part due to this drain of men, Lesotho has remained relatively undeveloped. Its main industry of note is tourism, as border "entertainment centers" catering to white South African men have developed. Ironically, the development of this industry has led to women dominating internal rural-urban migration flows in Lesotho, as young women come to these centers to work as prostitutes.

Thailand has also developed a profitable tourism industry. Sex tourism there had a big rise in the 1970s; in 1978 tourism earned about $408.3 million. About two-thirds of the visitors are Japanese – mostly men. Prostitutes in Bangkok numbered about 20,000 in 1970, increased to 100,000 in 1977, and by 1981 totalled 200,000. Another 300,000 to 500,000 prostitutes in the rest of the country bring the total prostitution workforce to about 10 percent of the female population ages 14 to 24, many of whom are rural migrants to the cities.[63] One analyst notes that the "flexible working hours are important to single mothers."[64]

Heavy rural-urban migration flows have placed a strain on city services and living conditions in many places, leading authorities to attempt reduction of these flows. These attempts can take several forms: outright banning of migration for all but selected groups of migrants; attempts to make city life more difficult (generally in the form of reduced provision of city services, which tends to occur anyway on a per capita level as migrants enter cities); and attempts to make rural life more appealing by funneling more investment there. Migration flows, both internal and external, show that people respond to economic incentives. The task for policymakers is to counteract these incentives when the flows lead to costs that are not taken into account by individuals in their migration decisions (i.e., negative externalities).

Summary

Nonindustrialized traditional societies display many of the same patterns that are to be seen in industrialized societies: higher rates of male labor force participation than female labor force participation, high levels of sex segregation, and a gender earnings ratio of less than one (subject to sample selection bias due to the lower rate of female participation in many of these countries). They are also characterized by higher rates of nonmarket work for women. The least economically developed societies, the forager societies, are characterized as the most egalitarian, while male dominance, both social and economic, tends to rise with the level of preindustrial economic development.

*E*ndnotes

1. World Bank, *World Development Report 1996* (Tables 1, 6, 9, 28, 29). Some small countries – namely Barbados, the Bahamas, Cyprus, and Malta – are included in this chapter even though their level of development is relatively high. The countries included in this chapter range in scores on the U.N. Human Development Index from 23 to 174, although some included countries have no score due to their small size.
2. Some countries that calculate rates for all persons 15 years and over are included where their old population is a small percentage of total population.
3. Moshe Semyonov, "The Social Context of Women's Labor Force Participation: A Comparative Analysis," *American Journal of Sociology* 86, no. 3 (November 1980): 534–550. Here the measure of inequality is the percentage of national income received by the top 5 percent of the country's population.
4. Andrew Collver and Eleanor Langlois, "The Female Labor Force in Metropolitan Areas: An International Comparison," *Economic Development and Cultural Change* 10, no. 4 (July 1962): 367–385. See also Alma T. Junsay and Tim B. Heaton, *Women Working: Comparative Perspectives in Developing Areas* (Westport, Conn.: Greenwood, 1989).
5. For historical background, see Leila Ahmed, *Women and Gender in Islam: Historical Roots of a Modern Debate* (New Haven, Conn.: Yale University, 1992).
6. Sharon Stichter, "Women, Employment and the Family: Current Debates," *Women, Employment and the Family in the International Division of Labour*, eds. Sharon Stichter and Jane L. Parpart (London: Macmillan, 1990): 11–71.
7. See Chapter 6 for the segregation index formula and discussion of its range. The same occupational categories are used as in Chapter 10, Table 10.3.
8. Jerry A. Jacobs and Suet T. Lim, "Trends in Occupational and Industrial Sex Segregation in 56 Countries, 1960–1980," *Work and Occupations* 19, no. 4 (November 1992): 450–486.
9. Joyce P. Jacobsen, "Workforce Sex Segregation in Developing Countries: General Patterns and Statistical Relationships for Developing Countries in the Western Hemisphere," Janet Rives and Mahmood Yousefi (eds.), *Economic Dimensions of Gender Inequality: A Global Perspective* (Westport, Conn.: Greenwood, 1997): 35–56.
10. See also Katherine Terrell, "Female-male Earnings Differentials and Occupational Structure," *International Labour Review* 131, no. 4–5 (1992): 388–389, for a set of earnings ratios from the 1980s collected from a variety of sources.
11. United Nations Development Programme, *Human Development Report 1990*: 32.
12. Javed Ashraf and Birjees Ashraf, "Estimating the Gender Wage Gap in Rawalpindi City," *Journal of Development Studies* 29, no. 2 (January 1993): 365–376.
13. William J. House, "Occupational Segregation and Discriminatory Pay: The Position of Women in the Cyprus Labour Market," *International Labour Review* 122, no. 1 (January-February 1983): 75–93.
14. Studies cited in Terrell, *op. cit.*: 393; Nasra M. Shah and Sulayman S. Au-Qudsi, "Female Work Roles in a Traditional, Oil Economy: Kuwait," *Research in Human Capital and Development* 6 (1990): 213–246; Bruce J. Chapman and J. Ross Harding, "Sex Differences in Earnings: An Analysis of Malaysian Wage Data," *Journal of Development Studies* 21, no. 3 (April 1985): 362–376.

15. J. B. Knight and Richard H. Sabot, "Labor Market Discrimination in a Poor Urban Economy," *Journal of Development Studies* 19, no. 1 (October 1982): 67–87.

16. F. Thomas Juster and Frank Stafford, "The Allocation of Time: Empirical Findings, Behavioral Models, and Problems of Measurement," *Journal of Economic Literature* 29, no. 2 (June 1991): 476.

17. H. R. Barrett and A. W. Browne, "Time for Development? The Case of Women's Horticultural Schemes in Rural Gambia," *Scottish Geographical Magazine* 105, no. 1 (April 1989): 4–11.

18. Sylvia Chant, "Women and Housing: A Study of Household Labour in Querataro, Mexico," *Women's Role in Changing the Face of the Developing World*, eds. J. H. Momsen and J. Townsend (Durham, United Kingdom: Women and Geography Study Group of the Institute of British Geographers, Durham University, 1984): 1–39.

19. John P. Robinson, Philip E. Converse, and Alexander Szalai, "Everyday Life in Twelve Countries," *The Use of Time: Daily Activities of Urban and Suburban Populations in Twelve Countries*, ed. Alexander Szalai (The Hague, Netherlands: Mouton, 1972): 114.

20. Sandy Cairncross, "Domestic Water Supply in Rural Africa," Douglas Rimmer (ed.), *Rural Transformation in Tropical Africa* (Athens, Ohio: Ohio University, 1988): 46–63.

21. Richard Anker, "Female Labour Force Participation in Developing Countries: A Critique of Current Definitions and Data Collection Methods," *International Labour Review* 122, no. 6 (November-December 1983): 709–723. See also Richard Anker, "Methodological Considerations in Measuring Women's Labor Force Activity in Developing Countries: The Case of Egypt," *Research in Human Capital and Development* 6 (1990): 27–58, which is a case study illustrating the difficulties inherent in collecting labor activity data.

22. Togolese Foundation of Women in the Legal Profession, "Women's Participation in Development: The Case of Togo," *Women and Economic Development: Local, Regional, and National Planning Strategies*, ed. Kate Young (New York: Berg/UNESCO, 1990): 171–208. The sample pertains only to Northern Togo, but the writers claim that it is representative of the routine found in other Togolese rural areas.

23. Togolese Foundation of Women in the Legal Profession, *loc. cit.* (Table 5.3).

24. Anker (1983): 719.

25. Richard Anker, preface to Luisella Goldschmidt-Clermont, *Economic Evaluations of Unpaid Household Work: Africa, Asia, Latin America and Oceania* (Geneva, Switzerland: ILO, 1987): vi.

26. Cf. United Nations Department of International Economic and Social Affairs, Statistical Office, and International Research and Training Institute for the Advancement of Women, "Methods of Measuring Women's Participation and Production in the Informal Sector," *Studies in Methods* Series F no. 46 (1990).

27. See Luisella Goldschmidt-Clermont, *Economic Evaluations of Unpaid Household Work: Africa, Asia, Latin America and Oceania* (Geneva, Switzerland: ILO, 1987); and Luisella Goldschmidt-Clermont, *Unpaid Work in the Household: A Review of Economic Evaluation Methods* (Geneva, Switzerland: ILO, 1982).

28. United Nations Development Programme, *Human Development Report* (1995): 89. Estimates are similar for industrial countries, except a larger share of male work is uncounted (34 percent) and women account for 51 percent of total time spent in economy activity.

29. Although see Susan Himmelweit, "The Discovery of 'Unpaid Work': The Social Consequences of the Expansion of 'Work'," *Feminist Economics* 1, no. 2 (Summer 1995): 1–19, for a critique of how work and nonwork have been defined and dichotomized.

30. This section draws on standard anthropological references, in particular, Ernestine Friedl, *Women and Men: An Anthropologist's View* (New York: Holt, Rinehart & Winston, 1984), and Charlotte G. O'Kelly and Larry S. Carney, *Women and Men in Society, Second Edition* (Belmont, Calif.: Wadsworth, 1986).

31. See Susan C. Bourque and Kay Barbara Warren, *Women of the Andes: Patriarchy and Social Change in Two Peruvian Towns* (Ann Arbor, Mich.: University of Michigan, 1981): Chapter

Two, on "Analyzing Women's Subordination: Issues, Distortions, and Definitions; and Alternative Frameworks."

32. Walter L. Williams, *The Spirit and the Flesh: Sexual Diversity in American Indian Culture* (Boston, Mass.: Beacon, 1986), discusses primarily berdaches; Carolyn Niethammer, *Daughters of the Earth: The Lives and Legends of American Indian Women* (New York and London: Collier Macmillan, 1977): 229–232, discusses lesbianism; Evelyn Blackwood, "Sexuality and Gender in Certain Native American Tribes: The Case of Cross-Gender Females," *Signs* 10, no. 1 (Autumn 1984): 27–42, discusses "cross-gender females," which Williams refers to as amazons.

33. For description and discussion of these groups see Serena Nanda, *Neither Man Nor Woman: The Hijras of India* (Belmont, Calif.: Wadsworth, 1990).

34. Martin King Whyte, *The Status of Women in Preindustrial Societies* (Princeton, N.J.: Princeton University, 1978): 167–168.

35. Peggy Sanday, *Female Power and Male Dominance: On the Origins of Sexual Inequality* (Cambridge, United Kingdom: Cambridge University, 1981).

36. See James G. Scoville (ed.), *Status Influences in Third World Labor Markets: Caste, Gender, and Custom* (Berlin and New York: Walter de Gruyter, 1991), for some essays related to these ideas.

37. Ansley J. Coale, "Excess Female Mortality and the Balance of the Sexes in the Population: An Estimate of the Number of 'Missing Females'," *Population and Development Review* 17, no. 3 (September 1991): 517. Data in this focus are from most recent available year, taken from International Labour Office and U.S. Bureau of the Census, International Database tables.

38. For discussion of such factors, see Coale, *op. cit*:: 517–523.

39. Cf. Marcia Guttentag and Paul F. Secord, *Too Many Women: The Sex Ratio Question* (Beverly Hills, Calif.: Sage, 1983). For another view on what can cause marriage patterns, see Hanan G. Jacoby, "The Economics of Polygyny in Sub-Saharan Africa: Female Productivity and the Demand for Wives in Côte d'Ivoire," *Journal of Political Economy* 103, no. 5 (October 1995): 938–971, for an interesting argument linking the practice of polygyny to the productivity of women in agriculture; i.e., men have more wives when women are more productive and therefore cheaper to maintain.

40. See Sarah Blaffer Hrdy, "Daughters or Sons," *Natural History* 97, no. 4 (April 1988): 63–83. This pattern has been studied widely for animal groups.

41. Matt Ridley, "A Boy or a Girl: Is It Possible to Load the Dice?" *Smithsonian Magazine* 24, no. 3 (June 1993): 115.

42. Nancy E. Williamson, *Sons or Daughters: A Cross-Cultural Survey of Parental Preferences* (Beverly Hills, Calif.: Sage, 1976): 103–115.

43. Ridley, *op. cit.*: 120.

44. *Ibid.*

45. Ridley, *op. cit.*: 121.

46. Lourdes Benería, "Gender and the Dynamics of Subcontracting in Mexico City," *Gender in the Workplace*, eds. Clair Brown and Joseph A. Pechman (Washington, D.C.: Brookings, 1987): 159–188.

47. A. Dasgupta, *Women and Silk Industry in Bengal – 18th–20th Century* (New Delhi, India: Centre for Women's Development Studies, 1987).

48. Vina Mazumdar and Kumud Sharma, "Sexual Division of Labor and the Subordination of Women: A Reappraisal from India," *Persistent Inequalities: Women and World Development*, ed. Irene Tinker (New York and Oxford: Oxford University, 1990): 193–194.

49. Narayan Banerjee, Lokenath Ram, and Barati Sengupta, *Women's Work and Family Strategies: A Case Study from West Bengal* (New Delhi, India: Centre for Women's Development Studies, 1987).

50. Dasgupta, *op. cit.*

51. Government of India, *Towards Equality: Report of the Committee on the Status of Women in India* (New Delhi, India: Ministry of Education and Social Welfare, Department of Social Welfare, 1974).

52. Mira Savara, *Changing Trends in Women's Employment: A Case Study of the Textile Industry in Bombay* (Bombay, India: Himalaya Publishing House, 1986).

53. *Ibid.*

54. Government of India, *loc. cit.*

55. This section draws on material in Mari H. Clark, "Woman-headed Households and Poverty: Insights from Kenya," *Women and Poverty*, eds. Barbara C. Gelpi, Nancy C. M. Hartsock, Clare C. Novak, and Myra H. Strober (Chicago, Ill.: University of Chicago, 1985): 103–119.

56. Similar patterns appear among female-headed households in other societies; cf. A. Lynn Bolles, "Economic Crisis and Female-Headed Households in Urban Jamaica," *Women and Change in Latin America*, eds. June Nash, Helen Safa, and contributors (South Hadley, Mass.: Bergin and Garvey, 1985): 65–83.

57. Regina Oboler, "Is the Female Husband a Man: Woman/Woman Marriage Among the Nandi of Kenya," *Ethnology* 14, no. 1 (1980): 69–88; see also Regina Oboler, *Women, Power, and Economic Change: The Nandi of Kenya* (Stanford, Calif.: Stanford University, 1985).

58. Janet Henshall Momsen, *Women and Development in the Third World* (London: Routledge, 1991): 21.

59. *Ibid.*

60. Graciela Taglioretti, *Women and Work in Uruguay* (Paris, France: UNESCO, 1983).

61. There are also active markets for female domestics in large cities in Asia; see Yasmeen Mohiuddin, "Female-Headed Households and Urban Poverty in Pakistan," *Women's Work in the World Economy, Issues in Contemporary Economics* 4, proceedings of the Ninth World Congress of the International Economic Association, Athens, Greece, eds. Nancy Folbre, Barbara Bergmann, Bina Agarwal, and Maria Floro (New York: New York University, 1992): 61–81, for a detailed discussion of Karachi's labor market for female domestics.

62. Clive Wilkinson, "Women, Migration and Work in Lesotho," *Geography of Gender in the Third World*, eds. Janet Henshall Momsen and Janet G. Townsend (Albany, N.Y.: State University of New York, 1987): 225–239.

63. Wendy Lee, "Prostitution and Tourism in Southeast Asia," *Working Women: International Perspectives on Labour and Gender Ideology*, eds. Nanneke Redclift and M. Thea Sinclair (New York and London: Routledge, 1991): 80.

64. Lee, *op. cit.*: 89.

65. See Vijayendra Rao, "The Rising Price of Husbands: A Hedonic Analysis of Dowry Increases in Rural India," *Journal of Political Economy* 101, no. 4 (August 1993): 666–677; and/or "Dowry 'Inflation' in Rural India: A Statistical Investigation," *Population Studies* 47, no. 2 (July 1993): 283–293.

66. Radhakrishna Rao, "Move to Ban Sex Determination," *Nature* 331 (February 11, 1988): 467.

*F*urther reading

Anker, Richard and Catherine Hein (eds.) (1986). *Sex Inequalities in Urban Employment in the Third World*. New York: St. Martin's Press. Overview chapters plus case studies of Cyprus; Lucknow, India; Colombo, Sri Lanka; Accra-Tema, Ghana; Mauritius; and Lima, Peru.

Brydon, Lynne, and Sylvia Chant (1989). *Women in the Third World: Gender Issues in Rural and Urban Areas*. New Brunswick, N.J.: Rutgers University. Chapters on gender issues in various topic areas, including migration, rural production, urban planning, and reproduction.

Bullwinkle, Davis A. (1989). *African Women: A General Bibliography, 1976–1985*. Also *Women of Eastern and Southern Africa* and *Women of Northern, Western, and Central Africa*. New York: Greenwood. Guides to sources on African women.

Duley, Margot I., and Mary I. Edwards (eds.) (1986). *The Cross-Cultural Study of Women: A Comprehensive Guide*. New York: Feminist Press, City University of New York. Chapters on India, China, Oceania, sub-Saharan Africa, Latin America, and the Middle East/North Africa.

Dwyer, Daisy and Judith Bruce (eds.) (1988). *A Home Divided: Women and Income in the Third World*. Stanford, Calif.: Stanford University. Essays dealing with inequality and negotiation in households; theoretical critiques of economic modeling and case studies.

Feminist Economics (1996). Vol. 2, no. 3 (Fall). Special issue in honor of Margaret Reid (an influential specialist on economics of household production), concentrating on household production measurement issues.

Gelpi, Barbara, Nancy C. M. Hartsock, Clare C. Novak, and Myra H. Strober (eds.) (1985). *Women and Poverty*. Chicago, Ill.: University of Chicago. Essays on poor women in various societies.

Kahne, Hilda, and Janet Z. Giele (1992). *Women's Work and Women's Lives: The Continuing Struggle Worldwide*. Boulder, Colo. Westview. Overview essays and three chapters on modernizing regions, including Sub-Saharan Africa, Latin America and the Caribbean, and the Middle East and North Africa.

Leacock, Eleanor, Helen I. Safa, and Contributors (1986). *Women's Work: Development and the Division of Labor by Gender*. South Hadley, Mass.: Bergin & Garvey. Essays on historical development of industrial capitalism, nonindustrial societies, and Third World and socialist societies.

Momsen, Janet Henshall, and Janet G. Townsend (eds.) (1987). *Geography of Gender in the Third World*. Albany, N.Y.: State University of New York. Case studies from various societies in Africa, Asia, South America, and the Caribbean.

O'Kelly, Charlotte G., and Larry S. Carney (1986). *Women and Men in Society: Cross-Cultural Perspectives on Gender Stratification, Second Edition*. Belmont, Calif.: Wadsworth. Good survey textbook using anthropological terms to discuss societal types.

Psacharopoulos, George and Zafiris Tzannatos (1992). *Women's Employment and Pay in Latin America: Overview and Methodology*. Washington, D.C.: World Bank. This and a companion volume report findings for 15 Latin American and Caribbean countries.

Rives, Janet M. and Mahmood Yousefi (eds.) (1997). *Economic Dimensions of Gender Inequality: A Global Perspective*. Westport, Conn.: Greenwood. Overview chapters and case studies of South Korea, Turkey, Mexico, Nigeria, Pakistan, and India, among others.

Schultz, T. Paul (ed.) (1995). *Investment in Women's Human Capital*. Chicago, Ill.: University of Chicago. Overview chapters and case studies from Indonesia, Côte d'Ivoire, Brazil, Kenya, and India, among others.

Discussion questions

1. Is it useful to develop typologies of societies or cultures, or do the exceptions prove the rule? How important is it to systematize one's thinking about cross-cultural comparisons?

2. In Table 12.2, why do you think sex segregation is so much lower in the Asian countries? Why is it so much higher in the Middle East?

3. Consider the Focus on rural Togolese women's time use. How could economic development affect their time use patterns? Can you suggest some concrete ways in which their housework could be reduced through development aid? How could you measure the value of housework reduction?

4. Consider the various ways suggested for measuring labor force activity. Is there any danger in using too broad a definition? Would it be possible to develop such a broad definition that all persons would be considered as engaging in labor force activity? Would this be a bad thing?

5. Consider the various ways suggested for valuing unpaid work. Which ways appear to be most defensible (by a principle of economic theory or by some other principle)? Which ways would tend to lead to either an overestimate or an underestimate of the value of unpaid work?

6. In some societies, dowries are traditional; in others, bride prices are traditional. Is the choice of one or the other custom a reflection of the relative scarcity or plenitude of marriageable women in the society?

7. In South Asia, the real value of dowries (which can be thought of as groom prices) have been rising steadily over the past forty years.[65] This may surprise you, since, according to the Focus on sex ratios, there are fewer women than men in this region, so the price of men in the marriage market should fall! Explain how the facts that men tend to marry younger women and that population growth has been high in this region allow one to reconcile this pattern with basic supply and demand theory.

8. Consider the Focus on the flexible gender roles in Native American societies. Are there any reasons why such roles could not develop in industrialized societies?

9. How might a relative scarcity of women in a society lead to decreased female labor force participation? How might it lead to increased female labor force participation? How might a relative abundance of women in a society lead to decreased female labor force participation? How might it lead to increased female labor force participation?

10. Consider the Focus on sex ratios. Use of amniocentesis to determine fetal sex has become widespread in India.[66] What do you think would happen if this use of the procedure were banned?

11. Consider the discussions of subcontracting in Mexico and the textile industry in India. Is it discriminatory against women to impose protective legislation on industries in developing countries?

12. If you were mayor of a city in an undeveloped country facing a large inflow of migrants, what policies, if any, would you attempt to put into place to deal with this flow? What if you were president of a country with large internal rural-urban migration flows? What if you were president of a country with large external rural-urban migration flows? Would it affect your decisions if you knew the flows were mainly men or mainly women?

Effects of the Development Process on Gender Differences

CHAPTER 13

While the preceding three chapters have considered sets of societies, grouped roughly by level of industrialization and form of social organization, this chapter attempts synthesis by considering how the development process affects women and men differently. The chapter begins by attempting to define and illustrate development by comparing a set of social and economic indicators across countries. Then the question of whether development tends to create more or less gender equality is considered, along with the effects of development on family structure. Case studies of specific development programs within particular countries are of interest, both as a source of ideas for projects that may be translated to other countries and as a way to see how potential drawbacks may be avoided. The general areas of land reform, education, and expansion of credit are considered, with examples drawn from various countries. The chapter closes with a consideration of how to avoid male bias in development programs.

What is development?

Development has been defined throughout this section of the book in both social and economic terms. Social development indicators include those relating to improved health and education, such as declining infant mortality and rising literacy rates. Reduced fertility is generally considered a sign of development, although some people may find this trend undesirable. Other more controversial and difficult-to-measure indicators of social development, such as measures of democracy and income inequality, have been tracked by many observers of development processes. Economic development indicators include rising national product and national income, rising labor productivity and wages, and a higher proportion of the labor force involved in manufacturing and services rather than in agriculture – all leading to a higher living standard.

Economic development generally begins through changes in the rural economy that increase the productivity of labor in agriculture, thereby freeing labor for use in other activities. Changes in the rural economy can be structural (e.g., land reform), technical (e.g., the Green Revolution of new seeds and breeds, new pesticides and herbicides and mechanization), and/or institutional (e.g., formation of cooperatives, setting up of credit institutions).[1]

TABLE 13.1 Development indicators for 174 countries grouped by quartile on the human development index

	LFPR – M/F	Active F/ population	Per capita income ($)	World population (%)
1st quartile	1.52	0.41	15,803	16
2nd quartile	2.21	0.38	3,265	14
3rd quartile	2.27	0.35	1,040	42
4th quartile	3.71	0.36	595	28

	Urbanized population (%)	Fertility rate	Infant mortality rate
1st quartile	76	1.9	9
2nd quartile	61	2.9	26
3rd quartile	44	4.1	53
4th quartile	27	6.0	106

	Life expectancy (years)			Illiterate (%)	
	F	M	Total	F	M
1st quartile	79	73	76	—	—
2nd quartile	73	67	70	28	18
3rd quartile	65	61	63	42	28
4th quartile	51	50	52	70	59

	Primary education rates			Secondary education rates		
	F/M	F	Total	F/M	F	Total
1st quartile	95	103	103	108	89	87
2nd quartile	94	99	100	114	56	58
3rd quartile	93	98	106	90	41	43
4th quartile	73	57	68	58	12	16

Sources: Index: United Nations Development Programme, *Human Development Report 1996*; labor market data: ILO, *Yearbook of Labour Statistics* (1991–96) (Table 1); other data: World Bank, *World Development Report 1996* (Tables 1, 1A, 27–29, 31–32). Fertility rates are lifetime births per woman; infant mortality rates are deaths per 1000 live births. Education rates for females and total are defined per 100 school-age population; rates exceed 100 if people above the traditional school age are enrolled.

Development continues with the increase in various manufacturing activities, both for import substitution and for export production. Overall trade volume tends to increase for a country as it becomes more developed and is better able to exploit and develop patterns of comparative advantage.

Relative development has been determined in this book using the relative scale of the Human Development Index (HDI), calculated by the United Nations Development Programme on the basis of a weighted combination of country data on per capita income (or gross domestic product), life expectancy, and educational attainment. Table 13.1 shows data for the 174 rated countries, grouped into quartiles by index value. Clear patterns occur, showing a lessened formal economic role for women, lower life expectancy and

TABLE 13.2 Development indicators for 196 countries grouped by geographic region

	LFPR – M/F	Active F/ population	Per capita income ($)	World population (%)
Eastern Europe	1.23	0.46	3,591	7.0
United States/Canada	1.24	0.46	22,695	5.3
Australia/New Zealand	1.29	0.44	15,675	0.4
Caribbean	1.39	0.44	5,101	0.7
Western Europe	1.45	0.41	20,296	5.5
South Pacific	1.57	0.38	3,365	0.1
South America	1.79	0.37	2,827	5.8
Asia	2.11	0.35	5,796	56.4
Central America	2.30	0.32	1,899	2.2
Sub-Saharan Africa	2.89	0.38	1,012	10.5
Middle East/North Africa	4.28	0.22	6,281	6.1

	Urbanized population (%)	Fertility rate	Infant mortality rate
Eastern Europe	63	1.7	16
United States/Canada	77	2.0	7
Australia/New Zealand	86	2.0	7
Caribbean	61	2.8	29
Western Europe	71	1.6	6
South America	75	3.2	36
Asia	43	3.3	51
Central America	53	3.9	36
Sub-Saharan Africa	31	6.0	96
Middle East/North Africa	61	4.5	39

	Life expectancy (years)			Illiterate (%)	
	F	M	Total	F	Total
Eastern Europe	75	66	70	—	3
United States/Canada	80	74	78	—	—
Australia/New Zealand	80	74	77	—	—
Caribbean	71	66	73	26	17
Western Europe	80	74	77	—	—
South Pacific	—	—	67	—	—
South America	72	67	69	14	11
Asia	66	62	64	46	34
Central America	72	67	70	24	24
Sub-Saharan Africa	53	51	54	65	51
Middle East/North Africa	70	67	69	46	35

	Primary education rates			Secondary education rates		
	F/M	F	Total	F/M	F	Total
Eastern Europe	95	93	95	135	82	85
United States/Canada	94	105	106	95	104	104
Australia/New Zealand	95	105	106	98	84	83
Caribbean	97	96	97	98	56	54
Western Europe	95	103	102	107	99	97
South America	96	105	107	121	52	51
Asia	85	90	96	80	43	46
Central America	95	98	98	103	45	39
Sub-Saharan Africa	80	66	74	67	17	20
Middle East/North Africa	91	92	98	89	56	58

Sources: Same as Table 13.1.

education rates, and higher fertility, infant mortality, and illiteracy rates in less developed countries. Additionally, the female-male gap widens for education, but narrows for life expectancy as we move down the quartiles.

Table 13.2 presents tabulations of the same indicators by geographic region to emphasize regional differences in development. Regions are ranked in increasing order of the first indicator, relative male-female labor force participation rates, to draw attention to gender differences across regions and by development level. It is notable that countries which rank high on the development index have the greatest levels of female labor force participation.

The United Nations Development Programme also calculates the gender-related development index (GDI), which is the HDI adjusted for gender inequality, and the gender empowerment measure (GEM), which focuses on variables that reflect women's participation in political and economic spheres.[2] The GDI is always lower than the HDI as there is gender inequality in every country. However, as countries move up the HDI scale, the GDI and GEM rankings also tend to rise. But – particularly in the low and medium HDI groups – there is disparity in GDI and GEM rankings among countries with similar HDIs. For example, Kenya and Pakistan rate similarly low on the HDI, but their female-male disparities are very different, with the GDI at 98 percent of the HDI in Kenya, but only 75 percent in Pakistan.[3]

Many additional development measures make it clear that a notable gender disparity exists in many less-developed countries. About 70 percent of the world's poor are female.[4] Women's literacy is 74 percent of the male literacy rate.[5]

Health indicators are particularly telling. In Bangladesh, for example, acute malnutrition is found among 10 percent of the girls but only 7 percent of the boys. Adult women are more likely than men to suffer from malnutrition. Maternal mortality rates provide the most telling story of the effects on women's health of underdevelopment; they are 600 per 100,000 live births in Sub-Saharan Africa, and 295 in South-East Asia and the Pacific, as compared to 10 in the industrial countries. A pregnant woman in a developing country is 9 times more likely to die from complications of pregnancy and childbirth than is a woman in a developed country.[6]

Why development might lead to greater gender equality

The origins of the burgeoning subfield in development studies of gender effects can be roughly dated to the publication of Ester Boserup's 1970 book, *Woman's Role in Economic Development*.[7] Since that time, the field has moved away from a corrective focus on women to a broader gender differences framework, and has developed through both the collection of case studies concerning the effects of economic development on women in many societies and the development of general theoretical frameworks (no one paradigm has yet risen to dominance). These frameworks tend to vary, in particular, by whether they consider economic development a potentially equalizing force or a process that is inherently male biased.

One question is whether economic development leads to social development, particularly in ways that allow women to catch up with men in measures such as health and education. It is clear from Table 13.1 that development does tend to lead to improvement of social indicators and to reduce the gender gap in measures such as education. One study, using data from 1973 to 1987 for 68 countries, finds positive and statistically significant correlations between national income growth and declines in infant mortality, decreases in the female-male education gap, and increases in the overall education level and the female education level. It also finds a strong correlation (0.63) between an index of political and civil liberties and the female education level.[8] All these results imply that women may gain more than men from economic development. However, it is not obvious that the causality runs from economic to social development. These correlations may indicate complicated interactions between these various indicators, as well as complex underlying forces driving the indicators.

Some proposed interactions are noncontroversial. It is widely accepted that higher overall education levels improve infant mortality and fertility indicators, but that countries with a large gender gap in enrollment rates are worse off at any level of male enrollment rates, indicating that mainly the increase in female education is driving these improvements.[9]

Another relatively noncontroversial hypothesis is the convergence hypothesis regarding labor force participation rates: high female labor force participation rate and low female labor force participation rate countries both converge through the development process to medium female labor force participation rates. For men, the development process appears to reduce labor force participation in entry and retirement age groups; this happens faster if the country had high levels of labor force participation in these age groups to begin with.[10] Higher wages, reflecting increased labor productivity from economic development, lead to both an income and a substitution effect: domination of the income effect causes some women and men to concentrate on nonmarket work (or true leisure), while domination of the substitution effect causes others – particularly women – to increase their market work. Since potential income is higher in either case (whether or not the person is actually engaging in market work), these persons are better off. While it is more difficult to determine whether or not men or women are helped more, the extent to which women's wages rise more than men's is a strong indicator that they might be made better off.

Why development might lead to greater gender inequality

Many analysts have made the case that economic development, as currently practiced, both affects the division of power and resources between the sexes and systematically improves men's lives more than women's. For instance, in considering structural, technical, and institutional changes in rural economies, one analyst generally sees all of these as potentially bad for women in that their decision-making ability and status may decline, even if their living standard increases.[11]

Anthropologists Susan Bourque and Kay Warren have proposed four alternative perspectives in order to explain the contemporary perpetuation of sexual division of labor and female subordination and to identify factors contributing to changes in subordination patterns:[12]

1. *Separate spheres perspective:* Women control the domestic sphere of activity and therefore have parity with men.
2. *Sexual division of labor perspective:* Constraints on female involvement in the economy shape women's subordinate position.
3. *Class analysis perspective:* Subordination is an outcome of the transformation of prestate societies into class-stratified, state-organized societies.
4. *Social ideology perspective:* Patriarchy is deeper than class and sexual division of labor, and it cannot be corrected by control in the domestic sphere, women's acquisition of economic positions, or movement to alternatives to class-based capitalist societies.

Both for their own research on people in the Andes and as an overall perspective, they favor a combination of (3) and (4), both of which imply either a negative effect on women's status through development or no effect at all.

Several analysts have concentrated on the effects of the recent debt crisis experienced by many developing nations.[13] This study involves discussion of the costs of economic restructuring and the redistribution caused by these nations' attempts to switch from production of nontradeables to production of tradeables in order to increase foreign exchange flows for debt repayment. One possible effect is an increasing burden of both unpaid and underpaid work on women, so that they may end up bearing more of the costs of restructuring and general belt-tightening.

The broader question of the relative effects on women of the global shift in development strategies towards export-led development (rather than import-substitution) has also been addressed by analysts.[14] In nations that are not in a crisis situation but instead are moving more smoothly towards this system, based on comparative advantage (generally lower labor costs leading to more labor-intensive industries such as apparel and electronics assembly), this change should lead to an increase in overall well-being. However, whether women are relatively helped or hurt by such a switch in strategy may depend on the type of export – e.g., commodities or manufactured goods. Additionally, as new technologies come into use, the interactions of both sexes with machines in the workplace can affect the structure and pay of their work in offsetting ways. For instance, factory work may pay better than alternative forms of employment, but the work may be less pleasant and work-time less flexible.

The industries that have become global, such as electronics assembly and textiles, appear to lead to increased female employment and earnings. For example, about 80 percent of the electronics work force is female.[15] Since developing countries have readily available male labor, a strong preference on the part of these industries for women is indicated. Such work has greatly expanded paid work opportunities for women, even as commentators have complained about the preponderance of low-paid jobs (relative both to developed countries and to many male-dominated, often unionized jobs within developing countries).

While neoclassical economic theory leads to the argument that such development patterns must be of benefit to women by increasing their potential income, critics have argued that rising female wages are not unequivocally positive for women. For instance, if women are barred through custom from deciding the use of their monetary contributions to the family, then a view of family bargaining that says that equal contributions to the household leads to equal power within the household will not hold. Women may increase their market work with no corresponding reduction in nonmarket responsibilities and no additional control over family resources that could be used to ease the burden, such as hiring domestic help. Daughters may be compelled to forego formal schooling in order to work in jobs with relatively high starting wages but no possibility of earnings improvement.

FOCUS

Two Brazilian factories

A case study of two factories in Sao Paulo, Brazil, underlines the trade-offs for women and their families in the current process of development.[16] One factory was large and foreign-owned, with 867 employees, 24 percent of whom were women. The other factory was small and foreign-owned, but the owners lived locally and the capital was local as well. This factory had 53 employees, 57 percent of whom were women.

The small factory made knitted garments using craft-based production techniques, mostly non-automated, although machinery was used. The factory ran for one daytime shift, and the workers were mostly older women. The labor force received low wages, but there was low turnover. Many of the workers had been with the firm for many years, taking pregnancy leaves when necessary. The workers did not consider the work to be monotonous and there was fraternization among the women.

The large factory manufactured cotton fabric, using automated processes, and ran continuously, with three shifts. The women were predominantly single, and almost half were under 18. The labor force received high wages and had a high turnover rate. The workers found the work easy, but they expressed dissatisfaction with the monotony and the working conditions. The work environment was dirtier, as cotton fibers were floating around in the air, and noisier.

In both cases, the women were able to improve the quality of their lives in the domestic sphere. The workers reported high rates of owning various physical energy-saving appliances, such as floor waxers and cake mixers. They also had high rates of owning leisure-related appliances, like radios and televisions. But while the work at home might become less burdensome due to these appliances, the married women still generally bore primary responsibility for home management and upkeep.

The women working in the large factory were in families with lower per capita income, and their income was a larger share of total family income than that of the women working in the small factory. Many of the women in the small factory worked to supplement the income of their parents, brothers, or husbands, while the women in the large factory were often primarily responsible for the survival of their families.

It appears that a family strategy with multiple wage-earners, in which the wage-earner with primary domestic responsibilities has the pleasanter job with lower wages while the other wage-earners have less pleasant, often more physically rigorous jobs with higher wages, may be an optimal, but often unattainable position. If development proceeds along the line of phasing out small factories of the type described herein, younger women will not have the option of switching out of the high-paying rigorous jobs into lower-paying, less rigorous work environments when their family responsibilities increase.

Development effects on family structure

One of the hottest topics in the field of gender effects on development is the question of how the family is affected by economic development.[17] The general prediction is that the family unit plays a decreased role, both economically and socially, as development increases. As Ester Boserup wrote recently:[18]

> As economic development proceeds, family production for its own use diminishes and a larger and larger share of goods for family consumption is produced outside the family in specialized enterprises. Moreover, most of the services that family members in subsistence economies produce for each other (including physical protection, health care, and education) are taken over by public institutions, or specialized private enterprises. During this process, the family gradually is stripped of most of its original functions. This causes radical changes both in the relation of family members to the outside world and in the relations between family members.

Predictions that follow from this viewpoint include:

- reduced individual dependence on the extended family for financial and social support
- higher divorce rates
- later marriages
- smaller household and family sizes
- more female-headed households[19]
- fewer children, with more resources invested per child

It is interesting to study societies that have experienced rapid economic development to see how family structures have adjusted to these accelerated changes. These societies include the "Asian Tigers": Hong Kong, Singapore, South Korea, and Taiwan (not to mention Japan, the biggest Asian Tiger of all). These societies rank just below the OECD countries on the HDI, and they have had phenomenal per capita GNP growth since World War II.

The general pattern in these societies is that traditional family structures have not yet been superseded by structures found in developed countries. Families are still internally reliant, continuing to pool resources; and children, particularly daughters, continue to defer to parents. One researcher studying women workers in Hong Kong concludes: "Working women accede to ongoing family control of their wages, as is expected of all dutiful daughters in Chinese families."[20] This may be partly because governmental social safety nets of the type found in Western Europe are not found in these societies. Also, except for Japan, companies in these societies cannot be relied upon for extended periods of employment or for post-employment support; turnover rates are high and pensions are not a widespread phenomenon. Therefore, the family still has critical risk-spreading and old-age pension functions in these societies.

Singapore is notable among these countries for its highly developed system of social control and government intervention into traditionally family-based concerns. Singapore has been the success story of Asia for many years. Since becoming independent from Great Britain in 1959, this small island city-state has become as successful as Hong Kong without the accompanying income inequality: there is virtually no poverty in Singapore. The educational system is intensive and advanced, and a large percentage of both sexes finish college. However, rapid social and economic changes have led to a mismatch between the sexes: men, regardless of education level, prefer "controllable" wives, while educated women do not want to marry men with lower educational attainment. As one analyst observed: "Unless they marry or have a steady dating partner before their mid-twenties, women professionals and managers in Singapore often fail to find compatible marital partners."[21] Statistics from the mid-1980s indicate that fewer than half of male college graduates choose to marry female college graduates, and fewer than one in ten of women graduates decide to "marry down." If the trend continues, around 40 percent of women graduates and over 25 percent of women with upper-secondary ("A" level) qualifications might remain unmarried in the future. Since the government wants women to have traditional roles as wives and mothers in addition to using their education, this is considered a potential crisis situation.[22]

In 1984 a set of novel social engineering measures began in an attempt to reverse these trends. The Social Development Unit was created to operate as matchmaker for educated Singaporeans. The National University of Singapore adjusted its entry requirements so that men would have an easier time getting in to make up for their tendency to have more difficulty than women in meeting the second language requirement.[23] And home economics became a compulsory course for all girls in secondary school.[24] However, it does not appear that these measures have succeeded in significantly reducing the number of unmarried educated women (or the number of unmarried uneducated men).

FOCUS

The marriage market in Singapore

New Yorker reporter Stan Sesser, who visited Singapore in 1991, describes the workings of the Social Development Unit (S.D.U.):[25]

> Only college graduates are eligible [for the S.D.U.'s services]; they fill out personal-data forms, and a computer then provides the names of potential partners. "In our culture, there are no singles bars, and it's hard to meet people socially," Ang Wai Hoong, the S.D.U.'s director, told me. "Girls read these lovely romantic novels, and our guys are practical-minded technocrats. So when the two get together it's a mismatch." The S.D.U. sponsors lectures on how to date women, along with a variety of other activities, including evening cruises to nowhere that are dubbed "love boats."

Once people marry, they are offered a variety of government incentives to have children, some of which are related to the couple's measured intellect. For instance, mothers who have achieved a certain level on tenth grade intelligence tests can take a tax deduction, which increases with the number of children they have.

Development policy topics

This section considers three areas of development: agrarian reform; education; and provision of credit. These areas are considered with emphasis on how programs may have differential impacts by sex.

Agrarian reform

Agrarian reform, which has been particularly widespread in Latin America in the recent past, is a drastic measure that can both help and hinder development, as well as redistribute resources between women and men. The breaking up of large commercial farms and traditional haciendas (family-owned estates) into many smaller holdings clearly has a strong redistributive impact across income classes. It may hinder achievement of agricultural productivity to the extent that innovation is more likely to occur on larger farms and takes longer to filter down to a large number of small farms, and to the extent that economies of scale are important in farming. However, some of these negative effects can be combated through increased institutional support for agriculture, such as agricultural education programs, and through formation of cooperatives that jointly own capital equipment and coordinate production and marketing activities.

One study contrasts the Peruvian, Chilean, and Cuban reforms and finds that in the Peruvian and Chilean cases, the criteria used to define beneficiaries of the reform process constituted the single most important factor in limiting the participation of rural women.[26]

These criteria included the requirement that one be the head of a household that includes dependents. This requirement automatically excluded the great majority of women, including most of those who had been agricultural workers on the large farms and haciendas. In general, only men became members of the new cooperatives, and in Peru, only men were given title to individual land parcels. Also, because the primary beneficiaries in each case were permanent agricultural workers who had been employed at the time of expropriation and because women were more likely to participate only seasonally in agriculture, they were less likely to benefit. However, in Cuba, agricultural cooperative membership was extended to all adults within farm households, and support structures were developed in an attempt to increase both women's participation in decision-making processes and their participation as permanent agricultural workers. The greater level of state support for agricultural cooperatives in Cuba, including attention to provision of both basic services such as electricity and running water and social services such as child care, appears to have been important in freeing women from household responsibilities so that more of them could make the transition from temporary to full-time agricultural workers (although their full-time participation rates are still below those of men).

Another aspect of land reform that also directly impacts women is the question of whether women have rights to inherit and/or utilize land. Economist Bina Agarwal has documented the ongoing estrangement of women from land in South Asia due to laws restricting women's property rights, gaps between law and practice in situations where women have legal claim to inheritance shares, and gaps between ownership and control in situations where women do have ownership of the land, but are hindered in managing it.[27]

Provision of education

An ongoing pattern in the poorest, least developed countries is low school enrollment and literacy rates, combined with a sizable gender gap in rates.[28] However, much progress has been made in reducing gender differences in access to education. While there were 19 countries in 1965 in which female primary enrollment rates were less than 42 percent of males, only Chad and Yemen still had such low female rates by 1985.[29] As shown in Table 13.2, some regions now have higher enrollment rates for women than for men at the primary and/or secondary levels. However, higher education has tended to incorporate men more than women, although increased expansion of higher education is correlated with a narrowing of the gender difference in enrollment rates. This can be seen in Table 13.3, which presents tertiary (postsecondary training, generally college or technical institute training) enrollment rates by sex (per hundred school-age persons) for several geographic regions. Where overall rates are low, women have notably lower rates, with female enrollment rates below 40 percent of males in Sub-Saharan Africa and South Asia. However, in regions where overall rates are higher, the gender differential shrinks notably to between 73 percent and 99 percent of the male enrollment rate. And in all regions, expansion of higher education has increased the relative access for women.

Why do such gaps continue? To the extent that educational resources are scarce in developed countries, planners might rationally attempt to determine an optimal rationing scheme, particularly at the secondary and tertiary education levels. If it is believed that women are less likely to have long worklives due to their family responsibilities, then the system may be skewed towards men in order to receive greater payoffs to investments in human capital.

TABLE 13.3 Tertiary education enrollment rates by sex and ratio of female to male rates, 1965 and 1988

	1965			1988		
	Females	*Males*	*Ratio*	*Females*	*Males*	*Ratio*
Sub-Saharan Africa	0.1	0.6	0.17	1.1	3.3	0.33
South Asia	0.6	2.0	0.30	2.0	5.2	0.38
Middle East and North Africa	2.1	5.6	0.38	11.8	16.2	0.73
Latin America and the Caribbean	3.1	5.7	0.54	16.2	16.4	0.99
East Asia	4.1	6.7	0.61	14.6	18.9	0.77

Source: UNESCO data as reported in M. Anne Hill and Elizabeth M. King, "Women's Education in Developing Countries: An Overview," *Women's Education in Developing Countries: Barriers, Benefits and Policies*, eds. Elizabeth M. King and M. Anne Hill (Baltimore, Md.: Johns Hopkins University, 1993): 12. 1988 Data are from most recent year, 1985–89.

However, it is not obvious that education should be provided to males instead of females. It appears that social returns to increased female education are very high. Higher female literacy and education levels are associated with lower infant mortality, better family nutrition, reduced fertility, and lower population growth.[30] For example, in Bangladesh, child mortality is five times higher among children of mothers with no education than among children whose mothers have seven or more years of schooling. And in the Philippines, as women's earnings capacity rises, more resources are allocated to their children's food intake.[31] Better-educated women also have smaller families, reducing the strain on developing societies of above-replacement birth rates. In Colombia, women who have achieved the highest education levels have approximately four fewer children than women who have completed only their primary education.[32]

Regardless of the social benefits accruing to a more equal division of education by sex, families in developing countries may opt to educate sons rather than daughters. There are many reasons why this may be a rational decision for the family to make:[33]

1. Out-of-pocket expenses of attending school may be higher for girls (e.g., attire costs).
2. Concern for moral and physical safety of girls may deter parents from sending them to attend distant schools or may cause higher lodging and boarding costs for them.
3. The opportunity costs of educating girls are higher, because they do nonmarket work for the family, such as housework and child tending.
4. There is concern that girls will miss important training in nonmarket skills if they attend school.
5. There is concern that highly educated women are less likely to make a good marriage.
6. There is concern that delay of marriage for schooling reduces the present value of the bride price families may receive for their daughters.
7. There is concern that expenses incurred by the family will not be recovered in societies where the woman affiliates with her husband's family after marriage.

A strong concern regarding formal schooling in less developed countries is that it is irrelevant to the future work that both sexes – but women, in particular – will likely be doing and, worse still, that it may actually reduce their probability of getting a useful job. While education, particularly at the secondary and tertiary levels, is a necessary precondition to entering higher-paying jobs, the general shortage of high-paying jobs means that receipt of a degree is not an automatic ticket to employment. Women, who generally have a lower probability of receiving a job after degree conferral, may be better served by receiving some form of practical training, such as agricultural training, rather than the liberal arts type of training that many schools in developing countries offer (partly as a holdover from colonial days).[34] Instead, women are generally excluded from whatever formal practical agricultural education is available, often relying, instead, on informal apprenticeships with other women in order to learn agricultural practices.[35]

Expansion of credit

One strategy for aiding the poor is to provide low-interest credit to self-employed persons so that they can expand their enterprises, overcome short-term cash flow problems, and/or consolidate high-interest-rate loans, often made by local moneylenders at usurious rates.[36] There is evidence that these programs are among the most successful of development strategies.

One much-publicized program is the Grameen ("village") Bank of Bangladesh, founded by an economist in 1976.[37] This bank specializes in very small average loans: $67, or about half of an average year's income in Bangladesh. The loans must be paid back within one year, and 98 percent of them are repaid, as contrasted to the country's average repayment rate of 30 to 40 percent. Evaluations of the broader social effects triggered by the existence of this bank have found that villages where the bank has lent money have registered improvements in education, health care, and women's status. The bank's strategy for success is peer lending: to obtain a loan, a person must band together with four neighbors. The group meets with a loan officer and then chooses one or two of the five to be eligible for an initial loan. Before another group member can receive a loan, the first borrowers must make regular repayments. All loans must be repaid before anyone becomes eligible for a second, larger loan. This strategy of using peers to provide mutual information and monitor each other solves two problems inherent in all capital markets: (1) a lack of information on the borrower of a small-scale loan, the cost of obtaining which in a usual bureaucratic way would make the loan unprofitable; and (2) reduction of the problem of moral hazard (which is when people fail to act in optimally risk-minimizing ways). While Grameen currently requires a subsidy to meet operation costs – its rapid expansion rate has precluded the erasure of its operating deficit – it is predicted to go into the black in a few years.

A rural bank program in Ghana has also been very successful. There are over 100 such banks, each of which is independent and run by the community. Growth in both total deposits and number of users has been very rapid. Local savings represent well over 90 percent of total available funds. Funds mobilized locally are used locally, loan approvals are based on the requester's reputation in the community, and loan recipients tend to be owners of small businesses or farms. Administrative costs are kept low through use of simple, standard procedures and use of local staff.[38]

A third small-scale lending strategy has been successful in the Philippines. The "money shops" of the Philippine Commercial and Industrial Bank make small loans (between $125 and $1250) to market stall-holders at a reasonable rate. The key to their success is, again, proximity to and close interaction with borrowers. The money shops meet short-term (30 to 60 days) credit needs of commercial customers and accept deposits. The loan recovery rate has been 98 percent. A money shop often consists of a wooden stall with about four employees. They operate in fairly large urban markets; there must be at least four hundred businesses at the market site to justify placement. About 70 such shops were in operation by 1979.[39]

These programs may be particularly helpful in providing credit for women, who may be less able to get loans from family members or from larger commercial establishments.[40] In fact, 92 percent of the Grameen Bank's clients are women who want to start their own businesses. In this case, a successful development program also appears to have high benefits for women. However, concerns have arisen that a significant proportion of these loans to women are actually controlled by male family members, and that loans may not be of sufficient magnitude to raise women's incomes out of the poverty range.[41]

FOCUS

Bank loans in Bombay

Scholars Jana Everett and Mira Savara studied Bombay women's participation in the nationalized banks' Differential Rate of Interest (DRI) program, in which banks lend 1 percent of the previous year's advances to the poor at the low rate of 4 percent (as compared with the usual bank rate of 12.5 to 16 percent annually and the moneylenders' rates of 12 to 25 percent per month!).[42] Their enumeration of the six primary types of activities such loans go to finance for the women borrowers illustrates the limitations of this strategy in bringing persons into the modern work world:[43]

1. broom makers, who make brooms and baskets out of a particular kind of grass from the jungles of Karnataka, the state to the south of Maharashtra, where Bombay is located, and sell the brooms to lower-class households with dirt floors and the baskets to wholesale markets.
2. glassmakers, who buy used bottles, cut off their tops, file and wash them, glue the tops on as stems and paint designs on the glasses, which they then sell on the street.
3. makers of hand-rolled cigarettes, who are "outworkers" since merchants supply the raw materials and buy the finished products.
4. vegetable vendors, who buy produce at the wholesale market and sell it on the street.
5. utensil barterers, who buy stainless steel cooking utensils and trade them to middle-class housewives, exchanging the utensils for old clothes to sell to merchants.
6. *knannawallis* (food providers), who cook meals for male workers who come to Bombay without families.

Even though it was mainly women who were borrowers, they received smaller loans on average than the male participants. This disparity is related to the types of businesses women are in, most of which the bankers perceive as needing less capital. The authors mention three reasons why more women than men receive these loans: (1) they are more likely to run lower-earning businesses and, therefore, are more likely to be eligible for the DRI program; (2) self-employed women are more likely to have male family members who draw a regular wage than are self-employed men, and bankers may be more willing to sanction DRI loans to women with access to male wages; and (3) bankers discriminate against lower-class men, thinking that they are more likely to spend their money on entertainment.

The authors conclude that it is difficult to tell whether the bank loans actually improved women borrowers' well-being, measured in terms of their income, their power, or their consumption. While small increases in income appear to have occurred, most borrowers are still below the poverty line.

Policy Application: Foreign aid practices

How could economic development aid women as much as men? While this chapter has presented examples of programs that appear to benefit women and men, a recent line of thought in the analysis of economic development is that economic development inevitably strengthens patriarchy.[44] Nonetheless, even if one believes that male bias is inherent in the development process, one could still consider how to lessen the effects of male bias.

Male bias in development planning and funding may take many forms, including:[45]

- evaluating an export-led development strategy as a failure because it mainly provides jobs for women rather than men
- evaluating a drop in financial support for social programs as a valuable cost-cutting measure without considering the hidden costs as measured in such factors as declining health and nutrition, particularly for women and children
- emphasizing austerity measures without considering the long-term effects on health and nutrition, particularly if the prices of basic food items rise substantially, and the possible increased nonmarket work burden on women

To the extent that international development agencies have become sensitized to gender issues in development, these forms of bias are less likely to occur. In particular, stipulations placed on countries in order to improve their financial solvency and make them eligible for additional loans may now be more likely to be analyzed with respect to distributional effects, both between women and men and by income group. However, it may be more important to run a proactive foreign aid policy. To the extent that funding of small-scale development projects appears to help women relatively more, recent shifts toward this type of development approach (e.g., funding agricultural and handicraft cooperatives in villages) are a promising move both towards equalizing development funding to women and men and towards giving women and men equal control over means of production and equal access to capital.

Finally, while development is generally considered a failure, or at best a qualified success if the economic components of development are not progressing, the Indian state of Kerala provides an interesting example of how social development may occur without correspondingly high levels of economic development.[46] This very poor area in a very poor country is notably more egalitarian than other regions in India – and it has better quality of life indicators, as well. While Kerala's per capita GNP is 63 percent of India's, its life expectancy is 19 percent higher (68 instead of 57 in 1988), the adult literacy rate is 81 percent higher (78 instead of 43 in 1981 in Kerala and in 1985 in India), and infant mortality and birth rates are substantially lower (in 1988, 27 infant deaths per thousand in Kerala vs. 86 in India; 22 births per thousand in Kerala vs. 32 in India). Widespread land reform in 1969 and a series of leftist state governments with a strong commitment to equality set Kerala apart institutionally from other Indian states. Minimum nutrition standards are guaranteed through rationing of staples at fixed prices, and the government funds a daily school lunch program. Kerala devotes a higher proportion of its budget to health concerns than any other Indian state, and hospitals and clinics are spread evenly throughout the region.

It may be that the worst development bias is to emphasize economic growth, assuming that social development will automatically follow. If women benefit relatively more from social development, but men benefit more from economic development, this emphasis can be viewed as an example of male bias in development practices. But Kerala also provides a lesson about the trade-offs inherent in running advanced social programs in resource-poor systems. Tax rates are higher than in other states, agricultural productivity is stagnant, and unemployment is rampant, causing a massive out-migration of Keralans to other parts of India and to the West.

Summary

The construct of development, both economic and social, provides a way of comparing all countries along a spectrum indexing development levels. As countries move up the spectrum, the question of whether women are relatively hurt or helped remains open. At the top end of the spectrum, the indicators show relatively small gender gaps and high levels of development in matters of particular importance to women, such as lower infant and maternal mortality rates, but economic development may lead to consolidation of control over the means of production in male hands and reduce female status and decision-making power. However, recent trends towards export industries with heavy female employment representation, interest in small and medium-scale economic development following well-publicized setbacks from large-scale economic development enterprises, and increased sensitivity towards gender issues on the part of development planners and foreign aid agencies may counter sources of male development bias.

Endnotes

1. Janet Henshall Momsen, *Women and Development in the Third World* (London: Routledge, 1991): 52–54 (Table 4.2).
2. See United Nations Development Programme, *Human Development Report 1995*: 130–133, for how these indexes are calculated.
3. United Nations Development Programme, *op. cit.*: 72–86.
4. Robin Wright, "Engines Out of Poverty," *Los Angeles Times* (May 29, 1997): A1.
5. United Nations Development Programme, *op. cit.*: 33–34.
6. United Nations Development Programme, *op. cit.*: 16; 25–28; 35.
7. (London: Allen & Unwin, 1970; reissued by Aldershot, United Kingdom: Gower, 1986).
8. World Bank, *World Development Report 1991*: 50. See endnote 70 in Chapter 6 for the correlation coefficient formula and discussion of its range.
9. World Bank, *op. cit*: 55.
10. John Dana Durand, *The Labor Force in Economic Development: A Comparison of International Census Data, 1946–1966* (Princeton, N.J.: Princeton University, 1975): 152–155.
11. Momsen, *loc. cit.*
12. Susan C. Bourque and Kay Barbara Warren, *Women of the Andes: Patriarchy and Social Change in Two Peruvian Towns* (Ann Arbor, Mich.: University of Michigan, 1981).
13. See the articles in *World Development* 23, no. 11 (November 1995); Lourdes Benería and Shelley Feldman, *Unequal Burden: Economic Crises, Persistent Poverty, and Women's Work* (Boulder, Colo.: Westview, 1992); and Haleh Afshar and Carolyne Dennis (eds.), *Women and Adjustment Policies in the Third World* (London and Basingstoke: Macmillan, 1992).
14. Cf. Kathryn Ward (ed.), *Women Workers and Global Restructuring* (Ithaca, N.Y.: ILR, 1990).
15. Susan Joekes, *Women in the World Economy: An INSTRAW Study* (Oxford: Oxford University, 1987): 41.
16. Heleith I.B. Saffioti, "Technological Change in Brazil: Its Effect on Women and Men in Two Firms," *Women and Change in Latin America*, eds. June Nash, Helen Safa, and contributors (South Hadley, Mass.: Bergin and Garvey, 1985): 109–135.

17. Cf. Sharon Stichter, "Women, Employment and the Family: Current Debates," *Women, Employment and the Family in the International Division of Labour*, eds. Sharon Stichter and Jane L. Parpart (London: Macmillan, 1990): 11–71.

18. Ester Boserup, "Economic Change and the Roles of Women," *Persistent Inequalities: Women and World Development*, ed. Irene Tinker (Oxford: Oxford University, 1990): 14.

19. For a discussion of issues regarding female-headed households, see Nancy Folbre, "Mothers on Their Own: Policy Issues for Developing Countries," The Population Council, International Centre for Research on Women Working Paper (1990).

20. Janet W. Salaff, *Working Daughters of Hong Kong: Filial Piety or Power in the Family?* (Cambridge, United Kingdom: Cambridge University, 1981): 9.

21. Audrey Chan, "Women Managers in Singapore: Citizens for Tomorrow's Economy," *Women in Management Worldwide*, eds. Nancy J. Adler and Dafne N. Izraeli (Armonk, N.Y.: M.E. Sharpe, 1988): 67.

22. *Ibid.*

23. Momsen, *op. cit.*: 34. Quotas had already been operating at the medical school since 1979, restricting entering classes to be no more than one-third women.

24. Chan, *op. cit.*: 68.

25. Stan Sesser, "A Nation of Contradictions," *The New Yorker* (January 13, 1992): 65–66.

26. Carmen Diana Deere, "Rural Women and Agrarian Reform in Peru, Chile, and Cuba," *Women and Change in Latin America*, June Nash, Helen Safa, and contributors (South Hadley, Mass.: Bergin and Garvey, 1985): 189–207.

27. Bina Agarwal, *A Field of One's Own: Gender and Land Rights in South Asia* (Cambridge, United Kingdom: Cambridge University, 1994).

28. For a comprehensive assessment of these issues, see Elizabeth M. King and M. Anne Hill (eds.), *Women's Education in Developing Countries: Barriers, Benefits and Policies* (Baltimore, Md.: Johns Hopkins University, 1993). The book contains overview chapters, as well as chapters focusing on particular regions, including sub-Saharan Africa, the Middle East and North Africa, Latin America and the Caribbean, South Asia, and East Asia. See also M. Anne Hill and Elizabeth M. King, "Women's Education and Economic Well-Being," *Feminist Economics* 1, no. 2 (Summer 1995): 21–46, for an update and expansion on some of the book's topics.

29. M. Anne Hill and Elizabeth M. King, "Women's Education in Developing Countries: An Overview," *Women's Education in Developing Countries: Barriers, Benefits and Policies*, eds. Elizabeth M. King and M. Anne Hill (Baltimore, Md.: Johns Hopkins University, 1993): 13.

30. See Shireen J. Jejeebhoy, *Women's Education, Autonomy, and Reproductive Behaviour: Experience from Developing Countries* (Oxford: Clarendon Press, 1995) for a comprehensive survey of the evidence.

31. Benjamin Senauer, Marito Garcia, and Elizabeth Jacinto, "Determinants of the Intrahousehold Allocation of Food in the Rural Philippines," *American Journal of Agricultural Economics* 70, no. 1 (February 1988): 170–180.

32. United Nations Development Programme, *loc. cit.*

33. See Hill and King, *op. cit.*: 21–30, for an expanded discussion of this topic.

34. See Sue Leigh-Doyle, "Increasing Women's Participation in Technical Fields: A Pilot Project in Africa," *International Labour Review* 130, no. 4 (July-August 1991): 427–444, for suggestions on how to remedy this situation.

35. Claire Robertson, "Women's Education and Class Formation in Africa, 1950–1980," *Women and Class in Africa*, eds. Claire Robertson and Iris Berger (New York: Africana/Holmes & Meier, 1986): 92–113.

36. In many communities persons have set up rotating savings and credit associations (ROSCAs), which are funded internally by the participants; see Shirley Ardener and Sandra Burman (eds.), *Money-Go-Rounds: The Importance of Rotating Savings and Credit Associations for Women* (Oxford and Washington, D.C.: Berg, 1995). However, it appears that most ROSCAs do not

operate on a large enough scale or with a clearly business-oriented nature to serve as a sufficient credit source to increase members' incomes significantly.

37. Marguerite Holloway and Paul Wallich, "A Risk Worth Taking," *Scientific American* 267, no. 5 (November 1992): 126. See also David Bornstein, *The Price of a Dream: The Story of the Grameen Bank and the Idea That Is Helping the Poor to Change Their Lives* (New York: Simon & Schuster, 1997).
38. United Nations Development Programme, *op. cit.*: 64.
39. United Nations Development Programme, *op. cit.*: 65.
40. Sharon L. Holt and Helena Ribe, "Developing Financial Institutions for the Poor and Reducing Barriers to Access for Women," World Bank Discussion Paper no. 117 (February 1991).
41. Anne Marie Goetz and Rina Sen Gupta, "Who Takes the Credit? Gender, Power, and Control Over Loan Use in Rural Credit Programs in Bangladesh," *World Development* 24, no. 1 (January 1996): 45–63.
42. Jana Everett and Mira Savara, "Bank Loans to the Poor in Bombay: Do Women Benefit?" *Women and Poverty*, eds. Barbara C. Gelpi, Nancy C.M. Hartsock, Clare C. Novak, and Myra H. Strober (Chicago, Ill.: University of Chicago, 1986): 83–101.
43. Everett and Savara, *op. cit.*: 90.
44. There now appears to be the start of a correctional wave of writings; cf. Margrethe Silberschmidt, *Rethinking Men and Gender Relations: An Investigation of Men, Their Changing Roles Within the Household, and the Implications for Gender Relations in Kisii District, Kenya* (Copenhagen, Denmark: Centre for Development Research, 1991), which is billed as a monograph that "challenges the tendency within women's studies to see men as winners and women as losers in the process of socioeconomic change" by presenting male circumstances and dilemmas.
45. Diane Elson, "Male Bias in the Development Process: An Overview," *Male Bias in the Development Process*, ed. Diane Elson (Manchester, United Kingdom: Manchester University, 1991): 1–28.
46. Richard Franke and Barbara Chasin, *Kerala: Radical Reform as Development in an Indian State* (Institute for Food and Development Policy, 1989).

*F*urther reading and statistical sources

Aslanbeigui, Nahid, Steven Pressman and Gale Summerfield (eds.) (1994). *Women in the Age of Economic Transformation: Gender Impact of Reforms in Post-Socialist and Developing Countries.* London and New York: Routledge. Includes case studies of Zambia, Singapore, South Korea, Chile, Mexico, and Nicaragua.

Benería, Lourdes, and Shelley Feldman (1992). *Unequal Burden: Economic Crises, Persistent Poverty, and Women's Work.* Boulder, Colo.: Westview. Case studies of the Caribbean, Mexico, Bangladesh, Bolivia, Tanzania, South Asia, Italy, and Nicaragua.

Birdsall, Nancy, and Richard Sabot (eds.) (1991). *Unfair Advantage: Labor Market Discrimination in Developing Countries.* Washington, D.C.: World Bank. Eight papers examining magnitude and type of labor market discrimination in low-income countries.

Dasgupta, Partha S. (1995). "Population, Poverty and the Local Environment," *Scientific American* (February): 40–45. Thought-provoking discussion of interlinkages between child labor, environmental degradation, fertility, and poverty.

Elson, Diane (ed.) (1991). *Male Bias in the Development Process.* Manchester: Manchester University. Essays, including case studies of Chinese peasants, Zimbabwe, Nigeria, and Mexico border industries.

Folbre, Nancy, Barbara Bergmann, Bina Agarwal, and Maria Floro (eds.) (1992). *Women's Work in the World Economy,* Vol. 4 in *Issues in Contemporary Economics.* New York: New York University. Proceedings of the Ninth World Congress of the International Economic Association; contains papers on the Philippines, Turkey, and Pakistan and on issues in developed countries.

Joekes, Susan (1987). *Women in the World Economy*. New York: Oxford University. Synthesis of results from a number of studies, commissioned by the International Research and Training Institute for the Advancement of Women (INSTRAW), a United Nations agency.

Momsen, Janet Henshall (1991). *Women and Development in the Third World*. London: Routledge. Short textbook written by a geographer.

Quibria, M. G. (ed.) (1995). *Critical Issues in Asian Development: Theories, Experiences, and Policies*. Oxford: Oxford University. See in particular chapters by Deaton and Hart on inequality within and between households and gender issues in household behavior.

Review of Radical Political Economy (1991). Vol. 23, nos. 3 and 4 (Fall and Winter). Issue on "Women in the International Economy."

Stichter, Sharon, and Jane L. Parpart (eds.) (1990). *Women, Employment and the Family in the International Division of Labour*. London: Macmillan. Chapters on the Caribbean and newly industrialized countries in Asia, Ireland, Nigeria, Algeria, Peru, and India.

Tinker, Irene (ed.) (1990). *Persistent Inequalities: Women and World Development*. Oxford: Oxford University. Essays on general issues in considering gender aspects of development, as well as essays focusing on situations in particular countries.

Townsend, Janet (1988). *Women in Developing Countries: A Selected, Annotated Bibliography for Development Organizations*. Sussex: Institute of Development Studies.

United Nations. *Women's Indicators and Statistics Database (Wistat)*. CD-Rom containing a comprehensive set of United Nations agency data. The UN maintains a publications list and some data at its website (www.un.org; to track down a specific UN agency, use www.unsystem.org).

—— (1995). *The World's Women 1995: Trends and Statistics*. Printed compendium of United Nations agency data.

United Nations Development Programme. *Human Development Report*. Oxford: Oxford University. Annual report on human development, including a useful statistical appendix of human development indicators, including literacy, income distribution, and life expectancy statistics. The 1995 report focuses on gender equality issues. UNDP maintains a publications list and some data at its website (www.undp.org).

UNESCO (1983). *Bibliographic Guide to Studies on the Status of Women: Development and Population Trends*. London and Reading: Eastern Press. A set of annotated bibliographies by geographic region. UNESCO maintains a publications list and some data at its website (www.unesco.org).

——. Occasional reports on the status of women in various countries, including Wali M. Rahimi, "Status of Women: Afghanistan" (1991).

Ward, Kathryn (ed.) (1990). *Women Workers and Global Restructuring*. Ithaca, N.Y.: ILR. Essays on how export-led development affects women.

World Bank. *Social Indicators of Development*. Baltimore, Md.: Johns Hopkins. Annual report, contains tables with basic data on each country where data are available. The World Bank maintains a publications list and some data at its website (www.worldbank.org).

——. *World Development Indicators* Oxford: Oxford University. Statistical compendium of world development indicators; expanded version of the appendix for the report listed below. Available in CD-Rom and printed versions.

——. *World Development Report*. Oxford: Oxford University. Annual report on development around the world, with a different subject focus each year. Always has a useful statistical appendix of selected world development indicators, as well as special statistics on the focus for the year.

——. Series of country study reports on the role of women in economic development, including: "Kenya: The Role of Women in Economic Development" (1989); Ann Duncan, "Women in Pakistan: An Economic and Social Strategy" (1989); "Bangladesh: Strategies for Enhancing the Role of Women in Economic Development" (1990); "Gender and Poverty in India" (1991); "Turkey: Women in Development" (1993).

World Development (1995). Vol. 23, no. 11 (November). Special issue on gender, adjustment, and macroeconomics.

Discussion questions

1. Draw a household production possibility frontier as in Figure 3.1. How would you represent the effect of economic development on this frontier? (Hint: look at Figure 4.10.) How would you represent changes in household division of labor on this graph (same hint)?

2. Why might higher female education levels reduce infant mortality rates? Why might they reduce fertility rates?

3. Consider the four perspectives proposed by Bourque and Warren. How might an economist restate these perspectives? Why do the different perspectives imply different effects of economic development on improving women's position?

4. Consider the Focus on factories in Brazil. Which factory would you choose to work in, and why?

5. When might a family rationally decide to educate a daughter rather than a son (assuming that their resources are limited so that they cannot educate both)?

6. Consider the Focus on government matchmaking in Singapore. Is a government-sponsored voluntary matchmaking agency for college graduates really such a silly idea? What about pronatalist policy that favors the higher-educated?

7. How might the structure of the formal education system in developing countries hinder women's achievement of economic equality?

8. Consider the Focus on bank loans in Bombay and the section on development programs that expand small-scale credit opportunities. Can you think of any bad aspects of such programs?

9. If small-scale credit programs are so successful, why had commercial banks not considered them commercially viable and instituted them decades ago? If they continue to be successful, why might commercial banks still decline to take on such programs?

10. Is male bias in development inevitable?

11. Consider the advantages and disadvantages of having different regions or states in a country attempt different development strategies.

Historical Comparisons: How Do Gender Differences Vary over Time?

PART

V

*T*his part of the book attempts to answer three questions. How have economic gender differences changed in the United States since before World War II? How do these patterns vary by race, ethnicity, and class? And, how might we expect them to change in the near future, particularly if new policies were undertaken with the goal of achieving gender equality?

Chapter 14 covers the period from the colonial era through World War II, focusing on the European-American experience. Chapter 15 covers the same period, focusing on variations from these European-American experiences for different racial and ethnic groups. Particular emphasis is placed on considering the changes over time for immigrant groups, as well as consideration of the Native American and African-American experiences. The chapter also addresses the general question of how important it is to consider differences in gender patterns by race, ethnicity, and class in modern data as well as in historical data, as well as how these differences might influence policy.

Chapter 16 summarizes the various types of policies that affect economic gender differences that have been illustrated throughout this book. It then considers various new policy directions for modifying social and economic structures so as to achieve economic gender equality.

Gender Differences in U.S. Economic History

*T*his chapter discusses gender-related topics in U.S. economic history. The main focus is on European-Americans, particularly those who are active in the labor market – i.e., the working class. After an overview of economic gender roles in distinct eras in U.S. economic history, the available quantitative data is considered in an attempt to extend backwards and analyze changes in the time series on variables such as labor force participation and the gender earnings gap. Measurement of the extent of sex discrimination in earlier eras is considered, along with the difficulties inherent in applying economic analysis to historical data. The chapter concludes by considering particular policy measures that arose during the early twentieth century, such as protective legislation and marriage bars, and institutionalized sex discrimination.

Overview by era

This section characterizes five periods, divided roughly by stage of industrialization: (1) the preindustrial period, from colonial times up to 1820; (2) the introduction of industrialization, from 1820 to 1860; (3) the transitional period, from 1860 to 1890; (4) the period of full-fledged industrialization, from 1890 to 1939; and (5) the World War II years, 1939 to 1945.

Preindustrialization: colonial times to 1820

To a large extent, due to its heavy reliance on quantitative data, economic history only comes into being as an industrial – or, at least, a market – economy emerges. Much of the economic history of women and men prior to industrialization concerns the discussion and description of their roles in an agricultural economy.[1] While earlier writers extolled the colonial period as a "Golden Age" for women, stressing their economic importance to a farm-based economy both as agricultural labor and in maintaining the household through a wide array of nonmarket activities, this characterization has been increasingly debunked.[2] The newer view is that women's economic contribution was not sufficient to guarantee them equal political and social status.

Few data exist from the seventeenth century concerning such factors as earnings and the occupational composition of those women who did do market-oriented work. Quantitative data from the eighteenth century are also rare, although there is some evidence on occupations of widows and their late husbands from the late eighteenth century that implies that widows often took over their husbands' occupations, such as various retail and craft occupations.[3] Other countries register a similar lack of historical quantitative economic data.[4] The 1841 and 1851 British censuses record occupation, age, and sex, but no prior comprehensive data exist.

Introduction of industrialization: 1820 to 1860

The period from 1820 to 1860 marked the evolution in America towards an industrial economy. In 1820, 28 percent of the workforce was in manufacturing; by 1860, 41 percent.[5] Women were increasingly drawn into manufacturing industries,[6] reflecting the increased value of their labor in these enterprises, and they quickly developed a wide occupational representation. Writer Harriet Martineau supposedly made the off-the-cuff remark on visiting the United States in 1836 that there were only seven occupations open to women: teaching, needlework, keeping boarders, work in cotton-mills, typesetting, bookbinding, and domestic service. In response to this remark, economist Edith Abbott has shown that women were represented in more than 100 different industrial occupations prior to 1837 (using data back to 1822), citing long lists of occupations from New York, Connecticut, and Massachusetts documents. Shoemaking was an important industry for female employment, as was hatmaking.[7]

This period may mark the status devaluation of nonmarket work in American society, as America began the move away from an agricultural society and more people became wage-earners rather than artisans and farmworkers. One study that considers housework prior to the Civil War argues that nonpaid labor was systematically devalued by society as wages rose to become the measure of work through the rise of capitalism[8] However, that does not mean that there was less nonmarket output; a recent study argues that per capita nonmarket output continued to grow steadily during this period, and that, "the demand for housewives' services expanded even as the demand for home-produced goods fell."[9]

The textile industry, which also marked the beginning of the industrial revolution in England, was the major manufacturing industry in early nineteenth-century America. Before the Civil War, Lowell, Massachusetts was the largest textile center and the center of industry innovation.[10] The industry also primarily employed women. Nevertheless, the male jobs in the mills were higher paid: a study of one mill found that in July 1836, the mean daily pay was $0.60 for women and $1.05 for men, for a gender earnings ratio of 0.57.[11] Men and women were in different jobs within the mill, and the male jobs paid better than the female jobs. Men also had lower turnover, although tenure was low for both sexes, with an average employment length of 2.17 years for the men and 1.75 years for the women.

Prostitution in cities, particularly New York City, appears to have risen substantially during this period.[12] As the number of young women drawn to cities in search of jobs increased, they were drawn into this activity in large part due to economic causes; one writer asserts that "the major factor inducing young women to sell their bodies was the low wages for female labor."[13] Both nondomestic and domestic labor in cities were low-paying, and some young women worked part-time as prostitutes to supplement their meager earnings as servants or seamstresses.

Transition: 1860 to 1890

During the transition from initial industrial development to full-fledged capitalism, several major social shifts occurred: the westward push, the Civil War, and changing antebellum roles, particularly in the South, as regions that had lagged in industrialization began to catch up. Although the move westward had started earlier, the ambitious were pulled west as opportunities opened up there. The pronounced depression following the Civil War pushed many more westward in search of economic opportunities. Migrants being primarily male – at least, in the early phase – caused sex ratios to be somewhat skewed, particularly in frontier areas. Still, there was a relative shortage of young women in both the East and West – due to high maternal mortality rates, for one thing. Therefore, young women in both the East and West still had relatively little time before marriage to work in paid labor and seek higher education.

FOCUS

Mill towns in New England

In the early 1800s, the textile factories in Lowell, Waltham, and other New England towns located on rivers, were staffed primarily by women. Young women poured off of New England farms into boarding houses in these towns, where they lived in close quarters with each other, worked 12- to 14-hour days six days a week, and saved their wages to generate a dowry or to pay for a male family member's college education. Their pattern was to stay a few years before returning home and marrying. Weekly wages were lower than in other work opportunities. A survey of 284 young women in Waltham in 1821 found the majority making only two to three dollars a week, from which they had to pay for room and board.[14] But the mill girls felt they had more "culture" and independence than domestic work, their main alternative, offered.[15] Lowell was famous for the number of clubs, lectures, and reading groups available.

In the 1830s, the mill workers, who had formed "protective associations," held several spontaneous factory walkouts and discussed holding formal strikes.[16] This rising militancy, along with the increased availability of immigrants of both sexes, led to a shift in the 1840s by factory owners towards using immigrant labor to run the mills. Working conditions and wages deteriorated and the New England farm girls left the mills. A study of one Lowell mill found that whereas in July 1836, 97 percent of the employed women were native-born,[17] by August of 1850, 41 percent of the women were immigrants.[18]

Civil War casualties increased work rates for women by reducing the supply of men for the labor force and by reducing the male source of income for women. The war's aftermath also had the effect of increasing the number of black women and men available for industrial labor as freed slaves moved northward.

After the Civil War, there was a notable rise in the size of the urban working class in Northern cities such as Pittsburgh,[19] as industrialization continued in industries like steel. Unionism rose during this period, but did not prove particularly helpful to women in getting higher wages. The history of American trade unionism dates back to shortly after the Revolutionary War: in 1786, Philadelphia printers struck for a one dollar daily wage. But American women were not welcomed with open arms by unions, which saw them as low-wage competition. In 1867 the Cigarmakers Union made history by becoming the first national union to allow women to become members on an equal basis with men. However, still unable to get into most unions, women began to form their own, including the Collarmakers and Laundry Workers Union, and the Daughters of St. Crispin, a shoemakers' union.[20]

The demand for teachers accelerated in the 1880s and 1890s, increasing the demand for female labor, as the benefits of formal education for individual and social economic progress increased and became more obvious.[21] However, most nonagricultural jobs for women (and men) were still found in the manufacturing sector.

In the early twentieth century, University of Chicago-educated economist Edith Abbott churned out articles on female earnings and employment in different industries, much of which research also appeared in her 1909 book, *Women in Industry*.[22] She concentrated on the nineteenth-century industries in which women were found in the greatest numbers: cotton; boots and shoes; cigarmaking; clothing; and printing. Her discussions of shoemaking[23] and cigarmaking[24] considered whether the introduction of machinery in particular industries had the effect of displacing male/skilled labor, while proving complementary to female/unskilled labor. In shoemaking, sewing and stitching machines proved to be critical innovations. Shoe production switched from an at-home to a factory system. However, women did not enter the male jobs in the manufacturing process; it remained a male-dominated, native-dominated industry. The cigarmaking industry provides a contrast to this tale of industry evolution: here, women comprised 9 percent of employees in 1860, but 40 percent in 1900,[25] with an even greater proportion of women in large factories. However, no gain in weekly median wages for women appears; rather, the reverse. In 1890, men earned $11.00 and women $6.00; in 1900, men earned $11.50, and women $5.50.[26]

Full-fledged industrialization: 1890 to 1939

Starting at the turn of the century, America embarked upon a period of continued industrialization, punctuated by business upturns and downturns, World War I, and waves of immigrants. Along with a general rise in literacy and affluence, concern over social differences – including gender differences – became widespread. This era marked the development of more concern over fair labor practices and a greatly increased number of labor regulations, leading to the use of the term Progressive Era.

While discussion of economic gender issues, i.e., the "Woman Question" is found in the writings of earlier authors such as John Stuart Mill and Harriet Martineau (in the early nineteenth century), this period witnessed increased discussion of such issues by economists and other commentators, both in England and the United States.[27] Debates over equal pay for equal work started in 1890 and continued into the early 1920s.[28] Extensive occupational sex segregation hindered the development of equal work comparisons. Writing in 1891, Sidney Webb surveyed a variety of data on men and women workers in Great Britain and the United States and noted the difficulty of making "equal work" comparisons due to the rarity of occupations that contained both sexes, but he found women workers making less anyway.[29] Progressive Era writers had the same explanations for low female wages that we use now (save for compensating differentials): an oversupply of women to some occupations; geographical and other immobilities, leading to relatively inelastic labor supply; sex discrimination; a lack of skill and education; intermittent work experience; lack of physical strength; relative youth and inexperience; and low unionism rates.[30]

The era also marked the beginning of the phenomenon of populist feminist writers on economic issues, of which Charlotte Perkins Gilman is the best known today.[31] This was not a field of particularly revolutionary thinking. Gilman was not antiman, but rather saw the sexes as complementary: "... *women* are not undeveloped *men*, but the feminine half of humanity is undeveloped human."[32] However, these writers were concerned that the middle class phenomenon of constraining women to the domestic sphere was both harmful to their mental and physical health and wasteful of their potential public contributions.

This period marked the emergence of reliable, steady statistical data collection – e.g., the 1890 Census. Analysts were interested in demographic as well as economic trends, and they were aware of the long-term demographic trends illustrated in Chapter 5, such as the rise in divorce, the fall in the birth rate, and the declining median age at first marriage (which dropped fairly steadily from 26.1 for men and 22.0 for women in 1890 to 24.3 for men and 21.5 for women in 1940).[33] For instance, a 1909 article commenting on a Census Bureau report on divorce from 1887 to 1906 noted the worrying fact that divorce was three times as frequent as it used to be, along with noting a slower, but rising, divorce growth rate in Europe.[34]

The service sector became an increasingly important employer of women workers during this period, and by the 1920s a larger percentage of employed women were in service-sector jobs than in manufacturing. Prostitution became a less attractive earnings option for many women as female wages and working conditions improved in both manufacturing and the service sector.[35]

World War II

The scale of World War II and the extent of U.S. involvement led to a large shift in employment patterns during the war. As men were conscripted and production of war-related goods increased, women entered manufacturing in large numbers, both to fill the slack in labor supply left by the men and as a response to both reduced income and reduced nonmarket work responsibilities. War industries hired 1.3 million women of the 2.5 million who entered the labor force for the first time, as well as hiring about 700,000 out of other industries.[36] Nonfamily child care became available for the first time on a widespread basis, as factories producing war-related products set up 24-hour child care centers so that women could work full-time, including swing shifts. Female wages rose relative to male wages and sex segregation diminished temporarily as women took on higher-paid manufacturing jobs.[37] Women also found increased work opportunity in the increased number of military support positions.

However, women were not so optimistic as to assume that their new roles would continue in peacetime; nor, in many cases, did they want to continue in their new economic roles. Feminist commentators were concerned by both the example of gender relations set by Hitler's Germany and the possibility of reversion after the war ended in the gains made by women. One popular-press maven, Elizabeth Hawes, commented: "I am terrified we may not start soon enough to avert the Hitlerian routine of children-kitchen-church for the next generations of Common American women and do away with economic slavery for their husbands."[38] The end of the war did lead to wholesale reduction of female industrial employment, both voluntary and involuntary, as men returned from their wartime roles. However, while the late 1940s and early 1950s marked social reversion in some measures, such as the drop in age at first marriage and rise in fertility, other trends that had been present before the war's onset continued and even accelerated, including the rises in divorce and married women's employment. While the majority of wartime labor force entrants exited between 1944 and 1950, half of all married women who were working in 1950 had also been working in 1940, and half of the 1940s' married women labor force entrants joined after the war.[39] The view of this period as a watershed in gender relations[40] has recently fallen out of favor, replaced by the view that the rise in women's labor supply after World War II is due primarily to longer-run factors, including increased clerical employment and female education.[41]

Long-run trends in labor markets

In an examination of historical data, the usual questions about wage and employment trends arise. Are these trends driven by labor demand or supply? Do they reflect cohort effects or effects that are shared across cohorts? What are their relationships to demographic changes? In this section, we consider data on labor force participation, occupational sex segregation, and the gender earnings ratio, applying the same general analysis to these data that was applied to data gathered after World War II (Parts II and III of this book).

Labor force participation

Table 14.1 displays decennial labor force participation rates by sex and women's proportion of the labor force from 1800 to 1940, charting upward trends in all three series (although men's participation peaks in 1910). Figure 14.1 shows these labor force trends from 1800 until the present. Here one can observe three distinct periods in female labor force participation and percentage female: a period of gradual rise over the nineteenth century, followed by a plateau or even a slight drop in the early twentieth century (1910 to 1940), followed by a sharp rise since World War II. Male participation rose up to 1910 (with a dip following the Civil War), dipped during the Depression years, rose in the mid-twentieth century, and has been declining since 1950.

The most notable participation rate change from 1890 to current times occurred for married women, rising from 4.6 percent in 1890 to 61.0 percent in 1995. Over the same time span, the labor force participation rate for single women rose from 40.5 to 66.8 percent. However, the rise from 1890 to 1940 was only to 13.8 percent for married women and 45.5 percent for single women (who had a higher rate in 1930 of 50.5 percent).[42] Cohort patterns are similar in age-specific participation rates, but shift up over time.[43] Labor market turnover of married women was not particularly high in these years; it was mostly the more highly educated married women who stayed in continuously. The other major worklife pattern for women was to exit the labor force at the time of marriage and only re-enter much later in life.

Historical calculations of female labor force participation are subject to some of the same problems encountered in dealing with current data from nonindustrialized societies: adjustments to female labor force participation for married women, in particular, would push these rates up. For example, the 1890 white, married women labor force participation rate rises from 2.5 percent to 12.5 percent if boarding house keepers and unpaid family farm agricultural workers are included; there is also evidence of an undercount of women in manufacturing.[44] However, the view that the rise from 1890 to 1940 is an artifact of data collection procedures has fallen out of favor.

TABLE 14.1 Labor force participation rates by sex and proportion of labor force that is female, 1800 to 1940

Year	Labor force/population (%)		Women/labor force
	Women	*Men*	
1800	4.4	72.6	0.04
1810	7.6	73.0	0.06
1820	6.0	73.4	0.05
1830	6.5	74.4	0.06
1840	8.0	74.4	0.07
1850	9.7	75.8	0.08
1860	9.6	76.2	0.08
1870	13.1	74.8	0.15
1880	14.7	78.7	0.15
1890	17.4	79.3	0.17
1900	18.8	80.0	0.18
1910	23.4	81.3	0.21
1920	21.0	78.2	0.21
1930	22.0	76.2	0.22
1940	25.4	79.0	0.24

Sources: 1800–60 – Thomas Weiss, "Revised Estimates of the United States Workforce, 1800–1860," *Long-Term Factors in American Economic Growth*, eds. Stanley L. Engerman and Robert E. Gallman (Chicago, Ill.: University of Chicago, 1986): 657 (Table 12.A.1), 658–659 (Table 12.A.2); 1870–1940 – U.S. Bureau of the Census, *Historical Statistics of the United States* (Washington, D.C.: Government Printing Office, 1976): Series D13. Data for 1800–1930 are for persons ages 10 and over, for 1940 are for persons ages 14 and over. Data for 1800–60 are for free persons only.

Valerie Oppenheimer,[45] in discussing the gradual rise in the female labor force participation rate from 1890 to 1940, emphasizes demand over supply shifts as the main force behind the increase, although both are considered important. She argues that the economy shifted to depending on "female occupations" that needed skill but not commitment or specialized location. She prefers a "replacing of men" to a "displacing of men" interpretation.

Women in the early twentieth century appear to have responded to the same underlying economic incentives in deciding whether or not to participate in paid work as have post-World War II women. One study applies a standard economic labor supply model to 1901 survey data on women (in which women choose how to allocate their time between market work, nonmarket work, and leisure) and concludes that it fits, although it requires augmentation with the alternatives of sending children out to work and taking in paying boarders.[46]

Meanwhile, male labor force participation rates have declined over the twentieth century, though not smoothly. The decline has been fueled mainly by a decline in participation among older men. During the late nineteenth century, the rate for men 65 and over declined from 76 percent in 1860 to 70 percent by 1900.[47] After a period of accelerated decline from 1900 to 1930, their rate dropped from 54 percent in 1930 to 41 percent by 1950, and was down to 19 percent by 1980. The main cause of this decline is the recomposition of the labor force from agriculture to manufacturing; rates for farm workers in rural areas remained constant from 1860 to 1900, but demand for older workers in

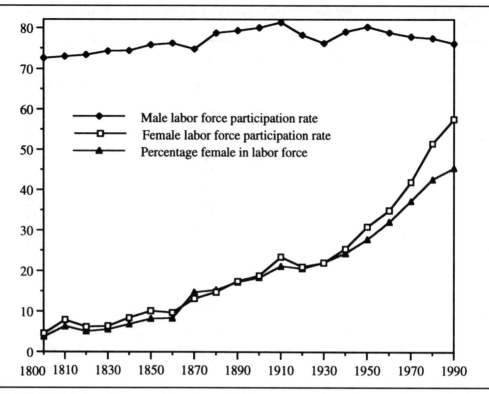

FIGURE 14.1 Labor force participation rates by sex and percentage of labor force that is female, 1800 to 1996

Sources: 1800–1940 – as Table 14.1; 1950–70 – U.S. Bureau of the Census, *Historical Statistics of the United States* (Washington, D.C.: Government Printing Office, 1976): Series D13; 1980–96 – *Economic Report of the President 1997*: 340 (Table B-34), 343 (Table B-37). Data for 1950–60 are for persons ages 14 and over, for 1970–96 are for persons ages 16 and over.

industrial settings was limited. The big decline in the male labor force participation rate between 1930 and 1950 is generally attributed to the creation of the Old Age Assistance program established by the Social Security Act of 1935; more recent declines are due to the Old Age and Survivors Insurance program and to growth in private pension programs.[48] There were also declines for young men over this long time-frame, due to higher rates of participation in schooling.[49] Young and older women also have declining participation rates over this period for apparently the same reasons: more schooling in earlier years and more financial support available in later years over the life cycle.[50]

Economic historians have also addressed the question of what caused the rise of part-time work: supply or demand shifts? Part-time work emerged only in the 1950s; before then, jobs requiring less than 35 hours a week of work were virtually nonexistent. The nineteenth-century work norm was six days a week, over ten hours a day. The Great Depression of the late 1920s and 1930s appears to have led to the idea of a five-day, forty-hour workweek as a worksharing institution. Before then, the only flexibility in work-time lay in occupations and industries where outwork/piecework was an option – at large pecuniary penalties.[51] The movement towards part-time appears to have been driven by declines in the number of hireable single women, due to less immigration, earlier marriage, and greater participation in higher education. Employers were forced to reorganize work so as to make jobs more compatible with the nonmarket responsibilities of married women. This change in the organization of work may have then led to increased numbers of women workers after the 1950s.

Occupational segregation

Systematic data on occupational sex segregation are available from 1870 onward on a decennial basis. There is strong agreement across studies that occupational sex segregation has remained virtually unchanged since the end of the nineteenth century. One economist reports that for a consistent set of 300 occupations, the Duncan index of segregation equals 66 in both 1900 and 1960.[52] This basic result is corroborated by a number of other studies.[53] However, there is a decline in segregation relative to the mid-nineteenth century. One analyst[54] uses three methods of computing the Duncan index for 1870 to 1900 as a robustness check:[55] (1) use all current occupations, (2) use a consistent subset of occupations (eliminate), and (3) back-aggregate (collapse and eliminate). She also does back-aggregation decade-to-decade and across all decades. Using U.S. Census data to calculate the index values, she finds that segregation declined from approximately 71 in 1870 to 64 in 1900 for all occupations, and declined from 87 in 1870 to 74 for nonagricultural occupations.[56] She argues that the reduction in sex segregation over this period was primarily due to changes in the sex composition of occupations, not to gender shifts among occupations. The reduced need for domestic servants was an important cause, along with the rise and integration of clerical labor. Among domestics, there was also increased substitution of male (and female) blacks after the Civil War.[57]

While overall sex segregation levels have remained relatively constant, there have been significant shifts in gender employment patterns between occupations. Several analysts have documented shifts across occupational classes.[58] Economist Rudolph Blitz has studied changes within the professions from 1870 to 1970, a period of rapid growth for them.[59] Occupations that were male-dominated in 1870 (no more than 5 percent female) experienced a large increase in women; those that were female-dominated (over 60 percent female) had an increased or continued high proportion of women; and those that were in the intermediate category showed no clear trend, save a hump in the 1920s and 1930s. Blitz finds the 1920s and 1930s to be a period of progress for women in these occupations, which was followed by a flattening-out in the 1950s.

A more pessimistic view would be that increases in female employment signaled a concurrent devaluation of these occupations – i.e., "women will make gains, but the 'professional' jobs they enter will be such in name only."[60] These jobs may experience increased routinization, de-skilling, and lower pay, either as a cause of feminization or as a result. One article points out examples of these phenomena in college teaching, medicine, and law as their proportion of women rises. Dentistry is a contrasting example of a profession that has remained predominantly male and has apparently experienced little erosion of professional power.[61]

Clerical occupations have been extensively studied. Originally a male-dominated group, these occupations have since become stereotypically female occupations. The Civil War labor shortage had led to the first hiring of female clerks as government employees.[62] But still, in 1870, most stenographers were men, and few stenographers worked in business.[63] Business stenography, however, quickly became female-dominated:[64] in 1880 this job area was about 40 percent female; by 1900 it was over 75 percent female, and by 1930 was over

95 percent female. As 1900 to 1930 was a real growth period for clerical work as well as for female dominance of it,[65] this occupation soon became the most significant source of employment for women since the advent of manufacturing.

Can the increased proportion of women in clerical work be explained by a change in technology favoring those persons (predominantly women) with more manual dexterity? While older studies had found that girls exceed boys in manual dexterity, recent studies find that they score higher on speed measures and better in finger dexterity, but debate continues over whether there is a sex difference in overall manual dexterity.[66] Some analysts have suggested that the typewriter was a gender neutral technology when introduced, so it could have become associated with either sex's labor.[67] Another analyst has suggested that the nonpecuniary attractions of clerical work (e.g., clean, nonphysical work) compensated for falling relative earnings; additionally, the secular decline in the family economy and the rise in education led to increased female labor supply, which increased female employment but drove down the wage. Since many other occupations were barred to women and a rise in labor demand occurred concurrently in clerical employment, women flowed into clerical jobs.[68]

FOCUS

Bank tellers and the tipping phenomenon

The occupation of bank teller shifted from virtually all male in 1935 to virtually all female by 1980. This tipping occurred relatively slowly. In 1935, a survey of 50 banks found no female tellers. By 1943, 37 percent of bank tellers were women, and by 1950, 45 percent. The rise in percentage female continued to 60 percent in 1960, 89 percent in 1970, and 91 percent in 1980.

Several reasons for this shift have been suggested. During World War II, many women found work in positions emptied by men in military service. But after the war, men did not appear in large numbers to reclaim the teller jobs, although in other industries they did displace women. The argument that women were hired instead of men because they could be paid lower wages does not explain the time path of the change; women received lower wages than men before the tipping began, as well as afterwards. Finally, the argument that de-skilling occurred through automation of the teller job also is inconsistent with the time path. Much of the automation that could have contributed to de-skilling of the occupation took place after the shift had occurred (for example, the widespread use of automated teller machines) and therefore cannot be considered a cause.

Analysts Myra Strober and Carolyn Arnold argue that men did not return to bank teller jobs because they were less attractive to them than other occupations.[69] They argue that changes in the banking industry that occurred during the 1930s would have led to the departure of men from the occupation before the War had it not been for the Depression, and that the de-skilling was a result of the bank teller job becoming "declassed."

Comparison of a 1922 description of the teller job with the 1939 Dictionary of Occupational Titles description implies that tellers had much more responsibility in the 1920s. At that time, a distinction was drawn between paying tellers, who cashed checks and paid out money to deposit holders, and receiving tellers, who accepted money for deposit. Paying tellers had more responsibility, and the job was considered to be "important, complicated, and dignified."[70] By 1929, banks were beginning to combine the two functions into one job. Then, in the 1930s, a hierarchical pay and position structure was developed in which head tellers supervised ordinary tellers, and note tellers took over the task of loan arrangements. Promotional opportunities out of teller positions into management became more limited, and pay dropped for the lower-level teller positions.

Strober and Arnold argue that these changes were brought about by changes in the nature of bank clientele. In the 1930s, banks changed from primarily serving companies and wealthy individuals to serving a larger section of the population. They reduced the cost of having a checking account, developed the use of consumer installment loans, and began receiving utility and telephone payments. Bank workload grew enormously: from 1939 to 1952, the number of checking accounts increased from 27 million to 47.1 million. Bank employment increased, and the percentage of employees who were tellers increased as well. Although the tasks of the teller did not change, mass retailing of banking was a lower-status job than catering to the wealthy. Strober and Arnold conclude that "the image of the teller job, rather than the tasks associated with it, was probably the main source of the decline in status and wages relative to other white-collar jobs for men. . . ."[71] A supporting piece of evidence is that the gender shift of the teller job has been accompanied by an age shift: a disproportionate share of bank tellers are ages 16 to 24. Many tellers may view their job not as a first step into a career in banking but as a short-term way of getting money while preparing for a more lucrative career through higher education.

Earnings differentials

Measures of the gender earnings gap are available intermittently for a fairly long way back in time.[72] In 1815 the wage ratio in agricultural and domestic activities was 0.29; in 1820, at the onset of the industrial revolution, the ratio in manufacturing was between 0.30 and 0.37. By 1832 the manufacturing wage ratio had risen to 0.44, and by 1850, in the Northeast, had risen still further to 0.50. By 1885 the manufacturing wage ratio had leveled out at 0.56, which was still the case nation-wide in 1905. Manufacturing wage ratios fluctuated in the range of 0.57 to 0.70 from 1914 to 1935, with evidence of a rise towards the middle of the 1930s, but by the 1950s they had fallen below 0.60 and fluctuated in the range of 0.50 to 0.58 during the 1950s and 1960s. Data on the overall earnings ratio are available since 1890; they show a rise from 1890 to 1930 of 0.46 to 0.56.[73]

Why did the ratio rise in the mid-nineteenth century? The rise coincided with the advent of manufacturing employment. Increasing division of labor and use of machinery led to rapid increases in labor productivity and a reduction of the importance of physical strength as a factor affecting earnings, both because machinery was substituted for physical labor and because fewer people were needed in the more physical agricultural occupations. Increased demand for unskilled manufacturing labor led to a rise in relative wages for women.

Why did the manufacturing wage ratio remain stable in the late nineteenth century? The growing heterogeneity of the female work force may be responsible for this development, as the more educated, higher-skilled women did not enter the manufacturing sector, while the lower-skilled women did. Another theory is that the introduction around 1900 of large-scale, continuous-process production technologies in manufacturing, gradually replacing small-scale, batch-process production technologies, led to a halt in the reduction of gender gap that had been going on as manufacturing initially moved from homes and artisan shops to early factories, which tended to be small and idiosyncratically managed.[74]

Why did the ratio rise in the early twentieth century? The rise was due more to changes in relative earnings within occupations than to changes in the distribution of women across occupations, but some of it is due to increased representation of women in higher-paying occupations. Additionally, narrowing of skill premia occurred with the general increase in

TABLE 14.2 Percentage female of high school graduates, and bachelor and first-professional degree recipients, end of each school year, 1870 to 1950

Year	High School	Bachelor's and First-Professional
1870	56.2	14.7
1880	54.2	19.3
1890	56.8	17.3
1900	60.0	19.1
1910	59.6	22.7
1920	60.4	34.2
1930	55.0	39.9
1940	52.7	41.3
1950	52.4	23.9

Source: Digest of Education Statistics (1991): 105 (Table 95).

the population's schooling levels, reducing men's wages on the top end and bringing up women's wages from the bottom.

Among women in manufacturing occupations during this period, there appears to have been little relationship between human capital differences and earnings differences. One study, using data from a 1907–1908 Labor Bureau survey of 3434 unmarried women workers 16 years and over in the silk, cotton, textile, and glass industries, uses earnings regressions to conclude that human capital variables (years of schooling, age and age-squared, which are common proxies for years of work experience) accounted for about one-quarter of earnings variance among women. However, occupation was important within industries. The authors lean towards occupational segregation (where women are found in semiskilled jobs with flat earnings profiles) and geographical immobility as the causes of low women's wages (which, as usual, does not allow us to discern whether these factors are due to discrimination or free choice on the part of women).[75] In measuring the effects of occupational segregation on the gender earnings gap, one can apply the counterfactual condition of applying female earnings by occupation to the male occupational distribution, and vice-versa. Using this method, differences in occupational distribution turn out to "explain" about one-fifth of the gap. If differences in industrial distribution are included, one can explain up to half of the gap.[76]

On the surface, nineteenth-century gender differences in the usual measures of human capital – particularly formal schooling – do not appear to be a major factor in explaining earnings differences. For example, Table 14.2 displays female high-school graduate per-centages from 1870 to 1950. Throughout this period, women were more likely to complete high school than were men. In fact, women comprise a higher proportion of high school graduates in the late nineteenth century than in the mid-twentieth century. However, the payoff to education, for women in particular, may have been lower. Women did comprise a small proportion of bachelor and first-professional degree graduates, as is also shown in Table 14.2 and therefore were less likely to receive the higher returns related to attainment of these degrees; however, such persons comprised a much smaller portion of the labor market during this period than they do currently.

Differences in work experience by sex in the nineteenth century also appear to have been too small to explain earnings differences. Turnover rates were high for both sexes.

A study of California manufacturing workers, using data from 1892, finds that differences in tenure at firm by sex are too small to have warranted differences in firm-specific training for young men and women; rather, both sexes had low rates of return on general occupational training.[77]

As with contemporary data, attempts to fit regression equations to earlier data show a significant large unexplained portion of the gender earnings gap. In comparison with recent data (1970), however, a larger percentage of the wage gap in both 1890 and 1930 is explained by differences in human capital. This indicates a possible secular increase in discrimination by 1970, but this difference can alternatively be explained by the increasing importance of excluded explanatory variables, such as ability.[78] This increase in discrimination appears to date from before World War II, at least in particular sectors, as economist Claudia Goldin finds an unexplained overall wage gap percentage of 20 percent in 1900 vs. an explained percentage of 55 percent in office work in 1940.[79]

Goldin advances a thesis of emerging wage discrimination from 1890 to 1940, occurring in the clerical sector, in particular, as contrasted to manufacturing. She argues that sex segregation was not intentional in manufacturing, but was defined by job requirements. Since much manufacturing labor – especially female labor – was paid by piece rates, there was no basis for pay other than productivity once the rate was set (although the piece rates could still be discriminatory, given occupational sex segregation). Additionally, much manufacturing labor was hired in spot markets, which operate more like neoclassical labor markets. However, a different organization of employment arose in the clerical sector, where wages were specified as part of the whole employment contract and had no direct relationship to workrates. Now internal job ladders existed rather than spot markets, and men were more likely to advance up these ladders to the higher-paying positions. Discrimination in promotion was now possible.

The second factor leading to wage discrimination in the early twentieth century was the rise of institutional constraints on labor markets that were discriminatory in nature. These included legislated sex differences, protective legislation, employer job restrictions, and marriage, training, and employment bars. Some of these restrictions are discussed below.

Policies affecting men and women differently

Many policies have been instituted with the explicit goal of treating the sexes differently. They may be instituted through court rulings,[80] through legislation, or through individual firm or industry practices. These policies often have the effect, whether explicit or implicit, of giving men an advantage in the labor market, whether it be a higher wage for equal work, a greater range of job opportunities, or a lower level of competition for a particular job. Prior to the twentieth century, practices existed that had these effects, but in the early part of the twentieth century, explicit policies yielding these effects became extremely common and may well have been more effective in giving men an advantage than earlier *ad hoc* discriminatory practices. A 1940 survey of firms found that sex restrictions were extremely widespread: 70 to 74 percent of all firms had at least one restricted job. Additionally, there were bars against women in many professions (e.g., medicine and law) for both training and employment. This section considers governmentally sanctioned workforce policies that affected women and men differently – i.e., legislated sex differences and protective legislation – as well as discussing the effects of unions pushing for such laws.

Legislated gender differences

Legislation regarding unequal treatment of women and men can take several forms, including establishment of lower wages for women and barring of women from particular types of employment. As discussed in Chapter 10 for the cases of Australia and New Zealand, lower wages for women were institutionalized in national wage-setting guidelines on the grounds of guaranteeing a family wage for men. Terms including "just" wage, "fair" wage, "family" wage, "living" wage, and "luxury" vs. "necessity" wage have all been used at various times to argue for setting a higher wage for men – particularly married men – than for women.[81]

Some historians, notably Alice Kessler-Harris, have argued that wages have meaning transcending economists' models, and that they are neither neutral nor natural, but reveal social constructs.[82] For instance, the term "woman's wage" is often considered a term of opprobrium.[83] To the extent that use of these terms can influence the formation of policy that restricts the free operation of labor markets, this appears to be true. A deeper question is whether social constructs can influence wage-setting in the absence of legislated policies regarding wages.

Protective legislation

Protective legislation is legislation ostensibly aimed at preventing the exploitation of those workers who are unable to stand up for themselves, particularly women and minors. Many current labor laws have historical roots in the move towards protective legislation. For instance, the minimum wage, when first adopted in 1910 by various states, was applied only to women and minors, who were viewed as not as able as men to negotiate higher wages, due partly to their lower skill levels and their lack of participation in unions.[84]

A number of social problems manifested themselves to reformers in the early twentieth century, leading to a call for protective legislation for women, in particular: (1) there were a large number of minors among the female workforce (about one-fifth between the ages of 10 and 20); (2) women comprised a transient workforce, for the most part, and were therefore unlikely to become unionized; (3) women appeared to have higher job-related and on-the-job illness rates than men. Even if advocates of protective legislation, as one writer of the time wrote, couched the grounds of protection in terms of protecting the most helpless, regardless of sex,[85] it appeared that the most helpless were usually women.

Some of the most effective advocates of protective legislation were members of the women's movement.[86] Josephine Goldmark, who greatly influenced the arguments of her relative, Louis Brandeis, in a landmark protective legislation case, was a member of the National Consumer's League, which was essentially a women's rights organization. In this famous 1908 Supreme Court case, Brandeis (later a Supreme Court justice) argued, using a number of contemporary medical sources, that women were physiologically inferior to men and that long working hours could render them sterile.[87] Over the next eight years, 41 states enacted new or updated laws restricting work hours for women. There was a concurrent notable decline in hours worked for all workers: in manufacturing, the percentage of workers working 60 or more hours a week declined from 39 percent to 12 percent from 1909 to 1919, while the percentage of workers working 48 or fewer hours per week rose from 8 percent to 49 percent.[88]

The role of unions

Unions were a major force in the development of legislation on sex differences and protective legislation (and, also, exclusionary policies against immigrants). The American Federation of Labor (AFL), a group of trade unions founded in 1886, was instrumental in these drives.[89] One analyst writes:[90]

> The AFL's short-term focus on increasing the wages of its members resulted in considerable ambivalence by the AFL toward organizing female workers. Despite rapid expansion in the numbers of working women in the industrial labor force between 1897 and 1920, the AFL was able to organize no more than 1.5 percent of the women engaged in industrial occupations by the year 1910. . . . The AFL's ambivalence derived from competing and conflicting concerns between a fear of being undercut by cheap female labor and a commitment to the patriarchal view of women's role as homemakers.
>
> . . . Even unions that did admit women sometimes directed exclusionary tactics at female members; these unions held meetings at late hours, in meeting places such as saloons.

In 1892 and 1894 the AFL urged special legislation concerning women.[91] It endorsed an eight-hour workday for women and prohibition of female employment on foot-powered machinery. In 1898 it introduced a resolution at the national convention to ask the U.S. Congress "to remove all women from government employment, and thereby to encourage their removal from the 'everyday walks of life and relegate them to the home.'"[92] The leading figure in the AFL's antiwomen worker campaign was none other than their president, Samuel Gompers. He remarked in 1887, "We know to our regret that too often are wives, sisters and children brought into the factories and workshops only to reduce the wages and displace the labor of men – the heads of families,"[93] foreshadowing his 1906 position paper on working women that also suggested that women should be relegated to the home.

FOCUS

The cigar industry

Cigarmaking was originally done by women in their homes. It was only with increased popularity and demand for cigars that it became a male-dominated trade, although women still did subsidiary aspects of the work. With large-scale immigration of Bohemian cigarmakers to the United States in the 1860s, and with technological change enabling the use of molds for cigar-forming (formerly the major skilled aspect of the trade), women were again used in all aspects of cigarmaking, and it became a basic tenement industry.

The percentage of women employees rose from 9 percent in 1860 to 17 percent in 1880, and to 37 percent in 1900.[94] Male cigarmakers reacted to this threat. In 1865 the Cigarmakers International Union established male-only membership. A year later members debated on whether to allow women to work in union shops. But in 1869, employers used women to break a cigarmakers strike in New York City, and women replaced men striking against molding machines in 1870. It thus became obvious that women were capable replacements for striking male cigarmakers. Accordingly, in 1875, the national union decided to end its policy of barring women.

> However, not all union members adhered to the new policy. Cincinnati cigarmakers, for example, objected to the national union's looser stand on women in the trade and struck to remove women from their shops. By 1878, however, the president of the national union conceded: "This state of affairs cannot be altered, it is better to unite than strike against them, because the latter course would prove futile, the employment of women having increased in alarming proportion."[95]
>
> But just one year later, the cigarmakers had developed a new strategy to fight women's working in the factories: "We cannot drive the females out of the trades but we can restrict this daily quota of labor through factory laws. No girl under eighteen should be employed more than eight hours per day; all overwork should be prohibited; white married women should be kept out of the factories at least six weeks before and six weeks after confinement."[96] Where direct exclusion had failed, the indirect route might succeed.[97]

Policy Application: Marriage bars

Marriage bars are rules dictating women employees' allowable family status. These rules relate to hiring and/or retention. In some cases, women who were hired when single and who subsequently married were not fired; however, women who became pregnant would sometimes be fired.[98] Marriage bars were often accompanied by preferential hiring of married men. These bars arose particularly in teaching and clerical work, and they became common practice in the late 1800s through the 1930s, a period of economic depression. A 1940 survey found that about 87 percent of local school districts and over 50 percent of office workers were working under some marriage or pregnancy bar.

Three hypotheses have been proposed as to why marriage bars came into being. The most commonly cited explanation is that they are an extension of the general patriarchal system that operates in all cultures.[99] Economists have proposed two alternative explanations. The first and most commonly cited economic explanation is that the bars encourage employee turnover, which is to the advantage of employers in situations where earnings rise more rapidly than productivity. The second, proposed by Goldin, is that an employment system involving employee turnover, along with rules dictating when such turnover will occur, is viewed by both employer and employee as a better system than one in which turnover is at the discretion of the employer. The increased use of marriage bars is tied to the rise of the use of institutionalized employment practices – i.e., the rise of personnel management as a distinct management field.

In the 1950s, firms started to state a preference for reliable older married female workers over young single women. This striking change in attitude appears to have been dictated to a large extent by the relative shortage of young single women, particularly as the age at first marriage dropped in the 1950s. This change led to the dropping of marriage and pregnancy bars. While there is still a pregnancy bar in some workplaces, the only marriage bar that persisted until recently in the United States was for airline stewardesses, although marriage bars were prohibited in Japan only in 1985.

Summary

With the advent of industrialism, the era of economic history began. Now we could begin to use statistical data to chart the increase in manufacturing employment and accompanying higher wages for both sexes, along with a reduced gender earnings gap, leading to increased female labor force participation. Various subsequent events, such as the use of systematic practices in managing personnel and changes in manufacturing technology, tended to reduce the rate of equalization in gender differences. Various instituted policies, including workhour limitations and marriage bars, formalized discrimination against women. However, long-run trends towards more education for both sexes and increased use of clerical labor led to the continued rise of female employment and eventual dropping or irrelevance of such policies.

*E*ndnotes

1. For a descriptive historical work on women, family, and work since colonial times, see Carl Degler, *At Odds: Women and the Family in America from the Revolution to the Present* (Oxford: Oxford University, 1980). Another historical reference is W. Elliot Brownlee and Mary M. Brownlee (eds.), *Women in the American Economy: A Documentary History* (New Haven, Conn.: Yale University, 1976).

2. Jeanne Boydston, *Home and Work: Housework, Wages, and the Ideology of Labor in the Early Republic* (Oxford: Oxford University, 1990).

3. Claudia Goldin, "The Economic Status of Women in the Early Republic: Quantitative Evidence," *Journal of Interdisciplinary History* 16, no. 3 (Winter 1986): 375–404.

4. See Bridget Hill, *Women, Work, and Sexual Politics in Eighteenth-Century England* (Oxford: Basil Blackwell, 1989), for a discussion of gender roles in England during this period.

5. Thomas Dublin, *Women at Work: The Transformation of Work and Community in Lowell, Massachusetts, 1826–1860* (New York: Columbia University, 1979): 5.

6. For a descriptive historical work on women since the early nineteenth century, see Lynn Y. Weiner, *From Working Girl to Working Mother: The Female Labor Force in the United States, 1820–1980* (Chapel Hill, N.C.: University of North Carolina, 1985). Other historical overviews of women's work history include Alice Kessler-Harris, *Out to Work: A History of Wage-Earning Women* (New York: Oxford University, 1982); and Susan Estabrook Kennedy, *If All We Did Was to Weep at Home: A History of White Working-Class Women in America* (Bloomington, Ind.: Indiana University, 1979). Also see Susan Estabrook Kennedy, *America's White Working-Class Women: A Historical Bibliography* (New York: Garland, 1987), for additional historical references back to colonial times.

7. Edith Abbott, "Harriet Martineau and the Employment of Women in 1836," *Journal of Political Economy* 14, no. 10 (December 1906): 614–626.

8. Boydston, *loc. cit.*

9. Nancy Folbre and Barnet Wagman, "Counting Housework: New Estimates of Real Product in the United States, 1800–1860," *Journal of Economic History* 53, no. 2 (June 1993): 275–288.

10. Dublin, *op. cit.*: 9.

11. Dublin, *op. cit.*: 184.

12. For interesting discussions of economic and other aspects of prostitution during this period in New York, see Marilynn Wood Hill, *Their Sisters' Keeprs: Prostitution in New York City, 1830–1870* (Berkeley, Calif.: University of California, 1993); Timothy J. Gilfoyle, *City of Eros: New York City, Prositution, and the Commercialization of Sex, 1790–1920* (New York: W.W. Norton & Company, 1992); and Christine Stansell, *City of Women: Sex and Class in New York, 1789–1860* (New York: Alfred A. Knopf, 1986).

13. Gilfoyle, *op. cit.*: 59.

14. Edith Abbott, *Women in Industry* (1909; reprinted in New York by Arno, 1969): 278.

15. Bettina Berch, *The Endless Day: The Political Economy of Women's Work* (New York: Harcourt Brace Jovanovich, 1982): 32.

16. Berch, *op. cit.*: 33.

17. Dublin, *op. cit.*: 26.
18. Dublin, *op. cit.*: 148.
19. Cf. S.J. Kleinberg, *The Shadow of the Mills: Working-Class Families in Pittsburgh, 1870–1907* (Pittsburgh, Pa.: University of Pittsburgh, 1989).
20. Jean Reith Schrodel, *Alone in a Crowd: Women in the Trades Tell Their Stories* (Philadelphia, Pa.: Temple University, 1985): 141–142.
21. Albert Fishlow, "Levels of Nineteenth-Century American Investment in Education," *Journal of Economic History* 26, no. 4 (December 1966): 418–436.
22. See Abbott (1969).
23. Edith Abbott, "Women in Industry: The Manufacture of Boots and Shoes," *American Journal of Sociology* 15, no. 3 (November 1909): 335–360.
24. Edith Abbott, "Employment of Women in Industries: Cigarmaking – Its History and Present Tendencies," *Journal of Political Economy* 15, no. 1 (January 1907): 1–25.
25. Abbott (1907): 8.
26. Abbott (1907): 15.
27. Cf. Michéle A. Pujol, *Feminism and Anti-Feminism in Early Economic Thought* (Cambridge, United Kingdom: Cambridge University, 1992); Peter Groenewegen (ed.), *Feminism and Political Economy in Victorian England* (Aldershot: Edward Elgar, 1994).
28. Cf. Eleanor F. Rathbone "The Remuneration of Women's Services," *Economic Journal* 27, no. 105 (March 1917): 55–68; Millicent Fawcett, "Equal Pay for Equal Work," *Economic Journal* 28, no. 109 (March 1918): 1–6; and F.Y. Edgeworth, "Equal Pay to Men and Women for Equal Work," *Economic Journal* 32, no. 4 (December 1922): 431–457.
29. Sidney Webb, "The Alleged Differences in the Wages Paid to Men and to Women for Similar Work," *Economic Journal* 1, no. 4 (December 1891): 635–662.
30. Mark Aldrich and Randy Albelda, "Determinants of Working Women's Wages During the Progressive Era," *Explorations in Economic History* 17, no. 4 (October 1980): 324.
31. Charlotte Perkins Gilman, *Women and Economics: The Economic Factor Between Men and Women as a Factor in Social Evolution* (Boston, Mass.: Small, Maynard & Company, 1898).
32. Charlotte Perkins Gilman, "Woman and the State," *Forerunner* 1, no. 12 (October 1910): 12.
33. "Marital Status and Living Arrangements: March 1990," *Current Population Reports Series P-20*, no. 450 (May 1991): 1 (Table A).
34. George Elliott Howard, "Is the Freer Granting of Divorce an Evil?" *American Journal of Sociology* 14, no. 6 (May 1909): 766.
35. Gilfoyle, *op. cit.*: 311.
36. William Henry Chafe, *The American Woman: Her Changing Social, Economic, and Political Roles, 1920–1970* (Oxford: Oxford University, 1972): 142.
37. See Ruth Milkman, *Gender at Work: The Dynamics of Job Segregation by Sex During World War II* (Urbana, Ill.: University of Illinois, 1987).
38. Elizabeth Hawes, *Why Women Cry or Wenches with Wrenches* (New York: Reynal & Hitchcock, 1943): xviii.
39. See Claudia D. Goldin, "The Role of World War II in the Rise of Women's Employment," *American Economic Review* 81, no. 4 (September 1991): 741–756.
40. Cf. Chafe, *op. cit.*: 195.
41. Goldin (1991): 755.
42. Claudia Goldin, *Understanding the Gender Gap: An Economic History of American Women* (New York and Oxford: Oxford University, 1990): 17 (Table 2.1).
43. Goldin (1990): 18–19 (Table 2.2).
44. Goldin (1990): 44 (Table 2.9).
45. Valerie Kincade Oppenheimer, *The Female Labor Force in the United States: Demographic and Economic Factors Governing its Growth and Changing Composition* (Westport, Conn.: Greenwood, 1976).

46. Martha Norby Fraundorf, "The Labor Force Participation of Turn-of-the-Century Married Women," *Journal of Economic History* 39, no. 2 (June 1979): 401–418.

47. Jon R. Moen, "Fewer Older Men in the U.S. Work Force: Technological, Behavioral, and Legislative Contributions to the Decline," *Economic Review* (Federal Reserve Bank of Atlanta) 75, no. 6 (November-December 1990): 16–31.

48. Donald O. Parsons, "Male Retirement Behavior in the United States," *Journal of Economic History* 51, no. 3 (September 1991): 657–674.

49. Labor force participation declines for young women and men are masked by the redefinition of the population for which labor force participation rates are calculated. The participation rates, which originally covered those persons ages 10 and over, were then changed to ages 14 and over, then to 15 and over, and currently to 16 and over.

50. Janet M. Hooks, "Women's Occupations Through Seven Decades," *Women's Bureau Bulletin* no. 218 (Washington, D.C.: U.S. Dept. of Labor, 1951): 34.

51. See Cynthia R. Daniels, "Between Home and Factory: Homeworkers and the State," *Homework: Historical and Contemporary Perspectives on Paid Labor at Home*, eds. Eileen Boris and Cynthia R. Daniels (Urbana, Ill.: University of Illinois, 1989): 13–32; also other articles in this collection.

52. See Chapter 6 for a definition of this index and discussion of its range.

53. Edward Gross, "Plus ça Change . . . ? The Sexual Structure of Occupations Over Time," *Social Problems* 16, no. 2 (Fall 1968): 202 (Table 2), using Census data at the detailed occupation level, finds a Duncan index of 67 in 1900, and 68 in 1960, with no values outside the range of 66 to 69 in the intervening Census years. Jerry A. Jacobs, "Long-Term Trends in Occupational Segregation by Sex," *American Journal of Sociology* 95, no. 1 (July 1989): 160–173, also finds very constant values of sex segregation indexes from 1900 to 1970, although there is a steady decline in nonfarm occupations. His results are not sensitive to the classification system or method of calculation.

54. Nancy E. Bertaus, "The Roots of Today's 'Women's Jobs' and 'Men's Jobs': Using the Index of Dissimilarity to Measure Occupational Segregation by Gender," *Explorations in Economic History* 28, no. 4 (October 1991): 433–459.

55. Development of this typology has been attributed to Paula England, "Assessing Trends in Occupational Sex Segregation, 1900–1976," *Sociological Perspectives on Labor Markets*, ed. Ivar Berg (New York: Academic Press, 1981): 276–277.

56. Bertaus, *op. cit.*: 440 (Table 1).

57. Bertaus, *op. cit.*

58. Cf. Goldin (1990): 64 (Table 3.2B).

59. Rudolph C. Blitz, "Women in the Professions, 1870–1970," *Monthly Labor Review* 97, no. 5 (May 1974): 34–39.

60. Michael J. Carter and Susan Boslego Carter, "Women's Recent Progress in the Professions, or Women Get a Ticket to Ride After the Gravy Train Leaves the Station," *Feminist Studies* 7, no. 3 (Fall 1981): 478.

61. Carter and Carter, *op. cit.*: 477–504. Thirty-one percent of professional dentistry degrees awarded in 1989–90 were to women – Digest of Education Statistics (1992): 268 (Table 244).

62. Margery W. Davies, *Women's Place Is at the Typewriter: Office Work and Office Workers 1870–1930* (Philadelphia, Pa.: Temple University, 1982).

63. Carole Srole, "A Blessing to Mankind and Especially to Womankind: The Typewriter and the Feminization of Clerical Work, Boston, 1860–1920," *Women, Work, and Technology: Transformations*, eds. Barbara Drygulski Wright et al. (Ann Arbor, Mich.: University of Michigan, 1987): 88.

64. Davies, *op. cit.*: 52.

65. See also Sharon Hartman Strom, *Beyond the Typewriter: Gender, Class, and the Origins of Modern American Office Work, 1900–1930* (Urbana, Ill.: University of Illinois, 1992).

66. Eleanor Emmons Maccoby and Carol Nagy Jacklin, *The Psychology of Sex Differences* (Stanford, Calif.: Stanford University, 1974): 38.

67. Davies, *op. cit.*

68. Elyce J. Rotella, *From Home to Office: U.S. Women at Work, 1870–1930* (Ann Arbor, Mich.: University Microfilms International, 1981).

69. Myra H. Strober and Carolyn L. Arnold, "The Dynamics of Occupational Segregation Among Bank Tellers," *Gender in the Workplace*, eds. Clair Brown and Joseph A. Pechman (Washington, D.C.: Brookings, 1987): 107–148.

70. Glenn G. Munn, *The Paying Teller's Department* (New York: Bankers Publishing Company, 1922): 9.

71. Strober and Arnold, *op. cit.*: 132.

72. Goldin (1990): 60–61 (Table 3.1).

73. Goldin (1990): 62.

74. Susan B. Carter and Peter Philips, "Continuous-Process Technologies and the Gender Gap in Manufacturing Wages," *New Developments in the Labor Market: Toward a New Institutional Paradigm*, eds. Katharine G. Abraham and Robert B. McKersie (Cambridge, Mass.: Massachusetts Institute of Technology, 1990): 213–239.

75. Aldrich and Albelda, *op. cit.*

76. This method ignores the dynamic of how earnings within occupations and industries would change if they became more feminized (where one might generally expect a decline, based on the discussion in Chapter 6).

77. Susan B. Carter and Elizabeth Savoca, "Gender Differences in Learning and Earning in Nineteenth-Century America: The Role of Expected Job and Career Attachment," *Explorations in Economic History* 28, no. 3 (July 1991): 323–343.

78. Claudia Goldin and Solomon Polachek, "Residual Differences by Sex: Perspectives on the Gender Gap in Earnings," *American Economic Review* 77, no. 2 (May 1987): 143–151.

79. Goldin (1990). See also Gavin Wright, "Understanding the Gender Gap: A Review Article," *Journal of Economic Literature* 29, no. 3 (September 1991): 1153–1163.

80. See Leo Kanowitz, *Sex Roles in Law and Society: Cases and Materials* (Albuquerqe, N.M.: University of New Mexico, 1973), for discussions of famous historical lawsuits dealing with gender issues.

81. Alice Kessler-Harris, *A Woman's Wage: Historical Meanings and Social Consequences* (Lexington, Ky.: University Press of Kentucky, 1990): 2.

82. Kessler-Harris, *op. cit.*

83. Kessler-Harris, *op. cit.*: 3.

84. Carol Kleiman, "Progress on Pay Equity Is Slow but Sure," *Chicago Tribune* (January 21, 1991); interview with Alice Kessler-Harris.

85. Elizabeth Faulkner Baker, *Protective Labor Legislation: With Special Reference to Women in the State of New York* (New York: AMS, 1969; reprint of 1925 Columbia University edition).

86. By the mid-1920s, an increasing number of women were arguing that protection was prejudicial rather than advantageous.

87. See *Women in Industry: Decision of the United States Supreme Court in Curt Miller vs. State of Oregon Upholding the Constitutionality of the Oregon Ten Hour Law for Women and Brief for the State of Oregon by Louis D. Brandeis, Assisted by Josephine Goldmark* (New York: Arno, 1960; reprinted from the 1908 case).

88. Baker, *op cit.*: 398; original source is *Monthly Labor Review* 15, no. 2 (August 1922): 89.

89. Marion Crain, "Feminizing Unions: Challenging the Gendered Structure of Wage Labor," *Michigan Law Review* 89, no. 5 (March 1991): 1161.

90. Crain, *op. cit.*: 1161–1162.

91. Berch, *op. cit.*: 41.

92. Quoted in Gladys Boone, *The Women's Trade Union Leagues in Great Britain and the United States of America* (New York: AMS, 1968): 54.

93. Samuel Gompers, *Labor Movements and Problems in America, Vol. II: Labor and the Employer* (New York: E.P. Dutton & Co., 1920): 118.

94. Abbott (1969): 195.

95. Quoted by French Eugene Wolfe, *Admission to American Trade Unions* (Baltimore, Md.: Johns Hopkins, 1912): 81; from *Cigar Makers' Official Journal* (May 10, 1878).

96. Quoted in Boone, *op. cit.*: 94.

97. For additional discussion of the cigar industry in the early twentieth century, see Patricia A. Cooper, *Once a Cigar Maker: Men, Women, and Work Culture in American Cigar Factories, 1900–1919* (Urbana, Ill.: University of Illinois, 1987).

98. For a thorough discussion of marriage bars, upon which this discussion draws heavily, see Goldin (1990): 160–178.

99. Cf. Kessler-Harris (1982).

Further reading and statistical sources

Goldin, Claudia D. (1990). *Understanding the Gender Gap: An Economic History of American Women*. New York and Oxford: Oxford University. A thorough review of what is known about the extent of female labor force involvement up through modern times, using modern econometric analysis.

Huls, Mary Ellen (1993). *United States Government Documents on Women, 1800–1990*. Westport, Conn.: Greenwood. In two volumes; Volume I covers social issues and Volume II covers labor issues. Annotated entries for around 7000 documents produced by the United States Government on or related to women.

Matthaei, Julie A. (1982). *An Economic History of Women in America: Women's Work, the Sexual Division of Labor, and the Development of Capitalism*. New York: Schocken. Provides much useful information on the economic status of women in America in the pre-World War II stages. Analysis is carried out in the Marxist tradition, stressing class considerations and worker exploitation.

U.S. Department of Labor. *Bureau of Labor Statistics Publications 1886–1971*. Retrospective listing; includes annotation.

———. *Women's Bureau Bulletins*. Starting in 1918 and continuing through the 1980s, an occasional series of publications, many of which are unique studies, using establishment data, of women's work in particular industries or states.

Discussion questions

1. How is economic history different from the history of work?

2. Consider the Focus on mill towns. Do you think that the replacement of native-born women workers by immigrants would have happened even if the women had not agitated for better wages and working conditions?

3. Consider the Focus on bank tellers. Can you think of another currently female-dominated occupation that used to be primarily male? Does a similar story based on dropping skills and status work to explain the change in this occupation?

4. Consider the data in Table 14.2. Why did percent female among bachelor's and first-professional degree recipients drop so precipitously from 1940 to 1950? Explain how this illustrates one of the problems with using infrequently collected data to illustrate long-term trends.

5. Can you give an example, similar to the one in question (4), where knowing something about historical events would be helpful to an economist studying long-term trends?

6. Can you give an argument that an economist would be willing to agree with for why early twentieth-century protective legislation (e.g., workhour limitations) might have been better for women than an unregulated labor market? Under your argument, is it still better to have such legislation in force now?

7. Do you think that the average work week length would have dropped anyway without protective legislation during the early twentieth century? Why or why not?

8. Consider the Focus on the cigar industry. What do you think happened after the cigar industry imposed protective legislation for women? As demand for cigars declined during the twentieth century, what do you think happened to female employment and earnings in this industry?

9. Do you agree or disagree with historian Kessler-Harris's argument that women's wages are currently affected by "custom"? What about historically affected? Can myths and custom be the main causes of the current U.S. gender wage gap?

10. Which of the three explanations for the implementation of marriage bars sounds most plausible to you? Does it matter which one is right in explaining why they fell out of use in the 1950s?

Race, Ethnicity, and Class Considerations in Interpreting Gender Differences

*I*n many respects, the economic history outlined in Chapter 14 was specific to the European-American experience and was couched not in terms of the experiences of recent immigrants but from the viewpoint of those who had "arrived on the first boat." This chapter addresses the question of whether the gender differences outlined in Chapter 14 and in Parts II and III of the book, as well, hold across the broad spectrum of groups found in the United States. After a short presentation of gender-related labor force patterns by racial/ethnic group, the chapter considers the question of whether these patterns display convergence over time or fundamental continual differences in labor market experiences of women and men by group membership. The continuing poor economic situations of Native Americans and African-Americans are compared with the apparent assimilation process for European, Asian, and Hispanic immigrants. The chapter closes with a consideration of relevant criteria for policy formation and implementation and the possible effects of racial- and/or ethnic-specific policies on gender differences within and between these groups.

Gender differences across groups

It is important to consider gender differences across groups, whether defined by race, ethnicity, and/or socioeconomic class, both to portray events in more detail and to uncover possible biases of economic agents. For instance, if employers treat white and black women differently, then these differences will likely be reflected in different economic outcomes for these two groups of women. However, we also need to consider whether the similarities in gender-related patterns across racial, ethnic, and class groups are more striking than the variations. While the cross-cultural comparisons in Part IV present evidence on similarities and differences in gender roles across societies, society is not synonymous with racial/ethnic group or class. This chapter considers differences among various groups within American society.

While there are many economics books and articles on racial differences and on gender differences, a much smaller economics literature considers these differences simultaneously.

TABLE 15.1 Female labor force participation rates, all and by marital status, race, and country of origin, 1890, 1930, and 1995

	1890	1930	1995
All	18.9	24.8	62.2
married	4.6	11.7	61.1
single	40.5	50.5	64.8
White	16.3	23.7	62.6
married	2.5	9.8	60.9
single	38.4	48.7	67.5
Nonwhite	39.7	43.3	59.8
married	22.5	33.2	62.5
single	59.5	52.1	56.7
Foreign-born women	19.8	19.1	53.6
married	3.0	8.5	52.6
single	70.8	73.8	56.5

Sources: 1890 – *Eleventh Census of the U.S.: 1890*, Parts I and II; 1930 – *Fifteeenth Census of the U.S.: 1930, Occupational Statistics, Abstract Summary of the U.S. Census*; 1995 – calculated by the author using data from the Current Population Survey, March 1995. 1890 and 1930 data are for persons 15 years and over; 1995 data are for persons 16 years and over.

Development of this literature has been hindered by a paucity of data, as well as by the difficulty of maintaining the more complicated analytical framework of stratifying by more than one variable, let alone by nondichotomous factors such as ethnicity. Many writers have concentrated on rectifying the underrepresentation of research on particular groups, such as black women, rather than on developing a general theoretical and empirical framework.[1] Class differences, while considered extensively in a radical economic framework, are generally not considered by neoclassical economists (other than as synonymous with income level), for both data-driven and conceptual reasons. Although class is important as a conceptual category in considering, for instance, differences in nonmarket work between women of different classes, class considerations are not as relevant a feature in this discussion to the extent that here we focus on measurement of labor market-related variables such as labor force participation and earnings. However, they will be considered in the following discussions of systematic differences between immigrant groups and in our examination of the possible confusion between racial categories and class categories, particularly with reference to African-Americans.

In order to coordinate the discussion in this chapter with preceding chapters, historical and contemporary data are presented for different racial/ethnic groups corresponding to measures of labor force activity used throughout the book. Table 15.1 presents an overview of variation in female labor force participation rates, overall and by marital status, for whites compared with nonwhites and foreign-born women for 1890, 1930, and 1995.

From 1890 to 1995, white women's rates have risen to meet the higher nonwhite women rates, although from 1890 to present, nonwhite rates are higher than white rates, both over time and for all age cohorts.[2] However, the nonwhite single rate drops below both the married nonwhite rate and the overall and single white rates; it is already lower than the single white rate by 1940, and drops below the married nonwhite rate by 1960.[3] In 1890 and 1930, immigrant women are less likely than native-born women to work if

TABLE 15.2   Labor force participation rates by sex, all and by racial/ethnic group, 1990

	Female	Male	Male/Female
All	56.8	74.4	1.31
African-American	59.5	66.5	1.12
Asians and Pacific Islanders	60.1	75.5	1.26
American Indian	55.1	69.4	1.26
European-American	56.4	76.1	1.33
Hispanic-origin	55.9	78.0	1.41

Source: 1990 Census of Population, "Social and Economic Characteristics" (1990-CP-2–1) (Table 44). For all persons 16 years and over.

TABLE 15.3   Median income, year-round full-time workers by sex, all and by racial/ethnic group, 1989

	Female	Male	Female/Male
All	19,640	28,600	0.69
African-American	18,020	21,690	0.83
Hispanic-origin	16,310	20,320	0.80
American Indian	16,680	22,080	0.76
Asians and Pacific Islanders	21,340	30,080	0.71
European-American	20,050	30,760	0.65

Sources: by group – Roderick J. Harrison and Claudette E. Bennett, "Racial and Ethnic Diversity," Reynolds Farley (ed.), *State of the Union: America in the 1990s, Volume Two: Social Trends* (New York: Russell Sage, 1995): 204–205 (Table 4A.1); all – *Current Population Reports Series P–60* no. 174 (August 1991): 106–107 (Table 24).

married, but much more likely to work if single, and their rates do not change as sharply from 1890 to 1930 as those of native-born women. However, by 1990, immigrant women are actually less likely to participate in the labor force than are native-born women.

While nonwhite figures are driven throughout this period by the largest minority group, blacks, it is instructive to consider variation between nonwhite groups, as well as for whites of Hispanic origin. Table 15.2 displays data for five racial/ethnic groups from the 1990 Census. African-Americans, as well as Asians and Pacific Islanders, have slightly higher female labor force participation rates than average, while African-Americans have a notably lower male labor force participation rate. The male-to-female ratio of labor force participation rates is notably lower for African-Americans.

One question is whether these relative participation rate differences are driven by different potential earnings by race-sex group. Table 15.3 displays 1989 median income data for year-round full-time workers for the same groups. While Asian women have both high income levels and the highest labor force participation rate among women, African-American women have relatively low income accompanying their above-average labor force participation rate. Hispanic-origin men, who have the highest labor force participation rate, have relatively low income.

The gender earnings ratios vary noticeably by racial/ethnic group, with African-Americans experiencing the smallest gender gap. All minority groups have a smaller gender gap

TABLE 15.4 Unemployment rates by sex, by racial/ethnic group, 1990

	Female	Male	Female – Male
All	6.2	6.2	0.0
American Indian	13.1	15.0	−1.9
African-American	12.1	13.1	−1.0
Hispanic-origin	11.2	9.6	1.6
Asians and Pacific Islanders	5.5	5.0	0.5
European–American	4.8	5.0	−0.2

Source: 1990 Census of Population, "Social and Economic Characteristics" (1990-CP–2–1) (Table 44). Data are for civilian persons in the labor force, 16 years and over.

than European-Americans. This pattern is still found in 1996 median weekly earnings data for white, black, and Hispanic-origin full-time workers, but the black and Hispanic-origin gender earnings ratios have converged to 0.88, while whites lag at 0.74.[4]

Table 15.4 contains unemployment rates by sex for various racial/ethnic groups at the same point in time. Here there is a wide disparity of rates across groups, as well as different gender gaps. African Americans and American Indians have higher male than female rates, as well as the highest rates of unemployment for both sexes.

It is clear from the data in these tables that convergence in gender-related employment and earnings patterns across racial/ethnic groups had not occurred by 1990. The question is whether these differences will persist, or whether convergence will occur in the foreseeable future.

Different conceptual frameworks for analyzing group differences

Is convergence by race/ethnicity for these labor market variables the most likely outcome? While many scholars argue that underlying factors influencing labor force participation and earnings become more similar over time across racial/ethnic groups within a country, others hold the alternative view that, for a number of reasons, convergence is quite unlikely, at least for all minority groups.[5] Those holding the alternative view have several ways in which to argue against convergence. First, historical differences may continue to affect current differences into the foreseeable future; hysteresis exists in the form of factors such as human capital and initial geographic location of the minority group. Second, the process of immigrant assimilation may differ crucially by the factors of: (1) size of the immigrant community, (2) racial/ethnic identity of the immigrant group, and (3) whether the immigrant group has tended to immigrate due to noneconomic factors such as political problems in the home country ("push") or due to their perceived economic advantage from immigration ("pull"). Third, discrimination on racial/ethnic grounds may continue. Fourth, if racial/ethnic identity is not empirically separable from class identity, then convergence is not to be expected unless the class composition of the racial/ethnic minority group matches the composition of the majority. This factor has been discussed at length concerning blacks, in particular, but it can also apply to groups of immigrants who may be primarily drawn from one class within the home country.

The degree of voluntarity among immigrants may have a large effect on their economic outcomes, relative both to native-born Americans and to those who remain behind. This self-selection bias may lead to the most work-oriented, opportunistic, Westernized persons being the ones who immigrate, which may mean that they are the most likely to achieve economic success. Those who migrate first, both within a group and across groups, may be the most self-selected for success, implying that future waves are destined by their individual characteristics to be less successful. Later immigrants can, of course, join existing ethnic enclaves, which has the positive aspect of easing their social and economic transition but the potential negative aspect of reducing the probability that they will go outside the enclave in order to achieve greater success in society's mainstream.

It is possible to sort between these views and determine which is more accurate for a particular racial/ethnic group by considering different minority group experiences, both historical and contemporary. In the following sections, we first consider two groups that appear to stand apart in U.S. history: the original natives of North America, the American Indians, and the only group subjected to wholesale importation against their will, African-Americans. Then we consider "voluntary" immigrants as a whole, as well as contrasting outcomes among waves of immigrants within the larger racial/ethnic categories of Asian-Americans and Hispanic-origin Americans.

FOCUS

Does the 1990 immigration law hurt women?

The U.S. Immigration Act of 1990 is a major revision of immigration policy intended to favor immigrants with higher levels of education and skills. While legal immigration is increased by 40 percent overall and the number of visas available for professional and skilled workers has almost tripled, the act drops the number of yearly visas for unskilled immigrants from 18,000 to 10,000.[6] Consequently, the Act appears to have created a booming underground labor market for unskilled illegal immigrants to do household help. Most of the demand in this market is for women to perform child care and domestic chores, implying that Americans would prefer to see the unskilled visa recipients be predominantly women. However, the law appears to have the effect of discriminating against women: about 64 percent of unskilled visa applicants are female,[7] while the majority of skilled visa applicants are male.

One could also argue that the law hurts professional American women, who are the most likely to want to hire home child care workers. Carolyn Killea, a Washington immigration lawyer, is quoted as saying: "the law not only promotes the age-old double standard for professional women, but it also demeans home care work by labeling it 'unskilled.'"[8]

Displaced populations – American Indians

American Indians, who currently comprise less than 1 percent of the U.S. population, have been little studied in a systematic way with regard to economic gender differences.[9] Tribes varied greatly in terms of economic orientation before the advent of European colonization. Tribes in the Southeast, Northwest, Great Basin, and California tended to band into small hunter-gatherer groups; Great Plains tribes formed groups of highly nomadic foragers; while tribes in the Southwest, and to a lesser extent in the Northeast, developed more settled, horticultural systems with larger population concentrations. While American Indians have often been characterized as having been relatively egalitarian social units with respect to class and gender, there were wide variations between tribes, basically corresponding to the division between the forager and horticultural societies discussed in Chapter 12.

The devastating effects, including huge population losses, that almost all tribes suffered from contact with Europeans led to a loss of social structure. While many American Indians live essentially apart from European-Americans on reservations, only on some of the Southwest reservations is there a semblance of the previously existing patterns of economic and social organization.

Repercussions of slavery: the African-American experience

Africans began arriving as indentured servants into America in the early 1600s, but by the mid-1600s this process had evolved into lifetime indentureship, or slavery. When slaves were brought to America, their male-to-female ratio was quite high, causing an initially skewed sex ratio, although the slave birthrate was high enough to lead to an eventual adjustment. This skewed ratio was driven by demand for women slaves within Africa; women brought higher prices therein mainly because they were valued for their productive, not their reproductive functions.[10] There were actually three distinct slave markets in terms of gender composition: the European and American export market was 2 to 1 for male slaves; the Muslim market of the Arab world was mainly female slaves; and the internal sub-Saharan African market was mainly women and children (while the men were killed in battle).[11] In America as well, women slaves were valued for their productive capabilities, and they both performed agriculture labor and worked as house slaves in domestic duties. It appears that male slaves, in contrast, were generally relegated to agricultural duty, and that they did not take care of nonmarket work in slave quarters, leading to slave women holding the traditional double shift.

Of all the minority groups in America, African-Americans have received the most scholarly attention, not only because of their numbers (12 percent of the population in 1980), but also because of their peculiar historical status as a slave population – a condition leading to much interest among scholars as to the lasting economic and social effects of this status.

Most work by economists prior to the 1980s concentrated on comparisons between black and white men. Only since 1980 have a number of works on black women's economic status appeared.[12] Much of both recent and earlier scholarly work on African-Americans has concentrated on discussions of African-American family structure and its apparent dysfunctionality, which is apparently manifested in high rates of birth out of wedlock, high rates of marital dissolution, and high poverty rates (which operate as both cause and effect of the demographic patterns). This vein of literature has come under scrutiny for methodological problems. Sociologist Bonnie Thornton Dill identifies four major problems in the existing literature on African-American families:[13]

1. Use of inadequate historical data and/or misinterpretation of that data; notably, the 1910 Census has since been declared unreliable in terms of its estimates of unmarried black women; widowhood was overreported, while marital turnover was higher than implied by Census reports at the time.[14]

TABLE 15.5 Percentage distribution of marital status for black and white women, 1940 and 1990

	Black		*White*	
	1940	*1990*	*1940*	*1990*
Never-married	15.7	38.3	21.7	20.8
Married	53.6	38.4	63.5	57.4
Divorced	13.7	11.4	6.0	9.4
Widowed	17.0	11.9	8.8	12.4

Sources: 1940 – Nadja Zalokar, *The Economic Status of Black Women: An Exploratory Investigation* (Washington, D.C.: U.S. Commission on Civil Rights, 1990): 28 (Table 2.13); 1990 – 1990 Census of Population, "General Population Characteristics" (1990-CP–1–1): 45–47 (Table 34).

2. Erroneous or partially conceived assumptions about the relationship of blacks to white society.
3. Differences in values between researchers and subjects; for example, paid work may have held less social stigma among black married women than among white women.
4. Confusion of class and culture; for example, Nicholas Lemann has argued that southern black family life was not particularly stable for a variety of reasons, including the general instability of the rural lower class in the South, regardless of race, and that the first generation of black immigrants to northern cities brought these patterns along with them, rather than the patterns arising as a response to urban living conditions for blacks.[15]

It is clear that black family patterns do vary considerably from white patterns, and that the variation has recently increased. Table 15.5 shows differences in marital status by race for women, using Census data for 1940 and 1990. While black women had lower rates of being currently married in 1940 and were much more likely to report being divorced or widowed, their marriage level dropped further by 1990, while their never-married rate more than doubled. Meanwhile, white women experienced much smaller changes in their marital status distribution, with a slight drop in the never-married category (partly reflecting their greater age relative to black women). By 1990, less than two-fifths of black women were currently married. This trend, combined with high birth rates for black women, has led to a high rate of female-headed family formation.[16]

While family structure is quite different by race, and therefore convergence may be less likely, evidence on human capital attainment by race lends mixed support to convergence theory. There have clearly been large gains for blacks relative to whites in terms of formal educational attainment. For instance, while illiteracy rates in the South in 1880 were 76.2 percent for blacks and 21.5 percent for whites, by 1930 these rates had dropped to 19.7 and 3.8, respectively. This was followed by an additional drop to about 11 percent by 1950 for blacks, and about 3 percent for whites.[17] Rates were lower for black females ages 10 to 24 than for black males throughout this period, although blacks ages 25 to 64 had higher rates for women, demonstrating the existence of higher illiteracy rates for black women than for black men prior to 1880.[18]

Table 15.6 provides another source of evidence on formal education gains: school attendance rates in the South. These data show convergence between race-sex groups from 1890 to 1950. Black males were the least likely of the four groups to receive schooling in

TABLE 15.6 School attendance rates in the South by race-sex group, by age group, 1890 and 1950

	Ages 10–14		Ages 15–20	
	1890	1950	1890	1950
White males	79.4	93.2	33.9	53.5
White females	76.6	96.5	30.1	49.1
Black females	53.1	94.6	18.4	45.0
Black males	48.6	93.5	17.1	45.4

Source: Robert A. Margo, *Race and Schooling in the South, 1880–1950* (Chicago, Ill.: University of Chicago, 1990): 10 (Table 2.2). Reprinted with permission.

TABLE 15.7 Decennial growth rates in real hourly earnings by race-sex group, 1939 to 1986

	Women		Men	
	Black	White	Black	White
1939–49	101.8	38.2	77.2	29.3
1949–59	27.0	26.8	35.1	40.4
1959–69	57.5	24.0	37.4	28.2
1969–79	21.0	−1.8	14.7	−0.6
1979–86	3.3	4.9	−6.7	−0.1
1939–86 average	44.7	20.3	33.4	21.0

Source: Nadja Zalokar, *The Economic Status of Black Women: An Exploratory Investigation* (Washington, D.C.: U.S. Commission on Civil Rights, 1990): 18 (Table 2.1).

1890. By 1950, convergence had essentially been achieved for the 10 to 14-year-old age group, but rates of higher education were notably higher for white males.

Given these convergences in education, however, why do racial groups continue to have different labor force participation rates and earnings levels? Some commentators argue that at least for employed blacks, convergence is occurring. Table 15.7 shows the notably higher earnings growth rates for blacks since the period before World War II. Blacks experienced particularly high earnings growth during the 1940s and 1960s, perhaps due both to expanding economic opportunities for all persons and to reduced discrimination, to labor shortages during the War years and to civil rights legislation during the 1960s. Over the full time period, black women experience the highest growth rate of all, followed by black men. However, growth has slowed since 1979 and has even reversed for black men, in particular, while black women lag behind white women in further gains.

It is notable that subsequent voluntary groups of black immigrants, including blacks from Caribbean islands such as Jamaica, and Africans, have higher earnings and labor force participation levels than native-born blacks. These groups are generally better-educated than native-born blacks and may emigrate with substantial financial capital as well. Nonetheless, their relatively positive economic outcomes subsequent to migration imply that race may not be the major factor preventing native-born blacks from improving their economic status. One must also look to cultural differences, class differences, and lower education and work experience levels in explaining differences in racial outcomes.[19]

FOCUS

Black progress in corporate America

A 1994 *Wall Street Journal* article reported the finding that black female professionals were much more numerous than black male professionals.[20] *Journal* researchers analyzed data for the 38,000 companies that report to the U.S. Equal Employment Opportunity Commission (EEOC). In 1982, there were 1.2 black female professionals for every black male professional; by 1992 this ratio had risen to 1.8. There were also substantially more black women than black men in the broader category of "white collar, excluding clerical": about 815,000 black women in the 1992 EEOC data, as compared to about 564,000 black men.

The article considered various reasons for this finding. One is that many black men are side-tracked through crime, drugs, and inadequate education, essentially rendered ineligible for admission into these positions. Another is that black men choose different career paths, in particular entering civilian government and military positions.

Another possibility suggested in the article is that white men, who still make up the majority of professionals, prefer working with black women over black men, both because they ascribe positive attributes to the women and because they are less threatening. One young black manager with NASA is quoted as saying: "Black women are taught from a young age to be multitalented, multifaceted and to be able to be a chameleon. And for industry that's very crucial. You need people you can put into a particular environment and know they'll thrive." A white senior vice-president who helped mentor a successful young black woman is quoted: "Based upon my interface with black males, the initial encounters will involve a chip on their shoulder, some obvious skepticism."

It is important, however, to put the relative success of black women into perspective. Black women are still less likely to receive a bachelor's, graduate, or professional degree than are white women or men. And blacks accounted for only 5.9 percent of professionals in the EEOC sample, less than half of their representation in the U.S. population.

*I*mmigrant experiences

While immigrants have always been an important labor source for the United States, the proportion of immigrants in the workforce has varied drastically from era to era.[21] Around the turn of the century, immigrants were particularly prominent. Between 1890 and 1910, about a quarter of the workforce was foreign-born, while almost another quarter was second-generation – i.e., native-born of foreign parents.[22] Subsequent waves of immigrants have dominated, and continue to dominate, particular sectors of the economy, particularly in the low-wage areas, including such service occupations as food preparation and domestic work.

Another test for convergence is to compare occupational distributions across racial/ethnic groups. Table 15.8 performs this comparison for 1980 by sex within seven distinct groups across six broad occupational classifications: clerical and sales; service, including domestic service; manufacturing; professional and technical; managerial; and agriculture.

Racial differences are less notable than sex differences in Table 15.8, but it is clear that within sex, occupational distributions had not converged by 1980. All groups of women had a high concentration of employment in the traditionally female occupations of clerical and retail sales, but European-American women were more likely to be in these areas. Hispanic-origin men and women and American Indian men had higher concentrations in manufacturing. Asian-Americans had above-average representation in professional/technical

TABLE 15.8 Percentage distributions of occupational group by sex, by racial/ethnic group, 1990

Women	Clerical/ sales	Service	Manufacturing	Professional/ technical	Manager	Agriculture
African-American	35.0	25.1	14.5	17.0	8.1	0.3
American Indian	36.2	23.4	14.2	15.7	9.4	1.1
Asians and Pacific Islanders	34.7	16.3	15.0	22.2	11.3	0.5
European-American	41.2	15.1	9.4	21.4	12.1	0.9
Hispanic-origin	36.4	23.5	18.7	12.1	7.6	1.6

Men	Clerical/ sales	Service	Manufacturing	Professional/ technical	Manager	Agriculture
African-American	16.2	18.8	45.0	10.0	7.3	2.7
American Indian	12.6	14.2	49.6	10.4	8.0	5.3
Asians and Pacific Islanders	20.5	13.5	24.6	26.0	13.6	1.8
European-American	18.6	8.5	38.1	16.8	14.5	3.6
Hispanic-origin	14.4	16.1	47.9	7.8	6.6	7.3

Source: 1990 Census of Population, "Social and Economic Characteristics" (1990-CP–2–1) (Table 45).

occupations. Within services, African-Americans had much higher rates of domestic service, with 5 percent of the women in this area.[23]

Another test for convergence is to compare the relative percentages in poverty and in affluence across groups. One study has compared racial/ethnic groups by their percentage below the poverty line and percentage affluent (the criterion used is pretax income six times the poverty line).[24] Using 1980 Census data, the study finds 11 percent of the population in poverty, and 12 percent affluent. Hispanic-origin groups (Cuban, Mexican, Puerto Rican, and other) ranged from 12 to 34 percent in poverty (where the low was Cuban, the high Puerto Rican) and 2 to 9 percent affluent (where Cuban was the highest, Puerto Rican the lowest). For Asian groups (Asian Indians, Chinese, Filipino, Japanese, Korean, Vietnamese, and other), the range was from 5 to 34 percent in poverty (where the low was Japanese, high Vietnamese) and 3 to 23 percent affluent (where the low was Vietnamese, high Japanese). Among American Indians, 25 percent were in poverty and 5 percent were affluent; among African-Americans, 27 percent were in poverty, and 4 percent were affluent. All white ethnic groups had low poverty rates, ranging from 4 to 9 percent, and high rates of affluence, ranging from 7 to 32 percent. It is notable that the two minority groups who did not undergo voluntary immigration had the lowest income measures, while among immigrant groups, the more recent arrivals had less favorable income status.

Asian-Americans

Starting around 1840, Asians were actively recruited to work in western America as low-wage labor.[25] They were crucial in building the intercontinental railroad and worked the mines in frontier centers such as Virginia City, Nevada. Immigration restrictions caused a severely skewed sex ratio among Chinese immigrants, in particular, as few men were allowed to bring their families along. Women comprised approximately 5 percent of the Chinese immigrant population from 1860 to 1880. The Chinese settled predominantly in California, into largely bachelor enclaves within larger cities such as San Francisco. They moved into service industries – in particular, running laundries – when they were no longer needed in large numbers in construction. The Japanese were more likely to enter farming and remain outside cities, moving in large numbers to the Northwest.

The Chinese experience provides a lesson about the relative substitutability of immigrant male labor for native female labor. A study of California employment patterns in the late 1800s found that as white women became more plentiful (where they initially had been quite scarce), the canning and woolen mills industries switched to using them in place of Chinese men, while the shoe and cigar industries continued to use Chinese men.[26] This pattern appears to be related to the level of competition across industries: shoe and cigar manufacture were more competitive industries with relatively easy firm entry, while the canning and woolen mill industries were less competitive due to higher barriers to entry, such as larger capital requirements. However, the authors of this study draw a distinction between discrimination and prejudice: where competition was strong, discrimination was constrained, but racism was virulent; racism was muted in the less competitive industries.[27]

While Asians, who currently comprise about 1 percent of the U.S. population, are often characterized as the "model minority," there is much dissatisfaction within the established Asian communities of Chinese and Japanese regarding progress to the top rungs of the American economic ladder. Notably, recent waves of affluent immigrants from Hong Kong have chosen to enter Canada rather than the United States, turning Vancouver, B.C. into a boomtown. Also, there has been a significant return wave of Taiwanese immigrants, who find that jobs for skilled workers such as engineers are better-paying in Taiwan than in the United States.

Particularly for the generation of Asian-Americans who came of age in the 1940s and 1950s, who were generally second-generation Americans and therefore not as hindered by language and cultural barriers as their parents, the existence of "glass ceilings" in firms was frustrating. This generation was well-educated, attending the excellent university system in California in large numbers. Ironically, it was actually easier for Asian women to become employed, particularly in the growing clerical sector, than for Asian men. Asian men often found themselves educationally overqualified for those jobs that were most open to them, such as laundry work, restaurant work, and running retail operations within Chinatown that serviced mainly other Chinese. Few men from this generation rose to upper-level managerial positions, even within the industries that did engage their services, such as those that made use of engineers.

The third generation of Asian-Americans has developed a wider occupational representation, including a heavy proportion of professionals, but it continues to be underrepresented in managerial occupations. However, Asian-American women have increased their representation in higher-paid occupations, and they may now also face frustration at the glass ceiling that relegates them to lower or middle management.

Not all Asian-Americans are in such a strong economic position that they need worry about bumping their head on upper-management ceilings. One question is whether the more recent waves of Asian immigrants, many of whom are from Vietnam, Cambodia, Laos, and Thailand (although many are ethnic Chinese rather than the native groups), will be able to assimilate as successfully. Another issue of current concern among Asian-Americans and other concerned parties is the practice of "mail-order brides," where young women from the Philippines, in particular, are recruited to marry European-Americans. Additionally, a large number of Asian women have been brought into the country as the wives of American servicemen. One apparent allure of these women to the men who marry them is their perceived relative docility and subservience to men as compared with native-born American women. These women, many of whom are not fluent in English and not well educated, are put in a vulnerable position by their lack of family ties in America and their inability to earn a living and to learn how to survive on their own.

Hispanics

Hispanic-origin groups together comprise about 5 percent of the U.S. population, but they are growing rapidly due to higher birth rates than the U.S. average and a relatively young population. Among Americans of Hispanic origin, contrasts can be drawn among four groups: the relatively affluent wave of Cubans who fled Cuba after Castro came to power; recent waves of relatively poor Central Americans, fleeing both political and economic problems in their home countries; the ongoing flow of relatively poor Mexicans, seeking economic opportunity; and Puerto Ricans, who inhabit a unique position of dependency vis-a\ag-vis the United States.

There are clear earnings-related differences among members of these four groups in income status prior to immigration and in educational attainment, both before and after immigration. The Cubans who left when Castro came to power – many of whom reside in the Miami area – were predominantly upper- and middle-class, and were able to leave with considerable assets. Even though they are a relatively recent immigrant group, this higher socioeconomic status prior to immigration has enabled them to attain a relatively affluent position in American society.

Mexican and Central American immigrants, in contrast, tend to be drawn predominantly from the lower classes in their home countries. Their main asset is their labor power, rather than any human capital or financial capital. While their earnings in this country may be low, their opportunities are better here than in the home countries. However, many potential Mexican immigrants have recently found better opportunities in the *maquiladoras*, or border factories, that have been drawn to Mexico by the lower wages and lower level of labor regulation. This has been a particularly strong source of employment for Mexican women, and it may generally dominate their options of domestic service and other service-sector jobs in Southern California and other U.S. locales, particularly for persons who can enter only as illegal immigrants.

Puerto Ricans are in a peculiar dependency position with the United States, due to their status as citizens of a protectorate and their close proximity to the United States. Approximately 40 percent of Puerto Ricans live in America, mostly in the New York vicinity, and many travel back and forth to Puerto Rico regularly. Their access to U.S. welfare provisions in Puerto Rico appears to be partially responsible for the lack of development of dependable industry there other than tourism. Puerto Ricans in both America and Puerto Rico represent the other end of the success spectrum from the Cuban immigrants.

Among all these groups, the preindustrial social structure – including heavy reliance on the precepts of Catholicism and the ongoing *machismo* tradition – have led to a lower rate of female labor force participation as well as relatively low female status in these societies.

These patterns have proved resistent to modification as these groups undergo economic development. However, among the poorer groups of immigrants, such as the Mexicans and Central Americans, women are working in large numbers in low-paying sectors, including migrant agricultural work. To the extent that family structure has been disrupted by the need to immigrate for economic or political reasons (often while some family members remain behind), migrant women appear to have been freed to some degree from traditional family responsibilities, and they have lower birth rates than those women remaining behind. The question is whether such patterns will persist when and if these immigrant groups achieve higher socioeconomic standing in subsequent generations.

Group membership considerations in formulation of policy

> The most sexist of all views is to treat women as a monolithic special-interest group. The only thing all women have in common is that they are not men. (Phyllis Schlafly)[28]

How are worthy groups defined, and should we define groups for policy purposes at all? Economist Lester Thurow has written: "Every society has to have a theory of legitimate and illegitimate groups, when individuals can be judged on group data and when they cannot be judged on group data."[29] Following this line of thought, such a theory is societally specific rather than universal. Thurow suggests two criteria for whether or not a group can legitimately make a claim for compensation for having been disadvantaged: (1) whether mobility out of the group is possible, and (2) whether members of the group can claim that they have been handicapped by past discrimination. By these criteria, for example, affirmative action for both blacks and women appears to be a defensible policy.

However, any compensation scheme is still defensible only to the extent that society considers it to be recompense for a legitimate complaint, rather than on absolute grounds of fairness, for one can argue that discrimination on any grounds by group rather than by individual is fundamentally unfair.[30] This premise clearly applies to discrimination in favor of a group as well, for even correcting a past wrong will involve some disadvantaging of those not covered. For instance, unless there is a one-to-one match between job types and individuals, comparable worth policies will treat like people unequally and different people equally. After all, there is no reason to assume that two persons filling the same job are equally productive. One might therefore argue that it is better to provide an environment that allows persons to find their best work niches on their own rather than to decide in some nonconsensus way what characteristics are and are not compensable.

Finally, *any* decision about what is a compensable factor may be fundamentally unfair from an income distribution point of view, whether it is the market or the government that sets wage scales. If we are concerned about society's income distribution, it is not even absolutely defensible to reward persons based on their own productivity. Philosopher Robert Nozick points out that in any society, there are fundamental assumptions about which human traits a person is allowed to hold title to.[31] In our society, we allow genetic gifts to be held as human capital, and we allow wealth to be passed down from generation to generation (albeit with some run-off through income and inheritance taxation). In this view, fairness is ultimately a relative concept; we set the rules for the market as to what may be traded and kept.

Does Title IX discriminate against black men?

Under the 1972 U.S. law known as Title IX, sex discrimination is barred at schools receiving federal funds. The number of females participating in high-school sports ballooned from 300,000 in 1971 to 2.24 million in 1994,[32] and many now go on to participate in college sports as well. While Title IX has been widely cited as greatly responsible for this enormous increase in the number of females playing organized sports, enforcement has often been controversial. Colleges have complied by creating women's teams, and have also reinstated women's teams in many cases after facing actual or threatened sex discrimination suits. However, in a time of budget reductions, maintaining or adding a women's team has often meant less money for other parts of a school's sports program.

One of the most prominent participants in the discrimination suits following passage of Title IX is lawyer Walter B. Connolly Jr., who has worked with several colleges on their defense. One tack he has taken is that Title IX is racially discriminatory. He has been quoted as saying that Title IX's "true beneficiaries are middle-class white women from suburban high schools. African-American males are directly hurt in disproportionate numbers by elimination of scholarships in football and basketball."[33]

Another prominent lawyer in Title IX proceedings, Arthur Bryant, found this approach novel, yet unsound, saying: "If they brought it up in court, they would get tossed out on their ear." He accused Brown University, one of Connolly's clients, of "trying to justify its sexist behavior by bringing up racial issues."[34]

Both Bryant and Connolly have been involved in an important class action lawsuit, *Amy Cohen et. al. vs. Brown University et. al.*, filed in 1992 by members of Brown's women's gymnastics and volleyball teams after the University decided to stop funding the two squads. In 1995, U.S. District Court found that Brown had violated Title IX, and in 1997 the Supreme Court refused to hear Brown's appeal.[35] Bryant, as one of the plaintiffs' lawyers, hailed this refusal as "a huge victory for everyone who believes in equality across the country."[36]

Policy Application: Quotas in educational programs and hiring

Implicit and explicit racial and ethnic quotas have existed and continue to exist for many firms and educational institutions. These quotas serve to limit entry for some groups (e.g., Jews in earlier decades and Asian-Americans currently, under implicit quotas, to institutes of higher education),[37] while simultaneously improving the probability of entry for other groups (e.g., African-Americans and Hispanics, under affirmative action programs, to firms and colleges). In the context of this book, one might consider whether such policies have had different effects on women and men, both within particular racial and ethnic groups, and overall, and whether such effects are intentional or unintentional byproducts of the quota system. Even though quotas may not include differentiation by gender, it turns out that they can nonetheless benefit one gender over the other, and that this can vary by racial group.

A particular quota program of interest is affirmative action in colleges, which currently favors black over white admission, holding the level of measured achievement constant. One study finds, controlling for academic credentials, that blacks are more likely to go to college than whites.[38] This result holds particularly for black women as compared with white women and black men. Nevertheless, the white rate of college attendance is higher due to higher status origins (e.g., family income) and measured ability (i.e., SAT scores, which, of course, may be racially biased). Family socioeconomic status has the largest effect on college attendance of all included variables, which the researchers interpret as a cultural rather than an economic effect.[39]

The researchers find a small but significant gender effect, with white men slightly more likely than white women to attend college, while black women are more likely than black men to attend. One could interpret these findings as saying that affirmative action has been particularly helpful for black women. This result could occur for several reasons that do not involve explicit intent to favor black women over black men, including: (1) black women may be more likely to apply to college than black men at any given measured achievement level; (2) black women may have a more favorable distribution of measured achievement levels than black men; and (3) black women may have a lower dropout rate from college than black men.

Notably, many private liberal arts colleges, where the female–male student ratios are becoming much greater than the national average for college students, are actually becoming concerned about gender imbalance as well as racial imbalance, but in terms of wanting to favor men over women. Whitman College in Walla Walla, Washington, which is about 59 percent women, sent out a second round of informational mailing in the spring of 1997 to 5,900 potential students in Washington, Oregon, and Idaho – all men. Edith Robles, a recent Whitman graduate, was not pleased to hear news of this, pointing out that Latinos comprise only 2.5 percent of the student body, but about 15 percent of the local population. She was quoted in the *Chronicle of Higher Education* as saying: "I consider the lack of ethnic diversity to be the biggest problem here. They shouldn't be concerned about the gender imbalance at all. Affirmative action for white men is really out of the picture, in my opinion."[40]

Summary

While some racial/ethnic groups, particularly those who immigrated longer ago and those who immigrated with more assets, have demonstrated a strong degree of convergence to national levels of labor market participation and earnings, other groups appear to have a slowed rate of convergence. The implication of these different patterns is that historical background continues to have a notable effect on current outcomes by group, particularly for those groups who had an especially disadvantaged historical status, such as African-Americans and American Indians. Therefore, discussions of historical and contemporary economic gender differences will not cover the range of outcomes for these groups unless specific differences in historical experiences by racial/ethnic group are considered.

Endnotes

1. Cf. Julianne Malveaux and Phyllis Wallace, "Minority Women in the Workplace," *Working Women: Past, Present, Future*, eds. Karen Shallcross Koziara, Michael H. Moskow, and Lucretia Dewey Tanner (Washington, D.C.: Bureau of National Affairs, 1987): 265–298. Elizabeth McTaggart Almquist, *Minorities, Gender, and Work* (Lexington, Mass.: Lexington Books, 1979), is an exception to this strategy; her book devotes chapters to characterizing the labor force participation of Indians and blacks, Spanish-heritage minorities, and Asians.
2. Claudia Goldin, *Understanding the Gender Gap* (Oxford: Oxford University, 1990): 18 (Table 2.2).

3. Goldin, *op. cit.*: 17 (Table 2.1).

4. *Employment and Earnings* 44, no. 1 (January 1997): 204 (Table 37).

5. Cf. the discussion of convergence in Malveaux and Wallace, *op. cit.*

6. Nicola Clark, "A Nannies' Advocate Argues Their Case," *Wall Street Journal* (January 26, 1993).

7. *Ibid.*

8. *Ibid.*

9. An exception is C. Matthew Snipp and Isik A. Aytac, "The Labor Force Participation of American Indian Women, *Research in Human Capital and Development* 6 (1990): 189–211.

10. Claire C. Robertson and Martin A. Klein, "Women's Importance in African Slave Systems," *Women and Slavery in Africa*, eds. Claire C. Robertson and Martin A. Klein (Madison, Wis.: University of Wisconsin, 1983): 3–25.

11. Robertson and Klein, *op. cit.*: 4.

12. Phyllis A. Wallace, *Black Women in the Labor Force* (Cambridge, Mass.: Massachusetts Institute of Technology, 1980), is the first significant work by an economist. Micheline R. Malson, Elisabeth Mudimbe-Boyi, Jean F. O'Barr, and Mary Wyer (eds.), *Black Women in America: Social Science Perspectives* (Chicago, Ill.: University of Chicago, 1990), is a set of articles originally published in *Signs* 4, no. 3 (Spring 1979). Jacqueline Jones, *Labor of Love, Labor of Sorrow: Black Women, Work and the Family, from Slavery to the Present* (New York: Vintage, 1985), is a comprehensive historical work on the subject of black women in America.

13. Bonnie Thornton Dill, "The Dialectics of Black Womanhood," *Black Women in America: Social Science Perspectives*, eds. Micheline R. Malson, Elisabeth Mudimbe-Boyi, Jean F. O'Barr, and Mary Wyer (Chicago, Ill.: University of Chicago, 1990): 66.

14. Samuel H. Preston, Suet Lim, and S. Philip Morgan, "African-American Marriage in 1910: Beneath the Surface of Census Data," *Demography* 29, no. 1 (February 1992): 1–15.

15. Nicholas Lemann, *The Promised Land: The Great Black Migration and How It Changed America* (New York: Alfred A. Knopf, 1991).

16. See the Policy Analysis of welfare reform in Part II for more discussion of this phenomenon.

17. Robert A. Margo, *Race and Schooling in the South, 1880–1950* (Chicago, Ill.: University of Chicago, 1990): 9 (Table 2.1).

18. *Ibid.*

19. See Jacqueline Jones, *The Dispossessed: America's Underclasses from the Civil War to the Present* (New York: Basic Books, 1992), for a historically based argument that explanations of black poverty rooted in black distinctiveness are invalid.

20. Dorothy J. Gaiter, "Black Women's Gains in Corporate America Outstrip Black Men's," *Wall Street Journal* (March 5, 1994): A1, A4.

21. For general background on immigrants and their effects on labor markets, see Guillermina Jasso and Mark R. Rosenzweig, *The New Chosen People: Immigrants in the United States* (New York: Russell Sage Foundation, 1990); and George J. Borjas, *Friends or Strangers: The Impact of Immigrants on the U.S. Economy* (New York: Basic Books, 1990). Borjas also analyzes earnings of immigrants and how these earnings change as groups assimilate.

22. Joan Younger Dickinson, *The Role of the Immigrant Worker in the U.S. Labor Force, 1890–1910* (New York: Arno, 1980): 21.

23. These occupational divisions likely conceal a significant movement of many tasks from the domestic service realm into the institutional service realm and an accompanying shift of low-wage minority workers; see Evelyn Nakano Glenn, "From Servitude to Service Work: Historical Continuities in the Racial Division of Paid Reproductive Labor," *Signs* 18, no. 1 (Autumn 1992): 1–43.

24. Reynolds Farley, "Blacks, Hispanics, and White Ethnic Groups: Are Blacks Uniquely Disadvantaged?" *American Economic Review* 80, no. 2 (May 1990): 238 (Table 1).

25. Ronald Takaki, *Strangers from a Different Shore* (Boston, Mass.: Little, Brown & Co., 1989) is a useful history of Asian immigration that includes discussion of subsequent waves of Japanese, Koreans, Asian Indians, and Filipinos.

26. Martin Brown and Peter Philips, "Competition, Racism, and Hiring Practices Among California Manufacturers, 1860–1882," *Industrial and Labor Relations Review* 40, no. 1 (October 1986): 61–74. Women as a percentage of the California population rose from 20 percent in 1860 to 44 percent by 1900, while the percentage of Chinese fell from 10 percent to 3 percent over this period; meanwhile women as a percentage of the California labor force rose from 6 percent in 1870 to 14 percent in 1900 (p. 62, Table 1).

27. Brown and Philips, *op. cit.*: 74.

28. Phyllis Schlafly, "A Conservative Vision of America: Lower Taxes, Less Government Regulation," *Radcliffe Quarterly* 78, no. 2 (June 1992): 9.

29. Lester C. Thurow, "A Theory of Groups: Which Age, Sex, Ethnic and Religious Groups Are Relevant?" *Income Inequality*, ed. J. Moroney (Lexington, Mass.: Lexington Books, 1979): 169–182.

30. Thurow, *op. cit.*: 171.

31. On the topic of distributive justice, see Robert Nozick, *Anarchy, State, and Utopia* (New York: Basic Books, 1974, reprinted 1980 by Basil Blackwell): Chapter Seven.

32. Jim Naughton, "Advocates on All Sides of the Title IX Debate Look to the Supreme Court," *Chronicle of Higher Education* 43, no. 33 (April 25, 1997): A41.

33. Wade Lambert, "Title IX Costs Black Men, Lawyer Says," *Wall Street Journal* (June 17, 1994): B7.

34. *Ibid.*

35. Andrew Goldsmith, "High Court Denies Title IX Appeal," *Brown Daily Herald* (April 22, 1997).

36. Jim Naughton, "Supreme Court Rejects Brown's Appeal on Women in Sports," *Chronicle of Higher Education* 43, no. 34 (May 2, 1997): A45.

37. Cf. Irvin Molotsky, "Harvard and U.C.L.A. Face Inquiries on Quotas," *New York Times* (November 20, 1988), Section 1: 35; Julie Johnson, "Asian-Americans Press Fight for Wider Top-College Door," *New York Times* (September 9, 1989), Section 1: 1.

38. Gail E. Thomas, Karl L. Alexander, and Bruce K. Eckland, "Access to Higher Education: The Importance of Race, Sex, Social Class and Academic Credentials," *School Review* 87, no. 2 (February 1979): 133–156. The study uses a subsample of the National Longitudinal Survey, combined with a follow-up survey conducted by the Educational Testing Service.

39. Thomas, Alexander, and Eckland, *op. cit.*: 148.

40. Ben Gose, "Liberal-Arts Colleges Ask: Where Have the Men Gone?" *Chronicle of Higher Education* 43, no. 39 (June 6, 1997): A35.

*F*urther reading

Amott, Teresa and Julie A. Matthaei (1996). *Race, Gender, and Work: A Multi-cultural History of Women in the United States, Revised Edition*. Boston, Mass.: South End. Comprehensive discussion of female work patterns by racial and ethnic groups, using Census data for 1900–1990 interpreted in a framework of radical political economics.

Bergmann, Barbara R. (1996). *In Defense of Affirmative Action*. New York: BasicBooks. Forceful arguments for expanding affirmative action and for the recognition that effective affirmative action requires use of quotas.

Farley, Reynolds (ed.) (1995). *State of the Union: America in the 1990s. Volume Two: Social Trends*. Includes two lengthy essays on racial and ethnic diversity, and immigration analyzing data from the 1990 Census in particular.

Farley, Reynolds, and Walter R. Allen (1987). *The Color Line and the Quality of Life in America*. New York: Russell Sage Foundation. Presents and analyzes a wealth of data from the 1980 Census and earlier sources, mainly focusing on black-white differences.

Federal Glass Ceiling Commission (1995). *Good for Business: Making Full Use of the Nation's Human Capital: The Environmental Scan.* Washington, D.C.: U.S. Government Printing Office. Fact-finding report from the Glass Ceiling Commission, established in 1991 to conduct a study and prepare recommendations concerning the advancement of women and minorities, particularly into management positions. Lists all commissioned reports in an appendix. All the reports are available for downloading at the School of Industrial & Labor Relations, Cornell University website (www.ilr.cornell.edu).

Discussion questions

1. Consider the data in Table 15.1 for whites and nonwhites. Do these data support the convergence hypothesis? Why or why not?

2. Consider the data in Table 15.1 for immigrants. Why would immigrant participation rates have changed so much since 1930?

3. Consider the data in Tables 15.2, 15.3, and 15.4. Do these differences in gender patterns across groups appear large or small to you?

4. Are race and class considerations naturally encompassed in multicultural studies of gender differences?

5. Is researcher subjectivity adequately dealt with in scholarly work by detailing race and gender differences?

6. How does awareness of potential sources of bias that would lead one to overlook important race and class differences influence the way research should be done and the ways in which policies should be constructed?

7. Consider the Focus on immigration. Does the current law appear discriminatory against women (both domestic and foreign)?

8. Consider the Focus on black women and men in corporations. Which of the explanations given for the apparent shortage of black men are supply-side? Which are demand-side? Can you think of additional potential explanations for either or both sides of the labor market?

9. Consider the Focus on Title IX. Do you agree that funding of one program means less money available to fund another program? If yes, then isn't Connolly's argument correct? Also, then is funding of athletic programs discriminatory against groups (i.e., white women and minorities) who are less likely to participate in college sports?

10. Do you think the existence of college sports scholarships is helpful or harmful, economically speaking, for minority males? What about for minority females?

11. In college affirmative action programs, should quotas be set up separately by racial/ethnic gender groups (i.e., have a different set of criteria for black men than black women to make up for their lower rate of college attendance relative to black women)? What about in employment affirmative action programs?

12. Why do you think the sex ratio in liberal arts colleges is skewed towards women? Should this skewing be addressed by favoring men in admissions policies? How might this type of policy affect minority students?

Policy Proposals

*T*his chapter presents a classification system, based on the stated aim of the policy, for organizing the many gender-related policies that have been presented throughout this book. Then it posits some general precepts for the formulation of sound policy and the generation of new ideas, and discusses some broad areas of social organization that may be venues for future, fundamental changes that would provide a greater chance for achievement of both equal opportunities and equal outcomes for women and men.

Summary of policy approaches to gender issues

In the broadest view, any economic or social policy that affects the sexes differently relates to gender issues. In the following sections, we consider four classes of policies relating to gender issues: (1) policies that aim at creating a balance between women and men, (2) policies that aim at shifting the balance in favor of women or men, (3) policies aimed at family issues that affect women and men differently, and (4) policies with no direct gender or family-related goal that affect women and men differently. Policies considered include business policies, governmental regulations, and governmental agency policies. Policies are classified below by how they are generally characterized, not by their actual effects.

Policies aimed at creating a balance between men and women

Policies falling into this category attempt to redress an existing perceived imbalance in female and male opportunities and/or outcomes. They include: (1) anti-discrimination legislation such as equal pay laws, (2) affirmative action programs, (3) comparable worth policies, and (4) programs that expand the amount of capital available to women, such as small-business loan programs targeted at women. In general, they try to counteract an existing perceived bias towards men without creating a net shift towards women.

Policies aimed at shifting the balance in favor of women or men

Policies in this category attempt to create an imbalance in women and men's opportunities and/or outcomes. They include: (1) unequal pay laws and (2) job and schooling restrictions, including marriage bars and quotas in educational programs and hiring. Although explicit national policies of this type in developed countries have been overturned by now, there are plenty of historical cases of them. Indeed, such policies still exist in some undeveloped countries, and implicit nongovernmental policies of this kind exist in all countries. An example is affirmative action, which can be construed as a quota system aimed at shifting the balance in favor of women.

Policies aimed at family issues that affect men and women differently

These policies have the explicit goal of affecting the constraints on family decisions, including who will work and how much, whether to form or dissolve a family, and how many children to have. They include: (1) family leave, both paid and unpaid, (2) no-fault divorce reform, (3) subsidized or employer-provided child care, (4) regulation of fertility through controlling access to abortion and contraception, (5) welfare programs, and (6) child allowances. These policies often have ambiguous effects on the relative well-being of women and men, along with ambiguous effects on such factors as female labor force participation.

Policies with no direct gender or family-related goal that affect women and men differently

The explicit goal of these policies is not construed in terms of gender or family effects. They include: (1) minimum wage laws, (2) macroeconomic employment policies, (3) earnings and income taxes, (4) job training programs, (5) workplace safety regulations, and (6) development aid policies. While these policies are not generally evaluated with an eye to differential effect by sex, they nonetheless can have a strong redistributional effect in one direction or the other.

General precepts for policy formulation

This section presents some general precepts for formation of policies to affect the gender balance, as well as giving some additional examples of specific policies. One general precept for sound policy formation is to create policies that open up possibilities for both sexes rather than serve to consolidate existing patterns. As economist Nancy Barrett has pointed out:[1]

> Many popular remedies to improve women's economic status paradoxically reinforce gender-based economic roles: the welfare system reinforces the expectation of female dependency; comparable worth pay admits gender distinctions; equal pay keeps women out of high-status jobs; wages for housework, part-time, flexitime, all reinforce traditional stereotypes while facilitating flexibility for women as homemakers, thereby reducing stress in traditional families and accommodating gender-role distinctions.

Potential policies should be reviewed to see whether or not they serve as enforcement mechanisms of existing gender roles.

Learning from others and from the past

While it is beneficial to come up with new policy options, the innovative policymaker need not neglect existing options that are or have been in use, though not necessarily widespread. One can consider examples from other countries of apparently successful policies, as well as consider lessons from the past (many of which are cautionary rather than helpful in terms of policies that might be readopted). However, it is not necessary to travel in time or outside the borders of one's country to find ideas that have not been widely adopted but that might be beneficial if implemented on a broader scale. For instance, many people may not be aware of the range of workplace benefits currently found in U.S. firms. Table 16.1 presents results from a 1993 employee benefit survey of medium and large private establishments. A wide range of benefits appears, although some policies are available only to a minority of workers. While some policies, such as paid vacations and holidays, are extremely widespread, it is notable that no one policy is available to all workers.

As of late 1993, formal family leave policies were mandated for employees fulfilling certain employment conditions, in companies with 50 or more employees; the offering of this benefit has risen substantially, from only 3 percent of workers covered in a comparable 1989 survey.[2] Some other fringe benefits, such as reimbursement accounts for medical and child care costs, have also become much more widespread. But other programs that have increased in cost, such as medical insurance and pension plans, have reduced coverage or, at least, lower benefit levels. And workers in small establishments (less than 100 workers) are much less likely to enjoy these benefits: a 1994 survey of employee benefits in small private establishments found lower provision rates on all of the items in Table 16.1. For instance, only 66 percent offered a medical insurance plan, only 15 percent had a defined-benefit retirement plan, and only 47 percent could take unpaid family leave.[3]

Consideration of new demographic trends

Policymakers need to be aware of demographic changes within societies and attempt to create policies that respond to these changes and are flexible enough to be open to further changes. One of the most – if not the most – important demographic shifts currently occurring in all developed countries is the shift towards a larger proportion of persons over 65, particularly towards the older age groups within this population, many of whom require new and more extensive forms of medical care.[4] The differing needs of older women and men may become more obvious, as well as the general increased diversity of the elderly population; policies directed at older persons need to be more responsive to this heterogeneity. Simultaneously, the proportion of young persons is shrinking, due to both lower birth rates and higher life expectancies. Policymakers must be resistant to the tendency to treat smaller groups in society as if they had greater homogeneity and to continue to consider whether young women and men face relatively different constraints and opportunities.

Policymakers also need to be aware of changes in human capital embodied in new entrants to the workforce. Along with changes in the amount and types of formal education that women, in particular, are receiving, it appears that the traditional transmission of household skills from mother to daughter may be breaking down. One study of household labor division finds that: "Children – particularly sons, but increasingly daughters – are not being taught the fundamental skills that underlie making a home. If men and women in the last generation have had difficulty sharing home tasks because of *men's* lack of training

TABLE 16.1 Percentage of employees receiving employee benefits in medium and large private establishments, 1993

Paid leave:			*Unpaid leave:*	
Vacations	97		Maternity leave	60
Holidays	91		Paternity leave	53
Jury duty leave	90			
Funeral leave	83			
Rest time	68			
Sick leave	65			
Military leave	53			
Personal leave	21			
Lunch time	9			
Maternity leave	3			
Paternity leave	1			
Insurance plans:				
Medical care	82			
Noncontributory	37			
Hospital/surgical	82			
Mental health care	80			
Alcohol abuse treatment	80			
Drug abuse treatment	80			
Home health care	71			
Extended care facility	67			
Dental	62			
Hospice care	53			
Vision	26			
In HMO's	19			
Life	91			
Noncontributory	87			
Accident/sickness	44			
Noncontributory	75			
Long-term disability	41			
Noncontributory	73			
Retirement and savings plans:				
Defined contribution	49			
Savings and thrift	29			
Deferred profit sharing	13			
Money purchase pension	8			
Stock ownership	3			
Defined benefit pension	56			
Earnings-based formula	40			
Additional benefits:				
Parking	88			
Educational assistance	72			
Travel accident insurance	44			
Employee assistance	62			
Reimbursement accounts	52			
Severance pay	42			
Bonuses, cash	38			

TABLE 16.1 cont'd

Wellness programs	37
Relocation allowance	31
Eldercare	31
Recreation facilities	26
Flexible benefits plans	12
Child care	7
Long-term care insurance	6

Source: Statistical Abstract of the United States (1996): 431 (Table 671). The sample is drawn from establishments with at least 100 workers.

and experience, it may be that the young men and women of the future will have even less confidence about their ability to take them on."[5] This suggests an interesting strategy, whether conscious or unconscious, of passive resistance on the part of mothers: don't teach girls homemaking skills, and thereby avoid the development of traditional comparative advantage patterns that effectively relegate women to the domestic sphere.

Younger workers of both sexes may find that, due to their reduced numbers, their comparative advantage increasingly lies in paid work. However, the demographic shift towards an aged population may cause women to retreat from the paid work force. Women are currently on the front lines of the aging trend, not only because they comprise a majority of the elderly, but because they are the main care providers, both unpaid and paid, for the growing numbers of frail and disabled very-elderly persons.[6]

The need for new ideas and perspectives

The potential policymaker needs to be open to new ideas and perspectives. Policymakers need broad training in a variety of analytical approaches – including, of course, economics. Within economics, students need to be aware of the different approaches that can be taken to gender issues, particularly feminist critiques of neoclassical economic theory as applied to discussion of household decision making.

One new approach is to move away from broad-based programs that affect all men and all women towards programs of more limited scope that target those most affected by current social structures. For instance, one idea is to set up programs that target particular disadvantaged subgroups of women. One writer suggests social credits for homemakers past the child-rearing stage that would be good for tuition or would confer an advantage on the federal jobs preference scale.[7] Since the scale currently recognizes veteran status, and most veterans are men, this approach would also help to alleviate the built-in federal job system bias towards men.

One might also consider programs that target disadvantaged population subgroups; although not conditioned on gender, such programs would have the effect of disproportionately helping women. For example, consider workplace literacy programs, particularly those targeted at various industries with high rates of illiteracy. It may be much more feasible for full-time workers to attend such classes at work-based locations than in settings such as community colleges, which may be far from workers' homes and workplaces. In a set of such projects in Massachusetts, about 60 percent of the adult learners were women, some of whom were literate in their native language but not in English, and many of whom

were literate in neither.[8] These projects have benefits beyond increasing people's employ-
ability and probability of receiving higher wages; they can generally empower people by
increasing their ability to function in modern society. Such programs could be industry- or
government-sponsored (they are unlikely to be sponsored by individual firms due to the
lack of expected return for the firm on provision of general human capital).

The need for a broader perspective

In considering how best to achieve redistribution across individuals, even if the individuals
belong to clearly defined classes such as women and men, economists have generally been
reluctant to advocate sweeping social change, preferring instead to advocate policies that
operate on the individual or family level. However, feminist economists, in particular, have
risen to critique this approach as ineffective. Nancy Barrett writes:[9]

> The economist's standard remedies for economic inequality have been income
> redistribution and human capital development. These are clearly not enough when
> they do not strike at gender roles in the family economy (a major use of women's
> economic time but not of men's) and at the gender-based property rights that tradi-
> tion has conferred to certain activities, property rights that do not necessarily enhance
> the economic welfare of the owner.

What kinds of changes could be made that would affect roles and rights? One
approach is to change the structure of daily life so as to ease the nonmarket work burden
on women by reducing the amount of nonmarket work to be done. We will consider four
areas of social organization in which fundamental changes would need to be made in order
to accomplish this goal: (1) transportation, (2) housing, (3) workplace, and (4) schools. The
suggested changes must be judged on other grounds as well, such as cost-efficiency and
desirability relative to other alternatives. While this discussion focuses on possible changes
in U.S. society, many of the suggestions could be helpful in other developed countries, as
well; indeed, in some cases, they are currently found – at least in limited usage – in other
countries.[10]

1. Transportation: The United States has developed a predominantly car-based transportation system, both within and between cities, that has clear disadvantages for those
who have trouble raising the capital to buy and maintain a car. To the extent that women
have lower family incomes than men, this is relatively more problematic for them. Because
much social capital (i.e., roads and vehicles) has been devoted to automotive transportation, it would be difficult and costly to switch quickly to a completely new system. Efficient
suggestions must utilize at least part of the existing capital stock.

Other countries have not only developed a more extensive public transportation system but, in some cases, businesses have stepped in to fill transportation needs. In Europe
it is not unusual for employers to provide bus or van service on a regular route to serve
commuting employees; company buses sometimes also transport employees' children to
nearby day care centers or schools. Some of these European concepts could be imported
to the United States, albeit with some modification. Companies located in clusters such as
industrial parks could pool resources to provide such services.

Another way to reduce the time spent in daily transportation is to create policies that
encourage the locating of housing closer to both workplaces and other often-visited sites.

Schools and after-school activities, as well, could be located near workplaces rather than in a distant location. The opportunity to create communities with greater integration of alternative uses would require relaxation of zoning laws regarding residential housing density and encouragement of mixed-use zoning, or no zoning. It is not, of course, a given that people would prefer this style of living to one in which home and work exist in separate locations. Also, greater reliance on public transportation would tend to reduce the amount of space required for roadways, allowing for higher-density communities.

2. **Housing:** One commentator has written: "Most American housing is based on Levitt's model of the home as a haven for the male worker's family."[11] In many ways, American housing represents a real break from the norm, for "the dream house is a uniquely American form, because for the first time in history, a civilization has created a utopian ideal based on the house rather than the city or the nation."[12]

Both the extent of suburbanization (which interacts with the transportation constraint on female labor force participation) and the type of housing commonly found, particularly in suburbs, are problematic for freeing women from nonmarket work. Houses (and many possessions) require much maintenance, and it is apparent that architects and designers are not driven to create designs that reduce maintenance. One could argue, however, that these variables reflect free choice on the part of households. But this argument both ignores zoning laws, which may not operate to the benefit of the majority, and the existence of a sizable housing stock, which codifies past decisions about housing style that may now be outmoded but is too costly to replace (as is the case with existing transportation systems). One's views on these issues depend on whether or not one believes that current practices represent free choice on the part of those who occupy housing – particularly, whether it represents free choice on the part of *both* sexes.

Numerous housing alternatives have been envisioned to alleviate some of the perceived drawbacks of the current housing stock.[13] These designs tend to incorporate two key features: reduced square footage per family and promotion of facilities to be shared across families. These features are considered desirable by the designers both because they reduce time spent in home maintenance and because they essentially push people into spending more time interacting with nonfamily members.

There is a clear trade-off in such designs between privacy and communality, as well as between cost-cutting and the desire to consume more household services; after all, having more housing space is not necessarily bad. Europeans and Japanese appear accustomed to having less space, but that does not mean they would not prefer more housing space if it were cheaper. Since space is more costly in European and Japanese cities, housing prices are higher for them than for Americans, so they consume relatively more of other goods. One could interpret the movement away from boarding houses in America as incomes rose as clear sign of preference for noncommunal living.

Various aspects of communal and cluster housing developments can reduce nonmarket work: communal eating facilities, where persons can take turns preparing meals for the community or can pool resources to hire a kitchen staff; rooms in a central facility for special occasions such as large dinner parties, so that families do not need so much space (which then requires upkeep) devoted to low-use areas (e.g., formal dining rooms) in their individual units; a central laundry facility, staffed or unstaffed; and an on-site child care center, possibly rotating child care responsibilities among parents in the complex. It appears that such systems are relatively more attractive to women. In Sweden, where there is a relatively long history of experimental communal multifamily living, the public housing authorities have introduced communal options into rental housing; those communal option projects that are not specifically for the elderly attract disproportionately higher numbers of women and single-parent households than public housing in general.[14]

To the extent that the small number of existing projects attracts those who are most highly motivated to live in such situations, the merits of extending such projects to a large proportion of the population may be overrated. Given the lack of ongoing private developments of this type, it appears that heavy communality appeals to a minority of persons. Although more are attracted in tight housing markets to the lower housing costs involved in these options (e.g., one very popular presubscribed community on Bainbridge Island outside Seattle), it is not obvious that communal living is considered a desirable feature. Certain subsets of the population have long congregated in publicly and privately developed living situations that are at least partially communal: dormitories for college students, elderly person care communities, condominiums with associations, and large rental housing developments (the last two of which tend to contain mostly younger, single people). All these environments tend to have smaller individual living units, combined with a central facility with larger meeting rooms and athletic facilities. Building and grounds upkeep are done by paid staff, and there are coordinated social and recreational activities and, in some cases, communally provided meal services. The question is whether or not the persons currently found in single-family detached dwellings would prefer a more communal style of life.

Another way to reduce nonmarket work is to set up service houses – locations near homes that serve as clearing houses for messages, package delivery, and repair calls. They can even serve as a place to drop off and retrieve laundry or to pick up hot meals upon returning home from work. Some gated single-family housing developments already provide some services of this nature. This approach may allow for a better integration of the desire for privacy and roomy housing with the desire for reduced housing upkeep.

3. Workplaces: Many observers have called for the development of more family-friendly work settings, both to accommodate the need of workers to attend to family responsibilities and to allow workers to bring some of those responsibilities into the office. Concrete policies already aimed in this direction include "personal days" and on-site child care centers. A more flexible attitude towards workers' family duties could be fostered in many offices. Indeed, family-friendly offices now exist where one can bring in infants or schoolchildren (as is the case in some nonprofit settings). Workplaces could create homework centers for children, an effort that could be as simple as setting aside a small room for children or as complex as developing small on-site libraries where children could do research for their homework. It is not apparent what the effects of such policies and practices would be on parent and coworker productivity.

Another trend that has been much noted is the evolution of the home into a high-tech workplace. While many women have engaged in paid homework in the past and continue to do so in lower-technology jobs such as assembly work, now – through the miracle of telecommunications – many white-collar jobs can be performed at least partially at home. Phones, beepers, faxes, modems, and personal computers all serve to liberate persons from workdays tied to the office. Additionally, it is possible in some occupations (college teaching, for one) to do some work at night and on weekends so as to free up blocks of time and maintain some flexibility during weekdays. There may, however, be trade-offs involved for those who use these work strategies. To the extent that they are not the norm, workers who spend greater periods of time away from the office may end up being penalized in terms of being considered less available for relatively inflexible assignments that can lead to promotions.

FOCUS

Why don't women get tenure?

Women have been increasingly entering postgraduate education. Figure 16.1 illustrates the notable jump in the percentage of female doctoral degree recipients. In 1993 42,000 persons received this degree, 16,000 of whom were women. Since 1969, the number of male recipients has remained essentially constant at 25,000, while the number of women has quadrupled.

These numbers mean that large numbers of women are available for teaching positions in colleges and universities. However, women have not been entering tenured positions at a proportional rate. For example, the American Economic Association's Committee on the Status of Women in the Economics Profession has tracked the share of women by rank since 1974. As of 1995, women are underrepresented at all levels of the academic job ladder except for nontenure track positions. Among Ph.D-granting economics departments, 24.2 percent of assistant professors, 12.9 percent of tenured associate professors, and 7.5 percent of full professors are women.[15] While part of these dropping percentages is related to the much lower proportion of women in earlier cohorts, the lower success rates of women in achieving tenure relative to men is also a factor. This pattern is also found in the natural science disciplines.

It is quite clear that earlier cohorts of women with doctorates were discriminated against in hiring and tenure procedures. In earlier decades women were often flatly informed that various institutions did not hire women, or they were only hired in adjunct researcher positions. Antinepotism rules – widespread at public universities in the 1950s and 1960s – were also problematic, as they could prevent women from working at the same institution as their husband.[16] Later the procedures became more circumspect. Prominent mathematician Mary Beth Ruskai relates this story from her 1972 academic job search as a postdoctoral researcher at MIT:[17]

> A visitor was vociferously holding forth in the mathematics department lounge about the pressure to hire women. He alleged that his department had no women applicants and he would gladly create a position if someone like me applied. So I asked for the name of his university – it turned out that I had just received a rejection letter from his chair in the mail I opened before lunch!

More recently attention has turned to women's lower publication rates and what the causes might be for that. Studies do show lower publication rates among women scholars,[18] and to the extent that the number of publications are an important determinant of receiving tenure, this is problematic.

But what are the causes of this lower publication rate? As usual, the economist looks at both supply and demand side factors in the "market" for scholarly books and articles. Perhaps women have more trouble getting their work published due to discrimination by the gatekeepers of the professions: the referees and editors of journals and books. Another leading explanation is that women, because of their double burden of market and nonmarket work, have less time available than men for research. While institutions have responded to this view, in part, by allowing for semester or year-long parental leaves and tenure clock extensions, it remains to be seen whether these policies improve the tenuring rate among women.

Working conditions still present a problem for women who consider entering and remaining in those professions that require much overnight travel. For some jobs, it seems unlikely that this dilemma can be solved through the reduction of such travel (without invention of instantaneous matter transporters *à la* Star Trek), although teleconferencing, either audio or video, is becoming both technically feasible and somewhat more popular. While hotels often provide child care referral services (the use of which could be subsidized

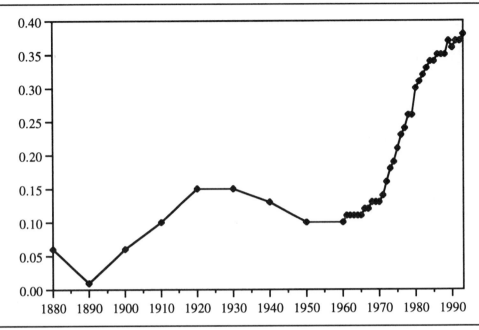

FIGURE 16.1   Percentage of doctoral degrees awarded to women, 1880 to 1993

Source: Digest of Education Statistics (1996): 253 (Table 239).

FOCUS

Part-time lawyers

A New York Times article in early 1991 focused on the trend of law firms towards accommodating lawyers who want to work part time, optimistically arguing that "part-time arrangements, which commonly have relegated women lawyers to the 'mommy track' with no hope of achieving partnership, may now merely delay partnership decisions."[19] The article quotes Lisa Hill Fenning, a judge on the U.S. Bankruptcy Court in Los Angeles and a member of the American Bar Association's Commission on Women in the Profession:

> Ten years ago large firms did not have part-time options available to their lawyers generally . . . Five years ago they did have the options, but they were experimental, limited and usually off partnership track. Today I think there's enough track record that being part time does not make you less a lawyer. It is becoming more acceptable to stay on partnership track.

However, while more than 86 percent of large law firms offer part-time schedules, only 2.4 percent of attorneys actually work part time.[20] And, belying the optimism of Judge Fenning, associates may be wise to avoid part-time schedules. Most partners at top law firms do not have any part-time experience, and less than half of first-year associates eventually make partner at the firms they begin work at. In such a competitive atmosphere, many associates are apparently loath to give up the edge they may attain by working the customary 16-hour days. Law firm Arnold & Porter's managing partner James Jones says:

> An associate, male or female, who goes into a part-time arrangement and stays for a long time may well be at a disadvantage for partnership consideration. It's not because it is thought that they haven't paid their dues. It's because they have been restricted in their opportunities.[21]

by employers), which make it theoretically possible for women to engage in business travel with young children, this approach is still difficult to coordinate. However, for two-parent households one spouse can choose not to have a traveling job, so as to stay home with children, and it need not be the woman who has the sedentary job.

4. Schools: The current school calendar, generally involving no more than 180 days of school, less than eight hours a day, with one three-month summer break, is a holdover from not only the agricultural past, when children were needed during the summer to do farmwork, but also from the days when mothers were less likely to be working full-time. These schedules currently do not operate to the advantage of all parents and children. Parents who are employed year-round full-time either must make plans for summer activities that will occupy the children during the day, as well as planning after-school care or activities, or face the spectacle of having unsupervised "latch-key" children.

School schedules that run more days, more hours per day, and stagger vacation time over the course of the year would be helpful to such parents. The limited amount of formal schooling currently offered – beginning in kindergarten, which is generally still a half-day program – seems surprising, given national concern over declining or stagnant educational achievement levels. There is much evidence, both from school systems in other countries such as Japan that run for more days per year, more hours per day, and from the small but growing number of systems in the United States than run year-round schools (often as an optional school within a large school district), that these innovations are welcomed by parents and are helpful in raising children's educational achievement levels. Given the growing number of children currently attending all-day year-round day care and preschool programs, this drop in time upon entry into kindergarten also seems unwarranted if based on the idea that children cannot bear a full day away from their parents. While formal teaching may be tedious if maintained over the full day, a more flexible schedule involving extended periods of play could be used (as it is in Japan).[22] Many schools, both public and private, have started optional after-school programs for children. This practice supplements the existing range of extracurricular activities, mainly for older children, such as music practice, dance lessons, and sports.

Dilbert / By SCOTT ADAMS

DILBERT © United Feature Syndicate: Reprinted by Permission

Policy Application: Family-friendly benefits

Firms are increasingly touting the availability of "family-friendly" benefits. These include many of the benefits discussed in this and previous chapters: child care, flextime, family leaves. Increasing one's ability to mesh work and family life more neatly is clearly a topic of great interest to many men and women. But it is difficult to analyze what the tradeoffs involved in the expansion of such policies might be.

One issue is how such policies affect persons who are not generally eligible for such policies. There are significant equity considerations generated by having noncafeteria plans, i.e., plans where employees can use a benefit, but do not receive an alternative form of compensation if they choose not to. In addition, if employers do not replace employees who take family leaves, this leaves the remaining workers to pick up the slack.

A second issue is whether use or availability of family-friendly benefits helps or hinders women's progression up the promotion ladder. One recent study by the *Wall Street Journal* finds that firms touting family-friendly benefits are not always the most likely ones to promote women (e.g., DuPont), while other firms that get low "family-friendly" ratings have a high proportion of women managers (e.g., Heinz and Monsanto).[23]

A final issue might be whether these family-friendly benefits have a negative effect on wages, which could conceivably reduce women's wages more than men's if women are more likely to seek employment with firms offering these benefits, and more likely to utilize these benefits. Two theoretical perspectives guide economists' view of the potential effects of these policies on wages. One, the compensating wage differential perspective (as outlined in Chapter 8), views there as being a trade-off between these benefits and wages (i.e., that the benefits are a quasi-fixed or variable cost for the employer). The second perspective argues that these benefits may have productivity-enhancing effects through allowing employees to operate more efficiently. Therefore, wages would stay the same or even increase. Interestingly, one recent study has found that the latter effect predominates.[24]

Summary

The variety of policy approaches to gender issues can be categorized by their explicit goals. Although actual effects could also serve as a categorization method, it is often difficult to evaluate the net effect of a particular policy on gender equality. Some general precepts regarding formation of sound policy include sensitivity to whether or not they tend to solidify existing gender roles, openness to a variety of approaches, and consideration of demographic changes. A variety of approaches can be attempted towards creating more fundamental changes in social organization that would tend to alleviate non-market workloads for all persons.

Endnotes

1. Nancy Barrett, "Obstacles to Economic Parity for Women," *American Economic Review* 72, no. 2 (May 1982): 164–165.
2. *Statistical Abstract of the United States* (1991): 420 (Table 686).
3. *Statistical Abstract of the United States* (1996): 431 (Table 671).
4. See Dorothy P. Rice, "Long-Term Care for the Elderly," *Women's Life Cycle and Economic Insecurity: Problems and Proposals*, ed. Martha N. Ozawa (Westport, Conn.: Greenwood, 1989): 170–193.

5. Frances K. Goldscheider and Linda J. Waite, *New Families, No Families? The Transformation of the American Home* (Berkeley, Calif.: University of California, 1991): 193.

6. Jessie Allen and Alan Pifer (eds.), *Women on the Front Lines: Meeting the Challenge of an Aging America* (Washington, D.C.: Urban Institute, 1993). See Nancy Folbre, " 'Holding Hands at Midnight': The Paradox of Caring Labor," *Feminist Economics* 1, no. 1 (Spring 1995): 73–92, for an interesting discussion of the valuation of caring labor.

7. Neil Gilbert, "In Support of Domesticity: A Neglected Family Policy Option," *Journal of Policy Analysis and Management* 2, no. 4 (Summer 1983): 628–632.

8. Paula Rayman, "The Meaning of Work in Women's Lives," *Radcliffe Quarterly* 76, no. 2 (June 1990): 13.

9. Barrett, *op. cit.*: 164.

10. For more suggestions, see Alice H. Cook, "Public Policies to Help Dual-Earner Families Meet the Demands of the Work World," *Industrial and Labor Relations Review* 42, no. 2 (January 1989): 201–215.

11. Dolores Hayden, *Redesigning the American Dream: The Future of Housing, Work, and Family Life* (New York: W.W. Norton, 1984): 12.

12. Hayden, *op. cit.*: 18.

13. See Dolores Hayden, *The Grand Domestic Revolution: A History of Feminist Designs for American Homes, Neighborhoods, and Cities* (Cambridge, Mass.: MIT, 1981); Leslie Kanes Weisman, *Discrimination by Design: A Feminist Critique of the Man-Made Environment* (Urbana and Chicago, Ill.: University of Illinois, 1992).

14. Alison E. Woodward, "Public Housing Communes: A Swedish Response to Postmaterial Demands," *Housing and Neighborhoods: Theoretical and Empirical Contributions*, eds. Willem van Vliet, Harvey Choldin, William Michelson, and David Popenoe (Westport, Conn.: Greenwood, 1987): 215–238.

15. "Report of the Committee on the Status of Women in the Economics Profession," *American Economic Review* 87, no. 2 (May 1987): 506–510.

16. Rita J. Simon, "On Nepotism, Marriage, and the Pursuit of an Academic Career," *Rabbis, Lawyers, Immigrants, Thieves: Exploring Women's Roles* (Westport, Conn.: Praeger, 1993): 3–16.

17. Mary Beth Ruskai, "Time for Advancement," *Focus: The Newsletter of the Mathematical Association of America* 14, no. 6 (July-August 1984): 25.

18. Rita J. Simon, "The Productivity of Female Scholars," *Rabbis, Lawyers, Immigrants, Thieves: Exploring Women's Roles* (Westport, Conn.: Praeger, 1993): 17–37.

19. "Time Trial: Firms Gradually Make Way for Part-time Lawyers," New York Times News Service article in the *Chicago Tribune* (January 6, 1991), Section 6: 4.

20. Jill Schachner Chanen, "In the Family Way," *ABA Journal* (July 1995). Statistics are from the National Association for Law Placement.

21. *Ibid.*

22. Harold W. Stevenson, "Learning from Asian Schools," *Scientific American* 267, no. 6 (December 1992): 70–76; for more details on Asian education systems, see Joseph J. Tobin, David Y.H. Wu, and Dara H. Davidson, *Preschool in Three Cultures: Japan, China, and the United States* (New Haven, Conn.: Yale University, 1989); Robert Leestma and Herbert J. Walberg, *Japanese Educational Productivity* (Ann Arbor, Mich.: University of Michigan, Center for Japanese Studies, 1992); and Harold W. Stevenson and James W. Stigler, *The Learning Gap: Why Our Schools Are Failing and What We Can Learn from Japanese and Chinese Education* (New York: Summit Books, 1992).

23. Rochelle Sharpe, "Family-Friendly Firms Don't Always Promote Females," *Wall Street Journal* (March 29, 1994): B1.

24. Nancy Brown Johnson and Keith G. Provan, "The Relationship Between Work/Family Benefits and Earnings: A Test of Competing Predictions," *Journal of Socio-Economics* 24, no. 4 (1995): 571–584.

*F*urther reading and statistical sources

Blau, Francine D. and Ronald G. Ehrenberg (eds.) (1997). *Gender and Family Issues in the Workplace.* New York: Russell Sage Foundation. Useful set of conference papers.

Bureau of National Affairs (1986). *Work and Family: A Changing Dynamic.* Contains case studies of various companies' programs, including day care, parental leave, and flex-time. BNA focuses on employment interests from a business and legal point of view and maintains a publications list at its website (www.bna.com).

Dornbusch, Sanford M., and Myra H. Strober (eds.) (1988). *Feminism, Children, and the New Families.* New York: Guilford. Essays by social scientists from a Ford Foundation-sponsored project at Stanford University entitled, "Public Policy Implications of Perceived Conflicts Between Children's Interests and Feminists' Interests."

DuRivage, V.L. (ed.) (1992). *New Policies for the Part-Time and Contingent Workforce* (Armonk, N.Y.: M.E. Sharpe. Discusses new trends in non-full-time work patterns.

Economic Policy Network. Provides links and a searchable topic database for a number of affiliated organizations with interests in economic and social policy (www.epn.org), including the Brookings Institution, the Economic Policy Institute, and the Russell Sage Foundation.

Folbre, Nancy (1994). *Who Pays for the Kids? Gender and the Structures of Constraint.* London and New York: Routledge. Argues that family and social policy cannot be disconnected from a larger framework of political economy and an understanding of comparative history. A wide range of historical and societal examples.

Institute for Women's Policy Research. The leading thinktank on economic policy issues of gender relevance maintains a useful website (www.iwpr.org).

Kalleberg, Arne L., Edith Rasell, Ken Hudson, David Webster, Barbara Reskin, Naomi Cassirer, and Eileen Appelbaum (1997). *Nonstandard Work, Substandard Jobs: Flexible Work Arrangements in the U.S.* Washington, D.C.: Economic Policy Institute.

*D*iscussion questions

1.   Classify each of the following policies into one of the four categories proposed in the chapter:
   (a)   Imposition of a national family wage, under which program married men receive more hourly pay than women or unmarried men.
   (b)   A national sales tax.
   (c)   Restrictions on allowing women into medical school.
   (d)   Subsidization of fertility treatments for infertile couples.
   (e)   Summer jobs programs that put teens in nontraditional jobs.

2.   Can you think of a policy not mentioned in the chapter for each category?

3.   What are the pros and cons of passing a national unpaid medical leave of *unlimited* duration for sickness or death of any family member (or housemate)?

4.   What are the pros and cons of passing a national year-long parental leave at three-fourths regular pay with full job security?

5.   What are the pros and cons of requiring all employers to provide child care payments or services for all their employees?

6.   Academics and others have complained that affirmative action makes it harder for couples to get jobs at the same university or other workplace (actually antinepotism rules in many workplaces used to make it impossible for both spouses to work in the same place). In your opinion, is this a good or a bad thing?

7. How might imposition of a national gasoline sales tax affect the sexes differently?

8. Is it society's responsibility to alleviate the burden on parents of providing transportation for the family? Why might society want to provide some child-related transport services? Can you think of any such services that are provided by the government?

9. If you were offered the opportunity to live in a cluster housing project, what would you see as the pros and cons of such a move for you?

10. Is the decision as to whether to live in cluster housing similar to the decision as to whether to live in a dormitory while attending school?

11. If you currently hold or have held a paid job or unpaid internship, comment on how the workplace you were in could be made more family-friendly. Were there any features of the workplace that made it particularly family-friendly?

12. Consider the Focus on professors. What differences do you note, if any, between the male and female professors at your school in terms of their work habits? Are you aware whether women have had difficulties at your school receiving tenure or in other ways proceeding up the academic job ladder?

13. Consider the Focus on part-time lawyers. What does it mean to have paid your dues, yet have been restricted in your opportunities?

14. Consider the Focus on part-time lawyers. Would you expect these practices to be successfully adopted in other high-paying, high-hour occupations, such as medicine, accounting, and investment banking? Why or why not?

15. How might the movement in many communities away from a purely neighborhood public school system towards a "magnet" school system or a free border school system, in which children are not constrained to attend the nearest school, affect male and female parents differently? Could it have differential effects on boys and girls?

16. Do you think people actively scout benefits plans in choosing employment? How important would the existence of family-friendly policies at a potential employer be to you in deciding where to work?

Author Index

Subject Index